95

Parenting— general

W9-BRI-748

THE GUINNESS BOOK OF

LESLIE DUNKLING

7TH EDITION

Facts On File®

AN INFOBASE HOLDINGS COMPANY

The Author

Leslie Dunkling is a freelance writer specialising in works of popular reference. Born in London in 1935, he left school at sixteen to become a copy-boy in a press agency. After a wide variety of other jobs he became a mature student, reading English at University College London. He later gained his MA in Linguistics at Stockholm University, where he also lectured in English in the 1960s.

In 1971 he joined the BBC as a producer of English-language teaching radio and television programmes. He remained in this post until 1991, writing several hundred radio scripts and two television series.

His special interest in names began in 1969. He founded the Names Society in 1971 and was for many years its Secretary and editor of the Society's journal. He has published eleven books on names of various kinds: other books include the *Guinness Book of Curious Phrases*, the *Guinness Book of Curious Words* and the *Guinness Drinking Companion*. He has also published a number of Readers for foreign students of English.

Cover photos (*left to right*): William (John Mitchell); Bobbie (Dave Turmaine); The Lobster Pot Restaurant (Irish Tourist Board); Map of New York; James (Christine Nuttall); Guinness logo; Frankie (Mark Taylor); The author, Leslie Dunkling (Lilleys of Hinchley Wood); Neil (Elaine Prenzlau); Jane (Elaine Prenzlau); Jessica (Dave Turmaine); Keanu Reeves (London Features International); Tusy Pie the cat (Carol Wright); Felix (Giles North); Frocks Restaurant (I.T.B.); Q Magazine; Jack Russell terrier (David Roberts); Thomas (Sallie Collins).

Copyright © 1995 by Leslie Alan Dunkling and Guinness Publishing Ltd.
'GUINNESS' is a registered trade mark of Guinness Publishing Ltd.

All rights reserved. No part of this book may be reproduced or utilized in any form or by any means, electronic or mechanical, including photocopying, recording, or by any information storage or retrieval systems, without permission in writing from the copyright owner. For information contact:

Guinness Publishing Ltd
33 London Road
Enfield, Middx, UK

CIP data for this book is available from the publisher.

ISBN 0-8160-3419-2

Facts on File books are available at special discounts when purchased in bulk quantities for businesses, associations, institutions or sales promotions. Please call our Special Sales Department in New York at 212/683-2244 or 800/322-8755.

Text design by Stonecastle Graphics Ltd.
Jacket design by Stonecastle Graphics Ltd.
Composition by Ace Filmsetting Ltd, Frome, Somerset
Manufactured by The Bath Press, Bath.
Printed in Great Britain.

10 9 8 7 6 5 4 3 2 1

This book is printed on acid-free paper.

Contents

Acknowledgements 4

Preface 5

1 **What's in a name?** *Introduction* 7

2 **First names first** *First name origins* 24

3 **Fashionable names** *First name fashions* 43

4 **Naming the baby** *First names – reasons for choice* 78

5 **First names appraised** *Reactions to first names* 92

6 **The gift of a name** *Given names around the world* 108

7 **The family name** *History of surnames* 118

8 **Making a name for yourself** *Psychology of surnames* 142

9 **Eking out names** *Nicknames* 153

10 **A local habitation and a name** *British place names* 165

11 **Names take their places** *New world place names* 177

12 **Neighbourly names** *Street names* 187

13 **Signing a name** *Pub names* 198

14 **Home-made names** *House names* 209

15 **Trading a name** *Trade names* 220

16 **No end of names** *Magazine names, pop group names, animal names, flower names, apple names, ship names, train and locomotive names, lorry names, dog names, cat names, yacht names, hat names, names of kisses* 229

17 **Name games** *Place name games, name anagrams, name rebus, name magic, name collecting, name stories, name poems, name jokes, hairy names* 244

Further Reading 258

Names Index 259

Acknowledgements

This book could not have been written without the helpful advice, comments and friendly assistance of a great many people. It is unfortunately not possible to mention by name the three thousand or more correspondents who have written to me in the last few years about names of one kind or another. Many of them are members of The Names Society; some are authors of books listed in the Bibliography; many others are members of the public who responded to newspaper appeals for information. I am most grateful to all of them.

A special word of thanks must go to the late C. V. Appleton, who made available to me the results of his very extensive first name researches.

Very specific help with the book has also been given by J. Bryan III, Jodi Cassell, Michael Darton, Cecily Dynes, Dr Cleveland Evans, John Field, John Foley, Darryl Francis, Beatrice Frei, William Gosling, Dr Kelsie Harder, David Henson, Susan Hibberd, George F. Hubbard, Alec Jeakins, Dr Terrence Keough, Anne Kirkman, Professor Edwin Lawson, Richard Luty, Pauline Quemby, Philip Riley, Adrian Room, Kathleen Sinclair, Gillian Skirrow, Elsdon C. Smith, Muriel Smith, John Smurthwaite, Rev Peter Sutton, Harvey Türkel, Helen Vnuk, A. A. Willis and Gordon Wright.

My wife, Nicole, has in her own way made it possible for the book to come into being. The poet was right: *a gode womman is mannys blys.*

Guinness

This Irish family name is a shortened form of **Mac Guinness** or **Maguinness,** also found as **Mac Genis, Magennis, Maguiness, Magennies, Maginniss.** It was earlier **Mag Aonghusa** or **Mag Aonghuis,** 'son of Angus'.

Angus in turn is a Gaelic personal name which was probably *Oino-gustu-s* in its earliest form, 'unique choice one'.

The usual Scottish form of the name is **MacInnes,** though it also occurs as **Mackinnes, Mackinness, MacGinnis, MacAngus** and **Macansh.** Manx forms of the name include **Kinnish, Keanish, Kennish, Kinch.**

Guinness, MacGuinness, etc., are not amongst those family names which are regularly used as first names (though the stirring tale of how **Maginnis Magee** received his name is related on page 56).

Mac, Gaelic 'son', is sometimes (wrongly according to the purists) contracted to *M'* or *Mc* in writing. In parts of Scotland, eg Arran, it is pronounced *Ac* by Gaelic speakers. The change to *Mag* before a vowel is a feature of Irish Gaelic. The Welsh equivalent is *Mab* or *Map,* usually shortened to *Ab* or *Ap* and still further to *B* or *P.* Thus **Mab Evan** becomes **Ab Evan,** then **Bevan. Map Howell** becomes **Ap Howell,** then **Powell.**

Preface

'A PREFACE,' wrote Isaac Disraeli, 'being the entrance to a book, should invite by its beauty. An elegant porch announces the splendour of the interior.'

It's a fine thought, but 'splendour' is not really what I want to offer in this book. Instead I have tried to bring together a mixture of information, entertainment, ideas and enthusiasm. The last of these I can at least guarantee to be present. Few authors can so have enjoyed immersing themselves in a subject, and I hope this will be clear on every page.

As for information, I asked myself at the outset what my potential reader would want to know about names. I thought he would certainly be interested in first names and surnames, in where those names came from and what they originally meant. In chapters on those subjects, therefore, I briefly summarise the historical and linguistic facts, and give the origins of as many names as possible. But I must say that, though I understand the interest in name origins, I think they are almost irrelevant in modern life. Far more to the point, it seems to me, is the consideration of why certain first names come into fashion or go out of fashion; why parents choose one name rather than any other at a given point in time; what associations are aroused in people's minds by certain names. There are a host of similar topics that concern the psychological and sociological aspects of names. I discuss such matters, having first presented firmly based tables of name frequencies that make a sensible discussion possible.

In these areas I try to offer a fresh approach, not merely to collate what is already in print. The usual books on first names are in any case very disappointing. I find no trace in any of them of an objective attempt to establish which names are currently being used. As a result they contain long articles about names such as Griselda and Letitia, while vital names such as Tracy, Joanne and Sharon are virtually ignored.

To complete the survey of personal names I deal with nicknames in a separate chapter. Nicknames have an inbuilt liveliness which makes them of special interest. The names are entertaining in themselves, whatever one says of them.

I thought my potential reader would next be interested in place names, and accordingly I turn in that direction. The interpretation of early English place names is a matter for the specialist, the scholar who has devoted a great deal of time to the study of certain languages and cultures. I received a preliminary training in philology, and my main hope is that this will have enabled me to interpret the findings of the experts without too much distortion. The place names of the New World have also been well studied by historians and linguists, and once again I summarise their work.

Personal and place names are the concern of a major part of this book, but the interest of names really does not end there. The rest of the book is concerned with street names and pub names, house names and trade names, boat names, locomotive names, animal names, and still more names. *All* names are fascinating, and I try to explain why. In this latter section of the book the scales are slightly loaded in favour of entertainment rather than information, especially in the chapter on 'Name Games'.

Finally, I include at the end of the book suggestions for further reading, including the book from which I borrowed my opening quotation, Isaac Disraeli's *Curiosities of Literature*. It is there because among dozens of other interesting essays it contains those on the 'Influence of a Name', the 'Orthography of Proper Names', 'Names of Our Streets' and 'Political Nicknames'. Disraeli was clearly a names enthusiast: I hope there are many more like him.

Leslie Alan Dunkling

What *is* a name?

'*The word(s) that someone or something is known by.*'

Longman Dictionary of Contemporary English

'*A proper name is a noun used in a non-universal function, with or without recognizable current lexical value, of which the potential meaning coincides with and never exceeds its actual meaning, and which is attached as a label to one animate being or one inanimate object (or to more than one in the case of collective names) for the purpose of specific distinction from among a number of like or in some respects similar beings or objects that are either in no manner distinguished from one another or, for our interest, not sufficiently distinguished.*'

Ernst Pulgram   *Theory of Names*

'*The name of a thing is its soul.*'

F. M. Cornford   *From Religion to Philosophy*

Naming Names

Names are usually defined more specifically by referring them to the set of names, or nomenclature, to which they belong. Thus we speak of a place name (toponym), house name (econym), first name (Christian name, forename, given name), etc.

Names can also be differentiated by origin. By primary origin every name is either:

a) descriptive, ie formed of a word or words which describe in some way what is being named,
b) converted, ie a word or words arbitrarily associated with what is being named and given name status,
c) invented, ie a newly-formed word or words, or group of letters, or combination of letters and numbers, of no known previous meaning, brought into being as a name.

Once a name exists it can be:

d) transferred, ie borrowed from one naming system for use elsewhere, as with Hamlet when used to name a cigar. There is a special set of names available for transfer to any group of persons or objects—see Number Names on page George (20),
e) linked, ie extended by the addition of another element, as Johnson from John,
f) blended, ie joined partly or totally with all or part of another name, as in the house name Patalan, where Patricia and Alan live.

1
WHAT'S IN A NAME?

THE MOST famous comment on names in the English language occurs in Shakespeare's play, *Romeo and Juliet*.

What's in a name? that which we call a rose
By any other name would smell as sweet.

Juliet's beautiful speech, which in context is a passionate plea for what is known to be a lost cause, is often misinterpreted. Juliet does not believe what she says even as she says it, and Shakespeare certainly did not believe it. He gives quite a different answer to his own question many times in his plays and poems. With his usual genius, however, he makes Juliet ask herself a timeless question which has an infinity of answers. The innumerable sub-editors who have echoed the question at the head of a thousand columns simply acknowledge the fact. We must also acknowledge it, and attempt to find some answers.

A name's meaning

A name has different kinds of meaning. To most people, for instance, **Romeo** means the character in Shakespeare's play. The name is so generally associated with that romantic young lover that it can be used humorously to describe any such person. The

---

. . . all bearers of the Forsyte name would feel the bloom was off the rose. He had no illusions like Shakespeare that roses by any other name would smell as sweet. The name was a possession, a concrete, unstained piece of property, the value of which would be reduced some twenty per cent at least.

John Galsworthy *In Chancery*

Her middle name was his mother's, Hannah. Who's in a name?

Bernard Malamud *Dubin's Lives*

---

original meaning of the name Romeo, which probably indicated a pilgrim to Rome, is quite another matter.

Names can have public meanings and private meanings. **Lamorna,** for example, is a place name. This simple fact about the name is a general meaning which is implied by its presence on a map or in a gazetteer. To somebody who was born in Lamorna, or who lives there, the name obviously means far more. It conjures up immediately memories and associations. The name has an extended, particular meaning as well for many married couples, since Lamorna happens to be well known as a honeymoon resort.

Some of those honeymoon couples transfer the name Lamorna to their houses, for it is often seen over porches in British suburbs. When such a transfer has taken place, a further extension of meaning is possible. A young couple who hope to have a house of their own one day see a house which is called Lamorna. For them that house is everything they dream about. Perhaps they fall in love with the name itself, with its form and sound. When they call their own house Lamorna some years later they may still be unaware of the name's public meaning as a place in the south-west of England. For them it has only a secondary, private meaning.

An even commoner example of secondary meaning occurs when parents use a particular name for their child to commemorate a friend or relation. In their minds the name is associated with the person who bore it, with that person's character and personality. The name means to them what that person means to them, rather than what a dictionary might say about the name's origin.

A name's origin

Just as many kinds of meaning are possible, so different kinds of name origins may be described. Primary origin refers to the way in which the name first becomes a name. For instance, if in the middle of a dark wood there is a clearing where the sun streams down, that spot might well be described by those who know it as 'the bright clearing'. A thousand years ago those words would have looked more like 'the sheer lea'. Such a description was applied to a place in southern England, and the general description gradually became a particular name. 'The sheer lea' is still so called today, though it has a slightly different pronunciation and is written **Shirley.**

But once such a name has come into being it can be transferred constantly from one entity to another. We spoke of Lamorna becoming a house name. By a similar process of transfer, Shirley became a surname. Then, as frequently happens with surnames, it began to be used as a boy's first name. In 1849 Charlotte Brontë wrote a novel in which the *heroine* was called Shirley, because:

> 'Her parents, who had wished to have a son, finding that . . . Providence had granted them only a daughter, bestowed on her the same masculine family cognomen they would have bestowed on a boy, if with a boy they had been blessed.'

The name was nevertheless rarely used for girls for many years, but in 1880 another transfer of the name occurred which was to prove helpful. The Reverend W. Wilks, who lived in the vicarage at Shirley, cultivated a new kind of poppy in his garden. He had grown it at Shirley Vicarage, so he quite naturally called the new flower Shirley. Soon afterwards it became fashionable to give girls flower names, such as Daisy and Violet, and Shirley was

now a candidate that could be considered. The final step was for Shirley Temple to come along in the 1930s and associate the name with an ideal little girl and international stardom. Shirley quickly became one of the most popular names for a girl. It enjoyed a brief spell in the limelight before retiring to a more modest position, but it is certainly established permanently now as a girl's name. For many people it must be that first and foremost, and some may be quite unaware of its place name, surname, boy's name and flower name connections.

With **Shirley**, then, we see how the principle of secondary origin applies. Names are passed from one naming system to another, just as words are passed from one language to another. It would be well to consider how many naming systems, or nomenclatures, surround us.

Name density

On a normal day—which can itself be identified by many different names—most of us meet a number of people who are known to us by name. We may know, and use, their first names, surnames or nicknames which are drawn from different, but overlapping, systems. We will also meet people whose names we do not know, and here we may have to make use of personal name substitutes. Professional titles such as 'driver', 'officer', 'waiter', are given temporary name status, or we use a general term such as 'sir'. Lovers are also fond of using name substitutes. A correspondent once told me that her fiancé addressed her variously as 'chunkie', 'porky', 'sloppy', 'floppy', 'big softie', 'hot chops', 'cuddly duddly', 'tatty head', 'rumble tum', 'kipper feet', 'twizzle', 'lucky legs' and 'lucky lips'.

In our newspaper (named) we will read of many more people who are known to us by name, but whom we have never met. We will read, too, of places

---

'. . . 'tis the same age our little bye would have been if we had had one six years ago. If we had, Jawn, think what sorrow would be in our hearts this night, with our little Phelan run away. . . .'

'Ye talk foolishness,' said Mr McCaskey. ''Tis Pat he would be named, after me old father in Cantrim.'

'Ye lie!' said Mrs McCaskey, without anger. 'Me brother was worth tin dozen bog-trotting McCaskeys. After him would the bye be named.'

O. Henry   *Between Rounds*

Name magic

Paris! Paris!! Paris!!!
*The very name had always been one to
conjure with, whether he thought of it as
a mere sound on the lips and in the ear,
or as a magical written or printed word
for the eye.*

George du Maurier   *Trilby*

*I have a passion for the name of Mary,
For once it had a magic sound to me.*

Lord Byron   *Don Juan*

*. . . thy name reminds me
Of three friends, all true and tried;
And that name, like magic, binds me
Closer, closer to thy side.*

H. W. Longfellow   *To the River Charles*

*'Who hath not owned, with rapture-
smitten frame,
The Power of grace, the magic of a
name?'*

Thomas Campbell   *Pleasures of Hope*

'Foxy?'
*'Yes, Piet?' Their simple names had a
magic, the magic of a caress . . .*

John Updike   *Couples*

'I am your father.'
*God knows what magic the name had for
his ears . . .*

Charles Dickens   *Barnaby Rudge*

*The accidental affinity or coincidence of a
name, connected with ridicule or hatred,
with pleasure or disgust, has operated like
magic.*

Isaac Disraeli   *Curiosities of Literature*

---

all over the world, most of whose names are familiar to us though we have not been to them.

When we leave our houses, which usually have number names but may have other names, we walk through named streets. In a town we will pass shops which have names and which are crammed with named products. In the country we will be passing named fields and natural features.

If we live near the sea, or near a river (named), we may be exposed to ship or boat names. In some parts of the English-speaking world we will almost certainly see the traditionally well-illustrated names of public houses.

Our job or profession will bring us into contact with still more names. They may be the names of other companies, or the names of products. If these products are simply components, not usually seen by the public, they may well have code names consisting of letters and numbers. The form will have changed, but these are still names.

Every occupation has its accompanying nomenclatures. The professional gardener must cope with vast numbers of plant names. A builder uses not just bricks but particular kinds of bricks that have names. A librarian becomes familiar with an ever-increasing number of names, though in his case they masquerade as book 'titles'.

All this only hints at the true name density which surrounds us. To stay with books for a moment, you are reading now a page that is identified by a number name, which has words printed by named type-faces (**Bodoni** and **Imprint**) on named paper (**Ashtead opaque**). The ink that has been used also has a name (**Onyx**).

A similar situation exists everywhere. Almost any generic term, even a word like 'table' or 'chair', conceals a naming system. A named chair may sound strange, but a company that manufactures chairs presumably makes several different models. A salesman from such a company might refer to the chair you are sitting on as an **Elizabethan**, say, or a **K52**. The simple word 'chair' would be meaningless on his order-forms.

So it is with specialists of all kinds. A man who works in a wholesale fruit market is probably surrounded by apples, but it is unlikely that he uses that word. He deals in boxes of **Coxes**, say, or **Granny Smiths**.

Such names differ from those that identify people, places, houses, boats and the like. They do not individualise, but serve to distinguish members of one group from those of another. There is obviously an important difference between generic names, such as **King Edward** for a potato, and what we may continue to call proper names, such as **Edward King** when it identifies an individual.

He kept reciting the names of cider apples:

'Coccagee and Bloody Butcher,

Slack-ma-girdle,

Red Soldier and Lady's Finger,

Kingston Black, Bloody Turk,

Fox Whelp, Pawson, Tom Putt,

Bitter Sweet and Fatty Mutt.'

His deep, rich fruity voice made them sound like poetry.

Humphrey Phelps   *Just Around the Corner*

Proper names are more important than generic names from one point of view, since man has always tended to bestow an individual name on something that he considers to have a personality. In the past a fighting man was quite likely to name his sword, because he looked upon it as a friend who helped him in times of trouble. Soldiers in the Second World War named their tanks and trenches in a similar way. Many modern car-owners bestow an individual name on their vehicles, and that by no means exhausts the possibilities of this personalised naming. One thinks of the characters in P. G. Wodehouse's *Buried Treasure* who name their moustaches, and of 'Tickler', the cane used by Mrs Joe Gargery on Pip in Dickens' *Great Expectations*. In rural areas local folk-tales can lead to the naming of individual trees, such as 'The Kissing Tree' which grows near the house of J. B. Priestley.

The 'name-print' theory

Linguists know that no two speakers of a language use the language in quite the same way. Because of where and when they were born they use one dialect or another; because of their educational, professional and social backgrounds they know and use different words, or use the same words in different ways. Every speaker of a language has a personal

dialect, an idiolect, which is like his linguistic fingerprint. Similarly, one can safely say that no two people know and use the same body of names. We have all what might be called an onomastic fingerprint, a 'name-print'.

This fact is sometimes exploited in general-knowledge tests. Candidates are shown a list of personal names, for example, and are asked to say whether the people concerned are engineers or writers, musicians, scientists or whatever. Properly applied, such a test can reveal very efficiently in which areas a candidate is well read, and how specialised his knowledge is.

An individual's 'name-print'—to use this playful term for a moment as shorthand for a highly complicated concept—is constantly changing. We hear a new song on the radio, see a new film, read a new book, and we add to our store of names or change the private meanings of old ones. We have no means of counting how many names a person knows at any one time, any more than we can count how many words he knows, but one's subjective impression is that whereas our store of words increases very slowly after the age of eighteen or so, we continue to add to our store of names at a steady rate all our lives. As we get older we are able to use our general vocabulary to talk of more and more specific entities—named entities. One wonders whether we reach a point where we know more names as such than words.

Here is a typical name-based quiz. Identify fully the literary characters whose unusual first names are listed below:

1 Hercule	5 Peregrine	8 Rawdon
2 Kimball	6 Pollyanna	9 Rhett
3 Lorna	7 Phileas	10 Robinson
4 Mycroft		

ANSWERS

1 Hercule Poirot in various Agatha Christie stories. 2 Kimball O'Hara in Rudyard Kipling's *Kim*. 3 Lorna Doone in R. D. Blackmore's novel of that name. 4 Mycroft Holmes, brother of Sherlock in the Conan Doyle stories about the great detective. 5 Peregrine Pickle in the novel of that name by Tobias Smollett. 6 Pollyanna Whittier in the Pollyanna stories by Eleanor H. Porter. 7 Phileas Fogg in Jules Verne's *Around the World in Eighty Days*. 8 Rawdon Crawley in William Thackeray's *Vanity Fair*. 9 Rhett Butler in Margaret Mitchell's *Gone With the Wind*. 10 Robinson Crusoe in Daniel Defoe's novel of that name.

Previous name studies

At first sight there appears to be general recognition of the importance of names because so much has been written about them. Elsdon C. Smith, in his excellent bibliography of works on personal names, listed nearly 3500 books and articles. That was in 1952, and he extends the list with newly published works and new 'discoveries' every year in *Names*, the journal of the American Name Society. An updated bibliography, *Personal Names and Naming*, compiled by Edwin D. Lawson, was published by Greenwood Press in 1987.

Geographical names have also received an enormous amount of attention, but there the matter virtually ends. It is possible to find the occasional books that deal with street names, house names, pub names, field names, ship names, pet names, nicknames, plant names, locomotive names and the like, but they are relatively few and far between. Details are given of as many as possible in the Bibliography at the end of this book.

What is serious about the situation is that statements about names, by writers on language and similar topics, invariably refer to personal and place names only or pay the merest lip-service to the existence of other nomenclatures. The position is thus very similar to the one that pertained 400 years ago in language studies, when it was only considered necessary to study seriously a handful of the world's languages. It was assumed that all other languages followed the same pattern as those few, and the then minor languages such as English were forced into a mould which was itself based on a misunderstanding.

Names—naming

As it happens, we cannot even claim that personal and place names have been thoroughly studied, in spite of the number of books about them. It is not just that a high proportion of those books are merely imitative, and often inaccurately so. Those studies which are sound and which make a real contribution to our knowledge are almost exclusively concerned with name origins. The psychology of naming has been made the subject of many short articles, but psychologists have on the whole left the field clear to the philologists.

A rare exception to this rule is *Nicknames: Their Origins and Social Consequences*, by Jane Morgan, Christopher O'Neill and Rom Harré, published in 1979 by Routledge and Kegan Paul. There is also a chatty book by Catherine Cameron called *The Name-Givers* (Prentice-Hall, 1983). But these two works are as nothing compared to the vast number of books on the subject published by philologists.

The result of this has been to give—in my own opinion—a totally wrong emphasis to name studies. The interpretation of philological data is obviously valuable for historians and the philologists themselves, but the interpretation of what the choice of names, for example, tells us about human thought processes would be equally valuable to scholars in many other fields.

To study the naming process one must have access to the namers as well as the names. The philologists have dominated name studies for so long that a myth seems to have grown up that only historically based name studies are academically respectable. We need to know about names *and* naming, just as when we study a language we need to know its vocabulary and its grammar. The one is virtually useless without the other.

The world of names

Because of the situation described above, our opening question: 'What's in a name?' can only be partly answered in this book. Just as an early cartographer, who wished to draw a map of the world, had very unevenly distributed information at his disposal, so a writer on the world of names is faced with an unbalanced situation. If a naming system is thought of as a country, then a few have been thoroughly explored and mapped—though in a specialist way. Others are almost virgin territories where one may wander for the first time. What follows must therefore be only a sketch-map at times—a first report. I hope that my traveller's tales will encourage others to visit these lands and fill in the details.

Any other name

'That which we call a rose', says Juliet, in Shakespeare's *Romeo and Juliet*, 'by any other name would smell as sweet.' Roses have hundreds of 'other names', as it happens, identifying the different varieties. I give below a personal selection of names taken from the useful publication *Find That Rose*, compiled by Angela Pawsey for the Rose Growers' Association.

Abundance	Black Lady	Cymbeline	Golden Promise	Lucetta	Rosy Cheeks
Ace of Hearts	Blesma Soul	Danse du Feu	Golden Showers	Maiden's Blush	Royal Romance
Adam	Blessings	Dapple Dawn	Golden Wings	Manuela	Royal Smile
Admired Miranda	Blue Moon	Dearest	Goldilocks	Margaret	Ruby Wedding
Agatha	Blue Peter	Deep Secret	Grandpa Dickson	Marlena	Satchmo
Agnes	Blush Damask	Dian	Grandpa's Delight	Martha	Saul
Air France	Bobbie Charlton	Dimples	Grouse	Mary	Scarletta
Albertine	Bonfire Night	Disco Dancer	Grumpy	Mary Rose	Schoolgirl
Alexander	Bonnie Scotland	Dopey	Gypsy Jewel	Masquerade	Scintillation
Alexia	Bonsoir	Doreen	Hannah	Maxima	Shepherd's Delight
Allgold	Boule de Neige	Double Delight	Happy Thoughts	Meg	Sherry
Aloha	Bountiful	Dreamgirl	Heaven Scent	Melinda	Shona
Alpine Sunset	Breath of Life	Dreaming Spires	Heidi	Mercedes	Silver Jubilee
Amanda	Bridal Pink	Dreamland	Helga	Mermaid	Silver Lining
Amberlight	Bright Smile	Easter Morning	Her Majesty	Message	Sleepy
Amelia	Buff Beauty	Eiffel Tower	Highlight	Michele	Smarty
Angela Rippon	Burning Love	Eleanor	Honeymoon	Mimi	Sneezy
Angelina	Busy Lizzie	Eminence	Hula Girl	Minnehaha	Soraya
Anna Ford	Butterfly Wings	Emma	Iceberg	Mischief	Stars 'n Stripes
Antonia	Can Can	English Holiday	Ilona	Monique	Stella
Apricot Brandy	Carefree Beauty	English Miss	Indian Sunblaze	Moon Maiden	Summer Wine
Apricot Silk	Carla	Eroica	Intrigue	My Valentine	Sun Blush
Apricot Sunblaze	Carmen	Escapade	Invitation	Nevada	Sunset Song
Ashwednesday	Carol	Ethel	Irish Mist	Nymphenburg	Sunsilk
Aunty Dora	Celeste	Evangeline	Irish Modesty	Oh La La	Super Star
Aurora	Celina	Evensong	Isabel	Oklahoma	Susan
Australian Gold	Cha Cha	Eyepaint	Jaquenetta	Olive	Sweet Promise
Autumn Fire	Chanelle	Fairy Prince	Jet Trail	Only You	Tallulah
Autumn Sunlight	Charmian	Father's Day	Jocelyn	Ophelia	Tatjana
Baby Darling	Cheerfulness	Felicia	Joy Bells	Orange Sensation	Tender Night
Baby Gold	Chicago Peace	Fervid	Just Joey	Orange Sunblaze	Thelma
Babylon	Chorus Girl	Fiona	Kathleen	Oriana	The Queen
Baby Masquerade	Cinderella	Fire Princess	Katie	Orient Express	Elizabeth
Ballerina	Claire	First Love	Kim	Peace	Thisbe
Baltimore Belle	Clarissa	Flora	King's Ransom	Peek A Boo	Topsi
Bashful	Cleo	Forever Amber	Lafter	Penelope	Tranquillity
Battle of Britain	Compassion	Forgotten Dreams	Laura	Perdita	Twinkles
Beautiful Britain	Congratulations	Fragrant Cloud	Lavinia	Piccadilly	Velvet Hour
Beauty Secret	Coral Dawn	Francesca	Leander	Pink Panther	Violette
Bees Frolic	Coralie	Frenzy	Leda	Polly	Wedding Day
Belle Amour	Coralin	Gabriella	Lilli Marlene	Prima Ballerina	Whisky Mac
Belle Blonde	Cordelia	Geraldine	Lindsey	Queenie	Yesterday
Black Beauty	Cornelia	Glenfiddich	Lovers Meeting	Rosina	

A lady who was flattered to have a rose named after her changed her mind when she saw the description of the rose in a gardener's catalogue. Against her name it said: 'shy in a bed but very vigorous against a wall.'

Naming the day

In theory every day of the year can be identified by the name of one of the saints allocated to it by the Roman Catholic Church. Use of such saints' names, however, is not always popular. One Anglican vicar who wrote to his bishop, heading the page 'St Timothy's Day', received a terse reply on a sheet headed 'Wash Day'.

In *The Egoist* George Meredith writes:

'There's a French philosopher who's for naming the days after the birthdays of French men of letters, Voltaire-day, Rousseau-day, Racine-day, and so on.'

'We might give alternative titles to the days, or have alternating days, devoted to our great families that performed meritorious deeds upon such a day.'

'Can we furnish sufficient?'

'A poet or two would help us.'

'Perhaps a statesman.'

'A pugilist, if wanted.'

'For blowy days . . . '

Meredith was no doubt referring to Auguste Comte, 1798–1857, the founder of Positivism. As part of his 'religion of humanity' Comte proposed dedicating the birthdays of those who had furthered the progress of human beings.

It would be an interesting exercise, no doubt, to name the days of the year along the lines proposed. We might also revive for our onomastic calendar some of the day-names that have been used in the past. I give a selection below, but have dealt more fully with nearly a thousand named days in *A Dictionary of Days* (Facts on File, 1988).

Admission day the day on which American states celebrate the anniversary of their admission to the Union.

Advent Sunday the first Sunday in Advent, ie 30 November or the Sunday nearest to it.

Alamo Day 6 March. The Mexicans slaughtered the defenders of Alamo Fort, Texas, in 1836. Amongst those killed was Davy Crockett, who had gone to help the Texans.

Alexandra Rose Day 26 June. Introduced by Queen Alexandra (1844–1925) in 1912 to celebrate her fiftieth year in England. The money collected goes to hospitals.

All Fools' Day 1 April. The traditional day for playing practical jokes.

All Hallow(s) Day 1 November. *All Saints' Day*.

Allhallowmass 1 November. *All Saints' Day*. 'We had kept Allhallowmass with roasting of skewered apples . . .' R. D. Blackmore, *Lorna Doone*.

All Saints' Day 1 November. Also known as *All Hallow(s) Day, Allhallowmass, Hallowmas*.

All Souls' Day 2 November. A day of prayer for the souls of all the departed.

Annunciation *Lady Day*.

Anzac Day 25 April. A holiday in Australia and New Zealand commemorating the landing of their troops in Gallipoli during the First World War.

Apple and Candle Night a local name for *Hallow-E'en*, eg in Swansea.

April Fools' Day 1 April. *All Fools' Day*.

Arbor Day a day on which trees are planted, usually observed in April in the USA.

Armistice Day 11 November. Commemorating the signing of the armistice in 1918 to end the First World War. In Britain it is now *Remembrance Day* (also in Canada). In the US it has become *Veterans Day* and is now associated with the Vietnam War.

Ascension Day the Thursday forty days after Easter, on which Jesus ascended to heaven.

Ash Wednesday the first day of Lent. Pope Gregory the Great sprinkled ashes on the heads of penitents on this day.

Assumption 15 August. Commemorating the death of the Virgin Mary.

August Bank Holiday in Britain the last Monday in August, formerly the first Monday.

Australia Day 26 January or the following Monday. Formerly *Anniversary Day, Foundation Day*.

Balaclava Day in military slang, formerly a term for pay-day.

Banian Day sometimes *Banyan Day*. A day on which no meat is eaten. Used, for example, in Jamaica, where it often becomes Ben Jonson's Day, and by sailors. The reference is to a Hindu sect.

Bastille Day 14 July. The bastille, or prison, in Paris was stormed by revolutionaries in 1789.

Battle of Britain Day 15 September.

Beltane one of the old Scottish quarter days, occurring on *May Day* (OS).

Binding Monday the day following *Low Sunday*, from the custom whereby women bound the men with ropes and demanded a forfeit before releasing them. The day following was *Binding Tuesday* when the men bound the women.

Black Friday applied variously to an examination day at school, the breaking up of the General Strike in 1926, and especially to 24 September 1869, when the Wall Street panic began.

Black Monday *Easter Monday*. Also the first Monday back at school after the holidays.

Blue Monday the Monday before Lent, when churches were decorated in blue. A later meaning was any Monday on which workmen preferred to drink rather than report for work.

Bonfire Night *Guy Fawkes' Day.*

Bounds Thursday *Ascension Day.* The parish bounds were traditionally traced on this day.

Boxing Day 26 December. Formerly the day on which Christmas boxes, containing money, were distributed among servants and tradesmen.

Bunker Hill Day 7 June. Also known as *Boston's Fourth of July.* Commemorating a famous battle in 1775.

Burns' Night 25 January. Scots honour their national poet, Robert Burns, 1759–96.

Bye Day an irregular and informal meet of hounds which is not mentioned on the hunt fixture card.

Cake Day 31 December. From the custom of giving children oatmeal cakes in Scotland.

Canada Day 1 July.

Candlemas Day 2 February. The feast of the purification of the Virgin Mary, celebrated with many candles in the churches.

Cantate Sunday *Rogation Sunday.* The introit for the day begins with the Latin word *Cantate,* 'sing'.

Care Sunday the fifth Sunday in Lent.

Carling Sunday *Care Sunday.* 'Carling' became the name for peas which were formerly eaten on this day.

Carnival Thursday the Thursday before *Shrove Tuesday.*

Childermas 28 December. Commemorates the slaughtering of the Holy Innocents by Herod.

Christmas Day 25 December.

Christmas Eve 24 December.

Circumcision 1 January.

Cobblers' Monday a Monday taken as a holiday. Cobblers were said to be unsure of which day to celebrate the feast of their patron saint, St Crispin. To be sure of not missing it, they celebrated it every Monday.

Collop Monday the Monday before *Shrove Tuesday,* the last day on which 'collops', or slices of meat, were eaten before Lent. Also known as *Shrove Monday.*

Columbus Day the second Monday in October, or 12 October. A US holiday commemorating the landing by Columbus in the Bahamas, 1492.

Commemoration Day at Oxford University, an annual celebration in memory of founders and benefactors.

Commonwealth Day 24 May originally, when it was known as *Empire Day.* Now second Monday in March.

Confederate Memorial Day celebrated on different days in various southern states of the US to commemorate the war dead.

Corpus Christi the Thursday after *Trinity Sunday.* The words are the Latin for 'body of Christ'.

Cussing Day formerly a dialectal name, eg in Somerset, for *Ash Wednesday.* Impenitent sinners were publicly cursed on this day.

Day of Atonement *Yom Kippur.*

D Day now the day on which any planned operation is due to begin. Originally 6 June 1944, when British, American, Canadian, French and Polish soldiers landed on the beaches of Normandy during the Second World War.

Decimal Day 15 February 1971. The day on which Britain changed to decimal currency.

Decoration Day same as *Memorial Day,* when graves are decorated with flowers.

Defenders' Day 12 September. A holiday in Maryland commemorating an unsuccessful attack on Baltimore by the British in 1812. It inspired Francis Scott Key to write the words of 'The Star-Spangled Banner'.

Derby Day the day in summer when the famous horse race is run on Epsom Downs in England, or when one of its namesakes is run in Kentucky, Santa Anita or elsewhere. Until 1891 the English Parliament adjourned on this day.

Devil's Night the night before *Hallow-E'en.* The term is used in Michigan and elsewhere, but

seems to be unknown in other parts of the US.

Dingaan's Day 16 December. A South African anniversary, now officially known as *Day of the Covenant.* It commemorates a victory in 1838 and is usually marked by sporting events.

Distaff's Day *Rock Day.*

Dog Days days between 3 July and 11 August, formerly considered to be the hottest and unhealthiest days of the year. The name links them to the heliacal rising of the Dog Star.

Dominion Day 1 July. An earlier name of *Canada Day.*

Easter Day *Easter Sunday.* 'Easter' derives from the name of a pagan goddess whose festival was celebrated at this time of the year.

Easter Monday the Monday following *Easter Day.* A day of parades, bonnets and the distribution of Easter eggs.

Easter Sunday *Easter Day.*

Egg Saturday the Saturday before *Shrove Tuesday,* when eggs were formerly eaten. The day following was also known as *Egg Sunday.*

Ember Days days of fasting appointed by the Council of Placentia (1095). They were the Wednesdays, Fridays and Saturdays following a) the first Sunday in Lent; b) Whitsunday; c) 14 September, d) 13 December. The four Fridays were called *Golden Fridays.*

Empire Day 24 May. This was Queen Victoria's birthday, which had been celebrated as a holiday for 60 years. After her death it became Empire Day, later *Commonwealth Day.*

Encaenia the day on which the anniversary of a church's dedication is celebrated.

Epiphany 6 January. From a Greek word basically meaning 'to show', with reference to the showing of the child Jesus to the Magi.

Fasten Tuesday a northern English name for *Shrove Tuesday.* The Monday is also known as *Fasten's E'en.*

Fat Monday the Monday before

Shrove Tuesday, which is known as *Mardi Gras*, 'Fat Tuesday' in eg New Orleans.

Father's Day UK: variable, usually early June. US: third Sunday in June.

Feast Day a saint's festival, eg that of the patron saint of a local church.

Feast of Stephen 26 December.

Field Day originally a day when troops were reviewed. Figuratively, a day of exciting events. In the US often a sports day at a school or college.

Fireworks Day *Guy Fawkes' Day*.

First Day *Sunday* for the Society of Friends, who wished to avoid references to pagan gods or objects of worship. *Monday* became *Second Day*, and so on.

Flag Day 14 June in the US, though the date may vary in some states. In Britain a general term for a day on which flags are sold to raise money for charity (*Tag Day* in the US).

Foundation Day a former name of *Australia Day*.

Founder's Day 29 May at the Royal Hospital in Chelsea, London. Applied to any day on which the founder of an institution such as a university is commemorated.

Fourth (of July) see *Independence Day*.

Fourth of June the birthday of George III and *Speech Day* at Eton College.

Frabjous Day a wonderful day, according to Lewis Carroll, in *Through The Looking Glass*.

Furry Day 8 May. 'Furry' is probably connected with 'fair'. A Cornish festival enlivened by dancing.

Gala Day in general terms, a day of local celebration. Also the occasion for a quip by Rufus T. Firefly (Groucho Marx) in *Duck Soup* when told that it was a gala day. 'A gal a day is enough for me. I don't think I can handle any more.'

Gang Monday the Monday in Rogation Week. 'Gang' means 'going', and refers to processions that took place. The same week had *Gang Tuesday* and *Gang Wednesday*.

Gaudy Day a day of celebration and relaxation at Oxford and Cambridge universities.

Glorious Twelfth 12 July. The day on which Orangemen celebrate the Battle of the Boyne.

Golden Friday see *Ember Days*.

Good Friday the Friday before *Easter Day*, the anniversary of Christ's death. 'Good' is used in the sense of 'holy'.

Gooding Day 21 December. A day when alms were collected.

Gowkie Day also *Gowkin' Day*. Scottish terms for *April Fools' Day*.

Grand Day an alternative for *Gaudy Day* in the Inns of Court.

Green Thursday *Maundy Thursday*.

Grey Cup Day mid-November. The Canadian football final between teams from east and west.

Groundhog Day *Candlemas*. The popular US legend is that if the groundhog (woodchuck) can see his shadow on this day, there will be six further weeks of winter.

Gule of August 1 August. The *Oxford English Dictionary* is unable to explain the origin of this ancient term.

Guy Fawkes' Day 5 November. In Britain the day on which Guy Fawkes' attempt to blow up the Houses of Parliament in 1605 is remembered with bonfires and fireworks.

Hallow-E'en 31 October. The eve of *All Hallows Day*. 'Hallow' means 'to make holy'.

Hallowmas *All Hallows Day*.

Handsel Monday the first Monday of the year, the day on which 'handsel', a gift or present which was meant to bring good luck, was given in Scotland.

Hock Monday the second Monday after Easter. Women bound the men with ropes and demanded payment to release them. 'Hock' is probably from a word meaning 'derision'.

Hock Tuesday the day following *Hock Monday*, when the men had their revenge on the women.

Hogmanay 31 December. The word is of disputed origin. Used mainly in Scotland.

Holy Cross Day 14 September.

Holy Innocents' Day *Childermas*.

Holy Rood Day *Holy Cross Day*.

Holy Thursday *Ascension Day*.

Hospital Day 12 May. Florence Nightingale's birthday. A day on which hospital rules are relaxed.

Huntigowk Day *April Fools' Day* in Scotland.

Inauguration Day 20 January following a presidential election in the US.

Independence Day 4 July. A US holiday, commemorating the adoption of the Declaration of Independence in 1776.

Ivy Day 9 October. An anniversary celebrated by some Irishmen related to the death of Charles Stuart Parnell.

Labor Day first Monday in September in the US.

Labour Day 1 May.

Lady Day 25 March. The Annunciation of the Virgin Mary. It is claimed that the British postal authorities once correctly delivered a letter addressed only to '25 March'. The recipient was a certain Lady Day, wife of a judge.

Laetare Sunday *Midlent Sunday*.

Lammas Day 1 August. Originally the 'loaf mass', at which the loaves made from the first ripe corn were consecrated.

League of Nations Day 10 January. Observed from 1920 to 1946.

Leap Day 29 February.

Lincoln's Birthday 12 February, or the first Monday in February. A public holiday in the US in honour of President Abraham Lincoln, 1809–65.

Long Friday *Good Friday*.

Love Day a day appointed for the settlement of disputes. Children born on such a day were sometimes named Loveday.

Low Sunday the Sunday following *Easter Day*.

Loyalty Day 1 May. US Veterans attempted to establish this title to combat what they saw as Communist propaganda disseminated on *May Day*.

Mad Thursday the Thursday before *Shrove Tuesday*.

M-Day a day when mobilisation is to begin. This is a military term similar to *D Day*.

Martinmas 11 November.

Maundy Thursday the Thursday before Easter. 'Maundy' is a 'mandate', or command, from the Latin version of John 13:34—'A new commandment I give you, that you love one another.' Originally princes washed the feet of poor people on this day. In Britain the king or queen distributes specially minted Maundy money.

May Day 1 May. The great rural festival of former times, now *Labour Day* in many countries.

Memorial Day the last Monday in May, or 30 May. A US holiday in memory of the war dead. Also called *Decoration Day*.

Michaelmas 29 September.

Midlent Sunday also known as *Mothering Sunday*.

Midsummer's Day 24 June.

Mothering Sunday originally the Sunday in the middle of Lent, now confused with *Mother's Day*.

Mother-in-Law Day 5 March. Initiated by the editor of a local newspaper in Amarillo, Texas, in 1934. It was observed by some families that year but does not seem to have caught on.

Mother's Day the second Sunday in May.

Nameday the feast day of the saint whose name one bears. Celebrated in many countries rather than the birthday.

Ne'er Day *New Year's Day*, Scottish.

Nettle Day *Oak-Apple Day*. In many parts of England children sting with nettles those who are not wearing a sprig of oak leaves.

New Year's Day 1 January.

New Year's Eve 31 December.

New Zealand Day 6 February.

Nickanan Night *Shrove Monday*, Cornish.

Nippy Lug Day Friday following Shrove Tuesday in parts of northern England. Children nip or pinch one another's ears.

No Smoking Day the custom of designating one day a year No Smoking Day appears to be taking hold in English-speaking countries.

Nut Monday the first Monday in August. A local British holiday.

Oak-Apple Day 29 May. The day on which Charles II was restored to the English throne. Oak-apples or oak leaves were worn to commemorate the incident when he hid in an oak tree to escape his pursuers (in 1651).

Open Day a day when members of the public can visit what is normally a closed institution.

Orange Day *Glorious Twelfth*.

Palm Sunday the Sunday before Easter. The palms in the church commemorate the palms strewn before Christ as he rode into Jerusalem.

Pan-American Day 14 April.

Pancake Day *Shrove Tuesday*.

Passion Sunday the fifth Sunday in Lent, the beginning of Passion Week.

Patriots' Day the third Monday in April. Celebrated in Maine and Massachusetts in commemoration of battles at Lexington and Concord in 1775.

Pentecost the seventh Sunday after Easter. 'Pentecost' is from Greek 'fiftieth (day)'.

Pinch-Bum Day *Oak-Apple Day*. A variant of the *Nettle Day* custom.

Plough Monday the first Monday after 6 January, the day on which farmers traditionally resumed their ploughing after the Christmas holiday.

President's Birthday *Washington's Birthday*.

Primrose Day 19 April. The anniversary of the death of Benjamin Disraeli, Earl of Beaconsfield. Queen Victoria sent a wreath of primroses, inscribed 'His favourite flower'.

Pulver Wednesday *Ash Wednesday*. From Latin *pulver* 'dust'.

Purification *Candlemas Day*.

Puss Sunday first Sunday in Lent. From Gaelic *pus* 'scowl'. In parts of Ireland unmarried people are thought to scowl on this day

because they feel sorry for themselves. Sometimes such people are marked with chalk on their backs.

Quasimodo Sunday *Low Sunday*. The introit for the day begins *Quasi modo geniti infantes*—'As newborn babes'.

Red Letter Day now any day of special significance. Originally a holy day marked on a church calendar in red.

Refreshment Sunday *Midlent Sunday*.

Remembrance Day 11 November. Formerly *Armistice Day*.

Rock Day 7 January. A 'rock' was another name for the distaff, the stick on which flax was wound when spinning.

Rogation Sunday the fifth Sunday after Easter, the beginning of Rogation Week. 'Rogation' is from a Latin word meaning 'to ask'.

Rood Day *Holy Cross Day*.

Rosh Hashanah the Jewish New Year's Day.

Royal Oak Day 29 May. See *Oak-Apple Day*.

Sabbath Day originally Saturday, now generally Sunday. Sabbath means 'rest'.

Sadie Hawkins Day 9 November, though now used of any day when the girls invite the boys to a dance. Introduced in the Li'l Abner strip cartoon in 1938 and now commonly celebrated in the US.

St Agnes' Eve 20 January. If young maidens fasted on this day they were said to dream of their future husbands. John Keats wrote his famous poem *The Eve of St Agnes* in 1819.

St Crispin's Day 25 October. The Battle of Agincourt was fought on this day in 1415, as Shakespeare reminds us in his *Henry V*.

St David's Day 1 March. Welshmen wear leeks to proclaim their nationality and honour their patron saint.

St Distaff's Day 7 January. The day on which the distaff side of the family, the women (who used distaffs for their spinning), resumed work after the Christmas holiday.

St George's Day 23 April. The feast of the patron saint of England.

St Lubbock's Day at one time a slang expression in England for a Bank Holiday. The reference was to Sir John Lubbock, whose Bank Holiday Act was passed on 25 May 1871.

St Patrick's Day 17 March. Irishmen wear the shamrock, a plant with trifoliate leaves which St Patrick used to illustrate the Trinity, and which became the national emblem of Ireland.

St Pompion's Day also *St Pumpkin's Day, Thanksgiving Day*. 'Pompion' was an earlier form of the word 'pumpkin'. Pumpkin pie is invariably eaten on this day.

St Swithin's Day 15 July. Ancient lore says that it will rain for forty days if it rains on this day.

St Valentine's Day 14 February. The day of the 'immortal go-between', as Charles Lamb called him. The modern custom of sending Valentine cards dates from the early nineteenth century, but there were much earlier traditions which involved drawing the name of a sweetheart by lot on this day.

Salad Days days of youthful inexperience.

Seventh Day Saturday for the Quakers, Seventh Day Adventists, etc.

Sheer Thursday *Maundy Thursday*. The 'sheer' means 'to shine', though early commentators thought that clergymen were meant to shear their hair on this day.

Shrove Tuesday the day before *Ash Wednesday*, or the beginning of Lent. The three days before Lent began are known as Shrovetide,

because people were 'shriven'—they confessed their sins and were absolved.

Simnel Sunday *Mothering Sunday*. Simnel cakes were traditionally eaten on this day.

Speech Day a day when prizes are distributed at a school or college after speeches by dignitaries.

Sports Day another day in the school calendar, normally near the end of the summer term, set aside for sporting events.

Spring Holiday an official British description of the holiday taken on 1 May or the first Monday following.

Spy Wednesday the Wednesday before Easter, the reference being to Judas. An Irish expression.

Still Days between Maundy Thursday and Easter Day, when bells were not rung.

Tag Day the US term for *Flag Day* in Britain.

Thanksgiving Day the fourth Thursday in November (USA) or second Monday in October (Canada). A holiday on which thanks are given for divine goodness.

Thanksgobble Day *Thanksgiving Day*. A humorous American reference to the turkeys consumed at Thanksgiving.

Three Kings' Day *Epiphany*.

Today Day 'This very day' in Jamaica.

Trafalgar Day 21 October. Commemorating Lord Nelson and the Battle of Trafalgar, 1805.

Trick or Treat Night *Hallow-E'en*.

Trinity Sunday the Sunday following *Whit Sunday*.

Turkey Day *Thanksgiving Day*. Not an official term, but much used by radio/tv commentators.

Twelfth see *Glorious Twelfth*. The reference is sometimes to 12 August, the opening of the

grouse-shooting season.

Twelfth Night 6 January. Formerly the day on which the pastrycooks excelled themselves with their fancy cakes, displaying them in their shop windows. Gentlemen who gathered to look at the displays were likely to have their coat-tails nailed to the shop-front, a traditional sport for boys on this day.

Tynwald Day 5 July. A day of celebration on the Isle of Man.

Union Day 31 May. Celebrated in South Africa.

Up Helly A' the last day of Yule, or *Twelfth Night*. Celebrated in the Shetlands.

Valentine's Day *St Valentine's Day*.

VE Day 8 May 1945. The day on which the Allies accepted Germany's surrender in the Second World War.

Veterans Day *Remembrance Day*.

Victoria Day *Empire Day*.

VJ Day 15 August 1945 (US 2 September). The day on which the Japanese surrendered to the Allies, bringing to an end the Second World War.

Waterloo Day 18 June. Commemorating the Battle of Waterloo in 1815.

Washington's Birthday the third Monday in February, or 22 February. A US holiday in honour of President George Washington, 1732–99.

Whit Monday the seventh Monday after Easter. 'Whit' is 'white'.

Whit Sunday the seventh Sunday after Easter.

Wrong Day usually mid-July. A time of celebration in the town of Wright, Minnesota.

Xmas Day *Christmas Day*. The 'X' represents the Greek letter *chi*.

Yom Kippur the Hebrew 'day of atonement' observed on the tenth day of Tishri.

Days which are special for one reason or another continue to be named. A few more recent examples are listed below:

Big Bang Day 27 October 1986. This was a day of significant change at the London Stock Exchange, marking amongst other things the

end of fixed commissions on stock exchange transactions. The financial centres often name particular days. **Contango Day**,

which probably corrupts **Continuation Day,** is an established term in London.

Comic Relief Day 5 February 1988.

Less formally known as **Red Nose Day**. This was a day of fund raising for charities where light entertainers donated their services on radio and television, while people in pubs and clubs throughout Britain told jokes in order to raise money. Plastic red noses were also sold and were worn at many a fund-raising event.

Super Tuesday 9 March 1988. The day on which primary elections took place in fourteen Southern and border states, as well as in six other states, in the run up to the election of the new American president. It was originally an attempt to give the 'South' a coherent say in national politics.

Personal-name words

Amp the usual form of *ampère*, from the name of André Ampère, 1775–1836, a French scientist.

Aphrodisiac from the name of the goddess of love, Aphrodite.

Atlas In Greek mythology Atlas was made to support the heavens on his shoulders. A 16th-century map-book showed him supporting the globe on its cover, and caused his name to be transferred.

Bakelite Synthetic resin invented by Leo Hendrik Baekland, 1863–1944, a Flemish chemist.

Begonia in honour of Michel Bégon, 1638–1710, a Frenchman known for his patronage of science.

Bloomers associated with Mrs Amelia Bloomer, 1818–1914, who wrote and lectured on women's rights.

Bobby Robert Peel, 1778–1850, was Home Secretary when the Metropolitan Police Act was passed in 1828.

Bowdlerise from the name of Dr Thomas Bowdler, 1754–1825, who edited (some would say vandalised) Shakespeare so that the poet could 'with propriety be read aloud in a family'.

Boycott The Irish Land League treated Charles Boycott in this way in 1880.

Braille the system of raised-point writing for the blind was invented by Louis Braille, 1809–52, himself blind from the age of three.

Caesarian Julius Caesar is usually said to have been born by means of what we now call a 'caesarian operation'. His name derived from a word meaning 'cut'.

Cardigan from the name of James Thomas Brudenell, 1797–1868, the seventh earl of Cardigan, who led the famous charge of the Light Brigade at Balaclava in 1854.

Casanova Giovanni Jacopo Casanova de Seingalt, 1725–98, an Italian adventurer was the original philanderer.

Cereal from Ceres, an Italian goddess of agriculture.

Chauvinistic Nicolas Chauvin of Rochefort was exaggeratedly loyal to Napoleon's France.

Collie probably from Colin, a popular first name in Scotland where these dogs originated.

Colt a pistol patented by Samuel Colt in 1835.

Cretin a Swiss dialect form of Christian, and therefore derived from Christ.

Dahlia Anders Dahl was a Swedish botanist in the 18th century. The flower was discovered in Mexico by Humboldt and named in Dahl's honour.

Dandy a form of Andrew.

Diddle Jeremy Diddler is a character in *Raising the Wind* (1803) by James Kenney. He is a cheat and swindler.

Diesel After its inventor Rudolf Diesel, 1858–1913, a German.

Eroticism from Eros, name of the Greek god of love.

Fuchsia for Leonhard Fuchs, 1501–66, a German botanist.

Gardenia for Dr Alexander Garden, Vice-President of the Royal Society, who died in 1791.

Guillotine invented by Joseph Guillotin, 1738–1814, a French doctor. His surname ultimately derives from Guillaume 'William'.

Guy from Guy Fawkes, whose first name appears in many European languages and may derive from 'wood, forest'.

Hooligan probably derived from an Irish family who lived in Southwark, London, actually named Houlihan.

Jacket from French jaquette, 'peasant's coat'. Peasants were often addressed as Jacques, the popular form of Jacob, regardless of their true names.

Jemmy pet form of James.

Jockey from Jock, northern form of Jack.

Jovial based on the name of the god Jove.

Lynch either from Lynch's law, after Charles Lynch, 1736–96, who presided over unofficial courts in Virginia, or from Lynch's Creek in South Carolina where groups of unofficial law-enforcers gathered.

Mackintosh patented in 1823 by Charles Mackintosh ('son of the chieftain').

Magpie the 'mag' is ultimately from Margaret and was added to the name of the bird.

Marionette a little Marian or puppet, ultimately from Maria.

Maverick Samuel Maverick neglected to brand his cattle. A maverick became a 'rover or stray', applied metaphorically to people as well as cattle.

Mesmerise Franz Anton Mesmer, 1734–1815, an Austrian physician, pioneered this early form of hypnotism, based on a false theory of animal magnetism.

Nicotine Jacques Nicot took some tobacco plants back to France in 1561. Nicot ultimately derives from Nicholas.

Ohm for Georg Simon Ohm, 1787–1854, a German physicist.

Pasteurise a method of sterilising milk, discovered by Louis

Pasteur, 1822–95.

Platonic from the name of the Greek philosopher, Plato.

Saxophone invented by a Belgian named Adolphe Sax, about 1840.

Silhouette originally a portrait rapidly traced on a wall, following a person's shadow. Satirically applied to Etienne de Silhouette, French Minister of Finance in 1759.

Teddy bear alluding to Theodore (Teddy) Roosevelt, 1859–1919, a great bear-hunter in his spare time.

Trilby ultimately from the name of George du Maurier's fictional heroine Trilby in the novel of that name.

Volt from the name of the Italian physicist Count Alessandro Volta, 1745–1827.

Wellingtons named in 1817 after the Duke of Wellington.

Yankee probably from Jan (John) Kes, referring to the original Dutch inhabitants of New York.

Place-name words

Airedale the breed of terrier, a cross between the Otterhound and a black and tan, was bred in the 19th century in the Airedale region of Yorkshire. 'Dale' is a mainly northern English word for 'valley'.

Angora the name of a fabric made from the long silky hair of the angora goat or rabbit. Angora wool is a mixture of sheep's wool and angora rabbit hair. Angora is now known as Ankara, the capital of Turkey.

Attic the name of the room under the roof of a house relates it to the Attic Order of architecture. The original reference was to a small decorative structure on top of a main facade. It was then transferred to the space enclosed by such a structure. Attic means 'of Attica, or its capital Athens'. The phrase 'Attic wit' or 'salt' refers to the refined, elegant wit for which the Athenians were once famous.

Badminton the game was popularised by the Duke of Beaufort at Badminton Hall, Great Badminton, Gloucestershire. At one time badminton was also well known as the name of a drink, claret and soda water, served by the Duke to his sporting guests.

Balaclava the woollen headgear which also covers the ears, neck and chin takes its name from a small port in the Crimea, near Sebastopol. The balaclava 'helmet', as it was originally known, was developed to help British soldiers during the Crimean War, which continued through two very severe winters.

Bunkum in the sense of 'nonsense' or 'humbug' derives from Buncombe County, North Carolina. In 1820 a politician who was making an irrelevant speech was frequently challenged. He explained that he was speaking not so much to Congress as to the people of Buncombe, who had elected him.

Canary the songbird is native to the Canary Islands in the Atlantic. The place name, however, derives from Latin *canis* 'dog'—a reference to the large dogs discovered there by the Romans. The canary drunk by Falstaff in the Shakespeare plays was a dry white wine which came from the Canaries.

Duffel the coarse woollen cloth used to make duffel coats, extensively worn by servicemen during World War Two. The cloth was originally manufactured at Duffel, in Belgium, some ten miles from Antwerp.

Gauze light transparent material originally made at Gaza in Palestine. Samson was blinded at Gaza, according to *Judges* 16:4, and pulled down the temple of Dagon, killing himself and 3000 Philistines. Aldous Huxley made use of Milton's *Eyeless in Gaza* phrase to name one of his novels.

Guinea the name of a gold coin last minted in 1813, though the term continued in use long afterwards to denote a value of 21 shillings. The gold came from the Guinea Coast of West Africa. Guinea pigs are native to Brazil not Africa. Professor Weekley surmised that they were introduced to England by sailors known as Guineamen. Their triangular voyages involved taking trade goods to the Guinea Coast, slaves from Africa to South America, other cargoes back to England.

Havana the capital of Cuba, famous for its tobacco industry and the high-quality cigars which are known as havanas.

Jodhpurs riding breeches, close-fitting from knees to ankles, designed for a Maharajah of Jodhpur in the 19th century. Jodhpur is the name of both a state and its capital city in India.

Lesbian the Greek island of Lesbos was the birthplace of Sappho, seventh century BC, a famous poetess who was later the centre of a female literary society. The sexual preferences attributed to Sappho and her followers led to lesbianism and associated words.

Milliner originally a Milan merchant, the city in northern Italy at one time being the centre of the fashion industry.

Rugby the version of football introduced in 1823 by William Webb Ellis, then a pupil at Rugby public school in Warwickshire. He picked up the ball towards the end of a frustratingly drawn game.

Serendipity coined by Horace Walpole in 1754 to mean 'the faculty of making pleasant unexpected discoveries by accident'. Serendip was an ancient name of Sri Lanka (Ceylon).

Number Names

IF WE say that there are seven days in a week we are using the number seven and are concerned with quantity. If we decide to identify the days in the week by calling them One, Two, Three, Four, Five, Six and Seven, then each of these becomes a number name.

Number names are a kind of free-floating set of names that can be used in any of the thousand and one nomenclatures that need to be established temporarily or permanently. There is a strong prejudice against using them for anything that has human connections, and some people feel insulted if they are identified in this way. Yet number names are probably the most efficient we have, with many advantages over other kinds of name. For instance:

a number name positively identifies a unique entity—natural duplication and transfer do not arise within a given nomenclature;

number names have a highly convenient shorthand form which is recognised internationally;

they are usefully descriptive, often, in the sequential information they give about what is being named;

they follow a regular, simple pattern of formation which is readily understood.

The computer that once calculated my pay knows me as 1199062. I was quite happy to acknowledge that particular pseudonym—or 'numbernym', as I should perhaps call it. That is not to say that I would like to be identified, on the cover of this book, for instance, as 1199062. For all its imperfections, the name that I bear because of parental whim and historical accident seems more appropriate, but that is only due to social convention. Noel Coward indicated the way things could go. When Lawrence of Arabia became an airman, Coward wrote him a letter which began 'Dear 338171, or may I call you 338 . . . .'.

The full advantages of number names can be demonstrated by substitution. It is a convention that we identify the pages of a book by number names. When a different kind of name is substituted, we realise what we have lost. This page I have called George, in honour of my father, but if I were to name every page in honour of relations and friends, much as that might please them, where would it leave my readers? Imagine being asked to refer to page Ethel or Nicole. Alphabetical order would help, but that would still be clumsy compared to numerical sequence.

This example is meant to seem absurd, but the fact is that in an average town we tolerate a system of street names that is even more ridiculous. A few street names give vague help in locating the streets concerned, as when all the streets named after poets or admirals are grouped on the same estate, but one might argue that this is only a help to a minority of well-educated people. We could probably change all that and devise number name systems that would effectively relate streets to each other in any given town, but we will not do it, of course. Nor are we likely to interfere with the charmingly haphazard situation that exists with our first names and surnames, our place names and trade names. We will allow simple efficiency to reign only in unimportant nomenclatures, such as the pages of a book. Number names will no doubt continue to be the norm in that context, but remember that you did once read a page named George.

I said I would call her Octavia. Both of them seemed to approve, although they said she wasn't my eighth at all, and ought to be called Prima, though that wasn't so pretty: one might as well call her Ultima, poor child, and have done with it.

Margaret Drabble   *The Millstone*

INTRODUCTION 21

Invented names

Journalists have long been in the habit of amusing themselves and their readers by inventing personal names. Sometimes the jokes are visual, as in a name like *C. A. Boose*. Initials are popular, leading to names like *M. T. Head*. Social and professional titles may help the name along: *Miss Fitt, Miss Print, Miss Trust*; *Sir Parr Stitt, Sir Tenly Knotte, Sir Vere de Pression, Sir Taxe*. We read of the clergyman who is a *Canon Ball*, the soldier who is a *Private Part*, and so on. Even academic letters after a name have been brought into the fold, to create a *Reverend Fiddle D. D.*

The names listed below are mostly phonetic puns and make use of first names that have not been invented for the occasion. Most of the examples are the inventions of writers, a few have been borne by real people whose parents were determined to display their sense of humour at all cost.

Aaron C. Rescue	Dinah Mite	Honor Bright	Lynn C. Doyle	Poppy Cox
Adam Swindler	Don Key	Hope N. Prey	Marius Quick	Ray Gunn
Agnes Day	Doris Shutt	Horace Cope	Mark Well	Reg Oyce
Al E. Gater	Doug Pitts	Hugh Raye	Martin Gale	Rex Cars
Alf A. Bett	Douglas Firr	Ida Down	Mary Christmas	Rhoda Camel
Amanda Lynn	Drew A. Head	Igor Beaver	Matt Adhoor	Rick O'Shea
Amelia Rate	Duane Pipe	Ima Hogg	Maud Lynne	Robyn Banks
Ames Hyer	Dustin Downe	Iona Mink	Max E. Mumm	Rose Dew
Anita Room	Earl E. Bird	Iris Tugh	May B. Dunn	Rosetta Stone
Ann Cuff	Eileen Dover	Isabel Tolling	Mel N. Colley	Rosie Bottom
Annie Seed	Ella Vater	Isla White	Melody Lingerson	Ruby Port
April N. Paris	Emma Nate	Ivor Headache	Mercy Lord	Russ Tinayle
Arty Fischel	Erna Living	Jack Pott	Mike Howe	Sally Forth
Barry D. Hatchett	Ernest N. Devour	Jay Walker	Miles A. Head	Salome Downe
Bea Holden	Esther Bunny	Jean Jerale	Minnie Buss	Sandy Beech
Bell E. Acres	Etta Carrott	Jerry Bilder	Moira Less	Sara Endipity
Ben Dover	Eva Brick	Jim Nasium	Molly Coddle	Sarah Nader
Bennie Factor	Evan Keel	Joan Novak	Mona Lott	Scarlett Feaver
Bess Toff	Faye Sake	Joe King	Moses Law	Sean Locks
Beverly Hills	Felix Cited	Joy Rider	Mustapha Fixe	Serge A. Head
Bill A. Dew	Ford Carr	Jules N. Gold	Nat E. Dresser	Shirley U. Care
Bing O. Winner	Frank N. Stein	Justin Thyme	Neil N. Prey	Sonny Enbright
Blaise A. Weigh	Freda Slaves	Kay Oss	Nick O. Teen	Stan Dupp
Bonnie Scotland	Gail Blows	Ken Tuckie	Noah Zark	Sue E. Seidl
Bunny Warren	Gay Cavalier	Kirsten Swore	Nora Bone	Tanya Hyde
Caesar High	Gerry Atrick	Kitty Hawk	Olive Green	Teddy Bear
Candy Kane	Gladys Canby	Lance Boyle	Oliver D. Place	Titus Zell
Carole Singer	Gilda Lily	Laura Norder	Ophelia Legge	Tom Katz
Celia Later	Gloria Mundy	Lee Vitoff	Orson Buggy	Tommy Gunn
Cherry Blossom	Gottfried Atlast	Leighton Early	Otis Goode	Topsy Turvey
Chester Minit	Gustave Wind	Lena Ginster	Owen Moore	Troy Waite
Chris Cross	Haile Delighted	Lettice Prey	Paddy Fields	Tudor Pyne
Claud N. Scratcht	Hank E. Panky	Levy Tate	Pat Ernal	Upton O. Goode
Cliff Hanger	Hans Zoffer	Libby Doe	Patty Cake	Valentine Card
Constance Noring	Hazel Twigg	Lionel Rohr	Paul Bearer	Victoria Falls
Coral Ireland	Hedda Hare	Lisa Wake	Pearl E. Handle	Wade Moore
Crystal Ball	Heidi High	Lois Price	Penny Nichols	Walter Loo
Dan D. Lion	Helen Hywater	Lori Driver	Persis Fuller	Wanda Toofar
Dawn O'Day	Herbie Hind	Lorne Mowers	Peter Owt	Warren Peace
Delia Cards	Hiram Young	Lotta People	Phil Landers	Will Power
Diane Decay	Holly Wood	Louis Dorr	Piers Inside	Willie Nilly
Dick Tate	Honey Potts	Luke Warm	Polly C. Holder	Yul B. Allwright

Converted names

The names listed below have all been officially bestowed as first names. One or two of them may be accidental mis-spellings (eg Murder for the Scottish Murdo); others may be transferred family names. Most are clearly *ad hoc* conversions from words to first name status.

Admiral	Crocus	Halcyon	Medium	Rice
Alias	Danke	Handy	Meek	Rosebud
Almond	Dark	Happy	Memory	Saffron
Alpha	Despair	Helm	Midsummer	Sapphire
Amorous	Diamond	Heron	Mimosa	Savannah
Anchor	Doctor	Home	Mine	Senior
Angel	Dolphin	Hymen	Mister	Sergeant
Anon	Duke	Ivory	Murder	Sham
Apple	Dusty	Jade	Mystic	Shared
Aria	Ebony	Jeans	Nova	Shed
Ark	Elder	Jewel	Oak	Silver
Arrow	Elderberry	Joie	Ocean	Silvery
Autumn	Elm	Jolly	Omega	Sir
Baby	Emit	Junior	Only	Slim
Berry	Energetic	Just	Orange	Smart
Beta	Esquire	Kaiser	Other	Snowdrop
Blossom	Evangelist	Khaki	Owner	Sonny
Blue	Fairly	Laddie	Peace	Squire
Bold	Farewell	Lady	Pepper	Star
Bonus	Fateful	Last	Pheasants	Stranger
Boy	Feather	Lavender	Pickles	Sunny
Brained	Fiancé	Liberty	Pinkie	Sunshine
Bridge	Free	Lilac	Pleasant	Swift
Briton	Freedom	Little	President	Syren
Buster	Friar	Lord	Princess	Tempest
Butter	Friend	Lovey	Quaver	Thistle
Captain	Gem	Low	Queen	Thorn
Charisma	General	Lucky	Rabbi	Treasure
Colonel	Gentle	Ma	Rainbow	True
Coma	Gipsy	Magnet	Rainy	Vale
Corky	Gladness	Major	Ramble	Vest
Corona	Glory	Maudlin	Raper	Virgin
Coy	Golden	Mayday	Raven	Worthy

Miss Pleasant Riderhood is a character in *Our Mutual Friend*, by Charles Dickens.

'Possessed of what is colloquially termed a swivel eye—she was otherwise not positively ill-looking, though anxious, meagre, of a muddy complexion, and looking twice as old again as she really was.'

'Why christened Pleasant, the late Mrs Riderhood might possibly have been able at some time to explain, and possibly not. Her daughter had no information on that point. Pleasant she found herself, and she couldn't help it. She had not been consulted on the question.'

What's Your Name?

'What's your name?' 'Nothing.' 'Nonsense!' retorted Quilp. 'What does your mistress call you when she wants you?' 'A little devil,' said the child.
Charles Dickens   *The Old Curiosity Shop*

Ferdinand: I do beseech you, chiefly that I may set it in my prayers, What is your name?
William Shakespeare   *The Tempest*

'And who might you be?' Yapp hesitated. He disliked being addressed so arrogantly.
Tom Sharpe   *Ancestral Vices*

'Now then, little man, and what may *your* name be?'
Hugh Maclennan   *The Watch that Ends the Night*

'I missed your name,' he said. Woermer paused. Was he meant to reply 'I didn't throw it' or something like that.
Tobias Wolff   *Ugly Rumours*

'What is your name? or what do they call you? – as North-country people would express it?'
Elizabeth Gaskell   *Wives and Daughters*

'I don't think I heard your name.' 'Horton,' said Ernest. 'Ernest Horton.' Mr Pritchard had a whole series of tactics for getting on with people. He never forgot the name of a man richer or more powerful than he, and he never knew the name of a man less powerful. He had found that to make a man mention his own name would put that man at a slight disadvantage. For a man to speak his own name made him a little naked and unprotected.
John Steinbeck   *The Wayward Bus*

'Might I be permitted to inscribe your name upon the tablets of my memory?' I asked.
Charles Dickens   *Bill-Sticking*

'How are you called?'
Ernest Hemingway   *The Sun Also Rises*

'We don't even know each other's names,' she remarked. 'Yours is the prettiest name in the world.' 'How do you know?' 'It must be – anyhow.' 'It *is* rather pretty, you know. It's Christabel.'
H. G. Wells   *The History of Mr Polly*

'I've a little bit of a message to deliver you from myself.' 'And may I beg to know who yourself is?'
Richard Cumberland   *The West Indian*

'You never heard my name before?' 'Never, and what is more, I do not think I know what it is now: I suppose I did not listen very attentively, but I do not think I caught it.' 'You talk as if it were a disease.'
Rhoda Broughton   *Nancy*

'As for your name – I am too discreet a *galantuomo* to ask. And, in any case, what *does* it matter? A rose by any other name . . .' 'But as a matter of fact,' she said, 'my name does happen to be Rose; or, at any rate, Rosie.'
Aldous Huxley   *Antic Hay*

'Friends should know each other's names. What is yours, pray?' 'Francis Goodman. But those who love me call me Frank. And yours?' 'Charles Arnold Noble. But do you call me Charlie.' 'I will, Charlie; nothing like preserving in manhood the fraternal familiarities of youth.'
Herman Melville   *The Confidence Man*

'Sir,' said Adams, 'may I crave the favour of your name?'
Henry Fielding   *Joseph Andrews*

'Please to favour me with your names, gentlemen.'
George Colman & David Garrick   *The Clandestine Marriage*

'Please kindly identify yourself.'
Bernard Malamud   *The Fixer*

Bottom: I beseech your worship's name.
William Shakespeare   *A Midsummer Night's Dream*

'It would be a convenience if we knew your name.'
Nathaniel Hawthorne   *The Blithedale Romance*

'*Your* name now will be – ?' 'Richard Carstone.'
Charles Dickens   *Bleak House*

'Hello,' he said, leaving a perceptible gap where her name might have fitted.
Kingsley Amis   *Girl 20*

'Well, well, come on – now we're friends – what's the darling little name?'
Sinclair Lewis   *Babbitt*

'Miss Francom. And Mr-er, Mr . . .' 'Julian Cohn,' he said. 'Ah, yes, of course.' It had been beautifully done again, but this time it had grated. Rex was certain de Fleury had known Cohn's name – he'd caught it the first time when Cohn had introduced himself, and he hadn't forgotten. It had been a tiny insult, but precisely calculated.
William Haggard   *The High Wire*

'Now – your name?' 'Front name or back name?'
Catherine Marshall   *Christy*

'What's your name?' 'Silas Wegg . . . I don't know why Silas, and I don't know why Wegg.'
Charles Dickens   *Our Mutual Friend*

2
FIRST NAMES FIRST

IT SEEMS to be a universal habit, and one as old as language itself, for human beings to name one another. The regular pattern today among the English-speaking peoples is for a child to be given at least two names at birth, a *first name* and a *middle name*. Of these the first name is normally by far the more important, and not just because it is the descendant of the original single personal name with which our remote ancestors were content. It is our first name that most of us will respond to throughout our lives and come to look upon as part of ourselves. It is therefore natural for us to ask such questions as:

where did our first names come from?

what did they originally mean?

which names do we make most use of today?

why do parents choose one name rather than another?

how should we ourselves choose a name for a child if we are given that responsibility?

What is a first name?

We shall be attempting to answer all the above questions in the next three chapters, but the apparently simple question: 'What is a name?' becomes surprisingly complicated when we come to the **Catherine/Katharine** kind of problem. Are we to treat such spelling variants as one name, or should we separate out each variant and refer to it as a new name? There is also the matter of diminutives. As everyone knows, names like **Margaret** have given rise to pet forms such as **Madge, Peggy, Greta, Maisie** and the like. Should all these be considered as separate names?

As we begin to answer such questions we see the widely differing viewpoints of the historically-based names student and the student who is more interested in the sociological and psychological aspects of names. For the etymologist Catherine and Katharine were originally the same name, as were Margaret and all its diminutive forms. Since he is concerned with origins, the etymologist takes all forms of a name in his stride provided he can explain why they occur.

But from another point of view the change of a single letter in a name is quite enough to differentiate it from all others. No one would convince a **Francis** that his name was the same as **Frances,** although an etymologist would be justified in bracketing them together. My own etymological training is instantly forgotten when someone writes my name as **Lesley** rather than **Leslie.** I do not easily forgive those who change my sex with careless orthographic surgery. The change from **Stephen,** say, to **Steven** may appear to inflict less damage, but no doubt those who bear one form of the name object to being given the other.

In cases such as **Tracy/Tracey** I find it hard to believe that parents are thinking of two names and carefully choosing between them. In my view they are choosing *a* name which happens to have genuinely variant spellings. I believe, therefore, that a modern researcher must fall back on his instinct as a native speaker and weigh up the relative importance of etymological, phonetic and orthographic factors. He must then decide in each case whether he is dealing with one or more names.

I once heard a father tell a registrar what name he wanted to give his daughter. He then surprised both the registrar and me by writing the name down as **Evon.** But it was the father who was surprised, not to say incredulous, when the registrar pointed out that the name was usually spelt **Yvonne.** He insisted on spelling it his way. All of us were thinking, it seems to me, of the same name, which is why I would personally bracket these two widely differing spellings as one name. I would also treat **Laurence** and **Lawrence** as one, though I admit that when another registrar recorded my son's name in the latter form my instinctive reaction was to tell her that she had written down the wrong name.

A single first name, then, like some words, can

occasionally have more than one 'official' spelling: perhaps because it started out in one language and eventually came to English-speakers both in its original form and in that of another language; perhaps because two or more forms of it were fossilised at a time when spelling was by no means standardised; perhaps because it is a new name that has not yet settled into one spelling; perhaps because some parents think that a different spelling will add a touch of novelty; perhaps because of a parent's or registrar's ignorance. In the following chapters I shall be grouping names by their main spellings, indicating variations only when opinion seems to be genuinely divided.

As for diminutives, it is clear that they eventually reach a point where they achieve full name status in their own right. If a girl is given the name **Elizabeth,** but her family and friends subsequently come to call her **Betty,** we could describe Betty as a link nickname.

But since the end of the 18th century, many pet names have been officially bestowed as if they were separate names. In some cases the names really have taken on a life of their own. It is no longer true to say that **Sally,** for example, is simply the pet form of **Sarah,** though that is how the name came into being. **Betty** is also frequently given as a name and must therefore be treated separately on those occasions.

Jacqueline has been a popular name in recent times, but many parents find it difficult to spell. Below are some of the ways in which it has been officially recorded on birth certificates. Should each spelling be treated as a separate name, or is it right to say that all the forms are variants of the same name?

Jacalyn, Jackalin, Jackaline, Jaclyn, Jaclynn, Jacolyn, Jacqualine, Jacqualyn, Jacqualynn, Jacquelean, Jacquelene, Jacquelin, Jacqueline, Jacquelyn, Jacquelyne, Jacquelynn, Jacquiline, Jacquline, Jacqulynn, Jaculine, Jakelyn, Jaqueline, Jaquelline.

Origins of first names

Sally and **Betty** represent developments of older names, but how did the older names come into being in the first place? We can usefully establish several different categories: the names began either as descriptions, or converted phrases, or they were inventions. They were formed by linking in some way to an existing name, or they were transferred from another naming system.

Let us look at each of those categories in turn and consider some examples:

Descriptive names include generic descriptions such as **Charles,** 'a man', **Thomas,** 'a twin', and direct descriptions such as **Adam,** 'of red complexion', **Algernon,** 'with whiskers or moustaches', **Crispin,** 'with curled hair', **Cecil,** 'blind'. Activity descriptions occur, such as **George,** 'a farmer', as do provenance descriptions: **Francis,** 'Frenchman'.

Sequential description led to names like **Septimus,** 'seventh', and **Decimus,** 'tenth'. **Original** and **Una** probably came into being as descriptions of first children, and **Natalie** and **Noël** were certainly temporal descriptions for children born or baptised on Christmas Day. Many names may have been either morally descriptive—**Agnes,** 'pure', **Agatha,** 'good'— or were commendatory conversions.

Converted names include those which seem to have reflected parental reaction to the birth. **Abigail,** 'father rejoiced', is an instance, as are **Benedict,** 'blessed', **Amy,** 'loved'. Commendatory conversions such as **Felicity** and **Prudence** merge with what were almost certainly descriptive names applied first as personal names to adults and subsequently transferred to children. Many Germanic names appear to be of this type, but **Cuthbert,** 'famous bright', **Robert,** 'fame bright', **Bernard,** 'stern bear' and the like may often have originated as blends, making use of standard name elements.

Invented names have often been introduced by writers. They include **Fiona, Lorna, Mavis, Miranda, Pamela, Thelma, Vanessa, Wendy.**

Link names were frequently formed with **Yahweh** as an element, as in **John, Joan, Joseph** and many others. **God** occurs in names like **Elizabeth,** 'oath of God'. Other names could be the basis, as with **Malcolm,** 'a disciple or servant of St **Columba**'.

Diminutive link names, of the Sally/Betty kind, later became a common source of new names, as did

'If you call me Anne, please call me Anne spelled with an "e".'
'What difference does it make how it's spelled?' asked Manilla.
'Oh, it makes so much difference. It looks so much nicer. When you hear a name
pronounced, can't you always see it in your mind, just as if it was printed out?
I can; and A-n-n looks dreadful, but A-n-n-e looks so much more distinguished.'

L. M. Montgomery   *Anne of Green Gables*

feminine links. These are names like **Louise, Roberta, Henrietta,** etc., from **Louis, Robert** and **Henry. Transferred names** have often been surnames which were themselves transferred place names. Examples are **Clifford, Graham, Keith, Leslie, Percy.** River names that have ultimately become first names by a long process of transfer include **Douglas, Alma** and more recently, **Brent.**

> By an interesting twist, 'middle name' has come to mean something for which a person is well known. 'Like fishing?' says a character in *Main Street*, by Sinclair Lewis. 'Fishing is my middle name', is the reply.

Middle names

Before looking at the more common first names in detail we must also say something about middle names. Firstly, it is statistically normal these days for children throughout the English-speaking world to be given one first name and one middle name. Two or more middle names are more usual than no middle name. While there is legally no upper limit on the number of middle names that may be given, most parents draw the line after four.

It has been the convention until very recently to give boys a 'safe', traditional first name and to be slightly more daring with the middle name, but to do the reverse with the girls. In the past many parents, having allowed their romantic fancy to run riot with their daughter's first name, felt that they must be more sober with the middle name. 'If she doesn't like X,' they would say, mentioning some exotic invention that they happened to have come across, 'she can always use her middle name'. There are signs that boys are now being treated in a similar way.

It is difficult to say how many people do in fact drop their first names and make daily use of their middle names as the result of a conscious decision. This involves a dramatic change, unlike the situation in which others find themselves, where the official first name—often the same as the father's or mother's name—has *never* been used in speech. Such middle names carried out the function of first names from the beginning. Perhaps one person in eight has a middle name which *is* used, for whatever reason. For other people, particularly those with common surnames, they mostly help to identify individuals more precisely on official forms. From an American point of view they also provide the essential middle initial.

Two American correspondents whose parents were thoughtless enough, as they humorously put it, not to provide them with middle names have commented to me in the past about the difficulties thus created. J. Bryan III (who at least has an interesting personal-name modifier) reports that his fellow countrymen absolutely insist on giving him a middle initial, and almost any seems to do. Mike Martin became M. Martin NMI ('No Middle Initial') when he joined the Army, and to avoid this disgrace he later legally adopted the middle initial **W.** The 'W' was, like the **S** in Harry S Truman, a letter name rather than an initial, not standing for any particular name. Mike was happy with his 'W' until his driving-licence arrived with his name written Michael **W (only)** Martin.

In some areas, such as Scotland, it is a custom for the wife's maiden name to become the child's middle name. The surnames of noble families in particular have long been used as first or middle names, so the precedent is there. Camden, writing in 1605, remarked that many were worried about what was then a new trend, thinking it would cause great confusion if surnames mixed with first names but we managed to absorb names like **Sidney, Howard, Neville** and **Percy** without difficulty. More recent transfers from surname to middle- or first-name status include

Scott, Cameron, Grant and Campbell—the Scottish influence being very noticeable. Such names often begin with very restricted use, used as middle names only where there is a family connection. After a probationary period as middle names they are promoted to first names. General recognition follows when they are used as first names by those who have no family reason for doing so.

It is always important to distinguish between first names and middle names. Historically it was first names, as individual personal names, which came first, to be followed in the Middle Ages by surnames, a large number of which were themselves derived from first names. Middle names, occupying a highly ambiguous area between the two more important nomenclatures and borrowing heavily from both of them, have been with us from the seventeenth century only. In terms of their social and psychological importance they are also totally overshadowed by the names that surround them. Middle names constitute what is almost a separate nomenclature, useful for minor purposes such as pacifying relations who want their names to live on, or perhaps genuinely acting as tokens of respect to namesakes. First names have the vibrancy which comes from daily use: middle names, and perhaps rightly so, are more like family heirlooms, necessary to preserve if only in the attic. The metaphor may be apt in another way. We have spoken of the middle-name arena as a proving ground for new names, but it is used to put old names out to pasture. John, George, Henry, Mary, Elizabeth, Frances, Ann(e) and Margaret currently appear to fall into that category. Ann(e), especially, is now used ten times as a middle name for every one use as a first name.

Perhaps you don't know what school-children are like. They're little devils. It's enough for them to know that your middle name, if you have one, is odd—I am called Jock Maconochie Campbell—and they give you no peace at all.

L. P. Hartley   *The Love Adept*

The central stock of first names

Having established our definitions of 'first name' and 'middle name', we may now turn to the question of how many first names there are in what might be called 'the central stock'. There is nothing to stop parents in the English-speaking countries giving *any* name to a child as its first name, but in practice the vast majority of parents make very great use in any one year of a relatively small number of names. In 1900, for example, the Smiths in England and Wales made really significant use of only 120 boys' names and 160 girls' names. In 1980 they made equally significant use—and by this we mean nine families out of ten made use—of 125 boys' names and 175 girls' names. In the case of the boys, about thirty 'new' names, such as Barry, Craig and Darren, had appeared by 1980, but twenty-five others had been left aside. The latter included names like Edmund, Herbert, Horace and Percy. Similarly, girls' names such as Deborah, Janice, Joanne and Karen were among the seventy or so 'new' names being used. The fifty-five names that had fallen by the wayside included Annie, Winifred, Nellie and May.

There is evidence of this central stock of names on all sides. In a supplement to the Registrar-General's Report for Scotland, 1958, the first names given to 52 882 boys and 50 204 girls that year were fully analysed. Every *spelling* of a name was counted as a separate name, whereas I would certainly have bracketed such pairs as Ian/Iain, Brian/Bryan, Alastair/Alistair, Ann/Anne, Lynn/Lynne, Carol/Carole, Teresa/Theresa. Even with each of these counted as a separate name, the hundred most frequently used boys' names accounted for 49 674 occurrences, or 94 per cent of the total. The top hundred girls' names accounted for 41 552 occurrences—83 per cent of the total.

This intensive use of a relatively small number of names in any given year is revealed by every survey based on *white* families. Black American families and the West Indians in Britain have different ideas about naming their children. They value individuality far more, and use a much greater range of names. A small percentage of them do follow white naming practices, and use the same names that are fashionable with white families. Another group may make use of what almost constitutes a central stock of names used exclusively by black Americans and West Indians. But the basic point is that black parents in general are more prepared than white parents to invent new names, to draw them from a wider variety of sources and restore old names to use, all in an effort to ensure that their children do not meet others who bear the same name.

At the end of this chapter I have included a mini-dictionary of first names, identifying the names which I think make up the central stock at the moment and giving their origins. I have tried also to identify the names which are especially popular with black families and comment on their sources. In both cases, the names which form the central stock today are not those which would have formed it a generation ago. Fashions in first names are always changing, and in the next chapter we shall go on to look at those changes in detail.

Name usage

There are fashions in name usage just as there are fashions in names. At the moment, first names are used very readily at every level of society between people who scarcely know one another. This has been the case now for at least fifty years, but as every reader of Victorian novels is aware, the situation in the 19th century was quite different. The 'lower orders', as they were then called, used first names amongst themselves, but polite society had a strict code of conduct which made them almost superfluous. Gentlemen addressed one another as Sir, before progressing to Mr with the last name. Later, if they were of equal rank, they might move on to using the surname on its own. Wives often addressed their husbands as Mr Jones, or whatever, and received the compliment of Mrs Jones in return.

It was young lovers of the time who attached great importance to the use of their first names. 'I would have leaped into the valley of the shadow of death, only to hear her call me John,' says a young man in *Lorna Doone*. To be allowed to call the young lady by her first name was also a great privilege.

The change towards less formal name usage began in America, and possibly reflected Quaker ideas of equality. By the 1930s the situation was also changing in Britain. C. Northcote Parkinson suggested in an article some years ago that the Duke of Windsor may have been influential in making first name usage acceptable at the highest levels of British society, having been influenced himself by American ways.

Name usage these days is generally simple, though particular relationships can still cause problems. Many people worry about what they should call their mother-in-law, for example. They feel that Mother or one of its variants is unsuitable, while Mrs followed by the surname is too formal. Use of the first name may also not feel right.

This can also be the case in a different kind of relationship. D. H. Lawrence interestingly remarks at one point that Lady Chatterley and her lover Oliver Mellors never use each other's first names.

Scottish lairds are traditionally addressed by the names of their properties, a fact which James Boswell stressed in his *Journal of a Tour to the Hebrides*. He commented on the problem of a laird who should correctly have been addressed as **Muck.** As Boswell says, this 'would have sounded ill, so he was called **Isle of Muck,** which went off with great readiness'.

The **Fred** Society was founded in 1983 by Fred Daniel. Members, who include those whose first or middle name is Fred and women who are **Winifred** and **Frederica**, receive a newsletter, the *Fred Connection*. They can also purchase Fred Society T-shirts, bumper stickers, coffee mugs and 'Freddy bears'.

Over 3000 Freds have joined forces in order to combat the 'caveman-nerd' image that the name invokes. The society, said an Associated Press report in 1987, 'tries to fend off images fostered by television's Fred Flintstone cartoons and advertisements depicting Freds as bumbling clerks and fast-talking salesmen'. The latest insult is the use of a term by cyclists in California. The people who crowd the bike lanes and get in the way of serious cyclists are now known as 'freds'.

Interested Freds should contact Fred Daniel, who is based in Palm Desert, California.

NAME CALLING

MOST of us are addressed in a variety of ways during a normal day. Friends will probably use our first names, or pet forms of those names, but they may also use personal name modifiers. Instead of: '*John*, how nice to see you!' someone says: '*My dear John*, how nice to see you!' They may also use a personal name substitute, otherwise known as a term of address, or a vocative: '*My dear*, how nice to see you!' Strangers, unaware of our names, are particularly apt to make use of these name substitutes. The shop assistant uses *Sir* or *Madam*, the motorist who has just had to take avoiding action because we stepped into the road in front of him uses *You stupid idiot!*

The variety of terms can be illustrated by reference to a character in *Anglo-Saxon Attitudes*, a novel by Angus Wilson. The central character of the book is Gerald Middleton, Professor Emeritus of Early Medieval History. Other characters, in the course of the novel, address him as follows:

family members—*Daddy, Father, my dear Father*

intimate friends—*darling, little Middleton, old dear, old thing*

friends—*dear, duckie, Gerald, Gerald dear, Gerald my dear, Middleton, my dear, my dear boy, my dear fellow, my dear friend, my dear Gerald, my dear Middleton, my dear Mr Middleton*

students and colleagues—*Professor, Professor Middleton, Sir*

an acquaintance—*Mr Middleton*

an angry friend—*you damned traitor*

Note how a term of address that begins with *my* is likely to be friendly, whereas one that begins with *you* is normally unfriendly. *Old* is also a friendly word: *old man* or *old lady* is affectionate where *young man* or *young lady* is probably reproving.

Friend, used as a term of address, is not necessarily friendly, any more than *pal* in an utterance such as: 'What's it got to do with you, *pal*?' The face value of any term can be reversed by the tone in which it is said.

As an experiment, try recording the different terms of address that others use when speaking to you. You might also note how many terms you use when addressing others, according to their status, age, sex, etc. Above all it is your attitude to the person you are speaking to which will decide what kind of name, name modifier or name substitute you use.

Those with a special interest in such matters should consult Leslie Dunkling's *Dictionary of Epithets and Terms of Address*, Routledge 1990. The Introduction to this book includes a theoretical discussion of the importance of vocatives. In particular it argues that the breakdown of the thou/you (earlier thou/yit/ye) pronoun system has led to the creation of a phrasal 'you' in English, with the term of address functioning as a particle which carries indications of both grammatical number and speaker-attitude.

Mrs. Millamant: And d'ye hear, I won't be called names after I'm marry'd; positively I won't be called names.

Mirabell: Names!

Mrs. Millamant: Ay, as wife, spouse, my dear, joy, jewel, love, sweetheart, *and the rest of that nauseous cant, in which men and their wives are so fulsomely familiar . . .*

William Congreve   *The Way of the World*

VIVE LA DIFFERENCE!

IT is now the custom of young people to shout at each other by their Christian names, or the abbreviations of their Christian names, or the most intimate substitutes for their Christian names, as soon as they know each other, or before they know each other. If (as you and I and all smart people are aware) the dashing and distinguished Miss Vernon-Vavasour was known in baptism as Gloria but among her most devoted friends as Gurgles, there is now no difference between those who call her Gurgles and those who call her Glory and those who would normally prefer, when suddenly presented to somebody they do not know from Eve, to call her Miss Vernon-Vavasour. As soon as she is seen as a distant dot on the other side of the tennis-court, a total stranger will yell at her as Gurgles, because he hears a crowd of other total strangers doing the same. He will use her nickname, because he has never known enough about her to have heard her name. Or he will use the first name, because he has not been in her company for a sufficient number of seconds to get as far as the last one.

Now there were many things in which the Victorians were quite wrong. But in their punctiliousness about etiquette in things like this, they were quite right. In insisting that the young lady should be called at one stage Miss Vavasour, and only at another stage Gloria, and only in extreme and almost desperate cases of confidence Gurgles, they were a thousand times right. They were maintaining a wholly superior social system, by which social actions were significant, and not (as they are now) all of them equally insignificant. Life is much more rich and interesting when there are individual initiations, special favours, and different titles for different relations of life.

G. K. Chesterton *On Calling Names –*
Christian and Otherwise

OUTWARD FORMS

'WHILE we are on the name matter,' said the captain, 'here is a resumé of our attitudes. First, Mrs Paradise. The hideous abbreviation "Florrie" may safely be used by you two, on account of your being creatures of tenderness, jollity, and enthusiasm. To me, however, as master of the house, she must always be Florence, no matter how deep my feeling for her may be. The reason for this double approach is that while Florence is fraught with grave, inhibitory influence, Florrie is suggestive of loose hair and even misappropriation. Thus, it will be for me, as it were, to suppress her rogue instincts with Florence, and for you two periodically to detonate the overcharged cannon with sparks of Florrie. It is a simple matter of balance, and if she shows signs of getting out of hand, you two can always start sticking in a few restorative Florences . . .

'Now, her brother. He is to be Jellicoe at all times to all three of us: his is not a name to conjure with. To make Jelly out of it, for instance, would be fatal. It must always be uttered gravely and deliberately, dwelt upon, even: in short, treated as the outward and audible form of his inward and spiritual grace.'

Nigel Dennis *Cards of Identity*

The central stock of boys' names

Aaron biblical; Hebrew or Egyptian; origin unknown.

Adam biblical; Hebrew; 'red skin' or 'red earth'.

Adrian papal; Latin; 'of the Adriatic'.

Alan Norman; Celtic, origin unknown. **Allan, Allen** are common variants.

Alastair see *Alistair*.

Albert Germanic; Old English/ German; 'noble bright'.

Alexander historical; Greek; 'defending men'. **Alec/Alex** occur.

Alfred royal; Old English 'elf-counsel'. **Alfie** is used independently.

Alistair (most popular modern spelling) translated; Gaelic form of *Alexander*.

Ambrose Greek 'immortal'.

Andrew biblical; Greek; 'manly'.

Anthony saint; Latin; origin unknown. **Antony** earlier and historically more correct.

Arnold Old German 'eagle-power'.

Arthur royal; possibly Celtic 'bear'.

Ashley surname/place name; Old English; 'ash wood or clearing'.

Austin saint; Latin *augustus*, 'venerable, consecrated'.

Barnaby biblical; Hebrew; 'son of encouragement'. Also as **Barnabas.**

Barry descriptive (?); Gaelic; based on 'spear'.

Basil saint; Greek 'kingly'.

Benedict saint; Latin; 'blessed'.

Benjamin biblical; Hebrew; 'son of the south', ie 'the right hand'.

Bernard Germanic; Old English/ German; 'brave as a bear'.

Bertram Old German 'bright-raven'. **Bertie** occurs independently.

Boyd Gaelic 'yellow (hair)'.

Bradley surname/place name; Old English; 'broad clearing'.

Brandon surname/place name; 'hill on which broom grows'.

Brendan saint; Gaelic; origin uncertain.

Brent surname/place name/river name; 'holy river' or 'high place'.

Bret(t) surname; Old French; 'a Briton'.

Brian historical; Celtic; origin uncertain. Also **Bryan.**

Byron aristocratic English surname, 'one who looked after cattle'.

Cameron surname; Gaelic; 'crooked nose'.

Carl anglicised *Karl*; German form of *Charles*.

Cecil Roman clan name; Latin 'blind'.

Chad saint; Gaelic; of uncertain meaning.

Charles historical; Germanic; 'a man'.

Christian commendatory; Latin; 'Christian'.

Christopher saint; Greek; 'bearing Christ'.

Clarence royal/literary; Latin 'of Clare'.

Clark English surname 'cleric'.

Clifford surname/place name; Old English; 'ford by a slope'.

Clive surname (historical); Old English; 'dweller by the cliff'.

Cody Irish surname of uncertain meaning.

Colin diminutive; Latin *columba* ('dove') or from *Nicholas*.

Conrad Germanic 'brave-counsel'.

Cornelius Roman clan name/biblical; Latin 'horn'.

Craig surname; Middle English; 'dweller by the crag'.

Dale surname; Old English; 'dweller in the dale'.

Daley Irish surname 'assembly'.

Damian saint; Greek; based on 'to tame'. Also **Damien.**

Daniel biblical; Hebrew; 'God is judge'.

Darren surname (?); origin uncertain.

Darryl, Daryl, Daryll surname of uncertain origin.

David saint; Hebrew; 'beloved'.

Dean surname; Old English; 'dweller in a valley'. Also Latin; 'son of the dean'.

Delroy also Elroy, Leroy Old French 'the king'.

Denis, Dennis saint; Greek; 'of Dionysos', (god of wine).

Derek Germanic; Old German; 'ruler of the people'.

Desmond surname; Gaelic; 'man from south Munster'.

Dirk pet form of **Diederick**, Dutch form of *Derek*.

Dominic(k) saint; Latin; 'of the Lord'.

Donald Celtic; Gaelic; 'world mighty'.

Douglas surname; Gaelic; 'dark blue' (originally a river name).

Duane, Dwayne surname; Irish; of uncertain meaning.

Dudley English place name/ aristocratic surname; 'Dudda's wood'.

Duncan surname; Gaelic; 'brown warrior'.

Dustin surname; 'dusty place'.

Edgar royal; Old English 'prosperity-spear'.

Edmond, Edmund royal saint; Old English; 'rich protector'.

Edward royal saint; Old English; 'happy guardian'.

Edwin royal; Old English; 'happy friend'.

Eliot, Eliott, Elliot, Elliott surname 'descendant of *Eli*'.

Elroy see *Delroy*.

Elvis phonetic form of Irish *Ailbhe*, name of patron saint of Munster.

Eric, Erik Danish; Old Norse; based on 'ruler'.

Ernest German 'earnestness'.

Eugene saint/Papal; Greek; 'noble, well-born'.

Felix saint; Latin 'happy'.

Francis saint; Latin; 'a Frenchman'. **Frank,** the diminutive, is as popular.

Frederick Germanic; Old German; 'peaceful ruler'.

Gareth literary; Welsh form of **Gerontius**; 'old man'.

Gary diminutive; from *Gareth* or *Gerard*.

Gavin literary; Celtic or Germanic; probably from **Gawain.**

Geoffrey Norman; Old German; based on 'peace'.

George saint; Greek; 'farmer'.

Gerald Norman; Old German; 'spear rule'.

Gerard Norman; Old German; 'firm spear'.

Gilbert Old German 'pledge-bright'.

Giles saint; Greek; 'young goat'.

Glen(n) surname; Gaelic; 'dweller in

the valley'. **Glyn(n)** probably derives from this name.

Godfrey Old German 'god-peace'.

Gordon surname (historical); Gaelic; 'great hill'.

Graham, Graeme surname; Old English; origin disputed.

Grant surname; Old French; 'great'.

Gregory saint; Greek; based on 'to be watchful'.

Guy Norman; Old German; origin uncertain.

Harold Old English 'army-power'. **Harry** is used independently.

Harvey surname; Old French; 'battle worthy'.

Haydn, Hayden, Haydon surname/place name, sometimes a variant of *Aidan*.

Hector Greek 'holding fast'.

Henry royal; Germanic; 'home ruler'.

Herbert Old German; 'army-bright'.

Howard surname; Old German, 'heart brave', also 'high warden', also 'ewe-herder'.

Hubert saint; Old German 'mind-bright'.

Hugh historical; Germanic; 'heart, mind'.

Ian translated; Gaelic form of *John*.

Ivan translated; Russian form of *John*.

Ivor Old Norse, meaning obscure.

Jack pet form of *John*, influenced by French **Jacques** (*Jacob*).

Jacob Arabic 'let God protect'. **Jake** is used independently.

James saint; Latin; form of **Jacob** 'let God protect' (Arabic).

Jamie diminutive; Scottish form of *James* and **Jimmy**.

Jared, Jarrod Hebrew; 'rose'.

Jason biblical; Greek; form of **Jesus** or **Joshua** 'Yah is generous' or 'Yah protects'.

Jeffrey see *Geoffrey*.

Jeremy, Jerry biblical; Hebrew form of **Jeremiah**, 'Yah raises up'.

Jesse biblical; Hebrew; 'man of Yah'.

Joel biblical; Hebrew; 'Yah is God'.

John biblical; Hebrew; 'Yah has favoured'.

Jon variant spelling of *John*.

Jonathan biblical; Hebrew; 'Yah has given'.

Jordan river name; Hebrew; 'to descend'.

Joseph biblical; Hebrew; 'may God add (other children)'.

Joshua biblical; Hebrew; see *Jason*. **Jeshua** and **Jesus** are other forms of this name.

Julian saint; Latin; form of **Julius**, possibly 'downy (beard)'.

Justin saint; Latin; 'just'.

Kane surname; Gaelic; 'warrior'.

Karl German form of *Charles*.

Keith surname; Celtic; 'wood'.

Kelvin Scottish river name.

Kenneth saint; Royal; Gaelic; usually taken to be 'handsome'.

Kevin saint; see *Kenneth*.

Kieran saint; Irish; 'little dark one'.

Kirk surname; Norse; 'dweller near a church'.

Kristian see *Christian*.

Kristopher modern form of *Christopher*.

Kurt pet name from *Conrad*; Germanic; 'bold counsel'.

Kyle Irish/Scottish surname, place name 'narrow piece of land'.

Lance Germanic; 'land'.

Laurence, Lawrence saint; Latin; 'of Laurentum'.

Lee surname; Old English; 'dweller by the wood or clearing'.

Leighton surname/place name; Old English; 'place where leeks were grown' or 'bright hill'.

Leon Greek 'lion'.

Leonard saint; Germanic; 'lion bold'.

Leroy see *Delroy*.

Leslie surname/place name; Gaelic; possibly 'garden or court of hollies'.

Lewis royal; Germanic; 'famous fighter'.

Liam pet form of *William* in Ireland.

Lionel Latin 'little lion'.

Lloyd Welsh 'grey'.

Louis see *Lewis*.

Luke biblical; Greek; 'of Lucania'.

Malcolm saint; Gaelic; 'servant or disciple of St Columba'.

Marcus Roman; Latin form of *Mark*. **Marc** is also becoming popular.

Mark biblical; Latin; possibly connected with Mars.

Martin, Martyn saint; Latin; 'of Mars'.

Matthew biblical; Hebrew; 'gift of Yah'.

Maurice saint; Latin 'Moorish, dark-skinned'.

Max, Maximilian Latin 'the greatest'.

Maxwell Scottish place name/surname, 'Macca's well'.

Melvin, Melvyn Gaelic 'smooth brow'.

Michael biblical; Hebrew; 'who is like the Lord'?

Miles Old German 'generous'.

Mitchell surname 'descendant of *Michael*'.

Nathan biblical; Hebrew; 'gift'.

Nathaniel biblical; Hebrew; 'God has given'.

Neil, Neal Irish; Gaelic; 'champion'.

Nevil, Neville Norman surname/place name, 'new town'.

Niall see *Neil*.

Nicholas saint; Greek; 'victory of the people'.

Nigel Latinised form of *Neil*.

Noël descriptive; French; for a child born on 'Christmas Day'.

Norman Germanic; Old English/German; 'northman'.

Oliver Norman; Old French; 'olive tree', but numerous other possibilities.

Oscar Old English 'god-spear'.

Owen literary; Welsh; taken to be from Latin **Eugenius**, 'well-born'.

Patrick saint; Latin; 'a nobleman'.

Paul biblical; Latin; 'small'.

Percival literary invention of uncertain meaning. **Percy** is used independently.

Perry pet form of **Peregrine**, Latin 'wanderer, stranger'.

Peter biblical; Greek (translation of Aramaic); 'stone'.

Philip, Phillip biblical; Greek; 'lover of horses'.

Piers medieval form of *Peter*.

Ralph historical; Old Norse; 'counsel wolf'.

Randal(l) historical; Old English; 'shield wolf'. **Randy** occurs.

Raymond Norman; Old German; 'wise protection'.

Reginald historical; Old English; 'powerful might'.

Reuben biblical; Hebrew; 'He has seen my misery'.

Rex Latin 'king'.

Richard Norman; Old German/English; 'stern ruler'. **Rickie** is also used.

Robert Norman; Old English/German; 'bright fame'.

Robin diminutive of *Robert*.

Roderick Old Germanic; 'fame rule'.

Rodney surname; Old English; 'Hroda's island'.

Roger Norman; Old English/German; 'fame-spear'.

Roland, Rowland literary; Old German 'famous land'.

Ronald Scottish form of *Reginald*; Old English; 'powerful might'.

Rory Gaelic; 'red'.

Ross surname; Gaelic; 'dweller at the promontory'.

Roy descriptive; Gaelic; 'red'.

Royston English place name/surname of several possible origins.

Rupert royal; old German form of *Robert*.

Russell surname; Old French, 'red'.

Ryan surname; Irish; 'red'.

Samuel biblical; Hebrew; 'name of God'.

Scott surname; Old English; 'a Scot'.

Sebastian saint; Latin; 'man from the city of Sebastia'. The city name meant 'venerable'.

Shane from **Sean**; Irish form of *John*.

Shaun, Shawn translated; Irish forms of *Sean = John*.

Sidney, Sydney aristocratic surname, 'wide well-watered land', but often associated with *Saint Denis*.

Simon biblical; Hebrew variant of **Simeon**, 'Yah has heard', but in Greek Simon is 'snub-nosed'.

Spencer surname; Old French; 'dispenser of provisions'.

Stanley surname/place name; Old English; 'stone field'.

Stephen biblical; Greek; 'crown'. Also as **Steven**.

Stuart surname; Old English; 'steward'. Also as **Stewart.**

Terence Roman; Latin; origin unknown. Frequently in form **Terry.**

Theodore saint; Greek; 'God's gift'.

Thomas biblical; Aramaic; 'twin'.

Timothy biblical; Greek; 'honoured by God'.

Toby biblical; Hebrew; form of **Tobias**, 'Yah is good'.

Todd surname; English; 'fox'.

Tony diminutive of *Anthony*.

Travis surname; Middle English; 'a toll-collector'.

Trevor surname; Welsh; 'big village'.

Troy surname/place name; Old French; from 'Troyes'.

Tyler surname 'tiler'.

Vaughan Welsh 'little, junior'.

Vernon surname; Old French; 'alder tree'.

Victor saint; Latin; 'conqueror'.

Vincent saint; Latin; 'conquering'.

Walter historical; Germanic; 'rule folk'.

Warren surname; Old French; from 'La Varenne'.

Wayne surname; Old English; 'wagon-maker'.

Wesley surname; English; 'west field' or 'field with a well'.

Wilfred saint; Old English 'will-peace'.

William Norman; Old German; 'will helmet'. Also **Willie.**

Winston English surname/place name, 'Wine's settlement'.

Zachary biblical; Hebrew, 'Yah has remembered'.

Boys' names used by black American families.

The names listed below have all been especially well used by black American families in recent years.

Alonzo pet form of **Alphonso;** royal; Germanic; 'noble + ready'.

Alvin surname; Germanic; 'noble friend'.

André French form of *Andrew*; Greek; 'manly'.

Antoine French form of *Ant(h)ony*. Also found as **Antwan.**

Arnold historical; Old German; 'eagle power'.

Bennie pet form of *Benjamin* or *Benedict*.

Bryant surname; 'descendant of *Brian* or *Bryan*'.

Byron surname; 'worker in a cowshed'.

Calvin surname; Latin; French; 'the bald one'.

Carlos Spanish form of *Charles*, 'man'.

Carlton surname/place name; 'settlement of free men'.

Cedric apparently a literary invention (Sir Walter Scott) of unknown meaning.

Clinton surname/place name; English; 'settlement on a hill'.

Corey surname; Irish; possibly connected with *Godfrey*, 'god peace'.

Cornelius Latin; 'horn'.

Cornell surname; 'man from Cornwall' or 'one who lived on a hill where corn was grown'. Several other origins are possible.

Curtis surname; French; 'courteous, well-educated'.

Damon a personal name which occurs in classical Greek literature, later used to denote a typical young lover. Known for his faithfulness to his friend Phintias.

Darius name of a Persian king, but of unknown meaning.

Darnell surname/place name; 'hidden nook'.

Darrell surname, indicating a man who came from a village in France called Airel.

Demetrius Greek; 'of Demeter, the Earth mother'.

Deon also **Dion**. Probably pet forms of *Dionysos* (*Denis*), name of the god of wine.

Derrick a modern spelling of *Derek*, 'ruler of the people'.

Deshawn apparently a new name based on *Shawn*, ie *John*.

Devin, Devon English county name.

Dion see *Deon*.

Dorian Greek; 'from the Dorian region', possibly indicating a Spartan. A male form of the name *Doris*.

Earl English; 'nobleman'.

Ernest Germanic; 'earnestness, vigour'.

Floyd surname; a variant of *Lloyd*.

Herman Old German; 'army man'.
Isaac biblical; Hebrew; 'God may laugh'.
Jamal Arabic; 'handsome'.
Jermaine possibly from a surname meaning 'German'.
Lamar probably from the surname, but the American writer Ashton Lamar was really Harry Sayler. The actress Barbara La Marr was born Reatha Watson, and Hedy Lamarr was formerly Hedwig Kiesler. There is a real French surname Lamare, indicating someone who lived near a pond.

Lamont surname, form of **Lamond;** Norse; 'lawyer'.
Marcus a Roman name connected with Mars, the god of war.
Marlon possibly from a French surname, ultimately meaning a 'blackbird', from a nickname given to one who liked to sing.
Marvin surname; from a Welsh name of unknown meaning.
Maurice saint; Latin; 'a Moor'.
Milton surname; English; 'settlement near a mill'.
Myron the name of a famous Greek sculptor.

Omar Arabic; 'most high', or 'first son', or 'follower of the Prophet'.
Quentin saint; Latin; 'fifth'.
Roosevelt surname; Dutch; 'rose field'.
Terrance a variant of *Terence*.
Terrell English surname/place name.
Tommie a diminutive of *Thomas*, 'twin'.
Tyrone from an Irish place name, 'Eoghan's land'.
Winston surname/place name; English; 'Wine's village'.

Some Irish first names for boys

Aidan Gaelic 'fire'.
Cathal Irish 'battle mighty'.
Ciarán Irish 'black'.
Colm Irish 'dove'.
Connor Irish 'high desire'.
Cormac Irish 'charioteer'.
Cornelius Latin 'horn', a Roman clan name.
Declan an Irish saint's name of unknown meaning.
Dermot Irish 'envy free'.

Diarmuid same as *Dermot*.
Donal Gaelic 'world mighty'.
Eamonn Irish form of *Edmond*, Old English 'rich protector'.
Enda Irish 'bird'.
Eoghan Irish form of *Eugene*, Greek 'well born'.
Eoin Irish form of *John*.
Fergal Irish 'man of strength'.
Flannan Irish 'of ruddy complexion'.
Garrett Irish form of *Gerard*,

Germanic 'firm spear'.
Niall Irish form of *Neil*.
Padraig Irish form of *Patrick*, Latin 'nobleman'.
Ronan Irish 'little seal'.
Seamus Irish form of *James*, itself a Latin form of Hebrew *Jacob* 'heel'.
Sean an Irish form of *John*.

Some Scottish first names for boys

Adair Scottish form of *Edgar*, Old English 'prosperity-spear'.
Alasdair a Scottish form of *Alexander*, Greek 'defending men'.
Alpin Gaelic 'white'.
Angus Gaelic 'unique choice'.
Arran Scottish place name.
Athol Scottish place name and family name.
Aulay Gaelic form of *Olave*, Old Norse 'forefather, ancestor'.
Blair Scottish place name and family name.
Broderick probably 'brother'.
Bruce Scottish family name, from Norman place name.
Calum, Callum from Latin *Columba*, 'dove', or pet form of *Malcolm*
Campbell Scottish clan and family name 'crooked mouth'.
Clyde Scottish river name.

Cosmo Greek 'order'.
Crawford Scottish place name and family name 'ford where crows gather'.
Denholm Scottish place name and family name.
Diarmid Gaelic 'envy free'.
Drummond Scottish family name.
Dugald Scottish form of Irish *Dougal* 'black stranger'.
Erskine Scottish place name and family name 'green ascent'.
Ewan form of Greek *Eugene* 'well born'.
Farquhar Gaelic 'very dear one'.
Fergus Gaelic 'supreme choice'.
Finlay Scottish family name 'fair hero'.
Forbes Scottish place name and family name 'field, district'.
Fraser Scottish family name from French place name.

Gilchrist Gaelic 'servant of Christ'.
Hamish phonetic form of *Seumas*, Gaelic form of *James*.
Keir Gaelic 'swarthy'.
Lachlan Gaelic 'fjord-land'.
Ludovic Latin form of German *Ludwig* 'famous in battle'.
Magnus Latin 'great'.
Maxwell Scottish place name and family name.
Mungo Gaelic 'amiable'.
Murdoch Gaelic 'mariner, sea warrior'.
Murray Scottish place name and family name 'from Moray'.
Ramsay place name and family name.
Rowan Gaelic 'red'.
Torquil Old Norse name of unknown meaning.
Wallace Scottish family name 'Celt, Welshman'.

Some Welsh first names for boys

Aled Welsh river name.

Alun Welsh form of *Alan*, a Celtic name of unknown origin.

Arwel an ancient Welsh name of unknown meaning.

Arwyn Welsh 'muse'.

Awen a variant of *Arwyn*.

Bleddyn Welsh 'wolf'.

Bryn Welsh 'hill, mound'.

Brynmor Welsh 'great hill'.

Carwyn Welsh 'blessed love'.

Cemlyn Welsh place name 'bent lake'.

Ceri Welsh 'love'.

Cledwyn Welsh river name.

Dafydd Welsh form of *David*, Hebrew 'friend'.

Deinol Welsh 'attractive, charming'.

Dewi Welsh form of *David*, Hebrew 'friend'.

Dyfan Welsh 'ruler of a tribe'.

Dylan name of a Welsh sea god, perhaps 'son of the waves'.

Edryd Welsh 'restoration'.

Eifion Welsh place name.

Eilir Welsh 'butterfly'.

Elfed Welsh 'autumn'.

Elgan Welsh 'bright circle'.

Elis Welsh form of *Elias*, Hebrew *Elijah* 'my god is Jehovah'.

Elwyn Welsh 'white brow'.

Emrys Welsh form of *Ambrose*, Greek 'immortal'.

Emyr Welsh form of *Honorius* 'honour'.

Eryl Welsh 'watcher'.

Eurig Welsh 'gold'.

Euros variant of *Eurig*.

Geraint Welsh form of Latin name meaning 'old'.

Gerlad Welsh name of unknown meaning.

Gerwyn Welsh name of unknown meaning.

Gethin Welsh 'dusky'.

Glyndwr Welsh family name.

Gruffydd Welsh 'powerful chief'.

Gwilym Welsh form of *William*, Germanic 'will-helmet'.

Gwyn Welsh 'fair, blessed'.

Gwynfor Welsh 'fair lord'.

Hefin Welsh 'summery'.

Huw Welsh form of *Hugh*, Germanic 'mind'.

Iestyn Welsh form of Latin *Justin* 'just'.

Ieuan Welsh form of *John*.

Ifan variant of *Ieuan*.

Iolo Welsh 'lord value'.

Iwan variant of *Ieuan*.

Llyr form of *Lear*, name of an ancient sea god.

Melfyn Welsh 'from Carmarthen'.

Morgan Welsh 'great and bright'.

Owain Welsh form of Greek *Eugene* 'well born'.

Rhodri Welsh 'circle-ruler'.

Rhys, Reece Welsh 'ardour'.

Wyn Welsh 'white, pure'.

Some biblical first names for boys

Unless otherwise stated these names are of Hebrew origin.

Abel 'vapour, smoke, ie vanity' or Accadian 'son'.

Abiel 'my Father is God'.

Abner 'the Father is the lamp'.

Abraham 'the Father loves'.

Absalom 'my Father is peace'.

Adlai 'my ornament'.

Ahab 'brother of the Father'.

Alvah 'height'.

Amon 'faithful'.

Amos 'strong'.

Ariel 'lion of God' or 'hearth of God'.

Asa 'myrtle' or 'healer'.

Asher 'what happiness!'.

Azariah 'Yah has helped'.

Azaziah 'Yah shows himself to be strong'.

Azel 'noble'.

Balaam Greek form of a Hebrew name probably meaning 'glutton'.

Barabbas 'son of the Father'.

Barak 'lightning flash'.

Bartholomew Aramaic 'son of Tolmai'.

Baruch 'blessed'.

Barzillai 'of iron'.

Becher 'young camel'.

Bela 'swallowed up'.

Boaz 'in him is strength'.

Cain 'blacksmith', though in Genesis explained as 'I have acquired'.

Caleb 'dog'.

Cephas 'rock'. (Aramaic.)

Cyrus 'shepherd'.

Darius Greek 'one who upholds the good'.

Dodo 'His beloved'.

Ebenezer 'stone of help'.

Elhanan 'God shows favour'.

Eli 'Yah is raised up'.

Eliakim 'God sets upright'.

Eliezer 'my God is help'.

Elijah 'my God is Yah'.

Elisha 'God has helped'.

Elkanah 'God has created'.

Elnathan 'God has given'.

Enoch 'inauguration, dedication'.

Enos 'man'.

Ephraim 'fertile'.

Er 'vigilant'.

Erastus Greek 'lovable'.

Esau 'shaggy, hairy'.

Ethan 'constant, permanent'.

Ezekiel 'may God make strong'.

Ezer 'help'.

Ezra 'God is helper'.

Gabriel 'man of God' or 'God is strong'.

Gad 'fortune, luck'.

Gershom 'an alien there'.

Gideon 'swordfish', or 'cutter'.

Goliath 'mighty warrior'.

Haggai 'born on a festival day'.

Ham of unknown meaning.

Hanan 'Yah has shown favour'.

Hananiah 'Yah has shown favour'. **Ananias** is another form of this name.

Heman 'faithful'.

Herod Greek 'noble'.

Hezekiah 'my strength is Yah'.

Hiram 'my brother is on high'.

Hod 'majesty'.

Hodiah 'Yah is majesty'.

Ichabod 'where is the glory?'.

Immanuel 'with us is God'.

Ira 'ass'.

Ishmael 'God hears'.
Jabal 'lead, guide'.
Japheth 'may he extend'.
Jared 'servant'.
Jedaiah 'Yah knows'.
Jehudi 'Jewish'. This name is sometimes written **Yehudi**.
Jeroboam 'may the people increase'.
Jethro 'superabundance'.
Joab 'Yah is Father'.
Job of disputed origin.
Jonah 'dove'.
Josiah 'Yah supports'.
Judah 'praised'. Also found as **Judas, Jude**.
Kish 'gift'.
Korah 'baldness'.
Laban 'the white'.
Lazarus 'God has given help'.
Lemuel 'who belongs to God'.
Levi 'united to'.
Malachi 'my messenger'.
Malchiah 'my king is Yah'.
Malluch 'king'.
Manasseh 'to forget'.
Melech 'king'.

Mesha 'God saves'.
Micah 'who is like Yah?'.
Mordecai 'of *Marduk*' (name of a Babylonian god).
Moses traditionally explained as 'drawn from the water'.
Moza 'issue, source'.
Nabal 'brute, fool'.
Nahor 'snorer'.
Nahum 'consoled'.
Naphtali 'I have fought'.
Nebuchadnezzar '*Nabu*, protect the son!' (Nabu was a god of writing and wisdom).
Nehemiah 'Yah consoles'.
Noah 'rest, console'.
Obadiah 'servant of Yah'.
Obed 'servant'.
Oren 'laurel'.
Pedaiah 'Yah ransoms, delivers'.
Ram 'height'.
Raphael 'God has healed'.
Rosh 'head'.
Rufus Latin 'red'.
Samson 'sun'.
Saul 'asked for'.

Seraiah 'Yah struggles'.
Seth 'God has raised up'.
Shelah 'request'.
Shelemiah 'Yah has completed'.
Shem 'name, renown'.
Shemaiah 'Yah has heard'.
Shephatiah 'Yah has judged'.
Solomon 'the peaceful'.
Tob 'good'.
Tobias 'Yah is good'.
Uri 'my light'.
Uriah 'Yah is my light'.
Uriel 'God is my light'.
Uzziah 'Yah is my strength'.
Uzziel 'God is my strength'.
Zabad 'He has given a gift'.
Zabdiel 'gift of God'.
Zadok 'justice'.
Zebadiah 'gift of Yah'.
Zebedee Greek form of *Zebadiah*.
Zechariah 'Yah remembers'.
Zedekiah 'Yah is my justice'.
Zephaniah 'Yah protects'.
Zuriel 'God is my rock'.

The central stock of girls' names

Abigail biblical; Hebrew; 'father rejoiced'. The short forms **Abbey, Abbie** and **Gail** are used independently.
Adelaide royal; Old German 'nobility'. Pet forms used independently include **Ada, Adela, Adele, Adelina, Adeline, Adelle, Alice, Heidi**.
Adrienne French; feminine form of *Adrian*.
Agnes saint; Greek 'pure, chaste'. Also found as **Annice, Annis, Agneta, Inez**.
Aimée modern; French; 'loved'.
Alexandra royal; Greek; feminine form of *Alexander*, 'defending men'.
Alexis saint; Greek; 'defender'. Formerly a male name. **Alexia** is also used.
Alice literary; Old German; 'nobility'. A contraction of *Adalheidis* = **Adelaide**.
Alicia Latin form of *Alice*. **Alisha, Alissa, Alyssa** also occur.
Alison, Allison literary; French;

diminutive of *Alice*.
Amanda literary; Latin; 'lovable'.
Amber literary; Arabic; used in sense 'precious thing'.
Amelia historical; Germanic; of unknown origin.
Amy historical; Old French; 'loved'.
Anastasia saint; Greek 'resurrection'. Pet forms **Stacey, Stacy** used independently.
Andrea feminine form of *Andrew*, 'manly'.
Angela saint; Greek; 'messenger'.
Anika Slavonic diminutive of *Ann*.
Anita Spanish diminutive of *Ann*.
Ann biblical; Hebrew; form of *Hannah*, 'God has favoured me'. French form **Anne**, Latin **Anna**.
Annabel, Annabelle possibly a reformation of Latin **Anabel**, 'lovable'.
Annemarie this blended name is also found as *Ann-Marie, Annmarie, Anne-Marie*, etc.
Annette French diminutive of *Anne*.
Annice, Annis See *Agnes*.
April the name of the month, also

used in its French form **Avril**.
Ashleigh mainly feminine form of *Ashley*.
Audrey historical; Old English; 'noble strength'. A contraction of Etheldreda.
Autumn the name of the season. Usage still confined to USA.
Avril see *April*.
Barbara saint; Greek; 'foreign'.
Beatrice, Beatrix literary; Latin 'she who makes happy'.
Becky diminutive of *Rebecca*.
Belinda literary; Old German; origin uncertain.
Bernadette saint; feminine form of *Bernard*.
Beryl name of a precious stone.
Beth pet form of *Elizabeth, Bethany*, etc.
Bethany biblical; Aramaic; 'house of poverty'. A place name in the Bible.
Betsy, Betty pet forms of *Elizabeth*.
Beverley, Beverly modern; probably from Beverly Hills, in California. Originally 'beaver meadow'.

Bianca Italian; 'white'. Now replacing French **Blanche**, Latin **Candida**.

Bobbie see *Roberta*.

Brittany English form of French place name.

Bonnie literary; connected with French *bonne*, 'good'. Used to mean 'looking well, healthy, cheerful'.

Brenda historical; Old Norse; 'sword'.

Bridget saint; Celtic; 'the high one'.

Brook(e) a modern use of the word as a name. Perhaps from a surname. Also used for boys.

Bryony the name of the flower, perhaps used to link with *Brian/Bryan*.

Caitlin see *Kathleen*.

Camilla literary; Etruscan; origin uncertain.

Candace, Candice biblical; Royal title in Ethiopia but meaning uncertain.

Cara Italian; 'dear one'. Diminutive **Carina** also used.

Carissa a diminutive of *Cara*.

Carla feminine form of *Carl*.

Carly a variant of *Carla*. **Carley** and **Carlie** occur.

Carmen Spanish form of *Carmel*, from title of Virgin Mary.

Carol(e) feminine form of *Charles*.

Caroline royal; Latin adjective formed on *Charles*, giving **Carolina**. Caroline is then the French form.

Carolyn(n) a modern variant of *Caroline*.

Carrie diminutive of *Caroline, Carol*, etc.

Cassandra literary; Greek; 'defending men'. **Cassey, Cassie** are used independently.

Catherine saint; Greek; 'pure'. This is the French form of *Katharine*.

Celia Roman clan name of unknown meaning. Irish form is *Sheila*.

Ceri from Welsh *caru* 'to love'.

Chantal saint; the French saint was Jeanne de Chantal, the name ultimately meaning 'stony place'. **Chantel, Chantelle**, etc, are found in English-speaking countries (not in France).

Charlene modern feminine form of *Charles*. Also **Charleen, Charline**, etc.

Charlotte royal; French feminine form of *Charles*.

Charmaine apparently from a 1920s song. Perhaps a form of **Charmian**, Greek: 'joy', though this is pronounced Karmian. Charmaine looks French but is not used in France.

Chelsea place name 'landing-place for chalk or limestone'. **Chelsie** occurs.

Chérie the French word for 'darling' used as a name.

Cherry the name of the fruit or a form of *Chérie*. Formerly a pet form of **Charity**.

Cheryl a modern diminutive of *Cherry*.

Chloë biblical; Greek; 'a young green shoot'.

Christa diminutive of *Christine*.

Christina Old English; 'christian'. **Christine** is the French form.

Christy diminutive of *Christina, Christine*.

Cindy diminutive of *Lucinda, Cinderella, Cynthia*, etc.

Claire saint; Latin; 'bright, clear'. Claire is the French form, **Clare** the Latin form (properly **Clara**). **Clair** occurs, though this is masculine in French.

Claudia biblical; feminine of *Claudius*, Roman clan name 'lame'.

Colleen the Irish word for 'girl' used as a name.

Colette diminutive of *Nicolette*, from feminine form of *Nicholas*. **Collette** occurs in English-speaking countries.

Constance Latin 'constancy'.

Coral Greek; used in the sense 'precious substance'.

Corey, Cory, Correy, Corrie forms of Irish surname linked with **Godfrey**, Germanic 'god-peace'.

Corinne French diminutive of Greek *cora* 'maiden'. **Corinna, Corrine, Corin, Corine, Korina**, etc., also occur.

Courtney a use of the surname, which derives from the French place name.

Crystal originally a Scottish diminutive of *Christopher*, then a surname. Perhaps also a 'jewel' name.

Cynthia Greek mythology; goddess of the moon.

Daisy from the flower name.

Danielle, Daniella French feminine forms of *Daniel*.

Daphne mythology; Greek 'laurel'.

Davina Scottish feminine form of *David*. **Davine, Davinia**, etc., also occur.

Dawn the word used as a name.

Deanna modern variant of *Diana*.

Debbie pet form of *Deborah*.

Deborah biblical; Hebrew; 'a bee'. **Debra** now occurs.

Denise French feminine form of *Denis*.

Desirée French; 'desired'.

Diana mythological; name of the moon goddess. **Diane** is the French form. **Dianne** now occurs.

Dolores Spanish 'sorrows', from a title of the Virgin Mary.

Dominique French feminine form of *Dominic*.

Donna Italian; 'lady'.

Doris mythology, Greek 'woman from Doris' (central Greece).

Dorothy Greek; 'gift of God'. Originally the elements of the name were in reverse order, giving **Theodora**.

Edith saint; Old English 'rich-war'.

Edwina feminine form of *Edwin*.

Elaine literary; French form of *Helen*.

Eleanor royal; another form of *Helen*. **Elinor** is found.

Elena Italian/Spanish form of *Helen*.

Elizabeth biblical; Hebrew; 'oath or fullness of God'. **Elisabeth** occurs.

Ellen English form of *Helen*.

Eloise probably feminine form of *Louis*.

Elsie pet form of *Elspeth* (*Elizabeth*).

Emily historical; Latin; the name of a noble Roman family of uncertain meaning. **Emilie** is found.

Emma royal; Old German; 'whole, universal'.

Erica Latin; scientific name for 'heather'. Used as a feminine form of *Eric*. **Erika** is common.

Erin poetic name for Ireland.

Estelle literary; probably connected with Latin *stella* 'star'.

Esther biblical; Persian; 'star' or 'myrtle'.

Ethel Old English 'noble'.

Eve, Eva biblical; Hebrew; 'lively, living'.

Evelyn historical; Old German; of uncertain meaning.

Fay perhaps a use of the obsolete word meaning 'faith' as a name. Fay is also a form of *fey*, 'fairy'. **Faye** occurs.

Felicity Latin; 'happiness'.

Fern from the plant name.

Fiona literary; Gaelic; 'fair, white'.

Fleur literary; French 'flower'.

Flora saint; Latin 'flower'.

Florence saint; Latin 'flourishing'.

Frances feminine form of *Francis*, 'Frenchman'. **Francesca**, the Italian form, is now popular.

Gabriella, Gabrielle Italian and French feminine forms of *Gabriel*. **Gabi, Gaby** are used independently.

Gail a pet form of *Abigail*. **Gayle** is now found.

Gaynor historical; a form of *Guinevere*. The short forms **Gay, Gaye** also occur.

Gemma Italian; 'gem'. **Jemma** is now frequent.

Georgia, Georgette, Georgina, Georgine feminine forms of *George*.

Geraldine feminine form of *Gerald*.

Gillian English form of *Juliana*, feminine of *Julian*.

Gina a pet form of *Georgina*.

Gladys literary; Welsh form of *Claudia*.

Glenda Welsh 'fair and good'.

Gloria literary; Latin 'glory'.

Grace the word used as a name.

Hannah biblical; Hebrew; 'God has favoured me'.

Harriet feminine form of *Harry* or *Henry*.

Hayley from a surname/place name, possibly meaning 'high clearing'.

Hazel the botanical name used as a first name.

Heather from the plant name.

Heidi a Germanic pet form of *Adelheid*, or *Adelaide*. See *Alice*.

Helen saint; Greek; 'the bright one'.

Helena is frequent.

Henrietta royal; feminine form of *Henry*.

Hilda saint; Old German 'battle'.

Hilary saint; Latin; 'cheerful'. **Hillary** occurs.

Holly the plant name used as a first name. **Hollie** is a modern variant.

Hope the word used as a name.

Imogen literary; probably Latin 'innocent'.

India literary; from the name of the country.

Ingrid old Norse; the name of a god Ingvi and a word of uncertain meaning.

Irene saint; Greek 'peace'.

Iris mythology; Greek goddess of the rainbow; plant name.

Isabel Spanish form of *Elizabeth*. **Isabelle, Isabella, Isobel**, etc, are also used.

Ivy plant name.

Jacqueline French feminine form of *Jacques*, or *Jacob*.

Jade from the precious stone.

Jaime Spanish form of *James*, now used with **Jamie** (also male until recent times) as a girl's name.

Jane Feminine form of *John*. **Jayne** occurs. **Janet, Janice, Janis, Janine, Jannine**, etc., are diminutives of Jane.

Jasmine literary; from the flower name.

Jean feminine form of *John*. Now more frequent in French form **Jeanne**. Diminutives **Jeanette, Jeannette**, etc., used independently.

Jemma see *Gemma*.

Jennifer a Cornish form of *Guinevere*, which may have meant 'white-cheeked'. Pet forms **Jenna, Jennie, Jenny** used independently.

Jessica biblical; Hebrew; 'God beholds'.

Jill pet form of **Jillian**, a variant of *Gillian*.

Joan contraction of Latin **Johanna**, feminine form of *John*. Now more frequent in forms **Joanna, Joanne, Jo-Ann, Jo-anne**, etc.

Jocelyn Old German, of uncertain meaning.

Jodi(e), Jody modern pet forms of *Judith* or *Judy*.

Josephine feminine form of *Joseph*. **Josie** is used independently.

Joy the word used as a name.

Joyce saint; Celtic; origin uncertain. Formerly a male name.

Judith Hebrew; 'a Jewess'. **Judy**, the pet form, is found as an independent name.

Julia, Julie feminine forms of *Julian* 'downy beard'. **Juliet** is the diminutive.

June the word used as a name.

Justine French feminine form of *Justin*, 'just'.

Kara see *Cara*.

Karen Danish form of *Katharine*, **Karin** is the Swedish form. **Karina** is now found.

Karla feminine form of *Karl*.

Kate pet form of *Katharine, Katherine*, used independently.

Katharine, Katherine saint; Greek; 'pure'. *Catherine* is the French form. The pet forms **Katie** and **Katy** occur often as names in their own right.

Kathleen Originally an Irish form of *Katharine*.

Kathryn a modern form of *Katharine*.

Katrina a modern variant of *Kathrina*, itself a short form of Germanic *Katharina*, or *Katharine*.

Kay(e) originally a pet form of names beginning with 'K'. Extended in modern times to **Kaylea, Kaylee, Kayleigh, Kayley, Kaylie**, etc.

Keeley from an Irish surname, one meaning of which is 'graceful'. **Keelie** and **Keely** are also used.

Kelly from the Irish surname. The meaning 'strife' has been suggested. **Kellie** and **Kelli** are now found.

Kelsey English place name/surname 'Ceol's island'. Originally a male name.

Kerry apparently a use of the Irish place name. In some instances a phonetic variant of *Carrie*. **Kerrie, Kerri, Keri** are found.

Kimberl(e)y a surname/place name used as a first name. The association of Kimberley in South Africa with diamonds may have influenced usage. **Kim**, the diminutive, occurs frequently as a name in its own right.

Kirsten Scandinavian form of *Christine*.

Kirsty Scottish pet form of *Christine*.

Kristina see *Christine*. The pet form **Kristy** also occurs.

Kylie a native Australian word for a 'throwing stick'.

Lacey from the (Irish) surname. Made well-known by the American television series *Cagney and Lacey*.

Lana short form of *Alana*, feminine of *Alan*.

Lara Slavonic form of *Laura*.

Laura feminine form of *Laurence*, 'person from the town of Laurentium'. **Lauren** is a diminutive.

Laurel from the botanical name.

Leah biblical; Hebrew; 'cow', a symbol of domestic virtue. **Lea** occurs.

Leanne possibly a blend of *Leigh* and *Anne*. Possibly a variant of *Lianne*, which appears to be a pet form of names such as *Julianne*, Italian *Giuliana*.

Leigh a place name element meaning 'meadow'. Also a surname. This form also used for boys, though *Lee* is more commonly the male name.

Leila, also **Lila** literary; Arabic '(dark as) night'.

Lena pet form of names like *Helena*.

Leona, **Leonie** feminine forms of *Leon*.

Lesley feminine form (in Britain) of *Leslie*.

Liane, **Lianne** see *Leanne*.

Lilian, **Lillian** from Italian *Liliana* 'lily'. Lily itself formerly popular.

Linda pet form of names like *Belinda*. **Lynda** is found.

Lindsay, **Lindsey** an English or Norman place name, then a surname and clan name in Scotland. Formerly used as a boy's first name, now mainly a girl's name. Much confusion as to its spelling. Forms include **Linsay, Linsey, Lyndsay, Lyndsey, Lynsay, Lynsey**.

Lisa pet form of *Elizabeth*. **Liza** is also used.

Lois biblical, origin unknown, in modern times often linked to *Eloise*.

Lori a modern variant of *Laura*.

Lorna literary; from the title of the Marquesses of Lorne.

Lorraine apparently from Jeanne de Lorraine, another name for St Joan of Arc, or from Mary, Queen of Scots who was also Mary of Lorraine. In either case the origin is the French place name. **Loraine** often occurs.

Louisa, **Louise** feminine forms of *Louis*.

Lucy saint; Latin, from *lux* 'light'. Latin form **Lucia**, French **Lucie** occur, together with diminutives **Lucille, Lucinda**.

Lydia biblical; Greek '(woman of) Lydia' (region in Asia).

Lynne diminutive of Linda. **Lyn** and **Lynn** occur.

Lynette literary; possibly a variant of linnet, the song-bird.

Mabel short form of **Amabel**, Latin *amabilis* 'lovable'. Reinterpreted as French *ma belle* 'my beautiful one'.

Madeleine biblical; Hebrew; 'woman of Magdala'. **Madeline** is found.

Maisie Scottish pet form of **Margery, Marjorie**, forms of Margaret.

Mandy pet form of *Miranda, Amanda*.

Marcia regarded as a feminine form of *Mark* or *Marc*.

Margaret saint; Greek; 'pearl'. **Marguerite** occurs.

Margot French/German form of *Margaret*.

Maria, **Marie** Spanish/Italian and French forms of *Mary*.

Marian, **Marion** French diminutives of *Marie*.

Marianne a modern blend of *Maria* and *Anne*.

Marilyn a blend of *Mary* and *Ellen*.

Marina feminine of *Marinus*, from *Marius*, but usually connected with Latin *mare* 'sea'.

Marlene blend of *Maria* and *Magdalene*.

Martha biblical; Aramaic; feminine of *mar* 'lord'.

Martina, **Martine** feminine forms of *Martin*.

Mary biblical; Hebrew; 'lady or

seeress'. **Miriam** is another form of the name.

Matilda royal; Germanic 'mighty in battle'. **Maud** is a contracted form of the same name.

Maureen an Irish diminutive of *Mary*.

Mavis literary; from a word meaning 'song-thrush'.

May pet form of names beginning with *M* or the name of the month.

Maxine a shortening of *Maximilian*, converted to female use.

Megan Welsh diminutive from *Margaret*. **Meghan** is found.

Melanie saint; Greek; 'black'.

Melinda literary; based on Latin *mel* 'honey'.

Melissa literary; Greek; 'a bee'.

Melody the word used as a name.

Meredith Welsh; originally a male name. Based on a word meaning 'greatness'.

Michaela feminine form of *Michael*.

Michelle, **Michele** French feminine forms of *Michael* (*Michel*).

Mildred saint; Old English 'mild strength'.

Miranda literary; Latin 'fit to be admired'.

Miriam biblical; a form of *Mary*.

Moira Irish/Scottish form of *Mary*.

Molly, **Mollie** pet forms of *Mary*.

Monica saint; of unknown origin.

Muriel Irish 'sea-bright'.

Nadine a diminutive of **Nadia**, Russian 'hope'.

Nancy originally a pet form of *Ann(e)*.

Naomi biblical; Hebrew; 'pleasant one'.

Natalie saint; Latin; 'Christmas Day'.

Natasha Russian pet form of *Natalie*.

Nicola Italian (male) form of *Nicholas* used (in Britain only) as a girl's name. In the US the French feminine **Nicole** is usual. Pet forms such as **Nicky, Nikki** are used independently. **Nichola** is frequent. The diminutives **Nicoletta, Nicolette** occur.

Nina Russian diminutive of *Ann(e)*.

Nora(h) pet forms of *Eleanora, Honora*, etc.

Norma Latin 'pattern, model'.

Olga saint; Russian 'holy'.

Olive from the tree, a symbol of peace.

Olivia saint; Latin; 'olive'.

Paige from the surname, meaning 'page (boy)'.

Pamela literary; Greek; 'all sweetness'.

Patricia feminine form of *Patrick*.

Paula Latin; feminine form of *Paul*. **Paola** is the Italian form. **Pauline, Paulette** are diminutives.

Pearl the word used as a name.

Peggy pet form of *Margaret* (**Maggie, Meggie**).

Penelope literary; Greek; of uncertain origin. The pet form **Penny** occurs independently.

Philippa feminine form of *Philip*.

Phoebe mythological, biblical; Greek 'pure, bright'.

Phyllis mythological; Greek 'leafy plant'.

Poppy the flower name.

Priscilla biblical; Latin 'primitive'.

Rachael, Rachel biblical; Hebrew; 'ewe'.

Rebecca, Rebekah biblical; same meaning as *Leah*.

Regina Latin; 'queen'.

Renée French; 're-born'.

Rita pet form of *Margarita, Dorita,* etc.

Roberta feminine form of *Robert*.

Robin originally a male name based on *Robert*, now identified with the bird. **Robyn** occurs.

Rochelle French 'little rock'. Unknown as a first name in France. The pet form is said to be *Shelley*.

Rose the flower name used as a first name. *Rosa* is Latin form. Diminutives include **Rosaleen, Rosalie, Rosalind, Rosaline, Rosalyn, Rosanna, Rosanne, Roseline, Rosetta, Rosie, Rosina, Rosita, Roslyn.**

Rosemary a flower name, associated with 'remembrance'.

Roxanne historical; Persian, but of unknown meaning. Name of the Persian wife of Alexander the Great (**Roxana**).

Ruby from the precious stone.

Ruth biblical; Hebrew; origin uncertain.

Sabrina literary; legendary river goddess.

Sadie pet form of *Sarah*.

Sally pet form of *Sarah*, but long used independently. **Sallie** occurs.

Samantha possibly Aramaic, meaning 'listener'.

Sandra pet form of *Alexandra*. **Sandy** and **Sandie** also occur.

Sara(h) biblical; Hebrew; 'princess'.

Selina probably from French **Celine**, a saint's name ultimately connected with the Latin word for 'heaven'. **Selena** occurs.

Serena Latin; 'serene'.

Shannon apparently a use of the river/place name.

Sharlene a modern variant of *Charlene*.

Sharon biblical; Hebrew; 'plain' in its place-name sense. This is a place name in the Bible, not a personal name.

Sheena a phonetic rendering of Gaelic *Sine* or *Jean*.

Shelley this looks like a transferred use of the surname, but it is more likely to be a pet form of names like *Michelle, Rochelle,* etc., given a new spelling. **Shelly** also occurs.

Sheri a phonetic variant of *Chérie*. **Sheree, Sherrie** are variants. **Sheryl** is a diminutive.

Shirley surname/place name; Old English; 'bright clearing'. *Shelley* is also used as a pet form of this name.

Simone French feminine form of *Simon*.

Siobhan Irish form of *Joan*. **Sian** also occurs.

Sonia literary; Greek; Russian diminutive of *Sophia*. **Sonja** and **Sonya** also occur.

Sophia, Sophie royal; Greek; 'wisdom'.

Stacey pet form of **Anastasia**. **Staci, Stacie, Stacy** also occur.

Stella literary; Latin 'star'.

Stephanie French feminine form of *Stephen. Stefanie* occurs.

Susan biblical; Hebrew; 'lily'. The full name is **Susannah**. **Susanne** and **Suzanne** are popular variants.

Sylvia literary; Latin; 'wood'.

Tamara Russian form of a Hebrew name meaning 'palm tree'.

Tammy pet form of **Tamsin**, itself from **Thomasin**, a Cornish feminine form of *Thomas*. **Tammie** is found.

Tania diminutive of *Tatiana*, name of a Russian saint. **Tanya** also occurs.

Tara use of a place name which occurs in Moore's *Irish Melodies* and the novel *Gone With the Wind*.

Teresa, Theresa saint; Greek; 'reaper'. **Terri, Terrie, Terry** occur as pet forms.

Tessa literary; pet form of *Theresa*.

Tina pet form of names such as *Christina*, used independently.

Thelma literary; Greek 'will-power'.

Tiffany form of **Theophania**; Greek 'manifestation of God'.

Toni pet form of *Antonia*, feminine of *Antony*. **Tonia** is frequent.

Tracey, Tracy formerly a pet name from *Teresa*. Later from the surname, which in turn derives from a French place name.

Trudi, Trudy pet forms of **Gertrude** where 'trude' means 'strength'.

Ursula saint; diminutive of Latin *ursa* 'bear'.

Valerie saint; Latin 'to be strong'.

Vanessa literary; invented by Jonathan Swift, using parts of the names Esther Vanhomrigh.

Vera Slavic 'faith' but associated with Latin 'true'.

Verity Latin; 'truth'.

Veronica saint; Latin; 'true image'.

Victoria royal; Latin; 'victory'. **Vicki, Vicky, Vikki,** etc., now occur as names in their own right.

Violet the flower name.

Virginia a Roman name, but associated with Elizabeth I, the Virgin Queen.

Vivienne literary, of uncertain origin.

Wendy literary; used by J M Barrie in *Peter Pan* and said to be taken from the phrase 'friendy-wendy'.

Winifred Welsh 'blessed reconciliation'.

Yasmin variant of *Jasmine*.

Yvonne French feminine form of **Yves**, 'yew tree'. **Yvette** is also used.

Zara an Arabic royal name of uncertain origin.

Zoe saint; Greek; 'life'. **Zowie** occurs.

Girls' names used by black American families

Aisha probably meant for **Ayesha**, favourite wife of the Prophet Mohammad.

Ayanna, Ayana of unknown origin.

Camille French form of *Camilla*, which is of unknown origin.

Carmen Spanish form of Hebrew *Carmel*, 'garden'.

Chandra the god of the moon in Hindu mythology.

Dionne probably meant for *Dione*, name of the mother of Venus.

Ebony the word used as a name.

Felicia a variant of *Felicity*, Latin 'happiness'.

Gloria Latin 'glory'.

Gwendolyn a Welsh name based on a word meaning 'white, fair'.

India the name of the country used as a first name.

Jaleesa Afro-American invention presumably based (phonetically) on *Lisa*. Associated with Jaleesa Vinson of tv series *A Different World* and found also as **Gelisa, Jaleisa, Jalesa, Jalisa, Jelisa, Jillisa**.

Janay respelling of *Janie*, diminutive of *Jane*. Found also as **Janae, Janaye**.

Katina one of the *Katharine* group of names, based on Greek 'pure'.

Keisha of unknown origin.

Kendra presumably a blend of *Ken(neth)* and *(San)dra*.

Kenya the name of the country used as a first name.

Kenyatta the surname of the African political leader Jomo Kenyatta, used as a first name. **Kenyetta** also occurs.

Kizzy Alex Haley claims an African origin for this name in *Roots*, which brought it back into use, but all the evidence suggests that it is a pet form of **Keziah**, a biblical name, Hebrew 'cassia'. **Kizzie** also occurs.

Lakeisha the popular prefix La- attached to a second element. Also well-used are **Lashawn, Latanya, Latonya, Latasha, Latisha, Latoya** and **Latrice**, most of which are probably blends of La- and a name (or pet name) that can also be used independently. Some writers draw attention to the Roman version of *Leto's* name, *Latona*—the mother of Artemis and Apollo by Zeus, but the resemblance to this name and Latonya is probably a coincidence.

Marlena a Germanic blend of *Maria* and *Lena*.

Mildred saint; Old English; 'mild power'.

Monique the French form of *Monica*.

Nakia of unknown origin.

Nakita this appears to be a diminutive of *Nakia*.

Patrice French form of *Patricia*.

Rasheda, Rashida Arabic 'pious'.

Raven the name of the bird used as a first name.

Renita perhaps a variant of *Renata*, Latin 're-born'.

Sade said to be a short form of **Folashade**, Yoruba 'honour confers a crown'. Singer of this name pronounces it *Sharday*. Name found in that spelling, also as **Charde, Shadae, Shardae,** **Shardai, Sharde.**

Shanice diminutive of *Shannon*, *Chanel(le)*, etc. Occurs also as **Chanise, Shanece, Shaniece, Shanise, Shenice, Shenise.**

Shayla possibly a phonetic variant of *Sheila*.

Sierra Spanish place-name. Usage influenced by popularity of *Pierre* for boys, *Tierra* for girls.

Tamike, Tamika, Tameke, Tomika, etc. The American name-expert Dr Cleveland Kent Evans suggests that these are forms of Japanese **Tamiko** 'people' with feminine ending. *A Girl Named Tamiko* was released in 1963.

Tanisha possibly linked to a Hausa (African) day name which indicates birth on a Monday.

Tasha a pet form of *Natasha*.

Tawanna, Tawana of unknown origin.

Tennille of unknown origin.

Tiara the word used as a name, conveying the idea of 'a precious adornment'.

Tierra appears to be Spanish 'land, earth' but probably a spelling variant of *Tiara* influenced by *Pierre, Sierra*.

Tiffany a form of *Theophania*, Greek 'manifestation of God'.

Toya 'toy' with a feminine ending?

Wanda a Slavic name of unknown meaning.

Whitney from an English surname 'white island'. Associated mainly with the singer Whitney Houston. Found also as **Whitnee, Whitni, Whitnie, Whittany, Whittney.**

Yolanda a variant of *Viola*.

Some Irish first names for girls

Aileen variant of *Eileen*.

Áine an ancient Irish name now linked with *Anna*.

Aisling Irish 'dream, vision'.

Aoife Irish form of *Eva, Eve*.

Bernadette feminine form of *Bernard*.

Bridget Irish 'the high one'.

Ciara probably feminine form of *Ciaran* 'black'.

Deirdre Irish 'fear' or 'one who rages'.

Eileen English form of Irish *Eibhlin*, itself a form of *Evelyn* or *Helen*.

Ethna Irish 'little fire'.

Fidelma blend of *Fidel* 'faithful' and *Mary*.

Gráinne Irish 'love'.

Ita Irish 'thirst'.

Mairead Irish form of *Margaret*.

Majella a reference to St Gerard *Majella*.

Maura a variant of *Mary*.

Muirne Gaelic 'beloved'.

Niamh Irish 'bright'.

Nuala pet form of *Fionnuala* 'white shoulder'.

Orla Irish 'golden lady'.
Róisín Irish form of *Rose*.
Sheila a form of *Celia* or *Cecelia*, ultimately from a Roman clan name.
Sineád Irish form of *Janet*.
Siobhán Irish form of *Joan*.
Sorcha Irish 'bright'.
Una usually linked with Latin 'one'.

Some Scottish first names for girls

Ailsa from the name of the island rock, *Ailsa Craig*.
Alana feminine form of *Alan*.
Alexina feminine form of *Alexander*.
Antonia Latin feminine form of *Antony*.
Beathag Gaelic 'life'.
Catriona Gaelic form of *Catherine*.
Christy pet form of *Christina*, *Christine*.
Edwina feminine form of *Edwin*.
Eilidh Gaelic form of *Helen*.
Elspeth Scottish pet form of *Elizabeth*.
Esmé French 'esteemed'.
Fenella form of *Fionnghal*, Gaelic 'white shoulder'.
Ina pet form of *Georgina*, *Clementina*, etc.
Innes Gaelic 'island'.
Iona Scottish island name.
Isla Scottish river name.
Ismay Scottish family name.
Jessie pet form of *Jessica, Janet*.
Katrine Scottish loch name.
Kirstie Scottish pet form of *Christine*.
Mairi Gaelic form of *Mary*.
Malvina Gaelic 'smooth brow'.
Morag Gaelic 'great'.
Morna Gaelic 'beloved'.
Morven Gaelic 'big mountain peak'.
Rhona Scottish place name 'rough isle'.
Senga back-spelling of *Agnes*.
Shona English form of Gaelic *Seonaid*, feminine form of *John*.
Thora Scandinavian 'Thor battle'.

Some Welsh first names for girls

Angharad Welsh 'much loved'.
Anwen Welsh 'very beautiful'.
Arwenna Welsh 'muse'.
Bethan pet form of *Elizabeth-Ann*.
Bronwen Welsh 'white breast'.
Carys Welsh 'love'.
Catrin Welsh form of *Catherine*.
Ceinwen Welsh 'beautiful and blessed'.
Cerian diminutive of *Ceri*, 'love'.
Cerys Welsh 'love'.
Delyth Welsh 'pretty'.
Eirlys Welsh 'snowdrop'.
Elen Welsh 'nymph, angel'.
Eleri Welsh river name.
Elin pet form of *Elinor* or variant of *Helen*.
Eluned Welsh 'idol, icon'.
Enfys Welsh 'rainbow'.
Ffion Welsh 'foxglove'.
Heulwen Welsh 'sunshine'.
Llinos Welsh 'linnet'.
Lona pet form of *Maelona* 'princess'.
Lora variant of *Laura*.
Lowri Welsh form of *Laura*.
Mai Welsh form of *May*.
Mair Welsh form of *Mary*.
Meironwen Welsh 'white dairymaid'.
Meriel variant of *Muriel*.
Mererid Welsh form of *Margaret*.
Myfanwy Welsh 'my fine one'.
Nerys Welsh feminine of 'lord'.
Nesta Welsh pet form of *Agnes*.
Nia legendary name of unknown meaning.
Olwen Welsh 'white footprint'.
Rhiain Welsh 'maiden'.
Rhiannon Welsh 'nymph, goddess'.
Sian Welsh form of *Jane*.
Sioned Welsh form of *Janet*.

Some biblical first names for girls

Unless otherwise stated these names are of Hebrew origin

Adah 'ornament'.
Athaliah '*Yah* is exalted'.
Azubah 'abandoned'.
Bathsheba 'daughter of opulence'.
Bernice Greek 'bringer of victory'.
Bithiah Egyptian 'queen'.
Carmel 'orchard'. A place name.
Cassia English form of *Keziah*.
Damaris possibly Greek 'calf'.
Delilah Old Arabic 'coquette, flirt'.
Dinah 'lawsuit'.
Dorcas Greek 'gazelle'.
Edna 'delight, pleasure'.
Eunice Greek 'fine victory'.
Jael 'antelope'.
Jemimah 'turtle dove'.
Jezebel 'control, domination'.
Kerenhappuch 'mascara'.
Keturah 'incense'.
Keziah 'cassia'.
Lilith Acadian, name of a devil.
Lois Greek, of unknown meaning.
Lydia Greek, 'woman from Lydia' (a place in Asia Minor).
Magdalene 'tower', a place name.
Marisa 'summit', a place name.
Martha Aramaic 'mistress'.
Naamah 'loved, pretty'.
Rhoda Greek 'rose'.
Salome 'safe and sound, peace'.
Sheba 'seven, fullness or oath'.
Tabitha Aramaic 'gazelle'.
Tamar 'palm tree'.
Tirzah 'pleasure'.
Zilpah Arabic 'with a little nose'.
Zipporah 'bird'.

3
FASHIONABLE NAMES

SEVERAL distinct first-name periods have occurred during the last thousand or so years. Before the Norman Conquest, for instance, the single personal names in use were mainly composed of Old English elements. Some of those names live on today in slightly altered form: **Alfred, Alwin, Edgar, Edith, Edmund, Edward, Herbert, Mervin, Norman.** Others survive mainly as family names. Examples are: **Algar, Coleman, Derman, Gladwin, Godman, Godwin, Harding, Osmund, Sperling, Watman, Wulmar, Wumond.** A fuller list of such names is to be found on page 125.

Since the Anglo-Saxons constantly formed new names by blending a series of traditional name elements, there was not at any time a central stock of names, only a stock of name parts which could be permutated. The names that were formed were meant to individualise their bearers, and duplication was avoided. This was partly because a name was felt to contain a person's spirit, and using his name for a new-born child might have drained that spirit from him. It was also partly because each person bore only one name, not a first name, middle name and last name, and that name was correspondingly more important for identification purposes.

Norman names

When the Normans conquered Britain in 1066 they brought with them a stock of new names and different ideas about naming. They were beginning to use the first name and last name system, which allowed the same first names to be borne by many different people at the same time. The names had also acquired a fixed form, they were not broken down and re-assembled for each new generation. Popular with the Normans were names like **Alan, Bernard, Brian, Denis, Everard, Geoffrey, Gerald, Gervase, Henry, Hugh, Louis, Maurice, Oliver, Piers, Ralph, Richard, Robert, Roger, Roland, Walter** and **Warren. William** was an outstanding

Twenty years ago, practically every other girl born in Gentilly must have been named Marcia. A year or so later it was Linda. Then Sharon.

Walker Percy   *The Moviegoer*

favourite. As for the Norman ladies, they were often **Adela, Alice, Amice, Avis, Constance, Emma, Jocelyn, Laura, Marjorie, Maud, Oriel, Rosamond** and **Yvonne.**

In the centuries that followed their arrival on British shores, it was the Normans and their descendants who formed the aristocracy. As has always been the case, those who were lower in the social scale aped the habits and customs of their superiors. This led to the steady disappearance of the Old English names and their replacement by the names the Normans had introduced. These names in their turn ceased to be 'new' and were thought by succeeding generations to be thoroughly English.

Christian names

The next naming period introduced Christian names in the true sense, for the Church encouraged parents to use names of Christian significance. In the 16th century the split between Roman Catholics and Protestants was reflected in name usage. The Protestants turned away from Catholic names such as **Mary,** and from the names of saints such as **Augustine** and **Benedict, Barbara** and **Agnes.** They preferred to use the Bible as a principal source of names, especially the Old Testament. It was now that Hebrew names such as **Aaron, Abraham, Adam, Benjamin, Daniel, David, Jacob, Jonathan, Joseph, Joshua, Michael, Nathan, Noah, Samuel, Saul, Seth** and **Solomon** were brought into use for boys, while the girls became **Abigail, Beulah, Deborah, Dinah,**

Esther, Eve, Hannah, Keziah, Leah, Miriam, Naomi, Rachel, Rebekah, Ruth, Sarah and Tamar. These names were later to become especially associated with the USA, when religious persecution forced the Protestant groups to emigrate.

Not all the Old Testament names, incidentally, were as familiar and pleasant as those mentioned above. At this time children also received biblical names such as Amaziah, Belteshazzar, Habakkuk, Jehoshaphat, Nebuchadnezzar and Onesiphorous (boys); Aholibamah, Eglah, Abishag and Maachah (girls).

It was also in the 16th and 17th centuries that the religious extremists known as Puritans appeared on the scene. For some of them, even the names that had biblical sanction were not pure enough. They gave their children slogan names, such as Be-Courteous, Faint-not, Fight-the-good-fight-of-faith, Fly-fornication, Make-peace, Safe-deliverance, Stand-fast-on-high, The Lord-is-near. Such names were much laughed at by the general public, of course, and sanity re-asserted itself. The more sensible Puritans had in the meantime managed to display their religious beliefs in less eccentric ways, creating a group of names which have survived to the present day. This naming layer featured the 'virtues', and it includes such names as Amity, Charity, Faith, Felicity, Grace, Honour, Hope, Joy, Mercy, Patience, Prudence and Verity.

The 18th century was marked by the emergence of diminutives as names in their own right. Until this time, women who might be known as Bess, Beth, Betty, Eliza, Elsie, Liz or Liza were all formally baptised as Elizabeth. Now the pet names began to appear in parish registers as official names. The names had perhaps been created centuries previ-ously; they simply achieved official recognition from 1750 onwards.

Flower names

The end of the 19th century brought flower names into fashion. Rose and Lily were amongst the earliest of such names to be used if one discounts names in other languages, such as Susanna, which happens to mean 'lily' in Hebrew. Hazel quickly became popular in the USA, while Ivy, Olive, Violet and Daisy appealed to British parents.

Once the idea of using flower names had established itself, more exotic names were used. A Bluebell Smith was named in 1902, an Eglantine Smith in 1890. When searching through birth records of the period it is not difficult to find examples of Blossom, Bryony, Cherry, Daffodil, Daphne, Fern, Heather, Holly, Iris, Laurel, Myrtle, Pansy, Poppy, Primrose, Snowdrop and Viola. An English clergyman who made a rail journey in 1890 commented on 'a perfect nosegay of children, all members of one family' that he met. Their names were Daisy, May, Lily, Violet and Olive. The same clergyman commented on a superstition that arose at the time—that children who bore flower names were supposed, like the flowers themselves, to live only a short time.

Other groups of names

Soon after the flowers came the jewel names. The main ones to be used were Pearl, Ruby, Beryl, Opal, Crystal, Amber, Coral, Amethyst, Jet, Onyx, Jade

---

They belonged to the Church of the Covenant community on Herkomer's Knob, the religious sect that had found its way from Kentucky into southern Illinois a hundred years ago. They were largely Indian stock though they bore English and Irish family names. Their given names were the source of much amusement. Some were taken from the Bible, but the larger number were from the two works that always accompanied the earliest adventurers from Virginia into the Wilderness: The Pilgrim's Progress *and* Plutarch's Lives. *There was many a Christian and a Good Works, and many a Lycurgus, an Apaminondas, a Solon, and an Aristides. The plantation owners in the East had drawn from Plutarch the tyrranicides and warriors – Cassius, Cincinnatus, Horatius, and Brutus.*

Thornton Wilder   *The Eighth Day*

Most of us are fairly certain to meet during our lifetime someone who bears the same first name as ourselves. From time to time I receive letters, however, from those who consider themselves to be nominally unique. A typical example of such a correspondent is **Harrianne** Mills, who writes from Gambier, Ohio. Miss Mills has borne her name since 1952. She explains the 'Harrianne' by saying simply: 'I was supposed to be a boy . . .' Not that all that many boys are called Harrianne, of course. I am compiling a list of these unique names, and would be glad to hear from those who bear them.

and **Diamond. Margaret** actually belongs in this group, since it also means 'pearl'.

Another distinctive layer of names began to appear in the 1930s. We might call this the 'fanciful spelling' period, for it has led to dozens of modern names like **Vikki, Mandi, Lynda, Jayne, Carolyn, Kristine, Debra**. It will be noticed that these examples are all girls' names. The attitude still persists that one may be frivolous or experimental in naming a girl, but tradition must rule when a boy is named.

Other groups of first names can be identified quite easily but it is not always possible to assign them to a period of time. We have the classical names, for instance, such as **Diana, Cassandra, Venus, Cynthia, Delia, Corinna, Sylvia, Anthea**. We must not forget **Alexander**, the most famous Greek name of all and the most popular name of this type to be taken into our own name stock. These names began to be used before the 17th century, since William Camden mentioned several of them in his *Remains*, published in 1605, but there was never a period of thirty years or so when they suddenly appeared in great numbers.

Similar groups of names, which do not link with a particular period, are animal names (**Leo, Leonard, Lionel**—lion; **Orson, Ursula**—bear; **Deborah, Melissa**—bee; **Jemimah, Jonah, Malcolm**—dove; **Rachel**—ewe; **Arnold**—eagle), and colour names (**Candida, Blanche, Bianca**—white; **Roy, Russell, Ginger**—red; **Electra, Amber**—amber; **Boyd, Flavia**—yellow; **Duncan, Dugald, Dougal**—brown; **Aurelia**—gold; **Melanie**—black; **Douglas**—blue). One cannot say of such groups that they suddenly became fashionable in the way that flower names obviously did.

The present stock of names contains examples from each layer, and the personal preference of each set of parents determines which kind of name is used. Nevertheless, as name-counts of all kinds clearly show, certain names become far more popular than others at a particular moment. One can only speculate as to the reasons.

It is not enough to say that a name becomes popular because a famous person bears it. Queen Victoria was certainly famous enough during her reign, yet **Victoria** was very rarely used during the 19th century. **Winston** Churchill was likewise famous in 1945, yet few boys were given his name at that time. **Elvis** Presley and **Errol** Flynn failed to have a significant impact on naming in spite of their fame and popularity.

A famous person may make a name known, but it has to have something about it which makes a general appeal. Its sound may be important, for instance. It is noticeable that **Karen, Darren, Sharon**—and to a lesser extent, **Aaron**—became

Pop drove happily . . . thinking of his six children and the splendid, handsome names he and Ma had given them. Jolly good names, perfick, every one of them, he thought. There was a reason for them all. Montgomery, the only boy, had been named after the general. Primrose had come in the Spring. Zinnia and Petunia were twins and they were the flowers Ma liked most. Victoria, the youngest girl, had been born in plum-time.

Suddenly he couldn't remember why they had called the eldest Mariette . . .

'I wanted to call her after that Queen,' Ma said. 'The French one, Marie Antoinette. But you said it was too long. You'd never say it, you said.'

H. E. Bates   *The Darling Buds of May.*

more fashionable at the same time, a phenomenon repeated in the case of **Vicky, Nicky** and **Ricky; Kerry, Terry, Sherri**. Then the name must have been little used for at least a generation. The name will be used at first by those who wish to get away from fashionable trends, but if they have chosen well, others will follow their lead. One can safely say that any name which is at the height of fashion at a given moment will go out of fashion within fifteen years, but it is impossible to predict which name will take its place. It does seem, however, that given time, every name will eventually have its day.

Changing Fashions

The fashion in Christian names [at the end of the nineteenth century] was changing; babies were being christened Mabel and Gladys and Doreen and Percy and Stanley; but the change was too recent to have affected the names of the older children. Mary Ann, Sarah Ann, Eliza, Martha, Annie, Jane, Amy, and Rose were favourite girls' names. There was a Mary Ann in almost every family, and Eliza was nearly as popular. But none of them were called by their proper names. Mary Ann and Sarah Ann were contracted to Mar'ann and Sar'ann. Mary, apart from Ann, had, by stages, descended through Molly and Polly to Poll. Eliza had become Liza, then Tiza, then Tize; Martha was Mat or Pat; Jane was Jin; and every Amy had at least one 'Aim' in life, of which she had constant reminder. The few more uncommon names were also distorted. Two sisters named at the font Beatrice and Agnes, went through life as Beat and Agg, Laura was Lor, or Low, and Edmund was Ned or Ted.

Laura's mother disliked this cheapening of names and named her third child May, thinking it would not lend itself to a diminutive. However, while still in her cradle, the child became Mayie among the neighbours.

There was no Victoria in the school, nor was there a Miss Victoria or a Lady Victoria in any of the farmhouses, rectories or mansions in the district, nor did Laura ever meet a Victoria in later life. That great name was sacred to the Queen and was not copied by her subjects to the extent imagined by period novelists of today.
Flora Thompson   *Lark Rise to Candleford*

In those old days the average man called his children after his most revered and historical idols; consequently there was hardly a family, at least in the West, but had a Washington in it—and also a Lafayette, a Franklin, and six or eight sounding names from Byron, Scott, and the Bible, if the offspring held out. To visit such a family, was to find oneself confronted by a congress made up of representatives of the imperial myths and the majestic dead of all the ages. There was something thrilling about it, not to say awe-inspiring.
Mark Twain   *The Gilded Age*

'Everybody in the next generation,' suggested Dick, 'will be named Peter or Barbara—because at present all the piquant literary characters are named Peter or Barbara.'

Anthony continued the prophecy: 'Of course Gladys and Eleanor, having graced the last generation of heroines and being at present in their social prime, will be passed on to the next generation of shop-girls—'

'Displacing Ella and Stella,' interrupted Dick.

'And Pearl and Jewel,' Gloria added cordially, 'and Earl and Elmer and Minnie.'

'And then I'll come along,' remarked Dick, 'and picking up the obsolete name, Jewel, I'll attach it to some quaint and attractive character and it'll start its career all over again.'
F. Scott Fitzgerald   *The Beautiful and Damned*

The top fifty first names* for boys, England and Wales

1700
1 John
2 William
3 Thomas
4 Richard
5 James
6 Robert
7 Joseph
8 Edward
9 Henry
10 George
11 Samuel
12 Francis
13 Charles
14 Daniel
15 Benjamin
16 Edmund
17 Matthew
18 Peter
19 Nicholas
20 Isaac
21 Christopher
22 Abraham
23 Stephen
24 Jonathan
25 Philip
26 Michael
27 Hugh
28 Joshua
29 Anthony
30 Ralph
31 Andrew
32 David
33 Simon
34 Roger
35 Alexander
36 Jacob
37 Laurence
38 Moses
39 Nathaniel
40 Walter
41 Aaron
42 Jeremy
43 Owen
44 Mark
45 Timothy
46 Adam
47 Martin
48 Josiah
49 Luke
50 Harry

1800
1 William
2 John
3 Thomas
4 James
5 George
6 Joseph
7 Richard
8 Henry
9 Robert
10 Charles
11 Samuel
12 Edward
13 Benjamin
14 Isaac
15 Peter
16 Daniel
17 David
18 Francis
19 Stephen
20 Jonathan
21 Christopher
22 Matthew
23 Edmund
24 Philip
25 Abraham
26 Mark
27 Michael
28 Ralph
29 Jacob
30 Andrew
31 Moses
32 Nicholas
33 Anthony
34 Luke
35 Simon
36 Josiah
37 Timothy
38 Martin
39 Nathaniel
40 Roger
41 Walter
42 Aaron
43 Jeremy
44 Joshua
45 Alexander
46 Adam
47 Hugh
48 Laurence
49 Owen
50 Harry

1850
1 William
2 John
3 George
  Thomas
5 James
6 Henry
7 Charles
8 Joseph
9 Robert
10 Samuel
11 Edward
12 Frederick
13 Alfred
14 Richard
15 Walter
16 Arthur
17 Benjamin
18 David
19 Edwin
20 Albert
21 Francis
22 Daniel
   Sidney
24 Harry
   Philip
26 Isaac
27 Herbert
   Peter
29 Alexander
   Frank
   Matthew
32 Stephen
   Tom
34 Abraham
   Elijah
36 Jacob
   Jonathan
   Joshua
39 Edmund
   Hugh
   Josiah
   Reuben
43 Amos
   Christopher
   Eli
   Ralph
47 Andrew
   Horace
   Israel
   Jesse
   Moses
   Seth

1875
1 William
2 John
3 George
4 Thomas
5 James
6 Henry
7 Charles
8 Frederick
9 Arthur
10 Joseph
11 Albert
12 Alfred
13 Walter
14 Harry
15 Edward
16 Robert
17 Ernest
18 Herbert
19 Sidney
20 Samuel
21 Frank
22 Richard
23 Fred
24 Francis
25 David
26 Percy
27 Edwin
28 Alexander
29 Peter
   Tom
31 Benjamin
   Harold
33 Daniel
   Isaac
35 Edgar
   Matthew
   Philip
38 Stephen
39 Andrew
   Sam
41 Abraham
   Christopher
   Oliver
   Willie
45 Alan
   Bertram
   Horace
   Leonard
   Ralph
50 Reginald
   Wilfred

1900
1 William
2 John
3 George
4 Thomas
5 Charles
6 Frederick
7 Arthur
8 James
9 Albert
10 Ernest
11 Robert
12 Henry
13 Alfred
14 Sidney
15 Joseph
16 Harold
   Harry
18 Frank
19 Walter
20 Herbert
21 Edward
22 Percy
23 Richard
24 Samuel
25 Leonard
26 Stanley
27 Reginald
28 Francis
29 Fred
30 Cecil
31 Wilfred
32 Horace
33 Cyril
34 David
   Norman
36 Eric
37 Victor
38 Edgar
39 Leslie
40 Bertie
   Edwin
42 Donald
43 Benjamin
   Hector
   Jack
   Percival
47 Clifford
48 Alexander
   Baden
50 Bernard
   Redvers

1925
1 John
2 William
3 George
4 James
5 Ronald
6 Robert
7 Kenneth
8 Frederick
9 Thomas
10 Albert
11 Eric
12 Edward
13 Arthur
14 Charles
15 Leslie
16 Sidney
17 Frank
18 Peter
19 Dennis
20 Joseph
21 Alan
22 Stanley
23 Ernest
24 Harold
25 Norman
26 Raymond
27 Leonard
28 Alfred
   Harry
30 Donald
   Reginald
32 Roy
33 Derek
34 Henry
35 Geoffrey
36 David
   Gordon
   Herbert
   Walter
40 Cyril
41 Jack
42 Richard
43 Douglas
44 Maurice
45 Bernard
   Gerald
47 Brian
48 Victor
   Wilfred
50 Francis

*Names with variant spellings are listed by their most frequent form

1935
1 John
2 Brian
3 Peter
4 Ronald
5 Michael
6 Alan
7 William
8 David
9 Kenneth
10 George
11 Derek
12 James
13 Robert
14 Donald
15 Colin
16 Raymond
17 Roy
18 Thomas
19 Anthony
20 Dennis
21 Joseph
22 Arthur
23 Edward
24 Frank
25 Norman
26 Geoffrey
27 Terence
28 Charles
   Frederick
30 Gordon
31 Eric
32 Albert
   Barry
   Leslie
35 Graham
36 Gerald
   Sidney
38 Leonard
39 Harold
40 Keith
41 Malcolm
   Reginald
43 Douglas
   Stanley
45 Bernard
   Ian
   Richard
48 Alfred
   Maurice
50 Henry

1950
1 David
2 John
3 Peter
4 Michael
5 Alan
6 Robert
7 Stephen
8 Paul
9 Brian
10 Graham
11 Philip
12 Anthony
13 Colin
14 Christopher
15 Geoffrey
16 William
17 James
18 Keith
   Terence
20 Barry
   Malcolm
   Richard
23 Ian
24 Derek
25 Roger
26 Raymond
27 Kenneth
28 Andrew
29 Trevor
30 Martin
31 Kevin
32 Ronald
33 Leslie
34 Charles
   George
36 Thomas
37 Nigel
   Stuart
39 Edward
40 Gordon
41 Roy
42 Dennis
43 Neil
44 Laurence
45 Clive
   Eric
47 Frederick
   Patrick
   Robin
50 Donald
   Joseph

1965
1 Paul
2 David
3 Andrew
4 Stephen
5 Mark
6 Michael
7 Ian
8 Gary
9 Robert
10 Richard
11 Peter
12 John
13 Anthony
14 Christopher
15 Darren
16 Kevin
17 Martin
18 Simon
19 Philip
20 Graham
21 Colin
22 Adrian
23 Nigel
24 Alan
25 Neil
26 Shaun
27 Jonathan
28 Nicholas
29 Stuart
30 Timothy
31 Wayne
32 Brian
33 James
34 Carl
35 Jeffrey
36 Barry
37 Dean
38 Matthew
39 William
40 Keith
41 Julian
42 Trevor
43 Roger
   Russell
45 Derek
   Lee
47 Clive
   Jeremy
49 Patrick
50 Daniel
   Kenneth
   Raymond

1975
1 Stephen
2 Mark
3 Paul
4 Andrew
5 David
6 Richard
7 Matthew
8 Daniel
9 Christopher
10 Darren
11 Michael
12 James
13 Robert
14 Simon
15 Jason
16 Stuart
17 Neil
18 Lee
19 Jonathan
20 Ian
   Nicholas
22 Gary
23 Craig
24 Martin
25 John
26 Carl
27 Philip
28 Kevin
29 Benjamin
30 Peter
31 Wayne
32 Adam
33 Anthony
34 Alan
35 Graham
36 Adrian
37 Colin
   Scott
39 Timothy
40 Barry
41 William
42 Dean
   Jamie
44 Nathan
45 Justin
46 Damian
   Thomas
48 Joseph
49 Alexander
   Alistair
   Nigel
   Shaun

1985
1 Christopher
2 Matthew
3 David
4 James
5 Daniel
6 Andrew
7 Steven
8 Michael
9 Mark
10 Paul
11 Richard
12 Adam
13 Robert
14 Lee
15 Craig
16 Benjamin
   Thomas
18 Peter
19 Anthony
20 Shaun
21 Gary
22 Stuart
23 Jonathan
   Simon
25 Philip
26 Darren
27 Carl
28 Martin
   Nicholas
30 John
31 Luke
32 Neil
33 Jason
34 Alexander
   Kevin
36 Dean
37 Ian
   Jamie
39 Ryan
40 Stacey
   Timothy
   Wayne
43 Alan
   Graham
   Oliver
46 William
47 Joseph
48 Gavin
   Nathan
50 Ben
   Edward
   Gareth

1995
1 Daniel
2 Thomas
3 Matthew
4 Joshua
5 Adam
6 Luke
7 Michael
8 Christopher
9 Ryan
10 Jack
11 Samuel
12 Benjamin
13 Alexander
14 Stephen
15 Joseph
16 Jordan
17 James
18 Aaron
19 Ashley
20 Andrew
21 Robert
22 David
23 Lewis
24 Oliver
25 Jake
26 William
27 Nathan
28 Connor
29 Jonathan
30 Sean
31 George
32 Richard
33 Nicholas
34 Anthony
35 Mark
36 Reece
37 Callum
38 Scott
39 Craig
40 Ben
41 Sam
42 Lee
43 Kieran
44 Edward
45 Martin
46 Kyle
47 Jacob
48 Karl
49 Philip
50 Paul

The top fifty first names for boys, USA

1875
1 William
2 John
3 Charles
4 Harry
5 James
6 George
7 Frank
8 Robert
9 Joseph
10 Thomas
11 Walter
12 Edward
13 Samuel
14 Henry
15 Arthur
16 Albert
17 Louis
18 David
Frederick
20 Clarence
21 Alexander
22 Fred
Howard
24 Alfred
Edwin
Paul
27 Ernest
Jacob
29 Ralph
30 Leon
Oscar
32 Andrew
Carl
Francis
Harold
36 Allen
Herman
Warren
39 Benjamin
Eugene
Herbert
Lewis
Maurice
Richard
45 Clifford
46 Earl(e)
Edgar
Elmer
Guy
Isaac
Leroy
Stanley

1900
1 John
2 William
3 Charles
4 Robert
5 Joseph
6 James
7 George
8 Samuel
9 Thomas
10 Arthur
11 Harry
12 Edward
13 Henry
14 Walter
15 Louis
16 Paul
17 Ralph
18 Carl
19 Frank
20 Raymond
21 Francis
22 Frederick
23 Albert
Benjamin
25 David
26 Harold
27 Howard
28 Fred
Richard
30 Clarence
Herbert
32 Jacob
33 Ernest
Jack
35 Herman
Philip
Stanley
38 Donald
Earl
Elmer
41 Leon
Nathan
43 Eugene
Floyd
Ray
Roy
Sydney
48 Abraham
Edwin
Lawrence
Leonard
Norman
Russell

1925
1 Robert
2 John
3 William
4 James
5 Charles
6 Richard
7 George
8 Donald
9 Joseph
10 Edward
11 Thomas
12 David
13 Frank
14 Harold
15 Arthur
16 Jack
17 Paul
18 Kenneth
19 Walter
20 Raymond
21 Carl
22 Albert
23 Henry
24 Harry
25 Francis
26 Ralph
27 Eugene
28 Howard
29 Lawrence
30 Louis
31 Alan
32 Norman
33 Gerald
34 Herbert
35 Fred
36 Earl
Philip
Stanley
39 Daniel
40 Leonard
Marvin
42 Frederick
43 Anthony
Samuel
45 Bernard
Edwin
47 Alfred
48 Russell
Warren
50 Ernest

1940
1 Robert
2 James
3 John
4 William
5 Richard
6 Thomas
7 David
8 Ronald
9 Donald
10 Michael
11 Charles
12 Joseph
13 Gerald
14 Kenneth
15 Lawrence
16 Edward
17 George
18 Paul
19 Dennis
20 Gary
21 Raymond
22 Daniel
23 Frank
24 Larry
25 Carl
26 Frederick
27 Allen
28 Walter
29 Anthony
30 Ralph
31 Philip
32 Leonard
33 Harold
34 Stephen
35 Roger
36 Norman
37 Arthur
38 Jack
Peter
40 Henry
Jerome
42 Douglas
Patrick
44 Eugene
45 Jerry
46 Louis
47 Harry
48 Francis
Howard
50 Bruce
Theodore
Timothy

1950
1 Robert
2 Michael
3 James
4 John
5 David
6 William
7 Thomas
8 Richard
9 Gary
10 Charles
11 Ronald
12 Dennis
13 Steven
14 Kenneth
15 Joseph
16 Mark
17 Daniel
18 Paul
19 Donald
20 Gregory
21 Larry
22 Lawrence
23 Timothy
24 Alan
25 Edward
26 Gerald
27 Douglas
28 George
29 Frank
30 Patrick
31 Anthony
32 Philip
33 Raymond
34 Bruce
35 Jeffrey
36 Brian
37 Peter
38 Frederick
39 Roger
40 Carl
41 Dale
Walter
43 Christopher
44 Martin
45 Craig
46 Arthur
47 Andrew
48 Jerome
49 Leonard
50 Henry

1960
1 Michael
2 David
3 Robert
4 James
5 John
6 Mark
7 Steven
8 Thomas
9 William
10 Joseph
11 Kevin
12 Richard
13 Kenneth
14 Jeffrey
15 Timothy
16 Daniel
17 Brian
18 Paul
19 Ronald
20 Gregory
21 Anthony
22 Donald
23 Charles
24 Christopher
25 Keith
26 Edward
27 Dennis
28 Gary
29 Lawrence
30 Patrick
31 Scott
32 Darryl
33 Gerald
34 Craig
35 Douglas
36 Alan
37 George
38 Dwayne
39 Peter
40 Matthew
41 Philip
42 Andrew
43 Bruce
44 Frank
45 Raymond
46 Eric
47 Carl
48 Randall
49 Martin
50 Larry

1970	1990 Whites	1990 Non-whites	1995 Whites	1995 Non-whites
1 Michael	1 Michael	1 Michael	1 Michael	1 Christopher
2 Robert	2 Christopher	2 Christopher	2 Joshua	2 Michael
3 David	3 Matthew	3 Brandon	3 Matthew	3 Brandon
4 James	4 Joshua	4 James	4 Jacob	4 Joshua
5 John	5 Andrew	5 Anthony	5 Zachary	5 James
6 Jeffrey	6 Daniel	6 Joshua	6 Christopher	6 Anthony
7 Steven	7 Justin	7 Robert	7 Tyler	7 Devonte
8 Christopher	8 David	8 David	8 Brandon	8 Jonathan
9 Brian	9 Ryan	9 Brian	9 Andrew	9 William
10 Mark	10 John	10 Jonathan	10 Nicholas	10 Justin
11 William	11 Steven	11 Justin	11 William	11 Jordan
12 Eric	12 Robert	12 Eric	12 Cody	12 Aaron
13 Kevin	13 James	13 Kevin	13 James	13 Darius
14 Scott	14 Nicholas	14 Steven	14 John	14 Eric
15 Joseph	15 Joseph	15 John	15 Joseph	15 Devin
16 Daniel	16 Brian	16 Marcus	16 Austin	16 David
17 Thomas	17 Jonathan	17 Derrick	17 Ryan	17 Marcus
18 Anthony	18 Kyle	18 William	18 Justin	18 Kevin
19 Richard	19 Sean	19 Darryl	19 Dylan	19 Antonio
20 Charles	20 William	20 Terrence	20 Jonathan	20 John
21 Kenneth	21 Brandon	21 Sean	21 Daniel	21 Derrick
22 Matthew	22 Eric	22 Joseph	22 David	22 Robert
23 Jason	23 Zachary	23 Antonio	23 Steven	23 Steven
24 Paul	24 Thomas	24 Daniel	24 Robert	24 Brian
25 Timothy	25 Anthony	25 Aaron	25 Alexander	25 Charles
26 Sean	26 Kevin	Ryan	26 Kyle	26 Darian
27 Gregory	27 Adam	27 Charles	27 Jordan	27 Joseph
28 Ronald	28 Tyler	28 Jeremy	28 Aaron	28 Corey
29 Todd	29 Jacob	29 Kenneth	29 Thomas	29 Jalen
30 Edward	30 Jeffrey	30 Andre	30 Adam	30 Cameron
31 Derrick	31 Jason	31 Andrew	31 Benjamin	31 Timothy
32 Keith	32 Timothy	Corey	32 Eric	32 Nicholas
33 Patrick	33 Benjamin	33 Matthew	33 Samuel	33 Tyler
34 Darryl	34 Corey	Jeffrey	34 Caleb	34 Ryan
35 Dennis	35 Aaron	35 Richard	35 Anthony	35 Shaquille
36 Andrew	36 Mark	36 Mark	36 Brian	36 Terrence
37 Donald	37 Alexander	37 Timothy	37 Timothy	37 Xavier
38 Gary	38 Richard	38 Antwan	38 Nathan	38 Dequan
39 Allen	39 Cody	39 Gregory	39 Sean	39 Jeremy
40 Douglas	40 Jeremy	Keith	40 Corey	40 Sean
41 George	41 Nathan	41 Donte	41 Jesse	41 DeAndre
42 Marcus	42 Travis	Travis	42 Dustin	42 Trey
43 Raymond	43 Derek	43 Devin	43 Kevin	43 Daniel
44 Peter	44 Jared	44 Jason	44 Charles	44 Matthew
45 Gerald	45 Patrick	45 Jamal	45 Christian	45 Christian
46 Frank	46 Scott	Ronald	46 Taylor	46 Tevin
Jonathan	47 Charles	Terrell	47 Patrick	47 Dominique
Lawrence	48 Dustin	48 Maurice	48 Jeffrey	48 Alexander
49 Aaron	49 Jordan	49 Phillip	49 Cameron	49 Deontae
Philip	50 Jesse	50 Edward	50 Jeremy	50 Gregory

The top fifty first names* for girls, England and Wales

1700	1800	1850	1875	1900	1925
1 Mary	1 Mary	1 Mary	1 Mary	1 Florence	1 Joan
2 Elizabeth	2 Ann	2 Elizabeth	2 Elizabeth	2 Mary	2 Mary
3 Ann	3 Elizabeth	3 Sarah	3 Sarah	3 Alice	3 Joyce
4 Sarah	4 Sarah	4 Ann	4 Annie	4 Annie	4 Margaret
5 Jane	5 Jane	5 Eliza	5 Alice	5 Elsie	5 Dorothy
6 Margaret	6 Hannah	6 Jane	6 Florence	6 Edith	6 Doris
7 Susan	7 Susan	7 Emma	7 Emily	7 Elizabeth	7 Kathleen
8 Martha	8 Martha	8 Hannah	8 Edith	8 Doris	8 Irene
9 Hannah	9 Margaret	9 Ellen	9 Ellen	9 Dorothy	9 Betty
10 Catherine	10 Charlotte	10 Martha	10 Ada	Ethel	10 Eileen
11 Alice	11 Harriet	11 Emily	11 Margaret	11 Gladys	11 Doreen
12 Frances	12 Betty	12 Harriet	12 Ann	12 Lilian	12 Lilian
13 Eleanor	13 Maria	13 Alice	13 Emma	13 Hilda	Vera
14 Dorothy	14 Catherine	14 Margaret	14 Jane	14 Margaret	14 Jean
Rebecca	15 Frances	15 Maria	15 Eliza	15 Winifred	15 Marjorie
16 Isabel	16 Mary Ann	16 Louisa	16 Louisa	16 Lily	16 Barbara
17 Grace	17 Nancy	17 Fanny	17 Clara	17 Ellen	17 Edna
18 Joan	18 Rebecca	18 Caroline	18 Martha	18 Ada	18 Gladys
19 Rachel	19 Alice	19 Charlotte	19 Harriet	19 Emily	19 Audrey
20 Agnes	20 Ellen	20 Susannah	20 Hannah	20 Violet	20 Elsie
21 Ellen	21 Sophia	21 Frances	21 Kate	21 Rose	21 Florence
22 Maria	22 Lucy	22 Catherine	22 Frances	Sarah	Hilda
23 Lydia	23 Isabel	23 Amelia	23 Charlotte	23 Nellie	Winifred
24 Ruth	24 Eleanor	24 Lucy	24 Lilly	24 May	24 Olive
25 Deborah	25 Esther	25 Clara	25 Ethel	25 Beatrice	25 Violet
Judith	26 Fanny	Esther	26 Lucy	26 Gertrude	26 Elizabeth
27 Esther	27 Eliza	27 Betsy	Rose	Ivy	27 Edith
Joanna	Grace	Isabella	28 Agnes	28 Mabel	28 Ivy
29 Amy	Sally	29 Eleanor	29 Minnie	29 Jessie	29 Peggy
Marjorie	30 Rachel	Matilda	30 Fanny	30 Maud	Phyllis
Phoebe	31 Lydia	Sophia	31 Caroline	31 Eva	31 Evelyn
32 Jenny	32 Caroline	Susan	32 Amy	32 Agnes	32 Iris
33 Barbara	33 Dorothy	33 Rebecca	Jessie	Jane	33 Annie
Bridget	34 Peggy	34 Anna	34 Eleanor	34 Evelyn	Rose
35 Fanny	35 Ruth	35 Agnes	35 Catherine	35 Frances	35 Beryl
36 Lucy	36 Kitty	Rachel	Maria	Kathleen	Lily
37 Betty	37 Jenny	37 Julia	37 Gertrude	37 Clara	Muriel
Eliza	38 Phoebe	Rose	38 Isabella	38 Olive	Sheila
Nancy	39 Agnes	39 Selina	39 Maud	39 Amy	39 Ethel
40 Emma	Emma	40 Kate	40 Laura	40 Catherine	40 Alice
41 Charlotte	41 Amy	Nancy	Lilian	41 Grace	41 Constance
42 Dinah	Jemima	Phoebe	42 Amelia	42 Emma	Ellen
Sally	43 Dinah	43 Annie	Esther	43 Nora	43 Gwendoline
44 Harriet	44 Barbara	Lydia	44 Beatrice	44 Louisa	Patricia
Jemima	45 Joan	Ruth	45 Bertha	Minnie	45 Sylvia
Kitty	46 Joanna	46 Priscilla	46 Susannah	46 Lucy	46 Nora
Mary Ann	47 Deborah	Rosanna	47 Lizzie	47 Daisy	Pamela
48 Caroline	Judith	48 Jessie	48 Henrietta	Eliza	48 Grace
Peggy	49 Bridget	49 Amy	Nelly	49 Phyllis	49 Jessie
Sophia	Marjorie	Grace	Rebecca	Ann	50 Mabel
		Helen			
		Henrietta			
		Jemima			

*Names with variant spellings are listed by their most frequent form

1935	1950	1965	1975	1985	1995
1 Shirley	1 Susan	1 Trac(e)y	1 Claire	1 Sarah	1 Rebecca
2 Margaret	2 Linda	2 Deborah	2 Sarah	2 Claire	2 Amy
3 Jean	3 Christine	3 Julie	3 Nicola	3 Emma	3 Sophie
4 Joan	4 Margaret	4 Karen	4 Emma	4 Laura	4 Charlotte
Patricia	5 Carol	5 Susan	5 Joanne	5 Rebecca	5 Laura
6 Mary	6 Jennifer	6 Alison	6 Helen	6 Gemma	6 Lauren
7 Sheila	7 Janet	7 Jacqueline	7 Rachel	7 Rachel	7 Jessica
8 Doreen	8 Patricia	8 Helen	8 Lisa	8 Kelly	8 Hannah
9 Sylvia	9 Barbara	9 Amanda	9 Rebecca	9 Victoria	9 Jade
10 Barbara	10 Ann	10 Sharon	10 Karen	10 Katherine	10 Emma
11 Audrey	11 Sandra	11 Sarah	Michelle	11 Katie	11 Emily
Maureen	12 Pamela	12 Joanne	12 Victoria	Nicola	12 Danielle
13 Brenda	Pauline	13 Jane	13 Catherine	13 Jennifer	13 Kirsty
14 Dorothy	14 Jean	14 Catherine	14 Amanda	Natalie	14 Katie
15 June	15 Jacqueline	15 Angela	15 Trac(e)y	15 Hayley	15 Rachel
16 Pamela	16 Kathleen	16 Linda	16 Samantha	Michelle	16 Samantha
17 Joyce	17 Sheila	17 Carol	17 Kelly	17 Amy	17 Chloe
18 Beryl	18 Valerie	18 Diane	18 Deborah	Lisa	18 Gemma
19 Eileen	19 Maureen	19 Wendy	19 Julie	19 Lindsay	19 Catherine
20 Ann	20 Gillian	20 Beverley	Louise	20 Samantha	20 Sarah
21 Kathleen	21 Marilyn	21 Caroline	21 Sharon	21 Joanne	21 Lucy
22 Valerie	Mary	22 Dawn	22 Donna	22 Louise	22 Holly
23 Pauline	23 Elizabeth	23 Nicola	23 Kerry	23 Leanne	23 Stephanie
24 Rita	24 Lesley	24 Michelle	24 Zoe	24 Helen	24 Natalie
25 Irene	25 Catherine	Sally	25 Melanie	25 Joanna	25 Hayley
Janet	26 Brenda	26 Claire	26 Alison	26 Hannah	26 Zoe
27 Betty	27 Wendy	27 Sandra	27 Caroline	27 Jodie	27 Victoria
Elizabeth	28 Angela	28 Lorraine	28 Lynsey	28 Charlotte	28 Natasha
Lilian	29 Rosemary	29 Janet	29 Jennifer	29 Kirsty	29 Jennifer
30 Marion	30 Shirley	30 Gillian	30 Angela	30 Lucy	30 Kelly
31 Marjorie	31 Diane	31 Elizabeth	31 Susan	31 Caroline	31 Chelsea
32 Gillian	Joan	32 Paula	32 Hayley	32 Elizabeth	32 Alexandra
33 Doris	33 Jane	33 Donna	33 Dawn	33 Ashley	33 Abigail
Elsie	Lynne	Jennifer	Joanna	Stephanie	34 Eleanor
Iris	35 Irene	Lesley	Lucy	35 Jessica	35 Jodie
36 Edith	36 Janice	Louise	36 Natalie	36 Emily	36 Stacey
Hazel	37 Elaine	37 Ann	37 Charlotte	37 Kerry	37 Kayleigh
Norma	Heather	38 Andrea	38 Andrea	Tracey	38 Georgina
39 Rosemary	Marion	39 Mandy	Laura	39 Charlene	39 Megan
40 Mavis	40 June	40 Elaine	40 Paula	Danielle	40 Ashleigh
41 Vera	41 Eileen	41 Denise	41 Marie	Zoe	41 Alice
42 Olive	42 Denise	42 Christine	42 Teresa	42 Kate	42 Claire
43 Evelyn	Doreen	Teresa	43 Elizabeth	Lauren	43 Nicole
Alice	Judith	44 Maria	Suzanne	44 Amanda	44 Georgia
45 Florence	Sylvia	Melanie	45 Kirsty	45 Alison	45 Kimberley
Frances	46 Helen	46 Julia	Sally	Anna	46 Louise
Phyllis	Yvonne	Lisa	Tina	Carla	47 Nicola
48 Gwendoline	48 Hilary	48 Tina	48 Jane	Carly	48 Naomi
Violet	49 Dorothy	49 Margaret	49 Ann(e)	Marie	49 Leanne
Winifred	Joyce	50 Lynn	Jacqueline	50 Alexandra	50 Melissa
	Julia			Melissa	Jasmine
	Teresa				

The top fifty first names for girls, USA

1875	1900	1925	1940	1950	1960
1 Mary	1 Mary	1 Mary	1 Mary	1 Linda	1 Mary
2 Anna	2 Ruth	2 Barbara	2 Patricia	2 Mary	2 Deborah
3 Elizabeth	3 Helen	3 Dorothy	3 Barbara	3 Patricia	3 Karen
4 Emma	4 Margaret	4 Betty	4 Judith	4 Susan	4 Susan
5 Alice	5 Elizabeth	5 Ruth	5 Carol(e)	5 Deborah	5 Linda
6 Edith	6 Dorothy	6 Margaret	6 Sharon	6 Kathleen	6 Patricia
Florence	7 Catherine	7 Helen	7 Nancy	7 Barbara	7 Kimberly
8 May	8 Mildred	8 Elizabeth	8 Joan	8 Nancy	8 Catherine
9 Helen	9 Frances	9 Jean	9 Sandra	9 Sharon	9 Cynthia
10 Katherine	10 Alice	10 Ann(e)	10 Margaret	10 Karen	10 Lori
11 Grace	Marion	11 Patricia	11 Beverly	11 Carol(e)	11 Kathleen
12 Sarah	12 Anna	12 Shirley	12 Shirley	12 Sandra	12 Sandra
13 Ella	13 Sarah	13 Virginia	13 Linda	13 Diane	13 Nancy
14 Clara	14 Gladys	14 Nancy	14 Diane	14 Catherine	14 Cheryl
15 Mabel	15 Grace	15 Joan	15 Janet	15 Christine	15 Denise
16 Margaret	Lillian	16 Martha	Joanne	16 Cynthia	16 Pamela
17 Ida	17 Florence	17 Marion	17 Joyce	17 Donna	17 Donna
18 Jennie	Virginia	18 Doris	18 Marilyn	18 Judith	18 Carol(e)
Lillian	19 Edith	19 Frances	19 Catherine	19 Margaret	19 Lisa
20 Annie	Lucy	Marjorie	20 Kathleen	20 Janice	20 Michelle
Edna	21 Clara	21 Marilyn	21 Carolyn	21 Janet	21 Diane
Gertrude	Doris	22 Alice	22 Ann(e)	22 Pamela	22 Sharon
23 Bertha	23 Marjorie	23 Eleanor	23 Dorothy	23 Gail	23 Barbara
24 Laura	24 Annie	Catherine	Elizabeth	24 Cheryl	24 Laura
25 Minnie	25 Louise	25 Lois	25 Geraldine	25 Suzanne	25 Theresa
26 Blanche	Martha	26 Jane	26 Donna	26 Marilyn	26 Julie
27 Bessie	27 Ann(e)	27 Phyllis	27 Susan	27 Brenda	27 Elizabeth
Elsie	Blanche	28 Florence	28 Gloria	28 Beverly	28 Janet
29 Emily	Eleanor	Mildred	29 Karen	Carolyn	29 Lynn(e)
Martha	Emma	30 Carol(e)	30 Betty	30 Ann(e)	30 Margaret
Nellie	Hazel	31 Carolyn	31 Dolores	31 Shirley	31 Christine
32 Marie	32 Esther	Marie	32 Elaine	32 Jacqueline	32 Brenda
33 Lillie	Ethel	Norma	33 Virginia	33 Joanne	33 Ann(e)
34 Ethel	Laura	34 Anna	34 Helen	34 Lynn(e)	34 Suzanne
Lulu	Marie	Louise	35 Phyllis	Marcia	Angela
36 Carrie	36 Julia	36 Beverly	36 Rose	36 Denise	Renee
37 Amelia	37 Beatrice	Janet	37 Jacqueline	37 Gloria	37 Sherry
38 Agnes	Gertrude	38 Sarah	38 Suzanne	38 Joyce	38 Jacqueline
Frances	39 Alma	39 Evelyn	39 Brenda	39 Kathy	39 Sheila
Harriet	Mabel	40 Edith	40 Frances	40 Elizabeth	40 Judith
Louisa	Minnie	Jacqueline	41 Ruth	41 Laura	41 Carolyn
Maud	Pauline	Lorraine	42 Alice	42 Darlene	42 Darlene
43 Ada	Rose	43 Grace	43 Janice	43 Theresa	Marie
Lucy	44 Fanny	44 Ethel	Marlene	44 Joan	44 Robin
Rose	45 Agnes	Gloria	45 Arlene	45 Elaine	45 Beverly
Stella	Carrie	Laura	46 Sally	46 Michelle	46 Andrea
47 Pauline	Edna	47 Audrey	47 Christine	47 Judy	Colleen
Rebecca	Evelyn	Esther	48 Gail	48 Diana	48 Anne Marie
49 Alma, Belle	Harriet	Joanne	Jean	49 Frances	49 Kathy
Charlotte, Dora	Ida	Sally	Marie	Maureen	Kim
Eleanor, Esther	Irene			Phyllis	Maureen
Eva, Fanny	Miriam			Ruth	
Ruth, Sophia					

1970	1990 Whites	1990 Non-whites	1995 Whites	1995 Non-whites
1 Michelle	1 Ashley	1 Brittany	1 Ashley	1 Jasmine
2 Jennifer	2 Jessica	2 Ashley	2 Jessica	2 Brianna
3 Kimberly	3 Amanda	3 Jasmine	3 Sarah	3 Brittany
4 Lisa	4 Sarah	4 Jessica	4 Brittany	4 Ashley
5 Tracy	5 Brittany	5 Tiffany	5 Kaitlyn	5 Alexis
6 Kelly	6 Megan	6 Erica	6 Taylor	6 Jessica
7 Nicole	7 Jennifer	7 Crystal	7 Emily	7 Chelsea
8 Angela	8 Nicole	8 Danielle	8 Megan	8 Courtney
9 Pamela	9 Stephanie	9 Christina	9 Samantha	9 Kayla
10 Christine	10 Katherine	10 Alicia	10 Katherine	10 Sierra
11 Dawn	11 Caitlin	11 Nicole	11 Amanda	11 Erica
12 Amy	12 Lauren	12 Latoya	12 Haley	12 Alicia
13 Deborah	13 Rachel	13 Jennifer	13 Lauren	13 Bria
14 Karen	14 Samantha	14 Sierra	14 Kayla	14 Amber
15 Julie	15 Heather	15 Stephanie	15 Rachel	15 Ebony
Mary	16 Elizabeth	16 Ebony	16 Elizabeth	16 Taylor
17 Laura	17 Danielle	17 Dominique	17 Hannah	17 Danielle
18 Stacey	18 Christina	Whitney	18 Kelsey	18 Tiffany
19 Catherine	19 Emily	19 Courtney	19 Amber	19 Destiny
20 Lori	20 Amber	20 Michelle	20 Courtney	20 Crystal
21 Tammy	21 Melissa	21 Amber	21 Chelsea	21 Shanice
22 Elizabeth	22 Tiffany	22 Amanda	22 Rebecca	22 Kiara
Shannon	23 Lindsey	Natasha	23 Nicole	23 Raven
24 Stephanie	24 Kristen	24 Shanice	24 Stephanie	24 Kiana
25 Kristin	25 Kayla	25 Tiara	25 Jennifer	25 Khadija
26 Heather	26 Rebecca	26 Candice	26 Allison	26 Kierra
Susan	27 Michelle	Kimberley	27 Victoria	27 Dominique
28 Sandra	28 Kelly	28 Tanisha	28 Brianna	28 Christina
29 Denise	29 Chelsea	29 Kendra	29 Kristen	29 Diamond
30 Theresa	30 Courtney	30 Melissa	30 Danielle	30 Asia
31 Christina	31 Crystal	31 Sarah	31 Lindsey	31 Tiara
Tina	32 Amy	32 Bianca	32 Morgan	32 Whitney
33 Cynthia	33 Laura	Latasha	33 Shelby	33 Bianca
Melissa	34 Kimberley	34 Lakeisha	34 Heather	34 Brandi
Patricia	35 Allison	35 Kayla	35 Mary	35 Tanisha
36 Renee	36 Erica	36 Andrea	36 Christina	36 Victoria
37 Cheryl	37 Alicia	Monique	37 Tiffany	37 Shaniqua
38 Sherry	38 Jamie	38 Sade	38 Alyssa	38 Tierra
39 Donna	39 Katie	39 Kristen	39 Anna	39 Andrea
40 Erica	40 Erin	40 Samantha	40 Jordan	40 Mariah
41 Rachel	41 Mary	Tierra	41 Alexandra	41 Ariel
Sharon	42 Alyssa	Victoria	42 Kelly	42 Kimberly
43 Linda	43 Kelsey	43 Felicia	43 Erica	43 Iesha
44 Barbara	44 Andrea	44 Chanel	44 Erin	44 Kendra
Jacqueline	45 Alexandra	45 Janay	45 Casey	45 Candace
Rhonda	46 Christine	46 Angela	46 Brooke	46 Stephanie
47 Andrea	47 Angela	47 Alexis	47 Kimberly	47 Maya
48 Rebecca	48 Jacqueline	48 Jaleesa	48 Alexis	48 Nicole
Wendy	49 Caseyn	49 Vanessa	49 Melissa	49 Desiree
50 Maria	50 Shannon	50 Shantel	50 Katie	50 Michelle

The top fifty first names in Australia

BOYS

1950

1 John
2 Peter
3 Michael
4 David
5 Robert
6 Stephen
7 Paul
8 Philip
9 Christopher
10 Ian
11 Gregory
12 Richard
13 Anthony
William
15 Geoffrey
16 Mark
17 James
18 Graham
19 Andrew
20 Gary
21 Colin
22 Alan
23 Bruce
24 George
25 Ronald
26 Keith
27 Terence
28 Thomas
29 Neil
30 Patrick
Stuart
32 Barry
Brian
34 Dennis
Raymond
36 Arthur
Joseph
Ross
39 Kenneth
40 Douglas
41 Trevor
42 Edward
43 Adrian
Bernard
Donald
Francis
Malcolm
48 Alexander
Frank
Russell
Wayne

1975

1 Matthew
2 Andrew
3 David
4 Michael
5 Paul
6 Adam
7 Christopher
8 Daniel
9 Mark
10 Scott
11 Steven
12 Simon
13 Jason
14 Benjamin
15 Bradley
16 Craig
17 Brett
18 Shane
19 Anthony
20 Timothy
Glenn
22 Alan
23 Cameron
24 Damian
25 Ronald
26 Justin
27 Dean
28 Travis
29 James
Peter
31 Luke
Stuart
Nicholas
34 Leigh
Shaun
36 Adrian
37 Brendan
Troy
39 Richard
40 Gregory
41 Ashley
42 John
43 Christian
44 Nathan
45 Aaron
46 Jeffrey
47 Gavin
48 Dale
49 Wayne
50 Kane

1995

1 Matthew
2 Thomas
3 Samuel
4 James
5 Joshua
6 Jack
7 Daniel
8 Benjamin
9 Nicholas
10 Jake
11 Michael
12 Alexander
13 Jordan
14 Luke
15 Christopher
16 Dylan
17 Mitchell
Ryan
19 Nathan
20 Andrew
21 Lachlan
22 William
23 Bradley
24 Adam
25 Sean
26 Anthony
Cameron
28 Jacob
29 Liam
Timothy
31 David
32 Jonathan
33 Patrick
Steven
35 Rhys
Scott
37 Aaron
Jarrad
Zachary
40 Joseph
41 Joel
42 Hayden
43 Jackson
44 Harrison
Henry
46 Alex
47 Tyler
48 Jason
49 George
50 Brayden

GIRLS

1950

1 Susan
2 Margaret
3 Ann(e)
4 Elizabeth
5 Christine
6 Jennifer
7 Judith
8 Patricia
9 Catherine
10 Helen
11 Kerry
12 Deborah
Lynette
14 Linda
15 Pamela
Robyn
17 Mary
18 Dianne
19 Sandra
20 Janet
21 Julie
Suzanne
23 Carol(e)
24 Barbara
25 Jane
Janice
27 Kathleen
Marilyn
Wendy
30 Jillian
31 Lynn(e)
32 Cheryl
Heather
Maria
35 Frances
Jill
Marion
Maureen
Roslyn
40 Gail
41 Joan
Lesley
Rosemary
Virginia
45 Michelle
46 Beverley
Lorraine
Penelope
49 Amanda
Kay

1975

1 Michelle
2 Catherine
3 Kylie
4 Nicole
5 Rebecca
6 Melissa
7 Lisa
8 Belinda
9 Rachel
10 Sarah
11 Kellie
12 Jodie
13 Emma
14 Melanie
15 Megan
16 Fiona
17 Sally
18 Amanda
19 Kate
20 Natalie
21 Danielle
22 Tania
23 Tracey
24 Joanne
25 Karen
26 Kim
27 Samantha
Jennifer
29 Narelle
30 Renee
31 Leanne
32 Claire
33 Elizabeth
Jacqueline
35 Jane
36 Simone
Julie
Alison
39 Sharon
40 Melinda
41 Carly
42 Deborah
43 Kristy
44 Kerrie
Susan
46 Donna
47 Christine
48 Vanessa
49 Angela
50 Andrea
Caroline
Naomi

1995

1 Jessica
2 Emily
3 Lauren
4 Sarah
5 Emma
6 Rebecca
7 Georgia
8 Stephanie
9 Madeleine
10 Caitlin
11 Hannah
12 Ashleigh
13 Amy
14 Nicole
15 Laura
16 Rachel
Taylor
18 Kate
19 Alexandra
20 Mikaela
21 Courtney
22 Alicia
23 Brittany
Chelsea
Katherine
26 Georgina
Samantha
28 Danielle
29 Megan
Sophie
31 Kayla
32 Amelia
Hayley
Lucy
Olivia
36 Madison
37 Melissa
38 Renee
39 Brooke
Chloe
41 Brianna
42 Claire
Jade
Kimberley
45 Ellen
Gemma
47 Alice
48 Abbey
49 Alana
Holly

A Bush Christening

On the outer Barcoo where the churches are
few
And men of religion are scanty,
On a road never cross'd 'cept by folk that are
lost,
One Michael Magee had a shanty.

Now this Mike was the Dad of a ten-year-old
lad,
Plump, healthy, and stoutly conditioned;
He was strong as the best, but poor Mike had
no rest,
For the youngster had never been christened.

And his wife used to cry, 'If the darlin'
should die,
St Peter would not recognise him.'
But by luck he survived till a preacher
arrived,
Who agreed straightaway to baptise him.

Now the artful young rogue, while they held
their collogue,
With his ear to the keyhole was listenin',
And he muttered in fright, while his features
turned white,
'What the divil and all is this christenin'?'

He was none of your dolts—he had seen them
brand colts,
And it seemed to his small understanding,
If the man in the frock made him one of the
flock,
It must mean something very like branding.

So away with a rush he set off for the bush
While the tears in his eyelids they glistened,
''Tis outrageous,' says he, 'to brand youngsters
like me;
I'll be dashed if I'll stop to be christened!'

Like a young native dog he ran into a log
And his father with language uncivil,
Never heeding the 'praste', cried aloud in his
haste,
'Come out and be christened, you divil!'

But he lay there as snug as a bug in a rug,
And his parents in vain might reprove him,
Till His Reverence spoke (he was fond of a
joke),
'I've a notion,' says he, 'that'll move him.'

'Poke a stick up the log, give the spalpeen a
prog;
Poke him aisy—don't hurt him or maim him;
'Tis not long that he'll stand, I've the water
at hand,
As he rushes out this end I'll name him.'

'Here he comes, and for shame!
ye've forgotten the name—
Is it Patsy or Michael or Dinnis?'
Here the youngster ran out, and the priest
gave a shout—
'Take your chance anyhow wid "Maginnis".'

As the howling young cub ran away to the
scrub
Where he knew that pursuit would be risky,
The priest, as he fled, flung a flask at his
head,
That was labelled "Maginnis's Whisky".

And Maginnis Magee has been made a J.P.
And the one thing he hates more than sin is
To be asked by the folk, who have heard of
the joke,
How he came to be christened Maginnis!

A. B. 'Banjo' Paterson [1864-1941], best-
known in his native Australia for having
written the words of 'Waltzing Matilda'.

First name profiles

The figures below, based on the Registrar General's Indexes of Births, show in detail the comparative use of first names in England and Wales since 1900. The numbers relate to 10000 births of the same sex in the year concerned. Thus '1' would indicate that one boy or girl of every 10000 born that year received the name.

Dates in brackets indicate approximately when a name began to come into general use in England and Wales, (though it may have been used elsewhere for centuries). Dates in square brackets refer to earlier isolated usage. Thus Tracey has *(1957)* against it to show when modern usage began. The *[1845]* date relates to occasional use of the name (for boys) in the 19th century. No date against a name means that it is known to have been in use before 1837.

	1900	1925	1935	1950	1955	1960	1965	1970	1975	1980	1985	1990
Aaron		4					6	7	26	30	52	124
Abbie								*(1966)*	2	2	2	
Abigail	4						4		24	20	30	114
Abraham	4	2				1	4	2				
Ada	166	26	18				2					
Adam	7	6			4	7	32	77	110	170	234	264
Adela			2				1	2				
Adelaide	11	3	2								1	
Adele			2	2	2	5	12	14	7	8	16	24
Adelle								*(1967)*		4	2	
Adrian	1	1	6	40	50	68	188	96	81	44	34	16
Adrienne		*(1902)*	1	1	6	6	2				1	2
Agnes	94	34	18	1	1		1					
Aidan		*(1904)*			1	1		1	2	6	2	16
Aiden *(1880)*							1	1	2	6	4	
Aileen *(1880)*	1	3	2	2		1		4	1			2
Aimee *(1873)*		1							1	2	26	30
Alan	12	126	234	324	224	182	126	82	71	80	38	12
Alana				*(1955)*	2	1			1	2	4	6
Alastair		*(1912)*	2	1	4	6	12	12	14	12	16	12
Albert	333	238	84	34	12	4	10	9	4		4	2
Alec *(1867)*	3	10	10	10	4	2	6	2	2	4	6	8
Alex *(1857)*			4				2	1	1	8	16	36
Alexander	27	24	20	16	10	9	14	35	48	50	60	178
Alexandra		2			6	2	4	10	9	29	14	28	74
Alexia				*(1951)*			2	1	1	4	4	2
Alexis *(1881)*				2		2	4	4	5	6	6	
Alfie						*(1965)*	2			2		6
Alfred	260	132	56	18	16	4	6	1	2			4
Alice	361	80	44	4	8	4	6	7	2	4	14	62
Alicia	1		4			4	2			2	4	12
Alick *(1864)*			2				2					
Alisha *[1846]*								*(1972)*	1	4	2	6
Alison			4	28	94	100	286	149	100	78	32	16
Alissa									*(1979)*	2		2
Alistair		*(1913)*		8	6	14	12	12	21	10	14	16
Alister *(1887)*			2		2			2		4		
Allan	4	24	28	52	32	27	20	9	10	12	4	
Allen	8	14	12	14	6	2	10	4	3	4	2	
Allison				4	2	4	42	30	7	2	4	
Allyson		*(1946)*			2	2	2	1			2	1
	1900	1925	1935	1950	1955	1960	1965	1970	1975	1980	1985	1990

	1900	1925	1935	1950	1955	1960	1965	1970	1975	1980	1985	1990
Alma *(1854)*	3	28	12	2	2	2						
Althea							2				2	
Alun *(1893)*				2		2	4	8				
Alwyn *(1888)*		1	2	1			2			2		
Alyson *(1946)*				1	2	2	12	8		2		2
Amanda				12	38	84	262	181	167	80	54	30
Amber *[1865]*			*(1944)*					2	4	8	4	36
Ambrose	12		2	2				2				
Ambrosine *(1856)*		2	2									
Amelia	18	2			4			2	2	4	4	24
Amos	5	4		2		2	2	2				
Amy	73	14	10	2	2	4		5	17	82	124	226
Anastasia										2		8
Andre *(1876)*							6	2	2	2	4	2
Andrea		*(1920)*	1	14	20	23	92	88	71	40	32	2
Andrew	13	16	8	124	274	338	682	428	421	312	292	206
Angela		4	14	92	92	168	186	123	90	58	34	6
Angelina	1	2				4		2	2			
Angeline *(1857)*				1	4		2					4
Angharad *(1943)*											2	4
Angus							2					6
Anika									*(1980)*	6	4	
Anita *(1863)*	1		12	28	20	36	54	37	14	2	6	
Ann	34	4	84	128	116	68	48	30	24	18	8	2
Anna	1	2		10	6	5	14	21	24	54	38	42
Annabel *(1862)*							4			8	2	14
Annabelle			*(1942)*				2				2	
Annamarie							*(1964)*	1	1	2		2
Anne	4	4	32	84	100	57	54	26	26	4	6	
Annemarie					*(1956)*		1	1	1	2		
Anne-Marie					*(1956)*		2	1	1	8		6
Annette	1		2	18	42	29	26	21	7	4	2	8
Annie	357	88	16	2	4							2
Annis		1	1							2		
Annmarie			*(1946)*			1	2		1	2	4	
Ann-Marie			*(1946)*				2	1	1	4	2	2
Anouska									*(1976)*	2		4
Anthea		*(1922)*	2	1	2	1	4		1			
Anthony	3	46	124	214	242	200	244	130	83	100	108	62
Antoinette *(1856)*						1		1	1	4	2	
Antonia				1			4	1		2	4	2
Antony		2	8	2	16	73	60	33	21	20	18	16
Anya								*(1972)*	1	2	2	
April		*(1917)*		4	2	2	6	2	14		4	10
Arlene *(1865)*			2		4	1			1			
Arnold	22	20	14	4	2	2	2	2				
Arran *(1943)*					2					2	4	18
Arron						*(1965)*	2				8	8
Arthur	367	224	118	32	18	13	14					2
Ashleigh			*(1947)*						1	2	4	40
Ashley *(1861)*	3	2	2	6		9	20	26	24	30	102	118
Ashton	1									2		4
Aubrey *(1856)*	8	6	4				2	1				
Audrey	9	152	180	24	10	14	4	6	2	2		
Austen *(1859)*		1								2	2	
Austin	7	2	2			2	4		2	2	4	2
	1900	1925	1935	1950	1955	1960	1965	1970	1975	1980	1985	1990

	1900	1925	1935	1950	1955	1960	1965	1970	1975	1980	1985	1990
Averil		1	4	1								
Avis		4	2			2						
Avril	(1904)	2	2	22	6	8	8	2	1			2
Barbara	13	162	194	216	130	71	32	11	2	6	4	2
Barnaby			(1948)					1	1	2	4	2
Barrie	(1918)	2	24	26	6	10	6	6	6	6	4	
Barrington	(1884)	4	2				6	2	2	2		
Barry	(1846)	4	60	132	90	82	84	35	60	34	18	6
Bartholomew		2			2						2	
Basil	5	26	16	2								
Beatrice	119	36	6	8	2					2		2
Beatrix		2			2							8
Becky										4	12	8
Belinda					6	18	28	9	7	4	2	4
Ben					2	4	2	2		30	46	90
Benedict							2	4	2		4	8
Benjamin	31	22	8	8			6	30	119	114	144	206
Berenice			4		2				2			
Bernadette		(1923)		4	12	14	6	5		2	4	2
Bernard	25	60	58	32	28	7	6	5		2	2	
Bernice	2	2	6	2	4			2				
Bert (1878)	7	14	2	2								
Bertha	36	10	6		2	2						
Bertie (1864)	42	16	2	2								
Bertram (1845)	18	10	4	2		2						
Beryl (1872)	7	82	130	20	6	5	4			4		
Beth									1	2		6
Bethany [1876]							(1967)			6	10	48
Betsy		1	2	4	2	4	2	2				
Betty	1	214	86	16	10	4	2					
Beulah		1	2				2					
Beverley		(1928)	2	8	48	129	126	25	40	12	22	2
Beverly			(1936)	6	10	20	24	4				
Bianca								(1973)	1	4	4	4
Bill							2	1		4	2	
Billy				1	2	1	8			2	10	16
Blaine					(1957)		2					4
Blair			(1903)				2					2
Blanche	16	8	2	2	4	2						
Blodwen (1889)		1	2									
Blossom (1894)						1	2					
Bobbie		(1917)			2							8
Bobby		(1903)								8	2	12
Bonita			(1946)	1	2		2				2	
Bonnie					(1959)					6	4	
Boyd (1891)					1		2					
Bradley						6	8	14	12	10	34	62
Brenda		42	180	88	50	18	12	2	2			
Brendan		(1905)	2		8	4	2	5	10	6	6	6
Brendon [1885]			(1941)		2		2			4	2	
Brent			(1940)				4		2	2	2	2	4
Brett			(1947)	2	4	8	4	8	10	14	14	12
Brian		36	458	240	152	95	94	53	29	32	10	8
Bridget	3	4	7	12	8	12	8	8	4		2	
Britannia		1	2									
Brittany											(1985)	4

	1900	1925	1935	1950	1955	1960	1965	1970	1975	1980	1985	1990

	1900	1925	1935	1950	1955	1960	1965	1970	1975	1980	1985	1990
Bruce	2	4		8	2	12	8	2		4		2
Bryan		20	34	26	20	23	24	7	7	2	6	
Bryony			(1941)				2	2	2		4	14
Byron (1850)				1	2	1	2	1			8	4
Caitlin										(1978)	2	8
Callum		(1922)									6	70
Calum						(1965)	2	2		2	4	32
Calvin (1868)					4	4		4	7		2	
Cameron [1844]		(1941)					4			2	8	18
Camilla					2	1		1	1	2	2	10
Candice [1875]				(1957)					1		6	
Cara [1873]		(1944)							14	8	10	6
Carey [1843]							4	2	2			2
Carina	(1916)				2	2				2	12	
Carl (1867)		6	4	16	14	20	62	56	86	92	78	36
Carla			(1941)	2		2	2	2	19	28	16	16
Carleton			(1951)		1	1	2					
Carley								(1973)	1	6	6	
Carlie (1910)						1			2	10	6	6
Carly								(1973)	2	52	36	28
Carlton (1886)					4		2	2				
Carmel (1886)				1	2		2	1	1		2	2
Carmen (1888)				1	1		2	1			4	4
Carol (1893)			10	244	212	204	126	25	20	6	6	
Carole	(1932)		1	68	88	105	44	7	7	2	2	
Caroline	24	8		38	54	120	118	100	107	78	36	30
Carolyn		(1932)		28	36	64	28	16	7	14	6	2
Caron			(1955)		2	2	2	2				
Carrie (1860)	3	4						4	10	24	12	6
Cassandra	3							1		12	10	4
Cassey (1861)											1	10
Catherine	60	44	18	40	58	70	124	82	81	56	42	68
Cathleen (1894)				1	2		1	1				
Cathryn		(1936)				1	4	2		4	4	2
Cathy				(1960)		1	2	1	2			
Catrina				(1955)	2		1	2	2	4		
Catriona			(1946)	1	4		2	2	1		2	6
Cecil	76	40	12					1	2			
Cecilia	13	20	2		2				5			
Cedric (1869)	2	8	8	2								
Celia	3		8	18	4	5	6	4	2			6
Ceri			(1940)			1	2	1		6	6	6
Ceridwen (1898)	1			1			2					
Chanel								(1979)		2		
Chanelle								(1979)		2		
Chantal				(1954)				1	1	2	4	4
Chantel					(1965)		2			6		12
Chantelle					(1963)			1	1	2	4	28
Charity	1	2	2						2			
Charleen								(1977)		6	2	
Charlene				(1952)						22	20	12
Charles	390	206	98	88	56	25	26	11	17	26	20	76
Charlie (1853)	13	6								2	4	26
Charline									(1980)	4	2	
Charlotte	28	14	4	14	2	7	18	39	74	92	110	300
Charmaine			(1943)	6	2	2	4	5	12	4	10	14
	1900	1925	1935	1950	1955	1960	1965	1970	1975	1980	1985	1990

	1900	1925	1935	1950	1955	1960	1965	1970	1975	1980	1985	1990
Charmian				(1955)	2				1			2
Chelsea								(1976)			2	68
Cherie		(1927)		1	2	1	2	1		2	4	2
Cherry (1893)					6	2		2		6		
Cheryl (1920)				14	24	39	56	35	29	32	36	10
Chloe								4	10	18	18	112
Christian	1	2			2	2	8	23	31	24	16	28
Christina	13	18	14	14	36	20	10	8	10	12	8	22
Christine	4	12	24	352	288	209	84	23	26	16	18	4
Christopher	7	24	16	200	216	196	268	230	276	302	368	380
Cindy				(1956)		2	6	3	2	4	2	
Clair (1887)								11	14	6	2	
Claire (1861)			2	2	10	13	88	123	310	212	184	80
Clara	76	16	4	2	2						2	
Clare (1868)		4	2		12	20	42	49	110	78	82	18
Clarence	21	12	8				1					
Clarice (1871)	8	8	2									
Clark								1		2	1	
Claud	1	1										
Claude	1	1	2	1								
Claudette			(1936)	1	2		1					
Claudia (1877)	1			2			2	2	5	2	10	6
Clayton						1		1	1	2		
Clifford	30	44	42	20	20	25	10	4		4	2	
Clint					(1960)	1			1	2		
Clive (1871)		2	22	46	58	54	50	12	21	6	4	4
Colette		(1928)		1	2	9	12	7	10	2		2
Colin	9	36	198	204	160	209	182	88	76	52	26	4
Colleen (1887)		1	4	2	8	2	4	2				2
Collette [1893]			(1940)					4		4		2
Connie (1885)		2			2							
Connor			(1936)		1					2	2	26
Conrad	1		1			2	2	6				2
Constance	46	78	8	2	4	2					2	4
Cora (1858)	2	4	2									
Coral (1880)		4	2	2	2	2	6	4	2	4	6	4
Corey						(1969)		1				8
Corin						(1965)	2	1	1			
Corinna			(1947)				2		1		4	2
Corinne (1861)			2	2	2	4	10	2	1	4	4	2
Cornelius	3			2	4	2	2				2	2
Corrine		(1922)							1			10
Courtney (1847)								2	1			16
Craig			(1945)	2	2	29	48	118	162	134	160	128
Crystal		(1906)							1	2	4	2
Curtis (1842)						1			1	12	6	14
Cynthia		36	34	16	24		4			2	2	
Cyril (1857)	57	104	32	10	2	7						
Dahlia		(1915)	1		4							
Daisy (1864)	58	28	6								2	18
Dale (1864)			2	2	4	14	28	11	17	40	28	32
Daley			(1950)	1						4	4	2
Damian			(1938)	4	2	2	4	23	38	12	4	20
Damien			(1944)					2	14	2	16	8
Damon					(1956)					2	12	4
Dane			(1943)						1	2	4	
	1900	1925	1935	1950	1955	1960	1965	1970	1975	1980	1985	1990

	1900	1925	1935	1950	1955	1960	1965	1970	1975	1980	1985	1990
Daniel	6	10	10	10	16	21	44	61	286	328	370	476
Daniela					(1959)	1	2	1	1			
Daniella						(1966)						20
Danielle		(1916)					2	4	10	42	68	134
Danny			(1930)	8	8	4	8	10	6	20	28	28
Daphne (1884)		38	36	12	36	7						
Daren					(1960)	1	24	10	2	2		
Darin					(1954)		6	1				
Darlene			(1937)							2		
Darran						(1961)	4	2		2	2	
Darrel		(1925)					1	4	1	4	2	
Darrell (1878)		2		1	2	2	6	2		4	4	6
Darren					(1960)	7	212	309	269	148	110	46
Darrin						(1964)	8					
Darron					(1960)	1	4	1	1			
Darryl			(1942)		2	4	10	16	10	6	8	16
Daryl		(1907)		1	2		12	14	8	12	14	16
Daryll					(1962)		2					2
David	52	106	270	832	638	625	706	386	369	340	328	154
Davina (1870)					2	1	6	3	1		4	
Dawn		(1928)	12	14	30	4	140	77	81	52	16	
Dean (1881)		2				16	76	82	64	102	78	50
Deanna			(1938)	1	2	1	2					3
Debbie				(1953)	2	9	30	23	14	18	6	
Debora							6					
Deborah	1	1	1	20	60	279	358	170	119	58	36	12
Debra		(1926)			14	86	118	23	14	16	6	4
Declan				(1948)								26
Deirdre		(1935)	1	10	8	4	10	2				
Delia		1		1	6	1	2			2		
Della		(1906)		1	1		8	1	1		2	
Delphine (1897)	1	2						1				
Delroy					(1960)	1	2	1		2	2	
Dene					(1961)		4	1				
Denis	3	60	20	20	6	2	2	2	1		2	
Denise	(1908)	4	4	56	96	102	86	25	14	6	6	
Dennis	3	128	110	38	26	23	18	2	12	2	2	
Denny (1868)									1	4		
Denzil (1894)	1						2					
Derek (1899)		60	176	122	76	64	56	25	14	14	6	
Derick	(1906)	8	10	10	4	4	2	2		2		
Dermot	(1909)			1	2							
Derrick (1896)		46	32	14	1	7	1	2	5	2	4	
Desmond (1892)	1	42	8	4	2	9	18	7	5	2	2	
Devon					(1962)		2	1				
Dewi			(1941)		1					2		
Dexter			(1940)		2	1			1			
Diana		8	28	28	14	21	14	4	7		2	
Diane (1887)			16	72	88	100	152	56	14	16	10	2
Dianne		(1935)	2	10	22	13	8	9	7			
Digby (1874)			2	1								
Dinah	1		4		2						2	
Dion	(1920)				2		2	1	1			
Dionne					(1964)		4	2	2	4	4	2
Dirk					(1961)		2	1				
Dolores	(1908)		1	1	6							
	1900	1925	1935	1950	1955	1960	1965	1970	1975	1980	1985	1990

	1900	1925	1935	1950	1955	1960	1965	1970	1975	1980	1985	1990
Dominic (1850)	1				1	1	10	14	33	12	12	30
Dominique					(1967)			1	1	2	8	8
Don		(1930)			2		1					
Donald	34	128	180	42	18	13	14		1	2		4
Donna	(1911)			2	4	25	104	91	124	100	58	18
Dora (1853)	36	34	2	1								4
Dorcas		1	2	1			4					
Doreen (1894)	1	190	214	60	14	7	4	7		2		
Dorian		(1918)	1		2						1	
Doris (1880)	266	278	66	10	2	2		2				
Dorothea	7	7	10									
Dorothy	246	350	166	48	32	7	4			4		3
Douglas	22	94	60	32	20	32	28	9	7	8	2	4
Drew				(1945)			2		1			
Duane				(1946)				4	10	6	2	8
Dudley (1847)	2	2	6				2					
Dulcie (1881)	5		4		2							
Duncan	1	6	2	18	12	30	36	28	26	16	16	6
Dwayne									(1971)		12	
Dylan					(1953)			4	12	2		3
Eamonn					(1956)	1	2					
Earl (1867)	1						2	1				
Eddie (1887)	1	1	2						1			
Eden			2				1					2
Edgar	42	12	6	2			2					
Edith	337	120	60	8	6	4	2				2	
Edmond			2	1								
Edmund	21	6	8	8	2	4	4				2	10
Edna	40	160	30	10	4		4	2				
Edward	166	228	116	70	60	43	40	49	43	30	46	82
Edwin	39	46	24	20	14	4	2	7		2	2	2
Edwina		2	4	6	2	4						
Eileen (1873)	10	192	120	62	40	16	18	2		2		
Elaine (1887)	1	8	8	68	180	109	88	54	24	10	10	2
Eleanor	34	14	14	4	8	4	22	4	10	18	24	60
Elena					1	1				2		
Elfreda (1880)		1	2									
Elijah			2						1			
Elinor	1			1		1	2				2	8
Elisabeth		1	2	1		1	2		1			4
Elisha							4			2		14
Eliza	60	4	2			2	4			2	2	4
Elizabeth	296	128	86	124	126	105	112	84	52	46	38	82
Ella			4						1	2	6	4
Ellen	176	78	28	14	6	11	8	7	10	14	6	10
Elliot								1	1	2	6	24
Elliott								1	1	2	2	14
Ellis	3	4			2							4
Eloise (1873)							2		1			6
Elsie (1857)	339	148	66	8	2				1			
Elvis			[1939]		(1958)							1
Emily	157	34	12	4		7	4	11	33	68	72	160
Emma	67	8	2	2			20	114	283	362	264	266
Emma-Jayne							(1970)	1		4		1
Emma-Louise						(1966)			1	4		6
Emmeline	1								1	2		
	1900	1925	1935	1950	1955	1960	1965	1970	1975	1980	1985	1990

	1900	1925	1935	1950	1955	1960	1965	1970	1975	1980	1985	1990
Emrys *(1896)*			2		1							
Ena *(1894)*	1	12	6		2							
Enid *(1877)*	8	32	20	8	2							
Enoch	3		2									
Eric	48	232	88	46	28	9	12	14	7	2	2	2
Erica *(1890)*			2	8	4	4	12	5	2	6		4
Erika		*[1903]*			*(1951)*		2	1		6	2	6
Erin							*(1978)*			4	6	8
Ernest	269	154	48	16	8	4	2					
Ernie *(1898)*					2		2			2		
Errol *(1890)*		2		2			2	1	1			
Esmé *(1884)*	2	8	8		2				1		1	
Estella *(1861)*		1					2	1				
Estelle *(1860)*					2	2	2	9	5	4		2
Esther	40	20	4	2			2	2	5	5	12	2	4
Ethel	246	82	12				1					
Euan *(1867)*					1					2		
Eugene		2	2	4	2	2	2	2				
Eunice	3	20	8	2	6	2						
Eva	97	28	10			4		2				6
Eve									1	6	2	4
Eveline *(1856)*	25	10	2			2			2			
Evelyn	63	96	44	20	6	9	6	4		4	2	
Ewan			*(1942)*	1				1		6	2	
Ewart *(1881)*	3		4									
Fanny	24	2				2					4	
Fay	*(1923)*	4	6	2	4	2	4	4	7			4
Faye		*(1926)*			2			4	12	10	16	38
Felicity	*(1912)*			1	2	1	2		1	8	8	14
Felix			2									14
Fenella					2							2
Fergus							2		1		2	2
Fern				*(1958)*								8
Fiona		*(1923)*		4	32	32	60	46	21	26	30	20
Fleur				*(1955)*	2			1		2		
Flora	15	4	2					2				
Florence	394	142	44	10	4			4			6	
Frances	79	44	44	46	32	23	8	19	7	14	8	12
Francesca *(1861)*				2			6	4	4	10	2	40
Francine			*(1937)*			1	4	1				
Francis	87	52	30	32	20	5	18	9	18	4	4	6
Frank	206	196	112	34	16	14	26	7	10	2	4	2
Frankie		*(1920)*					2		1			2
Franklin *(1857)*	1			2			2			2		
Franklyn			*(1939)*	1			2					
Fraser		*(1901)*			2	4	4	2	3	4	2	2
Fred	82	42	12	4	4	4						1
Freda *(1879)*	4	52	20	18	6	2						
Frederick	376	256	98	44	20	13	4	12	2	2	4	16
Gabriella			*(1957)*				1		1	2	2	8
Gabrielle *(1889)*	1						4			2		8
Gail			*(1939)*	12	26	36	58	28	10	14	2	
Gale			*(1936)*		2		2					
Gareth			*(1933)*		6	15	12	32	60	88	54	34
Garry		*(1929)*		8	20	43	30	35	33	10	16	
Gary		*(1931)*	4	20	106	250	324	161	128	100	96	42
	1900	1925	1935	1950	1955	1960	1965	1970	1975	1980	1985	1990

	1900	1925	1935	1950	1955	1960	1965	1970	1975	1980	1985	1990
Gavin		2	2	2	2	13	22	42	21	20	62	14
Gay			*(1941)*	4			2	1	1			
Gayle			*(1944)*				1	1	6			
Gaynor				8	8	13	34	19	7	6	2	2
Gemma					*(1956)*		2	7	19	68	280	94
Geoffrey	10	98	72	122	94	79	46	40	17	8	4	4
George	609	442	242	88	36	55	22	18	21	18	16	48
Georgia *(1882)*					2		4	2	2	4	8	30
Georgina	13	6	18	22	10	14	2	12	36	22	10	46
Gerald	6	60	80	32	44	13	14	4				4
Geraldine		4		34	26	13	12	5	2	6	2	
Gerard	2	10	10	6	22	18	8	10			4	4
Germaine		*(1935)*	2							2	2	
Gerrard			2		4							
Gertrude	112	26	10									
Gilbert	28	20	4	4			1					
Giles	1				2		6	9	12		2	2
Gillian			54	132	192	170	98	42	17	14	14	2
Gina		*(1926)*	2		6	2	2	4	2	2	6	2
Gladys *(1871)*	222	156	34	4	4							
Glen	1				10		8	22	21	8	18	4
Glenda		*(1933)*		10	10	7	4	2				
Glenis	*(1921)*	1	4	1	2	1						
Glenn		*(1934)*		6	22	21	16	7	14	14	6	14
Glenys	*(1906)*	4	2	8	8	2	2					
Gloria	*(1913)*	2	20	16	10	11						
Glyn *(1899)*		2	2	12	8	4	16	9	7	6	2	
Glynis	*(1924)*			14	14	7		2				
Godfrey	2	3	8	6	6	2						
Gordon	16	106	92	64	44	30	32	23	14	12	6	
Grace	70	64	14	1	6	1	1	2	1	2	8	36
Graeme	*(1901)*		2	6	16	30	12	17	12	16	2	
Graham	1	12	78	246	200	173	152	104	67	50	32	16
Grahame *(1899)*			4	4					1			4
Grant				4		4	8	11	12	12	12	28
Granville	1	1	2	2	4	1						
Gregory				12	14	21	42	16	43	16	22	24
Grenville *(1866)*			1		2	1						
Greta *(1887)*			12	2	4							
Guy	3	2	2		12	9	12	9	12	10	2	24
Gwen					2		1					
Gwendolen	1	2	4			2						
Gwendoline	15	72	36	8	10	2						
Gwendolyn	1	2	2		2							
Gwyneth *(1897)*		2	4		2		2					
Gwynneth *(1904)*		6	4	2								
Hadrian						*(1962)*	2	1				
Hamish			*(1932)*				4		1			1
Hannah	49	18					2	4	33	58	96	168
Harold	213	152	68	12	10	5	6	2				
Harriet	37	8	4	2			2	2		8	6	58
Harry	213	132	44	16	20	5		4		4	12	46
Harvey		2	4	12			8	16			2	2
Hayden *(1878)*							6	2		6	4	
Haydn *(1875)*					4	2	12	2		6	2	6
Haydon *(1850)*					2		2					
	1900	1925	1935	1950	1955	1960	1965	1970	1975	1980	1985	1990

	1900	1925	1935	1950	1955	1960	1965	1970	1975	1980	1985	1990
Hayley						(1961)	26	51	79	72	174	92
Hazel (1890)	3	38	60	44	20	36	32	16	24	6	8	2
Heather (1883)		6	18	68	70	66	50	26	15	20	30	28
Hector	31		2									
Heidi						(1958)	12	19	21	10	6	8
Helen	27	26	24	58	74	109	264	140	226	116	92	40
Helena	12	8	2	4	4	2	14	4	10	10	6	16
Helene (1880)							4		1			
Henrietta	9	6	2	2			2		2			4
Henry	261	114	54	38	12	16	24	2	2	4	16	36
Herbert	175	106	18	10	4	2			1			
Hilary (1864)		4	22	48	44	20	30	12	4		4	2
Hilda (1861)	231	142	32	6	6	2	2					
Hollie		(1923)									20	26
Holly (1878)	1	2							7	6	56	82
Hope												10
Horace	66	30	14	4	2		2		1			
Howard	12	12	16	26	26	29	28	9	10	6	8	4
Hubert	14	22	2									
Hugh	12	16	22	6	2	4		2	10	4	10	6
Hugo (1868)										2	2	6
Huw				(1946)			4	1			4	2
Hylton (1870)			2							2		
Iain		(1914)		2	2	10	12	14	16	18	10	6
Ian (1890)	6	8	58	152	294	270	384	196	150	82	78	30
Ida	31	30	8									
Imogen							2			2	2	18
India		(1901)										6
Iona (1850)												6
Irene (1854)	31	238	92	74	36	16	8	4		2		
Iris (1878)	7	94	66	4	4	5						
Isaac	10	12							2	2	2	2
Isabel	12	2	4	8	6		2	2	5	4	2	24
Isabella	36	10	10	2	2		2	2		2		12
Isabelle		1		1			2			2		4
Isaiah	1	1	2								1	
Ishmael										2		1
Isla		(1923)				1			1	2		4
Isobel	2	2		4	6		4				4	20
Ivan (1889)	1	14	16	4	8	5	2	7	5	2		1
Ivor (1847)	10	20	16	2	4	2	4					1
Ivy (1868)	112	120	32	8		4	2	2		2		
Jack	31	100	50	12	2	7	2	2	2	6	22	136
Jackie (1897)				1			2	1			2	
Jaclyn						(1966)				14	6	
Jacob	3	2	1	2		2	2				12	48
Jacqueline (1903)		2	18	160	208	205	282	98	45	16	18	20
Jacquelyn				(1936)	4	2		2				
Jade								(1974)	1	10	18	144
Jaime								(1973)		8	6	
Jake							(1967)	2	2	2	6	80
James	355	320	198	176	140	89	114	163	248	258	302	398
Jamie				(1945)		2	6	58	64	70	68	186
Jan (1900)	1			1		1				4	4	
Jane	96	148	26	76	80	127	146	95	38	18	12	10
Janet	12	18	82	262	270	157	106	30	19	8		
	1900	1925	1935	1950	1955	1960	1965	1970	1975	1980	1985	1990

	1900	1925	1935	1950	1955	1960	1965	1970	1975	1980	1985	1990
Janette (1845)		2	10	8	22	26	18	12	3		2	
Janice		(1932)	8	128	82	92	32	12	7	4		2
Janine		(1935)	1		2	9	26	21	7	8	8	4
Janis		(1916)		6	10	4	2					
Jannine					(1944)							8
Jaqueline		(1935)	2	2	2		1		1	4		
Jasmine [1885]			(1934)			1	2	1		2	4	6
Jason					2	7	14	454	207	98	70	48
Jay [1895]							(1964)	1	2	10	6	16
Jayne		(1942)	2		12	39	52	32	10	10	8	6
Jean		180	390	176	76	46	18	5		2	2	
Jeanette (1850)			14	12	24	38	40	9	12		2	1
Jeanne (1886)			8		4							
Jeannette (1856)			2		6		2					
Jeffery		2	4	8	4		4	1				
Jeffrey	1	8	28	54	42	55	48	30	17	12	8	4
Jemima	4	2	1							4		1
Jemma							(1963)		1	14	58	30
Jenifer			4	8	4		6	2		2		
Jenna								(1973)	1	12	42	16
Jennie	13	8	10				2	2	12			10
Jennifer		2	24	278	96	95	98	65	98	112	144	66
Jenny	9	2	2	2	4	7	12	4	19	18	22	12
Jeremy			6	20	38	48	50	35	29	10	8	10
Jermaine								(1973)		8	4	
Jerome				1	1		2	1	1	2		2
Jesse	1	1	1	1	2		2	1				8
Jessica	5	2	2	8	6	4	12	4		22	48	226
Jessie	97	62	10	2	4		2					10
Jill		2	30	20	24	32	26	10	6	2	2	
Jillian			14	8	14	18	18	2				
Jim	6	2	6	2	2	2				2		2
Joan		510	304	82	42	21	14	2				1
Jo-Ann						(1964)	4		1			
Joanna			4	16	6	27	44	32	29	52	52	24
Joanne			(1938)	2	12	39	192	309	271	152	116	26
Jo-Anne					(1960)	1	2		1	2	2	
Jocelyn (1894)		6		2	6	2	2	4		6		
Jodi							(1968)		1	8	14	6
Jodie							(1964)	4	20	42	32	72
Jody							(1965)	2	12	30	10	12
Joe	10	4			2		2	2		2	8	32
Joel							2	3	6	11	18	14	20
Johanna	6	2			4	4	4	2	10	2	4	2
Johanne				(1946)			8			2		
John	726	728	750	646	432	305	308	168	150	104	98	82
Johnathan			(1942)	1			2	1		8	4	6
Johnny (1848)							2	2		2	2	
Jolene						(1964)		1		4	4	
Jolyon			(1930)	1				1		2		2
Jon		(1929)	2	1		1	2	1		6	2	6
Jonas	1	1	2			1						
Jonathan	7		2	38	42	66	134	112	164	128	98	168
Jonathon [1859]		(1939)			2	2	6	2	3	6	4	24
Jordan			2							4	8	130
Jordana									(1980)	4	2	2
	1900	1925	1935	1950	1955	1960	1965	1970	1975	1980	1985	1990

	1900	1925	1935	1950	1955	1960	1965	1970	1975	1980	1985	1990
Joseph	221	174	120	42	28	32	32	30	50	40	72	156
Josephine	6	24	30	36	14	21	26	19	10	6	6	14
Josh *[1896]*									*(1980)*		2	8
Joshua	6								2		14	266
Josie		*(1909)*		1	2							10
Joy		8	12	20	22	7	6	5	4	4	4	
Joyce	3	390	154	48	16	5	2	2	2	4		
Juanita		*(1908)*	2	1				1				
Judith	1		6	60	56	57	34	19	7		4	
Judy			4	4	6	6	2	4			2	
Julia	15	10	18	48	48	59	80	44	33	2	14	12
Julian		4	2	12	10	18	66	39	17	6	4	
Julie *(1896)*			4	44	110	159	454	239	133	52	32	8
Juliet				4	7	16	12	2		16		4
Juliette *(1876)*		1				1	4		1			
June *(1919)*		38	160	66	44	36	14	4	7		2	
Justin *(1864)*						2	10	72	57	22	4	10
Justina *(1873)*									1	2		2
Justine *(1856)*			2				4	49	12	4	4	4
Kara							*(1966)*	4	10	2	4	6
Karen		*(1901)*		18	100	439	422	239	186	68	40	4
Karin			*(1921)*	1	8	1	4				2	
Karina			*(1946)*	2	1					10	2	4
Karl *(1878)*			2	2	2	11	48	26	45	30	36	34
Karla					*(1953)*				1	10	1	
Karly			*(1927)*							2	2	2
Karon				*(1948)*		1	8	1				
Karyn				*(1955)*	4	1						4
Kate	51	6			2	5	4	19	21	64	40	38
Katharine	3		2	6	2	4	8	14	7	14	4	16
Katherine	9	10		6	6	11	28	44	40	56	50	68
Kathleen	79	240	112	164	80	54	34	21	14	16	14	10
Kathrine					2		2					
Kathryn		*(1912)*		42	30	55	42	56	26	44	48	40
Kathy					*(1956)*		2			2		
Katie	6	2				2	4	18	52	98	144	142
Katrina		*(1909)*		2	6	9	10	16	21	14	14	16
Katy							2	4	10	18	36	24
Kay *(1883)*			2	8	18	32	28	12	14	6	8	2
Kaye *(1854)*					4	4	1	2	4	8	2	
Kaylea									*(1983)*		2	
Kaylee								*(1977)*		1		4
Kayleigh									*(1982)*		2	44
Kayley								*(1975)*		1		2
Kaylie									*(1985)*		2	4
Keeley						*(1962)*	2	10	7	24	8	2	10
Keely						*(1960)*	2	12	10	14	2	8	6
Keith *(1876)*		10	66	164	108	75	68	32	36	20	14	2
Kellie							*(1969)*	11	14	4	8	4
Kelly						*(1958)*	2	4	67	131	260	168	82
Kelsey *[1871]*									*(1971)*		2	22
Kelvin		*(1924)*		6	12	8	14	6	4	4	6	2
Kenneth	22	280	244	126	100	63	44	12	7	10	12	1
Kenny		*(1914)*								4	2	2
Keri				*(1939)*			2			4	2	4
Kerri						*(1963)*			4	4	10	2
	1900	1925	1935	1950	1955	1960	1965	1970	1975	1980	1985	1990

	1900	1925	1935	1950	1955	1960	1965	1970	1975	1980	1985	1990
Kerrie					(1951)	8	2	10	10	12	10	4
Kerry	(1920)					21	40	98	107	134	92	64
Kevan (1887)				4	8	6	4					
Kevin (1921)	(1921)	4	2	98	184	279	254	137	126	106	72	26
Kieran				(1943)						10	16	40
Kieron					(1951)		4			2	14	8
Kim			(1948)	2	10	84	36	23	19	16	28	4
Kimberley (1900)	3				2	2	6	2		12	94	74
Kimberly				(1955)	2			4			8	12
Kingsley (1859)			2	2		2						1
Kirk (1862)					2			2		2	10	4
Kirsten			(1948)					11	10	2	8	6
Kirstie							(1966)	8	5	2	6	18
Kirsty				(1955)	2			19	45	50	80	110
Kizzy										2		1
Kristian					(1960)	1		2	2	8	4	10
Kristina				(1952)				2		6	2	8
Kristy								(1970)		6		4
Kurt					(1958)			2			12	12
Kyle						(1964)				4	10	46
Kylie								(1974)		4	2	6
Lacey (1845)											2	8
Lana				(1943)		2				2	4	1
Lance				4			4	6	2			
Lara (1870)								6	6	8	6	6
Larry (1897)				2	2	2	6			2		
Laura	27	16	14	8	4	5	22	28	71	198	274	280
Laurel	2		2									4
Lauren				(1953)		6	2			12	76	192
Laurence	1	16	8	22	14	13	6	11	5	10	6	10
Laurie (1867)				2			4	2	2	4	4	8
Lavinia	14	4	2	4	4		2					1
Lawrence	15	18	24	26	2	5	10	5	2	4	8	12
Lawson (1850)		2					4	2				
Lea	6				2		6			2	2	
Leah		6			2		2	5	5	14	16	24
Leanne						(1963)	4	12	36	84	90	60
Lee	1	1	1	2	6	30	54	158	193	236	178	112
Leigh [1879]				(1951)	2	12	6	30	30	28	26	8
Leigh-Ann							(1969)			4		2
Leighanne									(1980)	4		
Leigh-Anne									(1976)	2		2
Leighton (1895)							2			2	4	
Leila (1855)		4		2	2			1	1	2		
Lena (1863)	8	8	4	2			2	2		8		
Leo	6	8					2				2	6
Leon (1857)		4	4	4	2	4	2	4	36	24	34	26
Leona (1878)		1					2		2	4	2	
Leonard	103	134	76	36	34	9	6	4	7	8	8	4
Leonie (1896)						1			1		2	24
Leroy		(1918)				2	2	4		2	2	2
Lesley (1882)	3	2	6	118	142	145	104	30	33	12	2	6
Leslie (1843)	40	204	84	94	78	50	26	5	10	6		4
Lewis	14	12	6	4	2	6	2	2		10	20	100
Liam		(1932)			2		2	2	4	12	34	152
Liane					(1960)	1	4	2		2	4	2
	1900	1925	1935	1950	1955	1960	1965	1970	1975	1980	1985	1990

	1900	1925	1935	1950	1955	1960	1965	1970	1975	1980	1985	1990
Lianne			(1946)					1	2	10		4
Lila (1890)					2		2					
Lilian (1853)	200	178	84	8	10	2	2	4				1
Lillian (1856)	16	12	4	6	6	6		1				
Lily (1856)	166	82	22	6	2	2					2	10
Linda (1849)	7	6	8	486	342	170	152	46	38	4	6	8
Lindsay (1845)	1	4		2	8	5	18	7	12	36	22	14
Lindsey (1857)					6	13	18	11	21	24	34	8
Linsey					(1962)			2	2	4	4	
Lionel	12	18	20	4	2	8	2	2				
Lisa [1893]			(1942)		1	5	80	249	224	228	134	54
Liza								2	2	2	8	1
Lloyd (1848)		2			2	8	6	4	5	12	10	12
Lois	6	2	4	4	2	2	2	2	2		6	10
Lola		(1919)		1	2							
Loraine (1870)				8	8	10	6	4				
Loren		(1946)								2		6
Loretta (1872)				2		2	2	2		2	2	2
Lorna (1876)	3	20	4	14	20	13	24	21	14	20	30	28
Lorraine (1873)				24	40	64	118	67	29	26	16	4
Louis	6	10	4	4	2	2		2		2	6	34
Louisa	63	16	6	4		4	10	7	12	20	10	10
Louise	3	2	2	6	14	34	104	121	133	152	128	60
Lucas		(1935)	2					1	1		2	2
Lucia (1855)					2		1					1
Lucie							2	1	1	2	10	6
Lucien		(1902)			2				1			
Lucille (1889)				4	2		2	2				
Lucinda						4	8	4	4	6	6	10
Lucy	61	22	2	4	2	4	10	19	71	66	82	142
Luke	1					4		16	24	52	92	218
Lydia	13	4				5	2	2	2	6	8	32
Lyn			(1936)	2		8	4	2				
Lynda (1896)		2		74	58	32	22	16	5	2		
Lyndon (1844)		2	1	2	2	4	18	6		4	2	8
Lyndsay				(1949)		1		1	2	4	4	
Lyndsey				(1948)		5	2	2	17	18	34	6
Lynette (1895)				2	8	9	14	4	4	12	6	
Lynn (1914)				30	60	54	40	11	17	4	2	
Lynne			(1939)	48	62	39	30	11	9	8		
Lynsey						(1958)			18	20	18	4
Mabel	106	58	12									
Madelaine				(1945)	2					2	2	2
Madeleine (1852)	1	2	6	4	2	5	8	2	7	4	10	14
Madeline (1852)	10	2		2	8		2	2	2	4		4
Maisie (1892)		20	12								2	4
Malcolm	1	2	62	158	98	77	34	26	7	12	14	2
Mandy			(1947)		4	55	90	49	24	18	10	2
Marc					(1956)		4	16	24	44	38	24
Marcia		4	4	6	4	2	8	2				
Marcus (1854)	1	2		2	2	2	14	35	29	10	12	16
Margaret	194	352	454	326	210	105	76	28	24	12	10	2
Margery	9	30	8	4								
Margot (1896)			4	1		1						
Marguerite (1867)	6	4	4									
Maria	25	6		20	22	18	82	21	24	22	20	16
	1900	1925	1935	1950	1955	1960	1965	1970	1975	1980	1985	1990

	1900	1925	1935	1950	1955	1960	1965	1970	1975	1980	1985	1990
Marian	9	24	30	16	14	5	2	2				
Marianne				4	2	4	6	2		8	2	
Marie *(1853)*	6	28	32	18	28	20	58	39	62	48	42	12
Marilyn		*(1930)*	2	128	38	7	4	4		2		
Marina *(1859)*			34	2	6	2	6	2		2	2	6
Marion *(1845)*	33	16	46	52	38	16	8	9		2		
Marissa					*(1954)*				2	4		
Marjorie *(1878)*	21	146	66	24	16	2	6	2				
Marjory *(1876)*	8	6	6									
Mark	6	6	4	12	98	398	516	467	426	272	232	96
Marlene		*(1932)*	24	16	8					2	1	
Marlon						*(1963)*		2	2	8		4
Marsha				*(1944)*					1	2		2
Martha	48	12	2				2					1
Martin	3	2	10	96	178	234	230	142	145	74	68	58
Martina *(1863)*					2	2	2	4	5	4		2
Martine				*(1947)*	2		2			8	4	
Martyn		*(1930)*		10	34	38	14	18	12	18	12	16
Mary	391	408	272	132	92	52	64	25	14	10	20	10
Mathew							2	12		22	24	34
Matilda	19	4	2		2	2		5		2		4
Matthew	22	6	4	6	8	27	76	211	288	358	334	400
Maud	22	12	4									1
Maureen *(1897)*		12	178	142	42	34	14	11		6		1
Maurice	15	66	50	28	16	5	2		5			1
Mavis *(1894)*	1	34	52	4	4					2		
Max *(1888)*			4	4			2				8	28
Maximilian *(1848)*							2				2	6
Maxine		*(1937)*		4	12	29	40	32	21	8	6	
Maxwell *(1850)*			2	6			2	1			4	10
May	130	46	16		4		4	2		2		
Megan	*(1911)*	4	2			8		2		2	8	52
Melanie				8	14	21	80	81	112	66	34	26
Melinda *(1842)*					2			4	5	4		8
Melissa *(1866)*							6	12	21	24	30	66
Melody					2	2	2	5	5	4	2	
Melvin *(1874)*	2		2	10	14	8	6			2		
Melvyn *(1874)*			2	20	16	4	4	2		2		
Meriel		*(1924)*			2		2					
Merle		*(1922)*	2									
Mervyn *(1870)*		6	6	6	4	4						
Michael	12	36	280	460	440	421	424	240	255	262	334	212
Michaela				*(1955)*	2		38	18	12	6	6	20
Michaella									*(1977)*	4		2
Michele			*(1943)*	8	6	6	34	8		4		
Michelle			*(1946)*	2	8	18	102	205	188	122	158	30
Mildred	22	14		2	2							
Miles							10	2			2	16
Milly		2					4					1
Milton	2	4	2			2	2			2		
Miranda		2			4	7	2	2	7	2	8	10
Miriam	9	12	8	2		4	2				2	1
Misty								*(1975)*	2			
Mitchell			2		2		2				6	20
Moira	*(1911)*	4	2	18	4		2	4				
Mollie	*(1901)*	6	12									
	1900	1925	1935	1950	1955	1960	1965	1970	1975	1980	1985	1990

	1900	1925	1935	1950	1955	1960	1965	1970	1975	1980	1985	1990
Molly *(1899)*	1	14	26					2				6
Monica		6	10	18	4	9	10					4
Montague	4	2	4									
Morris	6	2	6	2	4							
Muriel	18	84	38	8	4	4						
Murray *(1871)*			2		2		2			2	2	
Myra	3	4	6	8	2					2		2
Myrtle *(1857)*	3	6	6									
Nadia			*(1941)*							2	6	6
Nadine *(1895)*					2	4	4	11	5	16	8	8
Nancy	7	36	10	6	4	4	2	11	7	10	2	
Naomi	1		2	2	2	7	8	16	12	36	30	50
Natalie *(1886)*					2	2	10	37	69	124	192	146
Natasha		*[1906]*			*(1959)*			19	40	28	44	86
Nathan						2		19	57	62	40	118
Nathaniel	4	2			2		2	2		6	2	16
Neal			*(1941)*	2		8	6	6			4	4
Neil			4	48	42	107	142	114	195	126	76	6
Nellie *(1862)*	124	56	4									
Nelson	6	10	2	2		6				4	4	2
Nevil *(1873)*		2		2	2		2					
Neville *(1864)*		6	8	4	14	6	14	2			2	
Niall					*(1959)*		2			2		6
Nichola			*(1947)*		2		10	25	26	18	6	8
Nicholas	1	2		36	66	118	128	165	167	78	74	116
Nicky				*(1955)*	2					6		1
Nicola			*(1940)*	10	34	45	124	247	340	190	144	66
Nicolas			*(1936)*			4	4	4			4	4
Nicole			*(1937)*		2	5	2	5	14	2	8	34
Nicolette			*(1938)*	3	2	4	4	2			2	
Nigel *(1866)*	1	4	6	76	114	143	162	49	48	12	10	2
Nikki						*(1967)*		1	4	14	14	6
Nina *(1856)*	2	4	6	14	8	4	2	16		10	2	6
Noah	1	1		1	1	2	2	1				
Noel	2	8	8	4	8	2	4	8	4	2		
Nolan *(1881)*							1		1	2		
Nora	37	40	10	2	2					1		
Norah	56	52	20		4		2					
Noreen	*(1907)*	4	2			1						
Norma *(1879)*	2	36	60	10	10	8	4					
Norman	52	150	108	36	34	5	20	4	2		2	1
Nova		*(1935)*	2									
Olga *(1872)*	4	14	6				2				2	
Olive	73	140	48	6	2	2	2					
Oliver	9	2		4			4	5	24	74	66	114
Olivia	1	2	2	2					7	2	16	42
Olwen *(1892)*		4	2	6	4	2						
Olwyn *(1889)*		6	4	10		2						
Oonagh			*(1928)*				4					1
Oscar	2	2	2						1			6
Owen	6	2	6	4	2	7	6	5	14	2	10	14
Paige										*(1987)*		10
Pamela	1	66	158	186	134	154	26	18	21	16	2	
Pansy *(1882)*		2	2									
Patricia		76	304	258	242	136	60	35	24	14	6	2
Patrick	10	16	32	44	18	25	48	12	7	16	16	38
	1900	**1925**	**1935**	**1950**	**1955**	**1960**	**1965**	**1970**	**1975**	**1980**	**1985**	**1990**

	1900	1925	1935	1950	1955	1960	1965	1970	1975	1980	1985	1990
Paul		18	22	278	406	445	736	465	424	340	214	94
Paula		(1921)	2	12	32	18	110	95	67	62	34	8
Paulette		(1921)		2	2		12	2				
Pauline (1852)	1	22	104	186	138	93	70	23	10		2	
Pearl	3	22	12	10	8	4	2	4			1	
Peggy		110	34	10				2			1	
Penelope	1		2	34	48	41	28	12	10	6	4	
Penny [1846]			(1950)	2	4	4	2	7	12	2	2	
Percival	31	14	4	2								
Percy	131	34	8									1
Perry (1844)							2	4		4	4	8
Peta		(1934)								4	2	
Peter	24	194	390	534	410	343	312	135	119	132	114	54
Petra				(1957)			2					
Petrina			(1944)		2		2				2	
Petula			(1948)				2					
Philip	22	40	50	174	172	200	174	130	107	94	80	54
Philippa	1	2		6	6	7	26	14	33	6	8	22
Phillip		4	2	44	10	32	32	39	21	32	16	10
Phillippa					4						2	4
Phoebe	16	6	2		4		4				4	16
Phyllis	37	112	44	12	8	2						
Piers					4	2				1		1
Polly (1846)	6						2				4	6
Poppy (1895)		6					1			1		10
Primrose (1881)	2	2	2									
Priscilla	3	6	4	2	2	4					2	
Queenie (1891)	4	10	2		1		1					
Quentin (1880)					4		2					
Rachael		2			2		8	33	45	72	36	
Rachel	13	4	4	8	6	21	52	160	179	150	192	148
Rae		(1918)	2		2		2	4				
Ralph	21	44	28	12	10	4	4	4	2	4	2	
Ramon	(1925)	2	2		2							
Raphael										2		1
Ray	(1906)				4		2	3				
Raymond	12	138	176	136	70	68	42	21	26	8	20	
Rebecca	12	4		4	10	13	34	121	174	246	238	390
Rebekah							2	2	17	4	4	4
Reece		[1910]					(1966)					22
Regina (1869)			2									
Reginald	91	128	62	14	10	2			5			
Reiss											(1986)	6
Rena (1860)			2	3	2							
Rene (1899)	2	4	2	2								
Renee (1891)	2	6	12	4				2		1	1	
Reuben	22	8		2		2	4			6		4
Rex (1885)			6	2	2	2						1
Rhian				(1956)				3		2	4	2
Rhiannon				(1953)	2		2			2	6	16
Rhoda	16	8	4	2	2			4		2		1
Rhona (1870)		2	4	6	8		4			2		
Rhonda		(1917)		5	2	6	2		2			
Rhys			(1927)							2	8	12
Ria							(1961)			3	10	6
Richard	112	96	58	158	168	161	336	256	314	206	238	136
	1900	1925	1935	1950	1955	1960	1965	1970	1975	1980	1985	1990

	1900	1925	1935	1950	1955	1960	1965	1970	1975	1980	1985	1990
Ricky			(1947)			2	4	2		32	36	36
Rita (1895)		32	94	44	14	7	4	4				
Robbie			(1928)				2			4		12
Robert	267	284	186	356	344	161	342	239	231	210	142	188
Roberta	1	2	2	2	4	2	2	2	2	2	4	2
Robin			30	44	34	32	22	35	19	20	20	10
Robina	2	2		4	2		2					
Robyn			(1946)	2	2		2	5	2		4	22
Rochelle						(1958)			1			12
Roderick (1855)		2	2	6	20	14	4	2				1
Rodney (1857)		6	10	22	18	10	12	2		2		
Roger	1	8	46	134	62	63	62	19	26	12	6	4
Roisin		(1935)	1									2
Roland	9	30	16	6	6	11	10	2	10	8	2	2
Rona (1872)		4	4					2		2		
Ronald	21	308	362	96	66	27	40	11	2	4	6	2
Ronnie (1914)		2	2	2	2		2	2		2	8	
Rory			(1947)				2	2		2		28
Rosa	16	2	4									1
Rosalie (1857)	2		4	2	2						2	
Rosalind	3	4	2	26	18	16	20	11			4	4
Rosalyn (1925)		2		2	6	2	10	2		2	4	2
Rosamond			2									
Rosamund	2			2	2							
Rosanna	4						2			2	4	8
Rose	152	88	38	14	12	14	4	4	2	4		24
Roseanne						(1965)	2					4
Roselyn (1886)							2			2		
Rosemarie			2	12	8	2	4	5				1
Rosemary (1898)		14	52	78	54	38	30	14	2	4	16	6
Rosetta	4	6	4	2				2		2		1
Rosie (1869)	7	10							4	4	2	16
Rosina	12	20	10	12		5				2		4
Roslyn (1916)		2	2		6		2				2	1
Ross				2	4	6	4	6		24	18	42
Rowan				(1951)			2			2	6	4
Rowena			2		6	2	4	2	4			6
Rowland	12	12	2	6	6	2				2		
Roxanne									(1976)		16	8
Roy (1884)	3	122	152	62	68	29	42	11	12	10		1
Royston (1892)		5	24	6	8	6	6	4	1		1	
Ruby (1874)	21	32	10		2	4		2		1	1	8
Rupert		3	2	4	2	2	2	3		1		3
Russell	3	8	4	10	10	66	62	42	40	44	38	10
Ruth	22	38	26	16	18	11	26	14	26	16	10	20
Ryan			(1939)					7	21	44	102	156
Sabina			2				2					
Sabrina										1	6	6
Sadie (1895)						4	6		14	6	8	10
Sally		2	6	46	36	71	136	42	55	38	22	18
Sally-Ann			(1954)	2		5	4	6				
Sallyanne			(1950)	2		5	4	5		4		
Sam		12		2	2			2		16	12	52
Samantha [1892]						(1961)	58	168	152	98	162	126
Sammy (1849)										3	8	8
Samuel	106	38	8	2	8	11	12	5	24	46	42	202
	1900	1925	1935	1950	1955	1960	1965	1970	1975	1980	1985	1990

	1900	1925	1935	1950	1955	1960	1965	1970	1975	1980	1985	1990
Sandie						(1965)	2	1		6	4	2
Sandra		(1935)	6	192	150	120	126	18	17	10	6	2
Sandy (1843)							2	2		2	2	
Sara			2	6	10	5	24	32	24	30	24	6
Sarah	152	30	12	18	18	57	204	282	371	252	270	190
Sarah-Jane						(1968)		8	8	10	2	10
Sarah-Jayne						(1964)				3	4	
Scott (1882)				2		2	8	42	79	56	58	108
Sean		(1924)		4	6	9	66	47	17	26	54	54
Sebastian								2		2	6	16
Selena					1			2		1	4	
Selina	7	6		4	2		4	5	2	4	14	
Selwyn	2	2	4									
Serena (1852)					2					8	8	6
Shane			(1943)		2	11	14	23	38	38	40	44
Shannon			(1947)		2						2	6
Sharlene							(1970)			6		
Sharon		(1933)		20	60	161	224	286	119	28	22	4
Sharron		(1944)		2		4	10	19	4	2		
Shaun		(1942)			10	23	78	67	31	36	58	60
Shawn		(1948)					2			2	2	
Shayne					(1961)					3	2	
Sheelagh		(1930)	4	4			2					
Sheena		(1910)	8	4	5	2	2	4	4	6		
Sheila (1892)		78	242	150	66	41	30	9	7	6		
Shelagh (1906)		3		2	4		4					
Shelley (1860)				2	4	4	2	14	22	30	26	8
Shelly					(1961)		2	2	3	4	4	
Sheree				(1951)	4					2	4	
Sherrie									(1979)	3	2	
Sheryl		(1948)			6	5	4	4	5	4	4	
Shirley (1861)		8	484	84	102	46	30	14	5	8	4	2
Shona		(1943)					2	5	10	2	2	6
Sian		(1946)			2	2	6	6	7	10	12	42
Sidney	155	110	56	10	6	4	4	2		2		
Sigourney											(1990)	4
Simeon							4	2			2	
Simon	1		6	10	46	98	208	239	219	124	54	58
Simone			(1945)	2			4	4	4	18	8	12
Sinead								(1971)				22
Siobhan				(1953)			10	22	4	6	14	26
Sir (1846)		1		1	1		1					
Solomon	4							2		4	4	
Sonia	(1909)	4	8	6	4	7	28	19	14	8	10	2
Sonya			(1941)				4	2		4		
Sophia	10	2					4	2	2	2	4	20
Sophie (1863)		2				2		9	10	20	36	164
Spencer						2	6	14	21	6	2	2
Stacey		(1906)				2	6	16	21	40	74	140
Stacy							(1970)	1	4	8	12	8
Stanley	93	158	60	12	8	5	6	2	5		2	
Stefan			(1949)		1		1			1	10	8
Stefanie			(1943)							3	2	6
Stella	1	20	16	12	12	5	10	7	7	2	2	
Stephanie (1883)		2		28	14	27	30	35	43	36	50	138
Stephen	22	10	16	268	568	454	380	282	233	172	156	102
	1900	1925	1935	1950	1955	1960	1965	1970	1975	1980	1985	1990

	1900	1925	1935	1950	1955	1960	1965	1970	1975	1980	1985	1990
Steven				32	132	202	178	195	219	160	186	96
Stewart	4	6		18	8	32	26	21	21	16	8	8
Stuart	4	6	6	58	28	52	102	125	181	104	78	36
Sue (1873)										4		
Susan	19	8	14	654	692	446	406	102	86	30	28	4
Susanna							2			4	2	6
Susannah	18	2	2			2	8	2	12	2		4
Susanne (1869)				2	6	2	10	21	12	12	2	
Susie (1863)	2		2	4			4					4
Suzanna		(1937)					4			2	2	
Suzanne (1912)		2	2	14	22	25	50	32	45	24	26	12
Sydney	99	88	24	6	6							1
Sylvia	7	68	206	60	50	27	28	7	7	4	6	
Tamar			2							2		2
Tamara		(1938)						4	5			8
Tammy [1889]						(1961)	2	7	31	24	22	14
Tamsin		(1938)					2	2	10	4	4	12
Tania		(1939)				4	18	7	5	8		2
Tanya			(1943)		2	2	14	21	21	12	16	28
Tara						(1968)		21	17	16	10	22
Terence	1	30	96	154	106	88	42	9	14	10	12	4
Teresa		12	12	32	46	27	48	46	43	4	4	4
Terrence			4	10	2	8	2	4		2	6	
Terri			(1955)		2		2		2	4	14	14
Terrie			(1955)		2	1	2	1		4		
Terry (1849)		2	8	20	12	29	32	16	29	16	20	16
Tessa		(1903)	4	4	8	2	2	2	1	2		
Thelma (1894)	1	26	34	6	8							1
Theo (1888)												6
Theodora	4	4								2		1
Theresa	3	6	6	16	18	23	34	18	7	12	6	2
Thomas	452	254	150	82	64	39	40	44	52	120	160	362
Tiffany						(1966)		1	4	10		
Timothy	1	2	6	38	60	84	126	70	76	60	48	52
Tina		(1912)	2	2	30	80	78	74	55	22	6	
Tobias										6	6	
Toby				(1956)			2	12		6	14	12
Todd					(1962)		2			4	2	8
Tom	16	8	4	2					2	12	8	18
Tommy (1870)										8	6	10
Toni			(1944)		2	2	12	8		6	18	22
Tonia		(1932)				4	2	4		2	2	
Tony		(1912)	18	22	32	29	40	26	29	24	28	18
Tracey [1845]				(1957)		38	336	184	74	34	36	4
Tracie					(1961)		5	2			4	
Tracy [1851]				(1955)	2	50	250	198	88	52	14	2
Trevor (1862)	1	22	40	114	124	107	64	39	19	8	16	2
Trina			(1942)				6		2	2		
Tristan			(1956)					4	6	14	6	8
Troy				(1963)			4	8	4		2	1
Trudi			(1953)		4	4	4	10		2	2	6
Trudy		(1937)		8	10	8	8	10	6	4	8	
Tyler			(1942)						1			8
Tyrone			(1952)			6	4	4		2	4	4
Tyson (1861)												4
Una (1851)	4	8	2		2							
	1900	1925	1935	1950	1955	1960	1965	1970	1975	1980	1985	1990

	1900	1925	1935	1950	1955	1960	1965	1970	1975	1980	1985	1990
Ursula	3	8	2	2			2	4	2		4	
Valda		(1914)	2		2							
Valentine	4			4	2	2		2				
Valerie	1	6	108	150	126	50	28	7	5			
Vanda (1876)			2		2	1			1			
Vanessa (1923)				18	14	7	16	26	26	10	2	20
Vaughan (1881)				4	4	4	2				2	
Vera (1873)	28	190	50	12	2	5	2	5			1	
Verity (1935)			2				2			10	8	6
Vernon		22	6	2	4	6	2	6				
Veronica (1856)	3	24	16	26	20		10			6		
Vicki (1934)					4		6	12	12	10	8	4
Vickie (1952)							2		2			
Vicky (1952)				4	8	11	4	11	19	18	26	14
Victor	43	54	44	10	6	11	12	4	2		2	1
Victoria	12	2		22	20	20	46	181	176	184	180	154
Vida (1869)			4		2							
Vikki (1967)								4	5	14	6	10
Vincent	12	24	12	16	14	7	16	14	10	10	6	4
Violet	155	136	42	12		3	6	2	2	2		
Virginia				6		9	14	4	2	2	4	2
Vivian (1859)	2	4	8	4	6	4						
Vivien (1871)		2	8	18	10	8	12	2		2	2	1
Vivienne (1910)	6		18	20	8	6	8		6			
Wade (1854)					2		2					
Walter	187	106	44	12	6	5	6	4		2		
Wanda		(1944)			2		2					2
Warren			4	2	4	9	16	19	19	4	10	10
Wayne		(1940)		2	16	25	122	93	114	84	60	12
Wendy	(1920)	2	22	96	70	177	162	84	50	24	8	2
Wesley (1848)	2	4	2		2	2	4	2		16	16	6
Westley	(1910)								1	4		
Wilfred	49	50	14	2			2					
William	897	590	274	178	140	127	76	33	67	60	66	136
Willie	24	2	2		2		2					
Willow								(1978)		2		
Wilson			2		2							
Winifred	191	142	42	8	4	2				4		1
Winnie (1865)	8	2	8									
Winston (1900)	6				2		4	4				
Yasmin		(1927)					6		2	2	2	12
Yolanda				(1951)						2		2
Yvette			(1941)			4	10		6			
Yvonne (1899)		6	26	58	70	52	40	18	19	6	12	
Zachary										6		10
Zak						(1965)	1	1				6
Zara						(1968)		5	7	4	10	6
Zena (1894)			4		4		2					4
Zoe (1850)	2			2		2	12	30	107	50	52	92
Zowie								(1974)		4	2	
	1900	1925	1935	1950	1955	1960	1965	1970	1975	1980	1985	1990

4
NAMING THE BABY

I N THE last twenty years I have received several hundred letters from parents in all English-speaking countries, explaining why they chose the names they did for their children. The reasons they mentioned can be arranged under a number of headings.

Fashion

A great many parents began with the question of which names they believed to be currently fashionable, for this had affected their choice of names one way or the other. Parents who had chosen **Philippa** for their daughter, for instance, said that they had 'a major desire to avoid modern excesses of vulgarity and trend following'. It was perhaps an accident that 'vulgarity' occurred in such close context with 'trend following', but it should be emphasised that the two are not connected. Vulgarity presumably refers to a name's respectability, which I shall be discussing later. As for trend following, it is doubtful whether the majority of parents are really aware of what the trend is until several years after it has begun. When it becomes generally known which names are being used a great deal, there is ample evidence to show that most people hastily move away from them. This is true, at least, of names that have not had a high following for several generations. There is a fear that such names will not stand the test of time and that they will therefore 'date' a child.

Jason has been a typical example of such a name in recent years. It came in for a great many negative comments from my correspondents, many of whom said things like: 'I shall scream if I hear of another Jason.' There was a general feeling that the name was working class, a word which some writers equated with 'vulgar'. Others scoffed at it because of its associations with characters on television.

I believe there are working-class names, just as there are middle-class names, but Jason is *not* marked in this way. It clearly appealed to a wide

The reason I got called Tiffany is because when I was born, dear father Case was so sore I wasn't a boy he gave my mother a thousand bucks and a powder case from Tiffany's and walked out.

Ian Fleming *Diamonds Are Forever*

range of social levels. I also believe that some names are 'vulgar', but by my definition these are names which are totally unsuitable for use as first names which are given by publicity-seeking parents. Jason clearly does not fall into this class, either.

Nevertheless, the feelings reflected by my correspondents in the last few years have been equally well reflected in the popularity charts. Use of Jason has been declining rapidly, and it may be destined to return to obscurity.

A less dramatic swing of fashion than that which affected Jason can have a positive influence on a name, however. As one parent wrote about **Matthew**: 'Probably a few years ago I would never have dreamt of using this name, but simply for the fact that it has become popular one gets used to the sound of it and eventually likes it.'

This comment hints at another parental fear— that they will choose a name which is completely out of fashion. The majority of parents probably make a conscious attempt to steer between the two extremes. 'It isn't very common,' wrote a mother who had chosen **Timothy** during 1972, 'but it is not too unusual.' Other parents chose **Jessica** because it was 'not particularly fashionable, so wouldn't date her'. The parents of **John** considered the name 'not gimmicky, not easily dated'.

But if this conscious motivation is admirable in itself, how effectively do most parents achieve their aim? They tend to base their ideas about which names are popular and which names are not on their own social circle, which is a shaky base indeed. John,

The practice of romantic names among persons, even of the lowest orders of society, has become a very general evil: and doubtless many unfortunate beauties, of the names of Clarissa and Eloisa, might have escaped under the less dangerous appellatives of Elizabeth Deborah.

Isaac Disraeli   *Influence of a Name*

which seems to be a name that could not possibly be accused of dating a child, may well do so by the end of the century. It has suffered such an amazing decline on all sides that it is likely to become a rare name for future generations. Even now a John who is beginning school is likely to be the only boy of that name in the class—something which would have been out of the question a few years ago.

Social class associations

This is not the place to discuss the subtleties of what makes people 'working class' or 'middle class', or whether the labels can still be used meaningfully. Most of my correspondents clearly felt that there are still recognisable social strata and that the classes of people have different tastes in most things, including names.

Parents can certainly be influenced when choosing a name by their assessment of a name's social standing. Of **Benjamin** one parent wrote: 'It also appealed to the snob in me, seeming to be a name Hampstead-type people used.' On **Louise** another writer commented: 'it sounds very sophisticated', and a third parent said of **Alexandra**: 'I like regal

names', which I take to be another indirect reference to social class.

Not all names, needless to say, suggest one social class rather than another. When the associations are there, they can change drastically with the passing of time. **Abigail** went out of fashion completely because it had become almost a synonym for a lady's maid. It now seems to be coming back into fashion at the other end of the social scale. If it follows a normal course it will make its way slowly down the social grades until it fades away again, waiting for the whole mysterious process to bring it back to the top.

Euphony

The sound of a first name when placed alongside the surname is a common factor considered by parents. **Paul**, **Mark**, **Joanne** and **Tracey** may be popular generally, but as the birth registers reveal very clearly, there is an avoidance of such combinations as **Paul Hall**, **Mark Clarke**, **Mark Martin**, **Joanne Jones** and **Tracey Thomas**. **Jason** has never caught on with the **Jackson** family, for similar reasons.

Sometimes parents fall in love with the sound of an individual name. One parent commented on **Bronia** that 'it has an interesting sound', and another said of **Bryony**: 'short musical sound and the combination of an abrupt start and a subtle ending'. The reference by one mother to 'the beautiful name **Berengaria**' was presumably another comment on euphony.

Initials

The parents of Colin Cowdrey, an English cricketer of some renown, made sure when they named him that his full initials would be M.C.C. Amongst cricket lovers throughout the world these initials are

Are we naming our daughters too fancifully? I am inclined to sympathise with the feeling that makes poor parents who have perforce to live in some soulless slum, seek for something sweet and wholesome, even if it be only a name, and I have given up moralising when I hear such a one called Doris or Ivy. It is ever so much better than condemning them to the hackneyed Mary Ann which seems to rob them of all chance. I like the flowers and the gems, but I do not care about the mythological names such as Diana, Psyche, and the like—they seem too heathenish.

Anonymous article on the Woman's Page, in *Great Eastern Railway Magazine*, November, 1912.

In youthful London slang a girl who looks cheap and nasty is now likely to be described as 'a right Shaz'. In other words, she looks like a *Sharon*. This contrasts greatly with the 'rose of Sharon', the beautiful shepherdess who is passionately described in the Old Testament's Song of Songs. It was no doubt this reference which led to the use of Sharon as a girl's name. Its original meaning was simply 'flat land', specifically a fertile coastal plain between Carmel and Joppa.

famous as being those of the Marylebone Cricket Club. Colin Cowdrey was thus dedicated to cricket from the moment of his baptism.

Elsdon C. Smith has said that black Americans consider it lucky to create a set of initials for a child which make a meaningful word. Most parents would say that it rather depends what the word is. Amongst those who would seem to have begun life at a disadvantage in this respect are W. C. Fields and Sir Arthur Sullivan, of Gilbert and Sullivan fame. The latter gentleman began life as Arthur Seymour Sullivan.

Charles Dickens, who somewhere in his novels comments on every conceivable aspect of names and naming, was well aware of initial possibilities. In his *Pickwick Papers* he creates Peter Magnus, a man who thinks extremely highly of his own name. There is also the 'curious circumstance about those initials. You will observe—P. M.—post meridian. In hasty notes to intimate acquaintance, I sometimes sign myself "Afternoon". It amuses my friends very much, Mr Pickwick.' 'It is calculated to offer them the highest gratification, I should conceive,' is Mr Pickwick's reply.

Other surname influences

As we shall see when we come to discuss surnames in detail, there is a central surname stock just as there is a central first name stock. Some parents try to balance first names with surnames, the usual with the unusual or vice versa. In choosing **Guinevere**, for example, the **Day** family had in mind that this was 'a name to complement her surname', and **Jemima** was chosen as 'a fairly unusual name to go with **Brown**'. Another correspondent began by saying that they had had to find 'something unusual, because her surname is **Smith**'. This seems to be sensible thinking in principle, but all the evidence is that the majority of people with common surnames choose equally common first names.

Another factor that concerns the surname is the latter's meaning, or potential meaning when placed beside a first name. One comes across occasional instances of **Ann Teak**, **Handsome Mann**, **Orange Lemon** and the like, but one can safely say that the majority of parents are careful to avoid such combinations. Some may come later by marriage. There is a recorded instance of a **Rose** family who named their daughter **Wild**, thinking that they had hit on a beautiful combination. She later married a gentleman called **Bull**.

Respectability

This is felt to be conferred on a name when it has been in existence for some centuries, though parents who are concerned with such a point often use euphemistic expressions such as 'traditional' or 'old-fashioned' rather than 'respectable'. We are not necessarily talking about the use of a name by one social class rather than another here. We are talking about the choice of **Sarah**, say, rather than **Trac(e)y**— both of them immensely popular over a wide social range—simply because Sarah has been in use as an English first name for centuries whereas Trac(e)y has not.

Whether for practical considerations, such as the difficulties that can be caused for the bearer of a relatively unfamiliar name, for historical nicety, or simply for the usual reasons of snobbishness, one detects in many letters from middle-class parents a strong reaction against modern first names such as **Craig**, **Darren**, **Scott**, **Shane**, **Warren** and **Wayne** for the boys, **Beverl(e)y**, **Cheryl**, **Gaynor**, **Hayley**, **Kelly**, **Kerrie**, **Lorraine**, **Mandy** and **Trac(e)y** for the girls. **Lee/Leigh** should also be included in both lists.

Originality

As we have seen, black American families value individuality in names rather more than white families. They are therefore more ready to invent new names, convert words into names or transfer them from other sources. Some white parents feel equally strongly that they should invent a name for their child. Their thinking appears to be that they have created the child concerned, so they should also create the child's name.

The arguments for original names are that they avoid associations with other people who have borne the name and really do identify an individual. But very great care must be taken by parents who tread this dangerous path. Several studies by psychologists have shown that people who have names that are considered to be decidedly unusual or odd by those around them can experience great difficulties in their normal social relationships. This can apply to well-established, but very outmoded names as well as invented ones, for Harvard students classed **Ivy**, **Rosebud**, **Hope**, **Patience**, **Cuthbert**, **Reginald** and **Egbert** as 'odd' a few years ago. Another age-group in another place would naturally compile quite a different list of odd names and perhaps accept most of these as perfectly normal.

It is certain that there are misunderstandings between the black and white communities because of their different ideas about naming. It would help if white people bore in mind that black parents use different criteria and have their own sound reasons for doing what they do. On the other hand, black parents who know that their children will have to make their way in a multi-racial society should perhaps be extra cautious about the names they give. Their task is to retain originality while avoiding at all costs what might be called oddity.

Sexual characteristics

Parents frequently mention that certain names are particularly masculine or feminine and that this has affected their choice. Most of our first names give clear indications of a child's sex, and it is obviously felt to be important to preserve this situation. **Leslie** and **Lesley** are both fading away rapidly in the popularity charts, perhaps because of this sexual confusion. I would expect both **Lee** and **Leigh** to drop away if more boys as well as girls are given the name.

I also detect in many letters the belief that a strong, masculine name will make a boy into a 'real man', while a soft, feminine name will somehow produce a 'lovely lady'. I emphasise that these are letters being written by young parents of today. Ideas about the sexual roles clearly do not change overnight.

Religion

The parents' religious beliefs often influence the choice of first names. There are plenty of Christian first names available, so parents have a wide choice. The recent upsurge of **Christian** itself as a first name presumably reflects religious motivation, but with first names one can take nothing for granted.

Use of the name **Mary** has undoubtedly declined a great deal in the last twenty years or so, its very popularity having at last brought about its own downfall. Those parents who do continue to use it are probably keenly aware of its religious significance and regard it as a name of great potency. Earlier attitudes to it were well displayed in Montaigne's *Essays*, first published in John Florio's translation in 1603:

'A licentious young man had one night gotten a wench to lie with him, who so soone as she came to bed, he demanded her name, who answered Marie: The young man hearing that name, was suddenly so strucken with a motive of religion, and an awfull respect unto that sacred name of the Virgin Marie, the blessed mother of our Saviour and Redeemer, that he did not onely presently put her away from him, but reformed all the remainder of his succeeding life.'

She was named after Saint Therese of Lisieux, affectionately known as the Little Flower, a Carmelite nun who had died at the age of twenty-four in 1897 having apparently distinguished herself only by housework and obedience. But her autobiography found and published after her death, proved a document sweet, almost sickly, in its childlike influence. It became a runaway best-seller in the Catholic world and had been a favourite book in O'Halloran's boyhood home.

Bamber Gascoigne   *Murgatreud's Empire*

Personal associations

A name's associations with other people provide one of the most important reasons for choosing it or not choosing it. There can be both private and public associations.

Specific commemorative use of names, as we have seen, was normal for the naming of boys until the present century, with members of the family rather than public figures being honoured. A very large number of first names are still chosen in honour of friends and relations, particularly, it would seem, among the 'upper' classes. Such names are sometimes what Ian Hay once called 'sprats to catch testamentary whales'. But private or public associations of a name can just as frequently act against it. We all know of parents who reject names because they have known somebody unpleasant who bore it. A public taboo also operates against names like **Adolf**, not that this particular name was popular *before* the 1930s in the English-speaking world.

Origins

A few parents take account of a first name's origin when choosing a name for their child, but this tends to be a confirmatory rather than a deciding factor. If parents already have an inclination towards a certain name for other reasons, they are pleased to discover that it originally meant something favourable, as most of our first names did. But the parents of at least one boy who wrote to me were primarily influenced by the origin of the name they chose. Of **Selwyn** they wrote: 'an old English name meaning "house friend" . . . we liked its meaning.'

Fictional associations

Novels still continue to inspire parents when they are looking for names, though if a novel is made into a film it is obviously difficult to say which was the main source. *Gone With the Wind*, as both novel and film, was a major influence from 1939 onwards. **Melanie, Ashley** and **Bonnie** derived from that source, and other names which occurred in the story, such as **Scarlett** and **Careen**, have received some attention.

High Society, released in 1956, had Grace Kelly playing the part of Tracy Samantha Lord. **Tracy, Samantha** and **Kelly**, transferred to first name use, appeared almost from that moment. *High Society* was actually a re-make, with music, of *The Philadelphia Story*, released in 1939 and considered by many critics to be by far the better film. This version of the film, however, failed to influence parents-to-be.

A more recent film that had considerable impact on name usage was *The Graduate*, in which Dustin Hoffman played the part of **Benjamin**. That name has enjoyed a run of popularity ever since. It is interesting to note that it was the names of the fictional characters portrayed by Grace Kelly and Dustin Hoffman which became popular, not their own first names, as had been the case with **Shirley** Temple, **Leslie** Howard and the like in the 1930s.

Television series naturally have an effect on naming, in that they bring names to the public's attention. Probably the most outstanding television 'success' of recent times is that of **Emma**, reintroduced in *The Avengers* by Diana Rigg. Other names of this kind, used by parents because they admire the fictional characters bearing the names, are **Jason, Joshua, Fleur** and **Ricky**.

And now she was pregnant, and she laughed so much that she decided she would have to call her son 'Laughter'. 'Is there a name that means laughter,*' she asked Aubrey, and he told her he thought* Isaac *meant laughter. 'Isaac it is,' she said.*

Gwendolyn Macewen   *Day of Twelve Princes*

My father had combined diplomacy with the study of Anglo-Saxon history and, of course, with my mother's consent, he gave me the name of Alfred, one of his heroes (I believe she had boggled at Aelfred). This Christian name, for some inexplicable reason, had become corrupted in the eyes of our middle-class world; it belonged exclusively now to the working class and was usually abbreviated to Alf.

Graham Greene   *Doctor Fischer of Geneva*

One final name that deserves a mention in this section is **Jennifer**, which was decidedly unusual in North America—though it had been popular in Britain—until Erich Segal published *Love Story*. The film version of this, released in 1970, caused Jennifer to begin a swift ascent to the number one position amongst American girls' names. The film also showed that the real names of actors or actresses *could* still be noticed and copied, for **Ryan** O'Neal's name was also taken over.

Associated characteristics

Many people believe that everyone who bears a particular name will grow up to have the same characteristics. Laurence Sterne made superb fun of this idea in his 18th-century novel *Tristram Shandy*, expounding a 'philosophy of nomenclature' which was seized upon later by R. L. Stevenson in an essay of that name. More recently Roger Price and Leonard Stern had made suitable fun of the whole idea in their booklet *How Dare You Call Me That!* In the Introduction they say: 'Once you give a baby a name society begins to treat it as if it has the type of personality the name implies, and the child, being sensitive, responds consciously or unconsciously and grows up to fit the name.' The authors go on to give their own ideas about the public associations of a large number of names. A sample: '**Angus** is a giant who smiles a lot and looks as if he might have been

---

'I christened her Maria del Sol, because she was my first child and I dedicated her to the glorious sun of Castile; but her mother calls her Sally, and her brother Pudding-face.'

Somerset Maugham   *Of Human Bondage*

---

at Bannockburn. Be careful shaking hands with Angus. He'll dislocate all bones up to the elbow.'

There is a modicum of truth in this name-characteristics theory. If a large number of people from the same social group were asked to describe a **Cuthbert** or an **Agnes**, a **Fred** or a **Rita**, they might well show some kind of agreement in what they said. They would be drawing upon information stored in their minds about the social class, age and profession of people they had met who bore these names. It is also partly true that when two girls who both started life as **Elizabeth** or whatever have become **Liz** in one case and remained Elizabeth in the other by the time they reach their twenties, the two forms of the name may reflect to some extent their different personalities.

Some names, then, do have generally accepted associated characteristics, and these can influence parents' choices. It is hard to say where associated characteristics end and personal associations begin on occasions. Did Jerry Lewis choose **Wilbur** as the name for a silly person because of characteristics that he felt were already associated with it, or is the name now associated with Lewis's portrayals?

In our own society it is of course impossible to pin down seriously these 'meanings' of names, which can be positive or negative, which can vary from person to person, region to region, and which are constantly

---

Our oldest son was named George, after his uncle, who left us ten thousand pounds. I intended to call (my daughter) after Aunt Grissel, but my wife, who had been reading romances, insisted upon her being called Olivia. In less than another year we had another daughter, and now I was determined that Grissel should be her name; but a rich relation taking a fancy to stand godmother, the girl was, by her directions, called Sophia, so that we had two romantic names in the family, but I solemnly protest I had no hand in it.

Oliver Goldsmith   *The Vicar of Wakefield*

People always grow up like their names. It took me thirty years to work off the effects of being called Eric. If I wanted a girl to grow up beautiful I'd call her Elizabeth, and if I wanted her to be a good cook I'd choose something like Mary or Jane.

George Orwell (Eric Blair)   *Letters*

mutating with the passing of time and the arrival of new social influences.

In some other societies, however, far more specific beliefs exist and the effect of those beliefs can to a certain extent be measured. G. Jahoda, for example, has made an interesting study of Ashanti day names (whereby children are named according to the day on which they are born), and the characteristics associated with each name. He discovered that a child born on a 'bad' day was more likely to end up in the juvenile court than a child whose name advertised the fact that he had been born on a 'good' day. The bad day name would cause others to act towards its bearer in a certain way, and this would affect his personality.

Verbal associations

Many of the names that have been common in the past have come to have verbal associations. Everyone is familiar with expressions like: 'every **Tom**,

---

Now I wonder what would please her,
Charlotte, Julia or Louisa?
Ann and Mary, they're too common;
Joan's too formal for a woman;
Jane's a prettier name beside;
But we had a Jane that died.
They would say, if 'twas Rebecca,
That she was a little Quaker,
Edith's pretty, but that looks
Better in old English books.
Ellen's left off long ago:
Blanche is out of fashion now.

None that I have named as yet
Are so good as Margaret.
Emily is neat and fine.
What do you think of Caroline?
How I'm puzzled and perplexed
What to choose or think of next!
I am in a little fever
Lest the name that I shall give her
Should disgrace her or defame her.
I will leave Papa to name her.

Charles Lamb   *Naming the Baby* (1809)

Dick or **Harry**', 'simple **Simon**', 'a **Jack** of all trades'. Simon seems to have overcome its unpleasant associations recently, but the first name popularity tables indicate that some names are hampered by such idioms. The American use of 'the john' for the lavatory can hardly have helped the name **John**, and may have contributed to its recent spectacular downfall. Wise parents remind themselves of any verbal associations that may exist by checking a potential name in a good dictionary before finally deciding on it.

Other associations

Place names such as **Florence** and **Kent** have been used as first names because of a wish to commemorate the place of birth. American twins were given the names **Okla** and **Homa** for a similar reason. **Tulip** was chosen by the singer Tiny Tim to remind him of the song that made his fortune: 'Tip-toe through the tulips.' A more general transfer from a song in recent times is seen with **Michelle**, which the Beatles undoubtedly set on its way. It is also possible that the affectionate regard in the public's mind for the late Maurice Chevalier extended to his song 'Louise', and that the popularity of that name stems in part from the song. On the other hand one family wrote to explain that they had called their daughter **Louise** because 'this is the name of one of our cats, whom we love very much'.

Laura is another name which has been rising in popularity since the 1940s, when a song of that name made a big impact.

Nationality

Parents often want to proclaim their child's nationality in its name. Scottish, Welsh and Irish parents are especially fond of doing this—and I am speaking here of those who choose to do so. If one lives in Scotland, Wales or Ireland one is naturally exposed to a rather different central stock of first names and may pick a name from it without thinking of its national markings.

Various dictionaries of names which reflect different nationalities are listed in the Bibliography. My own special studies in this area bore fruit in 1978 when I published *Scottish Christian Names*.

Diminutive forms

The variant forms of a name are usually considered by parents, since it is accepted that many names are rarely used in their full forms by a child's friends. If parents do not like the usual diminutives and short forms they may well avoid a name altogether.

I have already commented on the difference between these formalised nicknames and names like **Jim** or **Bob** when the latter are bestowed as the legal names. With the development of the latter, it is possible that at some time in the future someone bearing a name like **Richard** will always remain Richard, since **Dick** will be looked upon as a completely separate name and not a diminutive.

Incidents at birth

Incidents that occur at or close to a child's birth often influence the name that is given to it. One little girl was called **Caroline** because 'she was born in the middle of a power cut, and as the power came on "Sweet Caroline" was being played on the radio'. A boy likewise became **James** because of 'a song, "St James' Infirmary" which my husband was playing just before I went to hospital'. I have also been told of a girl who was called **Sirene** because she was born during an air-raid and the siren was heard soon afterwards.

Perhaps one should include here the mother who 'had a dream two weeks before she was born that I had a baby girl and that we had named her **Jessica**.' This dream name was duly given to the daughter. Names that relate to the time of birth are also incident names in their way. **Noël**, **Avril**, **April**, **June** and **Natalie** are well established for this purpose. One parent wrote to say that **Octavia** was chosen partly because of an October birth, an interesting example of an incidental link name.

There is also a kind of verbal incident name. In *The Forsyte Saga* is a well-known example, when Annette looks down at her newly born daughter: '*Ma petite fleur!*' Annette said softly.

'*Fleur*,' repeated Soames: '**Fleur**! We'll call her that.'

Less poetic is the story reported in an American newspaper in 1975, to the effect that a baby boy had just been named **Bill** 'because he came on the last day of the month'.

Perhaps one should also set up a category called 'Incidents at conception', though none of my correspondents have mentioned such events. But Professor R. N. Ashley reported in an American Name Society *Bulletin* that **Margot** Hemingway received her first name because her parents thought she was conceived after they drank a vintage Château Margeaux. Nancy Mitford also has a character called **Northey** in her novel *Don't Tell Alfred*. It is explained that 'she was conceived in the Great Northern Hotel—hence her curious name'.

Description

A **Serena** received her name, according to a correspondent, because a friend of the family described her as 'so serene'. A **Daniel** received his name 'because he looked like a judge'. The choice of a first name for descriptive reasons is rare, however. The

---

Pride lives with all; strange names our rustics give
To helpless infants, that their own may live;
Pleased to be known, they'll some attention claim,
And find some by-way to the house of fame.
Some idle deed, some child's preposterous name,
Shall make him known, and give his folly fame.

George Crabbe   *The Parish Register* (1807)

The first name **Kylie** has been particularly well-used in modern times in Australia. It may well be the inspiration for **Kayleigh**, **Kayley**, etc., which is rapidly gaining popularity in Britain, and **Kyla**, which is popular in the US. Kayleigh has no doubt been influenced by **Hayley** and **Kelly**. Kylie itself was first given as a nickname to Kathleen Tennant (1912 – 88), the distinguished Australian novelist, who wrote as Kylie Tennant. It is an Aboriginal word and means 'boomerang'.

majority of names are decided on before birth, and it is recognised that a baby's appearance is hardly likely to remain that way for long.

Sibling influence

It should not be forgotten that a particular child may not be given a name because a brother or sister already bears it. Nevertheless, some families have been known to give all their sons the same name, and others like all the names of their children to begin with the same letter. Many parents consider whether a name they are thinking about for a later child will 'match' the names already in use in the family.

'Another flowery name!'

'What?' cried Jo. 'Come off it; I won't have no Carnations and such like in my family—and a boy, too!'

'He's William!' shouted Rosie 'Sweet William, and he is sweet.'

Eve Garnett   *The Family From One End Street*

Spelling and pronunciation

The rarer names may cause pronunciation problems. Looking through the birth registers for instance, I wonder myself how I would pronounce **Annarenia**, **Deion**, **Gyda** and the like. Parents sometimes try a name out on friends to see whether the pronunciation causes difficulty.

The spelling situation is far worse. Even very common names appear in strange forms, such as **Henery, Jonothon, Katheryne, Markk, Neal, Trever, Osker, Daved, Freada**. If these names, which should be familiar, cause problems, then one can be quite sure that anyone given a really unusual name will go through life constantly having to spell it out. Even then that person will have the irritating experience of seeing the name mis-spelled on countless occasions.

Family tradition

At one time it was common for families to have what were virtually hereditary first names which they passed on from generation to generation. A few of my correspondents still refer to family traditions, but these are tending to disappear along with the custom of naming children after their parents and grandparents.

Some conclusions

As the above notes are meant to illustrate, naming a baby can be a complicated affair. For parents who have yet to make a choice I have tried to provide help in the flow chart following this section. The golden rule that should always be observed was hinted at by Charles Lamb in the poem quoted earlier about choosing a name. 'I wonder what would please *her*,' he said. It was the right thing to wonder. When you choose a name for a baby you are acting on the child's behalf and doing something that is of great importance for its future. You are not simply satisfying a personal whim.

The responsibility is rather frightening, and it is all too clear that a minority of parents are not capable of exercising that responsibility properly. One can sometimes see the arguments in favour of an official bureau that would vet and advise on the choice of first names, a function which the more enlightened registrars unofficially perform already. In view of the undoubted psychological damage that can be caused to children by the bestowal of absurd names, such a bureau would have to have powers of veto. Naturally there would be no question of all names needing approval, but doubtful cases could be submitted by registrars.

We had a little baby girl
Who made our hearts to flutter.
We used to call her **Margarine**—
We hadn't any but her.

Herbert R. Allport

But let us not end this chapter on a sour note. First names are usually little volumes of social history in themselves as well as evocations of friends and loved ones. They provide a fascinating study, especially when we take into consideration, as we shall do in the next chapter, the names that are given at birth to children born into different cultures and religions around the world.

Naming the Baby

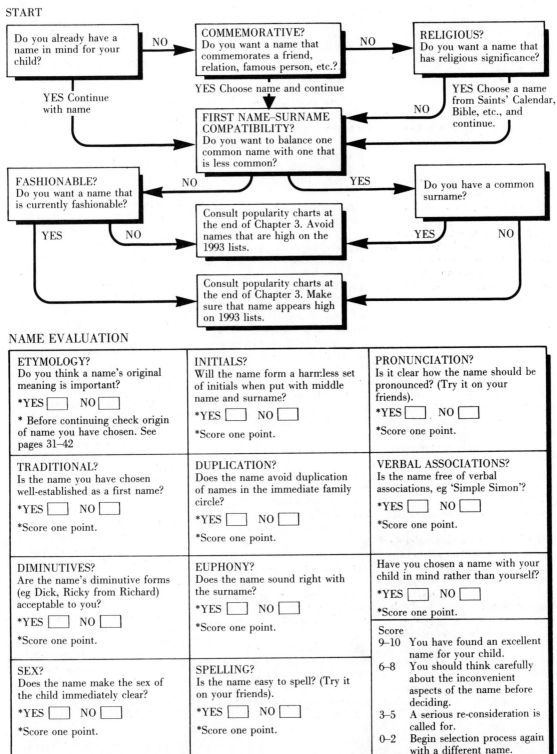

START

Do you already have a name in mind for your child?

NO →

COMMEMORATIVE?
Do you want a name that commemorates a friend, relation, famous person, etc.?

YES Choose name and continue

NO →

RELIGIOUS?
Do you want a name that has religious significance?

YES Continue with name

FIRST NAME–SURNAME COMPATIBILITY?
Do you want to balance one common name with one that is less common?

NO

YES Choose a name from Saints' Calendar, Bible, etc., and continue.

FASHIONABLE?
Do you want a name that is currently fashionable?

NO

YES

Do you have a common surname?

YES   NO

Consult popularity charts at the end of Chapter 3. Avoid names that are high on the 1993 lists.

YES   NO

Consult popularity charts at the end of Chapter 3. Make sure that name appears high on 1993 lists.

NAME EVALUATION

ETYMOLOGY?	INITIALS?	PRONUNCIATION?
Do you think a name's original meaning is important? *YES ☐ NO ☐ * Before continuing check origin of name you have chosen. See pages 31–42	Will the name form a harmless set of initials when put with middle name and surname? *YES ☐ NO ☐ *Score one point.	Is it clear how the name should be pronounced? (Try it on your friends). *YES ☐ NO ☐ *Score one point.
TRADITIONAL? Is the name you have chosen well-established as a first name? *YES ☐ NO ☐ *Score one point.	DUPLICATION? Does the name avoid duplication of names in the immediate family circle? *YES ☐ NO ☐ *Score one point.	VERBAL ASSOCIATIONS? Is the name free of verbal associations, eg 'Simple Simon'? *YES ☐ NO ☐ *Score one point.
DIMINUTIVES? Are the name's diminutive forms (eg Dick, Ricky from Richard) acceptable to you? *YES ☐ NO ☐ *Score one point.	EUPHONY? Does the name sound right with the surname? *YES ☐ NO ☐ *Score one point.	Have you chosen a name with your child in mind rather than yourself? *YES ☐ NO ☐ *Score one point.
SEX? Does the name make the sex of the child immediately clear? *YES ☐ NO ☐ *Score one point.	SPELLING? Is the name easy to spell? (Try it on your friends). *YES ☐ NO ☐ *Score one point.	Score 9–10 You have found an excellent name for your child. 6–8 You should think carefully about the inconvenient aspects of the name before deciding. 3–5 A serious re-consideration is called for. 0–2 Begin selection process again with a different name.

From the mailbag

ALISON – 'A friend of mine surnamed Harrison had a wife called Alison—OK, but they lived for a while in Hongkong and Singapore, and it's true what the Chinese do to the letters R and L!'
Paul Beale, Loughborough.

AUROLYN – 'Shame on you for not including my name in your book!'
Aurolyn Melville Horky, Tequesta, Florida.

DAVID – 'Regarding your researches into sexy names, I've been aware for many years that girls are turned on by the name David—perhaps because they learned as children in *Tales From The Bible* that it means 'beloved'. I heard of and was interested in my husband for years before I met him, because I liked the sound of David Dynes.'
Cecily Dynes, Cremorne, New South Wales.

GARETH – 'Those Welsh names which have been taken over by the English often have a different 'feel' for the Welsh. One example of this is Gareth, which my English friends consider 'on the posh side', whereas to me—born a Morgan of purish Welsh descent—it is just ordinary. In school with me in the late 50s, early 60s, were a Gus, a Gaga, a Garry and a Gareth—all Gareths in the school register.'
Elizabeth Horrocks, Stoke-on-Trent.

IRENE – 'In a souvenir booklet for the musical "Irene" the son of the composer says that his father was probably responsible for changing the pronunciation of the name in England. When he found the English chorus singing *Ireenee* in 1920 he told them he hadn't written a note for the final syllable and insisted on the pronunciation *Ireen*. I find most people today pronounce the name with two syllables, but there seems to be no agreement as to whether the stress should go on the first or second syllable.'
Irene Greatorex, Staines.

JUDITH – 'I was born in 1940 in Toledo, Ohio. I recently examined my high school yearbook and found that of the 255 girls in my graduating class, 30 were named Judith or Judy; that's one out of every 8.5 girls!
'I have always attributed the popularity of the name at that time to Judy Garland. "The Wizard of Oz" was released in 1939 and made quite an impact. However, the reason my mother selected it was that she once babysat for a child named Judy.'
Judith M. Deiulio, Fredonia, New York.

LECIA – 'When my sister was born my parents wanted to commemorate my grandparents, now dead. Working backwards, her second name became Roberta, for Robert, my maternal grandfather. My dad's mother was Celia, and they thought this was old-fashioned so they anagrammed it. Luckily (we think) they didn't notice that it made Alice, so instead they coined the name Lecia (to rhyme with *niece-ee-a*). For years as a child she hated it, but by her late teens it gained her a certain cachet.'
Joan M. Bagley, Guernsey.

NANCY – 'I dislike my own name, Nancy Jane—I was born in 1930 and named after my mother. When I went away to school I told everyone my name was Anne. But my mother was very hurt. Nancy seems OK for a little girl—like Sally—but not for an old lady. And whoever heard of a Lady Nancy or Queen Nancy? No dignity—always a sailor's lass or chambermaid, like Polly or Sukey.'
Nancy Thurston, Toronto, Ontario.

SIENA – 'My sister, Marsha Ann Williams, gave birth to her first child, a daughter, in February 1978, and named her Siena Rachel. No one in our family has ever been called Siena and we were familiar with the word only as the name of an Italian city.

My sister tells me that she read *Lust For Life*, the biography of Vincent Van Gogh. His mistress, Christine, was apparently known as Sien. Marsha thought that with an "a" added it had a very pleasant sound.'
Barbara Lynn Trick, Dayton, Ohio.

[Siena itself sometimes occurs in The Netherlands. It is usually a pet form of the French name Francine, borrowed by Dutch parents.]

SIRI – 'Being in a family of pure Norwegian ancestry, my parents have proudly managed to show the Viking blood in them by giving all their children good Scandinavian names: Erik, Kristian, Liv, Carrie and me, Siri.
Living in a country where my name is very uncommon, it can be frustrating and indeed a bit embarrassing to have to pronounce, pronounce again more slowly, spell and explain the origin of my name before the puzzled look is gone from the face of a newly-met person.
Deep down I know that if someone gave me the opportunity to change my name, I would not. Being the only Siri that most of my friends know gives me a strong feeling of individuality and a certain amount of confidence.'
Siri Marken (aged 15), Oxford.

SYLVIA – 'I don't particularly care for my own name Sylvia, even less now that I see it is a dated name listed among your names of those born before 1940! When it came to naming my own two sons I thought that the traditional names are best for boys as, in general, they seem to want to conform more than girls do. After all, if you go to a formal occasion, such as a wedding, you will see most of the men dressed more or less alike, but if two women turn up in identical dresses it is a disaster. So it is with names.'
Sylvia Ann Martin, Cheltenham.

....

Superlative first names

Shortest names Many families have used single-letter first names, such as **A**. The best-known example is the middle **S** of President Harry S Truman's name.

Longest names The longest 'normal' first name is probably **Alexanderina**, which is mainly found in Scotland. Mr E. G. Richards informs me of several 18th- and 19th-century Cornishmen named **Mahershalalhashbaz**. This odd Hebrew name, mentioned twice at Isaiah 8, means 'speedy-spoil-quick-booty'. Some of the extreme Puritans in the late 16th century were given, or adopted, 'slogan' first names. Two well-known examples were **Jesus-Christ-came-into-the-world-to-save** Barebone and his brother, **If-Christ-had-not-died-for-thee-thou-hadst-been-damned** Barebone. The latter, 'whose morals were not of the best' according to one commentator, was known to most people as Damned Barebone.

Oddest first name Probably the Norwegian name **Odd**. It is more familiar in its German form, **Otto**.

Funniest first name May well be **Joke**, a feminine Dutch name, ultimately a form of **John**.

Unluckiest names According to the 18th-century writer Laurence Sterne, **Tristram** was the worst name that could be given to a child. It would be sure to bring misfortune. The antiquarian William Camden had earlier reported that some names were generally considered to be 'unfortunate to princes'. He mentioned '**John** in France, England and Scotland; and **Henry** lately in France'.

Most racially marked names Black and white Americans theoretically make use of the same stock of first names, but some names are favoured by one group and virtually ignored by the other. Thus, young Americans who are called **Amy**, **Laura**, **Julie**; **Matthew**, **Scott**, **Todd** are almost certain to be white. Names used almost exclusively by black Americans include **Tamika**, **Kenya**, **Latonya**; **Jermaine**, **Reginald**, **Willie**.

Most popular 'insect' name There are more 'bees' buzzing around in the English-speaking world than ever before, due to the popularity in recent times of **Deborah** and **Melissa**, both of which mean 'bee'.

Most used 'place' name The Italian city of **Florence** has probably lent its name to more people in the English-speaking world than any other place, thanks to Florence Nightingale, who was born there.

Rudest name Perhaps the rudest first name is **Tacy**, which derives from Latin *tace*, 'be silent'. Every time a Tacy (**Tacey**) announces her name to someone she is saying 'Shut up!'

Most valuable first name Every American **Bill** knows that he is worth a hundred **Bucks**. **Richards** are often thought of as being **Rich**.

Most mysterious name According to Charles Dickens, who made use of it to name several characters, the most mysterious name for a girl was **Sophronia**.

Most popular 'animal' names Bears, lions and wolves are all very well represented in first names. The 'bear' is present in **Arthur**, **Bernard**, **Ursula**, **Orson**, **Björn**. The 'lions' include **Leo**, **Leonard** and **Lionel**. A 'wolf' occurs in names like **Adolph**, **Ralph**, **Randolph**, **Phelan**.

Fastest first names Perhaps those borne by **Jaguar Ferrari** Tonniges, of Nebraska, whose father is a car-freak.

Fruitiest first names The most used are **Cherry**, originally a form of **Charity**, and **Berry**, often from **Berenice**, or **Bernice**.

Highest numerical name Professor Weekley suggested that **Vicesimus** Knox, whose first name meant 'twentieth', was probably the record-holder in this area, leaving behind competitors such as **Septimus** ('seventh'), **Octavia** ('eighth'), **Decimus** ('tenth'). I have come across a lady whose name was **Mille**, which appears to be 'thousand' in French, but she was probably meant to be a **Millie**.

Lowest numerical name Zero Mostel made his nickname well-known by his many screen appearances. He said his name was given to him as a result of poor performances at school. The father of the South African athlete **Zola** Budd was determined to give his child a name beginning with Z, and in one interview said that had she been a boy, the name would have been Zero.

Most surprising name A British family named their daughter **Surprise** a few years ago. They had confidently expected a son.

Most musical names A music-loving family in Honolulu named their children **Dodo**, **Rere**, **Mimi**, **Fafa**, **Soso**, **Lala**, **Sisi** and **Octavia**.

Most colourful name Welsh parents are now using **Enfys** (rainbow) to name their daughters. **Rainbow** itself is occasionally used by English-speaking parents. I always enjoyed receiving a cheerful letter from the late Barbara Rainbow Fletcher, of Seattle, author of *Don't Blame the Stork* and avid collector of unusual names.

Most popular 'month' name **April** is the most popular month-name, thanks to the use of its French form **Avril** alongside April itself. **June** and **May** are runners-up.

Most popular 'time of day' names A birth at dawn or when stars are shining seems to be most likely to attract a special name. 'Dawn' names include **Dawn** itself, **Aurora**, **Oriana**, **Roxana**; 'star' names are **Estelle**, **Stella**, **Astra**, **Esther**.

Most odorous name Black American parents, especially, are now making good use of **Chanel**, which they sometimes spell **Channel**, **Shanel**, **Shanell**, **Shannell**. Madame Gabrielle Bonheur Chanel would no doubt have been pleased at the compliment. She herself was known to her intimates as **Coco**.

Most flowery names A very large number of flower names were used to name girls at the end of the 19th century. Perhaps the most flowery of all was **Carmel**, which means 'garden'.

Most prolific namer Several cases are known of parents who have given large numbers of names to an individual child, such as one beginning with each letter of the alphabet. The Reverend Ralph William Lionel Tollemache, born in 1826, married twice and had twelve children. Each was given a string of names, so that eventually 100 different names were distributed amongst them.

Sexiest names There have been several surveys designed to reveal the sex-appeal rating of different first names. In 1975 a British survey discovered that young men favoured **Susan**, **Samantha**, **Carol**, **Linda**, **Jennifer**, **Catherine**, **Amanda**, **Kerry**, **Claire** and **Natalie**. Girls would have willingly gone on a blind date with a **David**, **Stephen**, **Paul**, **Mark**, **Adam**, **Robert**, **Richard**, **Michael**, **Christopher** or **Philip**. Some ten years later a survey of *Daily Mirror* readers put **Samantha** as the sexiest girl's name, followed by a host of names with a French flavour—**Gabrielle**, **Dominique**, **Cerise**, **Nadine**, **Genevieve**, **Simone**, **Leonie**. **Michael** was voted sexiest male name, followed by **James**, **Stephen**, **David**, and **Clint**. A reader who was able to sign herself I. A. M. Bliss rightly claimed that her name must rank highly in sex appeal. In the early 1980s a survey in the US asked young men to rate girls' names by sexiness. **Christine** emerged as the clear winner, followed by **Cheryl**, **Melanie**, **Dawn**, **Heather**, **Jennifer**, **Marilyn**, **Michelle** and **Susan**.

Least sexy names The biggest 'turn-offs', according to the American respondents, were **Ethel**, **Alma**, **Florence**, **Mildred**, **Zelda**, **Myrtle**, **Silvana**, **Edna** and **Elvira**. *Daily Mirror* readers mentioned **Agnes**, **Gertrude**, **Agatha**, **Bessie**, **Enid**, **May**, **Nora**, **Maud**, **Freda**, **Ida**, **Edda** and **Margaret** in this category. They also condemned **Ivor**, **Basil**, **Cyril**, **Cuthbert**, **Willie**, **Horace**, **Norman**, **Alfred**, **Rupert**, **Percival**, **Cecil**, **Archibald**, **Herbert**, **Harold**, **Bernard**, **Sidney** and **Herman**.

Most stertorous name Borne by an ancestor of Abraham and also by Abraham's brother, **Nahor**, which means 'snorer', was perhaps a reference to a baby which snuffled.

Tastiest name R. A. Bullen writes from Reading, Berks., about the man he knew who was named **Delicious**. **Delicia** has also been used as a feminine name.

Most riotous name Born of British parents who were living at the time in Ceylon, and during a period of martial law when riots were taking place almost daily, **Rioty** M. Winter was given a name to commemorate the circumstances. His parents no doubt read the Riot Act to him when he misbehaved.

Most unexpected name According to journalistic report, a boy was named **Onyx**, after the precious stone, because he was onyx-pected.

Most original name The name **Original** was given in the early 16th century to the eldest son and heir of certain well-to-do families. Original Bellamy, for instance, who was buried at Stainton in 1619, aged eighty, had a son of the same name and a grandson Original, born in 1606. The name was no doubt meant to suggest that the boy concerned was carrying on the original stock. It did not come into general use because most people assumed that it referred to original sin.

Most common ananym An ananym is a word or name formed by spelling another word or name backwards. The most commonly-used first name of this type is **Senga**, found fairly frequently in Scotland, especially in former times when **Agnes** was being well used there. **Adnil** and **Azile** are other names of this type which occur in the records. Some Russian parents in the 1920s and 30s named their sons **Ninel**.

Most hesitant name There are three different men mentioned in the Bible whose name is **Er**, which actually means 'vigilant'. According to Luke (3:28) one of these Ers was an ancestor of Jesus.

Most frequent biblical name In one sense the most frequently-used biblical name is **Yahweh**, Hebrew *Yahveh*, the proper name of the God of Israel. In one form or another, eg as **Yah** in expressions like Alleluia, Hebrew **Hallelu-Yah** 'praise Yah!' it occurs over 6000 times and is the most frequently-used word (as well as name) in the Bible. Traditionally, to prevent the sacred name of God from being uttered during the reading of the Scripture, the artificial form **Jehovah** was used. Of the names used for people, **David** is the most frequently-occurring in the Bible, with 1150 mentions. However, all these mentions refer to the same man, whereas thirty *different* men bear the name **Zechariah**. There are some twenty-five **Johns** (or **Johanans**), twenty **Hananaiahs** (or **Ananiases**), eighteen **Simeons** (or **Simons**), sixteen **Joshuas** (or **Jesuses**), thirteen **Josephs**, ten **Michaels** and eight **Philips**. The name **Eve** is mentioned only five times. **Mary**, mother of Jesus, is mentioned by name only nineteen times, but there are references to seven other women who bear that name (or its alternative form **Miriam**). **Esther** occurs fifty-nine times, **Sarah** fifty-eight times.

Angriest name Paddy has come to mean 'a show of anger or temper', reflecting the frequency with which Irishmen named **Patrick** displayed such symptoms. In the Bible a man named **Maaz** 'anger' is mentioned. There are also three different men named **Ahimaaz** 'my brother is angry'. That might rank as the most puzzling name—why should my brother be angry?

Windiest name Gale is probably the windiest name in common use, though it is probably meant to be **Gail**, the pet form of **Abigail**. **Storm** Jameson, the novelist, has made her name well-known, but it has not been copied. **Tempest** is occasionally found in 19th-century records.

Sweetest Name Most people would probably vote for **Candy** as the sweetest name in use, though it came into being as a pet form of **Candace**. **Dulcie** is based on Latin *dulcis* 'sweet'. There are several names in use which contain a reference to 'honey', Greek *meli*, *melitos*, Latin *mel*, *mellis*. They include **Melita**, **Melinda**, **Melissa** and **Pamela**, the last of these meaning 'all honey'.

Most alcoholic name There is **Carling** Bassett, the tennis player, but the name most frequently used in modern times is **Brandy** (**Brandi**, **Brandee**, etc.). There also plenty of girls called **Sherry**, though this name probably began as *chérie*, French 'darling'.

Most popular 'day' name It is the child born on Christmas Day who is most likely to be given a name to commemorate the fact. **Noël**, **Noëlle**, **Natalie** and **Natasha** all mean 'Christmas Day'. In the 19th century parents might well have used **Christmas** itself as a first name. **Carol** is not a Christmassy name by origin, but is understandably popular at that time of year.

Dick Tracy, created by Chester Gould, was the best-known American detective in strip cartoons and films of the 1930s and 40s. A British policewoman whose first-name happens to be Tracy would prefer him to be forgotten. To her colleagues she has become Dick-less Tracy.

5
FIRST NAMES APPRAISED

ONE OF the things that makes names different from words is the way we react to them. If the word 'prudence', say, occurs in a conversation, we are unlikely to comment on whether we find it pleasant or unpleasant, or whether it is in or out of fashion. If instead we hear **Prudence** mentioned as a *name*, we may well find ourselves making an immediate instinctive comment along the lines of: 'That's nice,' or 'I don't like that'. The name may also conjure up an image which has nothing to do with the word's meaning.

Words do not always transpose easily into names, as some of the examples on page 22 reveal. Eleanor Cameron makes the point pleasantly in *A Room Made of Windows*: '**Felony** Franklinburg she'd named her doll, years and years ago when her father was alive, the most beautiful name she could think of and wished it might have been her own. But when she told it to a roomful of her mother's and father's friends, their mouths opened in round black pockets of laughter.'

Most of the first names we use do not also function as ordinary words; any overlap is accidental. Only in its pet form **Sue**, for example, does **Susan** become a rather threatening verb, hinting at a legal dispute. Puns which irritate the name-bearers are often the result of such name/word collisions, as indicated by Dickens in *Our Mutual Friend*: 'Being known on her own authority as Miss Abbey Potterson, some water-side heads, which (like the water) were none of the clearest, harboured muddled notions that she was named after, or in some sort related to, the Abbey of Westminster. But Abbey was only short for Abigail . . .'

A more normal reaction to a name has to do with emotion rather than meaning. We either like **Abigail** as a girl's name or we don't, though we might find it difficult in either case to say why. If we know an Abigail, we may be transferring our opinion of the person to the name, but we often have strong feelings

about names where we are unable to make such a connection. Our response is perhaps to nothing more than a pleasing sound, as was the case with the doll named Felony. It is interesting to note that had the child concerned chosen **Melanie** for a similar reason, there would have been no problem.

Literature is in many ways a reflection of life, and novels and plays provide plenty of evidence of our strong reaction to names. The name quotations which complete this chapter show the range of reactions that can occur, together with the varied reasons that can inspire a liking or loathing of a particular name. The quotations, of course, do not necessarily reflect the views of the novelists. Elizabeth Gaskell, for example, makes different characters in the same novel comment on **Molly** in very different ways. A snobbish gossip is made to disparage the name; another character comments favourably.

This reflects real life, where comments about a name reveal more about the person making them than about the name itself. When parents bestow ultimate approval on a name by choosing it for their child, they reveal in passing a great deal about their own social standing, educational level and aspirations for their child. It was this that William Faulkner had in mind when he commented, in *The Town*, on a father 'with a demagogue's capacity for using people to serve his own appetites, all clouded over with a veneer of culture and religion; the very names of his two sons, **Byron** and **Virgil**, were not only instances but warnings'.

Apart from their remarks about individual names, writers often have more general points to make about names and the naming process. Jane Duncan interrupts the narrative of *My Friend Muriel* to tell us: 'My family had a code of rules about names, especially Christian names. Roughly, these names fell into three classes: (a) names for people like us: **Janet, Elizabeth, Catherine, Isobel, Duncan, George,**

John (b) names for the gentry: **Victoria, Alexandra, Lydia, Deborah, Edward, Torquil, Anthony, Michael** (c) names silly and outlandish: **Gladys, Wendy, Muriel, Doris, Victor, Barry, Robin, Albert.**

'People like us could have names that the gentry were not using at the moment. Also, it was quite in order for the gentry to take a notion to call a girl **Jean**, although this name was truly the property of people like us, for the gentry had all sorts of licence, but it would not have been the thing for me to have been named **Eleanor** or **Eve**.'

This interestingly describes the effects of social-class on naming in Scotland in 1910. Mary McCarthy deals with some religious aspects of the same subject in *Memories of a Catholic Girlhood*: 'Names have more significance for Catholics than they do for other people; Christian names are chosen for the spiritual qualities of the saints they are taken from; Protestants used to name their children out of the Old Testament and now they name them out of novels and plays, whose heroes and heroines are perhaps the new patron saints of a secular age.'

Miss McCarthy goes on to comment on the **Mary Therese** she received at Baptism and the **Clementina**, for Saint Clement, which she adopted at Confirmation. The latter name she 'soon regretted on account of "My Darling Clementine" and her number nine shoes'.

Other name topics mentioned by writers include baptismal superstitions and the age-old need to display a loved one's name, scrawled on a wall or perhaps carved on a tree trunk. On the first topic

It is not only the effect that the sound of a name has on others which is to be thoughtfully considered; the effect that his name produces on the man himself is perhaps still more important. Some names stimulate and encourage the owner, others deject and paralyse him.

Max Beerbohm   *The Naming of Streets*

Graham Greene writes in *Brighton Rock*: 'Perhaps when they christened me, the holy water didn't take. I never howled the devil out.' On the second, Dickens talks in *The Uncommercial Traveller* of the notepads used by young clerks, which 'are taken into confidence on the tenderest occasions, and often times have I had it forced on my discursive notice that the officiating young gentleman has over and over again inscribed Amelia on the corners of his pad. Indeed, the pad may be regarded as the legitimate modern successor of the old forest tree: whereon these young knights engrave the names of their mistresses'.

But it is writers' comments on individual names which are perhaps the most interesting, as I hope my selection will prove. Such comments demonstrate that first names, especially, have 'meanings' for us which no dictionary could begin to explain. That is partly why they are so special.

'Pretty' names

'So what shall we call our little beauty?' 'Something pretty. Beautiful little girls should have names to match.'
Peter Ustinov   *Dear Me*

Algernon 'You'll like their names,' sighed Nancy. 'They're "Algernon", and "Florabelle" and "Estelle". I just hate "Nancy".' 'Why?' 'Because it isn't pretty like the others. You see, I was the first baby, and Mother hadn't begun to read so many stories with the pretty names in 'em, then.'
Eleanor H. Porter   *Pollyanna*

Arthur 'Arthur is charming tonight,' she whispered to Laura. 'Who?' said Laura. 'Arthur,' answered Blanche.

'Oh, it's such a pretty name.'
William Thackeray   *Pendennis*

Audrey 'Audrey, Audrey, Audrey! Do you know what a pretty name you have, child, or how dark are your eyes, or how fine this hair that a queen might envy?'
Mary Johnston   *Audrey*

Bevelina Some persons might object to the papers being signed occasionally with rather fine names, but this is an American fashion. One of the provinces of the state legislature of Massachusetts is to alter ugly names into pretty ones, as the children improve upon the tastes of their parents. These changes costing little

or nothing, scores of Mary Annes are solemnly converted into Bevelinas every session.
Charles Dickens   *American Notes*

Blanche 'My name is Blanche – isn't it a pretty name? Call me by it.' 'Blanche – it is very pretty indeed.' Miss Amory had been christened Betsy – but assumed the name of Blanche of her own will and fantasy, and crowned herself with it; and the weapon which the Baronet, her step-father, held in terror over her, was the threat to call her publicly by her name of Betsy, by which menace he sometimes managed to keep the young rebel in order.
William Thackeray   *Pendennis*

I looked down at her hair. It was amazingly black. I smiled at it softly. 'Why do they call you Blanche?' I said, 'when you're so black. Blanche means white.' 'How do you know I'm not white underneath?' I could not speak.
H. E. Bates   *The Kimono*

Celeste 'What are you going to name her?' 'Celeste.' 'That's a pretty name for a pretty girl,' he approved.
Erskine Caldwell   *Place Called Estherville*

Cerise 'Cerise,' repeated the lad. 'What a pretty name! Mine is not a pretty name. Boys don't have pretty names. My name's George.'
George Whyte-Melville   *Cerise*

Charlotte They suggested names endlessly, ranging from the dull to the fantastic; Joe came down finally in favour of January, while Lydia seemed to favour Charlotte, which I thought pretty but corny.
Margaret Drabble   *The Millstone*

Christal 'I know that child,' Olive said. 'I remember, too – for I asked – its singular and very pretty name, *Christal*.'
Mrs Craik   *Olive*

Clare 'Clarinda's pretty, but it's a little like a novel. Claribel I like. Names beginning with "Cl" I prefer. The "Cl's" are always gentle and lovely girls you would die for. Don't you really prefer the "Cl's"?' said Ralph, persuasively. 'Not better than the names ending in "a" and "y",' Richard replied. He read the words again and again: Clare Doria Forey. Why, Clare was the name he liked best – nay, he loved it. Doria, too. Clare Doria Forey – oh, perfect melody!'
George Meredith   *The Ordeal of Richard Feverel*

Cleodolinda 'You are St George who has saved me from the dragon.' 'Then you must be Cleodolinda.' 'Who's she?' 'St George's princess, of course. A pretty name, don't you think?' 'It's beautiful.'
Mary Lutyens   *Cleo*

Daisy 'Daisy! That's a pretty name. It's a flower, ain't it? Well – that's what you are – just a flower.'
Elmer Rice   *The Adding Machine*

Deirdre 'Deirdre Henderson,' said Poirot. 'Deirdre of the Sorrows. A pretty name . . .'
Agatha Christie   *Mrs McGinty's Dead*

Disastrous His name was Disastrous because his god-mother thought it such a pretty word. The parson said 'I cannot christen this child Disastrous, he must have another name,' so his name was Disastrous Thomas, we called him Sass.
Jean Rhys   *Wild Sargasso Sea*

Dolly 'Dorothea means a present – a present from God, which must be the best kind of present. Besides having a nice meaning, we like Dorothea because there's such a pretty way of shortening it. We're going to call your little sister Dolly.'
Mrs Molesworth   *Mary*

Dolores 'Her mother was a Spaniard, I believe: that accounts for her religion. But it is a very soft and pretty name.'
Elizabeth Gaskell   *North and South*

'She can wait, Lolly.' My mother's name was Dolores, and the 'Lolly' was a hangover from the days of her youth.
Evan Hunter   *Sons*

Doris 'I have actually forgotten your name, dear.' 'Doris Marlowe.' 'A pretty name. I don't think I ever heard it before.'
Charles Garvice   *Doris*

Ethel 'I must have your Christian name.' 'Ethel,' she told him. 'Ethel,' he said, and looked at her, gathering courage as he did so. 'Ethel,' he repeated. 'It is a pretty name. But no name is quite pretty enough for you, Ethel . . . dear.'
H. G. Wells   *Love and Mr Lewisham*

Fanny Fanny made a little curtsey, and put her hand under Arthur's

arm. 'Fanny's a very pretty little name,' he said.
William Thackeray   *Pendennis*

Fenella Jordan had never known a Fenella. It was light and soft and pretty.
Margaret Forster   *Fenella Phizackerley*

Flora 'I've decided on Flora,' she said suddenly. For a moment he was bewildered, but almost as quickly recovered himself. 'Yes, of course,' he said, 'the baby's name. How pretty!'
Barbara Goolden   *A Marriage of Convenience*

Florence Her name was as pretty as she was – 'Florence,' he said it to himself a great many times.
O. Henry   *Brickdust Row*

'I thought Florence was a place,' said Julius. 'So it is,' said the owner of the name. 'It comes of having a travelled father,' said Miss Lacy. 'It is a pleasant name,' said Tullia. 'Could you be called Paris or London?' said Dora. 'Oh, yes, I expect so,' said Florence, with a sigh. 'You might be called York or Constantinople,' said Julius.
Ivy Compton-Burnett   *Elders and Betters*

'At first I thought they were calling him "Florrie": then I remembered that Florence with its diminutive "Flurry" is not an uncommon Christian name for men in Ireland.'
Nicholas Blake   *The Private Wound*

Gianetta In the first place, I suppose, it was my parents' fault for giving me a silly name like Gianetta. It is a pretty enough name in itself, but it conjures up pictures of delectable and slightly overblown ladies in Titian's less respectable canvases.
Mary Stewart   *Wildfire at Midnight*

Gladys Gladys Bertha. Those were the names given to me when I was young and helpless. I have always pretended to dislike Gladys more

than in actual fact I do; it was in fashion as a pretty name when Mother picked it out for me [1890]: her own name was Elizabeth, and I still slightly resent that blindness of vision which made her discard Elizabeth as old-fashioned, along with Anne and Sophia and Harriet and Susan. All that group have now [1953] swung round into fashion again, whereas from 1910 onwards, Gladys was frequently disowned as the type of name associated with that slightly giggling girl of fiction, fond of cheap scent, high heels and whispering in corners.
G. B. Stern   *A Name to Conjure With*

Larita Husband: Larita's an extraordinarily pretty name.
Wife (acidly): It's all right – for musical comedy.
Noel Coward   *Easy Virtue*

Lawana 'My name is Lawana Neleigh,' the girl said. 'What a mighty pretty name for a girl!' Jenny spoke up. 'It makes you feel good just to think about a pretty name like that. I don't think I've ever heard a name exactly like that before, and now I won't be likely to forget it, neither. When you stop and think about all the common ordinary names for girls – like Ethel and Bertha and Nancy, and even Charlotte – it makes me feel real sad and downhearted. It's a sinning shame for girls to have to live with the names some of them get saddled with.
Erskine Caldwell   *Jenny by Nature*

Mary Ralph suggested that Mary might be considered a pretty name. Richard agreed that it might be; the housekeeper at Raynham, half the women cooks, and all the housemaids, enjoyed that name; the name of Mary was equivalent for woman at home.
George Meredith   *The Ordeal of Richard Feverel*

'I must say I think Mary is prettier than Molly, and quite as old a name, too,' said Mrs Hamley. 'I think it was,' said Molly, 'because mamma

was Mary, and I was called Molly while she lived.'
Elizabeth Gaskell   *Wives and Daughters*

Mellyora I called her Melly to myself, just to rob her of a little dignity. Mellyora! It sounded so pretty when people said it. I have never heard that Mellyora meant anything.
Victoria Holt   *The Legend of the Seventh Virgin*

(This name is usually spelt Meliora, adapting the Latin word for 'better', and is traditionally thought of as Cornish.)

Meredith Meredith's real name was Mary, but she wasn't having any of that. She needed something much more original and pretty, so she chose Meredith and it sounded suitably soft and caressing on the lips of her numerous boyfriends.
Margaret Forster   *Georgy Girl*

Mirabell ' "Mirabell"! What a pretty name!' 'No, it is a crazy name. My mother had it from a play. It is a man's name.'
Hugh Walpole   *Rogue Herries*

Prettyford 'Did they call you Pretty?' 'Yes, for Prettyford.'
Keith Colquoun   *Point of Stress*

Rachel 'I never used to care much for Rachel as a name. It always suggested a girl who made everyone uncomfortable by her indulgence of a weakness for self-sacrifice. I find I was wrong. Rachel is a very pretty name.'
H. B. Cresswell   *Rachel*

Robinetta 'A strange name that. I wonder what made your mother think of it.' 'It is because my second name is Wood. Robins live in woods. If I had been a boy mother would have called me Robin, but as I was a girl they called me Robinetta. I think it is a very pretty name.' 'It is better than Jane or Sarah, certainly; it is uncommon.'
L. E. Tideman   *Robinetta*

Rosamund 'Rosamund; Rose of the world,' said Beatrice, reflectively. 'It is a pretty name and a pretty meaning. I like my name, too. Beatrice, Blessed . . .'
Ivy Compton-Burnett   *A House and its Head*

Sylvia 'She might be called Bella.' 'I could ha' wished her to be called after thee.' 'Best be called after thy mother and mine.' 'Anything to please thee, darling.' 'Don't say that as if it didn't signify; there's a deal in having a pretty name,' said Sylvia, a little annoyed. 'I ha' allays hated being called Sylvia. It were after father's mother, Sylvia Steele.' 'I niver thought any name in a' the world so sweet and pretty as Sylvia,' said Philip, fondly . . .
Elizabeth Gaskell   *Sylvia's Lovers*

'Sylvia Doone?' Indeed! Yes. A soft name, a pretty name – and very like her!
John Galsworthy   *The Dark Flower*

'Why can't you just call me Sylvia? Don't you think that's a pretty name?' 'Sylvia's a girl in the Gardens already. Saliva, I call her.'
Richard Hughes   *The Fox in the Attic*

Theodore For the sake of a soft and pretty name (such as we of the literary sisterhood invariably bestow upon our heroes), I deem it fit to call him Theodore.
Nathaniel Hawthorne   *The Blithedale Romance*

Tregarvan The poor mother was absolutely thinking of calling the child Tregarvan Firmin, as a compliment to Mr Tregarvan, who had been so kind to them, and Tregarvan Firmin would be such a pretty name, she thought.
William Thackeray   *The Adventures of Philip*

Vespa 'I would have preferred Chlorian, that exquisite creature, but the word reminded her mother of chloroform, which she disliked, so we decided on Vespa, the name of the whole genus, including her.

Vespa, the wasp.' '*Wasp?* You don't mean to tell me you called your daughter after the most revolting, vicious, universally loathed – ' 'You speak from ignorance and prejudice. She is called after a superb creature. Vespa is a pretty and distinctive name, it suits her; but if you please we will forget its origin, which fortunately no one seems to know.'
Kitty Barne   *Vespa*

Vivien 'Vivien! It is a pretty name. *I* gave it to you, and took more trouble than if I had been choosing a name for myself. Only think – I could have called you Mary Ann if I had liked – always remember that. A nice name is a good start in life – I wonder if you will ever have Vivien's power. Never read *The Idylls of the King*? No, I don't suppose you have.
W. B. Maxwell   *Vivien*

'My name's Virginia – Virgin for short but not for long.'

Joseph Heller
Something Happened

Names in favour

Aglaia The delight of the miller's life was his little daughter, Aglaia. That was a brave name, truly, for a flaxen-haired toddler; but the mountaineers love sonorous and stately names. The mother had encountered it somewhere in a book, and the deed was done. In her babyhood Aglaia herself repudiated the name, as far as common use went, and persisted in calling herself 'Dums'.
O. Henry   *The Church with an Overshot Wheel*

Alexander . . . a classy name like Alexander. 'It's a good-sounding sort of name; it's not cheap like some.' She didn't feel bound to explain that so grand a name was compensation for the rest. She could not foresee how much blood, tears and sweat it would cost her grandchild, born into a world of Alfs and Berts and Freds.
Thelma Niklaus   *Lexy*

Some talk of Alexander, and some of Hercules
Of Hector and Lysander, and such great names as these . . .
Traditional song   *The British Grenadiers*

Algernon I really can't see why you should object to the name of Algernon. It is not at all a bad name. In fact, it is rather an aristocratic name. Half of the chaps who go into the Bankruptcy Court are called Algernon.
Oscar Wilde   *The Importance of Being Earnest*

Alice 'Her name is Alice?' 'A sweet name, is it not? it accords so well with her simple character.'
Lord Lytton   *Alice*

Anatole 'That's Anatole,' says one of the gentlemen. 'Anna who?' says my wife . . .
William Thackeray   *Cox's Diary*

Angelica Their one child was Angelica, a name her mother had thought beautiful even before she found it was a kind of cake decoration.
Penelope Gilliatt   *Catering*

Angus 'Angus? Is that his name?' Debbie sighed. 'Isn't it a lovely name?' 'North of the Tweed, maybe,' Maggie said.
Mollie Chappell   *A Wreath of Holly*

Anna 'Do you like the name: Anna?' 'It is a simple name,' replied Lady Isabel. 'And simple names are always the most attractive.'
Mrs Henry Wood   *East Lynne*

Anne 'Annie' is boisterous, where 'Anne' has style and dignity.
G. B. Stern   *A Name to Conjure With*

'What do you think they are going to name the baby? Anne; after her and her mamma. So very ugly a name.' 'I do not think so,' said Mr Carlyle. 'It is simple and unpretending. I like it much. Look at the long, pretentious names in our family – Archibald! Cornelia! And yours too – Barbara! What a mouthful they all are.'
Mrs Henry Wood   *East Lynne*

Archibald Archibald Jones had probably no rival. His Christian name helped him; it was a luscious, resounding mouthful for admirers.
Arnold Bennett   *The Old Wives' Tale*

Beatrice 'Her name is *Beatrice* and she is called *Trissie*. She has nothing, and to me she is everything.' 'What a very nice name!' said Joanna. 'Of course she would not have anything. *Beatrice* means "blessed", and naturally blessed people would not. They would be ashamed to.' 'And it is more blessed to give than to receive,' said Reuben.
Ivy Compton-Burnett   *A God and His Gifts*

Benjamin 'In my experience these late comers are the best loved of all. My "little Benjamins" I call them.'
James Balfour   *The Tiny Tots*

Blake 'I remember what you said your first name is. It's Blake. And it sounds so manly. That makes it so suitable for you. I like a man who looks like his name. And you can call me Medora, too. I always think my name suits me because it sort of sounds like me. That's because I am not beauticious but am bodily and bountiful. I always have feelings about names of people. Don't you, Blake?'
Erskine Caldwell   *The Earnshaw Neighbourhood*

Camille I used to think that was the loveliest name in the world. I knew a little girl who was named Camille, and the name fitted her. She had a skin with the softness of camellias.
John Steinbeck *To a God Unknown*

Cassandra 'She lets us call her Cassandra, or usually Cassie.' 'What a lovely Christian name! Am I allowed to use it?'
Ivy Compton-Burnett *A House and its Head*

Charis Charis! And I thought that never was anyone more aptly named, for it means 'grace', you know – from the Greek.
Georgette Heyer *Frederica*

Charles Whether it is a marvellous coincidence, or whether it is that the name itself has an imperceptible effect upon the character, I have never yet been able to ascertain; but the fact is unquestionable, that there never yet was any person named Charles who was not an open, manly, honest, good-natured and frank-hearted fellow, with a rich, clear voice that did you good to hear it, and an eye that looked you straight in the face, as much to say: 'I have a clear conscience myself, and am afraid of no man, and am altogether above doing a mean action.'
Edgar Allan Poe *Thou Art the Man*

(In the story a man named Charles is nevertheless revealed to be a murderer.)

Cherry 'Cherry's a nice name,' said Peg. 'I always wanted to be called Cherry. Or Candy. I was going to have a boy called Ralph and a girl called Cherry and then twins called Valerie and Patricia.'
Margaret Forster *Georgy Girl*

Chloe Her own name, Chloe, rare and strange, had elevated her from common status.
Jean A. Rees *Antonia*

Cordelia 'Such a perfectly elegant name . . .'

L. M. Montgomery *Anne of Green Gables*

Crystal I think Crystal's name meant a lot to her. Crystal Burde. It had been a talisman, a sort of strange consoling thing of beauty in her life: a significant fragment of a splendour past or to come.
Iris Murdoch *A Word Child*

Cytherea I had seen her name on a bag at the station and wondered what she would be like – Cytherea! A lovely name, anyhow.
H. G. Wells *Brynhild*

Delicia . . . the sweet, quaint name of 'Delicia'.
Marie Corelli *Delicia*

Désirée 'My name is Bernadine Eugenie Désirée. They call me Eugenie; I should much prefer Désirée.' 'All your names are beautiful.'
Anne Marie Selinko *Désirée*

Dirk The name Dirk had sounded to Selina like something tall, straight, and slim. Pervus had chosen it. It had been his grandfather's name. 'Oh, Mr DeJong,' they said, 'your name's Dirk, isn't it? What a slick name! What does it mean?' 'It's a Dutch name. My people were Dutch, you know.' 'A dirk's a sort of sword, isn't it, or poniard? Anyway, it sounds very keen and cruel and fatal.'
Edna Ferber *So Big*

Dorinda Dorinda! the name inspires me . . .
George Farquhar *The Beaux Stratagem*

Edith She who comes to me and pleadeth
In the lovely name of Edith
Will not fail of what is wanted.
H. W. Longfellow

Edmund 'There is nobleness in the name of Edmund. It is a name of heroism and renown; of kings, princes and knights; and seems to breathe the spirit of chivalry and warm affections.' 'I grant you the

name is good in itself, and *Lord* Edmund or *Sir* Edmund sound delightfully; but sink it under the chill, the annihilation of a Mr and Mr Edmund is no more than Mr John or Mr Thomas.'
Jane Austen *Mansfield Park*

Elizabeth James's own mother had been called Elizabeth, which was perhaps why he had a pro-Eliza-bethan bias. 'Elizabeth is almost a generic name for someone I like.'
L. P. Hartley *The Love Adept*

Emily Emily, in which all womanly sweetness seems bound up.
Mary Russell Mitford *Our Village*

Emma 'My name is Emma,' she told him childishly. 'That's a very fine name,' said Marshall benignly. 'It's a literary name.'
Judith Woolf *Emma With Objects*

Ernest 'My ideal has always been to love someone of the name of Ernest. There is something in that name that inspires absolute confidence.'
Oscar Wilde *The Importance of Being Earnest*

Eusdean 'I hope you children know that Eusdean's name is Gaelic for Hugh and a very fine name, I think.'
Jane Duncan *My Friend Flora*

Evangeline 'O Evangeline! rightly named' he said; 'hath not God made thee an evangel to me?'
Harriet Beecher Stowe *Uncle Tom's Cabin*

Felix I was a Sunday child, and, although I was brought up to reject every form of superstition, I have always thought there was a secret significance in that fact taken in connexion with my Christian name of Felix, and my physical fitness and attractiveness.
Thomas Mann *Confessions of Felix Krull*

'*You* like "Felix", don't you? Say you do. David moans on about it sounding poofy. He says that when he gets older (Felix, that is), he won't thank me for it. I think the

least you can do is to give someone a nice name.' 'I think it's a lovely name. I hope it's significant.' 'Oh, so do I. Imagine starting life saddled with Dolores. Or Perdita.'
Kathleen Conlon   *A Move in the Game*

Gerald 'At least you might have named one of them Gerald after Papa – and Gerald is such a lovely name.' A sissy name, Drake had called it.
Harlow Estes   *Hildreth*

Gerhart I was busy being in love. He was German (one more I couldn't bring home to my mother), with the romantic name of Gerhart.
Monica Dickens   *Kate and Emma*

Henry What a soft swain your Henry is, the proper theme of gentle poesy; a name to fall in love withal; devoted at the font to song and sonnet, and the tender passion; a baptized inamorato; a christened hero. Call him Harry, and see how you ameliorate his condition. The man is free again, turned out of song and sonnet and romance and young ladies' hearts.
Mary Russell Mitford   *Our Village*

Hercule 'I am Hercule Poirot.' The revelation left Mrs Summerhayes unmoved. 'What a lovely name,' she said kindly. 'Greek, isn't it?'
Agatha Christie   *Mrs McGinty's Dead*

Jacqueline All he knew about her was that her name was Jackie – there was something oddly exciting about having a girl with a boy's name . . .
Norman Collins   *London Belongs to Me*

Job 'What's your name, my patriarch?' 'Job.' 'And a wery good name it is; only one I know that ain't got a nickname to it.'
Charles Dickens   *The Pickwick Papers*

Kerensa My father wanted a Cornish name for her and he said that was a beautiful name because it meant peace and love which, he said, were

the best things in the world.
Victoria Holt   *The Legend of the Seventh Virgin*

Lanning The American boy's name was Lanning Budd; people called him Lanny, an agreeable name, easy to say.
Upton Sinclair   *World's End*

Louis 'Your lips have forgotten Louis.' 'No, Louis, no: it is an easy, liquid name; not soon forgotten.'
Charlotte Brontë   *Shirley*

Lowanna 'Everything about you seems, somehow, to fit,' she murmured. 'Name and all. It is a lovely name – Lowanna.'
Castleden Dove   *Lowanna*

Marguerite The pearl! the daisy! Oh!, name of romance and of minstrelsy, which brings the days of chivalry to mind, and the worship of flowers and of ladies fair.
Mary Russell Mitford   *Our Village*

Mercy Mercy! oh, what a charming name for such a pure-souled being as the youngest Miss Pecksniff. Her sister's name was Charity. There was a good thing! Mercy and Charity. And Charity, with her strong sense, and her mild, yet not reproachful gravity, was so well named, and did so well set-off and illustrate her sister.
Charles Dickens   *Martin Chuzzlewit*

Miriam Wells did, however, once go wildly wrong, when he called that most objectionable character who trapped and married Mr Polly by the name of Miriam, a name like rippling water and more musical than Minnehaha; no name could have been less suited to the home she came from, or to her own dreary, drudging nature.
G. B. Stern   *A Name to Conjure With*

Mordred 'Mordred,' murmured Miss Postlethwaite pensively. 'A sweet name.' 'And one,' said Mr Mulliner, 'that fitted him admirably, for he was a lovable sensitive youth with

large, faun-like eyes, delicately chiselled features and excellent teeth.'
P. G. Wodehouse   *The Fiery Wooing of Mordred*

Obadiah He designed himself Lieutenant Obadiah Lismahago, which she repeated with great emphasis, declaring it was one of the most noble and sonorous names she had ever heard. He observed that Obadiah was an adventitious appellation, derived from his great-grandfather, who had been one of the original covenanters; but Lismahago was the family surname, taken from a place in Scotland so-called.
Tobias Smollett   *Humphrey Clinker*

Owen 'What's your first name, Dr Tuby?' 'Owen. My mother was Welsh.' 'Charming and unusual, though it doesn't sound as clever as *you* are.'
J. B. Priestley   *London End*

Pandora 'I think it is the most evocative girl's name in the history of the world. Whenever I say it, or hear it, I get a bursting feeling behind my ribs.'
Sue Townsend   *The Growing Pains of Adrian Mole*

Persis 'I have discovered that your first name is Persis.' 'Yes,' she said humbly. 'I'm afraid it isn't a name I'd have chosen for myself if I'd had any say in the matter.' 'It is very beautiful,' Erik said. 'In Denmark we do not often use the pure Latin when we name our children.'
James Reid Parker   *The Merry Wives of Massachusetts*

(*Persis* is the Latin form of *Persia*.)

Phoebe 'Phoebe! H'm. Sounds as mild as a milkmaid. You can't judge a woman by her name.'
O. Henry   *Phoebe*

Ritchie Richard is his name but he uses Ritchie because it gets noticed. People see it, they remember you. Name recognition is important in sales.
Garrison Keiller   *Leaving Home*

Rupert 'Rupert, it's a lovely name.' Meg beamed. 'His father was a missionary in Prince Rupert's Land.'
Mazo de la Roche   *Variable Winds at Jalna*

Ruth 'I think your mother deserves a medal, incidentally, for giving you such an attractive first name. Ruth . . . For me that's always been the most poignant, the most evocative of the Old Testament names.'
Frederic Mullally   *Split Scene*

Sarah 'I think Sarah is a beautiful name.' She raised her brows and repeated the name after him. He thought her way of saying it was delightful. 'Sair-rah.' The syllables were like sweet stressed notes.
Mazo de la Roche   *Finch's Fortune*

Thelma 'Just the sort of name to suit a Norwegian nymph or goddess. "Thelma" is quaint and appropriate, and as far as I can remember there's no rhyme to it in the English language. Thelma!' And he lingered on the pronunciation of the strange word. 'There is something mysteriously suggestive about the sound of it; like a chord of music played softly in the distance.'
Marie Corelli   *Thelma*

Theophilus 'But we are in *America*, Theophilus. (What a beautiful name that is.) Here everybody calls everybody else by their given name after five minutes.'
Thornton Wilder   *Theophilus North*

Tony When they were alone, she usually called him Tony because, as she said, he looked like a Tony to her. Tonys were tough, handsome and virile, with a dash of ruthlessness thrown in.
Michael Underwood   *A Pinch of Snuff*

Vernon The chemist was amazingly beautiful and had a lovely name – Vernon.
Isadora Duncan   *My Life*

Violet Violet was as luscious and perfumed as her name.
Sinclair Lewis   *Cass Timberlane*

William 'Another flowery name!' 'What?' cried Jo. 'Come off it; I won't have no Carnations and such like in my family – and a boy, too!' 'He's William!' shouted Rosie, 'Sweet William, and he is sweet.'
Eve Garnett   *The Family From One End Street*

'William Edgeworth. By that name Baby Edgeworth may walk in our midst. And a good solid old name too, suitable from king to peasant.' 'I suspect it is as king that this young man will take his place in the house,' said Beatrice.
Ivy Compton-Burnett   *A House and its Head*

Touchstone: Is thy name William?
William: William, sir.
Touchstone: A fair name.
William Shakespeare   *As You Like It*

Annoying names

Adarene It was she who had been playing the piano. Adarene. One of those names that sounded made up.
Edna Ferber   *Giant*

Adney 'My name's Ad Locust – Jesus, think of it, the folks named me Adney – can you beat that – ain't that one hell of a name for a fellow that likes to get out with the boys and have a good time! But you can call me Ad.'
Sinclair Lewis   *Elmer Gantry*

Agnes It is a vulgar notion that every female of the name of *Agnes* is fated to become mad.
Isaac Disraeli   *Curiosities of Literature*

Ajax 'Ajax suggests somebody who defies lightning and fools about with a spear. It's a silly name. A maiden aunt persuaded my mother to give it me. I think she mixed it up with Achilles; she admired the statue in Hyde Park.'
William Locke   *Septimus*

Alf 'It's the *pretentiousness* of the name,' she retorted. 'I mean, calling yourself "Alf" just to show how democratic you are, pretending to be a costermonger when you know you're a duke.'
Pamela Hansford Johnson   *The Unspeakable Skipton*

Allegra 'What's her name?' 'Allegra. Like Lord Byron's daughter.' 'I should never dare to give a name like that to a child. It is too much of a challenge,' Robert said. 'She would be almost sure to grow up fat and flat-footed and terribly Andante.' 'Yes, like a girl at school called Honor Collins, who was an awful liar and told tales.'
Elizabeth Taylor   *A View of the Harbour*

Almeric Almeric, a tall, sallow youth of twenty-six with a look of sullen self-consciousness, whose grievance against the world began with his parents' choice of his name on the day of his birth.
Ivy Compton-Burnett   *A House and its Head*

Amos Amos got to Pasadena. He changed his name. Amos was too biblical and stuffy.
Henry Sutton   *The Exhibitionist*

Annabelle The Belles all through the alphabet, from Annabelle downward, are a generation of frights.
Mary Russell Mitford   *Our Village*

Uncle Tim had married a girl called Annabelle, who came from Southsea, and was not nearly as glamorous as her name.
Monica Dickens   *Mariana*

Annie Uncle Reuben would always call her 'Nannie'; he said that 'Annie' was too fine and Frenchified for us.
R. D. Blackmore   *Lorna Doone*

Ann-Marie 'What's that queer name your mother calls you?' 'Ann-Marie? It isn't queer. It's my name.' 'I couldn't call you that. I'm too insular.'
Richmal Crompton   *Westover*

Annunciata 'But then I got led astray, and went and did that awful thing to poor Annunciata. I think I must have been mad,' said Mrs Denham. 'And then they went and called her Nancy at school.'
Margaret Drabble   *Jerusalem the Golden*

Aphrodite She was christened by a very fine name – Aphrodite: so I and my father never called her anything but Afy.
Mrs Henry Wood   *East Lynne*

Arleena 'You'd rather live somewhere else, Arleena?' He pronounced it carefully, as seriously as if it were Joan. A few years in the juvenile court, and you can tackle any name.
Monica Dickens   *Kate and Emma*

Arlene Trust Lottie to pick a name like that, all ruffles, the same way she used to dress the girl so fussily.
Margaret Laurence   *The Stone Angel*

Arrow Mrs Sutcliffe had the odd first name of Arrow. When she was young and slender she had liked it well enough. It suited her; she was not disinclined to believe that it suited her character too: it suggested directness, speed and purpose. She liked it less now that her delicate features had grown muzzy with fat, that her arms and shoulders were so substantial and her hips so massive. The jests her name gave rise to were made behind her back and she very well knew that they were far from obliging.
Somerset Maugham   *Three Fat Women of Antibes*

Arthur One of the problems with the name was the two R's. In Scotland R isn't a letter, it's a goddam symbol. You have to roll your lousy R's to show you are goddam Scottish. The English are all right. In England the posh people say 'Aathah' and the Cockneys say 'Awhfa'. On top of all that you can't shorten the stupid name or make a diminutive out of it.
Gordon McGill   *Arthur*

Aurora My wife's name, I'm afraid, is Aurora. Since her majority she has gone as Audrey, which she regards as short for it though I take it to be an outright substitution. A woman's name ought ideally to steal over one, and not come up like thunder out of China 'cross the Bay.
Peter de Vries   *The Tunnel of Love*

Basil 'I must find a pet name for you. I don't like Basil.' 'Nor do I. It means kingly.' '*You* are my king.'
H. A. Vachell   *Averil*

Beatrice Her name was Beatrice, which was bad enough, and made worse by the fact that it had been shortened by ignorant foreigners to Treeshy.
Edith Wharton   *False Dawn*

'What's your name?' 'Beatrice,' said the girl. 'Pity about that . . . bad name . . . always imagine Beatrices with red faces.'
Ian Mowatt   *Just Sheaffer*

Bérénice It made him augur ill of a woman who bore the name of an Oriental princess without, apparently, being sensitive enough to live up to the name in matters of taste. If she had had some such name as Jeanne or Marie, he would not have given the matter a second thought. But Bérénice. How absurd one is about such things.
Louis Aragon   *Aurelien*

Bobby-May Julia's amusement again got out of hand. 'Bobby-May!' she managed to gasp. 'That name I was told but did not believe. Now I suppose I shall have to.' 'Perfectly true, it really is. The whole family has a sort of tennis fixation. It comes

out in the queerest ways.'
Colin Watson   *One Man's Meat*

Boyd One could hardly call anybody 'Boyd', though his mother persisted in doing so.
Patrick White   *The Twyborn Affair*

Braxton Mr Underwood, a profane little man, whose father in a fey fit of humour christened Braxton Bragg, a name Mr Underwood had done his best to live down. Atticus said naming people after Confederate generals made slow steady drinkers.
Harper Lee   *To Kill a Mockingbird*

Calla Calla's mother was exceptionally fond of white lilies, and christened her daughter after one variety of them. Calla detests her name and no wonder. Nothing less lily-like could possibly be imagined. She's a sunflower, if anything, brash, strong, plain . . .
Margaret Laurence   *Rachel, Rachel*

Caroline 'Of all abominable abbreviations I think *Carrie* the most repulsive.'
Georgette Heyer   *Frederica*

'*Fetch* and Carry I call her, or else Carryvan – she's so useful. Ain't you, Carry?'
William Thackeray   *A Shabby Genteel Story*

A great number of children, amongst the lower orders, are Carolines.
Mary Russell Mitford   *Our Village*

Cedric Pop put an arm round Mr Charlton's shoulder. 'You know, Charley boy,' he said, 'I wish your name was Charley instead of Cedric. It's more human. I can't get used to Cedric. It's like a parson's name. Can't we call you Charley?'
H. E. Bates   *The Darling Buds of May*

Cherry Now, who the hell would give a daughter that silly name? Nobody would. It's a fake, like the smile.
Judith Guest   *Ordinary People*

Clarence 'Alfred wants to call him Clarence, after his Dad.' '*Clarence!*'

He was almost too shocked to jeer.
Elizabeth Jane Howard   *After Julius*

Claud 'Claud – ' he began, then stopped. 'Do you like your own name?' 'No. It was my mother's fancy, and I never liked to change it; but it does seem to be in the facetious group of English names.' 'Think of it as a French one; it's not funny in French.'
Pamela Hansford Johnson   *A Summer to Decide*

Claudine 'His wife, Claudine (how the hell did a Lancashire lass come by a name like that?) is a snob.'
Stan Barstow   *The Right True End*

Comfort Her name was a very funny one – it was Comfort. 'How tired she must be of people saying to her that they hope she's a comfort to her father and mother,' said Leigh.
Mrs Molesworth   *Mary*

'I once knew a girl called Comfort and her life was a very sad one. Unhappy men were constantly attracted to her simply by reason of her name, when all the time, poor dear, it was really she who needed the comfort from them. She fell unhappily in love with a man called Courage, who was desperately afraid of mice, but in the end she married a man called Payne and killed herself in what Americans call a comfort station. I would have thought it a funny story if I hadn't known her.'
Graham Greene   *Travels with my Aunt*

Comus Francesca's husband had insisted on giving the boy that strange Pagan name, and had not lived long enough to judge as to the appropriateness, or otherwise, of its significance.
Saki   *The Unbearable Bassington*

Conrad . . . the pretentious name that his parents had fastened on him, like a badge of brains since birth.
Graham Greene   *It's a Battlefield*

Coral What's in a name? My family could have told you. No man could go calling his infant daughter Coral without being asked how he came to think of such a silly and outlandish name. Coral, for pity's sake! When the boy comes along call him Great Barrier Reef and be done with it. That was my family's attitude.
Jane Duncan   *My Friend Muriel*

Cynthia There had never been another Cynthia in the Josser family. And it had injured Mrs Josser more deeply than she could say that Ted's daughter, Baby, her own grandchild, should have been christened with the same absurd, irritating name.
Norman Collins   *London Belongs to Me*

Deirdre 'Her name's Durdree, D-E-I-R-D-R-E. Her mother got it out of a book. Sounds funny, doesn't it?'
Betty Macdonald   *The Plague and I*

Delia 'My parents . . . must I start with them? Let's just say they called me Delia. That's enough, surely? If you don't see what's wrong with Delia I can't explain.'
Thomas Hinde   *Bird*

Dinah . . . my great aunt Dinah, who, about sixty years ago, was married and got with child by the coachman, for which my father, according to his hypothesis of Christian names, would often say, she might thank her godfathers and godmothers.
Laurence Sterne   *The Life and Opinions of Tristram Shandy*

Duane 'It does give our Duane – and I might add the name sounds fishy to me too – a romantic air.'
Peter de Vries   *Into Your Tent I'll Creep*

Dunstable 'How on earth did you ever get yourself called Dunstable?' 'My mother's maiden name,' said I. 'But what's wrong with it?' 'It's hard to say, for one thing,' said she, 'and it sounds like a cart rumbling over cobblestones for another. You'll never get anywhere in the world named Dumbledum Ramsay. Why

don't you change it to Dunstan?'
Robertson Davies   *Fifth Business*

Edward His name was Eddie. She did not like the name and didn't know why. It seemed the name of a person who would never amount to much, though 'Edward' would have suited no better.
Alice Walker   *Meridian*

Eileen There had been no Eileens in our family at all, and it was considered at that time rather an outlandish name, Irish or Scottish rather than Welsh, and – by some – not even quite nice. Why not Gertrude, or Phyllis, or Helen, or Marjorie? But Mother clung obstinately to the name she liked, and so my second name had to be something acceptable to the neighbourhood – good solid Winifred.
Eileen Elias   *On Sundays We Wore White*

'Eileen O'Hara her name was.' 'Eileen as well as O'Hara. Almost too impossibly Irish, don't you think?'
Agatha Christie   *Partners in Crime*

Ellen 'What a dreary name "Ellen" is! It reminds me of a great-grandmother.'
Ivy Compton-Burnett   *A Father and his Fate*

Enoch 'Enoch means consecrated.' 'I don't like your name, Enie.' 'Nor do I, but it's a family name. The Dean is great on names.'
H. A. Vachell   *Vicar's Walk*

Erema Erema is popish and outlandish: one scarcely knows how to pronounce it.
R. D. Blackmore   *Erema*

Euphemia 'Euphemia; it isn't a name *common* people would give to a girl, is it?' 'It isn't the name any decent people would give to a girl,' said Buggins, 'common or not.' 'Lor'!' said Kipps. 'Why?' 'It's giving girls names like that,' said Buggins, 'that nine times out of ten makes 'em go wrong. It unsettles 'em. Euphemia indeed! What next?'
H. G. Wells   *Kipps*

Eustace There was a boy called Eustace Clarence Scrubb and he almost deserved it.
C. S. Lewis   *The Voyage of the Dawn Treader*

Evelyn My daddy had been proud of a couple of his ancestors – but is that any excuse for hanging 'Evelyn Cyril' on a male child? It had forced me to fight before I learned to read.
Robert A. Heinleim   *Glory Road*

Everbe Her name is Everbe Corinthia, named for Grandmaw. And what a hell of a name that is to have to work under. Over here, never nobody knowed about the Everbe and so she could call herself Corrie. So whenever I'm over here visiting her, since I know about the Everbe, she gives me five cents a day not to tell nobody.
William Faulkner   *The Reivers*

Fancy 'Fancy? Is that your real name?' 'Sure. My father had an unorthodox and poetic soul.' 'Your father had a tin ear. With a name like Hawkins, you ought to have a three-syllable first name.'
Robert Krepps   *Fancy*

'Now what might be your name?' 'I'm Fancy,' Fancy murmured. 'Damned right you are, but what's your name?'
Frank Yerby   *A Woman Called Fancy*

Fay How distressing it is to meet a middle-aged woman – one, say, of powerful build or masterful presence – saddled with such an unsuitable name as Joy, Winsom or Dawn. By all means let them call the little thing by any sentimental or whimsical pet-name they like, but for pity's sake do not have them baptised with a name they may be ashamed of when they grow up. An outstanding example of the thoughtlessness of parents in naming their children was the late Miss Lankester. She was built on a massive scale, which only tended to accentuate her fairy-like Christian name, Fay.
Philip Gosse   *An Apple a Day*

Fiona Her having been thus named had offended my uncle. Although 'Fiona' sounds eminently Scottish it is in fact scarcely a genuine name at all, having been invented in the eighteen-nineties by a man called William Sharp as part of a pseudonym under which to publish stories and sketches and poems of a Celtic Twilight character. Uncle Rory would have been incapable of estimating the literary quality of 'Fiona Macleod', but he did know that no woman of his acquaintance had borne that baptismal name.
J. I. M. Stuart   *A Memorial Service*

Flaude 'Flaude Stansburg. It's kind of a corny name, ain't it? My ma was romantic.'
Sinclair Lewis   *Gideon Planish*

Flora Floras are sure to be pale puny girls.
Mary Russell Mitford   *Our Village*

Florinda 'Is your maid called Florence?' 'Her name is Florinda.' 'What an extraordinary name to give a maid.' 'I did not give it to her; she arrived in my service already christened.' 'What I mean is,' said Mrs Riversedge, 'that when I get maids with unsuitable names, I call them Jane; they seem to get used to it.' 'An excellent plan,' said the aunt of Clovis coldly, 'unfortunately I have got used to being called Jane myself. It happens to be my name.'
Saki   *The Secret Sin of Septimus Snope*

Fred 'What's his name?' 'Fred. A very boring name. I keep asking him to change it, but he won't.'
Jennifer Johnston   *Shadows on our Skin*

'I won't ask you to call me "Fred," Miss Winthrop. Frankly, the older I get the more I dislike my own name.'
James Reid Parker   *The Merry Wives of Massachusetts*

Gail Your mother mentions as a constant companion of yours a girl called Gail – though what in the world such a name, whether

Christian or sur-, can be I cannot imagine, unless an abbreviation of Abigail, which would argue either Jewish ancestry or a conviction on the part of her parents (who should know) that she would be suited to domestic service, since Abigail was a Hebrew serving wench.
Dane Chandos   *Abbie*

Giulia Giulia was the kind of girl you'd imagine with a name like that, and I expect she encouraged him.
Eric Linklater   *Ripeness is All*

Grace Graces are usually awkward gawkies.
Mary Russell Mitford   *Our Village*

Gregory 'He's middle-aged and desiccated! His very name's dry and powdery! "Gregory," that's his name.'
E. H. Young   *William*

The name by itself is loaded. It conjures up for him nothing less than the entire history of Christianity.
Ellen Schwamm   *Adjacent Lives*

Guy 'I am tired of the sound of his name. One fifth of November is enough in the year.'
Charlotte M. Yonge   *The Heir of Redclyffe*

Harold Harold is Freckles's other name. But any boy that calls him Harold outside of the schoolhouse has got a fight on his hands, if that boy is anywhere near Freckles's size. Harry goes, or Hal goes, but Harold is a fighting word. His parents thought Harold was a name, or he guessed they wouldn't have given it to him; but it wasn't a name, it was a handicap.
Don Marquis   *Being a Public Character*

Harriet 'Why "Harry"?' 'It's what Flurry's always called me,' she replied indifferently. 'You're the last person who should have a man's name.' She gave no sign of being gratified by the compliment. '"Harriet" is so stuffy and old-fashioned. What's yours?' 'Dominic.'

'My God! That's worse. It makes me think of a pi little schoolboy.'
Nicholas Blake   *The Private Wound*

Helen Helen, so ridiculously not of Troy, waited . . .
G. B. Stern   *Mosaic*

Hephzibah 'Mrs White's name is that. Her husband calls her "Hep", and she doesn't like it. She says when he calls out "Hep-Hep!" she feels just as if the next minute he was going to yell "Hurrah!" And she doesn't like to be hurrahed at.'
Eleanor H. Porter   *Pollyanna*

Hjalmar 'What an ineffably ridiculous name! I bet he parts his hair in the middle.'
Richard Hughes   *The Fox in the Attic*

Horatio 'What a very odd name he calls you,' said Furlong, addressing young O'Grady. 'Ratty,' said the boy. 'Oh, yes, they call me Ratty, short for Horatio.'
Samuel Lover   *Handy Andy*

Hugh 'What's your name, young master?' 'Hugh,' he answered. 'Hugh,' said the man: 'Hugh! You won't never come to much, you won't.'
John Masefield   *Jim Davis*

Hyacinth 'Hyacinth! It's the silliest name I ever heard of; but it's hers, and I must call her by it. And the worst is, she's gone and perpetuated her own affected name by having her daughter called after her. Cynthia! One thinks of the moon, and the man in the moon with his bundle of faggots. I'm thankful you're plain Molly, child.'
Elizabeth Gaskell   *Wives and Daughters*

Ichabod Priss felt in awe of a person who could fasten a name like that on a baby. 'Aren't you afraid he'll be called "Icky" in school?' she said impulsively. 'He'll have to learn to fight his battles early,' philosophized Norine.
Mary McCarthy   *The Group*

Ida 'Ida,' she repeated thoughtfully, 'the name sure fits your description of her. Cosy and comfortable, especially flat on her back.'
R. F. Delderfield   *Come Home Charlie and Face Them*

Ina There was something funny about the child, something dark, stand-offish, classy. Ina: classy name, too classy. Cora didn't like it.
H. E. Bates   *The Landlady*

Irene Rex Hadley and that awful wife. Irene – what a dreadful name! And what a dreadful woman.
William Haggard   *The High Wire*

Jack 'There is very little music in the name Jack, if any at all, indeed. It does not thrill. It produces absolutely no vibrations. The only really safe name is Ernest.'
Oscar Wilde   *The Importance of Being Earnest*

Jane She had a trunkload of Jane epithets for me: 'Plain Jane.' 'Calamity Jane.' 'Pain.'
Gail Godwin   *The Odd Woman*

Janie 'She looks like a Janie – she is a Janie.' That gave her an obscure satisfaction; a Janie personality couldn't possibly be glamorous at all.
Jane England   *Janie*

Jasper Jasper Smarden, in spite of his rather sinister name, was the staunchest of Conservatives.
W. Gavin-Brown   *Their Village*

Jemima 'We will take the opportunity to change your name. You shall have a good English Christian name, Jemima, Jane or Sophy.' 'Jemima!' I cried. 'Oh, Mr Shovelin, save me from ever being called Jemima! rather would I never be baptised at all.'
R. D. Blackmore   *Erema*

Jemima, Euphemia and Angela. Terrible names. My grandad had been very religious and he reckoned that the names sounded biblical. The sisters must have had the same problem at school as I did, especially Euphemia and Jemima. All the girls

would have been Sadies, Audreys and Sallys.
Gordon McGill   *Arthur*

Joanne Her real name was Joanne. She changed it when she was thirty-eight because, as she said, what can you do with a name like Joanne? Too *nice*. She didn't dye her hair green or wear a safety pin in her ear but calling herself Jocasta was the equivalent.
Margaret Atwell   *Bodily Harm*

I can't help thinking, you know, of Jo-Anne. Pity about the child's name – so awful. If I had the nerve I'd suggest they should change it to Joanna.
Sarah Gainham   *Take-Over Bid*

Jocke 'Merry,' he said, 'this is Jocke Dunbar.' 'Yes, with an e,' he said. 'J O C K E. My mother had a lousy sense of humour.'
Henry Sutton   *The Exhibitionist*

Jonah She was bringing Jonah. Somewhere in Thea's mind was a whale. She pictured a fat young man. Long hair was inevitable, she knew, but Jonah, she felt sure, would turn out to be dirty.
Margaret Maddocks   *Thea*

Joyce Christopher *Joyce* Laker. It had taken the law to dig out his second name, and public reminder of it had come as an ugly jab in the ribs. It wasn't even as if it had any literary significance. It was simply his mother's maiden name which had, in one heedless moment, been tied round his neck at baptism. It had persuaded him at an early age that there could never be any real understanding between himself and a mother and father who had connived in such a purblind decision.
Michael Underwood   *The Silent Liars*

Julie Her name was not Julie; Julie was the name he chose for her. She despised it knowing that he wanted a wife who would fit that name, neat faced with a small pink mouth and a terrible tidiness in her and around her.
Martha Gellhorn   *Liana*

Junior 'You can't be named just Junior. You've got to be something Junior. Henry, or John, or James. Go ask them what his real name is.' 'He ain nothing Junior,' she said. 'He jes Junior. I name him myself.'
Mary Dutton   *Thorpe*

Kimberley Heifer calves born on the farm that year were given names such as Ladysmith and Bloemfontein. 'And as if the ent bad enough,' Jack said to Nenna, 'the Peter Luppits is calling their new baby son Kimberley.'
Mary E. Pearce   *Jack Merrybright*

(Set at the time of the Boer War)

Kirstie 'Kirstie, indeed!' cried the girl, her eyes blazing in her white face. 'My name is Miss Christina Elliott, I would have ye to ken.'
R. L. Stevenson   *Weir of Hermiston*

Kitty Miss Singleton had taught her the catechism. At the beginning it was deceptively easy. 'What is your name?' asked Miss Singleton on behalf of God. 'Kitty,' she had replied the first time. 'Catherine,' Miss Singleton had gently corrected her. 'God prefers us to use our full names.'
Margaret Bacon   *Kitty*

Laetitia She remembered the day on which the fourth form had discovered her christened name to be Laetitia; a shame that Lucy had spent her life concealing. The fourth form had excelled themselves, and Lucy had been wondering whether her mother would mind very much about her suicide, and deciding that anyhow she had brought it on herself by giving her daughter such a highfalutin name.
Josephine Tey   *Miss Pym Disposes*

Lauretta – Lauretta! aye, you would have her called so; but for my part I never knew any good come of giving girls these heathen Christian names: if you had called her Deborah, or Tabitha, or Ruth, or Rebecca, or Joan, nothing of this had ever happened; but I always knew Lauretta was a runaway name.

Richard Brinsley Sheridan   *St Patrick's Day*

Leila Privately, Edward thought Leila rather a silly name. But girls were silly in many ways, he reflected: one just had to put up with it.
Phyllis Bentley   *Leila*

Lenin 'What do you wish to name this child?' he asked Peppone's wife. 'Lenin Libero Alberto,' she replied. 'Then go and get him baptized in Russia,' said Don Camillo calmly, replacing the cover on the font.
Giovanni Guareschi   *The Little World of Don Camillo*

Lily Miss Thunder entered timidly, as became a young woman who had been christened Lily.
Horace Annesley Vachell   *The Actor*

Lionel 'I was born under the sign of Leo, though it's not my real name – it's Lionel. But don't tell anyone.' 'Why not?' 'Because it's rather a fancy name.' I saw her trying to probe the mystery of the schoolboy mind.
L. P. Hartley   *The Go-Between*

Lizzie 'She is named Lizzie, ma'am.' 'She can hardly be named Lizzie, I think, Mary Anne,' returned Miss Peecher, in a tunefully instructive voice. 'Is Lizzie a Christian name, Mary Anne?' 'No, it is a corruption, Miss Peecher.' 'Speaking correctly, we say, then, that Hexham's sister is called Lizzie, not that she is named so.'
Charles Dickens   *Our Mutual Friend*

Lolita Mrs Ewing had a daughter: Lolita. It is, of course, the right of parents to name their offspring what they please, yet it would sometimes be easier if they could glimpse the future and see what the little one was going to look like later on.
Dorothy Parker   *Lolita*

Lorna 'Lorna Doone . . . Ah, I shall remember it; because it is so queer a name.'
R. D. Blackmore   *Lorna Doone*

Louisa Is not your Louisa necessarily a die-away damsel, who reads novels, and holds her head on one side, languishing and given to love?
Mary Russell Mitford   *Our Village*

'Ay, ay, Miss Louisa Musgrove, that is the name. I wish young ladies had not such a number of fine christian names. I should never be out, if they were all Sophys, or something of that sort.'
Jane Austen   *Persuasion*

Lovejoy She was Lovejoy Mason. 'Nobody can be called Lovejoy,' Angela was to say, but Lovejoy was. What Vincent said was worse but he did not know lovejoy was listening. 'No-one who loved their child could give it a name like that.'
Rumer Godden   *An Episode of Sparrows*

Lucia 'It's Lucia.' How could he have forgotten the absurd pretentious name? She had confided to him in the corner of a warehouse that she had a brother called Roderick. Her father was responsible. He was a great reader of the obscurer classics.
Graham Greene   *England Made Me*

Lulu Lulu was christened Louise, and God knows why they gave her such a revolting nickname.
Charity Blackstock   *People in Glass Houses*

Madge Dear Amaryllis, – (may I call you that? Seeing I do not know your proper name;
And if I did, it might be something dull – like Madge).
A. A. Milne   *Reverie*

Maitland 'What's his name?' 'Maitland Fitzurgis.' 'Help!' said Adeline. 'What a name!' 'It is rather a mouthful.'
Mazo de la Roche   *Renny's Daughter*

Makepeace What a damned silly name to christen a boy! What a gratuitous handicap to fasten upon a stripling due to walk into an income

of several thousand a year once they trundled the old man away. Makepeace! The old man had told him that his son was named after the novelist, Thackeray, who was, it seemed, distantly related to Goldthorpe's hoity-toity wife.
R. F. Delderfield   *God is an Englishman*

Marah 'Gorsuch is my name – Marah Gorsuch.' 'Marah,' I said. 'What a funny name!' 'Is it?' he said grimly. 'It means bitter – bitter water, and I'm bitter on the tongue, as you may find.'
John Masefield   *Jim Davis*

Margaret Polly thought she should be called Margaret after her mother, but this suggestion had Jordan frothing at the mouth. Margarets were ten a penny, Margarets were ordinary, Princess or not.
Margaret Forster   *Fenella Phizackerley*

Marietta The student would not, I decided at once, make a good District Nurse. Her name was Marietta, which in itself was all wrong.
Joanna Jones   *Nurse is a Neighbour*

Marjorie I hated margarine. Everyone called me Marge at school.
Fay Weldon   *Female Friends*

His wife was a woman of one deception – the concealment of her Christian name. It had always been a grief to Marjorie that she was not called by a more biblical appellation. It vexed her greatly that so carnal a name as Marjorie should have been given her. Accordingly, she signed herself 'M. Harrison' only, hoping that it might appear to stand for Martha or Miriam.
S. McNaughton   *Selah Harrison*

Marvin Whoever chose Marvin for his name? Bram, I suppose. A Shipley family name, it was, I think. Just the sort of name the Shipleys would have. They were all Mabels and Gladyses, Vernons and Marvins, spent brown names, common as bottled beer.

Margaret Laurence   *The Stone Angel*

Matthew 'My name is Matthew Bramble, at your service. The truth is, I have a foolish pique at the name of Matthew, because it savours of those canting hypocrites, who, in Cromwell's time, christened all their children by names taken from the scripture.' 'A foolish pique indeed (cried Mrs Tabby) and even sinful, to fall out with your name because it is taken from holy writ.'
Tobias Smollett   *Humphrey Clinker*

Maud It sounds like a cow call. I'm Maudlin is what it amounts to. In grade school the kids made it 'Muddy' and now all I hear is 'Moody'.
Bernard Malamud   *Dubin's Lives*

Measag 'Her Christian name is Measag.' 'What?' Miss Cuffins had pronounced it 'Meesag', but even if she had pronounced it properly as 'mesac' Major Quiblick would probably have said 'what?' He regarded all Gaelic Christian names as a threat to Security Intelligence.
Compton Mackenzie   *Whisky Galore*

Meg 'You're at least twenty-three, Marguerite,' she said. She never called her friend Meg, pronouncing that name to be 'too domestic and altogether unlovely'.
Ethel Turner   *Seven Little Australians*

Melanie 'Melanie,' his mother-in-law is saying, 'what kind of a name is that? It sounds colored.' 'Oh, mother, don't drag out all your prejudices.'
John Updike   *Rabbit is Rich*

Melody She got a Southern name, one of those funny double names, Malarkey Betty-Lou or something like that . . .' 'The name Melody's not unusual in the South. I knew a girl in school from Kentucky whose name was Melody. She was a sweet little girl and after a while we got used to the name, it was kind of cute.'

Calder Willingham   *Providence Island*

Mercy Her name was Mercy, though she had none on me.
Charles Dickens   *The Uncommercial Traveller*

Mildred Her name was Mildred. He had heard one of the other girls in the shop address her. 'What an odious name,' said Philip. 'Why?' asked Dunsford. 'I like it.' 'It's so pretentious.'
Somerset Maugham   *Of Human Bondage*

Mimi The Langstreths were very affluent, and Mimi (what a name! and there was no getting around it as it was not short for anything else) already showed in some indefinable way that she was a child of wealth. 'Mimi has something to tell you.' The French poodle name sounded more out of place than ever on Miss Drew's lips, as though she had said something indecent.
Theodora Keough   *Meg*

Mira I knew I could never get on with anyone with a name like Mira.
B. S. Johnson   *Travelling People*

Moira 'What are you going to call her?' 'Moira, I believe.' 'Not Moira, darling, you can't. I never heard such an awful name.'
Nancy Mitford   *The Pursuit of Love*

Molly Her name is Molly too – which, as I have often thought, shows a low taste in them as first called her so; – she might as well be a scullery-maid at oncest.
Elizabeth Gaskell   *Wives and Daughters*

Monica 'I don't like your name. I've always classed it with the Muriels and Olives of this world. Ruby too – ' 'In a little time you'll be calling me "darling". That's much better because I don't like my name either.'
James Broom Lynne   *The Commuters*

'Funny thing about names – have you noticed that? They're more potent than we realise. Now Monica

. . . what image does that conjure up? The hockey-field. The swimming bath. The gymnasium. Tennis courts and netball and lacrosse.'
Andrea Newman   *A Bouquet of Barbed Wire*

Mortimer 'I wish my name were not Mortimer; it has such a reproachful sound.'
Ivy Compton-Burnett   *Manservant and Maidservant*

Muriel Muriel came floating towards me in the grey cloud of the unattractiveness of her name.
Jane Duncan   *My Friend Muriel*

She was named Muriel – after the rather peculiar name of John's mother.
Mrs Craik   *John Halifax, Gentleman*

Nancy 'You will treat him like a girl – you'll spoil his spirit, and make a mere Miss Nancy of him.'
Anne Brontë   *The Tenant of Wildfell Hall*

Nerissa Mrs Ellis thought Nerissa rather a high-flown name.
Phyllis Bentley   *On the Station*

Nigel 'Your mother wanted to call you Nigel,' he would say, 'a pansy name, like a duke.'
Gordon McGill   *Arthur*

Noah 'That's a terrible name to give a kid, Bruce.' 'We don't think so. He was named after my wife's father.' 'It's not even Jewish. Noah came before Abraham, and Abraham was the first. Noah was a drunkard. Why'd you ever name your kid after a Gentile drunk?'
Joseph Heller   *Good as Gold*

Olive 'The baby shall be christened Olive!' 'It's a strange, heathen name, Mrs Rothesay.'
Mrs Craik   *Olive*

Opal Opal Jessica – and I often wondered how my mother had come to give me such a frivolous name, because she was a far from frivolous woman.

Victoria Holt   *The Pride of the Peacock*

Orpheus I never discovered anything about him that would explain why his parents gave him such a pretentious Christian name; perhaps it ran in the family. He invited me to call him Orph.
Robertson Davies   *Fifth Business*

Pamela 'Pamela – did you say? A *queer* sort of name! Is it a Christian or a Pagan name? Linsey-woolsey – half one, half t'other, like thy girl.'
Samuel Richardson   *Pamela*

Percy He begged me to let him change his Christian name Percy to an abbreviation of his middle name, and become Rick, so they wouldn't tease him about having a sissy's name.
James Purdy   *Jeremy's Version*

'Funny thing with names. Most people think Percy's a pretty awful one, and yet it isn't all that different from Peter. They each have five letters and three of them in Common.'
Michael Underwood   *Shem's Demise*

'What a horrid little name. They might have called it something . . . well, grander, like Ulysses or Washington.' 'They never got beyond the P's.'
Raymond Hitchcock   *Percy*

Percy, somewhere in his Army experience, had thrown aside that name (which had become rather a joke, like Algernon) . . .
Robertson Davies   *Fifth Business*

His pals crowed with delight, tossing the name to each other on gales of laughter. Percy's name gave them a kind of purchase on him.
David Lodge   *Ginger, You're Barmy*

Phoebe Phoebe had early divined that her name had comic value . . .
Peter de Vries   *The Tunnel of Love*

Princess Prin's real name is Princess. Morag thinks this is the

funniest thing she has ever heard.
Margaret Laurence   *The Diviners*

Rain 'She has some pathetically comic name.' 'Rain Carter,' said Mor.
Iris Murdoch   *The Sandcastle*

Ramona 'Pregnant women shouldn't be allowed to read. I've never liked Helen Hunt Jackson.'
Lonnie Coleman   *Sam*

(Helen Hunt Jackson is the author of the novel *Ramona*)

Rance 'Your great uncle, Rance Joyner.' 'Rance! Rance! Gods! What a name! No wonder he smote fear and trembling to the Yankee heart!'
Thomas Wolfe   *The Web and the Rock*

Ravel His name was Ravel. Mrs Littlefield the First had been of a poetic temperament and she had conned this name from some languishing and romantic novel written by an English lady. Mr Littlefield had protested, for he had considerable common-sense of a rather cruder sort, but his wife had been determined.
Taylor Caldwell   *Melissa*

Reginald He was shy, and unwilling to own to the name of Reginald, as being too aspiring and self-assertive a name. In his signature he used only the initial R, and imparted what it really stood for to none but chosen friends, under the seal of confidence.
Charles Dickens   *Our Mutual Friend*

Richard Her father was a clergyman, without being neglected, or poor, and a very respectable man, though his name was Richard.
Jane Austen   *Northanger Abbey*

Robin . . . a tall English girl named, with a pertness that sat somewhat awkwardly on her mature body, Robin.
John Updike   *Still Life*

Rockmeteller He had this aunt in Illinois; and, as he had been named

Rockmeteller after her (which in itself, you might say, entitled him to substantial compensation) and was her only nephew, his position looked pretty sound.
P. G. Wodehouse   *Carry On, Jeeves*

Roderick 'His actual name is bad enough, as it is. Roderick!' Mrs Hammond winced. This was a painful subject with her. 'How often I pleaded with poor Lucy to call him Thomas.'
P. G. Wodehouse   *Bill the Conqueror*

Rosalind Jaques: Rosalind is your love's name? Orlando: Yes, just. Jaques: I do not like her name. Orlando: There was no thought of pleasing you when she was christened.
William Shakespeare   *As You Like It*

Runyon 'It's a terrible name, but Mother says I will like it when I grow up because it's distinguished, she says. The other boys call me Onion.'
Norman Corwin   *The Odyssey of Runyon Jones*

St John The letters were all 'my St John'. 'Whaurever did he get that name, fer Christ's sake?' 'Perhaps his Ma was a virgin,' said Lachlan. It was the one witticism of his life.
M. O'Donoghue   *Wild Honey Time*

Sandra All I have against Sandra is her name which, whether pronounced with a short or long first vowel, never ceases to jar on me.
V. S. Naipaul   *The Mimic Man*

Selene The heathenish given name of this young woman was pronounced as Say-lay-nay by herself and her father; Aaron later compromised as Say-lane; most people, including the Bois missionaries, called her See-lean. That it was an appellation of the swift moon goddess (something that Aaron never knew and Selene may not have known) was not too unsuitable.
Sinclair Lewis   *The God-seeker*

Sid The only thing about him she didn't like was his name. She always gave a small shiver of revulsion every time she used the name.
Michael Underwood   *A Pinch of Snuff*

Siegfried 'You can call me by my first name. But I ought to warn you that it's Siegfried.'
Brigid Brophy   *Flesh*

Stanhope 'I'm certainly not having him at a comprehensive. With a stupid name like Stanhope he'd only get laughed at, down there amongst the yobs.'
Fay Weldon   *Female Friends*

Tansy It was an impossible name! He wished he knew how old Father Conran had been persuaded into allowing such a heathenish title to be bestowed upon a Christian child.
Maureen Peters   *Tansy*

(The mother is said to have carried tansy flowers on her wedding day.)

Tetty . . . Mrs Johnson, whom he used to name by the familiar appellation of Tett, or Tetsy, which, like Betty or Betsy, is provincially used as a contraction for Elizabeth, her Christian name, but which to us seems ludicrous, when applied to a woman of her age and appearance.
James Boswell   *The Life of Dr Samuel Johnson*

Theodora . . . the baby, a tiny girl with a ridiculous name. What *was* her name, something barbaric, an empress, not Cleopatra – Theodora.
John Updike   *Marry Me*

Theodore 'Laurie Laurence – what an odd name!' 'My first name is Theodore, but I don't like it, for the fellows called me Dora, so I made them say Laurie instead.' 'I hate my name, too – so sentimental! I wish everyone would say Jo, instead of Josephine. How did you make the boys stop calling you Dora?' 'I thrashed 'em.'
Louisa M. Alcott   *Little Women*

Tobias 'What is his name?' 'An old-

fashioned name, I thought. For such a modern couple. Tobias.' 'That's not the cat?' 'Cotton is the cat. Tobias was Ken's grandfather.'
John Updike   *Couples*

Tom I knew his name was Thomas, but it's the first time I've ever heard of him calling himself Tom. Besides, a name like Tom doesn't sound dignified enough for a minister.
Erskine Caldwell   *Jenny by Nature*

Topaz She claims to have been christened Topaz. Even if this is true, there is no law to make a woman stick to a name like that.
Dodie Smith   *I Capture the Castle*

Trevor When he said 'Trevor' it was a statement of fact, not as it would have been with the others a statement of shame or defiance. Nor did anyone laugh except Mike.
Graham Greene   *The Destructors*

Victor 'It's your mother who chose Victor. I never liked the name. It sounded a bit like boasting.'
Graham Greene   *The Captain and the Enemy*

I thought his name, Victor, old-fashioned and pompous; unlike him and unworthy of him. I was saddened when I discovered his first name, I thought it so terribly unromantic. I don't mean I need him to have a name like Tristan or St John; any Tom, Dick or Harry would have done, or Michael or Paul or even Geoffrey, but I couldn't take Victor to my heart.
Siân James   *Yesterday*

Viola 'But what's your name? You didn't tell me last week.' 'Oh, it's a rotten name!' the girl said. 'I hate it.' 'But tell me what it is. I'd like to know.' 'It's Viola. It's silly. It's so pi.'
H. E. Bates   *The Man Who Loved Cats*

Wilfred Why are certain names funny? . . . My brother was christened Wilfred.
Pamela Hansford Johnson   *A Summer to Decide*

6
THE GIFT OF A NAME

S O FAR, names given to children born in English-speaking countries have been discussed. Those countries, of course, are *predominantly* English-speaking. In modern times the USA, Canada, Britain, Australia and the like are enriched by being multi-ethnic societies, with groups who continue to speak their own languages, practise their own religions and follow their own cultural traditions. Children born into such ethnic groups are likely to be named according to criteria which differ markedly from those I have so far outlined.

Since we also live in a time when travel between countries and continents has become commonplace, when modern communications have greatly increased our awareness of people and events elsewhere in the world, it is worth thinking about how names are bestowed at birth in other cultures. This chapter can only hint at the richness and complexity of naming customs throughout the world. Perhaps one day there will be a collection of authoritative essays on the subject written by name scholars from the countries concerned, but such a collection has yet to be assembled.

Chinese given names

Throughout this chapter, the term *given name* will be used for the name which a child receives at birth. *First name* is often inappropriate, as it is for example in China. If you are introduced to a Chinese person whose name, say, is **Liu Dai Lin,** then Liu is the family name. The name that occurs in the middle is sometimes a generation name, shared by all the children, or by all the children of the same sex, of a particular couple. The generation name, together with the third name of the group, becomes the child's personal name.

A traditional Chinese family may have adopted for naming purposes a poem of about twenty or more words, all of which are different. The words of this

'We named him [an adopted child] after the great Zen Master Po Chang. We dropped the Po.'

Nancy Mitford   *Don't Tell Alfred*

poem become, in sequence, the generation names. In Chinese all such words would be meaningful: purely grammatical words such as 'the' and 'a' would not occur. If there is no special generation name, parents usually choose two words as the child's name. What they do not do is turn to a ready-made stock of names, as do most western parents. They might, however, make use of certain words that frequently occur in personal names.

Typical words used to form names for boys include *Wen* (scholar), *Wu* (military), *Xiong* (hero), *Zhi* (ambitious), *De* (virtuous), *Dá* (high position), *Tai* (peace, healthy), *An* (peace), *Qiang* or *Chiang* (strong), *Dà* (big). Such elements can be permutated in almost any order. This Chinese method of forming names thus has much in common with the naming system of the Anglo-Saxons. They also permutated name-elements, usually those already present in the names of the parents, to make up the single personal names by which their children would be known. (For examples of such names see page 125.)

Flower names are not automatically feminine in China. **Ju Ao**, for example, means 'proud chrysanthemum'. The well-known Chinese actress Tsai Chin remarks in her autobiography that this name of the 'emperor of flowers', which is never considered as feminine, was given to one of her brothers. Her other brother became **Ying Hua**, 'heroic and magnificent'.

Names of Chinese girls are also formed on the permutation principle, but as in most cultures the feminine name elements tend to have more delicate and graceful associations. Popular name elements for Chinese girls include *Yue* (moon), *Hua* (flower), *Ying* (flower), *Mei* (beautiful), *Li* (beautiful), *Shu* (good), *Xia* (cloud), *Lian* (lotus), *Xiao* (small), *Qing* (blue), *Hong* (red), *Qin* or *Chin* (musical instrument). A girl might thus have a name meaning Moon-flower, Beautiful-moon, Precious-flower, Shining-cloud, etc. The sisters of Precious-flower might have names meaning Precious-dawn and Precious-peace.

> Chinese peasant families occasionally dress a boy in girl's clothes and give him a girl's name. Such families have always valued sons at the expense of daughters: the use of a girl's name and clothes for a boy is meant to fool the gods, who might otherwise take their son from them.
>
> A remark in Rudyard Kipling's *Kim* seems to indicate that such practices were also known in India; 'We changed his name when the fever came. We put him into girl's clothes.' This remark is made about an attempt to save a boy's life, it being assumed that the gods will not be so eager to take the life of a girl.

Having carefully named their children, Chinese parents are likely to do what parents everywhere do, and address them by a nickname. The Chinese actress Tsai Chin says in her autobiography that her father called her **Ah San**. The vocative prefix *Ah* is attached to the names of insignificant people, such as servants, though it can also be used affectionately to friends. *San* is simply the number 'three'. In a similar way, **Ah Si** might be use for a fourth child. The Chinese expression 'any Ah San, Ah Si' is the equivalent of 'any Tom, Dick or Harry.'

Japanese names

Number names for children are also found in Japanese, where the order of birth, as in many countries, is of importance. A first son could receive a name like **Taro, Ichiro** or **Kazuo**; a second son could become **Eiji, Jiro** or **Kenji**; a third could be **Saburo, Taizo** or **Shuzo**. Jack Seward says in his book *Japanese In Action* that the given name of one of his teachers was **Gohachiro**, which translates literally as 'five-eight-male'. The man concerned was the thirteenth child in his family. **Minako**, 'three-seven-child', would be a suitable name for a girl who was the tenth child.

When they are not making a simple statement about numerical position, Japanese given names indicate parental aspirations for their child. The parents of **Katsutoshi** hope that he will 'win cleverly'; and those of **Noboru** that he will 'rise' in social and professional status. A **Hideo** is meant to be an 'excellent male', a **Nagataka** to show 'everlasting filial duty', a **Chokichi** to have 'long-lasting good luck'.

One of my Japanese colleagues in the BBC World Service jotted down the following male names as being fairly common in 1990: **Kenichi** or **Kentaro** (healthy), **Toru** (accomplishment), **Minoru** (ripening), **Daisuke** (big man), **Shunsuke** (brilliant), **Masayoshi** (justice), **Makoto** (sincerity), **Shingo** (new oneself), **Takeshi** (stout), **Akira** (distinct). To these he added the common female names **Mami** (true beauty), **Michi** (beautiful and wise), **Yuko** (grace), **Kazuko** (gentle and peaceful), **Akiko** (distinct), **Junko** (purity), **Kyoko** (apricot), **Yuriko** (lily), **Sakura** (cherry blossom), **Hanako** (gorgeous). Some less common male Japanese names are **Kumakichi** (fortunate bear), **Torao** (tiger man), **Mima** (pretty horse), **Tobikuma** (flying cloud).

As can be seen from the above, *-ko* (child) is a common suffix in Japanese feminine names. Seward mentions also the feminine endings *-e* (inlet or tree branch) and *-yo* (generation), though such suffixes are of fairly recent origin. Male names often end in *-o* (male), *-zo* (storehouse), *-emon* (guarding gate), *-yoshi* (good), *-suke* (assistance), *-take* (filial duty), *-kichi* (good luck).

A few names, such as **Misao** (fidelity), **Sakae** (prosperity), **Nao** (honest, right), can be given to either sex, but a Japanese who sees a name like **Sachiko** recognises both its meaning (happy child) and the specific indication (*-ko*) of its femininity. Our own first names could be said to give some indication of sex, inasmuch as suffixes like *-a*, *-ia*, *-e*, *-ette*, *-elle*, *-ine*, *-ina*, *-een*, *-ene*, *-ice*, *-issa*, *-inda* and *-ita* are usually feminine, but unlike the Chinese and Japanese we rarely know a name's meaning. There must be many people in the western world who remain permanently unaware of what their own first name, or the name they have given to their child, actually means. Oriental given names mostly provide a constant reminder to those who bear them of the hopes their parents invested in them. The philosophy that gives rise to such names would have been familiar to the sixteenth-century Puritans, who introduced to our own naming system such 'virtue' names as **Faith, Hope, Charity** and **Mercy**.

Japanese parents often pay a great deal of attention to a name's written appearance. It is not a question of spelling, as it sometimes is in the West – **Anne** being preferred to **Ann,** say, or **Stephen** to **Steven**. The Japanese are concerned with the shape of the characters, or *kanji*, that are used to form the name, and the number of brush strokes which are required to write them. It is not unknown for Japanese, especially women, to amend their names in some way after consulting an astrologer or fortune-teller. The new name is usually composed of a more favourable number of brush strokes. The equivalent practice in our own society occurs when a letter is added to or subtracted from a name by an ardent believer in numerology (see page 228).

Hindu names

Numerology, astrology and suchlike arts are seldom major influences in the naming of a western child. Throughout Asia, by contrast, it is relatively normal to seek professional astrological advice when naming a child. The astrologer usually suggests the first syllable of the name or word which is based on it.

It is easy to understand why professional help is needed. In his booklet *Naming the Hindu Child*, Dwarka Nath writes: 'The name of a child may be fixed according to the Nakshatra under which he is born. The 12 signs of the Zodiac, which are called Rasis, are divided into 27 Nakshatras, two and a quarter Nakshatras representing one Rasi. Each Nakshatra is further divided into four parts, and the name is fixed according to the part of the Nakshatra under which the child was born.'

Mr Nath's notes become even more complicated after this introduction, but he does mention that the sub-divisions of the Nakshatras change approximately every 13 minutes. This, he says, is why two people who are born half an hour apart may have entirely different characters.

Mr Nath provides a list of Hindu names, as do the *Notes on the Names of Asian Immigrants* issued by the British Community Relations Commission some years ago. The two lists vary considerably, and neither provides English translations of the names concerned. Typical Hindu names for boys, however, appear to be **Aditya, Anand, Anil, Arun, Damodar, Devindra, Ganesh, Jitindra, Kanti, Kapil, Krishna, Naresh, Niranjan, Rajesh, Ram, Satish, Vijay**. Of the names for Hindu girls, only the following appear in both the list provided by Mr Nath and that of the Community relations Commission: **Aruna, Gayatri, Indira, Leela, Mohani, Rohini, Sumitra, Usha**.

Discussing Hindu given names in his *Treasury of Name Lore*, Elsdon C. Smith says that most of them 'contain names of gods or have religious connotations, relate in some way to nature, reflect abstract qualities or virtues, derive from words which designate common objects or refer to parts of the body'. That summary would apply equally well to the majority of first names used in the English-speaking world, if by 'parts of the body' one included references to complexion and colour of the hair.

Hindus, incidentally, write their names in the same order as we do. One or more given names precede a subcaste name (surname) which is shared by the whole family.

Sikh names

Most Sikh given names apply equally well to both sexes. When borne by a man, the name is followed by **Singh**, and then perhaps by a subcaste name, though the latter is often dropped. Singh literally means 'Lion', a reference to the well-known martial qualities of the Sikhs, but it has become the conventional indication of maleness. A Sikh woman uses **Kaur** after her given name. When she marries she will adopt the subcaste name of her husband if he uses it. If he is **Mohinder Singh Sandhu**, for instance, she will become **Gurmit Kaur Sandhu**; if he uses only Mohinder Singh then she remains Gurmit Kaur.

Common names among the Punjabi Sikhs in Britain, according to the notes provided by the Community Relations Commission, include **Ajit, Amarjit, Baljit, Daljit, Davindar, Dibag, Gurmit, Harbans, Joginder, Kuldip, Malkiat, Manjit, Mohan, Mohinder, Paramjit, Piara, Pritam, Rajinder,**

Ramindar, Ranjit, Ravinder, Sewa (males only), Sohan, Surjit, Swaran.

> In *The Netsilik Eskimo*, Asen Balicki writes: 'The Netsilik believed that a personal name had supernatural power closely associated with an individual's personality, and that the dead had a strong desire to reincarnate in newborn infants, irrespective of sex. If the mother was having a difficult childbirth, she called out various names of dead people in the hope of enlisting their help. The name proving most helpful at delivery was retained, the mother believing that that spirit had entered the infant's body.'

Muslim names

In an article on the naming of children in the Muslim world (*The Muslim*, November, 1974), Abdul Wahid commented on the great variety of current practices which, as he put it, reflected 'different levels of Islamic consciousness' in different parts of the Muslim world. Reverence for Islam was not always matched, said Mr Wahid, by a knowledge of Muslim tradition or of the Arabic language. He also commented on the effect of contact between Muslims and Europeans, which could lead to Muslim names such as **Saliha** (righteous, devout), **Zaynab** (name of the Prophet's daughter) and **Khadija** (name of the Prophet's wife) being transposed into **Sally, Jane** and **Dee**.

There are also devout Muslims who favour 'new' names. The Malaysian magazine *Dian* published an article in 1972 entitled 'Modern Names for Your Children'. Though aimed at a readership in Kelantan, one of the most Islamic states of Malaysia, it encouraged parents to form 'musical, flattering, beautiful names for children, especially baby girls'. Amongst the names it suggested, which it admitted had no specific meaning but merely sounded pleasant, were **Zizi, Nini, Mimi, Lili, Sisi, Tuti, Biba, Nani, Zuzi, Juju** and **Susi**. According to Mr Wahid, the new generation of Pakistani Muslims uses such names. He has also noted the use of **Simi** (silver) and **Ambreen** (Amber).

It is very easy for westerners to misunderstand Arabic names. One of the commonest mistakes concerns composite names in which *Abd* is used. This word simply means 'servant' and should always be followed by one of the names of Allah, eg **Abd al-Basit** (servant of the Withholder, the Enlarger). For westerners, a name like Abd al-Basit tends to be interpreted as **Abdul** Basit. In fact Abdul is not and has never been a separate name.

R. D. Chapman and A. Crump, authors of the Community Relations Commission *Notes on the Names of Asian Immigrants* which have been referred to above, make the same point. They list 'the names of the principal Muslim *titles*, which can never be personal names'. In addition to Abdul they mention **Allah, Mohammed, Quraishi, Shah, Syed** and **Ullah**. The inclusion of Mohammed will surprise many, but these authors say firmly that if a teacher 'were for example to make the mistake of calling Mohammed **Khalig** *Mohammed* just because this was the name which came first, the boy might well be offended. *Khalig* is his name; *Mohammed* could more properly be described as his Muslim title or forename.'

Other writers on Muslim names, such as Elsdon C. Smith, treat the name of the Prophet, which occurs in different spellings as Mohammed, Muhammad, etc., as a given name rather than title. Nevertheless, the warning that one should not assume that a name which occurs first is automatically the 'call name' of the person concerned obviously remains true. Even in the English-speaking world, after all, there are many who prefer to be known by one of their middle names. My own practice has long been to ask those I meet, wherever they come from, how they wish to be addressed if they have not already made that clear.

Muslim parents who need guidance in Islamic naming traditions, and those with a special interest in the subject, can turn to the attractively-produced *Book of Muslim Names*, available from the offices of the Muslim Education and Literary Services in London. The introduction to this booklet admits that the transliteration of Arabic names into English can cause difficulty. If it is to be done accurately, then diacritics, or marks placed above or below the letters, need to be used to indicate sound qualities. Even then, those who do not speak Arabic are unlikely to know exactly how to pronounce **Sajid**, say, or **Azizah**. The lengthening of the vowels is perhaps best indicated in other ways, using spellings such as Saajid and Azeezah. Correct pronunciation of both vowels and consonants is important, since the meaning of the name may be seriously affected. The name **Abd al-Haqq**, for example, means 'servant of God, the Truth'. Most native English-speakers would tend to pronounce it as Abd al-Hakk, which would make it the blasphemous 'servant of scratching'.

> Mis-hearing and mis-pronunciation of names by foreigners can affect us all. I have personally been converted into an animal on at least two occasions. At one time I had a German colleague who was convinced that I was **Lassie** rather than **Leslie**. As for my surname, I once received a letter from Nigeria from a young man who had heard me say on the radio that my name was **Dunkling**. His letter was addressed to Mr **Donkey**.

Muslims who live in English-speaking countries will probably continue to spell their names in simplified form, without the diacritics. I give examples of some typical names below, together with their English meanings.

Male names: **Abbas** (description of a lion; name of an uncle of the Prophet), **Abdullah** (servant of God), **Akbar** (greater, bigger), **Akram** (more generous), **Ali** (excellent, noble), **Amin** (reliable), **Ashraf** (most noble), **Aslam** (safer, sounder), **Aziz** (mighty), **Badr** (full moon), **Bashir** (bringer of good news), **Faruq** (distinguisher of truth from falsehood), **Habib** (beloved), **Hafiz** (protector), **Hanif** (true believer), **Hasan** (handsome, good), **Hashim** (generous; great-grandfather of the Prophet), **Hussain** (handsome), **Ibrahim** (name of a Prophet), **Iqbal** (responsiveness), **Jafar** (stream; cousin, companion of the Prophet), **Khalid** (glorious, eternal), **Latif** (fine, gentle), **Malik** (reigning) **Masud** (happy), **Muzzammil** (one who is wrapped up), **Nabil** (noble), **Qasim** (divider, distributor; name of a son of the Prophet), **Rafiq** (kind friend), **Rashid** (righteous), **Sadiq** (truthful, sincere), **Salim** (secure, free), **Sharif** (noble), **Sulayman** (name of a Prophet), **Sultan** (power, authority), **Zahid** (abstinent).

Female names: **Abir** (fragrance), **Afra** (dust-coloured), **Aisha** or **Ayesha** (living, prosperous; name of the wife of the Prophet), **Aminah** (trustworthy; name of the Prophet's mother), **Arub** (loving), **Azhar** (flowers, blossoms), **Basimah** (smiling), **Bushra** (good news), **Daliya** (dahlia), **Durrah** (pearl), **Farah** (joy, cheerfulness), **Faridah** (unique, precious), **Fatima** (weaning; daughter of the Prophet), **Hannah** (sympathy), **Hayfa** (slender, of beautiful body), **Inas** (sociability), **Jamilah** (beautiful, elegant), **Kamilah** (perfect), **Karimah** (generous, noble), **Lina** (tender), **Malikah** (queen), **Muna** (wish, desire), **Nadimah** (friend), **Nadirah** (flourishing, radiant), **Najmah** (star), **Nasha** (scent, perfume), **Nasimah** (gentle breeze), **Nawal** (gift), **Rabiah** (fourth), **Sabah** (morning, dawn), **Salma** (peaceful), **Thara** (wealth), **Uzma** (greatest), **Yasmin** (jasmine), **Zahrah** (flower, blossom), **Zinah** (adornment, beauty).

> What appears to be the same name can mean different things in different countries. *The Book of Muslim Names*, for instance, includes **Nada** as a name for a girl, and says that it means either 'generosity' or 'dew'. I have a friend of that name, but she is from Croatia. Her name is therefore a variant of the Russian **Nadya**, which means 'hope'. In many parts of the world, therefore, Nada is an acceptable given name, though for different reasons. It becomes a decidedly odd name in Spanish-speaking countries, where the word *nada* means 'nothing'.
>
> A similar fate befalls the male Arabic name **Kamil**, which means 'complete, perfect'. On hearing it pronounced, English-speakers tend to think that the person concerned is called 'camel'.

Sri Lankan names

In 1990 I had the pleasant experience of discussing Sri Lankan given names with Pandula Endagama, an anthropologist who works at the National Museum in Colombo. Mr Endagama and his wife are Buddhists, and he explained first of all how they had chosen two names for each of their daughters. They had begun by asking the advice of an astrologer for the auspicious syllable on which the main name should be based. They had then consulted a monk for specific name suggestions. For their eldest daughter they needed a name beginning with *Na*. She became **Nayana Priyadharshani**, 'one with eyes which are a delight to see'. That, at least, became her formal name. Like most Sri Lankan children she had another name for daily use, and at home her parents addressed her more simply as **Lokuduya**, 'big daughter'. (A son would have been **Lokuputa**.)

This use of a nickname is almost ritualistic. Mr Endagama mentioned that many Sri Lankans believe that a young person, especially, should not be addressed by his or her given name. Parents tend to 'hide the name,' as he expressed it, by the use of pet names.

The second Endagama daughter needed a name based on the syllable *Sa*. She became **Samadara Hasarangani**, 'one who has a smiling flower-like face', though once again, the name used in normal address was less formal. At home she was **Podiduya**, 'small daughter'. Her schoolfriends called her **Sama** or **Dara**.

The third daughter of the Endagamas became **Dilipa Manaranjani**, 'one who has a glittering mind', or **Dili** to her parents and friends. Her younger sister, whose name again needed to be based on *Na*, be-came **Nalinika Jayanadani**, 'all-purpose victory', or 'wherever you go victorious'. Her home-name became **Sudu** or **Sududuya**, 'daughter with the fair complexion'.

Discussing Sri Lankan names in more general terms, Mr Endagama said that there were often clues in a name as to the age and caste of the name-bearer. Families of superior caste still tended to use traditional names, or the full forms of those names. Thus an upper-caste name might be **Hetuhamy** 'lord of fortune'. The lower-caste version of this would be **Hetuwa**. In our own society we can compare the continued upper-class use, both in speech and writing, of traditional names like **Thomas** and **James**. Lower-class usage allows **Tom** and **Jim** not only to be used in speech, but to become the formally registered names.

Some modern Sri Lankan names mentioned by Mr Endagama were, for boys, **Arawinda, Arjuna, Asanka, Bandula, Dilip, Nimal, Padman, Prem, Sadun, Sena, Sepala, Sunil**. Names for girls included **Dilipa, Mihika, Nimala** or **Nimali, Nimalka, Padma, Prema, Punya, Sepalika, Soma, Upeksha**. Some names for boys and girls appear to be the same, but **Nayana, Chandra, Priya** and the like become feminine when the stress is placed on the final syllable. Names classified as 'lower-caste' by Mr Endagama were (male): **Baba, Babiya, Bayya, Kiribaba, Menika, Pediya, Pina, Silida, Ukkuwa**. Similar female names included **Babi, Bebi, Hinni, Kiribabi, Meniki, Pedi, Silidi, Sobani, Soida**.

Names of the previous generation tended to be permutations of popular name-elements. **Chandra** 'moon' was more likely to be found as **Chandrapala** 'moon-protector', **Chandraratna** 'moon-precious', **Chandrasiri** 'moon-brightness', **Chandradasa** 'moon-slave'. Similarly **Dharma** 'dispensation', **Ariya** 'noble' and the like were seen in the forms **Dharmapala, Dharmaratna, Dharmadasa, Ariyapala, Ariyaratna, Ariyasiri, Ariyadasa**.

Some of these names look strange to western eyes, but in my conversations with Mr Endagama I was struck by the similarities between Sri Lankan given names and our own first names. In both societies an informed observer can identify the fashions of different periods and see how attitudes to naming vary at different levels of society. Both naming systems clearly identify the sex of the name-bearer and reflect the need for a 'strong' name for a boy, a more graceful one for a girl. In both societies a form of name-magic operates, with parents believing that the qualities of the name will affect the nature of the child. Nicknames and pet names commonly replace official given names. It could even be said that most westerners also conceal at least one of the names given to them at birth, usually a middle name that has been given to them for family reasons.

As in the west, the less-educated Sri Lankan parents name their children instinctively, with little or no conscious awareness of cultural heritage. They are likely to corrupt and render meaningless names which were once of great significance. The names are changed, but the basic thinking of the namers reflects, as one would expect, age-old beliefs and attitudes. It would seem that wherever we look at naming customs, we are reminded that we belong to the family of man.

American Indian names

The statement in the previous paragraph might seem to be difficult to maintain when considering, for example, the traditional naming habits of the North American Indians. It is commonly said that the Indians changed their names fairly frequently—at puberty, at the time of a first war expedition, at the time of some notable achievement, on elevation to chieftainship, on retirement. If we say instead that Indians were addressed in different ways at different stages of their lives, the links with our own customs become clearer. In our own society a first name may give way as the normal form of address to a social title used with the family name, then to a professional title such as Doctor or Professor, then perhaps to a title of nobility. Retirement may not be marked, as it was in some Indian tribes, by an old man adopting the name of his own son, but it may well be signalled by the use of a term such as Grandpa.

The one name by which an Indian was unlikely to be addressed at any time in his life was his real name, which was often kept a closely-guarded secret. As with the Australian Aborigines, this real name was thought to be an almost tangible thing that contained the spirit of the person who bore it. In exceptional circumstances it could be loaned, pawned or given away, but it was certainly not for daily use.

> Some modern American Indians bear Scottish surnames which their forefathers bought from traders. The Indians would have assumed that once they bought a name, the original bearer could not possibly continue to use it. No doubt the traders thought otherwise.
>
> The Indian belief that a name is a tangible possession still continues. Chiefs have objected strongly in recent times to what they call the stealing of tribal names. **Blackfoot, Sawridge, Sarcee** and the like have been used as trade names by companies which wish to suggest they have a North American heritage.

Many Indian given names appear to have been of the 'incident' type, referring to something which particularly impressed the father or mother at the time of birth. A surprising number of western parents choose a name in a similar way, responding to a song that happens to be playing on the radio, or a more serious event linked with the day of birth.

Some of the Indian names best known to us are those of chiefs, and are really adopted titles. They often have a strange appearance and apparent meaning, though the latter may be due to misunderstanding or mis-translation. There is a Dakota chief whose name has often been recorded as 'Young-man-afraid-of-his-horses'. Later linguistic probing has shown that a more accurate version of his name would be 'Young-man-whose-very-horses-are-feared'. 'Stinking-saddle-blanket', the name of a Kiowa chief, is an accurate enough translation of the original but gives a misleading impression. We think only of an unpleasant smell and assume that the name was insulting. His own tribesmen knew that

the name referred honourably to his being so often on the warpath that he had no time to change his saddle blanket.

A Haida chief had the equally misleading name 'Unable-to-buy'. To the white man this would appear to be an indication of poverty. The name in fact commemorated a triumphal occasion when a rival chief had been forced to admit that he lacked the necessary funds to buy something offered to him.

In some cases the translation of an Indian name depended on one's point of view. **Chito Hajo**, a Creek chief who opposed the domination of the white man at the end of the 19th century, was recorded officially as '**Crazy Snake**'. To the Creeks themselves, the Hajo part of his name was a war title which meant 'brave to the point of recklessness'. One man's fearlessness is perhaps another man's craziness.

It is doubtful, though, whether a discussion of such names belongs in a chapter about given names. The real given names of American Indians, when not referring to incidents at birth, appear to have been religious (referring to totemic animals), commendatory (suggesting the wealth or status the name-bearer would acquire), commemorative (of an ancestor) or descriptive of the child concerned. They seem, in other words, to have conformed to the general categories of given names that are found elsewhere.

African day names

Tribal naming habits in Africa have never, to my knowledge, been thoroughly explored. There is a rich territory awaiting research students of the future, as I know from informal talks with African colleagues. Complex rites and ceremonies come into play when a child is named, reflecting the importance of the act itself.

One of the best-known naming customs in West Africa concerns the giving of day names, as western writers normally refer to them. In Ashanti they are called 'soul names', since it is thought that the day of birth is the day on which the soul is washed or purified. The names themselves in their Ashanti forms, are as follows:

	Boys	*Girls*
Sunday	**Kwasi**	**Akosua**
Monday	**Kwadwo**	**Adwoa**
Tuesday	**Kwabena**	**Abenaa**
Wednesday	**Kwaku**	**Akua**

	Boys	*Girls*
Thursday	**Yaw**	**Yaa**
Friday	**Kofi**	**Afua**
Saturday	**Kwame**	**Amma**

Day names, of course, are not unknown in our own society. A child born at a special time, such as Christmas, is likely to be named **Noel**, say, or **Carol** in commemoration of the fact. Catholic children may be named for the saint whose feast is celebrated on their birthday. The difference is that in West Africa, *all* children are given a day name.

In the days of slavery, very few Africans managed to retain their tribal day names when they reached the plantations. Slave-owners made no attempt to cope with strange names, and usually renamed their property for their own convenience. The forms **Cuffee, Cuffy** and **Coffee**, it is true, do occur fairly frequently in lists of slave names, presumably indicating men who were Kofi, but slaves were more normally given single-syllable English names which were easy to shout.

As far as days are concerned, in English we have the traditional nursery rhyme that begins 'Monday's child is fair of face, Tuesday's child is full of grace.' Children born on most days of the week, according to this rhyme, are accorded pleasant attributes of one kind or another. Wednesday's child is decidedly unlucky, being 'full of woe'. This is especially interesting in a West African context, for there is a very wide-spread belief there that a **Kwaku, or** Wednesday's child, is quick-tempered, aggressive and a trouble-maker.

> **A Kwaku**, in West Africa, is a boy born on a Wednesday, and therefore thought to be one with a bad character. During World War Two, it is said, some West Africans used to refer to Kwaku **Hitler**.

What does an African child do, one may ask, when his name instantly reveals that he is a trouble-making Wednesday's child? The answer to that, according to G. Jahoda, writing in the *British Journal of Psychology* in 1954, is that he responds to expectations and gets into more trouble than his friends who were born on more fortunate days. Mr Jahoda proved the point by consulting records of Juvenile Courts. Boys named Kwaku appeared there far more frequently than statistical normality would have predicted. By contrast, boys named **Kwadwo**, born on a Monday and therefore expected to be quiet and peaceful, generally lived up to expectations and kept out of trouble.

Mr Jahoda did not, of course, conclude from this that there was any truth in the premise that the day of birth actually affects a person's character. As he put it, his investigation showed that 'Ashanti beliefs about a connection between personality characteristics and the day of birth may be effective in selectively enhancing certain traits which otherwise may have remained latent.' Or as our proverb has it: give a dog a bad name and hang him.

In our own society it has been shown that giving a child a 'bad' name, one which other children will laugh at, can affect the child's assessment of his own character. Children tend to think that someone with an odd name must be odd in other ways. It can easily happen that a child then begins to think this of himself. In the case of day names, if we gave our own children names which clearly revealed the day of birth, a Wednesday's child would no doubt soon receive a playground name such as **Misery Guts**.

Names elsewhere

At the end of this chapter I provide some lists of names commonly used in various countries, mostly suggested by friends and colleagues from the countries concerned. The French, German and Dutch lists derive from published sources and represent Top Tens of recent years. It will be seen that names used in a particular country, such as Germany, are not necessarily Germanic by origin, any more than those used in Scandinavia always derive from Old Norse. Intense usage of names like Sarah and Daniel in English-speaking countries has, after all, caused them to be thought of as 'English' rather than Hebrew.

In the Christian countries, especially, the same name may appear in variant forms, but a given name is never genuinely translatable. At only the simplest level can one say that **John** is French **Jean**, German **Hans**, Spanish **Juan**, Italian **Giovanni**, Polish **Jan**, Irish **Sean**, Gaelic **Iain**, Russian **Ivan**. In each country the name has a different social history and arouses a different response.

As one would expect, there is plenty of evidence to show that parents everywhere attach great importance to the naming of their children, though in many countries they would not think in terms of 'choosing' a name. There is a widespread belief that when a child is born, a name already awaits it. The parental task—sometimes an arduous one—is to identify and bestow on their child that one special name.

Adrian Room, in an article which appeared in the *Journal of Russian Studies* in 1983, says that **Kim**, and a feminine form **Kima**, are occasionally found as Russian given names. They owe nothing to Rudyard Kipling's novel *Kim*, where the hero is **Kimball** O'Hara, or to Edna Furber's character Kim Ravenal in *Showboat*, supposedly born on the Mississippi at a point where *K*entucky, *I*llinois and *M*issouri meet. Russian Kim derives from the initial letters of *Kommunisticheskiy Internatsional Molodzhni*, or Communist Youth International, an organization which existed from 1919 to 1943.

My correspondent Oleg Leonovich, writing from Pyatigorsk in March 1990, tells me that all such invented names have been shunned by Russian parents for some time. His studies show that 80 per cent of Russian children now receive names which derive from the Russian Orthodox Church calendar.

The top ten given names (1980s)

FRANCE		GERMANY		NETHERLANDS	
Boys	*Girls*	*Boys*	*Girls*	*Boys*	*Girls*
1 Nicholas	1 Marie	1 Christian	1 Stefanie	1 Mark	1 Linda
2 Guillaume	2 Caroline	2 Michael	2 Christine	2 Dennis	2 Marieke
3 Thibaud	3 Charlotte	3 Daniel	3 Julia	3 Jeroen	3 Kim
4 Thomas	4 Sophie	4 Stefan	4 Sabina	4 Mertijn	4 Wendy
5 Pierre	5 Aurelie	5 Andreas	5 Melanie	5 Bart	5 Marloes
6 Edouard	6 Camille	6 Sebastian	6 Nadine	6 Jan	6 Suzanne
7 Antoine	7 Pauline	7 Matthias	7 Kathrin	7 Marcel	7 Sandra
8 Alexis	8 Emilie	8 Markus	8 Katherina	8 Peter	8 Bianca
9 Matthieu	9 Claire	9 Alexander	9 Nicole	9 Sander	9 Karin
10 Benjamin	10 Stephanie	10 Thomas	10 Anita	10 Patrick	10 Chantal

Some typical given names

FINLAND		HUNGARY		ICELAND	
Boys	*Girls*	*Boys*	*Girls*	*Boys*	*Girls*
Juha	Anu	Attila	Ágnes	Arni	Anna
Jyrki	Hanna	Balázs	Anna	Björn	Guthbjörg
Kari	Helmi	Gábor	Edit	Einar	Helga
Kimmo	Jenni	György	Éva	Gunnar	Jonina
Matti	Jonna	István	Flóra	Guthrun	Katrin
Mika	Kaisa	János	Judit	Jon	Kristin
Ossi	Minna	László	Júlia	Magnus	Margrét
Tomi	Riitta	Miklós	Mária	Óskar	María
Veli	Satu	Tibor	Piroska	Petur	Olafia
Vesa	Ulla	Zoltán	Sára	Stefán	Stefania

ITALY

Boys	Girls
Aldo	Alessandra
Alfredo	Anna
Arturo	Beatrice
Bruno	Caterina
Cesare	Claudia
Dino	Eleonora
Enzo	Fabia
Giuseppe	Laura
Mario	Maria
Pasquale	Tullia

NORWAY

Boys	Girls
Anders	Beate
Andreas	Birgitte
Joakim	Cecilia
Johan	Elisabeth
Josef	Frøydis
Mads	Kristine
Markus	Marianne
Martin	Patricia
Simen	Ragnhild
Svein	Sidsel

POLAND

Boys	Girls
Adam	Anna
Andrzej	Beata
Jan	Edyta
Jerzy	Elżbieta
Krzysztof	Ewa
Roman	Irena
Stanisław	Izabela
Stefan	Katarzyna
Tadeusz	Krystyna
Tomasz	Urszula

PORTUGAL

Boys	Girls
Antônio	Ana
Domingos	Branca
Félix	Catarina
Fernando	Filipa
Francisco	Isabel
João	Joana
Jorge	Leonor
José	Luísa
Luís	Maria
Tomás	Teresa

ROMANIA

Boys	Girls
Alexandru	Ana
Cosmin	Carmen
Damian	Delia
Eugen	Elena
Florin	Florica
George	Georgina
Jon	Joana
Petru	Oana
Radu	Patricia
Vasile	Stefania

RUSSIA

Boys	Girls
Alexey	Elena
Andrey	Galina
Dmitriy	Irina
Eugeniy	Larisa
Igor	Nadezhda
Nicolay	Natalya
Oleg	Olga
Sergev	Svetlana
Vladimir	Tatyana
Yuriy	Vera

SLOVAKIA

Boys	Girls
Antonín	Eva
František	Hana
Jan	Jana
Jaroslav	Jarmila
Jiří	Jitka
Josef	Lenka
Karel	Ludmila
Miroslav	Marie
Petr	Martina
Václav	Miroslava

SPAIN

Boys	Girls
Antonio	Ana
Felipe	Dolores
Francisco	Elena
José	Francisca
Juan	Juliana
Luis	María
Manuel	Patricia
Miguel	Petra
Pedro	Rosa
Ramón	Teresa

SWEDEN

Boys	Girls
Anders	Birgitta
Bo	Elisabet
Erik	Eva
Göran	Karin
Gunnar	Kerstin
Karl	Kristina
Lars	Margareta
Lennart	Marianne
Nils	Monika
Olof	Ulla

TURKEY

Boys	Girls
Ahmet	Ayşe
Barış	Çağdaş
Cemal	Çağrı
Halil	Elif
Ilhan	Esma
Ismet	Eylem
Kemal	Fatma
Remzi	Gönül
Salik	Gülsevin
Selim	Makbule

'Poor Alexey! You were quite right to give him a foreign name for no true Englishman would have behaved as he did.'

L. P. Hartley   *The Love Adept.*

7
THE FAMILY NAME

THERE was a time when no one had a hereditary surname. The Norman Conquest of 1066 is a convenient point at which we can note the appearance of the first family names, but the Normans certainly did not have a fully developed surname system. It was not yet their conscious policy to identify a family by one name, but the idea was soon to occur to them. There is every sign that it would also have occurred spontaneously to the people they conquered, but the Norman example no doubt helped speed things along.

Before we turn to modern surnames, let us look at the situation that existed before the 11th century. Our remote ancestors had single *personal names* which were quite enough to distinguish them in the small communities in which they lived. Personal names were either well-established name elements, or permutations of such elements. These in turn usually referred to abstract qualities such as 'nobility' and 'fame'. A new single-element name, or a new permutation, was given to every child, so that everyone in the community had a truly personal name. Natural duplication must have caused the same name to come into being simultaneously in different communities, but names were not deliberately re-used.

Some of the Anglo-Saxon personal names later made the change to become first names such as **Alfred, Audrey, Cuthbert, Edgar, Edmund, Edward, Harold** and **Oswald.** Many more of them survived long enough to form the basis of modern surnames. **Allwright,** for example, was once a personal name

---

I started schooling and was taught to write my name 'Chaplin'. The word fascinated me and looked like me, I thought.

Charles Chaplin   *My Autobiography*

---

composed of *aethel* and *ric,* or 'noble' and 'ruler'. **Darwin** was *deor wine,* 'dear friend', and **Wyman** was *wig mund,* 'war protection'.

Scandinavian names

When the Danes and later the Norwegians invaded England and settled in large numbers, they naturally took their own names with them. Still more important, they retained their own ideas about naming. The Scandinavian personal names sometimes resembled those of the Anglo-Saxons, so that both Old Norse *Harivald* and Old English *Hereweald* could lead to **Harold,** while similar pairs led to **Oswald** and **Randolph.** Many truly Scandinavian names survive today in surnames.

But it was the Scandinavian method of naming, rather than the names themselves, that eventually had the biggest effect on the English naming system. Among the Anglo-Saxons, personal names that had been made famous by distinguished ancestors had always been honoured by *not* using them for descendants. The Scandinavians, however, readily duplicated their personal names in different generations of the same family. It was also their common practice to name a son after a famous chief or a personal friend. They believed, as Sir Frank Stenton has explained, that 'the soul of an individual was represented or symbolised by his name, and that the bestowal of a name was a means of calling up the spirit of the man who had borne it into the spirit of the child to whom it was given'.

The natural result of consciously re-using the same personal names, apart from creating a far smaller central stock of names, was to make those names far less effective as identifiers of individuals. When exact identification was particularly necessary it became essential to add a second name which gave extra information about the person concerned. This did not lead to the immediate creation of surnames, but it was certainly a step in that direction.

Bynames

The new second names that came into existence at this period, at first among the Scandinavian settlers, were temporary surnames, similar to nicknames in many ways. It is useful to distinguish them as a historical phenomenon, however, from surnames or nicknames as we know them today. For this purpose they have often been referred to as 'bynames'. Bynames were meant to be added to someone's personal name to help identification, but sometimes they simply replaced it completely. As substitute personal names they were probably not always to their bearers' liking. Many men must have begun life with flattering traditional names, only to become at a later date **Drunkard, Clod, Idler, Short Leg, Shameless, Squinter, Clumsy** or **Miser**. These are all direct translations of names which occur in medieval records. When these bynames were common enough to be used frequently they sometimes became true surnames at a later date. Of those mentioned above, for instance, the first three subsequently became family names, though their meanings would fortunately not now be recognised. In a modern directory they might appear as **Gipp, Clack** and **Sling**.

The need for a supplementary name, then, had made itself felt in England before the Normans arrived, but the Normans, even more than the Scandinavians, believed in using the same personal names over and over again. They also needed second names to identify them properly, especially in legal documents. In the Domesday Book of 1086 almost all the Norman landowners have such names. An earlier version of this survey also gives bynames for many of the former English land-owners, and those Englishmen who managed to retain their lands under the new régime also have them. The Norman bynames were frequently the names of the villages from which they came or were the personal names of their fathers, but some described occupations and others personal characteristics. Many of the elements of modern surnames were thus present.

A major difference between bynames and surnames is that the former were not passed on from one generation to the next. They were meaningful names that were meant to apply to the individuals who bore them. The retention of a particular name as a family identifier may have been deliberate, but it could just as easily have happened accidentally at first. One way in which it could occur, for instance, was by the inheritance of property. If the father was known as 'of' followed by the name of his estate, the eldest son might logically take over both the estate and the name.

However it began, one can imagine how this passing of a name from one generation to the next was noted as an aspect of aristocratic behaviour—for it would certainly have begun at baronial level—and duly imitated.

> *'I wish, my dear, you would cultivate your acquaintance with Towneley, and ask him to pay us a visit. The name has an aristocratic sound.'*
>
> Samuel Butler   *The Way of all Flesh*

The officials who dealt with wills and the like must also have found what soon became a fashion of great convenience to them, and no doubt they encouraged the habit. Slowly bynames were turned into hereditary family names, a process which spread downwards through society until even the humblest person had one. It was to be 300 years, however, before that happened. At the end of that period, the concept of the single personal name had gone for ever. Bynames introduced a great many place names into the personal name system, but transfer of names between people and places had always seemed natural. This type of byname was probably readily

> *'Gabriel what?'*
>
> *'Oh, Lord kens that; we dinna mind folk's after-names muckle here, they run sae muckle into clans. The folks hereabout are a' Armstrongs and Elliots, and so the lairds and farmers have the names of the places that they live at . . . and then the inferior sort o' people, ye'll observe, are kend by sorts o' bynames, as Glaiket Christie, and the Deuke's Davie, or Tod Gabbie, or Hunter Gabbie.'*
>
> Sir Walter Scott   *Guy Mannering*

accepted, as were the patronymic link names. The latter simply described someone as '**John**'s son' or '**William**'s son', so that the new names contained an obvious personal name element. It was the descriptive names that must have had a harder time of it. One would expect it to take longer for phrases like 'the carpenter' or 'the short one' to convert to the names **Carpenter** and **Short**. Where some activity names were concerned, two factors would help the process. One of these would be the following of the same occupation by a succession of fathers and sons, thus enabling the same byname to remain in a family for a long period and appear to be a hereditary name.

A second factor that would have helped this group would be natural duplication. During the period we are considering, which is between 1066 and 1400, each community had its important and easily recognisable craftsmen, tradesmen, officials and other workers. It would have been natural for every village to have someone who was a smith, another who was a baker, and so on. All these medieval occupations are seen in modern surnames as we see on pages 130–31. We must not forget, however, that with each of these names there had to come a point when their status as names was finally accepted. When it was considered quite usual for a **John Carpenter** to be a baker or follow some other trade, 'carpenter' had in one sense lost its meaning. It had acquired, however, a new kind of referential meaning and had passed through the byname stage to become a surname.

Patronyms also had to get by this hurdle, though with names of the John **Andrews** type it is very easy to see how new generations could inherit it, with those around them slightly adjusting its meaning. At first they would have said to themselves that he was the son of **Andrew**, later, that he was the grandson, later still, that he was a descendant of someone called Andrew. Eventually this type of name, like the others, would no longer be interpreted at all in a literal sense, but as showing a connection with the Andrews family.

Locative bynames were easily inherited, too. A family that lived by the village green, on the hill, near the ford, or wherever, was likely to remain there for several generations. As for place names, when these indicated provenance rather than inherited property one can see how they were passed on. Even today a village community will remember for several generations that a family came from some other place.

But if one can understand how a great many bynames of different types developed into heredi-tary surnames, those which described an individual's physical or moral attributes are surprising. A father may rightly have been described as a drunk-ard, but surely this was not a suitable name for his descendants? Such names may have been another kind of patronymic to begin with, indicating 'son of the drunkard'. If they were bestowed as bynames late in the 14th century, by which time the majority of people had surnames, they may have been mistaken for surnames. Nevertheless, one would expect this kind of name to have survived less frequently as a surname and all the evidence points quite clearly to this being the case. The early bearers of such surnames must have occupied a very lowly social position and had no say in the matter. Later descendants who have been of higher standing have frequently rid themselves of such embarrassing family reminders.

We shall never know the exact details of how bynames became surnames, but from the beginning of the 15th century nearly all English people inherited a surname at birth and the word 'surname' was used with the meaning we give it today. It had been borrowed from the French *surnom*, deriving in turn from Latin *super-* or *supra-nomen*, and was used at first to mean simply 'an extra name', 'a nickname'. Modern French retains that meaning and translates 'surname' as *nom de famille*.

Spelling and pronunciation

Most of our surnames have, therefore, been in the family for 500 years or more, but that is not to say that the one name among many by which our ancestors finally came to be known is exactly the same as the name we bear today. The names came into existence, but they had no fixed forms. Our ancestors—and this probably includes any who were of the upper classes—were for centuries mostly illiterate. Their names were occasionally recorded by a parson or clerk when there was a birth, marriage or death in the family, and he wrote down what he heard using his own ideas about the spelling. He was obliged to do this, for though the spelling of ordinary words very slowly became standardised after the 15th century, there were no agreed forms for names. It was the printed books which helped to fix the words, but only a tiny proportion of names ever appeared in print.

The same name could be written down in many

Mr P. S. Clark of Sutton Coldfield writes to point out that he probably has a uniquely chemical name. It appears in correct sequence in the Periodic Table, where Elements with the atomic numbers 15–19 inclusive are respectively P (phosphorus), S (sulphur), Cl (chlorine), Ar (argon) and K (potassium).

different ways by different clerks, and even, as the parish registers clearly show, by the same clerk at different times. A further complication was provided by regional dialects. A sound which in the personal name period could be represented by 'y', for example, became 'i' in the North and East Midlands, 'e' in the South East and 'u' in the Central Midlands and other southern counties. These changes had occurred by the beginning of the surname period.

The influence of the French officials who later came to write down English names has also been felt in our surnames. They, too, spoke different dialects and had varying orthographic systems. All in all it is hardly surprising that what was once the same name can appear in a wide variety of modern forms. We normally refer to Sir Walter **Raleigh,** for instance, but **Rawley** probably captured the name's pronunciation more accurately. Other forms include **Ralegh, Raughley, Rauly, Rawleigh, Rawleleygh** and **Rayley.**

Almost every modern surname has its variant forms. Even the short man we referred to earlier whose byname lived on as a surname has become **Shortt** in some instances, acquiring a superfluous letter somewhere along the line. As a word this would long ago have been regularised; as a name it now remains fossilised in the form it accidentally took on.

Many names have acquired extra letters, but we should note that the initial 'ff' preserved by some families is rather different. This was a medieval scribal alternative for an 'F' and should always be written, therefore, as two small letters. P. G. Wodehouse, in *A Slice of Life,* made marvellous fun of such names:

'Sir Jasper Finch-Farrowmere?' said Wilfred.

'ffinch-ffarrowmere,' corrected the visitor, his sensitive ear detecting the capital letters.

In some cases the spelling of a name has remained artificially fixed while its pronunciation has changed. One finds the same lack of relationship between spelling and pronunciation in many place names. Well-known surname examples include **Cholmondeley,** 'Chumley', **Mainwaring,** 'Mannering', **Marjoribanks,** 'Marchbanks', **Beauchamp,** 'Beecham', **Featherstonehaugh,** 'Fanshaw'. With these names as with many others the pronunciation normally used by one family may differ from that preferred by another.

Irish names

As in England, bynames preceded surnames in Ireland. The earliest kind mentioned the name of the father, preceded by 'Mac', or that of a grandfather or earlier ancestor, in which case 'O' preceded the name. Later, names were formed by adding these prefixes to the father's byname, which could be of any of the kinds seen in England. The 'Mac' (or 'Mc', which means exactly the same) and 'O' prefixes were dropped during the period of English rule, but the 'O' especially has now been resumed by many families.

Other influences on Irish surnames include translation from Gaelic to English, abbreviation and absorption of rare names into common ones. By translation, which in many cases was demanded by the English authorities, families such as the **McGowan**s correctly became **Smith**s, but many mistranslations were made.

The Norman invasion of Ireland in the 12th century naturally carried many of their personal

---

'There's some devilish queer names, like that army doctor in the war that was called Major Marchbanks although to read it you would have said it was Marjory Banks.'

'A very queer name altogether, that,' Tom agreed. 'Major Marjory Banks, as if it was a lassie that was in it.'

Compton Mackenzie *Whisky Galore*

names and bynames there. Some of these, in the form of surnames such as **Burke**, **Cruise** and **Dillon**, are now thought of as essentially Irish, and with good reason. Later English settlement in Ireland also caused many English surnames to become well established.

Scottish names

In the Scottish Lowlands surnames developed along the same lines as in England, though at a slightly later date. In the Highlands the development of hereditary surnames was held back by the clan system. Many families voluntarily allied themselves to a powerful clan or were forced to do so, and in either case they assumed the clan name as their new surname.

The power of the clan names in their day is seen in the action taken by James VI against the **McGregor**s. By an Act of Council he proscribed and abolished the name altogether, because 'the bare and simple name of McGregor made that whole clan to presume of their power, force and strength, and did encourage them, without reverence of the law or fear of punishment, to go forward in their iniquities'. The proscription against the name was not finally removed until 1774.

Gaelic names from the Highlands began to spread south in the 18th century, and later throughout the English-speaking world. Mrs Cecily Dynes, who keeps records of the names used by parents in New South Wales, noted in 1972 'a sudden upsurge of "Mac" or "Mc" middle names'. Other typically Highland names, such as **Cameron,** are already being used as first names.

Welsh names

The many Welshmen who came into England in the byname period were treated like Englishmen as far as their names were concerned. A few Welsh personal names, such as **Morgan, Owen, Meredith**, thus became established as surnames centuries before hereditary surnames were normal in Wales itself. The usual custom there was for a man to be something like **Madog Ap Gryffyd Ap Jorweth**, with 'ap' meaning 'son of'. As late as 1853 the Registrar-General was able to say—using expressions that no one would dare use today—that 'among the lower classes in the wilder districts . . . the Christian name of the father still frequently becomes the patronymic of the son'.

Traces of the 'ap' system survive in names like **Price**, formerly **Ap Rhys**, and many of the original Welsh personal names have managed to live on, but the well-known preponderance in modern Wales of names like **Jones, Davies, Williams, Thomas, James, Phillips, Edwards, Roberts, Richards** and **Hughes** show all too clearly that the **John, David** and **William** type of first name became thoroughly established there. When formal surnames were eventually used, the traditional method of naming after the father was remembered but it was the new names that formed their base.

'My name is not spoken. More than a hundred years it has not gone upon men's tongues, save for a blink. I am nameless like the Folk of Peace. Catriona Drummond is the one I use.'

Now indeed I knew where I was standing. In all broad Scotland there was but the one name proscribed, and that was the name of the McGregors.

R. L. Stevenson   *Catriona*

'Ay, Macintosh is my name,' said the traveller . . .

Mr Brown felt inclined to say that it was a very good name to have on such a morning (it was pouring with rain), but having heard that the Celts lacked humour he decided to refrain.

Compton Mackenzie   *Whisky Galore*

'Tickler is a rather unusual name,' he said.

I made what has necessarily become a set speech.

'It's an Americanization of Tichelar,' I said, spelling it out. 'Tichel is the Dutch word for brick, tichelaar for tile-worker or bricklayer. . . . I might as well have been sea-changed into Jimmy Bricklayer—or James Mason—as Jimmy Tickler, which is simply a phonetic spelling of the way the name has always been pronounced here in this country anyway.'

Peter de Vries   *The Glory of the Hummingbird*

Other American family names

British surnames, as we have seen, are not without their complications. When those surnames have been taken to other countries and mixed with surnames from all over the world, the situation becomes almost impossible to cope with. A glance at a list of common surnames in America, for instance, shows that there are as many **Jorgensens** as **Cliffords**, as many people called **Lombardo** as **Dickens**. It is not that these common names cause difficulty, for a 'son of **George**' is not particularly difficult to recognise even in his Danish disguise, and a 'man from Lombardy' is not concealed by that final '-o', but for every common name there are a dozen unusual ones brought from the same country.

Elsdon C. Smith has made a heroic attempt to cope with the difficulties in his *American Surnames* and other works, in all of which he has collated information from a vast range of sources. His work has an added interest in that it compares surname development and types of modern surname in many countries. Not unnaturally he expands on **Smith**, which has its equivalent in many countries. Apart from the German **Schmidt** and French **Lefevre**, Gaelic **Gowan** and Latin **Faber**, it occurs as the Syrian **Haddad**, Finnish **Seppanen**, Hungarian **Kovacs**, Russian **Kuznetsov**, Ukrainian **Kowalsky**, Lithuanian **Kalvaitis**, and so on. One can see why Mark Lower, a highly entertaining writer on names in the 19th century, suggested that there should be a science called *Smithology* to deal properly with all aspects of this family name.

Many surnames in America have retained the form they had in other countries, but others were consciously adapted by immigrants so that English-speakers would find them easier to spell and pro-

In Spain, a married woman keeps her maiden name, but tacks on her husband's after a 'de'. Thus, on marrying Wifredo Las Rocas, our Majorcan friend Rosa, born an Espinosa, became Rosa Espinosa de Las Rocas—a very happy combination. It means 'Lady Thorny Rose from the Rocks'. Rosa was luckier than her maternal cousin Dolores Fuertes, who thoughtlessly married a lawyer named Tomás Barriga, and is now Dolores Fuertes de Barriga, or 'Violent Pains of the Stomach'.

Robert Graves   *A Toast to Ava Gardner*

nounce. The Dutch name **Van Rosevelt**, 'of the rose field', became **Roosevelt**; German **Huber**, 'tenant of a hide of land', became **Hoover**, while German **Roggenfelder**, 'rye field', became **Rockefeller**. The Finnish name **Kirkkomäki** was changed to **Churchill**.

Some such names, according to Elsdon C. Smith, have become particularly American 'because their bearers made such significant contributions to American life and history'. His full list of distinguished names is as follows: **Audubon, Barnum, Baruch, Carnegie, Edison, Eisenhower, Emerson, Franklin, Hancock, Hawthorne, Jefferson, Knickerbocker, La Fayette, Lincoln, Longfellow, McCormick, Penn, Pershing, Pullman, Rockefeller, Roosevelt, Thoreau, Wanamaker** and **Washington**. By origin, these names derive from many different national sources, but as Smith says, who can doubt that they are truly American?

Family names that link with first names

The following surnames mostly began by meaning 'son of' (later 'descendant of') or 'employee of' the person named.

Adam Adams, Adamson, Adcock, Addison, Addy, Adkins, Aitken, Aitkins, Atkin, Atkins, Atkinson.

Agatha Aggass, Tag.

Agnes Annis, Annison, Anson.

Alan Alcock, Allan, Allanson, Allen, Alleyn, Allinson.

Alexander Sanders, Sanderson, Saunders, Saunderson.

Amice Ames, Amies, Amis, Amison, Aymes.

Andrew Anderson, Andrews, Dandy.

Augustine Austen, Austin.

Bartholomew Bartle, Bartlet(t), Bate, Bateman, Bates, Bateson, Batkin, Batt, Batten, Batty, Tolley.

Beatrice Beaton, Beatty, Beet, Beeton.

Benedict Benn, Bennett, Benson.

Cassandra Case, Cash, Cass, Casson.

Cecily Sisley, Sisson.

Christian Christie, Christison, Christy.

Christopher Kitson, Kitt, Kitts.

Clement Clements, Clementson, Clemms, Clempson, Clemson.

Constance Cuss, Cussans, Cust, Custance.

Daniel Daniels, Dannet, Dannson.

David Dakins, Davidge, Davidson, Davies, Davis, Davison, Davitt, Dawe, Dawes, Dawkins, Dawson, Day, Dowson.

Denis Dennett, Dennis(s), Dennison, Denny, Dyson, Tennyson.

Donald Donald, Donaldson.

Durand Durant, Durrance, Durrant.

Edith Eade, Eady, Eddis, Eddison, Edis, Edison.

Edmund Edmond, Edmonds, Edmondson, Edmons, Edmund, Edmunds.

Edward Edwardes, Edwards.

Eleanor Ellen, Ellinor, Elson.

Elias Eliot, Elliot(t), Ellis, Ellison.

Elizabeth Bethell.

Emery Amery, Emerson.

Emma Emmett, Empson.

Evan Evans, Bevan, Bevin.

Geoffrey Jeeves, Jefferies, Jefferson, Jeffrey, Jephson, Jepp, Jepson.

Gerald Garrard, Garratt, Garrett, Garrod, Gerard, Jarrett, Jerrold.

Gervais Gervas, Gervis, Jarvie, Jarvis.

Gilbert Gibb, Gibbin, Gibbons, Gibbs, Gibson, Gilbart, Gilbertson, Gilbey, Gilpin, Gilson, Gipps.

Gregory Greer, Gregson, Greig, Grierson, Grigg, Grigson.

Hamo Hamblin, Hamlet, Hamley, Hamlyn, Hammett, Hammond, Hamnet, Hampson, Hamson.

Harvey Harvie, Hervey.

Henry Harriman, Harris, Harrison, Hawke, Hawkins, Henderson, Hendry, Henryson, Heriot, Parry, Perry.

Herman Armand, Arment, Harman, Harmon.

Howel Howell, Poel, Powell.

Hubert Hobart, Hubbard.

Hugh Hewes, Hewett, Hewitson, Hewlet, Hewson, Howkins, Howson, Hudson, Huggett, Huggins, Hughes, Hullett, Hullis, Hutchings, Hutchins, Hutchinson, Pugh.

Humphrey Boumphrey, Humphreys, Humphries, Pumphrey.

Isabel Bibby, Ibbotson, Ibson, Libby, Nibbs, Nibson, Tibbs.

Jacob Jacobs, Jacobson.

James Gemson, Gimson, Jamieson, Jimpson.

John Hancock, Hankin, Hanson, Jackson, Jaggs, Jenkins, Jennings, Jennison, Johns, Johnson, Jones, Littlejohn.

Juliana Gill, Gillett, Gillott, Gilson, Jewett, Jolyan, Jowett, Julian, Julien, Julyan.

Katharine Catlin, Caton, Cattling, Kitson.

Laurence Larkin(s), Laurie, Law, Lawrence, Lawrie, Lawson, Lowry.

Lewis Llewellyn, Louis, Lowis.

Luke Lucas, Luck, Luckett, Luckin, Lukin.

Mabel Mabbot, Mabbs, Mapp, Mappin, Mapson, Mobbs.

Magdalen Maddison, Maudling.

Margaret Maggs, Magson, Margerison, Margetson, Margretts, Meggeson, Meggs, Mogg, Moggs, Moxon, Pegson, Poggs.

Martin Martell, Martens, Martinet, Martinson.

Mary Malleson, Mallett, Marion, Marriott, Marrison, Marryat, Maryat, Mollison.

Matilda Madison, Maudson, Mault, Mawson, Mold, Mould, Moulson, Moult, Tillett, Tilley, Tillison, Tillotson.

Matthew Machin, Makins, Makinson, Matheson, Mathieson, Matson, Matterson, Matthews, Mattin, Maycock, Mayhew, Maykin.

Maurice Morcock, Morrice, Morris, Morrison, Morse, Morson.

Michael Michell, Michieson, Mitchell, Mitchelson, Mitchison.

Nicholas Cole, Collett, Colley, Collins, Collinson, Collis, Coulson, Nicholson, Nickells, Nicks, Nickson, Nicolson, Nixon.

Nigel Neal, Neilson, Nelson.

Pagan Paine, Pannel, Payne.

Patrick Paterson, Paton, Patterson, Pattinson, Pattison.

Peter Parkin, Parkinson, Parks, Parr, Parrot, Pears, Pearse, Pearson, Perkins, Perrin, Perrot, Person, Peters, Peterson, Pierce.

Petronella Parnell, Purnell.

Philip Filkins, Phelps, Phillips, Phillipson, Philpot, Phipps, Potts.

Ralph Rawkins, Rawle, Rawlings, Rawlins, Rawlinson, Rawlison, Rawson.

Randal Randall, Randolph, Rand(s), Rankin, Ransome.

Reynald Rennell, Rennie, Rennison, Reynolds, Reynoldson.

Rhys Rice, Reece, Price, Preece.

Richard Dickens, Dickinson, Dickson, Dix, Dixon, Hickie, Hicks, Hickson, Higgins, Higgs, Hitchens, Prickett, Pritchard, Pritchett, Richards, Richardson, Ricketts, Rix.

Robert Dabbs, Dobbie, Dobbs, Dobie, Dobson, Hobart, Hobbs, Hobson, Hopkins, Hopkinson, Nobbs, Probert, Probyn, Robbie, Robbins, Robens, Roberts, Robertson, Robey, Robinson, Robson.

Roger Dodd, Dodge, Dodgson, Dodson, Hodges, Hodgkinson, Hodgkiss, Hodgson, Hodson, Hotchkiss, Rogers, Rogerson.

Simon Simms, Simmonds, Simpkins, Simpson, Sims, Symonds.

Stephen Stenson, Stephens, Stephenson, Stevens, Stevenson.

Thomas Tamblin, Tamlin, Tampling, Thomason, Thompson, Tombs, Tomlinson, Tompkins, Tomsett, Tonkins, Tonks.

Walter Walters, Waterson, Watkins, Watkinson, Watson, Watts.

William Gilham, Gillam, Gilliam, Mott, Wilcock, Wilcox, Wilkie, Wilkins, Wilkinson, Williams, Williamson, Willis, Wills, Wilson.

Family names from Old English personal names

Some Old English personal names have survived as surnames. The meaning of these names is rather special. *Edrich*, for example, contained the elements *ead* and *ric*, the first meaning something like 'prosperity' or 'happiness', the second indicating 'power' or 'rule'. This is not to say that the name therefore means 'prosperous rule'. It may well have come about because the mother's name contained *ead* (in a name like *Edith*) and the father's name *ric* (in a name like *Kenrick*). Such names must often have been blended simply in order to show parentage. This accounts for the names where the elements seem to contradict each other. In their modern forms, many elements have more than one possible origin. *Al-* and *El-* could derive from 'elf' or 'noble', for instance. Alternative possibilities are indicated below.

Adlard noble—hard.
Alflatt elf/noble—beauty.
Allnatt noble—daring.
Alvar elf—army.
Alwin noble/old/elf—friend.
Averay elf—counsel.
Aylmer noble—famous.
Aylwin noble—friend.
Badrick battle—famous
Baldey bold—combat.
Balman bold—man.
Balston bold—stone.
Bedloe command—love.
Brightmore fair—famous.
Brunger brown—spear.
Brunwin brown—friend.
Burchard fortress—hard.
Burrage fortress—powerful.
Burward fortress—guard.
Cobbald famous—bold.
Cutteridge famous—ruler.
Darwin dear—friend.
Eastman grace—protection.
Eddols prosperity—wolf.
Eddy prosperity—war.
Ellwood elf—ruler.
Elphee elf—war.

Elsegood temple—god.
Elsey elf—victory.
Elvey elf—war.
Erwin boar—friend.
Frewin free—friend.
Frewer free—shelter.
Gladwin glad—friend.
Godwin good—friend.
Goldbard gold—bright/beard.
Goldburg gold—fortress.
Goldhawk gold—hawk.
Goldwin gold—friend.
Goodliffe good/God—dear.
Goodrich good/God—ruler.
Goodwin good—friend.
Gummer good/battle—famous.
Hulbert gracious—bright.
Kenward bold/royal—guardian.
Kenway bold/royal—war.
Kerrich family—ruler.
Lambrick land—bright.
Leavey beloved—warrior.
Leavold beloved—power/ruler.
Lemmer people/dear—famous.
Lewin beloved—friend.
Lilleyman little—man.
Litwin bright—friend.

Lovegod beloved—god.
Loveguard beloved—spear.
Milborrow mild—fortress.
Ordway spear—warrior.
Orrick spear—powerful.
Osmer god—fame.
Oswin god—friend.
Outridge dawn—powerful.
Quenell woman—war.
Redway counsel—warrior.
Seavers sea—passage.
Siggers victory—spear.
Stidolph hard—wolf.
Trumble strong—bold.
Wennell joy—war.
Whatman brave—man.
Whittard elf—brave.
Wilmer will—famous.
Winbolt friend—bold.
Winbow friend—bold.
Winmer friend—famous.
Winney joy—battle.
Woolgar wolf—spear.
Wyman war—protection.
Yonwin young—friend.
Youngmay young—servant.

Some additional American family names

Alvarez son of **Alvaro** 'the prudent one'.

Bauer farmer.

Berg dweller on or near a hill or mountain.

Berger shepherd.

Brandt farmer on land cleared by burning.

Camero dweller in or worker at a hall.

Carlson son of *Carl*.

Carson dweller near a marsh.

Castillo dweller near a castle, or a castle servant.

Castro see *Castillo*.

Chavez descendant of **Jaime**, or *James*.

Christensen descendant of *Christian*.

Cohen the priest.

Cruz dweller near a cross.

Diaz descendant of **Diego**, or *Jacob*.

Fernandez descendant of **Fernando**, 'the adventurer'.

Figueroa maker of statuettes.

Fischer fisherman or fish-trader.

Flores dweller in flowery place.

Friedman descendant of the peaceful man.

Garcia descendant of Garcia, or *Gerald*.

Garza dweller at the sign of the heron or dove.

Goldberg family from Goldberg 'gold mountain', name of various places in Germany.

Goldstein descendant of a goldsmith.

Gomez descendant of **Gomo**, or **Gomesano**.

Gonzales descendant of **Gonzalo** 'battle', name of an early saint.

Gora dweller on, or near, a hill or mountain.

Gross descendant of the large or fat man.

Gutierrez descendant of Gutierre, or Walter.

Haas dweller at the sign of the hare, or one who could run as swiftly as the hare.

Hahn dweller at the sign of the cock, or one who had the characteristics of the cock.

Hansen descendant of Hans, or *John*.

Hanson see *Hansen*.

Hartman descendant of the strong man.

Herman descendant of Herman 'army man'.

Hernandez descendant of **Hernando** 'the adventurer'.

Hess(e) family from Hesse 'hooded people' in Germany.

Hoffman farmer or farm-worker.

Hoover tenant of a hide of land, about 120 acres.

Jensen descendant of Jen, or *John*.

Katz descendant of a priest.

Kaufman descendant of a merchant or tradesman.

Keller worker in a wine-cellar.

Klein descendant of the small man.

Kline see *Klein*.

Koch descendant of a cook.

Kramer descendant of an itinerant tradesman.

Krause descendant of the curly-headed man.

Kruger descendant of an inn-keeper.

Lang descendant of the tall man.

Larsen son of Lars, or *Laurence*.

Larson see *Larsen*.

Levine descendant of the wine-dealer.

Levy descendant of **Levi** 'united'.

Lopez descendant of **Lope** or **Lupe** 'the wolf-like man'.

Maldonado descendant of *Donald*.

Mann descendant of a servant.

Marks dweller near the mark or boundary, or descendant of Mark, or family from Marck in France.

Martinez descendant of *Martin*.

Mayer descendant of the head-servant or farmer.

Medina dweller near the market, or worker in a market.

Meyer see Mayer.

Morales descendant of Moral, or family from Morales 'mulberry tree', the name of two places in Spain.

Moreno descendant of the dark-complexioned man.

Mueller descendant of a miller.

Mullen descendant of Maolan 'bald man'.

Myers see *Mayer*.

Nielsen descendant of *Niel* 'champion'.

Novak descendant of the stranger or newcomer.

Olsen descendant of Olaf 'ancestor'.

Olson see *Olsen*.

Ortiz descendant of Ordono 'fortunate one'.

Perez descendant of Pedro, or *Peter*.

Ramirez descendant of **Ramon** 'wise protector'.

Ramos descendant of Ramos 'palms'.

Reyes descendant of one of the king's household, or family from Reyes, name of places in Spain.

Rivera dweller near a brook or river.

Rodriguez descendant of **Rodrigo**, or *Roderick*.

Romero descendant of a pilgrim to Rome.

Rosenberg family from Rosenberg 'rose mountain', name of several places in Germany.

Ruiz descendant of **Ruy**, or *Rodrigo* (Roderick).

Sanchez descendant of **Sancho** 'sanctified'.

Santiago family from Santiago 'St James' in Spain.

Schaefer descendant of a shepherd.

Schneider descendant of the tailor or cutter.

Schoen descendant of the beautiful or handsome person.

Schroeder descendant of the tailor.

Schultz descendant of the magistrate or sheriff or steward.

Schwartz descendant of the swarthy man.

Silva dweller in or near a wood.

Snyder see *Schneider*.

Stein dweller near a significant stone or rock.

Torres dweller at or near a tower or spire.

Vandermeer dweller at or near a lake.

Vazquez a Basque family or descendant of a shepherd.

Wagner descendant of a wagon-driver or wagon-maker.

Weber descendant of a cloth weaver.

Weiss descendant of a man with white hair or skin.

Werner descendant of Werner 'protection-army'.

Zimmerman descendant of a carpenter.

Some Celtic names

The surnames of Scotland, Wales, Ireland, Cornwall and the Isle of Man have distinct characteristics, deriving as they do from Celtic languages such as Gaelic and old Welsh. Separate dictionaries exist which deal with them in detail (see the Bibliography). Some examples of common and well-known names are given below.

Agnew 'action'.
Aherne 'steed lord'.
Bane 'white'.
Bardon 'bard'.
Begley 'little hero'.
Behan 'bee'.
Berryman 'man from St Buryan'.
Bevan son of Evan (*John*).
Bosanquet 'dwelling of Angawd', a Cornish place name.
Boyd 'yellow-haired'.
Boyle 'pledge'.
Brennan 'sorrow/raven'.
Bruce from a Norman place name.
Burke probably from Burgh, a place name.
Burns 'dweller by the stream'.
Cameron 'crooked nose'.
Campbell 'crooked mouth'.
Cardew 'dark fort'.
Carrick 'rock mass'.
Craig 'dweller by rocks'.
Cunningham from Scottish place name, or descendant of Con (Ireland).
Daly 'assembly'.
Docherty 'the stern one'.
Douglas from the place name, 'dark stream'.
Doyle 'dark stranger'.
Duncan 'brown warrior'.
Dyer 'thatcher' (Cornwall).
Farrell 'man of valour'.
Ferguson son of 'man choice'.
Findlay 'fair hero'.
Forbes from the place name, 'field'.
Freethy 'eager, alert'.
Furphy 'perfect'.
Galbraith 'British stranger'.
Gale 'stranger'.
Gallacher 'foreign help'.
Gough 'red-faced or red-haired'.
Guinness son of *Angus*, 'one choice'.
Hamilton from place name.
Innes 'dweller on an island'.

Jago son of *James*.
Jory son of *George*.
Kelly son of Ceallach 'war'.
Kennedy 'ugly head'.
Kermode son of Diarmaid, 'freeman'.
Kerr 'dweller by the marsh'.
Lloyd 'grey'.
McFarlane son of *Bartholomew*.
McGregor son of Gregory, 'to be watchful'.
McIntosh son of the 'chieftain'.
McIntyre son of the 'carpenter'.
McKay son of Aodh, 'fire'.
McKenzie son of Coinneach, 'fair one'.
McLean son of the devotee of St John.
McLeod son of Ljotr, 'the ugly one'.
McMillan son of Mhaolain, 'the tonsured man', a religious servant.
McPherson son of the 'parson'.
Mundy 'dweller in the mine house' (Cornwall).
Munro from a place name, 'mouth of the River Roe'.
Murphy descendant of the 'sea warrior'.
Murray from the place name, 'sea settlement'.
Nance 'dweller in the valley'.
Negus 'dweller by the nut grove'.
Nolan descendant of the 'noble one'.
O'Brien descendant of Brian, from King Brian Boru.
O'Byrne descendant of the 'bear' or 'raven'.
O'Connor descendant of Connor, 'high will'.
O'Neill descendant of the 'champion'.
Opie descendant of **Osbert**.
O'Reilly descendant of the 'prosperous or valiant one'.
Pascoe 'Easter child'.

Pengelly 'dweller by the top of the copse'.
Penrose 'dweller at the top of the heath'.
Quiggin son of Uige, 'skill'.
Quirk son of Corc, 'heart'.
Rafferty 'prosperity wielder'.
Rafter 'decree'.
Ratigan 'decree'.
Reagh 'grey'.
Reavey 'grey'.
Reilly 'prosperity'.
Renehan 'sharp pointed'.
Ring 'spear'.
Ritchie son of *Richard*.
Ross from the place name.
Ryan descendant of Rian.
Sinclair from places called Saint-Clair in Normandy.
Stewart 'the steward'.
Sullivan part of the name means 'eye'. The other part could mean 'black', 'one', 'hawk', etc.
Sutherland from the place name, 'south land'.
Trease 'dweller in the homestead by a ford'.
Tremaine 'dweller in the stone homestead'.
Trevean 'dweller in the little homestead'.
Trevor from the place name, 'big village'.
Trewen 'dweller in the white homestead'.
Vaughan 'the little man'.
Vessy 'son of life'.
Weeney 'wealthy'.
Weir 'steward'.
Whearty 'noisy'.
Whelan 'wolf'.
Wogan 'frown'.
Wynn 'fair'.

TRACING THE ORIGIN OF A FAMILY NAME

I GIVE below the typical procedure for investigating the origin of a family name, using Dunkling as an example.

1 Is the modern spelling of the name reliable? The only way to find out is to check your family history to see how the name was recorded in earlier times. Such a check quickly revealed that before 1900 Dunkling had no final '-g'. My grandfather was illiterate, and the officials who recorded his name no doubt thought that when he said 'Dunklin' he was mispronouncing 'Dunkling'. They therefore 'corrected' the name.

2 To which language does the name belong? Again, a check into one's family history probably offers the best clue. My direct ancestors were settled in Buckinghamshire, England, by 1726. Dunklin also shows no obvious signs of being Gaelic, French, Dutch, etc. For both positive and negative reasons it is likely to be an English name.

3 Given that Dunklin represents fairly reliably the form of the name that probably became attached to the family in the surname-formation period (1066–1400), and that it is English, into which class of name does it fall? Does it

a describe an ancestor's trade or profession?

b describe his physical appearance or moral character?

c describe his relationship to another named person?

d describe where he came from?

4 The names of medieval trades were normal words, and as such were fairly well documented. Names of this kind are certainly amongst those which have been most convincingly explained and listed by scholars, and explanations can be found in either good surname dictionaries or the *Oxford English Dictionary*. A check of such reference works shows that Dunklin is not such a name.

5 English nicknames used in the Middle Ages were again normal words and have been thoroughly investigated by etymologists. A check on dictionaries shows that Dunklin could not have been a nickname.

6 Family names which link with other personal names have also been well studied. There appears to be no known personal name which could have led to Dunklin, meaning 'descendant of someone called Dunk, Dunkl or Dunklin'.

7 Family names of place name origin do in fact form the largest class, so there is every likelihood of Dunklin being a place name by origin. A check in reference works on place names for any name vaguely resembling the *sound* of Dunklin bears fruit in *The Place-Names of Worcestershire*, by A. Mawer and F. M. Stenton. The entry for Dunclent Farm, near the village of Stone, reveals that on Saxton's map of the county of Worcestershire, published in 1577, the farm-name was given as Dunklyn. Again, in Ogilby's *Itinerarium Angliae*, of 1699, it is mentioned as Dunklin. This is an indication of how pronunciation of the name had changed locally, and clear evidence that the family name Dunklin is the same as the place name Dunclent. The farm, which I visited in 1981, is a few miles from the Clent Hills. The 'dun' of the name means 'down', and the place name means 'settlement at the foot of the Clent Hills'. The family name simply means that the original Dunklins came from that place, since there appear to be no other places of a similar name in England.

8 A search for the origin of a family name should begin, then, with consultation of the main reference works (place name dictionaries as well as surname dictionaries). Research into one's own family history will always make the conclusions about the name more reliable.

Surnames that put a man in his place

A very large number of surnames originally indicated where a man lived, where he came from or where he worked. These names began as phrasal descriptions, often mentioning a specific place name. When a surname is the same as an English place name, this kind of origin is always possible. Other surnames made use of a topographical feature, such as a *Ford*, or a building, such as a *Hall*, to indicate residence or working place. The surnames below are among the most frequent of this kind.

Alston, Barton, Benton, Bolton, Burton, Carlton, Clayton, Clifton, Compton, Cotton, Dalton, Denton, Dutton, Eaton, Fenton, Hampton, Hilton, Hinton, Horton, Houston, Hutton, Melton, Milton, Morton, Newton, Norton, Pendleton, Preston, Shelton, Skelton, Stanton, Stapleton, Stratton, Sutton, Thornton, Thurston, Tipton, Walton, Washington, Winston, Worthington, Wotton.

Alford, Ashby, Bentley, Blackwell, Bradford, Bradley, Bradshaw, Brandon, Buckley, Caldwell, Churchill, Clifford, Conway, Crawford, Crosby, Davenport, Dudley, Durham, Farley, Hartley, Hastings, Hatfield, Holbrook, Holloway, Kirby, Langford, Langley, Lincoln, Mayfield, Moseley, Norwood, Oakley, Prescott, Ramsey, Rowland, Shipley, Stafford, Stanford, Stanley, Stokes, Ware,

Warren, Wells, Wesley, Westbrook, Whitaker, Willoughby, York.

Banks, Bridges, Brooks, Castle, Downs, Fields, Green, Grove, Hayes 'enclosure', **Heath, Hill, Holmes** 'island', **Holt** 'thicket', **House** 'religious house', **Knapp** 'hilltop', **Knowles** 'hilltop', **Lake, Lane, Lee** 'glade', **Meadows, Mills, Shaw** 'small wood', **Townsend, Woods, Yates** 'gate'.

Another way of assigning a man to his place was to describe his nationality. Some of the following names have more than one possible origin, but all could have indicated the nationality of the man who was so named.

Brittany
Breton, Brett, Britt, Britten, Britton.

Cornwall
Cornell, Cornish, Cornwall, Cornwallis, Cornwell

Denmark
Dence, Dench, Dennis, Denns.

England
England, English, Inglis.

Flanders
Flament, Flanders, Fleeming, Flement, Fleming, Flinders.

France
France, Frances, Francis, Frankish, French, Gascoigne, Gascoyne, Gaskain, Gaskin, Loaring, Loring, Lorraine.

Germany
Germaine, German, Germing, Jarman, Jermyn.

Ireland
Ireland, Irish.

Italy
Romain, Romayne, Rome, Room, Roome.

Netherlands
Dutch, Dutchman.

Norway
Norman, Normand (but also Norman French).

Portugal
Pettengale, Pettingale, Pettingell, Portugal, Puttergill.

Scotland
Scollan, Scotland, Scott, Scutts.

Spain
Spain, Spanier.

Wales
Walch, Wallace, Walles, Wallis, Walsh, Walsman, Welch, Wellish, Wellsman, Welsh.

Sign names

*I have heard of them which said they spake of knowledge that some in late time dwelling at the sign of the **Dolphin, Bull, Racket, Peacock**, etc., were commonly called Thomas at the Dolphin, Will at the Bull, Robin at the Racket; which names, as many other of like sort, became afterwards hereditary to their children.*

William Camden   *Remains Concerning Britain* (1605)

Surnames reflecting medieval life

The surnames given below are examples of the traditional 'occupational' group. Taken together they provide us with a wide-ranging picture of medieval life and activities.

Archer a professional archer, or perhaps a champion.

Arrowsmith responsible for making arrow-heads.

Bacchus a worker in the bakehouse.

Backer a baker.

Bacon he would have sold or prepared bacon.

Bailey a bailiff, a word that described (high) officials of several kinds.

Baker the bread-maker.

Barber he trimmed beards, cut hair, pulled out teeth and performed minor operations.

Barker he worked with bark for the leather trade.

Bayliss usually the son of a *Bailey*.

Baxter a female baker.

Bowman like *Archer*.

Brasher a brazier, brass-founder.

Brewer occasionally from a place name, but usually what it says.

Brewster a female brewer.

Butcher as now, though once a dealer in buck's (goat's) flesh.

Butler chief servant who supervised the bottles.

Campion a professional fighter, a champion.

Carpenter as now.

Carter driver, perhaps maker, of carts.

Cartwright maker and repairer of carts.

Carver a sculptor.

Castle(man) man employed at the castle.

Catchpole sheriff's official who seized poultry in lieu of debts.

Cater purveyor of goods to a large household.

Century belt-maker.

Chafer worker at a lime-kiln.

Chaffer merchant.

Chalker white-washer.

Challender seller of blankets.

Challinor as *Challender*.

Chalmers as *Chambers*.

Chamberlain once a nobleman's personal servant, but became a general factotum in an inn.

Chambers as *Chamberlain*.

Champion see *Campion*.

Chandler he made or sold candles.

Chaplin a chaplain.

Chapman at first a merchant, later a pedlar.

Chaundler as *Chandler*.

Clark(e) a minor cleric.

Coke a cook.

Collier he sold charcoal.

Cook(e) a professional cook. The extra -e acquired accidentally in such names or an attempt to disguise the name's meaning.

Cooper concerned with wooden casks, buckets, etc.

Cowper as *Cooper*.

Day often a worker in a dairy.

Draper maker and seller of woollen cloth.

Dyer a cloth-dyer. Dye was deliberately changed from die to avoid confusion.

Falconer in charge of the falcons used for hunting.

Falkner, Faulkner etc., as *Falconer*.

Farmer, the modern meaning came after the surname. He was a tax-collector before that, 'farm' once meaning 'firm or fixed payment'.

Farrar a smith or farrier.

Fearon an ironmonger or smith.

Feather a dealer in feathers.

Fisher a fisherman.

Fletcher he made and sold arrows.

Forester a gamekeeper.

Forster sometimes a cutler, scissors maker, or as *Forester*.

Fowler a hunter of wild birds.

Frobisher he polished swords, armour and the like.

Fuller he 'fulled' cloth, cleansing it.

Gardner, Gardiner, etc., a gardener.

Glover a maker and seller of gloves.

Goldsmith often a banker as well as a goldsmith.

Grave a steward.

Grieve manager of property, a bailiff.

Harper maker or player of harps.

Hayward literally a 'hedgeguard'. In charge of fences and enclosures.

Herd a herdsman.

Hooper he fitted hoops on casks and barrels.

Hunt, Hunter both 'huntsman'.

Kellogg literally 'kill hog', a slaughterer.

Kemp as *Campion*

Knight in the surname period the meaning was 'a military servant'.

Lander a launderer.

Lavender a launderer.

Leach a doctor.

Leadbeater, Leadbetter, Leadbitter, etc., worker in lead.

Leech a doctor.

Lister a dyer of cloth.

Lorimer a spur-maker.

Machin a mason, stoneworker.

Marchant a merchant.

Marshall a marshal, originally in charge of horses, rising to be a high official.

Mason a skilled stoneworker.

Mercer a dealer in silks and such-like fabrics.

Merchant a dealer, especially wholesale imports/exports.

Mills a miller.

Miller a corn-miller.

Milner as *Miller*.

Mulliner as *Miller*.

Naylor a maker and seller of nails.

Page a minor male servant.

Paget a little *Page*.

Paige as *Page*.

Parker keeper of a private park.

Parson a parson, rector.

Parsons servant or son of the *Parson*.

Pepper a dealer in pepper and other spices.

Piper a pipe-player, but may include the name *Pepper*.

Plummer a plumber, lead-worker.

Potter a maker and seller of earthenware.

Proctor a 'procurator', a steward, agent, tithe-farmer.

Redman sometimes from 'reed-man', a thatcher.

Reeve a high-ranking official, a bailiff, a steward.

Saddler a saddle-maker.

Salter a salt-worker, or seller of salt.

Sargent a domestic, legal, or military servant.

Sawyer a sawer of wood.
Shepherd, Sheppard, etc., a shepherd.
Singer a professional singer.
Skinner a preparer of skins, a tanner.
Slater a slate-layer.
Slatter as *Slater*.
Smith a metal-worker, maker of all-important weapons and implements.
Smithers son of *Smith*.
Smythe as *Smith*.
Spencer a dispenser of provisions, a steward or butler.
Spicer a seller of spices.
Spooner a spoon-maker, or roofing-shingle maker.
Squire a knight's attendant, usually a young man of good birth.
Steele a steel-worker.

Stringer a maker of strings for bows.
Tanner a tanner of hides.
Taylor a maker of clothes, though the Normans could also 'tailor' other materials, such as stone.
Thatcher 'thatch' is linked with the Roman 'toga' and means 'to cover'.
Thrower a potter.
Tiller farmer.
Tillman tile-maker or farmer.
Todd foxhunter.
Toddman officially appointed foxhunter.
Toller toll-collector.
Trainer trapper.
Tranter waggoner.
Trapp trapper.
Travers tollbridge-keeper.
Trinder wheelmaker.
Trotter messenger.

Tucker a cloth-worker.
Turner a wood-worker, but possibly a turnspit-operator, a translator, competitor in tournaments, etc.
Tyler maker and layer of tiles.
Vickers son or servant of a vicar.
Wainwright a waggon-maker and repairer.
Walker a cloth-worker, who trod cloth in order to cleanse it.
Waller sometimes a builder of walls, but other origins possible.
Ward a watchman, guard.
Weaver, Webb, Webber, Webster, all mean weaver.
Wheeler a maker of wheels.
Woodward a forester.
Wright a workman who made a variety of articles.

Some family names which are not what they seem

Allbones a form of *Alban's*.
Anguish descendant of *Angus*.
Ball descendant of *Baldwin*.
Batty descendant of *Bartholomew*.
Billion descendant of *William*.
Blackbird one with a black beard.
Blanket one with a white skin.
Body descendant of *Baldwin*.
Bone a good person.
Boosey dweller near a cow stall.
Bowell form of *ap Howell*, or *Powell*.
Brolly dweller near a wood or thicket.
Budd descendant of *Baldwin*.
Chessman seller of cheese.
Coffin a bald man.
Collie descendant of *Nicholas*.
Custard a round-headed man.
Deadman one from *Debenham*, Norfolk.
Devil French *de ville* 'of the town'.

Duck descendant of *Duke*, ie *Marmaduke*.
Eels descendant of *Elias*.
Earthy descendant of *Arthur*.
Eye dweller on an island.
Fear a proud man or a companion.
Foal a fool, jester.
Forty dweller on an island near a ford.
Fullman a foal man.
Gosling descendant of *Jocelyn*.
Gumboil descendant of *Gumbold*.
Ham dweller near a river meadow.
Handshaker one from *Handsacre*, Staffs.
Hogg descendant of *Roger*.
Hollyman a holy man.
Human servant of Hugh.
Jelly descendant of *Jilly* (*Juliana*).
Killer lime kiln worker.
Kisser maker of cuisses (armour).
Lush an usher.

Maggot descendant of Margaret.
Money one from *Monaye*, France.
Moneypenny 'many penny', a rich man.
Moody courageous man.
Pate descendant of *Patrick*.
Quail = *MacPhail*, son of Paul.
Salmon descendant of *Solomon*.
Shufflebottom dweller in a sheep valley.
Smellie dweller near a small enclosure.
Smoker maker of smocks.
Spittle worker at a hospital.
Swindle one from *Swindale*.
Tombs servant of *Tom*.
Tortoiseshell man from *Tattershall*.
Trollope a strolling man.
Whisky dweller near the river *Whiske*.
Woof descendant of *Wulf*.

Immigrants who spoke no English were often renamed by officials at Ellis Island. One bewildered man, who had been made to understand that henceforth he would be known by a new 'American' name, was asked by another official what it was. *'Schon vergessen,'* he said apologetically—('already forgotten'). He was duly registered as Sean Ferguson.

Some descriptive surnames

Arlott young fellow, rogue.
Armstrong as *Strongitharm*.
Ballard a bald man.
Bass a short man.
Bassett diminutive of *Bass*.
Beard a man who was bearded when beards were not fashionable.
Belcher a man who belched or had a 'pretty face'.
Bell (sometimes) the handsome man.
Bellamy handsome friend.
Best a man who was beast-like.
Biggs son of a big man.
Black with black hair, or darkish skin.
Blackbird with a black beard.
Blake usually as *Black*.
Blundell a blond man.
Blunt as *Blundell*.
Bossey a hunch-backed man.
Bragg a brisk man, or a proud one.
Brennan (English) a man whose job was to 'burn the hand' of a criminal, or a man whose hand was branded.
Brent (sometimes) a branded man.
Brown with brown hair.
Burnett with dark brown hair, or wearer/seller of cloth of that colour. Other meanings are also possible.
Carless free from care.
Cave (usually) a bald man.
Crippen with curly hair.
Cripps as *Crippen*. Also **Crisp** and **Crispin**.
Cronk a vigorous man.
Cruikshank with crooked legs.
Crump crooked, stooping.
Cuckow a cuckoo-like person, silly.
Curtis courteous/educated, or a wearer of short hose.

Doggett 'dog head'.
Dunn a swarthy man.
Dwelly a foolish man.
Fairchild a handsome young man.
Fairfax with beautiful hair.
Fortescue a strong shield.
Fry(e) free, generous.
Gay a cheerful man.
Giddy a madman.
Goodfellow a good companion, a **Goodman**.
Goolden with yellow hair.
Grant a tall man.
Gray or **Grey**, a grey-haired man.
Gulliver a glutton.
Hardy a tough man, courageous.
Hendy a courteous man.
Hoare a grey-haired man.
Jolliffe as **Jolly**, a cheerful man.
Keen a brave man.
Lang a tall man.
Lemon a lover.
Long a tall man.
Lovelace (sometimes) a man who loved the lasses.
Mallory an unlucky or unfortunate man.
Moody a bold man.
Moore (sometimes) swarthy as a Moor.
Noble of noble character.
Parfitt a man who was **Perfect**.
Pettit a small man.
Pratt a cunning man.
Prettyman as *Pratt*.
Proudfoot a man with a haughty walk.
Prowse a valiant man.
Puddifoot a man with a big paunch.
Pullen a frisky or lascivious person.

Quartermaine a man with 'four hands', wearing mailed gloves.
Rank a strong or proud man.
Read (usually) a man with red hair.
Reed as *Read*.
Russell as *Read*.
Savage a savage man. *Best* is the same type of name.
Shakespeare a shaker or brandisher of a lance or spear, a soldier.
Sharp a quick-thinking man.
Short a small man.
Shorthouse a wearer of short hose.
Simple an honest man.
Skegg a bearded man.
Small a thin or small man.
Smart as *Sharp*.
Smollett a man with a small head.
Snell a bold man.
Snow a white-haired man.
Sorrell with reddish-brown hair.
Strang a **Strong** man.
Swift a swift man.
Tait a cheerful man.
Thoroughgood a thoroughly good man.
Turnbull a strong man, able to turn a bull.
Wagstaffe similar to *Shakespeare*.
Whitbread (sometimes) a man with a white beard.
Whitehouse (sometimes) a man with a white neck.
Wild a man who behaved wildly.
Wise a wise man.
Worledge and **Woollage,** a distinguished man.
Wrenn a wren-like person, small or shrewd.
Yapp a deceitful or smart man.

. . . much of its greatness it owes to the Browns. For centuries, in their quiet, dogged, homespun way, they have been subduing the earth in most English counties, and leaving their mark in American forests and Australian uplands. Talbots and Stanleys, St Maurs, and such like folk, have led armies and made laws, time out of mind; but those noble families would be somewhat astounded, if the accounts ever came to be fairly taken, to find how small their work for England has been by the side of that of the Browns.

Thomas Hughes   *Tom Brown's Schooldays*

Henry Guppy's 'Peculiar' Names

In 1890 Henry Brougham Guppy published his *Homes of Family Names in Great Britain*. Guppy had made a particular study of the names of farmers, whom he described as 'the most stay-at-home class of the country', and discovered that in each county their surnames fell into various groups:

a) General—names found all over the country

b) Common—names found in 20–29 counties

c) Regional—names found in 10–19 counties

d) District—names found in 4–9 counties

e) County—names found in 2–3 counties

f) Peculiar—names found mainly in one county only.

I list below the names he considered to be peculiar to one county. They provide strong clues for those interested in their family history as to where further investigations should be made. I have retained the former county names, though many of these have now changed for administrative purposes.

Bedfordshire

Battams, Breary, Brightman, Buckmaster, Claridge, Cranfield, Darrington, Dillamore, Duncombe, Fensom, Foll, Hallworth, Harradine, Hartop, Inskip, Kempson, Malden, Mossman, Negus, Quenby, Scrivener, Scroggs, Stanbridge, Stanton, Timberlake, Whinnett.

Berkshire

Adnams, Benning, Buckeridge, Bunce, Corderoy, Corderey, Crockford, Dormer, Fairthorne, Freebody, Frogley, Froome, Halfacre, Headington, Izzard, Keep, Kimber, Lanfear, Lay, Lonsley, Lyford, Maslen, Napper, Pither, Poyey, Shackel, Tame, Tyrrell, Wilder.

Buckinghamshire

Belgrove, Boughton, Brazier, Dancer, Darvell, Darvill, Dover, Dwight, Edmans, Fountain, Fountaine, Ginger, Gomm, Holdom, Horwood, Ing, Kingham, Plaistowe, Purssell, Roads, Sare, Sear, Slocock, Stratford, Syratt, Syrett, Sirett, Tapping, Tattam, Tofield, Tomes, Tompkins, Varney, Viccars, Warr, Willison, Wilmer, Wooster.

Cambridgeshire

Bays, Chivers, Clear, Collen, Coxall, Dimmock, Dimock, Doggett, Elbourn, Frohock, Fullard, Fyson, Ground, Grounds, Haggar, Hagger, Hurry, Ivatt, Jonas, Maxwell, Murfitt, Mustill, Purkis, Ruston, Sallis, Shepperson, Skeels, Stockdale, Thoday, Vawser, Wayman, Yarrow.

Cheshire

Acton, Adshead, Allman, Ankers, Ardern, Astbury, Aston, Basford, Baskerville, Basnett, Bebbington, Birtles, Blackshaw, Boffey, Bolshaw, Bracegirdle, Braddock, Broadhurst, Broster, Callwood, Cash, Chesters, Done, Dooley, Dutton, Eden, Erlam, Etchells, Furber, Gallimore, Gleave, Goddier, Goodier, Gresty, Hankey, Hassall, Hassell, Henshall, Hickson, Hockenhall, Hockenhull, Hocknell, Hollinshead, Hooley, Hopley, Houlbrook, Huxley, Jeffs, Jepson, Kennerley, Kinsey, Leah, Leather, Littler, Major, Marsland, Minshall, Minshull, Mottershead, Mounfield, Mountfield, Mullock, Newall, Noden, Norbury, Oakes, Okel, Oulton, Pimlott, Pownall, Priestner, Rathbone, Ravenscroft, Rowlingson, Ruscoe, Sandbach, Scragg, Sheen, Shone, Shore, Siddorn, Snelson, Sproston, Stelfox, Stockton, Summerfield, Swinton, Tapley, Thompstone, Thornhill, Tickle, Timperley, Trickett, Trueman, Urmston, Wheelton, Whitelegg, Whitlow, Witter, Woodall, Woollam, Woollams, Wych, Yarwood.

Cornwall

Benny, Berriman, Berryman, Bice, Biddick, Blamey, Boaden, Boase, Bolitho, Borlase, Brendon, Brenton, Budge, Bullmore, Bunt, Burnard, Cardell, Carlyon, Carne, Carveth, Cawrse, Chenoweth, Clemow, Clyma, Clymo, Coad, Cobbledick, Cobeldick, Congdon, Couch, Cowling, Crago, Cragoe, Craze, Crowle, Cundy, Curnow, Dingle, Dunstan, Dunstone, Eddy, Eva, Freethy, Galtey, Geach, Geake, Gerry, Gillbard, Glasson, Goldsworthy, Grigg, Grose, Gynn, Hambly, Hawke, Hawken, Hawkey, Hayne, Hearle, Henwood, Higman, Hodge, Hollow, Hotten, Ivey, Jane, Jasper, Jelbart, Jelbert, Jenkin, Jose, Julian, Julyan, Keast, Kerkin, Kestle, Kevern, Kitto, Kittow, Kneebone, Laity, Lander, Lanyon, Lawry, Lean, Liddicoat, Littlejohn, Lobb, Lory, Lugg, Lyle, Mably, Maddaford, Maddiver, Magor, Mayne, Morcom, Morkam, Moyle, Mutton, Nance, Oates, Oats, Odger, Odgers, Old, Olver, Opie, Oppy, Pascoe, Paynter, Pearn, Pedlar, Pedler, Pender, Pengelly, Pengilly, Penna, Penrose, Peter, Pethick, Philp, Pinch, Polkinghorne, Prisk, Raddall, Raddle, Rapson, Retallack, Retallick, Rickard, Rodda, Roose, Roseveare, Rosewarne, Roskelly, Roskilly, Rouse, Rowse, Rundle, Runnalls, Sandercock, Sandry, Scantlebury, Seccombe, Skewes, Spargo, Tamblyn, Tinney, Tippett, Toll, Tom, Tonkin, Trebilcock, Tregear, Tregellas, Tregelles, Tregoning, Treleaven, Treloar, Tremain, Tremayne, Trembath, Trerise, Tresidder, Trethewey, Trevail, Treweeke, Trewhella, Trewin, Tripcony, Trounson, Trudgen, Trudgeon, Trudgian, Truscott, Tyack, Tyacke, Uren, Vellenoweth, Venning, Verran, Vivian, Vosper, Wearne, Wellington, Whetter, Wickett, Woodley, Woolcock, Yelland.

Cumberland and Westmorland
Beattie, Beaty, Burns, Carruthers, Dalzell, Dalziel, Donald, Faulder, Fearon, Fleming, Johnston, Martindale, Mossop, Mounsey, Pattinson, Routledge, Sim, Simm, Spotterswood, Thomlinson, Topping.

Derbyshire
Alton, Bark, Barnsley, Beardsley, Biggin, Boam, Bowmer, Briddon, Brocksopp, Broomhead, Burdikin, Byard, Chadfield, Clewes, Clews, Copestake, Crookes, Cupit, Cutts, Drabble, Dronfield, Eley, Else, Fearn, Fitchett, Foulke, Fowke, Fretwell, Gent, Gratton, Gyte, Hadfield, Handford, Hartle, Hawley, Henstock, Housley, Hulland, Jerram, Joule, Knifton, Knott, Limb, Litchfield, Longden, Ludlam, Lynam, Mallinder, Marchington, Marples, Maskery, Maskrey, Mortin, Murfin, Nadin, Oakden, Outram, Peat, Plackett, Pursglove, Purslove, Rains, Renshaw, Revell, Revill, Rowarth, Saint, Seal, Shacklock, Sherwin, Shirt, Sidebottom, Skidmore, Smedley, Spalton, Staley, Staniforth, Stoppard, Storer, Tagg, Towndrow, Townrow, Townroe, Turton, Tym, Tymm, Udall, Wager, Wallwin, Waterfall, Waterhouse, Wetton, Wheatcroft, Whittingham, Wibberley, Wigley, Winson, Wragg.

Devonshire
Addems, Alford, Amery, Anning, Arscott, Babbage, Balkwill, Balman, Balsdon, Bastin, Bater, Beedell, Beer, Besley, Bickle, Blatchford, Blowey, Bloye, Bolt, Boundy, Bovey, Bradridge, Bragg, Braund, Brayley, Breayley, Bridgman, Brimacombe, Broom, Bucknell, Burgoin, Burgoyne, Burrough, Burrow, Cawsey, Chaffe, Chamings, Chammings, Channin, Channing, Chave, Cheriton, Chowen, Chown, Chubb, Chugg, Cleverdon, Coaker, Cockram, Cockeram, Colwill, Coneybeare, Conybear, Connibeer, Coombe, Copp, Courtice, Crang, Crimp, Crocombe, Cuming, Dallyn, Damerell, Darch, Dare, Dart, Dayment, Densem, Densham, Dicker, Dimond, Dymond, Doble, Doidge, Dommett, Dufty, Earl, Earle, Easterbrook, Estabrook, Eggins, Ellacott, Ellicott, Elston, Elworthy, Endacott, Eveleigh, Evely, Fairchild, Fewings, Foale, Foss, Friend, Furneaux, Furse, Furze, Gammon, German, Gidley, Gillard, Gloyn, Gorwyn, Grendon, Halse, Hamlyn, Hannaford, Hartnell, Hartnoll, Hayman, Headon, Health, Heaman, Heard, Heddon, Heggadon, Helmer, Hext, Heyward, Heywood, Hillson, Hilson, Hockridge, Honniball, Hookway, Hurrell, Huxham, Huxtable, Irish, Isaacs, Jackman, Kerslake, Kingwell, Knapman, Lambshead, Lang, Langman, Langworthy, Lear, Lerwill, Lethbridge, Letheren, Ley, Lidstone, Littlejohns, Loosemoor, Loosmoor, Lovering, Luscombe, Luxton, Madge, Manley, Maunder, Melhuish, Melluish, Metherall, Metherell, Mildon, Mill, Millman, Milman, Mogford, Mugford, Mortimore, Mudge, Nancekivell, Nancekeville, Nankevil, Netherway, Newcombe, Norrish, Northam, Northmore,

Nosworthy, Oldreave, Oldreive, Paddon, Palfrey, Palk, Parkhouse, Pavey, Pearcey, Penwarden, Perkin, Perrin, Petherbridge, Petherick, Pinhay, Pinhey, Powlesland, Prettejohn, Prettyjohn, Pring, Pugsley, Pym, Quance, Rabjohns, Raymont, Raymount, Reddaway, Reddicliffe, Retter, Rew, Ridd, Routley, Seldon, Sellek, Sercombe, Seward, Shapland, Sharland, Shorland, Sherrill, Sherwill, Shopland, Slader, Slee, Sluggett, Smale, Smallbridge, Smallridge, Smaridge, Smerdon, Smyth, Soby, Soper, Spurrell, Spurle, Squance, Stanbury, Stidston, Stoneman, Tancock, Taverner, Toms, Tope, Tozer, Tremlett, Trick, Trott, Trude, Tuckett, Tully, Underhay, Underhill, Vallance, Vanstone, Venner, Voaden, Vodden, Vooght, Wadland, Wakeham, Ware, Waycott, Were, Westacott, Westaway, Westcott, Western, Westren, Wheaton, Whiteaway, Whiteway, Widdicombe, Willing, Withecombe, Witheycombe, Witheridge, Wonnacott, Woolland, Wotton, Wrayford, Wreford, Wroth.

Dorsetshire
Antell, Ballam, Bastable, Besent, Bowditch, Brickell, Brine, Bugg, Bugler, Caines, Cake, Chilcott, Cluett, Dominy, Dorey, Dunford, Durden, Ensor, Fifett, Fooks, Foot, Gatehouse, Genge, Gillingham, Guppy, Hames, Hann, Hansford, Hayter, Homer, Honeyfield, Hounsell, Jesty, Kellaway, Keynes, Kingman, Larcombe, Legg, Lodder, Loder, Mayo, Meaden, Meatyard, Meech, Milledge, Munckton, Peach, Pomeroy, Rabbetts, Ridout, Ross, Rossiter, Samways, Scutt, Shute, Spicer, Sprake, Studley, Swaffield, Symes, Topp, Trowbridge, Tuffin, Wakely, Walden, Wareham, Wrixon.

Durham
Applegarth, Beadle, Bruce, Bullman, Bulman, Burdon, Callender, Coatsworth, Eggleston, Greenwell, Heppell, Hepple, Hewitson, Hopps, Jameson, Jamieson, Kirkup, Kirton, MacLaren, Makepeace, Mallam, Pallister, Pease, Proud, Quelch, Shotton, Surtees, Tarn, Tinkler, Walburn, Wearmouth.

Essex
Basham, Beddall, Belcham, Bentall, Byford, Cant, Caton, Challis, Christy, Dowsett, Eve, Fairhead, Felgate, Fenner, Folkard, Gowlett, Halls, Hasler, Hockley, Housden, Hutley, Kemsley, Ketley, Kettley, Lagden, Littlechild, Lucking, Marriage, Maskell, Matthams, Meeson, Metson, Milbank, Millbank, Mott, Muggleston, Nottage, Pannell, Parish, Parrish, Patmore, Pegrum, Pilgrim, Pledger, Quilter, Raven, Rickett, Root, Ruffle, Savill, Scruby, Shave, Sorrell, Spurgeon, Staines, Stock, Strutt, Sweeting, Taber, Tabor, Thorington, Tilbrook, Tofts, Tween, Wenden, Wendon, Whitlock.

Gloucestershire
Arkell, Ballinger, Biddle, Blandford, Browning, Bubb,

Cadle, Clutterbuck, Comely, Cornock, Croome, Cullimore, Dobbs, Dowdeswell, Fawkes, Flook, Fluck, Flux, Garne, Gazard, Goulding, Goulter, Hanks, Hatherell, Hewer, Hignell, Holder, Iles, Kilminster, Kilmister, Limbrick, Lusty, Minchin, Minett, New, Niblett, Organ, Parslow, Pegler, Penson, Priday, Radway, Ricketts, Righton, Rugman, Rymer, Selwyn, Shields, Shipp, Shipway, Staite, Stinchcombe, Theyer, Till, Trotman, Tuffley, Vick, Vimpany, Wadley, Werrett, Wintle, Wintour, Witchell, Yeend.

Hampshire

Abbinett, Amey, Attrill, Ayles, Barfoot, Blackman, Broomfield, Budd, Clift, Cobden, Drewitt, Drudge, Edney, Fay, Fitt, Jolliffe, Lavington, Light, Mew, Poore, Portsmouth, Potticary, Rumbold, Seaward, Southwell, Stares, Stride, Turvill, Twitchin, Whitcher, Witt.

Herefordshire

Allcott, Apperley, Banfield, Berrow, Bodenham, Bounds, Bromage, Callow, Eckley, Embrey, Godsall, Godsell, Hancorn, Hobby, Hoddell, Maddy, Mailes, Mainwaring, Marfell, Meadmore, Monnington, Ockey, Orgee, Paniers, Panniers, Pantall, Scudamore, Sirrell, Skerrett, Skyrme, South, Tudge, Vale, Welson, Went.

Hertfordshire

Acres, Ashwell, Bonfield, Campkin, Chalkley, Chennells, Clinton, Hankin, Ivory, Kingsley, Kitchener, Mardell, Orchard, Overell, Parkins, Patten, Sears, Tittmuss, Vyse, Walby, Woollatt.

Huntingdonshire

Achurch, Bletsoe, Cheney, Corney, Ekins, Humbley, Jellis, Ladds, Lenton, Looker, Mash, Speechley, Spriggs.

Kent

Ballard, Barling, Belsey, Benstead, Bensted, Bing, Boorman, Boulden, Brenchley, Brice, Broadley, Buss, Chantler, Clinch, Coultrip, Coveney, Crowhurst, Curling, Dark, Dilnot, Dungey, Fagg, File, Filmer, Finn, Fremlin, Godden, Goodhew, Gower, Hambrook, Harden, Hartridge, Hickmott, Hogben, Hogbin, Holness, Honess, Hollamby, Hollands, Inge, Jarrett, Kingsnorth, Langridge, Larkin, Larking, Laslett, Leney, Love, Luck, Manwaring, Matcham, Maylam, Maxted, Millen, Milne, Minter, Miskin, Missing, Morphett, Murton, Neame, Offen, Orpen, Orpin, Oyler, Pidduck, Pittock, Pilcher, Prebble, Quested, Rigden, Scoones, Seath, Shorter, Solley, Solomon, Southon, Stace, Stickles, Stunt, Stuppies, Swaffer, Tassell, Thirkell, Tickner, Tomkin, Tompsett, Tuff, Usherwood, Wiles, Wyles, Witherden.

Lancashire

Alker, Almond, Alty, Aspinall, Aspinwall, Atherton, Bamber, Battersby, Bent, Bibby, Bleasdale, Bleazard, Blezard, Blezzard, Bonney, Bretherton, Brindle, Bulcock, Butterworth, Caldwell, Cardwell, Cartmell, Catlow, Catterall, Caunce, Charnley, Charnock, Collinge, Coward, Critchley, Crompton, Cropper, Culshaw, Cunliffe, Dagger, Dearden, Dewhurst, Drinkall, Duckworth, Dunderdale, Duxbury, Eastham, Eaves, Eccles, Entwisle, Entwistle, Fairclough, Fazakerley, Fish, Forrest, Forshaw, Gornall, Gorst, Greenhalgh, Gregson, Grimshaw, Hacking, Hakin, Halliwell, Halsall, Hardman, Haworth, Haydock, Hayhurst, Haythornthwaite, Hesketh, Hesmondhalgh, Higson, Hindle, Horrocks, Huddleston, Ibison, Iddon, Kellett, Kenyon, Kilshaw, Lawrenson, Leaver, Lever, Livesey, Livesley, Longton, Longworth, Lonsdale, Lyon, Lythgoe, Lithgoe, Maden, Margerison, Margerson, Marginson, Margison, Martland, Mashiter, Maudsley, Mawdsley, Mayor, Molyneux, Newby, Nutter, Ollerton, Pemberton, Pendlebury, Pickup, Pilkington, Pilling, Pimblett, Pollitt, Pomfret, Postlethwaite, Rainford, Ramsbottom, Rawcliffe, Rawlinson, Riding, Ryding, Rimmer, Rogerson, Rosbotham, Rosbottom, Rosebotham, Rossall, Rossell, Rothwell, Sagar, Segar, Salthouse, Scholes, Seddon, Sefton, Sephton, Shacklady, Shakelady, Sharples, Sharrock, Shorrock, Silcock, Singleton, Stanworth, Starkie, Stuart, Swarbrick, Tattersall, Threlfall, Topping, Townson, Tyrer, Unworth, Wallbank, Walmsley, Walsh, Wareing, Waring, Whipp, Whiteside, Winder, Winstanley, Worsley.

Leicestershire and Rutlandshire

Beeby, Berridge, Branson, Burnaby, Cobley, Dalby, Darnell, Dawkins, Dexter, Dowell, Drackley, Draycott, Eayrs, Eayres, Forryan, Frearson, Freestone, Geary, Gimson, Hack, Henson, Hollier, Jarrom, Jesson, Keetley, Keightley, Kirkman, Lacey, Leadbeater, Leadbetter, Loseby, Macaulay, Mackley, Matts, Musson, Oldacres, Orson, Paget, Pochin, Pretty, Royce, Scotton, Sheffield, Shipman, Toon, Toone, Wilford, Wormleighton.

Lincolnshire

Anyan, Bemrose, Bett, Blades, Blankley, Border, Borman, Bowser, Brackenbury, Bristow, Broughton, Brownlow, Brumby, Burkill, Burkitt, Butters, Cade, Cammack, Capes, Casswell, Chatterton, Codd, Collishaw, Coney, Cooling, Cottingham, Coupland, Cranidge, Cropley, Cutforth, Cuthbert, Dannatt, Daubney, Desforges, Dook, Dows, Dowse, Drakes, Drewery, Drewry, Dring, Drury, Dudding, Elmitt, Elvidge, Epton, Evison, Forman, Frisby, Frow, Gaunt, Gilliart, Gilliatt, Gillyatt, Goodyear, Goose, Grummitt, Hay, Herring, Hewson, Hides, Hildred, Hoyes, Hoyles, Hutton, Ingall, Ingle, Laming, Lamming, Leggett, Leggott, Lill, Lilley, Lynn, Mackinder, Maidens,

Marfleet, Markham, Mastin, Maw, Mawer, Merrikin, Minta, Mowbray, Odling, Overton, Palethorpe, Patchett, Pick, Pickwell, Pocklington, Ranby, Reeson, Rhoades, Riggall, Rippon, Sardeson, Sargisson, Scarborough, Scholey, Scoley, Scrimshaw, Scrimshire, Searson, Sergeant, Sharpley, Sneath, Stamp, Storr, Stowe, Strawson, Stuble, Temple, Thurlby, Trafford, Ullyatt, Vinter, Waddingham, Wadsley, Wass, Westerby, Westoby, Whitsed, Willey, Willows, Winn, Wroot.

Middlesex
Ewer, Woodland.

Norfolk
Abbs, Amies, Amis, Arthurton, Atthow, Attoe, Banham, Batterham, Beales, Beanes, Beck, Bettinson, Boddy, Brasnett, Bunn, Cannell, Case, Claxton, Copeman, Cossey, Cubitt, Culley, Curson, Duffield, Dyball, Dye, Eglinton, Failes, Flatt, Gamble, Gapp, Gayford, Gaze, Gedge, Gooch, Goulder, Greenacre, Heading, Howes, Huggins, Ingram, Kerrison, Lain, Land, Larwood, Leeder, Leeds, Lewell, Mack, Mallett, Milk, Minns, Mullinger, Nurse, Plumbly, Poll, Purdy, Ringer, Rising, Rivett, Rix, Roofe, Sands, Savory, Scales, Sheringham, Shreeve, Slipper, Soame, Spink, Spinks, Starling, Stimpson, Thrower, Tooley, Utting, Warnes, Whalebelly, Whittleton, Woolston, Wortley.

Northamptonshire
Aris, Barford, Bazeley, Bazley, Bellairs, Bellars, Borton, Brafield, Britten, Bromwich, Buswell, Butlin, Chew, Dainty, Drage, Dunkley, Gibbard, Goff, Golby, Goode, Gulliver, Hales, Heygate, Holton, Hornsby, Judkins, Kingston, Linnell, Mackaness, Main, Mawle, Measures, Montgomery, Newitt, Panther, Roddis, Scriven, Siddons, Spokes, Stops, Turnell, Vergette, Warwick, Westley, Whitton, Whitney, Woolhouse, Wrighton, Wyman, York.

Northumberland
Alder, Allan, Annett, Arkle, Aynsley, Bewick, Bolam, Borthwick, Bothwick, Brewis, Brodie, Bushby, Cairns, Carmichael, Cockburn, Common, Cowan, Cowen, Cowing, Craig, Dand, Dinning, Embleton, Fairbairn, Gallon, Gilhespy, Glendinning, Harle, Herdman, Hindmarsh, Hogg, Howey, Howie, Jobling, Laidler, Lumsden, Middlemas, Middlemiss, Morrison, Nevin, Nevins, Ormston, Phillipson, Pringle, Renton, Renwick, Roddam, Shanks, Shield, Stewart, Stobart, Stobert, Straughan, Telfer, Telford, Usher, Wanlace, Wanless, Weddell, Weddle, Younger.

Nottinghamshire
Annable, Barrowcliff, Bartram, Beardall, Beecroft, Billyard, Binge, Bingley, Blatherwick, Broadberry, Buttery, Byron, Carver, Challand, Cheshire, Chettle, Collingham, Corringham, Cumberland, Darwin, Derry,

Doncaster, Duckmanton, Eddison, Esam, Farnsworth, Fenton, Footitt, Footit, Gagg, Gelsthorpe, Gunn, Hardstaff, Harpham, Hempsall, Herrick, Herrod, Hickton, Holbrook, Howett, Howitt, Hurt, Huskinson, Keyworth, Leavers, Leivers, Lindley, Merrills, Millington, Norwood, Ogle, Oliphant, Olivant, Paling, Payling, Paulson, Peatfield, Pell, Pickin, Plumtree, Quibell, Radley, Redgate, Roadley, Selby, Staples, Stendall, Straw, Stubbins, Templeman, Truswell, Weightman, Wombwell, Woombill.

Oxfordshire
Akers, Aldworth, Arnatt, Batts, Blencowe, Breakspear, Buller, Calcutt, Chaundy, Clapton, Clare, Coggins, Deeley, Edginton, Filbee, Florey, Hatt, Hutt, Hobley, Hone, Honour, Loosley, Louch, Lovegrove, Luckett, Midwinter, Neighbour, Nevell, Padbury, Paxman, Paxton, Pether, Pettipher, Rowles, Sabin, Savin, Shrimpton, Spurrett, Stanbra, Turrill, Tustain, Widdows, Wilsdon, Witney, Woolgrove.

Shropshire
Ashley, Back, Bather, Batho, Beddoes, Benbow, Blakemore, Boughey, Bowdler, Breakwell, Brisbourne, Broughall, Cadwallader, Cleeton, Corfield, Cureton, Duce, Eddowes, Everall, Felton, Fowles, Growcott, Gwilt, Heatley, Heighway, Hinton, Home, Hotchkiss, Inions, Instone, Jacks, Kynaston, Lawley, Madeley, Mansell, Mellings, Millichamp, Minton, Munslow, Nock, Onions, Paddock, Pinches, Pitchford, Podmore, Ravenshaw, Rodenhurst, Sankey, Shuker, Tipton, Titley, Warder, Wellings.

Somerset
Amesbury, Aplin, Ashman, Arney, Baber, Badman, Bagg, Banwell, Barnstable, Barrington, Batt, Bicknell, Binning, Bisdee, Board, Bowering, Brimble, Burch, Burston, Carey, Cary, Chard, Churches, Clapp, Clothier, Coate, Cogan, Coggan, Corner, Corp, Cosh, Counsell, Croom, Crossman, Dampier, Denman, Denning, Derrick, Dibble, Dicks, Diment, Dyment, Durston, Evered, Farthing, Fear, Floyd, Gare, Giblett, Greed, Haggett, Hatch, Hebditch, Hembrow, Hockey, Horsey, Hurd, Hurley, Isgar, Keedwell, Keel, Keirl, Kidner, Look, Loveybond, Lovibond, Loxton, Lutley, Mapstone, Meaker, Oram, Padfield, Perham, Phippen, Pople, Pottenger, Pow, Puddy, Rawle, Reakes, Rood, Rugg, Say, Sealey, Sealy, Singer, Speed, Sperring, Spratt, Stallard, Steeds, Stuckey, Sully, Summerhayes, Swanton, Sweet, Tarr, Tatchell, Tazewell, Teek, Tilley, Toogood, Treasure, Tyley, Vigar, Vigors, Vowles, Walrond, Wescott, Winslade, Winstone, Withey, Withy, Wookey, Yeandle.

Staffordshire
Ash, Averill, Bagnall, Bakewell, Baskeyfield, Batkin, Beardmore, Bickford, Boden, Boon, Bott, Bould, Boulton, Bowers, Brindley, Brunt, Cantrell, Cantrill,

Chell, Clewlow, Clulow, Clowes, Colclough, Corbishley, Cumberledge, Deakin, Durose, Eardley, Elsmore, Fallows, Farrall, Fern, Forrester, Goldstraw, Hambleton, Hammersley, Heler, Hodgkins, Hollingsworth, Hollins, Howson, Jeavons, Jevons, Keeling, Kidd, Lakin, Leese, Leighton, Lindop, Lovatt, Loverock, Lymer, Limer, Malkin, Marson, Mayer, Mottram, Myatt, Orpe, Parton, Pyatt, Sharratt, Sherratt, Shelley, Shemilt, Shenton, Shirley, Shoebotham, Shoebottom, Stoddard, Swetnam, Tomkinson, Torr, Tunnicliff, Turnock, Warrilow, Whitehurst, Wilshaw, Wint, Wooddisse, Woodings.

Suffolk
Aldous, Alston, Aves, Baldry, Bendall, Blowers, Borrett, Button, Calver, Catling, Cattermole, Cobbold, Colson, Cracknell, Cutting, Debenham, Deck, Feaveryear, Feaviour, Finbow, Fincham, Fisk, Fiske, Flatman, Fulcher, Garnham, Gooderham, Grimsey, Grimwood, Hadingham, Haward, Hitchcock, Hurren, Ingate, Jillings, Juby, Keeble, Kemball, Kerridge, Kerry, Kersey, Last, Meen, Nesling, Newson, Pendell, Pendle, Sawyer, Sheldrake, Sheldrick, Southgate, Squirrell, Stannard, Steggall, Sturgeon, Thurman, Tricker, Whitmore, Wolton, Woollard.

Surrey
Caesar, Charlwood, Chuter, Gosden, Puttock, Smithers, Tice, Wenham.

Sussex
Akehurst, Allcorn, Ayling, Aylwin, Barham, Bodle, Boniface, Botting, Bourner, Challen, Chitty, Churchman, Coppard, Corke, Cornford, Diplock, Dumbrell, Dumbrill, Etheridge, Evershed, Fogden, Funnell, Gander, Gates, Goacher, Gorringe, Haffenden, Head, Heaver, Hide, Hoadley, Hoath, Hobden, Hobgen, Honeysett, Hook, Isted, Joyes, Killick, Leppard, Longley, Mannington, Message, Newington, Packham, Pankhurst, Penfold, Pennifold, Rapley, Sayers, Sinden, Sparkes, Stay, Sturt, Suter, Tester, Tobitt, Towes, Towse, Tribe, Verrall, Wakeford, Walder, Wickens, Woodhams, Wren, Wrenn.

Warwickshire
Arch, Boddington, Burbidge, Chattaway, Crofts, Currall, Edkins, Elkington, Fitter, Grimes, Hands, Hicken, Hickin, Hollick, Ibbotson, Jeffcoate, Jephcott, Keyte, Knibb, Ledbrook, Moxon, Murcott, Rainbow, Tibbetts, Tidy, Trippas, Truelove, Warden, Weetman, Wilday, Willday.

Wiltshire
Awdry, Beak, Bracher, Breach, Compton, Cottle, Cuss, Cusse, Doel, Eatwell, Frankcombe, Frankcome, Freegard, Freeth, Garlick, Ghey, Greenaway, Greenhill, Grist, Hathway, Henley, Howse, Hulbert, Jupe, Keevil, Kemble, Kinch, Knapp, Manners, Maundrell, Melsome,

Milsom, Mintey, Minty, Morse, Newth, Ody, Parham, Pickett, Pinchin, Puckeridge, Ruddle, Rumming, Russ, Sidford, Sloper, Taunton, Titcombe, Whatley.

Worcestershire
Albutt, Allbutt, Allington, Amphlett, Blakeway, Boucher, Boulter, Byrd, Careless, Cartridge, Doolittle, Essex, Firkins, Follows, Gabb, Ganderton, Granger, Grove, Guilding, Hadley, Halford, Harber, Hemus, Hingley, Hollington, Holtom, Huband, Hyde, Merrell, Moule, Munn, Mytton, Newey, Nickless, Penrice, Purser, Quinney, Quinny, Smithin, Spiers, Stinton, Tandy, Tipping, Tolley, Tongue, Willets, Willetts, Winnall, Winwood, Workman, Wormington, Yarnold.

Yorkshire, North and East Ridings
Agar, Blenkin, Blenkiron, Bosomworth, Botterill, Bowes, Brigham, Bulmer, Codling, Coverdale, Creaser, Danby, Dinsdale, Duck, Duggleby, Elgey, Elgie, Ellerby, Foxton, Galloway, Garbutt, Goodwill, Grainger, Harker, Harland, Hawking, Hebron, Heseltine, Hick, Holliday, Holyday, Horsley, Hugill, Iveson, Jacques, Jordison, Judson, Kendrew, Kettlewell, Kilvington, Kipling, Knaggs, Lamplough, Lamplugh, Laverack, Laverick, Leak, Leake, Leaper, Leckenby, Matson, Matterson, Mattison, Medforth, Megginson, Meggison, Megson, Monkman, Nornabell, Nottingham, Outhwaite, Parnaby, Petch, Pickersgill, Plews, Porrett, Porritt, Precious, Prodham, Prudom, Pybus, Raw, Readman, Rennison, Rider, Rodmell, Rounthwaite, Routhwaite, Rowntree, Scarth, Sedman, Sellars, Sellers, Severs, Spenceley, Spensley, Stainthorpe, Stavely, Stockhill, Stockill, Stokell, Stonehouse, Sturdy, Suddaby, Suggett, Suggitt, Sunter, Tennison, Tweedy, Tyerman, Tyreman, Ventress, Ventris, Weighell, Weighill, Welburn, Wellburn, Welford, Whitwell, Wilberforce, Wilberfoss, Witty, Wray, Wrightson.

Yorkshire, West Riding
Addy, Ambler, Appleyard, Armitage, Balmforth, Bamforth, Barraclough, Batty, Battye, Beever, Beevers, Beevors, Bentham, Binns, Blakey, Bottomley, Bramall, Brear, Brears, Broadbent, Broadhead, Butterfield, Capstick, Clapham, Clough, Cockshott, Crapper, Crawshaw, Demain, Demaine, Denby, Denison, Dibb, Dyson, Earnshaw, Emmott, Feather, Firth, Garside, Geldard, Gelder, Gledhill, Gott, Haigh, Hainsworth, Haley, Hampshire, Hanson, Hardcastle, Helliwell, Hepworth, Hey, Hinchcliff, Hinchcliffe, Hirst, Hobson, Holdsworth, Houldsworth, Holroyd, Horsfall, Houseman, Ingleby, Jagger, Jowett, Jubb, Kenworthy, Laycock, Lodge, Longbottom, Lumb, Mallinson, Mawson, Midgley, Moorhouse, Murgatroyd, Myers, Newsholme, Newsome, Noble, Peel, Popplewell, Poskitt, Ramsden, Redmayne, Rishworth, Rushworth, Robertshaw, Roebuck, Sedgwick, Shackleton, Sheard, Stansfield, Sugden, Sunderland, Tatham, Teal, Teale,

Thackery, Thackray, Thackwray, Thornber, Thwaites, Tinker, Townend, Umpleby, Uttley, Varley, Verity, Wadsworth, Watkinson, Weatherhead, Whiteley, Whitley, Widdop, Widdup, Woodhead, Wrathall.

North Wales
Bebb, Bellis, Colley, Foulkes, Ryder, Tudor.

South Wales
Beynon, Duggan, Harry, Matthias, Mordecai, Ormond.

Monmouthshire
Crowles, Duckham, Ellaway, Gwynne, Jeremiah, Moses, Rosser.

(Some surnames appear in more than one of Guppy's Scottish groups)

Scottish Border Counties
Aitchison, Armstrong, Beattie, Bell, Calder, Carruthers, Douglas, Edgar, Elliot, Grierson, Hogg, Hope, Hyslop, Irvine, Irving, Jardine, Johnston, Johnstone, Kelly, Kerr, Laidlaw, Little, Maxwell, Milligan, Moffat, Nicholson, Nicolson, Oliver, Purves, Purvis, Rae, Richardson, Robson, Rutherford, Scott, Tait, Turnbull.

Scottish Lowlands
Adamson, Aitken, Allan, Arthur, Baird, Barbour, Barclay, Barr, Bell, Blair, Boyd, Brodie, Brown, Buchanan, Cairns, Caldwell, Cowan, Craig, Crawford, Cunningham, Currie, Dalgleish, Dalziel, Dick, Dickie, Dickson, Dodds, Dods, Dunlop, Dunn, Dykes, Findlay, Finlay, Forrest, Forsyth, Fullarton, Fulton, Gemmell, Gibson, Gillespie, Gilmour, Graham, Gray, Hall, Hamilton, Hood, Howie, Inglis, Jack, Jackson, Johnston, Johnstone, Kay, Lang, Laurie, Lawrie, Lawson, Lennox, Lindsay, Logan, Lyon, McCulloch, McKie, Mackie, McNeil, McNeill, Mair, Marshall, Martin, Morton, Muir, Murdoch, Neil, Neilson, Nisbet, Nisbett, Orr, Park, Paton, Pollock, Pringle, Rankin, Richmond, Scott, Shanks, Sloan, Smith, Somerville, Steel, Stevenson, Stoddart, Struthers, Swan, Templeton,

Tennant, Thomson, Tod, Todd, Turner, Waddell, Wallace, Watson, Welsh, White, Whyte, Wilson, Young.

Central Scotland
Balfour, Baxter, Burns, Cameron, Campbell, Dawson, Dewar, Dickson, Donaldson, Drummond, Drysdale, Duff, Duncan, Edward, Edwards, Finlayson, Forbes, Galbraith, Galloway, Gordon, Gow, Graham, Hall, McArthur, McDougall, McEwan, McEwen, McFarlane, McGregor, McIntosh, Mackintosh, McIntyre, McLaren, Maclaren, McClean, Maclean, McMillan, Macmillan, McNab, Macnab, McNaughton, McNeil, McNeill, Marshall, Menzies, Ogilvie, Ogilvy, Paton, Sharp, Stirling, Tod, Todd, Wallace.

The Highlands
Cruikshank, Cumming, Duncan, Farquhar, Farquharson, Forbes, Geddes, Gordon, Grant, Innes, Low, Lumsden, McDonald, McIntosh, Mackintosh, McKay, Mackay, McKenzie, Mackenzie, McKie, Mackie, McLeod, Macleod, McPherson, Macpherson, McRae, Macrae, Middleton, Milne, Munroe, Rennie, Ross, Stephen, Strachan, Sutherland, Urquhart, Watt.

Throughout Scotland
Adam, Alexander, Anderson, Baillie, Ballantyne, Black, Bruce, Burnett, Carmichael, Chalmers, Christie, Clark, Crichton, Davidson, Donald, Ewing, Ferguson, Fisher, Fleming, Fraser, Gardiner, Gardner, Gibb, Gilchrist, Glen, Greig, Grieve, Guthrie, Hardie, Harper, Harvey, Hay, Henderson, Hill, Hunter, Hutchison, Jamieson, Kennedy, Kidd, King, Laing, Lamont, Law, Leslie, McAdam, Maitland, Malcolm, Matheson, Mathieson, Meikle, Millar, Miller, Mitchell, Moir, Morrison, Muirhead, Murray, Nicol, Nicoll, Paterson, Patterson, Philips, Ramsay, Reid, Ritchie, Robb, Robertson, Rodger, Russell, Shaw, Shepherd, Simpson, Sinclair, Stewart, Stuart, Taylor, Thom, Walker, Webster, Weir, Wilkie, Williamson, Wood, Wright, Wylie, Wyllie.

Superlative surnames

Bearers of certain surnames are used to hearing jokes about them. Those who bear the names below will, I hope, forgive the punny introductions. The accompanying notes attempt to set matters right.

Most tear-jerking name – Onion/Onions. Some of those who bear a form of this name had an ancestor who grew or sold onions, but most owe their name to a Welsh ancestor named Einion.

Good, better, best names – Families called Good, Goodbody, Goodfellow, Goodfriend, Goodhew (= 'good servant'), Goodlad, Goodman, Goodson, Goodswen (= 'good servant') and Goodwill had an ancestor who really was a good person. Better is a rarer surname, though N. I. Bowditch records it in his *Suffolk Surnames*. It probably indicates an ancestor who was a Bartholomew, Beatrice or Elizabeth. The Best people usually take their name from someone who looked after beasts or who acted like a beast.

Most painful name – Ouch. James Pennethorne Hughes, in his book *Is Thy Name Wart?*, mentions this name. He links it with Zouch (as in the place-name Ashby-de-la-Zouch). A commoner form of the name is Such, which derives from someone who lived near a tree stump or who was of stumpy build. Pain is another contender for this title. Its various forms (Paine, Payne, etc) usually indicate a man who was a 'pagan' – which originally meant a country-dweller rather than a townsman. Later the word came to designate a non-military man, a civilian, and later still, someone who was not enrolled in Christ's army, a heathen.

Laziest name – Gotobed. A late friend of mine bore this surname, which is unusual in that it probably means what it says. It would have begun as a nickname, bestowed on a lazy person.

Most ungainly name – Waddle. A variant of Waddell, and indicating an ancestor who came from Wedale, near Edinburgh.

Most macho name – Manly. Found more frequently as Manley and Manleigh, which give a more accurate indication of the place-name origin. H. B. Guppy, in his *Homes of Family Names*, found this surname only in Devonshire. This fact caused Basil Cottle, in his otherwise excellent *Penguin Dictionary of Surnames*, to surmise that the name must mean 'manly, brave', since the only Manley known to him was in Cheshire. He overlooked East and West Manley, Devonshire villages named because of a 'clearing shared by the community'. Either of them could have led to this name.

Most laugh-provoking name – Tickle. This is really the place name Tickhill, South Yorkshire, which was where the earliest bearers of the name originated.

Most disapproving name – Tutt. There was an Old English personal name Tutta, but no one has been able to explain its meaning.

Sprucest name – Neat. Actually a name for a herdsman, since *neat* in Old English meant an ox or cow. The word meaning clean and tidy came into English from French, long after surnames had become hereditary. Another contender for this title would be Tidy, originally a highly complimentary nickname for a handsome man.

Most bashful name – Coy. From an Old French *coi*, Latin *quietus*. A nickname given to a quiet, unassuming person.

Most fiery name – Burns. In reality, from one who lived near a burn or burns, as small streams are called in Scotland and the North of England.

Most revealing name – Streaker. Probably a variant of Streek, a nickname given to a stern or obstinate person.

Most footsore name – Bunyan. This name derives from Old French *bugne*, 'swelling', and possibly indicates an ancestor who was a hunchback. Scholars are surprisingly reluctant to derive the bunion that grows on the toe from the same word.

Most playful name – Toy. The surname is thought to indicate an ancestor who was light-hearted and frivolous, or who indulged in 'amorous sport'. The modern sense of toy as a child's plaything appeared only in the late 16th century. The surname was recorded 300 years earlier.

Nicest name – Nice. Not such a nice name when it was bestowed. Instead of expressing general approval (a very modern sense), it indicated someone who was foolishly simple. Ultimately 'nice' is from Latin *nescius*, 'ignorant'.

Most accident-prone name – Careless. The variant Carless is frequently found, suggesting careless driving to the modern mind, but these names indicate an ancestor who was a cheerful, unconcerned person. Careless originally described someone who was what we would now call carefree.

Most hollow-eyed name – Haggard. When surnames were coming into being, the word 'haggard' meant wild, untamed. It was applied especially to a wild hawk that was captured and trained after it had reached adulthood, rather than being reared in captivity. *A Dictionary of Surnames*, by Patrick Hanks and Flavia Hodges, suggests that it might therefore have been a name for a professional falconer. The English writer Sir H. Rider Haggard (1856–1925), however, was descended from a Danish nobleman, Andrew Ogard, whose surname was a variant of a Danish place-name. J. K. Stephen, in his poem *To R.K.*, was responsible for the immortal lines:

When the Rudyards cease from Kipling
And the Haggards ride no more.

Most villainous name – Lawless. This nickname is likely to have been given originally to a man who indulged himself in animal passions, though Professor Reaney, in his *Origin of English Surnames*, thinks it could also have indicated an outlaw.

Most punctual name – Early. Most Early families originally came from one of the many places called Earley, Earnley or Arley. All of these were named because of woods with eagles (ernes) in them. Early can occasionally be traced back to Old English *eorlic*, earl-like. It then becomes a nickname given to a man of noble qualities.

Most trade unionist name – Striker. An occupational surname, in spite of appearances. To strike corn was to pass a flat stick across the brim of the measure, levelling out any heaps.

Strangest name – Strange. A name given to someone who was a stranger, a newcomer to the area.

Most regular name – Daley or Weekly. Daley (Daly, O'Daly, Dailey, Dalley, etc) represent Irish O Dalaigh, 'descendant of Dalach'. Dalach is in turn linked with Irish *dail*, 'assembly'. Weekly is more often found as Weekley, the place from which early bearers of the name would have come. The place name means '(Roman) settlement near a clearing' or 'wych-elm wood', according to different reference sources. It would have been good to have the opinion of Ernest Weekley on the matter, but he modestly did not speculate about his own name in either his *Romance of Names* or his *Surnames*.

Most talkative name – Chattaway. Another place-name-turned-surname, thought to contain an Old English personal name *Ceatta* and 'way, path'.

Most effective name – Greenhouse. A family which lived in a house by the village green would have received this name. Garden greenhouses have only been with us since the late 17th century. The greenhouse effect, referring to the progressive warming-up of the earth's surface due to carbon dioxide in the atmosphere, has been identified even more recently.

Politest name – Manners. A word used by some to excuse an eructation or other socially-unacceptable noise. Such usage probably does not please the bearers of this decidedly aristocratic Norman-French name, derived from *Mesnières*, a habitation in Seine-Maritime.

Most fidgety name – Shufflebottom. The -bottom surnames are far too common in the North of England to give rise to sniggers, but such names can still cause problems. It has even been claimed that they are disappearing because women are reluctant to marry men who bear them. Bottom, or as it is also legitimately spelt, Botham, refers to the broad bottom of a valley. The Shuffle- of this name is more correctly Shipper-, and refers to a spring where sheep were washed.

Most scientific name – Boffin. It is not known why backroom military scientists began to be known in British slang as boffins. The origin of the surname, which clearly appealed to Charles Dickens, has also puzzled many scholars. Early writers, such as Charles Wareing Bardsley in *A Dictionary of English and Welsh Surnames*, thought it was a French nickname. Professor Dauzat finds no room for it in his dictionary of French surnames, nor does it appear to be a French place name, as Barber states in his *British Family Names. The Oxford Dictionary of Surnames* is probably correct in deciding that it is a variant of Welsh Baughan, or Vaughan 'little'.

Fifty most common surnames

ENGLAND AND WALES		USA		SCOTLAND	
1 Smith	26 Harris	1 Smith	26 Nelson	1 Smith	26 Morrison
2 Jones	27 Clark	2 Johnson	27 Wright	2 Brown	27 MacLeod
3 Williams	28 Cooper	3 Williams	28 Baker	3 MacDonald	28 Fraser
4 Taylor	29 Harrison	4 Brown	29 Hill	4 Thomson	29 Henderson
5 Davies	30 Davis	5 Jones	30 Scott	5 Wilson	30 Gray
6 Brown	31 Ward	6 Miller	31 Adams	6 Stewart	31 Cameron
7 Thomas	32 Baker	7 Davis	32 Green	7 Campbell	32 Graham
8 Evans	33 Martin	8 Wilson	33 Lee	8 Robertson	33 Duncan
9 Roberts	34 Morris	9 Anderson	34 Roberts	9 Anderson	34 Hamilton
10 Johnson	35 James	10 Taylor	35 Mitchell	10 Johnston	35 Kerr
11 Robinson	36 Morgan	11 Moore	36 Campbell	11 Miller	36 Hunter
12 Wilson	37 King	12 Thomas	37 Phillips	12 Murray	37 Davidson
13 Wright	38 Allen	13 Martin	38 Carter	13 Scott	38 Ferguson
14 Wood	39 Clarke	14 Thompson	39 Evans	14 Reid	39 Simpson
15 Hall	40 Cook	15 White	40 Turner	15 Clark	40 Martin
16 Walker	41 Moore	16 Harris	41 Collins	16 MacKenzie	41 White
17 Hughes	42 Parker	17 Jackson	42 Parker	17 Paterson	42 Kelly
18 Green	43 Price	18 Clark	43 Murphy	18 Taylor	43 Allan
19 Lewis	44 Phillips	19 Lewis	44 Rodriguez	19 MacKay	44 Grant
20 Edwards	45 Watson	20 Walker	45 Edwards	20 MacLean	45 Bell
21 Thompson	46 Shaw	21 Hall	46 Morris	21 Young	46 Black
22 White	47 Lee	22 Robinson	47 Peterson	22 Ross	47 Wallace
23 Jackson	48 Bennett	23 Allen	48 Cook	23 Walker	48 Russell
24 Turner	49 Carter	24 Young	49 Rogers	24 Mitchell	49 Marshall
25 Hill	50 Griffiths	25 King	50 Stewart	25 Watson	50 MacMillan

Mayflower names

The 102 passengers on the *Mayflower*, who sailed to America from Plymouth in 1620, bore the following family names:

Alden	Carter	Ellis	Howland	Priest	Tilley
Alderton	Carver	English	Langemore	Prower	Tinker
Allerton	Chilton	Fletcher	Latham	Rigdale	Trevor
Billington	Clarke	Fuller	Leister	Rogers	Turner
Bradford	Cooke	Gardiner	Margeson	Samson	Warren
Brewster	Cooper	Goodman	Martin	Soule	White
Britteridge	Crackston	Holbeck	Minter	Standish	Wilder
Browne	Dotey	Hooke	Moore	Story	Williams
Button	Eaton	Hopkins	Mullins	Thompson	Winslow

The Indexes at the General Register Office in London list all births, marriages and deaths registered in England and Wales since 1837. My colleague C.V. Appleton once made an investigation to see who would be placed first and last if all the names were combined into a single list. Contenders for first place included those with the surnames Aaron, Aarkins, Aargan, Aarah, Aansell, Aanensen, Aal, Aafers, Aackerman, Aablaster and Aab, but they were beaten by two men named Aa. Peter Aa married in 1841; Louis Aa was married at Westminster in 1939. Both were presumably Dutch.

Last-place contenders included those named Zurrap, Zursman, Zyers, Zyscherk, Zytogorski, Zywyno, Zyznarski, Zyzyk, Zzaman and Zzoha. None of these could match Jokine Zzuppichine, whose death at the age of 68 was registered at Liverpool in 1929.

8
MAKING A NAME FOR YOURSELF

A GREAT many people have a burning ambition to make a name for themselves. Although 'name' here is used for 'reputation', the name itself remains of great importance. If it is to be widely used and remembered, other people must be able to say it and spell it easily, and it must not suggest anything undesirable or silly. At the same time, a slight dash of the unusual is welcome to provide the necessary individuality. Many of our surnames, casually bestowed centuries ago and badly treated since, do not fulfil these criteria. Bearers of such names are left with little alternative but to change them if they really are set on a public life. They must begin quite literally by making a name for themselves.

Stage names

The world of entertainment naturally comes immediately to mind. Stage names are an accepted part of the profession. Among those who have adapted their real surnames to some purpose are Dirk **Bogarde**, otherwise Derek Gentron Gaspart Ulric van den **Bogaerde**; Fred **Astaire**—Frederick **Austerlitz;** Danny **Kaye**—David Daniel **Kaminsky;** Jerry **Lewis**—Joseph **Levitch;** Greta **Garbo**—Greta **Gustafsson.** The smallest possible change was made by Warren **Beatty,** formerly **Beaty.** His sister, Shirley Maclean Beaty, emerged as Shirley **Maclaine. Liberace** is one who retained his real surname but dropped the **Wladziu Valentino** that preceded it. Others have preferred to take more drastic action and forget the old surname completely. Well-known examples include Diana **Dors,** formerly Diana **Fluck;** Judy **Garland**—Frances **Gumm;** Kirk **Douglas**—Issur Danielovitch **Demsky;** Engelbert **Humperdinck**—Arnold **Dorsey**

Politicians can hardly be described as entertainers, but they also need names that the public can cope with. Spiro **Agnew** understandably adapted his Greek family name, **Anagnostopoulos,** for this

'Alan Bolt? Nothing. Let's get a name for him, somebody. A long one. That one is too short. It's over before you know it. I like long names. They look bigger on the billing. People think they are getting more for their money. Like Rudolph Valentino, now there's a good name.'

Garson Kanin *Moviola*

reason. Such changes differ from the adoption of political pseudonyms, which have been used in countries such as Russia. **Stalin,** 'steel', was chosen by **I. V. Dzhugashvili**, whose real name derived from a word meaning 'dross'. **Lenin**'s name was meant to be a reminder of political disturbances on the River **Lena,** in Siberia, though it exists as a real name, derived from **Alexander**. Lenin's real name was **Ulyanov.**

Mention of Russian names brings us back to stage names, for in certain circles, such as the ballet, they have great prestige. Those not as fortunate as Rudolf **Nureyev**, who was able to use his real name, have sometimes adopted one that has a suitably Russian-sounding flavour. Alice **Marks** became Alicia **Markova,** while Patrick **Healey-Kay** changed to Anton **Dolin.** The dignity and romanticism of such names contrasts interestingly with the names of some other dancers, who appear in the Parisian Crazy Horse Cabaret. The latter appear under such evocative names (and little else) as Pamela **Boum-Boum,** Polly **Underground** and Rita **Cadillac.**

Pen names

Writers' pseudonyms have been used far longer than stage names and often for different reasons. The desire is not necessarily to escape from an unfortunate name, but genuinely to conceal the writer's true identity. In the past it was sometimes thought that readers would be prejudiced against women writers, so many of them wrote as men or tried to conceal their sex in non-committal names, such as those used by the Brontë sisters, **Currer, Ellis** and **Acton Bell**. Other authors have been ashamed of their works for one reason or another and have not wished anyone to know their true identities. In modern times there are authors who would flood the market if they used their own name all the time, and a string of pseudonyms becomes necessary. A single pen name can, on the other hand, conceal the fact that several different authors are writing the stories concerned. Finally, if an author has made himself something of an authority in one area, he may feel that another name is required when he turns to pastures new.

About this time, to her more familiar correspondents, Charlotte Brontë occasionally calls herself 'Charles Thunder', making a kind of pseudonym for herself out of her Christian name, and the meaning of her Greek surname.

Elizabeth Gaskell   *The Life of Charlotte Brontë*

(In fact Brontë was a form of Prunty or Pronty, Irish Proinntigh, 'bestower, generous person', the change to Brontë having been made by Charlotte's father. He was probably more influenced by the fact that Lord Nelson had been made Duke of Brontë, a place in Sicily, in 1799, than by *bronte*, Greek for 'thunder'.)

One would expect authors to choose pen names that have linguistic point to them. **Lewis Carroll** has a suitably etymological connection with **Charles Lutwidge Dodgson**, its inventor. Lutwidge is a form of **Ludwig**, which can be directly translated as Lewis. Charles is **Carolus** in Latin, and Carroll simply adapts it slightly. The 19th-century writer **Ouida** looks as if she transferred her name from the city of

---

Her real name wasn't Lois Angeles, it was Linda Peabody, which struck him as a damn good reason for changing it to almost anything else you could think of.

L. J. Davis   *Walking Small*

---

that name in Morocco, but she herself explained it as a natural linguistic development. It represented her own attempt as a child to pronounce her middle name, **Louise**.

Aliases

These last examples once again retain a definite link with the real name, which many people who adopt a new name consider to be necessary. Traces of name magic are revealed here, for this hints at a deep-rooted belief that one's real name is somehow part of one's real self, and that complete abandonment of it will have evil consequences. Criminal records support this contention strongly, for an analysis of aliases that have been used shows that the adopted surnames normally have the same initial, number of syllables and basic sound as the originals. What appears to be a totally new name is more often drawn from the namer's immediate onomastic environment. It will be the mother's maiden name or the surname of a close friend, or a name transferred from a street or place that has strong personal associations. The link with the real past is maintained.

As we have seen, immigration into an English-speaking country can be another reason for name change and here again an attempt is often made to link with the original name. The Ukrainian Vasyl **Mykula** who became William **McCulla** showed one way of doing it. Other Russian-English pairs are **Prishchipenko—Price, Chernyshev—Chester, Grushko—Grey.** Direct translation, eg of German **Müller**, French **Meunier**, Hungarian **Molnar**, Dutch **Mulder** into English **Miller** achieves a similar result. But by far the commonest reason for a surname change is marriage. Here, of course, there is no question of a woman consciously choosing a new name; she is simply re-exposed to the complex of accidental factors that gave her a surname in the first place. As for the name that has been so much a part

---

'Under what name did you make your appearance here?'

'I used my own.'

'I would have preferred Polkinghorne or Gooch or Withers,' said the Bishop pensively. 'They sound more legal.'

P. G. Wodehouse   *Cats Will Be Cats*

Maiden names

'I offer you my name and hand, Laetitia!'

George Meredith   *The Egoist*

Mr Alfred Cortez married her and gave her his name and the two foundations of her family, Alfredo and Ernie. Mr Cortez gave her that name gladly. He was only using it temporarily anyway. His name, before he came to Monterey and after he left, was Guggliemo.

John Steinbeck   *Tortilla Flat*

Nancy kept her own name for all purposes, refusing to be called 'Mrs Graves' in any circumstances. She explained that as 'Mrs Graves' she had no personal validity.

Robert Graves   *Goodbye to all That*

'I sometimes think of marrying old Maltravers,' said Mrs Beste-Chetwynde, 'only "Margot Maltravers" does sound a little too much, don't you think?'

Evelyn Waugh   *Decline and Fall*

of her life for many years, she finds that it becomes a mere maiden name. It is instantly reduced to at best middle-name status, and perhaps even less.

The implications of this marital name change have been much commented on, but although one reads at regular intervals of women who insist on using their maiden names after marriage, no general protest seems to be made. Suggestions that both husband and wife should take on a new name at marriage—perhaps blending parts of their surnames—are not taken very seriously. The blocking up of both surnames with hyphens between them has unfortunate connotations of pretentiousness, apart from leading to some very unwieldy combinations. Perhaps the problem will only be solved if we finally abolish hereditary surnames altogether. They are already superfluous in many ways. If we were allocated an individual number name at birth and used that for all official purposes, we could probably get by very well with one other personal name.

Other surname changes

Meanwhile, however, a large number of ordinary people who are not seeking public fame or trying to conceal their identities, change their surnames every year. They make use of a very simple legal process

to rid themselves of a name which for one reason or another is an embarrassment to them. Who can possibly blame the Mr **Bugg** who became a **Howard**, or the gentlemen called **Bub, Holdwater, Poopy, Piddle, Honeybum, Leakey, Rumpe** and **Teate** who quietly dropped these surnames a century ago? Curiously enough, they were criticised at the time, though the criticisms were directed at the names they adopted, thought to be too high and mighty for ordinary citizens.

Personally, I can only wonder why more people do not follow the sensible example set by these name-changes. Why on earth do *I*, for example, put up with **Dunkling**, which is frequently converted into **Dumpling** by the hard-of-hearing or malicious? I

If I say that a man is a wealthy Boston banker, automatically in your mind you assign him a high-prestige rating.

But if I add that his name is Lazienki *, a new dimension has been added, even though you may still agree he deserves a high-prestige rating.*

Vance Packard   *The Status Seekers*

have had its replacement standing by for years, an easy-to-spell, easy-to-say, pleasant-sounding name with the most respectable literary and other associations, and not, to my knowledge, at present attached to any other family. If I do not adopt it, is it because—not being an actor by nature—I would not be able to live out my life behind an onomastic disguise? Or am I conceited enough to think that I can overcome the natural disadvantages of my name and win through anyway?

You have a name and one thing after another happens to you, and you behave in various ways and do things, so that soon the name begins to have a meaning. Things have accumulated around the name. If it is bad and you have a bad reputation, then you can't jump out of your name and escape like that. And if it is good and you have a good reputation, then you should be content and satisfied.

Carson McCullers   *The Member of the Wedding*

Ideas about what is unusual also change with the passing of time. At one time somebody named **Petard**, which derives from a word meaning 'to break wind', would presumably have wanted to change it: today his friends might simply associate him vaguely with a passage in *Hamlet* and he would not feel under attack. A **Belcher,** on the other hand, was quite happy when others interpreted his name as *bel chiere*, 'pretty face'. The forgetting of this early meaning has left him sadly exposed.

Other men are quite happy with their names until they reach adulthood and take up a profession. They then fall victim to the inevitable comments about their being **Berriman** the undertaker, or **D. Kaye,** the dentist. Partnership names such as **Reid** and **Wright** for Belfast printers, and **Doolittle** and **Dally** for estate agents are also much commented on, though they do have the advantage of attracting publicity.

If you are seriously thinking of changing your surname you would do well, for your descendants' sake, to begin it with a letter near the front of the alphabet. The custom when groups of people are gathered together for any purpose of working through them in alphabetical order has had a serious effect on people named **Young** and the like, psy-

chologists tell us. They are constantly made to feel insignificant because they are dealt with last.

If you ever have occasion to write to me, would you mind sticking a P at the beginning of my name? P-s-m-i-t-h. See? There are too many Smiths, and I don't care for Smythe. I've decided to strike out a fresh line. In conversation you may address me as Rupert (though I hope you won't), or simply Smith, the P not being sounded.

P. G. Wodehouse   *Mike*

Psychological effects of surnames

If you are *not* thinking about a surname change, perhaps you should be. At the very least you should make an honest evaluation of your surname to see whether it is a definite hindrance to you, or whether it will be so for your children. As an adult you may be well aware that your surname is totally irrelevant in any evaluation of your total worth as a human being, but your children will spend many important years in a group where there is no such awareness. Studies such as that made by Christopher Bagley and Louise Evan-Wong ('Psychiatric Disorder and Adult and Peer Group Rejection of the Child's Name') prove beyond all reasonable doubt that children who consider a surname derisive will transfer their feelings about the name to the person who bears it. The attitude of his class-mates is likely to reinforce a child's negative opinion of himself,

I ought to explain that it was not the peculiarity of Mr Loggerhead's name that produced the odd effect. Loggerheads is a local term for a harmless plant called the knapweed, and it is also the appellation of a place and of quite excellent people, and no-one regards it as even the least bit odd.

Arnold Bennett   *Why the Clock Stopped*

Richard **Vlk,** of Pittsburgh, had often thought of changing his surname, which is of Czech origin and means 'wolf'. Most people had no idea how to pronounce it ('Velk'), and spelled it wrongly. Many simply laughed at it.

In 1983 Mr Vlk and his wife Kathy had the last laugh when they won over twenty thousand dollars in a contest run by the Pepsi-Cola Bottling Co. of Pittsburgh. They collected flip tops with letters on them that spelled their name. Consonants were easy to come by, vowels were hard to get. The Vlks suddenly found that a short, vowel-less name was just the thing to have.

which will have been influenced by his own assessment of his name.

A point not pursued in the above-mentioned article is that if children evaluate unusual names, they presumably evaluate *all* names. How does a **Smith** child react, one wonders, when he realises that he has a very common name? It could conceivably lead him to think that he must be a very ordinary person. And what effect does it have on a child who discovers that he happens to possess a rather distinguished name? I can personally recall, as a child, envying a boy in the class *because of his name*, which happened to be **Nelson.** Surely I am not the only one to have known such feelings? And was the young Nelson so self-confident and assured partly because of his name?

I am not advocating a change of surname as a way of adjusting a person's psychological balance, or as a way of instantly improving his self-image. It appears to be a belief of the Kabalarians, founded in 1926 by Alfred J. Parker and based in Vancouver, that the one will automatically lead to the other. An article in *The Province*, December 1972, gives several examples of name changes advised by this organisation. They include **Jennifer Lulham** to **Alannah Matthew, Dorothy Rayner** to **Dhorea Delain, Marian Birch** to **Natallia Hohn.**

The very existence of the Kabalarians, and their ability to attract adherents, proves that a belief in the association of name with character can be carried into adult life. The name-changers clearly believe that mystic qualities of the new name will rub off on to them. They speak in the newspaper article of immediate and beneficial results of taking on a new name, and in this one can readily believe. But one can believe, too, that it boosts a normal person's morale to be well groomed and dressed. The effects of the new name will last no longer than the effects of make-up if the underlying attitude is wrong.

The name-makers

Where should those who are considering changing their name turn for guidance? Should they begin, for instance, with the most practised and prolific name-makers in our society, the writers of fiction? Novelists as name-makers provide an interesting study. The writers still occasionally fall back on the literary convention of type-names, the **Shallow** of Shakespeare or the Mrs **Slipslop** of Fielding, but when they do so the characters concerned are usually personifications of abstract ideas rather than ordinary people. At their best, novelists have a feeling for a name's associated characteristics—for surnames have these just as first names do—and use a name that works below the conscious level to achieve the desired result. Dickensian characters such as **Pickwick** and **Scrooge** seem to be perfectly named. One wonders whether Pickwick appealed to the author because it partly echoed his own name, or did he simply see the name somewhere and jot it in his notebook, as he frequently did with names. Scrooge seems to be a made-up name, based on the word 'screw' as in the sentence used by Thackeray: 'I must screw and save in order to pay off the money.'

'Quilp is my name. You might remember. It's not a long one—Daniel Quilp.'

Charles Dickens   *The Old Curiosity Shop*

'I'm surprised and rather disappointed that you like Scarp. I know it simply means a steep descent, but as a name it suggests somebody small, hard and mean— perhaps a dwarf moneylender in a Victorian novel.'

J. B. Priestley   *Out of Town*

I always judge a young author by the names which he bestows upon his characters. If the names seem to be weak or to be unsuitable to the people who bear them, I put the author down as a man of little talent, and am no further interested in the book.

Emile Zola   *Dr Pascal*

One of the subtler difficulties that confront an author's name-sense arises from the necessary re-naming of such characters who have been adapted from real life, and whose own names cling to them closely as a wet bathing-costume.

G. B. Stern   *A Name to Conjure With*

But authors are not always objective in their naming. They often seem to have a liking for particular sounds, and they return to these again and again. Thackeray clearly fell in love with the surname **Crump,** which actually exists and originally meant 'stooping'. He used it for three different characters. He has another character named **Crampton.** Dickens, as it happens, has a **Crumpton** and a **Crupp.** Both Dickens and Thackeray made use of **Crawley** as a character name, and between them they cover a wide range of other names beginning with 'Cr-'. Those they omit are accounted for by Sir Walter Scott, George Eliot, Jane Austen, Thomas Hardy, John Galsworthy and Anthony Trollope, all of whom begin the surnames of more than one character with these letters. Perhaps they pay a subconscious tribute to the first fictional character in English literature, **Robinson Crusoe,** but they may be revealing what a linguist might call their 'phonaesthetic preference'.

An analysis of any writer would probably reveal quite quickly his particular likes in this respect. Graham Greene, for example, has characters called **Rank, Rolt** and **Rowe, Rennit, Rimmer** and **Robinson.** If we ourselves were faced with the problem of naming a series of characters in different books we, too, would no doubt fall into some kind of pattern. If we tried to make a name for ourselves we would make use again of our linguistic preferences. This would be something to beware of, for it would be subjective. There is no point, surely, in changing one's name unless one is totally objective about it. The name would be meant to appeal to other people, not oneself.

Namesakes

Which surnames *do* please people? There have been no studies made that I am aware of which could answer that question. The names of popular people presumably have a head start on others, but it would be an error for anyone to turn himself into a namesake. I can think of nothing more depressing than having to answer the constantly repeated question: 'Not *the* **James Stewart?**' (or whoever) with 'No', or a wan smile.

Some people evidently enjoy being namesakes. The Jim Smith Society was founded in 1969 and has annual gatherings in America. One object of the society, according to a letter from its founder, James H. Smith, Jr, of Camp Hill, Pennsylvania, is to seek 'background information about acts of heroism by Jim Smiths'. Such as founding a Jim Smith Society, perhaps. I gather that a lot of fun is had by all concerned at the annual meetings, and perhaps we shall see more societies of this type in the future.

'Tis but thy name that is my enemy;
Thou art thyself, though, not a
Montague.
What's Montague? It is nor hand, nor
foot,
Nor arm, nor face, nor any other part
Belonging to a man. O, be some other
name.

William Shakespeare   *Romeo and Juliet*

Becoming a partial namesake of someone famous might be an answer to the name-change problem. A little glory will rub off, possibly, and one will avoid the jokes. Reflected glory of a kind has been turned to commercial advantage in recent years by the firms which supply coats of arms. What happens here is that a coat of arms which has been awarded to a family is treated as being attached to the surname rather than the family concerned. In fact, a coat of arms in its 'undifferenced' form can be used only by the head of the family to which it was granted. Other members of the family use it too, but incorporate cadency marks. A man cannot sell his coat of arms or give someone else permission to use it, so there is absolutely no question of another family, which happens to have the same name, having the right to use it. This does not deter a great many people from displaying in their homes someone else's coat of arms with the shared family name written beneath it. There is little doubt that many people confuse coats of arms with clan tartans as far as usage is concerned, though the firms concerned usually explain the situation fairly clearly in the small print of their advertisements.

Perhaps no harm is done, other than to the occasional outraged head of a family who sees his personal property being trampled on, as it were. He might console himself with the thought that those meaningless little plaques are exerting a little name magic, enabling some anonymous people to feel somehow more dignified and content with the names they bear. If name magic is to continue having an influence, even in our apparently civilised society, it might as well have some positive effects as well as negative.

I have talked at some length about changing

A name—if the party had a voice
What mortal would be a Bugg by choice,
As a Hogg, a Grubb or a Chubb rejoice,
Or any such nauseous blazon?
Not to mention many a vulgar name
That would make a doorplate blush for shame
If doorplates were not so brazen.

Thomas Hood

names, but my main object has been to stimulate a few thoughts about the meaning in modern times of the surnames that we inherit. Changing one's name is easy from a legal point of view, but it is understandable that many people are reluctant to do it. Those of us who put up with what we have must console ourselves with the thought that a change might not bring about the desired result in any case. Our bright new name might be brushed aside in favour of a nickname, and nicknames are not always complimentary as we shall see in the next chapter. Or perhaps our new names would simply fail to convince. Mr A. A. Willis makes this point in a story he passed on to me about a gentleman named **Brown** who applied to change his name to **Smith.** He was asked why he wanted to make this change, as he had changed his name only six months previously from **Gorfinckel** to **Brown.** His reply was: 'Becos ven pipple say to me: "Vot vas your name before it was Smith?" I vant to be able to say: "It was Brown—so there." '

Caller: 'Oh, hello. Do you have a Sexauer in your company?'
Telephone operator: 'Sexauer? We don't even have a coffee break.'

Some people who made a name for themselves

Anouk Aimée Françoise Sorya.
Woody Allen Allen Stewart Konigsberg.
Julie Andrews Julia Elizabeth Wells.
Pier Angeli Anna Maria Pierangeli.
Mary Astor Lucille Langehanke.
Lauren Bacall Betty Joan Perske.
Brigitte Bardot Camille Javal.
Eva Bartok Eva Sjöke.
Jack Benny Benjamin Kubelsky.
Irving Berlin Israel Baline.
Sarah Bernhardt Rosine Bernard.
Scott Brady Gerald Tierney.
Dora Bryan Dora May Broadbent.
Richard Burton Richard Walter Jenkins.
Michael Caine Maurice Joseph Micklewhite.
Rory Calhoun Francis Timothy Durgin.
Phyllis Calvert Phyllis Bickle.
Eddie Cantor Edward Israel Iskowitz.
Jeannie Carson Jean Shufflebottom.
Jeff Chandler Ira Grossel.
Lee J. Cobb Lee Jacoby.
Claudette Colbert Lily Claudette Chauchoin.
Gary Cooper Frank J. Cooper.
Lou Costello Louis Cristillo.
Constance Cummings Constance Halverstadt.
Tony Curtis Bernard Schwartz.
Vic Damone Vito Farinola.
Bebe Daniels Virginia Daniels.
Bobby Darin Walden Robert Cassotto.
Doris Day Doris Kappelhoff.
Yvonne de Carlo Peggy Yvonne Middleton.
Marlene Dietrich Marie Magdalene Dietrich von Losch.
Douglas Fairbanks Julius Ullman.
José Ferrer José Vincente Ferrer Otero y Cintrón.
Gracie Fields Grace Stansfield.
W. C. Fields William Claude Dukinfield.
Bud Flanagan Chaim Reuben Weintrop.
Sam Goldwyn Samuel Goldfish.
Cary Grant Alexander Archibald Leach.
Nadia Gray Nadia Kujnir-Herescu.
Kathryn Grayson Zelma Hedrick.
Jean Harlow Harlean Carpenter.

Rex Harrison Reginald Carey Harrison.
Laurence Harvey Larushka Mischa Skikne.
Susan Hayward Edythe Marriner.
Hy Hazell Hyacinth Hazel O'Higgins.
Audrey Hepburn Edda Hepburn van Heemstra.
William Holden William Franklin Beedle.
Judy Holliday Judith Tuvim.
Leslie Howard Leslie Stainer.
Rock Hudson Roy Harold Fitzgerald.
Tab Hunter Arthur Andrew Gelien.
Burl Ives Burl Icle Ivanhoe.
Elton John Reginald Kenneth Dwight.
Al Jolson Asa Yoelson.
Boris Karloff William Henry Pratt.
Buster Keaton Joseph Francis Keaton.
Veronica Lake Constance Ockleman.
Hedy Lamarr Hedwig Kiesler.
Dorothy Lamour Dorothy Kaumeyer.
Mario Lanza Alfredo Arnold Cocozza.
Wilfrid Lawson Wilfrid Worsnop.
Gypsy Rose Lee Rose Louise Hovick.
Peggy Lee Norma Dolores Egstrom.
Vivien Leigh Vivian Mary Hartley.
Herbert Lom Herbert Charles Angelo Kuchacevich ze Schluderpacheru.
Sophia Loren Sofia Scicolone.
Dean Martin Dino Crocetti.
Tony Martin Alvin Morris.
Virginia Mayo Virginia May Jones.
Ethel Merman Ethel Zimmerman.
Ray Milland Reginald Truscott-Jones.
Carmen Miranda Maria de Carmo Mirando de Cunha.
Marilyn Monroe Norma Jean Baker.
Anna Neagle Marjorie Robertson.
Kim Novak Marilyn Novak.
Ivor Novello David Ivor Davies.
Merle Oberon Estelle Merle O'Brien Thompson.
Maureen O'Hara Maureen Fitzsimmons.
Jack Palance Walter Palanuik.
Cecil Parker Cecil Schwabe.
Jean Parker Mae Green.

Mary Pickford Gladys Mary Smith.
Jane Powell Suzanne Burce.
Chips Rafferty John William Goffage.
Ted Ray Charles Olden.
Debbie Reynolds Mary Frances Reynolds.
Cliff Richard Harold Roger Webb.
George Robey George Edward Wade.
Ginger Rogers Virginia Katharine McMath.
Roy Rogers Leonard Slye.
Mickey Rooney Joe Yule.
Romy Schneider Rosemarie Albach-Retty.
Randolph Scott Randolph Crane.
Mack Sennett Michael Sinott.
Moira Shearer Moira Shearer King.
Tommy Steele Thomas Hicks.
Connie Stevens Concetta Ann Ingolia.
Gale Storm Josephine Cottle.
Jacques Tati Jacques Tatisceff.
Robert Taylor Spangler Arlington Brough.
Terry-Thomas Thomas Terry Hoar-Stevens.
Mike Todd Avrom Hirsch Goldbogen.
Sophie Tucker Sophia Abuza.
Lana Turner Julia Turner.
Twiggy Lesley Hornby.
Rudy Vallee Hubert Prior Vallee.
Odile Versois Militza de Polakoff-Baidarov.
Erich von Stroheim Hans Erich Maria Stroheim von Nordenwall.
Anton Walbrook Adolf Wohlbrück.
Jean Wallace Jean Wallasek.
Jack Warner Jack Waters.
John Wayne Marion Michael Morrison.
Clifton Webb Webb Parmelee Hollenbeck.
Shelley Winters Shirley Schrift.
Jane Wyman Sarah Jane Fulks.

'You're a disgrace to our family name of Wagstaff, if such a thing is possible.'

Groucho Marx in *Horse Feathers*

SIGNS OF THE TIMES

A PERSON'S signature is thought to reveal far more than the name of the person concerned. Psychologists seem to agree that the larger the signature, the greater the person's self-esteem. Studies have shown that men normally have larger signatures than women, reflecting the greater status they have traditionally enjoyed. Individuals are also likely to increase the size of their signature if they happen to be feeling satisfied with themselves because of something they have just achieved, or because their status has been advanced by long-term achievement. Richard L. Zweigenhaft, for instance, in an article published in *Social Behaviour and Personality*, 1977, shows how one man's signature steadily became larger as he advanced from being a student to a member of the faculty. Zweigenhaft also reports on students who were asked to sign their names as themselves, then while imagining themselves to be President of the United States. The imaginary status was enough to cause an increase in signature size. Self-esteem, however, is not necessarily linked to real status. Conceited people are found at all levels of society.

The style of signature is also thought to be revealing. The average person, who has a first name, middle name and last name, has to choose between six possible styles:

a) *J. Smith* Use of the initial suggests an unwillingness to disclose oneself to others, and hints at emotional, possibly sexual, repression.

b) *John Smith* The style of a conventional conformist, but one who is easily approachable. Tends to be informal and frank, and of liberal views.

c) *J. D. Smith* An insecure person who wishes to present a mature image to the world. Possibly repressed emotionally or sexually. Has a strong preference for traditional ways of behaviour.

d) *John D. Smith* Very conventional, likely to have right wing views. Believes in strict rules and punishments. Inclined to be religiously dogmatic.

e) *J. David Smith* A narcissistic person, obsessed with his own image. Considers himself highly individualistic and is determined that others should think so too.

f) *John David Smith* The sign of an exhibitionist who likes to publicise himself. Certainly does not suffer from low self-esteem.

The above comments are based on a newspaper interview with a Canadian psychologist, Dr Elizabeth Willett.

Individuals will, of course, change their signature according to circumstances. To test your friends, give them a blank sheet of paper and ask them to sign their names in the way they prefer.

Claud Morris's signature was large, in blue ink, clear to read, emphasized by a flowing hooked line beneath it. I deduced that this Claud Morris believed he had a name to be proud of. He underlined his own importance.

Edith Courtney   *My Feet are Killing Me*

'I have signed my name,' said Louis, 'already twenty times. I, and again I, and again I. Clear firm, unequivocal, there it stands, my name . . . all the furled and close-packed leaves of my many folded life are now summed in my name.'

Virginia Woolf   *The Waves*

Literary surnames

Aziz 'Aziz! What a charming name!'
E. M. Forster   *A Passage to India*

Bedworth 'Here's a damned impertinent letter from God knows who – calls himself Piddlebed, or some such.' 'Bedworth,' I said. 'Bedworth, Bedpan – I don't give a fart for the fellow's name.'
J. I. M. Stuart   *A Memorial Service*

Blight The office door was opened by the dismal boy, whose appropriate name was Blight.
Charles Dickens   *Our Mutual Friend*

Brass The legal gentleman, whose melodious name was Brass . . . The dwarf glanced sarcastically at his brazen friend.
Charles Dickens   *The Old Curiosity Shop*

Brownjohn 'Mr Brownjohn's a good man.' 'Unbelievable name, that. I do very much wonder how he came by it – I should say, how his ancestor came by it.'
Kingsley Amis   *Ending Up*

(The name indicates a man named John who had brown hair)

Bucket 'My name's Bucket. Ain't that a funny name?'
Charles Dickens   *Bleak House*

Bullock 'Mr and Mrs Bullock's compliments, sir, and they hope you are pretty well after your journey.' 'Who would have expected such kindness from such an unpromising name?'
Elizabeth Gaskell   *Mr Harrison's Confessions*

Butts 'Mr Butts of the Life Guards.' 'Mr Butts – *quel nom!*'
William Thackeray   *The Newcomes*

Carlyon He was absolutely devoid of all ambition, save a desire to have his surname pronounced correctly. 'Car-lee-on,' he would say, with polite emphasis, 'not Car-ly-on. Our

name is an old, historical one, and like many of its class is spelt one way and pronounced another.'
Marie Corelli   *Delicia*

Christian A beggar woman, repulsed from door to door as she solicited quarters through a village of Annandale, asked in her despair if there were no Christians in the place. To which the hearers, concluding that she inquired for some persons so surnamed, answered: 'Na, na, there are nae Christians here; we are a' Johnstones and Jardines.'
Sir Walter Scott   *Guy Mannering* (note to text)

Chuzzlewit 'Then Martin is your Christian name?' said Mr Pinch thoughtfully. 'Of course it is,' returned his friend: 'I wish it was my surname, for my own is not a pretty one, and it takes a long time to sign. Chuzzlewit is my name.'
Charles Dickens   *Martin Chuzzlewit*

Finching 'Who ever could have imagined Mrs Finching when I can't imagine it myself!' 'Is that your married name?' asked Arthur. 'Finching?' 'Finching oh yes isn't it a dreadful name but as Mr F said when he proposed to me, he wasn't answerable for it and couldn't help it could he . . .'
Charles Dickens   *Little Dorrit*

Fitz-Adam She had always supposed that Fitz meant something aristocratic. Fitz-Adam! – it was a pretty name, and she thought it very probably meant 'child of Adam'. No one, who had not some good blood in their veins, would dare to be called Fitz; there was a deal in a name – she had had a cousin who spelt his name with two little ffs – ffoulkes – and he always looked down upon capital letters and said they belonged to lately-invented families. When he met a Mrs ffaringdon, at a watering place, he took to her immediately. Mr ffoulkes

married her; and it was all owing to her little ffs.
Elizabeth Gaskell   *Cranford*

Glubb 'I wish you'd tell old Glubb to come and see me, if you please.' 'What a dreadful low name!' said Mrs Blimber. 'Unclassical to a degree. Who is the monster, child?'
Charles Dickens   *Dombey and Son*

Grant . . . the senior chaplain. His name was Grant, which caused restrained smiles during services when he intoned prayers that began Grant, O Lord, we beseech Thee.
Paul Scott   *The Jewel in the Crown*

Grey Our surname was Grey: I wished it had been Shelmerdine, or de Courcy, ffrench with two small 'ff's or double-barrelled like Stuyvesant-Knox, but it was, simply, Grey. 'Better than Bullock,' said Joss. We had not quite escaped that; Uncle William was a Bullock, William John Bullock.
Rumer Godden   *The Greengage Summer*

Hoggins The name of these good people was Hoggins. Mr Hoggins was the Cranford doctor now; we disliked the name and considered it coarse; but, as Miss Jenkyns said, if he changed it to Piggins it would not be much better. We had hoped to discover a relationship between him and the Marchioness of Exeter whose name was Molly Hoggins; but the man, careless of his own interests, utterly ignored and denied any such relationship, although, as dear Miss Jenkyns had said, he had a sister called Mary, and the same Christian names were apt to run in families.
Elizabeth Gaskell   *Cranford*

Hogsbotham Mr Hogsbotham had to be a bachelor, because it was not plausible that any woman, unless moved by a passion which a man of Mr Hogsbotham's desiccated sanctity could never hope to inspire, would consent to adopt a name like Mrs

Hogsbotham.
Leslie Charteris   *Follow the Saint*

Maarbjerg 'Isn't that a funny-sounding name? I mean – Americans often think so.' 'Morebeer?' said Mrs Minturn, experimentally.
James Reid Parker   *The Merry Wives of Massachusetts*

Maradick His name was Maradick – Sir James Maradick. A strange, unreal kind of name for so real and solid a man.
Hugh Walpole *Portrait of a Man with Red Hair*

Moneypenny I did not like pushing myself upon strangers, who perhaps had never heard of my mother's name, and, such an odd name as it was – Moneypenny.
Elizabeth Gaskell   *Cousin Phillis*

Mouldy Falstaff: Is thy name Mouldy?
Mouldy: Yea, an't please you.
Falstaff: 'Tis the more time thou wert used.
Shallow: Ha, ha, ha! most excellent, i' faith! Things that are mouldy lack use. Very singular good.
William Shakespeare   *Henry IV Part 2*

Mozart Although it would be an exaggeration to say that Arnold Green fell in love with Bessie Mozart because of her surname, he was certainly influenced by it. 'After all,' he told his parents, 'a name like that's historic. It's an omen. It's a name with class.' 'Mozart, schmozart! Omens, schmomens!' his mother growled. 'As for class, any name's got class when there's money in the bank. Believe me, Green would also be the classiest name in the world if we had the money of the Rothschilds. Class in a name yet!'
Cyril Kersh   *The Soho Summer of Mr Green*

Muchbetter There was a family named Muchbetter, who didn't seem to mind. They took it in their stride.
Peter de Vries   *Let Me Count the Ways*

Peel He bore the almost sacred name of Peel. His family had been distinguished in the district for generations. Peel! You could without impropriety utter it in the same breath with 'Wedgwood'. And 'Swynnerton' stood not much lower.
Arnold Bennett   *The Old Wives' Tale*

Pensil 'Pensil. It's an odd name, but it isn't a bad one.' 'I think one name's as good as another.'
Henry James   *The Portrait of a Lady*

Pidgeon 'His name was Pidgeon.' Eddie tittered at this.
Elizabeth Bowen   *The Death of the Heart*

Pitsner There was probably no such person as Mr Pitsner. The very name shattered conviction.
J. B. Priestley   *The Good Companions*

Potts 'I had a great friend called Potts.' '*Potts!*' said Lady Circumference, and left it at that.
Evelyn Waugh   *Decline and Fall*

Pugh His opponent is a Welshman who calls himself apHugh (affectation, a Pugh is a Pugh the world over).
Dane Chandos   *Abbie*

Quarles 'The president, old Quarles – quarrels is right, by golly, ha, ha, ha!'
Sinclair Lewis   *Elmer Gantry*

Shatwell 'A chap with the name of Shatwell,' he explained, 'learns rather early on that things are likely to go against him, you understand. I thought of changing the old name once, but I'd become rather attached to it, you understand, so I decided to make do.'
Hugh Maclennan   *The Watch that Ends the Night*

Skinner 'Take Jock Skinner's name, now. Skinner is not a bonnie word at a-all. Do you think that is because Jock himself is not bonnie or is it

chust an ugly word whateffer?' 'It is not a bonnie noise of a word,' Tom concluded, 'besides making you think on beasts being skinned at the slaughter-house, poor craiturs. Of course, there might be some very nice people off the name off Skinner for all that.'
Jane Duncan   *My Friend Flora*

Smith A mere Mrs Smith, an every day Mrs Smith, of all people and of all names in the world, to be the chosen friend of Miss Anne Elliot. Mrs Smith, such a name!
Jane Austen   *Persuasion*

Smithson 'Do not think,' he had once said to her, 'how disgracefully plebeian a name Smithson is.' 'Ah, indeed – if you were only called Lord Brabazon Vavasour Vere de Vere – how much more I should love you!'
John Fowles   *The French Lieutenant's Woman*

Starbuck 'My mother's grandmother was a Starbuck.' Coffin had always thought that the name Starbuck had been made up by the guy who wrote *Moby Dick* – or at least by the guy who wrote the movie script for *Moby Dick* – and not even made up very well.
L. J. Davis   *Walking Small*

Sunnyfarebrother The name 'Sunnyfarebrother' struck me as almost redundant in its suggestion of clear-cut, straightforward masculinity. It seemed hardly necessary for Peter to add that someone with a name like that had 'done well' in the war, so unambiguous was the portrait conjured up by the syllables.
Anthony Powell   *A Question of Upbringing*

Towneley 'I wish, my dear, you could cultivate your acquaintance with Towneley, and ask him to pay me a visit. The name has an aristocratic sound.'
Samuel Butler   *The Way of all Flesh*

9
EKING OUT NAMES

WITH his first name, middle name and surname it might seem that the average person was adequately identified, but far from it. We are all given additional names for official purposes—mostly number names or code names—and most of us acquire an unofficial extra name as well. We use the term 'nickname' to describe the latter, which is usually friendly. The word 'sobriquet', which we borrowed centuries ago from the French, is also useful. It describes a name which is decidedly unfriendly, meant to cut a person down to size. The etymology of the word seems to hint at a 'taming', for the original meaning was 'a chuck under the chin', as when a horse is reined in.

'Nickname' itself simply means 'an additional name', with no bias towards a good or bad name and no indication as to whether a person, place or thing is involved. The word derives from the expression 'an eke name', which later became 'a nekename'. This is the 'eke' we use when we say that we must 'eke out our supplies'. Traced back far enough it probably links up with the Latin word *augere*, which is the root of words such as 'augment'.

This explanation of 'nickname' is fairly modern, by the way. Dr Johnson thought it must derive from the French nique, which means a gesture (but not a name) of mockery. Harry Long, a 19th-century

I became almost conical in shape. My nickname was Podger or Binge.

David Niven   *The Moon's A Balloon*

writer on names, appears to have connected it with the German nicken, which means 'to nod', for he explains it as 'a name given with a contemptuous nick of the head'. Long also explained 'sobriquet' wrongly, but he can perhaps be forgiven because of his fine comment that nicknames and sobriquets are 'biographies crowded into a word'.

To-names

We have already separated out bynames as a special kind of nickname, acting as a temporary surname. There is another special kind of personal nickname which is sometimes called a *to-name*. This is an extra name that becomes necessary for identification purposes in communities where many people bear the same surname. John McPhee, for example, in his book about the Scottish island of Colonsay (*The Crofter and the Laird*) describes the substitute surnames taken on by the McNeills and McAllisters.

'Swidge' is the appellation by which they speak of Mrs William in general, among themselves, I'm told; but that's what I say, sir. Better be called ever so far out of your name, if it's done in real liking, than have it made ever so much of, and not cared about! What's a name for? To know a person by. If Mrs William is known by something better than her name—I allude to Mrs William's qualities and disposition—never mind her name, though it is Swidger, by rights. Let 'em call her Swidge, Widge, Bridge—Lord! London Bridge, Blackfriars, Chelsea, Putney, Waterloo or Hammersmith Suspension—if they like!

Charles Dickens   *The Haunted Man*

Many of them are known by place names, of which there is an ample supply. Only 138 people lived on the island when McPhee was there, but there were 1600 recorded place names—with the most minor landmarks being counted as places.

Another system is for a husband and his wife to borrow each other's first names. **Peter McAllister** is known as **Peter Bella,** his wife as **Bella Peter.** Such a system might be very useful at an ordinary social gathering, such as a cocktail-party, and it would certainly add a touch of charm. The more usual kind of patronymic nickname is seen in **Mary Calum Coll,** Calum being the lady's father, Coll her grandfather. **Donald Gibbie** is the son of Gilbert, but his cousin is **Angus the Post.**

. . . four inhabitants called Andrew, or Dandie, Oliver. They were distinguished as Dandie Eassil-gate, Dandie Wassil-gate, Dandie Thumbie and Dandie Dumbie. The two first had their names from living eastward and westward in the street of the village; the third from something peculiar in the conformation of his thumb; the fourth from his taciturn habits.

Sir Walter Scott   *Guy Mannering*

Welsh nicknames

This last example naturally reminds us of Wales, where the commonness of **Jones** traditionally necessitated nicknames. An article in the London *Times* (December 1970) by Trevor Fishlock, however, claimed that names like **Jones the Meat, Flat Nose Jones, Jones King's Arms, Jones Popbottle** and **Jones the Bread** were fast disappearing. In modern times people know fewer of their neighbours than they did in the older communities, and there is less need to distinguish between individuals. One hopes that the folk-wit displayed in the names will be recorded before it is too late. **Dai Piano,** for instance, was not the musician his nickname might suggest. He was for ever cadging cigarettes and saying that he had left his own at home on the piano. **Amen Jones** and **Jones Hallelujah** were men who responded over-enthusiastically in chapel.

Sartorial as well as verbal habits could provide nicknames, as in **Jones Spats** and **Harry Greensuit.** A favourite food or drink could lead to names like **Jones Caerphilly** and **Dai Brown Ale.** The phrasal equivalents of activity surnames—**Jones the Milk, Eddie Click-Click** (for a photographer)—were found everywhere, as were locative names—**Jones Cwmglo, Jones Craig-Ddu** (from farms), **Will Plough, Huw Railway Inn** (from public houses).

In any community where surnames failed to distinguish individuals, nicknames were formerly added or substituted. In the 19th century the shop-keepers in towns like Peterhead would write down the 'fee-names' of their customers. Their account-books reveal names like **Buckie, Beauty, Bam, Biggelugs, The Smack, Snuffers, Toothie, Doodle, Carrot** and **Nap.** The novelist Henry Treece has described Black Country nicknames that were applied to the many **Fosters** and **Wilkes.** A character in *The Rebels,* himself nicknamed **Bacca Chops** because of his habit of chewing plug tobacco, remarks on **Ode Mouldyhead,** whose hair grew in patches, **Ode Foxy, Gentleman, Whackey, Dragon, Bullet, Brick End,** and **Soft Water Jack.**

In the case of royal nicknames, a similarity of first names may be one of the reasons that brings them into being. The kings took on a sequential surname, **The First, The Second,** etc., but their subjects usually replaced this with a descriptive nickname. **Richard Lionheart** was more fortunate than **Richard the Coxcomb** and **Richard the Boar.**

The Georges likewise varied from **The Turnip-Hoer** and **Farmer George** to **Augustus** and **George the Greater.** In France the eighteen kings called

---

Jubilee town was the name of the settlement; and when the schoolmaster announced his own, David King, the title struck the imitative minds of the scholars, and turning it round, they made 'King David' of it, and kept it so.

Constance Fenimore Woolson   *King David*

King James' real name was James King; but the people reversed it because it seemed to fit him better, and also because it seemed to please his majesty.

O. Henry   *The Last of the Troubadors*

Louis naturally attracted nicknames. **Baboon, The Foolish, The Universal Spider, The Fat** and **The Indolent** were among the less complimentary, but one or two were rather better favoured. The last Louis had a nickname which is impossible to translate, punning on his liking for oysters (*des huîtres*) and his sequential surname, 18 (*dix-huit*).

Other reasons for nicknames

It would be foolish, however, to imply that personal nicknames are always to-names, given because they are genuinely needed for identification purposes. They arise for a number of other reasons, reflecting such human habits as ornamenting what is plain, being clever, showing dislike or affection, being funny, being secretive, showing group membership. Most of these reasons could be applied to the use of slang, with which nicknames have a great deal in common.

Tommy's real name was Tommy Flynn, but he was younger than any of them so that neither he nor they were ever quite sure that he ought to belong to the gang at all. To show it they called him all sorts of nick-names, like Inch because he was so small; Fatty because he was so puppy-fat; Pigeon because he had a chest like a woman; Gong Gong because after long bouts of silence he had a way of suddenly spraying them with wild bursts of talk like a fire alarm attached to a garden sprinkler.

Sean O'Faolain   *The Talking Trees*

Family members naturally share a special knowledge of one another, and this may well extend to nicknames. They are frequently bestowed on children by the parents, though more often by the father than the mother, it would seem. A teacher friend discovered recently that his ten-year-olds were known at home as **Crunchy, Boo, Squitface, Popsy Dinkums, Woo, Moonbeam, Muff** (girls), and **Dilly, Dump, Hug, Longlegs, Luscious Legs, Bigpants** (boys). It is much rarer for children to have a nickname for

---

'Flopsy's a lovely name. It comes from the Flopsy Bunnies in Peter Rabbit.*'*

'It does not,' said Hamish, entering the room. 'It is taken from the immortal English surrealist Edward Lear and his Mopsikon-Flopsikon bear.'

Angus Wilson   *Crazy Crowd*

---

either parent, but Angus Wilson, in his *Anglo-Saxon Attitudes*, may be reflecting a real-life situation known to him when he makes **Thingy** the mother's nickname.

Other nicknames connected with children are those that arise at school. Children invariably seem to nickname one another and their teachers, sometimes following intricate paths to arrive at the final name. The point is illustrated in a letter from Mr James B. Fryer, commenting on **Whiskers Bowles.** He writes: 'Bowles became "bowels". The Latin for "bowels" is *viscera*. Pronouncing the "v" in Latin as "w" we get *wiscera*, whence the easy transfer to "whiskers".' One can compare the French headmaster who became **The Doe** (*La Biche*). Trying to maintain his dignity as he crossed the playground he stuck his chest out and looked rather haughty. A pupil remarked quietly that he was 'as proud as Artaban', a normal French simile that refers to a character in a play. **Artaban** became his nickname, but was soon changed to the more agreeable sounding **Artabiche.** This was finally shortened to **Biche.**

If anything like these complications led to the formation of medieval bynames, the philologists clearly have an impossible task before them where the elucidation of some surnames is concerned.

Most first names have conventional pet forms, such as **Debbie** for **Deborah, Frank** for **Francis.** Occasionally, first names lead to more individual nicknames: **Bilge** from **Jill** (*via Jill* **Baby, Jill Bab, Bill Jab**); **Dustbin** from **Dustin; Feeble** from **Phoebe; Gladeyes** from **Gladys; Gnat** from **Natalie; Jinx** from **Virginia; Lousy** from *Lucy*; **Patch** from **Patricia; Oggi** from **Olga; Tin Bum** from **Nicholas** (*via* **Nickle-arse**); **Zobo** from **Zoe.**

'Why is he called Sunny?' I asked.
'Because his Christian name is Sunderland,' said Peter.

Anthony Powell   *A Question of Upbringing*

He was known by intimates and strangers as Ace. The original name, like a scar, he reopened each morning, while shaving. 'I am Eustace,' he would mumble into the mirror.

James Purdy   *Eustace Chisholm and the Works*

Some of the bynames, one would think, must have been inspired in some way by whatever personal name an individual already had. Nicknames of this type are certainly very frequent. Mr **Fryer,** for instance, remarks that he himself became **Tuck,** which one might call an *associated transfer.* A colleague whose surname is **Snow** is known as **Fairy** because of the soap powder *Fairy Snow.* Dr T. Keough has also told me of a friend in his Canadian home-town who was **Twenty Below** because his name was **Ozero.** His sister was called **Scratch Below** for a slightly different reason.

Abel Sampson, commonly called, from his occupation as a pedagogue, Dominie Sampson.

Sir Walter Scott   *Guy Mannering*

He called her Dreary sometimes instead of Deirdre and it seemed to make her a little cross.

Penelope Gilliatt   *A State of Change*

Dubby was the ordinary name by which, among friends and foes, Mr Daubeny was known.

Anthony Trollope   *Phineas Finn*

Link nicknames are even more common. Those based on first names we usually refer to as 'diminutives' or 'pet names', but **Maggie** from **Margaret** is just as much a nickname as **The Barrow Boy** from **Nabarro.** A newspaper correspondent, commenting on the nicknames of her classmates, reveals that her own is **Ballbag,** based on her surname **Ball.** I am sometimes obliged to answer to **Dunkers,** and my son tells me he is **Dunks** to his friends.

Miss Ball goes on to say that her girl-friends have such nicknames as **Bun, Bondy, Snuff, Crunk, Melon, Twiggy** and **Spindle,** while the boys in the class are known by such names as **Primrose, Flapper, Squelch, Haggis, Leggy, Reverend, Fizz** and **Ribs,** all of which reveal a cheerful friendliness. Some of these are clearly descriptive, others might be further examples of surname links. With names like **Crunk** one suspects a verbal incident, perhaps a slip of the tongue one day when another word was intended.

Incident nicknames

Verbal incidents are well represented in nicknames, in the adult world as well as at school level. **Azzerwuz, Juicy, Banjo** and **Rabbit** have come into being in this way, from the favourite expressions 'As I was saying' and 'D'you see?'; because of a constantly repeated remark about being 'highly strung', and because of a teacher's remark about a certain family breeding 'like rabbits'. A comment by the head of a typing-pool: 'Let's have no bloomers today, girls', immediately earned her the nickname **Naughty-Naughty,** and a favourite remark, 'Leave it to me', was the reason for **The Pawnbroker.**

G. B. Stern, in her book *A Name To Conjure With,* tells of the house-party she attended at which all the guests adopted nicknames for the week-end. H. G. Wells was already **Jaguar,** but Miss Stern was unnamed. She remarked that she would like to be something between a tigress and a sphinx, whereupon he dubbed her **Tynx.**

A few pages later Miss Stern describes an incident name of another kind, perhaps what one might call an 'internal incident'. Her eight-year-old friend, Naomi,

'swallowed a penny and was seriously ill and away from school for several months. When she returned . . . she was greeted callously and a little

Laura: He used to call me Blue Roses.

Amanda: Why did he call you such a name as that?

Laura: When I had that attack of pleurosis—he asked me what was the matter when I came back. I said pleurosis—he thought I said Blue Roses!

Tennessee Williams   *The Glass Menagerie*

'It ain't going too far to say he is a pudd'n-head.'

Mr Wilson stood elected. The incident was told all over the town. Within a week he had lost his first name. Pudd'n-head took its place. In time he came to be liked, and well liked too; but by that time the nickname had got well stuck on, and it stayed.

Mark Twain   *Pudd'n-head Wilson*

cruelly by Upper and Lower School with "Hello, **Moneybox!**", while reeling from our own wit, we would beg her to cough up a penny to buy a bun, and keep the halfpenny change.'

Children *would* reel with their own wit, of course. They love playing with words and names and are delighted with names like **Woolly, Wog, Ruby Nose** and **Lumber Bonce** for their sound alone. Where meanings are concerned, they have little time for euphemism, preferring to be simple and direct. Those who are named usually take no offence. Another of my own nicknames, **Pug**, was hardly complimentary, but I distinctly recall sharing the joke when it was proposed. There is a degree of pleasure gained *in being named* which offsets the thought of insult, and if one accepts the nickname it tends to lose its force in any case.

Descriptive nicknames

In a classroom situation, one or two of the brighter children will probably be throwing suggestions for nicknames into the continuous flow of group conversation. There will be instant acceptance, or counter-suggestion, or rejection. If the whole class is present and can see the steps that have led to the name, it will have point to the whole group. A larger community, such as a village, may have to use simpler names, based on characteristics that will be obvious to all. Many of these will be visual names, for just as locative names began by being a person's address, so these names are often verbal portraits. A summary of their origins was given in 1682 by Sir Henry Piers, writing about the Irish:

'They take much liberty, and seem to do it with delight, in giving of nicknames; and if a man have any imperfection or evil habit, he shall be sure to hear of it in the nickname. Thus if he be blind, lame, squint-eyed, gray-eyed, be a stammerer in speech, be left-handed, to be sure he shall have one of these added to his name, so also from the colour of his hair, as black, red, yellow, brown,

At Sandy Bar in 1854 most men were christened anew. Sometimes these appellations were derived from some distinctiveness of dress, as in the case of 'Dungaree Jack'; or from some peculiarity of habit, as shown in 'Saleratus Bill', so-called from an undue proportion of that chemical in his daily bread; or from some unlucky slip, as exhibited in 'Iron Pirate', a mild, inoffensive man, who earned that baleful title by his unfortunate mispronunciation of the term 'iron pyrites'. Perhaps this may have been the beginning of a rude heraldry; but I am constrained to think that it was because a man's real name in that day rested solely upon his own unsupported statement.

Bret Harte   *Tennessee's Partner*

etc, and from his age, as young, old, or from what he addicts himself to, or much delights in, as in draining, building, fencing or the like; so that no man whatever can escape a nickname, who lives amongst them.'

Traditional nicknames

Nicknames *ought* to be tailor-made and meaningful, but there are some which are hand-me-downs, others which come as almost meaningless accessories with one's surname. The former arise partly because there are a number of human features which are always commented on, and a limited number of ways in which the allusions can be made. Baldness, for example, begins by attracting a name like **Baldy** or **Patch,** or is immediately contradicted with a name like **Curly.** Metaphorical descriptions then begin to apply, such as **Dutchy** (because of the appearance of some Dutch cheeses) and **Skating Rink,** shortened to **Skates.** There is a tendency to pass on such names, particularly in the Services, to each new generation

---

'How are things, Lightning?' He got his nickname ironically of course, but not because of the speed with which he yields a hammer, but because he never strikes twice in the same place.

Peter de Vries   *Let Me Count the Ways*

---

of bald-headed men. There is still room for wit, of course, and not every bald-headed man needs to be dubbed with a cliché. A former teacher of mine was, I hope, grateful for his own **Cue-Ball,** bestowed by some unknown wag.

A list of nicknames used by school-children, collected by Iona and Peter Opie and published in

---

There were the nicknames of her friends: Poody and Pip and Pebble, Shrimp and Brute and Tug, Squeck, Bumpo, Baba— it sounded, I said, as though she had gone to Vassar with Donald Duck's nephews.

Philip Roth   *Portnoy's Complaint*

The Lore and Language of Schoolchildren, shows how these avid nicknamers deal with a number of features. A fat person may be **Balloon, Barrel, Barrel-Belly, Billy Bunter, Buster, Chubby, Chunky, Diddle-Diddle Dumpling, Falstaff, Fat Belly, Fatty Harbuckle, Football, Guts, Piggy, Podge, Porky, Steam-Roller, Tank, Tubby** or **Two Ton Tessy** among others. But wide as this selection may appear to be, there is a great deal of duplication, for probably every class in every school has at least one person whose obesity calls for comment. The Opies make the interesting point that when children use names like Fatty Harbuckle (as they spell it) they are usually unaware that they are commemorating a real person, Roscoe **Arbuckle,** a star of the silent screen until his career ended in a scandal. It is unlikely, too, that many of them have actually read the Bunter stories or know of the original Two-Ton Tessie. Such evidence clearly shows the traditional nature of these nicknames.

Clan nicknames

But though traditional and formalised, such names are at least still meaningful, telling other people something about the person named. Another class of personal nicknames, which have sometimes been described as 'inseparables', have almost no meaning at all. They are treated as if they were clan nicknames, applicable to anyone bearing a certain surname. The system leads to men called **Martin** automatically being nicknamed **Pincher** when they join the Royal Navy. Originally the nickname applied to Admiral Sir William F. Martin, a disciplinarian who had ratings put under arrest ('pinched') for the smallest offence. His name is still so well known in naval circles that associated transfer of his nickname follows.

Criminal nicknames

Tradition dictates the use of clan nicknames, but a more practical reason for the use of nicknames is to conceal one's identity, especially from officials such as the police. It is very noticeable that criminals, both great and small, are very fond of nicknames. Their great ambition seems to be to achieve the fame, or notoriety as we would call it, of such figures as **Scarface, Al Capone** or **Jack the Ripper.** The public accepts the right of criminals to have nicknames, and is quick to bestow one on someone whose

> *'Your name isn't Skip,' Pomeroy had replied.*
>
> *'It's my nickname.'*
>
> *'No, it isn't. People don't give themselves nicknames, Lieberman. They inspire them in others. Whatever you are now, Lieberman, or ever hope to be, you are not now and never will be a Skip.'*
>
> Joseph Heller   Good as Gold

identity is unknown. A **Charlie Chopper** was terrorising New York in the early 1970s, the name apparently having been coined by local children. Most people remember **The Boston Strangler,** who will probably go down in criminal history under that nickname rather than under his real name, Albert De Salvo.

Elsdon C. Smith reports that the FBI has a Nickname File containing at least 150 000 entries as part of its background material, and presumably police forces everywhere are obliged to make similar collections. The New York file contains examples like **Gold Tooth Frenchy, Clothesline Slim, Wild Cat Alma** and **Iron Foot Florence. Fire Alarm Brown** was so named from his habit of raising a fire alarm, then picking pockets among the crowd that gathered. **Step Ladder Lewis** would pretend to be a painter and enter houses through upper windows.

Names like Wild Cat Alma for the women bring to mind the nicknames used by their sisters in what have been called 'houses of horizontal refreshment'. Bill Carmichael has listed many of them in his *Incredible Collectors*, and they are best left to speak for themselves: **The Roaring Gimlet, Sweet Fanny, Glass-Eyed Nellie, Tin Pot Annie, Rotary Rosie, The Galloping Cow, Smooth Bore, Madam Moustache, Madam Butterfly.** This last name was given a totally new meaning, of course, by Puccini but it was a genuine non-Japanese nickname for a prostitute before he made use of it.

Political nicknames

At such a level nicknames are simply amusing, but one should not forget that they can have more serious significance. Nicknames can help make public figures seem friendly and accessible, however remote they remain in reality. **Dizzy** and **Old Hickory** performed this function for Benjamin Disraeli and Andrew Jackson. Gladstone, Disraeli's rival, was never given an affectionate nickname,

which reflects his different kind of reputation. Some modern politicians consciously try to become known by a nickname in order to make an emotional appeal to the public.

> *Brevity is the soul of wit; and of all eloquence a nickname is the most concise, of all arguments the most unanswerable. It is a word and a blow.*
>
> *A nickname is the heaviest stone that the devil can throw at a man.*
>
> William Hazlitt   *On Nicknames*

Just what can happen to a politician's name is exemplified by Sir Robert Peel, British Home Secretary in the early 19th century. He acquired several nicknames, including the inevitable **Orange Peel** when he displayed anti-Catholic tendencies. He later became **The Runaway Spartan** when he changed his mind and worked in favour of the Irish Emancipation Bill. His surname was also adapted to **Peeler** and applied as a generic nickname for a policeman

> *I should explain that Maria Spaghetti-maker had never made any spaghetti; it was her great-grandmother who plied the trade, but the nickname persisted in the female line. Similarly, Sentiá Dog-beadle inherited his nickname from an ancestor whose task had been to keep stray dogs from taking sanctuary on hot days in the cool of Palma Cathedral. Sentiá is short for Sebastian.*
>
> Robert Graves   *The Viscountess and the Short-Haired Girl*

I had heard his mother tell my mother that when he was a dear little fellow, just learning to talk, his best version of his name, Percy Boyd, was Pidgy Boy-Boy, and she still called him that in moments of unbuttoned affection. I knew that I had but once to call him Pidgy Boy-Boy in the schoolyard and his goose would be cooked; probably suicide would be his only way out.

Robertson Davies   *Fifth Business*

when he founded the Metropolitan Police in 1829. An alternative form, **Bobby**, was derived from his first name. This has lasted longer and has gone on to become a word.

When we remember that bynames are a kind of nickname, and that surnames are all derived from bynames, we can well understand. Ernest Weekley's comment that 'every family name is etymologically a nickname'. In spite of this Weekley himself appears to have made no serious attempt to collect the nicknames of his time together with evidence about how the names had come into being. In his many books on names he stays well within his chosen philological area, rarely venturing past the Middle Ages. Other writers of equal eminence on surnames have dutifully nodded in the direction of modern nicknames, but once again none of them has made anything like a real attempt to get to grips with what is, in effect, the only living personal name system. There is an obvious need for a full-scale linguistic inquiry into personal nicknames and nicknaming today. The conclusions that would emerge from a thorough study could not fail to help the philologist in the interpretation of his data.

Previous works on nicknames

Julian Franklyn's *Dictionary of Nicknames* (1962) contains about 1500 entries, but the examples are all of the institutional type. They apply to anyone who has a certain surname or first name, fits a descriptive category or fills a particular role. We learn that **Trugs,** for instance, is a nickname given to a lazy man and that it is 'Scottish dialect'; that **Enzedder** is an Australian way of referring to a New Zealander, and so on. These are fossilised nicknames, generic names that border on being common names.

Within this rather restricted area Franklyn's work is valuable for reference purposes, an advance in many ways on studies such as Latham's *Diction-*

ary of Names, Nicknames and Surnames and Albert Frey's *Sobriquets and Nicknames*. Both of these do actually contain truly individual nicknames—those borne by major historical figures—but there are not enough of them. Latham also goes beyond personal nicknames to take in some of those attached to towns, states, battles, institutions, newspapers and anything else. But both writers restrict themselves to names that occur in polite literature and are careful not to descend to the level of everyday speech.

It is precisely that, of course, that is needed. It may only be of anecdotal interest to know that a nurse was nicknamed **Tonsils** because several doctors wanted to take her out, or that a young man was called **Yankee** because he doodled all day, but enough examples like this gathered together would soon reveal patterns of name formation, related to statistics, for worthwhile statements to be made about certain linguistic habits. The vast majority of names, obviously, would not be amusing puns, but they would have their own interest. Whoever does eventually take on the task will not find it a dull one. Nicknames comment, and always have done, on every conceivable aspect of human behaviour.

In facetious homage to the smallness of his talk, and the jerky nature of his manners, Fledgeby's familiars had agreed to confer upon him (behind his back) the honorary title of Fascination Fledgeby.

Charles Dickens   *Our Mutual Friend*

Obsolete nicknames

One must not be misled by the relatively simple types of nickname that developed into our surnames. Our ancestors did not name everyone by the colour of his hair, his job, his father's name or where he lived. These are, it is true, the types of name that

The real name of the little man was Harris, but it had gradually merged into the less euphonious one of Trotters, which, with its prefatory adjective Short, had been conferred upon him by reason of the small size of his legs. Short Trotters, however, being a compound name, inconvenient of use in friendly dialogue, the gentleman on whom it had been bestowed was known among his intimates either as 'Short', or 'Trotters,' and was seldom accosted at full length as Short Trotters, except in formal conversations and on occasions of ceremony.

Charles Dickens   *The Old Curiosity Shop*

have mainly survived, but a great many others that are now obsolete are recorded in medieval Subsidy Rolls, Tax Returns and the like. The following examples were all solemnly written down, in their Middle English form, in documents of this kind in order to identify individuals. They allow us to gain some idea of the names that must have been in colloquial use: William **Breakwomb**, William **Catchmaid**, Simon **Cutpurse**, Hugo **Lickbread**, Leofric **Lickdish**, Geoffrey **Lickfinger**, Robert **Eatwell**, John **Skipup**, John **Spillwater**, Emma **Spoilale**, Muchman **Wetbed**, John **Leavetoday**, Serle **Gotochurch**, Adam **Hangdog**, Adam **Fairarmfull**, Elias **Overandover**, Robert **Moonlight**, Arnold **Pokestrong**. Dozens more like this, including many that are rather too obscene to reproduce here, occur in the documents. Fuller lists of them are cited by Dr Reaney in his *Origin of English Surnames* and Professor Weekley in his *Surnames*.

Range of nicknames

Mention of Latham's *Dictionary* a moment ago serves to remind us that nicknames are not restricted to people. They can replace any proper names, ranging from those of football teams such as **Arsenal (The Gunners)**, to regiments—**The 11th Hussars (The Cherry-pickers** or **Cherubims)**; newspapers—**The Times (The Thunderer)**; cities—**Portsmouth (Pompey)**; States—**Pennsylvania (The Keystone State)**; shops—**Marks and Spencer (Marks and Sparks)**; periods of time—**The Silly Season**; musical works—**Haydn's Symphony No. 96 (The Miracle)**; railways—**Somerset and Dorset (Slow and Dirty)**, and many others.

Where there is not an obvious linguistic connection between name and nickname, there is usually an anecdote to be told. 'The Thunderer' was originally the personal nickname of Edward Sterling, a contributor to *The Times*, but was extended to the newspaper itself. 'The Miracle' was named at the first performance of the symphony, when the audience miraculously escaped injury from a falling chandelier. Nicknames of all kinds do as they claim; in other words—they eke out real names, augmenting them with wit, biographical detail or anecdote. They are a fascinating study, jewels in the great treasury of names, and we should be grateful for them.

The merchants [in Kashmir] leant forward with glistening smiles, holding out their cards. They called themselves names like Suffering Moses, Patient Job, Long John. Sophie's friend, Profit David, had meant to be different. 'I have respect for the Bible,' he said. He particularly admired the psalms and called himself after David whom he always spoke of as a prophet. 'Prophet David,' he said often, with reverence, but his spelling of English was muddled and he had 'Profit David' on his cards. Sophie thought it suited him much better.

Rumer Godden   *Kingfishers Catch Fire*

Clan nicknames

Some examples of nicknames that have become associated with particular surnames.

'Birdy' for **Sparrow, Wren,** etc.

'Blacky' **White.**

'Blanco' **White,** from the trade name of a whitener.

'Bodger' **Lees.**

'Bogey' **Harris.**

'Bricks(an)' **Morter.**

'Bronco' **Rider.**

'Buck' **Taylor,** from a member of Buffalo Bill's team.

'Bunny' **Warren.**

'Bushey' **Fox.**

'Butch(er)' **Lamb.**

'Captain' **Kettle** or **Kidd.**

'Chalky' **White.**

'Chippa' **Wood.**

'Chunka' **Wood.**

'Daisy' **Bell,** from the music hall song.

'Dick(y)' **Richards,** or **Bird.**

'Ding-Dong' **Bell.**

'Dodger' **Long.**

'Doughy' **Baker.**

'Drawers' **Chester.**

'Duck(y)' or 'Ducks' **Drake.**

'Dusty' **Miller,** or **Rhodes** (roads).

'Dutchy' **Holland.**

'Fanny' **Adams,** from the name of a murder victim originally.

'Fishy' **Pike, Chubb,** etc.

'Foxy' **Reynolds,** because of Reynard.

'Ginger' **Beer.**

'Happy' **Day.**

'Hopper' **Long.**

'Jelly' **Pearson.**

'Johnny' **Walker,** because of the whisky.

'Jumper' **Cross.**

'Knobby' **Coles.**

'Lefty' **Wright.**

'Muddy' **Waters,** or **Walters.**

'Ned' **Kelly.**

'Needle' **Cotton.**

'Nick' **Carter,** for a fictional detective.

'Nigger' **Brown.**

'Nobby' **Clark,** said to be because clerks had to look as if they were 'nobs' or gentlemen in spite of being poorly paid.

'Nocky' **Knight.**

'Norman' **Conquest.**

'Nosey' **Parker.**

'Nosmo' **King,** from 'No Smoking' signs.

'Nutty' **Cox.**

'Peeler' **Murphy,** probably from 'peel a spud'.

'Peggy' **Legg,** from Peg-Leg.

'Piggy' **May.**

'Poppy' **Tupper.**

'Powder' **Horne,** from a character in a strip cartoon.

'Rabbit' **Hutch, Hutchins** or **Hutchinson.**

'Rattler' **Morgan.**

'Reelo' **Cotton.**

'Rusty' **Steele.**

'Sandy' **Brown.**

'Schnozzle' **Durrant,** because of Schnozzle Durante.

'Sharky' **Ward,** possibly from a pirate so named.

'Shiner' **Bright,** thence to **Wright** and **White.** Also **Black** because a 'black-eye' is a 'shiner'. Also **Bryant** because of 'shine a light' being associated with Bryant and May on match-boxes.

'Shoey' **Smith.**

'Shorty' **Long** or **Little.**

'Shover' **Smith.**

'Slide' **Overett.**

'Slider' **Cross.**

'Slinger' **Wood(s).**

'Smitty' **Smith.**

'Smokey' **Holmes,** perhaps a reference to Sherlock Holmes's famous pipe.

'Smudger' **Smith.**

'Smutty' **Black.**

'Snip' **Taylor.** Also **Parsons,** from parsnip.

'Snowball, -drop, -flake' **Snow.**

'Snowy' **Baker,** referring to white flour.

'Soapy' **Hudson, Pears, Watson,** from names associated commercially with soap.

'Spider' **Webb.**

'Spike' **Sullivan,** possibly because itinerant potato-pickers gave the name Sullivan when working on the 'spike'. Or from a prize-fighter.

'Splinter' **Wood.**

'Spokey' **Wheeler.**

'Spongey' **Baker.**

'Spud' **Murphy,** both 'spud' and 'murphy' being slang terms for a potato.

'Swank' **Russell.**

'Sticker' **Leach.**

'Stitch' **Taylor.**

'Stormy' **Gale.**

'Sugar' **Cain** or **Kane.**

'Timber' **Wood(s).**

'Tod' **Hunter,** 'tod' being a fox.

'Topper' **Brown.**

'Topsy' **Turner,** a play on 'topsyturvey'.

'Tottie' **Bell.**

'Tubby' **Martin.**

'Tug' **Wilson.**

'Wheeler' **Johnson.**

'Wiggy' **Bennett.**

'Youngy' **Moore,** a joke based on *Old Moore's Almanack.*

The Canadian author W. P. Kinsella informed readers of *The Globe and Mail* in 1988 of SPAN, the Society for the Prevention and Annihilation of Nicknames. The nicknames concerned were actually pet forms of first names, which is why SPAN members said things like: 'I'll be totally francis with you' and talked of being 'unable to pay the william.' As non-sexists they gave one another either patricks or patricias on the back. The Society, according to Mr Kinsella, was founded by an Oxford donald.

Some famous nicknames

'The Admirable Crichton' a Scottish scholar who gained his Master of Arts degree at the age of fourteen.

'Beau' or 'Buck Brummel' patronised by George IV until Brummel's 'Who's your fat friend?' remark deliberately insulted him.

'Bloody Mary' Queen Mary, daughter of Henry VIII, who persecuted the Protestants.

'Blue Beard' Possibly meant to refer to Giles de Retz, Marquis of Laval.

'Boney' Napoleon Bonaparte.

'Bozzy' James Boswell.

'Capability (Launcelot) Brown' who always saw 'capabilities' in the gardens he looked at.

'Conversation (Richard) Sharpe' a critic.

'Crum-Hell' One of the nicknames of Oliver 'Cromwell', whose name was pronounced Crum-ell in his own time. Also known by names such as the 'Almighty Nose', 'King Oliver'.

'Dizzy' Benjamin Disraeli.

'Elocution (John) Walker', author of a pronouncing dictionary and teacher of elocution.

'Farmer George' George II, said to have the dress, manners and tastes of a farmer, and to have referred more to his farming problems than matters of State when opening Parliament.

'Goldy' Oliver Goldsmith.

'Hotspur' Henry Percy, son of the Earl of Northumberland, so named because of the fiery temper he could not control.

'Iron Duke' The Duke of Wellington. An iron steam-boat named after the Duke was known as the *Iron Duke*. The nickname was later jokingly applied to the Duke himself.

'Ironside' Edmund II, from his iron armour.

'King Coll' Colley Cibber.

'King of Bath' or 'Beau Nash,' who managed social events at Bath.

'Lionheart' Richard I, for his courage, though one writer tells of his plucking out the heart from a lion.

'Log-Cabin Harrison' an insulting reference to a log cabin was turned into a successful election slogan by President Harrison.

'Long Hair' General Custer's name among the Indians.

'Man in the Iron Mask' The great historical mystery man in France. Guessing his identity is as much a sport as deciding who wrote Shakespeare's plays for him. A summary of the theories appears in Frey's *Sobriquets and Nicknames*.

'Merry Andrew' Andrew Borde, Physician to Henry VIII.

'Merry Monarch' Charles II.

'Old Harry' and 'Old Nick' are the best-known nicknames of the devil, who is also known as 'Auld Clootie', 'Auld Hangie', 'Nickie-Ben', 'Old Scratch', etc.

'Old Hickory' Andrew Jackson, because he was as tough as old hickory.

'Old Rough and Ready' Zachary Taylor, twelfth President of the USA.

'Prince of Showmen' Phineas Barnum.

'Railway King' George Hudson of Yorkshire, but also applied to William Vanderbilt.

'Rob Roy' Robert Macgregor, later Campbell, the Robin Hood of Scotland.

'Sixteen-String Jack' John Rann, a highwayman renowned for his stylish dress, especially the eight tags on each side of his breeches which gave him his name. Hanged in 1774

'Stonewall (Thomas) Jackson', so called after another general remarked that he was standing there in front of the enemy like a stone wall.

'Swedish Nightingale' Jenny Lind, later Jenny Goldschmidt, the singer.

'Tumbledown Dick' Richard Cromwell, son of Oliver.

'Turnip-Hoer' George I, who talked of planting turnips in St James's Park.

'The Unready' Ethelred II, who was without 'rede' or counsel.

'The Venerable Bede', ecclesiastical historian of the 8th century.

'Virgin Queen' Elizabeth I.

'Water Poet' John Taylor, who worked as a Thames waterman.

'The Witch-finder' Matthew Hopkins, who toured England in the 17th century finding witches. His own test—he floated in water—eventually proved him a wizard and he was executed.

Self-generated nicknames

In his booklet *Welsh Nicknames*, D. Leslie Chamberlain tells of the minister of a chapel in Rhos, near Wrexham, who told the deacons of his many degrees and theological works and added: 'But I want to be called Reverend, pure and simple.' **Reverend Pure and Simple** he immediately, and permanently, became.

Jones Balloon was likewise so-called because of his appeal to his workmen when an important visitor was about to visit the factory: 'Now don't let me down, boys.'

Literary nicknames

'Agony'
Mike ('Agony') Lammermoor, so nicknamed because of the suffering he went through with and over women.
Comfort Me with Apples Peter de Vries

'Bat'
Bat got his name at school, possibly from the whimsical, peering expression in his eyes.
Thomas H. B. Cresswell.

'Beany'
'Now, Beany—for they called me by that name, having begun by calling me Beanpole, I always being spare-made, boy as well as man. . . .'
Night Rider Robert Penn Warren

'Black Peter'
He was known in the trade as Black Peter, and the name was given him, not only on account of his swarthy features and the colour of his huge beard, but for the humours which were the terror of all around him.
Black Peter A. Conan Doyle

'Chicken'
Chicken was a 'hobo'. He had a long nose like the bill of a fowl, an inordinate appetite for poultry, and a habit of gratifying it without expense, which accounts for the name given him by his fellow vagrants.
The Passing of Black Eagle O. Henry

'Demi'
His real name is John, but they call him Demi-John, because his father is John too.
Little Men Louisa M. Alcott

'Dinger'
The new master, Edwin Bell—already 'Dinger' to the whole school.
Darkness Visible William Golding

'Doodle-calf'
Everything came to pieces in his hands, and nothing would stop in his head. They nicknamed him Jacob Doodle-calf.
Tom Brown's Schooldays T. Hughes

'Duke'
James Mears, better known as 'Duke'

Mears, because he was always smartly dressed in correct riding costume.
The Web and the Rock Thomas Wolfe

'Flap-Fanny'
His buttocks spread and jounced flabbily in the saddle. For this reason he was known to the soldiers as Captain Flap-Fanny.
Reflections in a Golden Eye Carson McCullers

'Flopper'
The legendary Flopper, so-called because of the inimitable manner in which he had once minded the nets for the Boston Bruins.
Joshua Then and Now Mordecai Richler

'Glory'
A rather sentimental headmaster once referred to his exploits as 'glorious', and from that arose his nickname.
Lost Horizon James Hilton

'Handy Andy'
Andy Rooney was a fellow who had the most singularly ingenious knack of doing everything the wrong way; disappointment waited on all affairs in which he bore a part, and destruction was at his fingers' ends: so the nickname the neighbours stuck upon him was Handy Andy.
Handy Andy Samuel Lover

'Honey'
Honey Wilkes, so called because she indiscriminately addressed everyone from her father to the field hands by that endearment.
Gone With the Wind Margaret Mitchell

'Hoofer'
Mr Prout, whose school name, derived from the size of his feet, was Hoofer. . . .
Stalky & Company Rudyard Kipling

'Jampot'
Old Jampot, the nurse (her name was Mrs Preston and her shape was Jampot). . . .
Jeremy Hugh Walpole

'Jules'

I invented the name for him on account of Vernon=Verne=Jules of *Round the World in Eighty Days*.
Absolute Beginners Colin MacInnes

'July'
She was called July by all, although she was named Ada. She had a slightly older sister named June.
The Children Sing Mackinlay Kantor

'Lousy'
Scripps had a daughter whom he playfully called Lousy O'Neil. Her real name was Lucy O'Neil.
The Torrents of Spring Ernest Hemingway

'Magnet'
A term of affection the sailor often used in allusion to his niece's personal attractions.
The Pathfinder James Fenimore Cooper

'Mop'
He had been nicknamed 'Mop' from this abundance of hair, which was long enough to rest upon his shoulders.
Life's Little Ironies Thomas Hardy

'Old Stut'
'Old Stut' stuttered. . . .
Lark Rise Flora Thompson

'Scud'
Scud was East's nickname, or Black, as we called it, gained by his fleetness of foot.
Tom Brown's School Days Thomas Hughes

'Smiler'
She calls him Smiler, because he has a sad, rejected face, like a dog pressed against a locked door on a cold night.
Kate & Emma Monica Dickens

'Stuffy'
His name is George, but we call him Stuffy 'cause he eats so much.
Little Men Louisa M. Alcott

'Trout'
'Trout' they used to call her, because her fair skin was speckled with freckles.
Joshua Then and Now Mordecai Richler

10
A LOCAL HABITATION AND A NAME

SO FAR we have talked mainly about the names of people—the names they inherit, are given or adopt. Men have obviously named one another from time immemorial. After themselves they named their gods, then they named the places in which they lived and the rivers, hills and natural features around them.

The earliest place names

The English-speaking countries in the modern world contain layers of place names which stretch back century by century into the remote past. The oldest names are those given by the earliest inhabitants of each country and which have managed to survive in one form or another. In Britain some names are thought to be pre-Celtic, which would take them back to before 500 BC. The name of the River **Wey,** for example, cannot be explained by Old English or Celtic scholars, and they assume it to be older than names in either of these languages. Other words were added much later to give place names such as **Weybridge** and **Weymouth**.

In America it is impossible to date accurately the Indian names that were taken over by settlers, but these are certainly the earliest names there. With nothing known at the time of Indian languages or customs, it was inevitable that such names should change their sound and form considerably. **Chicago** may well have been the Algonquian word 'stinking' originally, but if so one cannot be sure whether the reference was to wild onions, stagnant water or skunks.

Australia has its ancient names such as **Murrumbidgee** and **Woomera,** and here again there are often difficulties of interpretation. While these two names are normally translated as 'big water' and 'throwing stick', **Paramatta** might have meant anything from 'the dark forest' to 'the head of the river' or 'the place where eels lie down' when it was first given. The Aborigines had a great many languages which they did not write down, and even intelligent guesses are difficult to make in such circumstances.

In New Zealand the Maori names are relatively numerous and quite well preserved. As the New Zealand writer Mrs C. M. Matthews points out, in her *Place Names of the English-Speaking World*, there is only one Maori language. Then Captain Cook took with him from Tahiti a boy called Tupia, who discovered that the Maoris could understand his own Polynesian words. Cook was able to talk to the natives through Tupia and record their place names, while later missionaries learned Maori and interpreted them well. Sometimes the words seem simple, but the original meaning was a metaphorical one. **Rangi** means 'sky', and by extension 'light' or 'day', **Rangitoto** is therefore 'day of blood', not 'sky of blood', and is a reference to the wounding there of a folk-hero.

Maori names were more fortunate than native names elsewhere. European settlers from the 16th century on had a strong tendency to rename their colonies in Africa, North America and elsewhere by

Maori place names often record historical or mythological incidents in complete sentences. This tends to make them rather long, though not all equal the length of Taumatawhgakatangihangakoauauotamateaturipukakapikimaungahoronukupokaiwhenu-akitanatahu. Known more usually as *Taumata*, the name of this hill in New Zealand means 'the place where Tamatea, the man with the big knee who slid, climbed and swallowed mountains, known as Traveller, played on his flute to his loved one'.

transferring familiar names to them or describing them as they themselves saw them. A respect for the original names only arose in the later 19th century, and they began to appear on maps as well as being heard in native speech. The new attitude affected the Victorian explorers of Central Africa, who mostly made an effort to record the names they found rather than impose new ones. Even then, patriotism revealed itself in **Lake Victoria** and the like.

In general we must remember that countries are usually settled or taken over by highly practical men rather than scholars. They are concerned with convenience and their own pride when they name places, and are not inclined to stand back and take an enlightened historical view. The Romans and Normans look like exceptions to this rule, for they made very few changes to the place names they found in Britain, but both groups lived as a separate, ruling class and had a rather different attitude from the normal settler.

Difficulties of place name studies

One way to examine place names is to take them layer by layer according to age, but it is best to stay within definite geographical boundaries when doing this. Names which may have come into being at roughly the same time, but in different parts of the world, are likely to have very little in common. The beliefs and attitudes of the namers are more important than the time of naming, and these—perhaps more so in the distant past than now—varied considerably from tribe to tribe, nation to nation. Since it is usually easier to assign a place name to its language, and therefore to the people who gave the name, rather than to an exact period, we will do well to follow familiar paths through the place name jungle.

The jungle, as it may justly be called, is primarily a linguistic one. In Britain the number of languages concerned is relatively small, with Celtic—or Primitive Welsh, Gaelic, Old English, Old Norse, Latin and Norman French being the more important. In America there are the many Indian tribal languages, which began to receive serious attention only in recent times. As one travels round the world, African, Polynesian and Aboriginal languages make their appearance. With each language one has to do also with the culture that lies behind it.

This linguistic jungle, however, has had its

Spekes and Livingstones. England has been especially fortunate, for a determined army of scholars, mostly gathered together in The English Place Name Society, has been hacking away at the undergrowth for over fifty years. Names like Stenton, Mawer, Gover and Ekwall are mostly unknown to the general public, but these are a few of the men who first penetrated into really difficult areas. Other men and women now use the methods they established to explore new areas and refine our knowledge of the others, but the quantity and quality of work done by the pioneers was quite outstanding. In America George R. Stewart has also made a particularly noteworthy contribution to place name studies, though as a social historian rather than a philologist.

Paths, then, have been established and made familiar. A fuller list of the scholars who have helped lay them appears in the Bibliography of this book, but some may be overlooked. Scholars know that is the fate of road-builders to make travel easy for others and be forgotten themselves.

When the Anglo-Saxons invaded Britain it is clear that they took over many place names *as names*, without understanding their meaning. The evidence is to be found in names like **Penhill**, where Old English *hyll* was added unnecessarily to a word which represented Old Welsh *penn,* 'hill'. A Penhill in Lancashire developed into **Pendle** and was later expanded to **Pendle Hill**, a name which means 'hill-hill-hill'. England also has a **Torpenhow Hill**, or 'hill-hill-hill-hill'.

Celtic place names

Let us start out, then, along the first main path. It is as well to begin with British place names because, as with surnames, so many of them were later transferred to other countries. The first layer of names that have a known meaning are those left by the Celts, who came to Britain from central Europe from about 500 BC onwards. **London** is one of their many place names that remains in use today, but opinions differ as to its exact meaning. It is likely to have been 'the settlement of **Londinos**', a man (or god) whose name in turn meant 'the bold one'.

One of the mysteries about **Loch Ness**, in Scotland, is the origin of its name, or the name of the river that flows into it, at least. Professor W. F. H. Nicolaisen has tentatively suggested that it might derive from Nessos/Nessa, earlier Nestos/Nesta, from Nedtos/Nedta, linking with an Indo-European word meaning 'to flood'. This would make it a pre-Celtic name.

As for the name of the monster which is said to lurk in the depths of the lake, **Nessie** is doubly suitable. Apart from the river name connection, Nessie was formerly the common abbreviation for **Agnes**, once a popular name in Scotland.

Carlisle is another Celtic name, its modern form having been influenced by French-speaking clerks who adapted what they heard to fit their own spelling system. What they heard was **Cair Luel,** with *cair* being an earlier version of the Welsh *caer*, 'fort'. The Venerable Bede noted in the 8th century that Luel was how the Latin name **Luguvallium** was then being pronounced. The Latin version of the name indicates what the Romans had heard the natives saying centuries before, an original name which may have meant 'strong in Lugus', Lugus being a popular god. The links in this complex chain, from Carlisle back to Luguvallium, happen to exist in this case, but with many names there is no such help available.

Carmarthen contains the word 'fort' twice, for besides beginning with *caer* it ends with what was once *din*, which had the same meaning. The name was originally the 'fort near the sea', represented by the Romans as **Mari Dunum**. The Welsh made it **Myrddin**. Just as we might now talk of Carmarthen Castle, unaware that Carmarthen already twice refers to a castle, so by the 8th century it was forgotten that Myrddin contained the word. *Caer* was added, and **Caer Myrddin** was interpreted four centuries later by Geoffrey of Monmouth as 'the castle of Myrddin'. The non-existent Myrddin became *Merlinus* in Latin and has been part of the Arthurian legend ever since.

The Anglo-Saxons who invaded Britain from the 5th century onwards did not immediately occupy the whole of England, and a study of place names enables their progress across the country from the east to the west to be traced. They appear to have killed or driven away most of the people in the eastern area, for very few of the original Celtic names remain. As they slowly pushed west, leaving behind settlers, they took over or adapted more and more names. The adaptations often appear as *hybrids*, with elements of more than one language joined together. The density of Celtic names or elements increases all the time until one comes to Wales and Cornwall, where we have as much proof as we want that the Britons continued to live their own lives and speak their own language.

The Angles pushed north into Caledonia, but this area was later over-run by migrants from Ireland, called 'Scots'. The Scots gave their name to Scotland, and eventually displaced or absorbed the mysterious Picts, who lived in the Highlands. Gaelic, Old English and Pictish names are found in Scotland today, together with Scandinavian and Norman names that were introduced later. It is hardly surprising that many names remain unexplained. **Edinburgh,** for example, has a second element meaning 'fortress', but 'Eidyn', which is the first element, cannot be interpreted. All that can be said with any certainty is that Edinburgh does *not* mean 'Edwin's fortress' as is popularly supposed. The evidence for the refutation is best set out in *The Names of Towns and Cities in Britain*, by Nicolaisen, Gelling and Richards.

Ireland's place names derive mainly from Gaelic, but their forms have been much distorted by non-Gaelic-speaking officials. P. W. Joyce says in his *Irish Names of Places* that it was necessary to ask

In 1865 a couple named their son after the place where they had first met. The name later became world-famous when the man concerned won the Nobel Prize for Literature, yet no other parents seem to have been attracted to it. **Rudyard** Kipling is possibly the only man to have borne that Christian name. It derives from **Rudyard Lake**, in Staffordshire, and may have meant 'pond in which rudd were kept'. An alternative explanation is 'lake near a garden in which rue was grown'.

local people how they pronounced the names before the origins became at all clear. **Dublin** is well known to be *dubh linne*, an exact translation of which appears in the English name **Blackpool**. **Belfast** takes its name from its proximity to a natural sandbank formed near the mouth of a river by the opposing currents and able to be used as a *farset*, or 'ford'.

To return to England, one of the place name facts that most people know is that 'caster', 'chester' or 'cester' in a name indicates Roman connections. This is true, but it was not the Romans themselves who named places in this way. For them *castra* was a military camp, but they did not bother to add this word to the names of the camps. It was the Anglo-Saxons who did so, having taken the word into Old English as *ceaster*.

The Romans had actually withdrawn from England before the Anglo-Saxons invaded, but wherever the newcomers went they would have found the very distinctive signs of Roman occupation. One must assume that the Celts had taken *castra* into their language and were able to pass it on to the Anglo-Saxons. The latter made full use of it, sometimes attaching it to a Celtic name, as in **Gloucester**, where the first element meant 'bright'; sometimes adding another of their own words, as in **Chesterfield**, with 'field' originally meaning 'open land'. The Romans had frequently referred to camps by the names of nearby rivers, and this led to place names like **Doncaster, Lancaster** and **Exeter**, from the rivers **Don, Lune** and **Exe**. By no means every Roman settlement, however, had a *ceaster* added to it, and some names that were given it lost it again quickly. London was referred to as **Lundenceaster**, for instance, but this was clearly felt to be too unwieldy.

The Romans themselves had attempted to call London **Augusta**, but like most of their attempts at bestowing place names in Britain, this failed. To all intents and purposes, the Romans left behind them in Britain no place names of their own invention. What they did during their long stay of over three centuries was to record in Latin the Celtic names

they heard, but it was not these written forms that were passed on to the Anglo-Saxons. The Celtic names the latter took over—mostly the names of larger settlements and rivers—would have been passed to them by word of mouth. Many others had to be given, and this the Anglo-Saxons proceeded to do.

Anglo-Saxon clan names

The earliest Anglo-Saxon names reflect the fact that they were moving across new territory. What was important to them at the time was their own identity as a group, which was the one thing that remained constant. They travelled as bands, each with a leader whose name they took. If the leader was Reada, then they were *Readingas*, his followers and dependants. Eventually, when they decided to settle, that place would be known as 'The Readingas' place', **Reading** as it is today. Some names of this kind also add a '-ham' or '-ton' to indicate a settlement.

Not every English place name that contains 'ing' can automatically be given this kind of meaning. The suffix '-ing' can also mean 'place' or 'river', and sometimes it refers to an Old Norse *eng*, 'meadow'. A '-ridding' is a 'clearing', a '-ling' often a 'bank' or 'ridge'. A place name student must have evidence that the '-ing' was once a plural before he can say that it refers to a clan name. In a few cases this plural has survived, as in **Hastings** and **Cannings**.

The clan names were in use at the end of the 5th century. Although at that time they described people and not places they changed their nature completely long before the byname period. Once they had permanently settled the small groups who had borne these names gradually joined together and formed larger kingdoms. The later place names of the Anglo-Saxons were obviously true place names from the beginning, but the existence of these early transferred names is a great help to historians. Plotting them on a map helps to show not only where the Anglo-Saxons went but when they went there.

It has long been a popular pastime to invent explanations for place names. Thus it is said that **Purfleet** received its name on the day that Queen Elizabeth I stood by the river and saw her battered war-ships returning from the fight against the Spanish Armada. Seeing their battered condition, she is said to have exclaimed: 'My poor fleet.'

The name was in existence, however, at least three hundred years before the sea-battle took place. Its second element means 'stream', while the first part of the name probably contains an obscure personal name.

London has several botanical connections. *London pride*, for example, is another name for the Sweet William, perhaps because that flower was formerly much grown in the city's window boxes. Foxgloves have also been known as *London buttons*. After the Great Fire of London in 1666, a plant (*Sisymbrium irio*) sprang up abundantly amongst the ruins. It became known as *London rocket*.

London ivy, on the other hand, was once a slang name for the clinging London fog (also known as a London particular). But when Cockneys refer to a 'London fog' in their rhyming slang they mean a dog.

The clan names (sometimes called '-ing names' or 'folk names') often contain the personal name of the clan leader, but it is not only these names, transferred to places, that contain personal names. Thousands more link the name of an individual farmer or landowner with his property. These are not the great names of history, but the names of ordinary people. As we saw when we looked at the history of first names the typical Anglo-Saxon names—**Eanwulf, Helmheard, Cynewulf, Beornred** and the like—were later replaced by names of foreign origin, though many are known to us from coins and charters. Many others, however, live on only in place names such as **Hauxton, Hawkesbury** and **Hawksworth,** all of which mention a man called **Hafoc.**

There were other ways of describing in a place name the people who lived there without using a personal name. **Sussex** uses the tribal name, describing the 'South Saxons', and **Grantchester** the name of a river. The '-chester' here is a modern form of Old English *saete*, meaning 'dwellers', not the usual *-ceaster*, so the name meant 'dwellers on the River Granta'. The *-ingas* of the clan names can also occur attached to a generally descriptive word instead of a personal name. **Epping** was once the 'people of the upland', not the 'followers of Yppe'. **Norfolk** and **Suffolk** are other obvious descriptive names of people, dividing them into northern and southern groups.

Other Anglo-Saxon place names

The Anglo-Saxons appear to have done little conscious naming of the places in which they came to live. Most of the names clearly began as phrases in normal speech and gradually became fossilised. In the place names that arose during the Anglo-Saxon period there is therefore a true picture of England as it was, filled in with many fine details. Apart from the country itself, many names tell us about the people, their beliefs and customs. The Anglo-Saxons came to Britain as pagans, for instance, but were slowly converted to Christianity. We know this from other sources, but the change can be seen in the place names. Some early names contain references to heathen temples, as in **Harrow-on-the-Hill** and **Weedon,** or are theonymic links, as in **Tuesley** and **Wednesbury.** The latter names naturally remind us of the day names **Tuesday** and **Wednesday** in which the names of the gods **Tiw** and **Woden** again appear. Pagan customs such as sacrificing animals and burying the dead alongside their weapons and domestic items are probably hinted at in names like **Gateshead,** 'goat's head', and **Hounslow,** 'Hund's burial mound'.

Christian place names often mention a monastery or church, as in **Warminster** and **Cheriton,** 'minster on the River Were' and 'village with a church'. Saints' names also occur: **Felixstowe, Bridstow,** St Felix and St Bridget being linked with '-stow', which often meant 'holy place'. 'Holy' itself, Old English *hālig*, is seen in **Halliwell** and the like, while many other names refer to priests, canons, abbots, nuns, monks and bishops.

Lay society is also reflected in many place names. **Kingston, Queenborough, Aldermanbury** are self-explanatory, but modern Englishmen no longer refer to 'churls' in the sense of 'free peasants'. **Charlton** and **Chorlton** refer to farms held by such men. 'Knights' are still with us, but this word has been considerably upgraded. The Anglo-Saxons used it to refer to a youth, and **Knightsbridge** was therefore a bridge where young men met.

All this is very proper, but the Anglo-Saxons had their thieves and other criminals whom they dealt with in no uncertain manner. **Shackerley** was a 'robbers' wood', **Warnborough,** 'felon stream', a stream where they were drowned. The gallows are referred to in many local names, often the names of the fields where the executions took place. **Dethick** is thought to derive from a name given to a particular tree, 'the death oak', where no doubt Anglo-Saxon justice was frequently carried out.

Scandinavian names

The Anglo-Saxons settled and named their places, and the time of their coming receded into the past. In the 9th century it was the turn of new invaders, the Vikings, to establish a permanent foothold in Britain. By 886 King Alfred had signed a treaty with Guthrum, the Danish leader, and the Danelaw came into being. The newcomers responded exactly as the Anglo-Saxons had done before them to the place names they found—accepted them as they found them, adapted their pronunciation to suit their own language (usually called 'Old Norse'), added words of their own to existing names, thus creating new hybrids, or gave entirely new names. Naturally their own personal names, and those of their gods, were also linked to their place names, which are especially concentrated in Yorkshire and Lincolnshire.

Old Norse and Old English had far more in common with each other than with Celtic or Gaelic, but there were differences of vocabulary and usage. The distinctive word of the Danes was *by*, used instead of Old English *tun*. They also made frequent use of *thorp*, whereas the Anglo-Saxons were not fond of their equivalent *throp*, both of which meant an 'outlying farm'. Typical pronunciation preferences are reflected in **Keswick**, the Scandinavian way of saying **Chiswick** 'cheese farm'; **Skipton** and **Shipton**, 'sheep farm'. Once again, the plotting of Scandinavian place names on a map of Britain provides evidence of where they settled and in what numbers.

Norman influence

Invasion and settlement did not end with the Vikings, but place name scholars tend to talk of the Norman influence on English place names rather than French names. The Normans came to England 200 years after the Vikings, and by then place names were thick on the ground and well established. Not many Normans came and they did not settle in the same way as the Vikings and Anglo-Saxons. They became rulers, not farmers, and were concerned with the building of castles rather than cottages.

When they did give names they were frequently subjective descriptions rather than the down-to-earth factual descriptions of the past. **Bewley** is another form of **Beaulieu,** 'beautiful place'. **Merdegrave,** an Anglo-Saxon name probably referring to 'martens', they hastily changed to **Belgrave,** an interesting early example of whitewashing a name (*merde* in French meaning 'faeces'). Rather similar was their change of **Fulepet,** 'foul pit', to **Beaumont,** 'beautiful hill'.

The ordinary Englishman, as the Normans must have quickly realised, could not cope with French names, which had sounds and spellings totally strange to him. But the same was true of the Norman clerks who tried to write down English names. They wrote what they heard, but in their own spelling system. When English sounds did not exist in French they wrote the nearest thing. Often they turned the '-chester' ending into '-sester', spelling it '-cester', as in **Gloucester, Cirencester.**

There have been many other changes to place names in Britain since the Middle Ages, apart from changes in pronunciation. Names have been changed by folk-etymology, the process that turns the unfamiliar into the familiar. **Chartreuse,** for instance, was turned into **Charterhouse,** which seemed more meaningful to Englishmen. Names have been shortened over the centuries, but they have also been lengthened. **Ditton,** 'a farm by a dyke or ditch', split into **Thames Ditton** and **Long Ditton,** two more precise locations. They might have become North and South, Great and Little (*Magna* and *Parva*), High and Low. They could have taken the names of different landowners, as has frequently happened in English place names. Instead one took a simple adjective, the other became linked to one of the world's most famous river names.

The origin of **Thames,** incidentally, which was mentioned a moment ago, is not known. It is possibly a simple description, 'dark river', parallel to a tributary of the Ganges, **Tamasa.** The older river names are mostly of this type, many of them simply meaning 'water' or 'river', with no qualification of any kind. **Avon, Dore, Dover, Lent, Esk, Axe, Exe, Don, Ouse, Arrow** and others all have such an origin.

What a natural, simple county, content to fix its boundaries by these tortuous island brooks, with their comfortable names— Trent, Mease, Dove, Tern, Dane, Mees, Stour, Tame, and even hasty Severn.

Arnold Bennett   *The Old Wives' Tale*

I find it easy to understand this. Like everyone else who lives near a river I go down 'to the river' for a walk without ever specifying it more exactly. When Thames *is* used for any reason, the 'h' is not pronounced of course. The letter was artificially inserted centuries ago, as a 'b' was in words like 'doubt' and 'debt', but has never been pronounced.

The study of river names is a special aspect of place name studies. Eilert Ekwall spent several years looking for early forms of the names in unpublished medieval documents and travelled round England looking at the rivers themselves. The results of his researches are to be found in his *English River Names*, but this is primarily a book by a philologist for other philologists. (See pages 158–9.)

Field names

Among the many other specialised aspects of place name studies may be mentioned that of field names. Town-dwellers rarely hear these names, and are perhaps unaware that they exist, but countless thousands of them are there. They were applied first to open stretches of country cleared of trees, for this was the earliest meaning of 'field'. Later they identified the furlongs of open fields and finally they were applied to the enclosed fields we think of today.

Just as street names usually contain a word that means some kind of street, so field names usually contain a substitute for 'field', such as 'bottom', 'erg', 'jack', 'slang'. The first of these is used for land in a valley, the second for pasture used only in summer. 'Jack' refers to common land while a 'slang' describes the narrowness of the field.

Accompanying the wide variety of 'field' words are descriptions of the land's size and shape, its distance or direction from the village, its soil or crop, its plants or animals, its buildings or natural features. The names of the owners are often linked to them, and there are transferred names such as **Bohemia** and **Zululand** as light-hearted references to remote fields. A humorous reaction to unproductive land leads to names like **Bare Arse, Muchado, Pinchgut, Cain's Ground** and the like. Names given after the 18th century may be arbitrary conversions, reflecting the whim of the namer but saying nothing about the fields themselves.

One interesting aspect of field names is that there is scope for the amateur researcher. In many areas the names have not been collected yet and a real contribution to a worthwhile study can be made. The names often fall within the bounds of local history

Some samples of English field names:

Bangland land on which beans were grown.
Botany Bay a distant field in which hard labour was needed.
Catsbrains a common name for a field with mixed clay and pebbles.
Cupid's close a corruption of 'coalpit's close', a field near a coalpit.
Gallantry bank a field in which there was once a gallows.
Greedy guts a field needing a lot of manure.
Hoppit a small enclosure.
Nackerty a field with many corners.
Pickpocket an unprofitable field.
Pudding acre a field with soft, sticky earth.
Shivery sham a field with an unstable surface.
The Wong an enclosed area in an open field.
Zidles 'side hills', a field with hilly land at the side.

rather than philology, though the interpretation of older names needs the help of an expert. Field names often repay in themselves the time that has been spent searching for them. I am rather fond, personally, of some Scottish names—**Knockmarumple, Glutty** and **Gruggle O' the Wud**, but English field names offer similar pleasures. Many examples are to be found in John Field's *English Field Names*.

'Territorial names,' Oscar explained, gravely, 'have always a "cachet" of distinction; they fall on the ear full toned with secular dignity. That's how I get all the names of my personages, Frank. I take up a map of the English counties, and there they are. Our English villages have often exquisitely beautiful names. Windermere, for instance, or Hunstanton.'

Frank Harris   *Oscar Wilde*

The amateur can often interpret field names, but it must be said once again that the interpretation of place names must on the whole be left to the specialist. This has not prevented a great many mythological explanations being offered by sages of the past. H. G. Stokes quoted a favourite place name legend in his *English Place Names* concerning the village of **Kirkby Overblow,** where the second half of the name actually refers to early smelters. The locals tell the tale of a lovelorn maiden flinging herself from a nearby cliff in despair, but floating harmlessly down when her petticoats and skirts acted as a parachute. It is surprising that the legend does not extend to the invention of the parachute itself.

Pleasures of place names

Legends of this kind are one of the pleasures of place names if one is not too deadly serious about the whole subject. Another pleasure is to be found in many of the names themselves. Many people collect interesting place names that have a happy combination of sounds and hinted meanings. Stokes let his imagination run riot with **Bursteye** ('What an address for a film studio!') and delighted in names like **Bouncehorn, Rhude, Furtherfits, Badnocks, Shambelly, Undy, Snoring, Nobottle, Nicknocks, High Harpers.** A. A. Willis, another ardent collector, listed such names as **Shavington-cum-Gresty, Stank End, Dottery, Snoreham in Ruins, Maggots End, Great Fryup** and **Finish.** Surely we all recall, when we speak these names aloud, the time when language was new to us, when every word acquired was a linguistic toy waiting to be played with? The speaking aloud is important, for as our eyes run over the printed page we do not always translate into sound.

Poets, as we have seen, may respond to place names in a different way:

Our maps are music and our northern titles
Like wind among the grass and heather, grieve.

Ivor Brown begins his poem 'The Moorland Map' with those fine words. John Betjeman has played poetically with Dorset place names, and many other poets have sensed the poetry inherent in ancient names.

We are not all place name specialists, humorists or poets, but there is something in certain place names for us all. There are names which have for us that private meaning that we spoke of at the beginning of this book, a thousand and one personal associations. Some names spoken aloud will be like pebbles thrown into a pool of memory, recalling our childhood or other periods of our lives. One must never forget this quality of names, which may make them hardly meaningful to some people but very meaningful indeed to others.

When the Great Age of Discovery began in the 16th century, British place names already had these intense personal meanings for the explorers and colonists. It is hardly surprising that they frequently transferred those names to the new lands. Even without being attached to new places, many of the names would have spread round the world, for they had now become the names of the emigrants themselves. On the *Mayflower*, for example, were men named **Allerton, Billington, Bradford, Britteridge, Chilton, Crackston, Eaton, Holebeck, Howland, Leister, Rigdale, Standish, Tilley, Warren** and **Winslow,** all of which remain to this day in one form or another as English place names. There, too, among the names on the land are **Cromwell** and **Raleigh, Lincoln** and **Washington.** Our place names may have had humble beginnings, but they have sometimes become the proudest names of all.

Professor Albert Dauzat, in his *Dictionnaire Étymologique des Noms de Famille et Prénoms de France*, informs his readers that **Oldham,** as a French surname, derives from English immigrants whose name meant *vieux jambon*, literally 'old ham'. (The name indicates ancestors who came from Oldham—'old holm'.) One is reminded of a hamburger, so-called because it came from **Hamburg,** 'town on an inlet'. The apparent assumption that hamburger meant 'burger with ham in it' led to cheeseburger, eggburger, and so on.

County names

Present and former county names of the United Kingdom.

Aberdeenshire 'mouth of the Don' (formerly Devona, 'goddess').

Anglesey 'Angles' island'.

Angus (belonging to) 'Aeneas', brother of Kenneth II.

Antrim 'Aentrebh', name of a monastery in the 5th century.

Argyll 'boundary of the Gaels'.

Armagh (Queen) 'Macha's height'.

Ayrshire from the Ayr, 'running water'.

Banffshire 'young pig' (possibly alternative name for the Deveron). Or 'Banba/Banbha', a poetic name for Ireland used as a district name in Scotland. Animal names for rivers do occur, but the young pig reference might also be to totemism.

Bedfordshire 'Bieda's ford'.

Berkshire 'hilly'.

Berwickshire 'barley farm'.

Breconshire 'Brychan's territory'.

Buckinghamshire 'land belonging to Bucca's clan'.

Bute 'beacon' or 'hut, bothy'.

Caernarvonshire 'the fort in Arfon, opposite Mona (Anglesey)'.

Caithness 'ness of the Cataibh'.

Cambridgeshire 'bridge on the Granta'. (Grantabridge became Crantbridge, Cantbridge, Canbridge, Cambridge.)

Cardiganshire 'land of Ceredig'.

Carmarthenshire 'fort near the sea'.

Cheshire 'Roman camp'.

Clackmannanshire 'stone of Manau'.

Cornwall 'the Welsh (foreigners) in the land of the Cornovii tribe'.

Cumberland 'land of the Cumbrians (Britons)'.

Denbighshire 'little fort'.

Derbyshire 'village or farm near a deer park'.

Devon 'territory of the Dumnonii'.

Dorset 'dwellers in the Roman town of Durnovaria' ('fist play'—with reference to a nearby amphitheatre).

Down 'fort'.

Dumfriesshire 'fort of the copses'.

Dunbarton 'fortress of the Britons'.

Durham 'island with a hill'.

East Lothian from a personal name.

Essex 'East Saxons'.

Fermanagh 'Monach's men'.

Fife presumably from a personal name.

Flintshire 'the flinty (rocky) place'.

Glamorgan 'Morgan's territory'.

Gloucestershire 'Roman town of Glevum (bright)'.

Hampshire 'estate on a promontory'.

Herefordshire 'army ford'.

Hertfordshire 'hart ford', ie crossing-place for stags.

Huntingdon and Peterborough 'huntsman's hill' and 'St Peter's town'.

Inverness-shire 'mouth of the Ness'.

Isle of Wight possibly 'that which juts from the sea; an island'.

Kent 'coastal area'.

Kincardineshire 'at the head of a wood'.

Kinross-shire 'head of the promontory'.

Kircudbrightshire 'St Cuthbert's Church'.

Lanarkshire 'glade'.

Lancashire 'Roman fort on the Lune'.

Leicestershire 'Roman town of the Ligore tribe'.

Lincolnshire 'Roman settlement (*colonia*) by the lake'.

London, Greater based on 'Londinos', a personal name.

Londonderry 'London (because of a charter granted to the Livery Companies of the City of London) + oak wood'.

Merionethshire based on personal name 'Marion'.

Middlesex 'Middle Saxons'.

Midlothian probably based on a personal name.

Monmouthshire 'mouth of the Mynwy'.

Montgomeryshire after a castle built by Roger de Montgomery, a Norman.

Moray 'territory by the sea'.

Nairnshire 'the river'.

Norfolk 'northern people'.

Northamptonshire 'north settlement'.

Northumberland 'land north of the Humber'.

Nottinghamshire 'settlement of Snot's clan'.

Orkney 'whale islands'.

Oxfordshire 'oxen ford'.

Peebleshire 'shiels, huts'.

Pembrokeshire 'end land'.

Perthshire 'copse'.

Radnorshire possibly based on 'red' (referring to colour of land?).

Renfrewshire 'flowing brook'.

Ross and Cromarty 'moor' and 'crooked bay'.

Roxburghshire 'Hroc's fortress'.

Rutland 'Rota's land'.

Selkirkshire 'hall church'.

Shetland based on a personal name.

Shropshire 'fortified place of Scrobb's clan', or 'in the scrub land'.

Somerset 'dwellers at the summer village'.

Staffordshire 'ford by a landing-place'.

Stirlingshire no satisfactory explanation can be proposed.

Suffolk 'southern people'.

Surrey 'southern district'.

Sussex 'land of the southern Saxons'.

Sutherland 'the southern land'.

Tyrone 'Owen's territory'.

Warwickshire 'dwellings by the weir'.

West Lothian as *Midlothian*.

Westmorland 'land of the people west of the (Yorkshire) moors'.

Wigtownshire 'dwelling-place'.

Wiltshire 'village on the Wylye'.

Worcestershire 'Roman settlement formerly inhabited by the Weogora tribe'.

Yorkshire 'estate of Eburos'. *Riding* is 'thridding', a 'third'.

The re-organisation of local government in England and Wales led to the adoption of the following 'new' county names. Most of the names are, in fact, restorations of ancient names or transferred river names.

Avon from the river name.
Cleveland 'the hilly district'.
Clwyd from the river name.
Cumbria the name of an ancient tribe.
Dyfed name of an ancient province.
Gwent name of an ancient province.

Gwynedd name of an ancient province.
Humberside based on a river name.
Manchester, Greater 'the Roman town *Mamucium*', of uncertain meaning.
Merseyside based on a river name.

Midlands, West descriptive.
Powys name of an ancient province.
Salop from *Salopesberia*, a Norman-French version of *Scrobesbyrig*, or *Shrewsbury*.
Tyne and Wear from two river names.

Place name elements

A selection of elements that occur in place names throughout Britain is given below. The elements were originally words in Celtic (Old Welsh), Gaelic, Old English and Old Norse. In their passage through the centuries they have undergone many changes, and what was once the same word may exist in many modern forms. It is never possible to explain the original meaning of a British place name on the basis of its modern form alone. Only by examining the earliest forms known to be recorded can a philologist give a judgment as to the intended meaning; even then he must always consider topographical information about the natural features as well as linguistic facts.

In the list an element that normally occurs as a prefix is shown thus: *Aber-; Ac-; Aird-*, etc. An element that is normally a suffix is shown thus: *-beck; -borne; -by*, etc. Elements that can occur as names in themselves, or as prefixes or suffixes, are shown thus: *Barrow; Firth; Haigh*, etc.

Aber- 'river mouth'.
Ac- 'oak'.
Aird- 'height'.
Ard- 'height'.
Auch(in)- 'field'.
Avon- 'water, river'.
Bally- 'farm, village'.
Bar- 'barley'.
Barrow 'hill, tumulus, grove'.
-beck 'stream'.
Ber- 'barley'.
-ber 'grove'.
-berry 'burial mound'.
Bold- 'building'.
-borne 'stream'.
-borough 'fortified place'; 'burial mound'
-bourne 'stream'.
Bryn- 'hill'.
Bur- 'fortified place'.
Burn- 'stream'.
-burgh 'fortified place'.
-bury 'fortified place'.
-by 'farm, village'.
Cam- 'crooked'.
Car- 'fortified place'.
Carl- 'churl'.
Carn- 'heap of stones'.
-caster 'Roman settlement'.
Charl- 'churl'.

Chat- 'wood'.
Chep- 'market'.
Chester 'Roman settlement'.
Chip- 'market'.
Coat- 'cottage'.
-combe 'deep valley'.
Comp- 'deep valley'.
-cot(e) 'cottage'.
Crick- 'small hill'.
Dal- 'dale; meadow by a stream'.
Darwen- 'oak tree'.
Dean- 'valley'.
Den- 'valley'; 'fortress'.
Din- 'fortress'.
-don 'hill'.
Down- 'hill'.
Drogh- 'bridge'.
Drum 'ridge'.
Dub- 'black'.
Dun- 'hill'; 'fortified place'.
Ea- 'water, river'; 'island'.
Eglo- 'church'.
Ey- 'island'.
-ey 'water, river'; 'island'.
-fell 'hill'.
Firth 'fiord'.
-ford 'ford'; 'fiord'.
Gal 'stranger'.
Garth 'enclosure'.
-gethly 'wood'.

-gill 'narrow ravine'.
Glais- 'stream'.
Glas- 'stream'; 'greeny blue'.
Graf- 'grove'.
-grave 'grove'.
-greave 'grove'.
-guard 'enclosure'.
Hag- 'hedge, enclosure'.
Haigh 'hedge, enclosure'.
Hal(e) 'corner'.
-hall 'corner'; 'hall'.
Ham 'homestead'; 'water-meadow'.
-haugh 'hedge, enclosure'.
Hayle- 'salt water'.
Hel- 'salt water'.
-hithe 'landing-place'.
Holme 'small island'.
Holt 'thicket'.
Hoo 'high land'.
Hop- 'valley'.
Hough 'high land'.
How(e) 'mound, hill'.
Hurst 'wooded hill'.
Hythe 'landing-place'.
Inch 'island'.
Innis 'island'.
Inver- 'river mouth'.
Kil- 'monastic cell, church'.
Killi- 'wood'.
Knock- 'small hill'.

Kyle 'strait'.
Lan- 'enclosure, church'.
-law 'mound, hill'.
Lee 'glade'.
Leigh 'glade'.
Lin 'lake, pool'.
Lis- 'court, hall'.
-low 'mound, hill'.
Lyn(n)- 'lake, pool'.
Magher- 'coastal plain'.
Mar- 'lake'.
Mal- 'hill'.
-mel 'sandbank'.
Mel- 'hill'.
Mer 'lake'.
-mere 'lake'.
Mine- 'mountain'.
Mon- 'mountain'.
Mor- 'sea'.
Moy- 'coastal plain'.
Mynd 'mountain'.
-ness 'cape'.
-ock 'oak'.

Oke- 'oak'.
Or- 'bank'.
Pen- 'head'.
Pol- 'pool'.
Rath- 'fort, court'.
-rith 'ford'.
Ros(s) 'moorland'.
-rose 'moorland'.
Ru- 'slope'.
-ryn 'cape'.
-scar 'rock, reef'.
Sel- 'sallow (a tree)'.
-set 'hill pasture'.
Shaw 'small wood'.
Sher 'bright'.
Shir- 'bright'.
Sil- 'sallow (a tree)'.
Skerry 'rock, reef'.
Slieve 'range of hills'.
Stain- 'stone'.
Stan- 'stone'.
-stead 'place'.
-sted 'place'.

-ster 'place'.
Stock 'holy meeting-place'; 'tree-stump'.
Stoke 'holy meeting-place'.
Stow(e) 'place'.
Strat- 'Roman road'.
Strath- 'a wide valley'.
Stret- 'Roman road'.
Thorp(e) 'farm, village'.
Thwaite 'glade, clearing'.
-tire 'land'.
-ton 'farm, village'.
Tre- 'farm, village'.
-try 'shore, sands'.
Ty- 'house'.
Tyr- 'land'.
Usk 'water'.
Wal- 'foreigner, Briton'.
Wen- 'white'.
-wich 'dwelling, farm'.
Wick 'dwelling, farm'; 'sea inlet'.
Win- 'white'.
Worth(y) 'enclosure, farm'.
Wyke 'dwelling, farm'.

English river names

The names of rivers are often amongst the most ancient known to us. Interpreting them is exclusively a matter for the trained philologist, as a glance into *English River-Names*, by the Swedish scholar Eilert Ekwall, will clearly reveal. This book was first published in 1928 by the Oxford University Press and is still available. It is a remarkable labour of love and a model piece of research. Those interested in the meanings of English river names, as far as they can be ascertained, should consult the above-mentioned book, which also gives their precise locations. Below I list a selection of the names themselves.

Adur	Belah	Cary	Dacre	Fal	Hail
Allen	Bell	Char	Dane	Fleet	Hamble
Aller	Biddle	Cherwell	Dart	Flitt	Hamps
Allow	Biss	Chess	Dee	Flyford	Hannon
Alwin	Blackwater	Chet	Deer	Font	Hayle
Amber	Bleng	Chew	Dent	Foss	Hel
Anker	Blyth(e)	Chid	Derwent	Foulness	Hems
Ann	Borrow	Churn	Devon	Freshwater	Humber
Ant	Bourne	Claw	Dewey	Frome	Hundred
Anton	Boyd	Cocker	Don	Gade	Idle
Ark	Brain	Cole	Douglas	Gaunless	Inny
Arrow	Bray	Colne	Dove	Gelt	Irk
Arun	Brent	Connor	Duddon	Gilpin	Irthing
Ash	Bride	Coquet	Earn	Glem	Irwell
Avon	Brock	Corve	Eden	Glen	Isis
Axe	Brue	Cover	Ellen	Glendermackin	Isle
Bain	Burn	Craddock	Erewash	Glyme	Itchen
Ball	Cad	Crake	Erme	Gowan	Ive
Beal	Calder	Crane	Esk	Granta	Keer
Beam	Cam	Crouch	Evenlode	Greet	Kemp
Beane	Camel	Cunkel	Exe	Greta	Kenn
Bedwyn	Can	Curry	Eye	Gussage	Kennet

Kensey	Luney Stream	Noe	Ribble	Swift	Wear
Kent	Lyd	Ore	Roach	Tala Water	Weaver
Kenwyn	Lyde	Orwell	Rom	Tamar	Welland
Kex Beck	Lyme	Otter	Rother	Tame	Went
Key	Lyn	Ottery	Rye	Tavy	Were
Kyle	Mad Brook	Ouse	Sark	Taw	Wey
Kym	Manifold	Pang	Sem	Team	Wharfe
Lambourn	Marden	Pant	Sence	Tees	Whitsun Brook
Lark	Mardle	Parret	Seph	Teign	Wiley
Laver	Medina	Penk	Shooter	Test	Wimborne
Lea	Medway	Peover	Sid	Thames	Windrush
Leach	Meon	Perry	Silk Stream	Thrushel	Wiske
Leam	Mere	Piddle	Silver	Tiddy	Wissey
Leen	Mersey	Pilling	Skerne	Till	Witham
Lemon	Mimram	Pipe	Skippool	Tone	Woburn
Len	Mint	Plym	Skitter Beck	Tory Brook	Wolf
Lew	Mite	Pont	Slea	Trent	Worf
Lickle	Mole	Pow	Smite	Ure	Worm Brook
Loose	Morda	Quarme	Soar	Valency	Wreak
Loud	Must	Quinny	Sow	Ver	Wye
Low	Nadder	Rattle Brook	Sprint	Wampool	Wyre
Lox	Nanny	Ray	Stiff key	Wandle	Yare
Lud	Nar	Rea	Stour	Wash	Yarrow
Lugg	Nent	Rede	Swale	Waveney	Yarty
Lune	Nidd	Rib	Sway	Waver	Yealm

PLACE NAME OVERTONES

HUMORISTS have managed to find ingenious new answers to the question: what's in a place name? It was the British writer Paul Jennings who first seems to have noticed that place names 'carry wonderful overtones—they seem to have been drawn from some huge, carelessly profuse stock of primal meaning'. Mr Jennings began to assign his own meanings to place names, as if they were normal words. Thus **Woking** became 'the present participle of the verb *to woke*, an obsolete word meaning "to day-dream"'.

In 1983 Douglas Adams and John Lloyd came along with *The Meaning of Liff*, in which they also made use of some of the spare words 'doing nothing but loafing about on sign-posts'. They found place names useful to name 'experiences, feelings, situations and even objects which we all know and recognise, but for which no words exist'. **Farnham,** for example, became a noun meaning 'the feeling you get at about four o'clock in the afternoon when you haven't got enough done'.

Adams and Lloyd even tampered with one of the most literary of all place names, **Adlestrop.** They made it 'that part of a suitcase which is designed to get snarled up on conveyor belts at airports'. Commuters and other travellers might care to compile their own 'travel dictionaries', using the place names encountered *en route*.

11
NAMES TAKE THEIR PLACES

THE PLACE names of the English-speaking countries other than Britain reflect the histories of those countries as clearly as British place names tell the story of the Celts, Gaels, Romans, Anglo-Saxons, Vikings and Normans. A historial approach to them has accordingly been made by writers such as George Stewart and Mrs C. M. Matthews, both of whom bring a literary elegance to name studies that is very refreshing. Details of their books, together with others on which this chapter is based, are given in the Bibliography.

My own approach will not be primarily historical, for when the Age of Discovery began in the 15th century it seems to me that we entered a new era of place naming that was quite unlike anything that had happened previously. Broadly speaking, place names that came into existence before the 10th century evolved naturally in the midst of descriptive speech. Place name transfers did not occur, and those place names that contained personal names were accidentally evolved links. People wanted to distinguish between one habitation and another and one natural way for them to do it was to link them to their owners' names. 'Ecga's homestead', say, and 'Ceabba's homestead' gradually became the accepted labels for those two places, surviving even after **Ecga** and **Ceabba** were forgotten. **Egham** and **Chobham** had taken the first step to becoming real place names. At no time had Ecga and Ceabba done the naming—it was their neighbours who made use of their names.

Signs of conscious naming appeared with the Normans, when the names they gave to their castles indicated an interest in the names themselves. **Beaurepaire,** later **Belper,** meant 'beautiful retreat', and was clearly never intended to be descriptive in a functional way. British place names would have changed in kind as well as language had the Normans done far more naming, but Britain had most of the names it needed by the time they came. There was, therefore, a gap of several centuries before the naming of places began again in earnest on the other side of the ocean, and this time the name giving was

normally deliberate. Often the same names as those that had arisen in Britain were given to new places, but those names had changed in kind. Their origins had usually been forgotten, but they had acquired new 'meanings'.

Transfer of place names

It is easy to see why the principle of name transfer was taken for granted by the Europeans when they went to the New World. (We must obviously say Europeans rather than British, for many of the place names now in the English-speaking world were given by Spanish, Portuguese, French and Dutch explorers and settlers.) These men all had far more place names as part of their total vocabulary than had been the case with their ancestors. They knew their own countries more thoroughly, and knew more about one another's countries.

Secondly, they had all become used to name transfer in other nomenclatures. The development of first names and surnames had been roughly parallel throughout Europe, and both systems established a stock of names which was re-used as required. Finally, and perhaps most importantly, many place names had become usable almost as words because of their meanings. **Plymouth**, for example, must have meant almost the same as 'home' to a 17th-century Englishman when he was far from home himself. A settlement of that name could bring security and familiarity to a strange land. The name might no longer be relevant to the new place that bore it, in that it was not 'the mouth of the River **Plym**', but it was very meaningful to the namers.

There seem to be no signs of this kind of place name transfer in the earlier naming period, though another kind of transfer had its faint beginnings with the Anglo-Saxons and Vikings. We have seen how they occasionally linked the names of their gods to places, as in **Grimsdyke** and **Grimsbury (Grim** being

The naming of **America** is well described by George R. Stewart in his *Names on the Globe*. The basic facts about the naming are:

a. Columbus missed his opportunity to name the new continent because he failed to realise that the continent *was* new.

b. It was left to the Florentine **Amerigo** Vespucci (whose name in its Latin form was **Americus** or **Albericus** Vesputius) to insist that the lands he, and earlier Columbus, had visited did in fact constitute a New World.

c. A German scholar called Waldseemüller, who in the fashion of the 16th century used a classical form of his name, Hylacomylus, then suggested that the new continent should be named Americus—or since Europe and Asia were named for women, and since countries were always feminine in Latin grammar, the name might take its feminine form and become America. He entered this name on a map published in 1507, applying it to the present-day South America.

d. When it was realised that two continents had been discovered, the second one became North America. Subsequently the name of the continent was applied to the country.

The USA is thus named for a man, but uses the feminine form of his name, which seems a fair compromise.

an alternative form of **Woden**). This linking *between nomenclatures* obviously increased as time passed and affected name transfers. By the 16th century the present-day situation, whereby names can be transferred with almost total freedom from one naming system to another, had been established. The great explorers of the period lived with a constant reminder of this fact, for the very ships in which they sailed often had transferred names.

Columbus and Columbia

Columbus made early use of the name of a flagship, the **Marie Galante**, by transferring it to an island which has kept the name to this day. He may have been the first to take a name from a ship and root it firmly on the land, but he was certainly not the last. Captain Cook, for example, named a strait and a river after his ship, the **Endeavour**. When America had at last discovered Columbus (as Professor Stewart brilliantly puts it) another ship was sailing round the American coast with Robert Gray as its master. This ship's name commemorated Columbus himself in the form **Columbia**, and when Gray found a new river, he transferred his ship's name to it.

Columbia almost became the name of the United States of America. Poets of the 18th century referred to the new country by this name, but the statesmen failed to ratify the choice. The opportunity was missed, for others were quick to seize on a name

which was historically apt and pleasant in sound. It was given to a city and to the **District of Columbia** as well as the river. **British Columbia** and **Colombo** came into being subsequently, as did towns called **Columbus, Columbiana** and **Columbiaville**.

Long before all this Columbus was revealing his own deeply religious convictions by naming islands after churches, which had already been named after saints. **Santa Maria La Antigua De Sevilla** was one such name, though it was later shortened to **Antigua**, 'ancient'. This was as far from Columbus's original intention as **Rum Cay**, which he had named **Santa Maria De La Concepción**. British seamen were responsible for the renaming, which incorporates a local word meaning 'sandy island'. They also changed **St Christopher**, which he named in honour of his patron saint, into its diminutive form, **St Kitt's**.

Royalty in place names

Columbus dutifully tried to bestow some names in honour of his royal patrons, but names must live in the mouths of men in order to survive, not just on charts and maps. Most of these early royal names disappeared, but during the 17th century new ones appeared in profusion, especially when **New England** was founded. Prince Charles, for instance, was invited by John Smith to strike out native names that had temporarily been inserted on the map and give more suitable names. The young Prince responded

> The Puritans who named **Boston**, in Massachusetts, thought they were simply transferring the name from Boston in the English county of Lincolnshire. They were later disconcerted to discover that the meaning of the original name was 'St **Botulf**'s stone', indicating a stone church or cross, or a boundary stone used by the saint as a meeting place. The 'saintly' connection was a great embarrassment.
>
> Later developments of the place name, in which it came to mean a kind of card game, a dance and a type of cream cake, would certainly not have pleased them.

to the invitation with pleasure. **Cape Elizabeth, Cape Anna** and **Cape James** were immediately named after his sister, mother and father. Cape James did not survive, for local people had already been speaking of it as **Cape Cod** for a long time, and the fish were still there to make the name a suitable one.

Charles named the **Charles River** after himself and was later to honour himself yet again, in Latin, with **Carolina.** His wife's name was linked to **Maryland.** A glance at the map will show many other royal names that have been transferred or linked to places. **Georgia, Georgetown, Williamsburg, Annapolis, Frederick County, Fredericksburg, Augusta, Orangeburg, Cumberland** and **New York** represent a small selection. The last of these was after the Duke of York, later James II. **Victoria** naturally appeared everywhere during the 19th century. French royalty was similarly commemorated in names like **Louisiana**, and at least one American town called **Isabella** was named after the Spanish queen of that name.

Royalty established a naming fashion that was to be extensively imitated. Kings and queens might give their names to large areas of land, but there were a million smaller places to be named. The early explorers naturally put their own names on the maps, though many of them were extremely modest about it. **Cook, Tasman, Vancouver, Cabot, Cartier, Drake, Flinders** and the like are all attached to places which show where they travelled, but since all of them needed a great number of names to identify the places they came across, they made use of all the names they knew. They had a golden opportunity to please other people, such as their superior officers, shipmates, friends and relations, at no cost to themselves, and it was natural for them to do so.

Sometimes the people whose names found a permanent place on the maps had a real connection with the places they named. Captain Cook buried a seaman named **Sutherland** and gave the name to that area. It lives on as a suburb of Sydney. **Sydney** itself, however, was named after Lord Sydney, an English statesman. The city has made his name known throughout the world, but he himself was never to set eyes on Australia.

Names of people great and small have been transferred or linked to place names since the 16th century. In more recent times men have gone a long way from the relative dignity of royal first names or noble surnames. **Sniktaw**, in California, reverses the name of a local journalist; **Squeaky Creek** in Colorado incorporates the nickname of an earlier settler; **Ekalaka** in Montana comes from the name of the Sioux wife of a settler. Such names somehow seem to be quite at home in states that are rather more poetically named themselves.

But in spite of all the names of people in place names, still more are simple transfers from other places. **Plymouth** was mentioned earlier, a name that can be found today in twenty-five American states. Contrary to popular belief, the Pilgrim Fathers did not actually name their new settlement: it had already been done for them by Charles Stuart. When he ran out of family names that could be used for place names on John Smith's map, he inserted the names of some English towns. The *Mayflower* was thus able to sail from Plymouth to Plymouth. Later settlers arrived at the same port, then went inland to found new towns which needed naming. It was natural for many of them to turn to the name of the last town they had seen in the homeland and the first in the new.

The duplication of so many British names in America, Canada, Australia, New Zealand and other

> Some political commentators believe that John F. Kennedy lost Washington's electoral vote in 1960 because he referred in a speech to *Spoke-Ayne,* instead of *Spoke-Ann,* which is how people in Washington pronounce the name **Spokane.**

countries has an odd result for present-day travellers. They are likely to find clusters of familiar place names strangely rearranged as if by a giant earthquake. The pronunciation of the same names can also differ from country to country. In Britain an old name will usually have an unstressed ending, so that **Chatham** becomes 'Chat-em'. Elsewhere it is likely to be pronounced as spelt, with the '-ham' given its full value.

Other names transferred to places

It should be stressed that there are many possible sources of transfer for place names. Saints' names were often bestowed because a place was first seen on their feast-days. **Garryowen** in Montana was named for the regimental tune of the 7th Cavalry; the Bible has supplied names like **Shiloh** and **Bethesda**; **Buccaneer Bay** in Canada was named after a race-horse; poetry led to **Hiawatha** and **Avoca**; **Kodak** was borrowed from the trade name for places in Kentucky and Tennessee. The endlessness of the possibilities is perhaps best exemplified by **Truth or Consequences** in New Mexico. The name was transferred in 1950 from a radio programme as a result of certain inducements to the citizens, who voted on the matter.

While few transferred or linked place names come into being because of such specific advantages, most of them at least do so for positive reasons. It is hard to imagine a hated name being bestowed on a place, but this happened in Canada. The towns of **Luther** and **Melancthon** were named by a Roman Catholic surveyor because 'as it was the meanest tract of land he had ever surveyed he would name the country after the meanest men he ever heard of'.

Charles II also had vindictive intentions when he insisted on William Penn's name being linked to the suggested **Sylvania**. He knew perfectly well that **Pennsylvania** would greatly distress the modest Quaker, making him seem proud before his followers. Penn made desperate attempts to get the name changed, but perhaps it is as well that he did not succeed. Time has made the name a fine memorial, with the original unpleasant motive forgotten.

Mention of Penn brings number names to mind (for reasons which will become clear when we deal with street names). There is a group of such place names, and they show that such names can be as evocative as any other names. **Seventy-Six**, for instance, is a place in Kentucky which reminds everyone of the year of Independence. **Fortynine Creek** links the place with 1849, when wagon-trains poured through it. **Forty Fort** is a reminder of the number of settlers who built the stockade. In West Virginia the name **Hundred** arose because Henry Church and his wife both lived to be over 105 years old. **One Hundred and Two River**, in Missouri, translates the French name **Cent Deux**, but this probably represented a mis-heard Indian word that meant 'upland forest'.

Another group of North American place names are not quite what they seem to be. **Battiest, Loving, Kilts, Breedlove, Schoolcraft** and **Buncombe** are all perfectly straightforward transferred surnames from early settlers and the like, whatever else they might suggest. Similarly, **Otter Point** in British Columbia contains the surname 'Otter' rather than a direct reference to the animal. When a very unusual surname becomes a place name, however, later residents may adapt it in an effort to make sense of it. **Swearing Creek** in North Carolina is from the Swearington family, while **Due West** in a neighbouring State shows what can happen to a name like **De Witt**.

Folk-etymology can accidentally conceal a transferred name, but there can also be deliberate concealment at the time of naming. **Subligna** in Georgia is an attempt to translate the surname 'Underwood' into Latin, while **Irvona** in Pennsylvania vaguely Latinises the name 'Irvin'. A place **Neola** in West Virginia owes its name to **Olean** in New York, but the namer preferred to mix up the letters. Back-spellings are even commoner in the USA than anagrams, **Remlap** and **Remlig** being examples from Alabama and Texas.

Link place names

Place names which are blends of other names are links rather than transfers, but once again they usually conceal their origins. Parts of names may be used, or parts of names coupled with other elements. The results look like **Clemretta, Texhoma, Ethanac, Fluvanna, Cresbard** and **Ninaview**. The various paths leading to such names include putting together parts of two cow names, Clementine and Henrietta, for a place in Canada; blending the state names Texas and Oklahoma because a town borders on both; using parts of Ethan A. Chase, the name of an early landowner; putting part of the Latin *fluvius*, 'river', next to Anna (a similar name being

She had been christened Bethany, after the town in Connecticut her mother had come from.

Thomas Tryon   *Harvest Home*

'Georgia?' his mother said. 'Why in the world would a mother want to give her daughter such an outlandish name?'

'Georgia's named for a whole state.'

'How'd thee like to be called Ohio?' his mother said.

'Thee was born there.'

Jessamyn West   *Except for Me and Thee*

Rivanna); joining parts of two surnames, Cressey and Baird; adding a common element to the name Nina.

Incident place names

Another way of arriving at names that was known to our remote ancestors was description or conversion arising out of an incident. In the place names of the English-speaking world there are many that recall incidents connected with the places concerned. One of the best known is **Cannibal Plateau** in Colorado, where a certain Alfred Packer kept alive through the winter by eating the five companions he had killed. Other place names refer to a **Murder, Suicide, Earthquake** or **Battle.** An island called **Naked** supposedly received its name from a crazed Indian woman who was found wandering there, but the name may originally have referred to the lack of vegetation. One of the problems with names of this type is sorting out the genuine explanations from the later myths.

The names just mentioned were almost certainly given by early settlers, who were a hardy breed. Their rawness is aptly reflected in many other names they gave, which are among the most genuine on the map. Genteel residents who come later, however, are apt to change such names. Both Cook and Flinders, when they were sailing round the coast of Australia, were much influenced by incidents when they were giving names. Cook, for example, changed his mind about **Stingray Harbour**, a name he had just decided on, when the botanists who were sailing with him, including the famous Joseph Banks, came back to the ship in high excitement. They had found a great number of previously unknown plants. Cook thought of Botanists' Bay, and finally decided on **Botany Bay.** Banks himself was remembered by **Cape Banks,** and he was later to give his name to the genus of flowers that so excited him.

Flinders named **Cape Catastrophe** and **Memory Cove** after the loss of a boat and its crew. A meeting with a French ship, which might have led to a battle, caused him to name **Encounter Bay**. One entry in his log reads: '**Anxious Bay**, from the night we passed in it.' Incident names are all of this type, in fact—sudden glimpses into the diaries of the namers. They are the least formal of place names, recalling the intimacy of some nicknames. They are the names on the map which stir even the dullest imagination with their suggestion of real-life drama.

Invented place names are unlikely to have such an effect. **Tono**, in Washington, was first connected with a railway, but no one can be sure what was in the namer's mind when he gave the name. One suggestion is that it is taken from 'ton of coal'. If so, it is not a particularly attractive part-conversion. **Sob**

Some of the place names in Hawaii commemorate mythological incidents. **Puuenuhe**, for instance, literally means 'caterpillar hill', but the local story is of a legendary caterpillar who married a girl when he assumed human form. He fed his wife on his own food, sweet potato greens, and she wasted away. The caterpillar husband was then cut into pieces by Kane. The pieces became the caterpillars of today, which Hawaiians are careful not to injure.

Lake in Canada has done rather better, especially when one thinks that it began as the phrase 'son of a bitch', used to describe a trapper who had a cabin there.

Another kind of converted place name is far less arbitrary, for it represents a deliberate attempt to supply a name of good omen. **Accord, Concord, Optima, Utopia** and **Paradise** are all found in several English-speaking countries. Oklahoma has a place name **Fame** which was intended to bring just that. Florida has a **Niceville.** This seemingly French blend is all American, for 'ville' was extremely popular as a place name element in America from the end of the 18th century. Even the German immigrants who lived in Pennsylvania liked it, and were not averse to creating place names such as **Kleinville** and **Schwenkville.** The suffix '-ville' is the truly American equivalent of '-ton', a distinctive element in settlement names. As for being French, it is said that there are more places in America which end in '-ville' than there are in France.

Indian place names

Each of the English-speaking countries has its own special kind of place names which help to add interest to a world gazetteer. The other typical American names are naturally those taken over from the Indians, though they may have changed their form somewhat. **Suckabone**, for example, represents an Algonquian *suc-e-bouk*, which meant a place in which either potatoes or groundnuts grew. **Minnehaha** is a Siouan name, 'waterfalls', and in this case it is the meaning rather than the form of the name which has been changed in the popular imagination. The '-haha' was assumed to mean 'laughing' for obvious but unfounded reasons, and Longfellow took it over as 'laughing waters'.

Other tribal languages that have led to American names include Choctaw—**Seyoyah Creek;** Potawatomi—**Shabbona;** Ojibway—**Sha-Bosh-Kung Bay;** Aleut—**Einahnuhto Hills;** Muskogean—**Egoniaga;** Athapascan—**Mentasta;** Iroquoian—**Sacandaga.** The variety of languages and corruption of the names often makes their interpretation difficult or impossible, but most Indian place names appear to be topographical descriptions or incident conversions.

Canada also has its Indian names, such as the rivers **Illecillewaet**, which apparently means 'swift water', and **Incomappleux**, 'fish'. Its French names are both important and distinctive. **Montreal** cap-

tures 'royal mountain' in an early form of French, the mountain being the extinct volcano on whose slopes the city stands. **Frontenac** is a form of **Frontignac**, a place in France which gave its name to the Duke of Frontenac. Governor of New France for twenty-seven years. It is said that he asked to be sent to North America in order to escape his shrewish wife.

Australia's Aboriginal place names are a fine heritage, and the national accent also seems to come through in names like **Bargo Brush, Bong Bong, Blue's Point, Broken Hill, Cobbity, Diggers' Rest, Gippsland, Kissing Point, The Paroo, Pretty Sally's, Violet Town** and **Yackandandah.** New Zealand is rightfully proud of its Maori names, many of which can be accurately translated. **Waimakiriri** is beautiful either in that form or as 'snow-cold water'. **Taupo Nui A Tia**, 'the big cloak of Tia', names the country's largest lake by poetic metaphor.

Wherever one looks, the place names of a country manage to individualise it in spite of the vast number of duplicated British names. Countless languages have contributed to the great reservoir of names, from the Polynesian **Hawaii**, 'place of the gods', to English, German and French, as in **Applebachsville.** New names continue to appear, some disappear, others are consciously changed.

The changes may be regrettable from an onlooker's point of view, but they are understandable. **Skull Creek** in Colorado is now **Blue Mountain,** for instance. The former name conjures up a vivid picture of early reality, the present one suggests a reproduction painting for a popular market, but this is no criticism of the people who made the change. Just as we admitted the need to change some surnames because of the image they create, so we must admit that some place names, in the ordinary run of daily life, give a false impression of a place and its inhabitants. It is the inhabitants who matter. The name of the place in which they live is, in a sense, their collective name, and they have a right to adjust it.

Some name changes manage to satisfy everyday interests and those of the scholar at the same time. These are the old names that are restored after being out of use for a long time. **San Salvador** is a name of this kind, for though it was one of the first names given by Columbus when he arrived in the West Indies (it means 'holy saviour') the name did not survive. It was restored fifty years ago after careful research had established which island had been so named. Other changes satisfy everyone by being pleasant jokes. Local residents can enjoy the collec-

Some places have known multiple name-changes. **Babcock's Grove** was named in 1833 after its first settlers, but by 1834 it had become **DuPage Center**. In 1835 it changed again to **Stacy's Corner**, but in 1849 it emerged as **Newton's Station**. Two years later it was re-named **Danby**, only to become **Prospect Park** in 1882. Since 1889 it has been **Glen Ellyn**. **Portland, Maine**, was formerly **Machigonne**, **Indigreat, Elbow, The Neck, Casco** and **Falmouth**.

tive impression they give of being wits. The best example is the community in West Virginia that made a **Mountain** out of a **Mole Hill**.

We shall be looking in a later chapter at the further possibilities offered by place names for light-hearted games. We have already seen how some place names can take on very special meanings and pass into the ordinary language. For the moment we must remember that 'places' are often towns and cities which have a complex internal structure of neighbourhoods and streets. Naturally, all these have names, and it is to these names within place names that we will now turn.

When the meaning can be made out at all, the native Alaskan names are most commonly simple descriptives. Like other primitive peoples, also, the various tribes labored under no sense of obscenity. Thus Anaktuvuk Pass on the Arctic watershed is a narrow gap which forces the migrating herds of caribou to concentrate thickly. The name means something to the effect of 'dung-all-around-everywhere'.

George R. Stewart   *Names on the Land*

Some national names

Algeria Arabic 'the islands'. The name of the country was transferred from the name of Algiers, the city.

Argentina Latin 'silvery'.

Australia Latin 'southern (land)'.

Austria Latin 'eastern (land)'.

Bahrain Arabic 'two seas'.

Belgium Celtic 'brave, warlike'.

Bolivia based on the name of Simon Bolivar.

Brazil Portuguese 'heat'.

Burma Sanskrit 'strong ones'.

Cameroon Portuguese 'prawns' which were seen in the River Cameroon.

Canada Iroquois 'cabin'.

Chile Araucanian 'cold, winter', but not connected with the English word 'chilly'.

China from the Ch'in dynasty.

Colombia for Christopher Columbus

Denmark Germanic 'territory of the Dane tribe'.

Dominican Republic Spanish 'holy Sunday'.

Ecuador Spanish 'equator'.

El Salvador Spanish 'the saviour'.

England 'Angles' land'. The Angles came from Germany.

Ethiopia Greek 'people with sunburnt faces'.

Finland Swedish 'land of the Finn tribe'.

France Germanic 'Franks, freemen'.

Germany Latin form of tribal name, possibly meaning 'strong hands'.

Greece possibly 'venerable people'.

Haiti Native word for 'mountainous'.

Honduras Spanish 'depths', ie of sea off the coast.

Hungary 'tribe who lived by River Ugra'.

Iceland 'Land of ice'.

India from name of River Indus.

Indonesia *India* + Greek word for 'island'.

Iran Sanskrit 'worthy'.

Iraq Arabic 'shore, lowland'.

Ireland Erse 'western' or 'green'.

Israel Hebrew 'god Isra'.

Italy 'land of Vitali tribe'.

Ivory Coast for the ivory-trading that occurred.

Jamaica Arawak 'island of springs'.

Japan Chinese 'land of rising sun'.

Jordan from River Jordan.

Kuwait Arabic 'the enclosed' or 'little port'.

Lebanon Hebrew 'white mountain'.

Liberia Latin 'free'.

Malawi Chichewa 'flames'.

Malta Phoenician 'shelter, refuge'.

Mauritania Greek 'black-(skinned people)'.

Mexico Aztec 'moon-water', name of a lake.

Monaco Greek 'monk'.

Mongolia native word meaning 'brave ones'.

Netherlands 'low-lying lands'.

New Zealand 'new Zeeland' (Dutch province).

Niger from River Niger, 'flowing water'.

Nigeria same as *Niger*.

Norway Norse 'northern (sea)-way'.

Pakistan an acronym/blend from the Moslem states Punjab, Afghanistan, Kashmir, Iran and Baluchistan.

Paraguay from river name meaning 'water'.

Peru from River Biru.

Philippines for Philip II of Spain.

Poland Slavonic 'plain dwellers'.

Portugal Latin 'warm harbour', formerly Roman name for what is now Oporto.

Romania 'people from Rome'.

San Marino 'Saint Marinus', a 4th-century Italian.

Saudi Arabia from the name of King Ibn-Saud.

Scotland 'Scots land', the Scots possibly being 'wanderers'.

Sierra Leone Spanish 'lion mountains'.

Singapore Sanskrit 'lion town'.

Spain Carthaginian 'rabbit' or Basque 'shore'.

Sudan Arabic 'country of the black people'.

Sweden Swedish 'Svea kingdom'.

Switzerland from the canton name Schwyz.

Tanzania a blend of Tanganyika and Zanzibar, which united to form it in 1964.

Thailand native words 'country of the free'.

Trinidad Spanish 'Trinity'. Perhaps named on Trinity Sunday, or with reference to three peaks which Columbus saw from the sea.

Venezuela Spanish 'little Venice'.

Vietnam Annamese 'land of the south'.

Wales 'foreigners'.

Yemen Arabic 'right', ie on the right as one faces Mecca.

Yugoslavia Slavonic 'southern Slavs'.

Zambia from River Zambezi.

The Koreans' own name for their country means Morning Calm. A charming name . . .

Han Suyin   *A Many Splendoured Thing*

'Luxembourg. Don't you think that's a lovely name?' Berenice roused herself. 'Well, baby—it brings to my mind soapy water. But it's a kind of pretty name.'

Carson McCullers   *The Member of the Wedding*

Names and nicknames of the American states

Alabama An Indian tribal name of unknown meaning, its form influenced by Spaniards. Also: 'Heart of Dixie', 'Cotton State', 'Yellowhammer State'.

Alaska An Aleutian word for 'mainland'. Also: 'The Last frontier', 'Land of the Midnight Sun'.

Arizona Papago for 'place of the small spring'. Also: 'Grand Canyon State', 'Apache State'.

Arkansas An Indian tribal name, pronounced Arkansaw. The 's' was erroneously added by the French to make a plural. Also: 'Land of Opportunity', 'Wonder State', 'Bear State'.

California An invented name for an imaginary island. Cortés is said to have transferred the name to the state. Also: 'Golden State'.

Colorado Spanish 'reddish', for the colour of the Colorado river. Also: 'Centennial State', because it was admitted to the Union a hundred years after the Declaration of Independence.

Connecticut Algonquian 'long river'. The second 'c' has never been pronounced. Also: 'Constitution State', 'Nutmeg State'—because of the alleged manufacture there of wooden nutmegs for export.

Delaware For Thomas West, Lord de la Warr (1577–1618). Also: 'First State', 'Diamond State'—ie a rich state.

Florida Spanish 'flowered, flowery', but also suggesting Easter, when the name was given. 'Sunshine State', 'Peninsula State'.

Georgia For George II. Also: 'Empire State of the South,' 'Peach State'.

Hawaii 'Place of the Gods' with particular reference to the volcanoes. Also: 'Aloha State', from the local word for 'love', used as both greeting and farewell.

Idaho An Apache name of uncertain meaning. Also: 'Gem State', 'Gem of the Mountains'.

Illinois Algonquian 'men, warriors'. Also: 'Prairie State'.

Indiana Latinised name in honour of Indian tribes. Also: 'Hoosier State'. Many anecdotes purport to explain the nickname, eg local habit of saying 'Who's yere?' when someone knocks on the door. Other explanations are equally ingenious and unreliable.

Iowa An Indian tribal name of uncertain meaning. Also: 'Hawkeye State'—for an Indian chief of this name.

Kansas Based on the name of an Indian tribe. Also: 'Sunflower State', 'Jayhawk State'—from a fictitious bird according to some, others say a corruption of 'the gay Yorker', applied to Colonel Jennison of New York, then to his soldiers.

Kentucky Iroquois 'meadow land'. Also: 'Bluegrass State'.

Louisiana For Louis XIV of France. Also: 'Pelican State', because of the pelican in its coat of arms;

'Creole State', 'Sugar State', 'Bayou State'.

Maine The word 'mainland', later altered by the French to conform with the name of a French province. Also: 'Pine Tree State'.

Maryland For Henrietta Maria, wife of Charles I. Also: 'Old Line State', because of the Old Maryland line of troops; 'Free State'.

Massachusetts Algonquian 'at the big hills'. Also: 'Bay State', 'Old Colony State'.

Michigan Algonquian 'big lake' or 'forest clearing'. 'Wolverine State'—wolverines once trapped there.

Minnesota Sioux 'cloudy water'. Also: 'North Star State', 'Gopher State'.

Mississippi Algonquian 'big river'. Also: 'Magnolia State'.

Missouri From an Algonquian name for the river, possibly meaning 'muddy'. Also: 'Show Me State', because of the local insistence on proof.

Montana Spanish 'mountainous'. Also: 'Treasure State'.

Nebraska Sioux 'flat water', referring to the River Platte. Also: 'Cornhusker State', 'Beef State', 'Tree Planter's State'.

Nevada Spanish 'snowed upon, snowy', with reference to the Sierra Nevada mountains. Also: 'Sagebrush State', 'Silver State', 'Battle Born State'.

New Hampshire Named by a settler, John Mason, who came from the English county of Hampshire. Also: 'Granite State'.

New Jersey Named by Sir George Carteret, who came from the Channel Island Jersey. Also: 'Garden State'.

New Mexico Named in the hope that the territory would prove to be as rich as Mexico. Also: 'Land of Enchantment', 'Sunshine State'.

New York For the Duke of York, brother of Charles II. Also: 'Empire State'.

North Carolina For Charles IX of France, then Charles I and Charles II of England. (A Latin feminine form of 'Charles'.) Also: 'Tar Heel State', from the tar industry, 'Old North State'.

North Dakota Indian tribal name 'alliance of friends'. Also: 'Sioux State', 'Flickertail State', for its squirrels.

Ohio Iroquoian 'beautiful river'. Also: 'Buckeye State', from the trees that grow there.

Oklahoma Choctaw 'red people'. Also: 'Sooner State', for the settlers who anticipated the official opening.

Oregon Possibly from a mis-reading of the river name. Wisconsin, spelt Ouaricon-sint on an 18th-century map, with the last four letters on the next line. Also: 'Beaver State'.

Pennsylvania For William Penn, plus a Latin word meaning 'woodland'. Also: 'Keystone State', because its name appeared on the keystone of the bridge between Washington and Georgetown.

Rhode Island Likened to the Greek island of Rhodes. Also: 'Little Rhody'.

South Carolina Derivation as for *North Carolina*. Also: 'Palmetto State' because of the palmetto tree in the seal of the Commonwealth.

South Dakota Derivation as for *North Dakota*. Also: 'Coyote State', 'Sunshine State'.

Tennessee From a Cherokee river name of unknown meaning. Also: 'Volunteer State'.

Texas Possibly the name of an Indian tribe, or an incident name arising from a misunderstanding of a greeting, meaning 'good friend'. Also: 'Lone Star State' because of the star in the centre of its flag.

Utah An Indian tribal name of unknown meaning. Also: 'Beehive State'.

Vermont Based on French words meaning 'green mountain'. Also: 'Green Mountain State'.

Virginia For Elizabeth I, the Virgin Queen. Also: 'The Old Dominion', 'Cavalier State'.

Washington For George Washington, first President of the USA. Also: 'Evergreen State', 'Chinook State'.

West Virginia Derivation as for *Virginia*. Also: 'Mountain State', 'Panhandle State', because of its shape.

Wisconsin Algonquian 'long river'. Also: 'Badger State', because miners are said to have made homes for themselves by burrowing into the ground.

Wyoming Algonquian 'broad plains'. Also: 'Equality State', with reference to the early acceptance of women's suffrage.

'Georgia?' his mother said. 'Why in the world would a mother want to give her daughter such an outlandish name?' 'Georgia's named for a whole state.' 'How'd thee like to be called Ohio?' his mother asked. 'Thee was born there.'

Jessamyn West   *Except for Me and Thee*

Fifty capital names

Addis Ababa (Ethiopia) 'new flower'.
Algiers (Algeria) 'the islands'.
Ankara (Turkey) 'angled' or 'gorge, ravine'.
Amsterdam (Netherlands) 'dam on the River Amstel'.
Asunción (Paraguay) '(Our Lady of the) Assumption'.
Athens (Greece) after Athene 'queen of heaven', patron goddess.
Baghdad (Iraq) 'God's gift'.
Bangkok (Thailand) 'wild-plum village'.
Beijing/Peking (China) 'northern capital'.
Brussels (Belgium) 'buildings on a marsh'.
Buenos Aires (Argentina) 'good winds', alluding to the Virgin Mary, patron saint of sailors.
Cairo (Egypt) 'victorious', part of full Arabic name 'Mars the victorious', Mars being visible when city was founded.
Canberra (Australia) 'meeting-place'.
Caracas (Venezuela) name of an Indian tribe.
Copenhagen (Denmark) 'merchants' harbour'.
Delhi (India) 'threshold'.
Dublin (Ireland) 'black pool or lake'.
Freetown (Sierra Leone) 'town for liberated slaves'.
Georgetown (Guyana) for George III.
Harare (Zimbabwe) name of a hill, itself named for a chief Neharare.
Islamabad (Pakistan) 'Islamic city'.

Jakarta (Indonesia) 'place of victory'.
Jerusalem (Israel) 'foundation of (the god) Shalem'.
Kabul (Afghanistan) from river name.
Khartoum (Sudan) 'elephant's trunk', referring to shape of country.
Kingston (Jamaica) for William III.
Kuala Lumpur (Malaysia) 'mud-yellow estuary'.
Kuwait (Kuwait) 'enclosed'.
Lagos (Nigeria) 'lagoon'.
La Paz (Bolivia) '(Our Lady of) peace'.
London (England) from the name of Londinos tribe.
Lusaka (Zambia) from Lusaakas, name of a village chief.
Montevideo (Uruguay) 'I saw the mountain'.
Nairobi (Kenya) river name 'water'.
Nicosia (Cyprus) 'place of victory'.

Oslo (Norway) 'mouth of River Lo' or 'forest clearing'.
Ottawa (Canada) from name of an Indian tribe.
Paris (France) from Gaulish tribe.
Quito (Ecuador) name of Indian tribe.
Rabat (Morocco) 'fort'.
Rangoon (Burma (Myanmar)) 'end of strife'.
Rome (Italy) named for the River Ruma, former name of the Tiber.
San Salvador (Salvador) 'holy saviour'.
Santiago (Chile) '(in honour of) Saint James'.
Sofia (Bulgaria) 'wisdom'.
Tehran (Iran) 'warm place'.
Tokyo (Japan) 'eastern capital'.
Tripoli (Libya) 'three towns'.
Washington (USA) for George Washington, first president.
Wellington (New Zealand) for the Duke of Wellington.

The most famous pun involving a place-name concerned the annexation to British India in 1843 of Sind. At the time Sir Charles Napier reported his conquest of the province in a single Latin word: *Peccavi* 'I have sinned'. Sind (Sindh), which includes Karachi, is now part of southern Pakistan. The name is from Sanskrit *sindhu* 'river'.

12
NEIGHBOURLY NAMES

THE NAME of the street in which we live can take on a deep personal significance. It can evoke an area that we know in detail and a small community of people whom we know well. Another street name that we have known in the past might instantly recall our childhood and a thousand small incidents, reminding us of friends and neighbours and the passing years.

Street names can have this private meaning, but they are also felt to have a more public meaning. As with place names, street names reflect on the people who live in the streets concerned, particularly on their social status. Few people, therefore, care to live in **Thieves Lane**, say, or **Cowdung Street**, though such names almost certainly indicate that the street has been there since the Middle Ages. For that matter, few people, it seems, care to live in a street that is actually called a street.

'Street'

This curious fact has impressed itself on estate-developers everywhere. A few years ago an estate agent complained in a British newspaper: 'Streets have gone out of fashion and no one wants to live in one. You can call them roads, avenues, lanes, groves, drives, closes, places—anything but streets.' It was about this time that a builder was complaining of customers who were cancelling orders for new houses. They had learned that the street in which they stood was going to be referred to as a 'street' in its name.

As it happens, there are plenty of euphemisms available nowadays. They have a certain interest in themselves, and I have listed them as street name elements on pages 178–9. But this sensitivity to the generic word in a street name is a sure indication that residents will look very closely indeed at the element attached to it to see whether that reflects on their status. The result is a steady flow of applications to local councils asking to change existing names to

Famous street names are sometimes used allusively, having acquired a separate 'meaning'. 'What makes you so **Park Avenue** today?' asks a character in *Gideon Planish*, by Sinclair Lewis. 'Or are you being English?' he adds.

In England the **M25** motorway, encircling London, soon became notorious for its densely-packed, slow-moving traffic. A review of a play in *The Times* (1988) was therefore able to refer to 'a lacklustre adaptation and an M25 pace'.

something that 'sounds better'. Sometimes the local authority itself quietly 'loses' certain names in the cause of respectability.

What sort of name disappears? A few that have disappeared from London include **Foul Lane, Stinking Lane, Hog Lane, Bladder Street, Grub Street** and **Pudding Lane**. Of these 'foul' and 'stinking' were accurate descriptions no doubt in medieval times, while hogs and bladders would have been sold in the streets concerned. 'Puddings' were the entrails of animals which were carried along Pudding Lane to be dumped in the Thames. Grub Street probably included the name of an early resident, though a reference to caterpillars or worms is just possible. The street may have been infested with them.

Grub Street is now **Milton Street,** which shows an especially interesting change. The original name had come to be associated with low-quality writing because of the hack-writers who lived there in the 17th century. In the 19th century the residents deliberately decided to use the name of the poet in an attempt to raise the street's status.

The loss of Foul Lane and the like for general purposes is inevitable, though such names are carefully examined by the historian. Like obsolete

Among the Liverpool docks occur the names of the King's and Queen's. At the time, they often reminded me of the two principal streets in the village I came from in America, which streets once rejoiced in the same royal appellations. But they had been christened previous to the Declaration of Independence; and some years after, in a fever of freedom, they were abolished, at an enthusiastic town-meeting, where King George and his lady were solemnly declared unworthy of being immortalised by the village of L-.

Herman Melville   *Redburn*

surnames and place names they can help to paint an accurate picture of medieval life. Non-historians are quite happy for the names to be in records of the past, but they do not want to see them displayed on the street corner. They are also not fond of names like **Foundry Street,** which blatantly implies that manual work goes on in the district.

A similar kind of reaction to street names is discernible in the United States. Estate agents know that a suburban house will be easier to sell if the street name contains an element suggestive of rural peace, such as 'Hayloft' or 'Corncrib'. Streets laid out in strict geometric patterns are no longer popular, nor are the efficient number names that went with them. **Seventh Avenue** may be easier to find than **Rosemont Drive,** but there is actually prestige to be gained these days in being difficult to find.

Number names for streets

Such names, however, are thoroughly established both in the USA and Canada. They owe their existence, primarily, to William Penn, who was far from being the non-literary person such names might suggest. He was a classical scholar who used a Greek name for the city he founded in 1682—**Philadelphia,** 'brotherly love'. Had he wanted to he could certainly have suggested similar names for the streets.

When Penn came to Philadelphia many houses had already been built. People were referring to the existing streets by the name of the most important person living there. But Penn was founding a Quaker colony, and the last thing he could allow was a street name system that raised some people above others. Like all Quakers he objected strongly to any social custom that emphasised different ranks of people. He had deeply offended his father, for

instance, by refusing to take off his hat in his presence.

The Quakers referred even to Sunday as **First Day,** thus removing the pagan reference, and this may have inspired Penn to use a similar system to identify the streets of his city. These were not the haphazard sprawl of a typical English town, but were laid out at right angles to one another at regular intervals. Penn began at the eastern boundary with **First Street** and continued with his simple sequential names from there. For the streets which crossed from north to south he decided on verbal names, but once again he was careful to avoid links with people. He turned to nature and 'the things that spontaneously grow in the country'. **Chestnut Street, Walnut Street, Spruce Street, Pine Street** and the like were created. For a road that faced the river Penn wrote of **Front Street,** and he allowed the use of such names as **Market Street.**

Whether there was a general appreciation of the high principles which had led to the Philadelphian street name system, or whether the practicality of at least having a system of some kind made its appeal, we shall never know, but other towns quickly followed suit. Not only were the number names

The Quaker William *Penn* was strongly opposed to the practice of naming streets after people. The number names and nature names he used in Philadelphia were much copied by other cities, but the general fondness for commemorating people in street names remained. Perhaps the best proof of this is the fact that by the beginning of the 20th century, over a hundred streets and avenues in various US cities were named after Penn himself.

The Street Directory of the Principal Cities of the United States (1908 edition, republished by Gale Research Co. in 1973) reveals the curious fact that there are many more *Second Avenues* in the US than there are *First Avenues*. It also shows that New York has more numbered streets than any other city, the system continuing to *262nd Street*.

Streets which were laid down after number names had already been allocated, caused many ½ *streets* to come into being. Apart from the ½ Street in Washington, DC, and Wabash, Indiana, many cities have *1½ Street, 2½ Street, 3½ Street*, etc. In Moline, Illinois, is *15¾ Street*.

transferred elsewhere—often the tree names were borrowed, too, regardless of whether the trees concerned grew in the area. Yet with all its apparent simplicity, the number name system posed problems for the towns that adopted it in Ohio, Kentucky, Louisiana, Virginia, Tennessee and elsewhere. Where was First Street to be, for example, and would it remain First Street?

St Joseph had a **First Street, Second Street** and **Third Street** at one time, but the land caved into the river and left **Fourth Street** to begin the sequence. A more frequent occurrence was for towns to develop later beyond the original boundary, causing no problems at the open end of the number sequence but considerable problems at the beginning. Number names were always interpreted as being sequential in space, not time, and an **Eighty-seventh Street** could not be placed out of order on the basis that it merely recorded that eighty-six streets had been built previously. The usual solution was for suburban streets to take on verbal names and remain outside the general system.

When Washington was laid out at the beginning of the 19th century the street names included the usual number names in one direction. Letter names were introduced, however, for the streets that crossed them, and important streets, called 'avenues' for the first time, were linked to the names of states. **A Street, B Street** and the like did not appeal to other city-planners, but some copied the idea of using the names of the states. What really caught on everywhere was the use of 'avenue', though even this may have been influenced as much by New York as Washington. A few years later, when New York was extended, the ultimate in street name systems was devised. The **First Street, Second Street,** etc., from Philadelphia were there, but crossing them were **First Avenue, Second Avenue** and so on. A few streets that lay outside the grid became **Avenue A, Avenue B, C** and **D.** There were also occasional, survivals of established street names,

such as the Dutch **De Bouwerij,** 'the farm', in its anglicised form **The Bowery,** and **Breede Wegh,** which easily became **Broadway.** These were mostly streets which ran diagonally and thus cut across the basic grid pattern.

New York's system would no doubt have been widely followed, but it came late in the day. One other city that influenced American street names because it gave an example from an early date was Boston. Here one cannot talk of a system unless one calls it the English non-system. All streets were named, either by description as in **Commercial Street,** by conversion, as in **Congress Street,** after national and local figures, or from the places the streets led to. Other towns followed Boston's example, or the English example as it may have been in many cases, if local usage established street names before the City Fathers turned their minds to the matter. Occasionally there must have been a deliberate rejection of number names, the reason for their use not being known or respected. There must also have been occasions when the people who were in a position to influence street names already had their own family names linked to them. In such cases they would obviously have been tempted to allow them to remain undisturbed.

Medieval street names

Britain had no William Penn who could start a national street name fashion with a single flash of original thinking, and there were not, of course, cities to be founded in the same way. Towns and cities had been growing naturally for centuries, and the streets within them acquired the same kind of naturally descriptive names as the places themselves had done. The principal street in medieval times was the **High Street** in Southern England, **High Gate** in the North. 'Street' had been borrowed from Latin in Anglo-Saxon times to describe the Roman roads which were far superior to anything previously known in Britain. The Northern 'gate' was not the kind of gate one opens and shuts but the Old Norse *gata*, 'street'. The ordinary 'gate' also occurred in medieval street names to indicate the entrance to a walled town or the presence of a water-gate.

The name 'High Street' was taken at first to the New World, but 'high' tended to be interpreted as 'elevated' rather than 'important'. In most cases **Main Street** came to replace it. 'Main' is also used in Britain, but usually in connection with a road rather than a street. The original distinction between a 'road', which was an unmade way along which horses were ridden, and a paved 'street' lasted until at least the end of the Middle Ages. 'A main road' tends to be a descriptive phrase rather than a name.

Early English street names commented on their relative positions, as in **North Street,** etc., **Upper Street** and **Nether** ('lower') **Street**; on their surfaces, as in **Chiswell** ('pebble') **Street** and perhaps **Featherbed Lane,** a reference to soft mud. **Summer Road** in Thames Ditton would have been **Summer Lane** or **Summer Street** in medieval times, but the meaning would have been the same—a road which was unusable in winter. Other old names were of the type **Bollo Lane,** where a 'bull hollow' is referred to, and **Woodgate,** a road along which wood was transported. Commodities sold in the streets often gave those streets their names, the usual items being salt, pepper, milk, fish and bread.

There were formerly several **Love Lanes** in London, and as in any city these also referred to something being sold rather than a romantic lovers' walk. In his *London Lanes* Alan Stapleton suggests humorously that **Huggin Lane**, which was near a Love Lane, might be connected with it and not derive its name from an early resident called Huggin or from the sale of hogs. In several towns there is a **Grope** or **Grape Lane,** which really is a synonym for Love Lane. One writer has explained the name as 'a dark, narrow alley through which one groped one's way', but the full medieval forms of the name make it quite clear that another meaning was intended.

Other common street names in medieval times mentioned where the street led, including either a place name or a generic term such as 'ferry' or 'castle'. **Gallows Street** survives in some places as a reminder of the grim realities of earlier times, but **Dead Lane,** which has usually been 'lost' as a street name, was a simple reference to a cemetery. The residents of a street were often described in its name, as with **Lombard Street** and **Walker Lane,** the latter being where the walkers, who processed cloth, lived and worked.

> In at least two American cities it is possible to live on *Easy Street* (Boston, Mass, and Johnstown, Pa). Three cities have a tongue-twisting *Treat Street*. Of the streets which have Christian names attached to them, *John Street* is the most popular, followed by *Elizabeth Street* and *Mary Street*. I am unable to confirm the report that somewhere in California, because of a prominent member of the Chinese community, there is a *Wong Way*.

These medieval street names throughout Britain have obviously received attention from historical students of place names. They often supply much incidental information about medieval urban life. But relatively few of the names survive in living use. They were bestowed casually by people who always called a spade a spade, and they were doomed when the guardians of public morality began to appoint themselves in the 19th century.

London street names

The street names of London, like those of several other European capital cities, have received a great deal of attention. By 'London' the City of London is primarily meant, but several dictionaries have included some of the main suburbs. All writers on the subject begin with a reading of Stow's *Survey of London*, which was first published in 1598. Stow

Snow Hill! What kind of place can the quiet town's-people who see the words emblazoned on the north-country coaches, take Snow Hill to be? All people have some undefined and shadowy notion of a place whose name is frequently before their eyes, or often in their ears, and what a vast number of random ideas there must be perpetually floating about, regarding this same Snow Hill. The name is such a good one.

Charles Dickens   *Nicholas Nickleby*

In London it is still possible to visit *Bleeding Heart Yard*, though the name is perhaps more interesting than the place. Charles Dickens was attracted to it and featured it in *Little Dorrit*:

The opinion of the Yard was divided respecting the derivation of its name. The more practical of its inmates abided by the tradition of a murder; the gentler and more imaginative inhabitants, including the whole of the tender sex, were loyal to the legend of a young lady of former times closely imprisoned in her chamber by a cruel father for remaining true to her own true love, and refusing to marry the suitor he chose for her. The legend related how the young lady used to be seen up at her window behind the bars, murmuring a love-lorn song of which the burden was, 'Bleeding Heart, Bleeding Heart, bleeding away,' until she died.

Neither party would listen to the antiquaries who delivered learned lectures in the neighbourhood, showing the Bleeding Heart to have been the heraldic cognisance of the old family to whom the property had once belonged. And considering that the hour-glass they turned from year to year was filled with the earthiest and coarsest sand, the Bleeding Heart Yarders had reason enough for objecting to be despoiled of the one little golden grain of poetry that sparkled in it.

Dickens does not mention an even commoner legend concerning Lady Hatton, who sold her soul to the devil. At one time London children knew that as the devil bore her off he dropped her shoe in *Shoe Lane*, her cloak in *Cloak Lane*. Her bleeding heart was found in Bleeding Heart Yard.

As for the truth of the matter, the name certainly derives from an inn sign. There was one which showed the heart of the Virgin Mary pierced with arrows, for instance. The inn sign could also have shown a bleeding 'hart', or male deer. Heraldic experts have been unable to trace a family coat of arms which contains a bleeding heart.

There are perhaps some who will prefer, like the Dickens characters, to stay with the legends and forget the dullness of reality. As with the explanations of so many romantic names, truth is unfortunately *not* stranger than fiction.

himself knew 16th-century London well, and he was also a student of early records. This showed him that many street names had already changed their form. **Belliter Lane,** for instance, had earlier been **Belzettars Lane,** which indicated more clearly its connection with the bell-makers. There was a large group of such men, for the bells in the many London churches were much used. The lane still exists as **Billiter Street.**

The first actual street name dictionary for London, however, appears to have been *London Street Names*, by F. H. Habben. This was published in 1896, so that it had to rely mainly on Stow. In his introductory remarks Habben states sensibly that names cannot usually be dismissed 'with a curt etymological sentence and nothing more'. He talks of the 'facts or circumstances round about the name' which need to be given, and he gives them himself.

Nothing is known of Habben, but his frequent quotations of Chaucer, Milton, Longfellow and other poets, and his willingness to guess at an Old Norse personal name origin for names like **Snow Hill** makes one think that the 'B. A.' mentioned on the title-page was probably a degree in English.

Louis Zettersten's *City Street Names* was published in 1917, but the author does not seem to have been aware of Habben's *Dictionary*. Zettersten was a Swedish businessman who worked in London, and once again he was obliged to accept the explanations of Stow and one or two others as facts. His great strength, however, was to produce an attractive little dictionary that could easily be read by a layman, and there seem to be very few instances where he would seriously mislead his readers. In his article on **Fleet Street,** for instance, he says that the name derives from a bridge over the River Fleet rather than the river itself, a comment based on a 13th-century reference to *vicus de Fletebrigge.* As it happens, later writers have unearthed a still earlier reference which would make the explanation 'street leading to the Fleet River', but this is hair-splitting. When a real problem occurs, as it definitely does with the **Snow Hill** (earlier **Snore Hill**) already mentioned, Zettersten makes it clear that there is a problem and that suggestions as to the original meaning can only be tentatively made.

In many ways Zettersten's little book is more satisfying than that of his compatriot, Eilert Ekwall, who published *Street Names of the City of London* in 1954. Ekwall is a pure philologist of the highest quality writing for other specialists, and for him a street name's origin is all that matters. Subsequent associations of a street, which may have given it a meaning that is recognised throughout the world, are totally ignored. He does not mention journalism, for example, when he deals with Fleet Street. He says quite clearly that he is interested only in names 'which go back to medieval times', and could have added that his interest even in those names is highly restricted.

The point perhaps needs stressing for Ekwall, as the heavyweight scholar, has tended to over-shadow Zettersten, the intelligent amateur, and others like him. The amateurs respond instinctively to street names and see them as meaningful wholes rather than linguistic specimens under a microscope. I believe very firmly that the 'amateur' approach is the right one, the linguistic facts forming only a part of the whole story.

In between Zettersten and Ekwall several other studies of London street names appeared. These were mostly imitative of the earlier works, but in 1935 E. Stewart Fay published *Why Piccadilly?* in which he abandoned the dictionary style in favour of a discursive work. He begins by writing of **Piccadilly** for three pages, attributing it to the 'pickadills', or ruffed lace collars, made by the tailor Robert Baker in the 17th century. Baker made enough money from these highly fashionable articles to buy a house, which others quickly named **Pickadilly Hall.** The name eventually spread to the area, and has survived several official attempts at various times to change it.

Stewart Fay states his view of street names immediately after the Piccadilly explanation. For him the names lead directly to human anecdotes, the

'hundreds of such stories hid behind the often prosaic names of London streets, squares and localities. To search these out is to lay bare a cross-section of the pageant of London from the earliest times down to the living present . . . **Spring Gardens** will inform us of a royal practical joke. **Hatton Gardens** conceals a scandal concerning the frailty of Elizabeth. . . .'

He gives further examples designed to whet the appetite, and it is difficult not to read on. The 'royal joke' he refers to was a sundial which stood in **Spring Gardens.** It had a concealed spring tap nearby on which people stepped when they went to look at the dial. A jet of water would then spurt out and soak them. In spite of this, Spring Gardens is far more likely to have got its name because of the 'spring' of young trees formerly planted there, but who would sacrifice the anecdote? The **Hatton Gardens** story is made into a playlet by Stewart Fay and is rather overwritten, but the essential facts about Elizabeth I and her 'dancing Chancellor' are given. Sir Christopher Hatton danced his way into the Queen's favour, then persuaded her to let him take over most of the Bishop of Ely's house and gardens. Hatton gave his name to the gardens, and later—in rebus form—to a nearby public house, the **Hat and Tun.**

The style of *Why Piccadilly?* is often successful and is a good example of an imaginative writer's approach to names. Although no philologist the author is generally able to sort out fact and fiction in the works he has consulted. On **Snow Hill,** which is always something of a test case, he mentions the story of stage-coach passengers snoring by the time they arrived at the Saracen's Head public house only in order to dismiss it. For a man who was clearly deeply fascinated by names, he also has many sensible things to say about American number names for streets. After praising the functional advantages of the New York system he goes on to say that number names can take on a meaning and value like any other names. Names do not have, he reminds us, 'an inherent stamp of quality; their reputation is derived solely from the nature of their associations'. He gives the example of **Mayfair,** which was notorious at the beginning of the 18th century because of the riotous celebrations which took place at the beginning of May each year but which later changed its meaning completely.

Stewart Fay's discursive method was partly emulated in 1952 by Hector Bolitho and Derek Peel in

Of all the streets that have been named after famous men, I know but one whose namesake is suggested by it. In Regent Street you sometimes think of the Regent; and that is not because the street is named name after him, but because it was conceived by him, and was designed and built under his auspices, and is redolent of his character and time. From this redolence I deduce that when a national hero is to be commemorated by a street we should ask him to design the street himself. Assuredly, the mere plastering-up of his name is no mnemonic.

Sir Max Beerbohm   *The Naming of Streets*

In streets, the names of which are matters of history, I should like to see a simple inscription, in full view, within the range of all mental capacities, recording the memorable events or public services connected with the memory of the illustrious man named, or enumerating his literary labours, if an author. Nothing beyond bare facts should be admitted into these inscriptions; and no inscription should be awarded to a man during his lifetime, or to a prince whose dynasty has not expired, so that flattery might not be substituted for history.

Eusebius Salverte   *History of the Names of Men, Nations and Places*

Without The City Wall. Their sub-title refers to 'an adventure in London street names, north of the river', and their aim is to take the reader on a series of excursions—which are mapped out—explaining the names encountered. It is an interesting idea, and shows yet another approach to street names. These authors too make it clear that they are not scholars, but they have gone to respectable sources of information and then applied their own common sense. Wherever possible they checked 'facts' in their own way, so when told that **Chiswell Street** took its name from Old English *ceosel*, 'gravel', they telephoned the Borough Engineer to ask about the geological strata in that area. He confirmed that there were large deposits of flint and gravel there.

And still books on London street names appear. A London taxi-driver, Al Smith, brought out his *Dictionary of City of London Street Names* in 1970. It is a personal selection of historical material gathered from standard sources. Gillian Bebbington's *London Street Names* appeared in 1972. It covers a wider area than previous dictionaries and makes a further useful contribution by displaying the family trees of important landowners. For general reference purposes it is probably the best dictionary of its kind. It has nevertheless been succeeded by *London Street Names*, 1977, by John Wittich and *The Streets of London*, 1983, by S. Fairfield.

Johannesburg street names

An interesting contrast to London street names is provided by those of Johannesburg. They have been carefully studied by Anna H. Smith, whose monumental *Johannesburg Street Names* was published in 1971. At that time the city was still only eighty-five years old, and it might be thought that in such a case there are no difficulties for the researcher. These names were given, however, by a large number of early landowners and surveyors, who usually kept no records of why the names had been chosen. Naming was not taken very seriously, and sometimes the draughtsmen preparing maps were left to select names. They usually made them as short as possible for their own convenience.

Miss Smith omits number names from her dictionary as being self-explanatory, but mentions in her Introduction that there are 'forty or so **First Avenues, Lanes, Roads** or **Streets** in Johannesburg'. This reflects, presumably, the parallel development of different areas by early pioneers. There was certainly no attempt made to evolve an over-all street name system, though the City Council now tries to exercise control.

As with most towns in Britain, a wide variety of people are commemorated in Johannesburg street names. There they include entertainers, admirals, artists, authors, sportsmen, prominent city residents—including landowners, musicians, kings and queens, scientists and inventors, prominent persons in South African history, surveyors and government officials. Street names that link with first names—usually those of women—were often meant to honour the relations of the namers. Place names are usually meant to be reminders of the pioneers' home-towns. One pioneer, at least, must have come from very close to where this book is being written, for he named an **Esher Street** and **Surbiton, Kingston, Hampton, Molesey** and **Ditton Avenues**, all of which places are within a mile or two of my house.

It was a place of pleasant sounding old names, richly English, and romantic. The names of the streets fascinated Christopher: Green End, Lombard Street, Baileygate, Golden Hill, The Tything, Market Row, Vine Court, Barbican, Angel Alley.

Warwick Deeping   *Sorrell and Son*

Other names linked to the street names include those of battles, churches, companies, farms, hotels, mines, mountains, mythological figures, rivers, saints and ships. Transferred names from ships show particularly well the dangers that lie in wait for a researcher less thorough than Miss Smith. **London Street, Suffolk Road, Dunrobin Street, Ivanhoe Street, Mars Street** and **Zebra Street** are names that one would naturally be inclined to explain as being other than ship names, which they happen to be. It is never possible to take a name purely at its face value. Even **Winning Way** turns out to be named after a Mr Winning.

Other street name dictionaries

In a more modest way, there is great scope for local historians and others to compile street name dictionaries in their own areas. An excellent method is to make use of the local newspaper, publishing a series of articles street by street giving the facts so far known. Earlier forms of older names are vital, and with more modern names it is essential to know

---

A suitable address for a traditional English policeman—**Letsby Avenue**.

---

when the names were given. Local residents will usually respond by giving further information which can be included when the material is published later in more permanent form.

The earliest example I have seen of such articles, leading to a discursive work in this case rather than a dictionary, is *Greenock Street Names*, by Gardner Blair. This was published by the *Greenock Herald* itself in 1907. A more recent example is *Warrington and the Mid-Mersey Valley* by G. A. Carter. Several newspapers are currently publishing articles about local street names. The *Winnipeg Tribune*, for example, has a long-running series written by Vince Leah. It is quite clear that readers of the *Tribune* enjoy having their memories stimulated by such articles.

Local historians working independently have produced very satisfying street name dictionaries for places like Lewes, Bristol, Watford, Stevenage, Acton and Shrewsbury. Articles on the street names of other areas have appeared from time to time in specialised magazines. In the *Maryland Historical Magazine* for June 1948, for example, is an article by Douglas H. Gordon, *Hero Worship As Expressed in Baltimore Street Names*. Similar topics have been discussed in *Names*, the journal of the American Name Society. Public libraries often have a collection of index cards on which street name information is given, but in other areas the basic research has still to be done.

I have no doubt that it is worth doing. Sir Max Beerbohm once wrote that every street had its character, like individual human beings, and that he was affected by that character when he walked there. In older towns and cities especially, the names of the streets have character, and they are well worth investigating.

Minto Square, Great Clive Street, Warren Street, Hastings Street, Ochterlony Place, Plassy Square, Assaye Terrace ('Gardens' was a felicitous word not applied to stucco houses with asphalt terraces in front, so early as 1827).

William Thackeray   *Vanity Fair*

A street by any other name

Many of the following words occur in street names as substitutes for the word 'street' itself. In some cases the original meanings of the words have been considerably stretched, but others are genuine synonyms.

Acre(s)

Alley

Approach

Arcade also used of an avenue of trees forming an arch.

Archway

Ascent

Avenue

Backs behind buildings.

Bank a raised shelf or ridge of land.

Bend

Billet

Bluff

Bottom land in a valley.

Boulevard

Broadway

Bullring

Butts usually transferred from a field name where it referred to land at the boundary of the field, or land covered with tree-stumps.

By-Pass

Carfax from Latin *quadrifurcus*, 'four-forked', used where four or more roads meet.

Causeway raised way across a marsh or a paved way.

Centre

Chase originally unenclosed land reserved for hunting.

Circle

Circus where there is a circular ring of houses.

Cliff

Close an entry or passage.

Common(s) common land.

Coombe a small valley.

Coppice plantation of young trees.

Copse = coppice.

Corner

Cottages

Court

Covert

Cranny a narrow opening.

Crescent

Croft an enclosed field.

Cross for a cross-roads.

Cut where an excavation has been made to allow road to pass.

Cutting = cut.

Dale a valley.

Dell

Dene (also *Dean*) a wooded valley.

Drang (dialectal) an alley.

Drift a track.

Drive

Droke (dialectal) a narrow passage.

Drove a road along which cattle were driven.

Embankment

End

Esplanade = promenade.

Estate

Expressway (USA)

Extension (USA)

Fair on former fair-ground.

Farrow a path.

Fennell (dialectal) an alley.

Field(s)

Flyover

Fold

Freeway

Front

Furlong

Gardens

Garth (dialectal) an enclosure.

Gate Old Norse *gata*, 'road'.

Ginnel (dialectal) narrow passage.

Glade

Glebe land assigned to a clergyman.

Glen

Green

Ground

Grove

Gully

Hangings a steep slope on a hill.

Harbour

Hard a sloping roadway or jetty.

Hatch fenced land.

Hays

Hey fenced land.

Highway

Hill(s)

Hollow

Houses

Hundreds

Jigger (dialectal) an alley.

Jitty (dialectal) an alley.

Knoll

Lane

Lawn = 'laund', a stretch of untilled ground.

Lea untilled land.

Line (USA)

Link

Loke (dialectal) an alley.

Main

Mall where pall mall, a game with mallet and ball, was played.

Marina

Market

Mead = meadow

Meadow(s)

Mews stables.

Midway (USA)

Mile

Moat

Motorway

Mount

Narrows

Nook

Ope an opening.

Orchard

Oval

Paddock

Pantiles properly roofing-tiles but sometimes used to describe paving-tiles.

Parade

Park

Parkway

Pass

Passage

Pastures

Path(way)

Pavement a roadway in USA.

Pickle a small enclosure.

Piece

Pightle = pickle.

Pike

Pines

Place

Plain

Plaisance (USA) a pleasure-ground.

Plaza (USA) Spanish, 'market-place'.

Pleasaunce

Poultry a poultry market.

Promenade

Prospect a place affording a view.

Quadrant a square.

Quay

Range

Retreat a secluded place.

Ride

Ridge

Riding(s)
Ring
Rise
Road
Roundabout
Row
Rue (USA)
Scarp the steep face of a hill.
Side
Skyway (USA)
Slip
Slope
Slype a covered way, especially one leading from the cloisters of a cathedral.
Sneck (dialectal) a narrow passage.
Sneckett = sneck

Snicket = sneck
Square
Steps
Strand
Sward
Sweep
Terrace
Thoroughfare 'thorough' is an old form of 'through'.
Throughway
Tollway (USA)
Turn
Turnpike a toll-gate.
Twitchel (dialectal) a narrow passage.
Twitchet = twitchel.
Twitten = twitchel.

Twitting = twitchel.
Tyning land enclosed with a fence.
Usage a public right of way.
Vale
Valley
Viaduct
View
Villas
Walk
Wall a footpath next to a wall.
Way(e)
Wharf
Wood
Wynd (dialectal) a narrow street.
Yard

A selection of London street names

Adelphi Terrace from the group of buildings The Adelphi (Greek *adelphoi*, 'brothers') designed by the Adam brothers.

Aldwych possibly 'old wick' or settlement.

Baker Street after William Baker, once controller of the Marylebone estate. Sherlock Holmes lived at 221B according to Conan Doyle.

Barbican a word brought back from the Crusades. An outer defensive wall and watch-tower.

Bayswater Road Bayard's (or Baynard's) watering-place.

Belsize Square from the manor of Belassis, 'beautifully situated'.

Berkeley Square where the nightingale sang. Baron Berkeley had a house there.

Bevis Marks earlier Beris Marks. Land within the marks 'boundaries' of the Abbots of Bury.

Birdcage Walk where Charles II kept birdcages.

Blackfriars Road for the Dominicans who settled there.

Bow Street the famous police court is in this street shaped like a bow.

Cannon Street formerly the street where the candle-makers lived.

Carmelite Street the friars of Our Lady of Mount Carmel, or 'Whitefriars' lived there.

Carnaby Street famous in the 1960s as a fashion centre. From Carnaby in Yorkshire (?).

Charing Cross Road 'Charing' refers to a turning of the Thames; the cross commemorated Queen Eleanor, whose funeral procession passed this way.

Clerkenwell Road a well where parish clerks gathered annually.

Cockspur Street in the days of cockfighting the cocks wore spurs, which were sold in this street.

Cornhill a hill where corn was grown.

Dean Street for the Dean of the Royal Chapel.

Downing Street the official residence of the Prime Minister. Sir George Downing, an unpopular diplomat, was an early leaseholder.

Farringdon Street from the surname of an early Sheriff of London.

Gower Street for the first Earl Gower.

Gracechurch Street the church was St Benet's; 'grace' was formerly grass, perhaps with reference to a turf roof, or to a fodder market.

Gray's Inn Road The inn was a hostel for law students owned by the Grey family.

Great Windmill Street a windmill was there in the 17th century.

Grosvenor Square otherwise 'Little America' because of the Embassy, etc., was owned by the Grosvenor family.

Hanover Square honoured George I, son of the Elector of Hanover.

Harley Street famous as a gathering-place for the élite of the medical profession, is on an estate owned by the Harley family.

Haymarket was a hay market.

High Holborn from the bourne ('stream') in the hollow.

Kingsway for Edward VII.

Leadenhall Street for a hall that had a leaden roof.

Liverpool Street in honour of Lord Liverpool.

Marylebone High Road the church St Mary Bourne, the 'bourne' being the Tyburn stream. Later thought to be *Mary la Bonne*.

Middlesex Street the official name that is rightfully ignored by every Londoner, who knows that petticoat-makers who worked here in the 17th century caused the street to become Petticoat Lane.

Moorgate a gate led to the moor, 'marshy wasteland', outside the north wall of the City.

Old Bailey often used as a synonym for the Central Criminal Court which is situated there. The bailey was once a mud rampart just outside the city wall.

Old Bond Street after Sir Thomas

Bond, who owned the land.

Oxford Street formerly **Tyburn Way,** leads to Oxford but was named after Edward Harley, second Earl of Oxford, the landowner.

Park Lane runs beside **Hyde Park,** once a 'hide' or measure of land.

Pentonville Road was owned by Henry Penton.

Petticoat Lane see *Middlesex Street.*

Piccadilly see page 175.

Portland Street the Dukes of Portland owned land here.

Portobello Road to commemorate the capture of Porto Bello in the Gulf of Mexico, 1739.

Praed Street after the banker William Praed.

Procter Street after a former inhabitant, Bryan Procter, solicitor and poet.

Regent Street after the Prince Regent, later George IV, and meant to link Carlton House and Regent's Park.

Rosebery Avenue the fifth Lord Rosebery was the first Chairman of the London County Council, and this street was named after him.

Russell Square owned by the Russell family, Dukes of Bedford.

St Giles High Street a leper colony was established here in medieval times, the hospital and church being dedicated to St Giles.

St James Street from a hospital dedicated to St James.

Shaftesbury Avenue in honour of the seventh Earl of Shaftesbury who did much philanthropic work for the people who formerly lived in this area.

Sloane Square after Sir Hans Sloane, a distinguished physician whose library formed the nucleus of the British Library.

Soho Square 'So-ho' was a hunting cry like 'tally-ho'. There may have been an inn in this area which took the cry as an incident name.

Southampton Row the owner was Thomas Wriothesley, Earl of Southampton.

Theobalds Road led in the direction of Theobalds, in Hertfordshire, where Lord Burghley had his home and lavishly entertained Elizabeth I and James I.

The Strand was formerly the 'strand' or shore of the Thames.

Threadneedle Street from a sign of a house or inn with three needles on it, perhaps the arms of the Needlemakers' Company. But one writer mentions the folk-dance Threadneedle, where dancers form arches for one another.

Tottenham Court Road the court of 'Totta's ham' or village.

Wardour Street now mainly linked with the film industry. Sir Edward Wardour was former owner.

Watergate a rather insignificant London street bears this highly significant name. There was once a gate giving access to the Thames.

Whitefriars Street see *Carmelite Street.*

Whitehall Cardinal Wolsey owned the palace of this name, which passed to Henry VIII.

Wigmore Street one of the Harley family, the landowners, was Baron Harley of Wigmore, in Herefordshire.

NOT IN THE SAME STREET

THERE are certain streets where no one would want to be. 'Queer Street is full of lodgers just at present!' says Fledgeby, in Charles Dickens's *Our Mutual Friend.* In Britain people still talk about being in **Queer Street** when they are short of money, perhaps unaware that they are obliquely referring to **Carey Street**, in London, the former home of the Bankruptcy Court.

Skid Row, on the other hand, 'the eponymous habitat of the down-and-out in every American city, owes its name to Skid Road, a district near the Seattle sawmill where timber workers and drifters used to hang around in the late 19th century'. (*Observer* newspaper 10.12.89.)

No writer would want to be known as a Grub Street hack. This London street was notorious in earlier times because of the impoverished writers who lived there. Its residents changed the name to **Milton Street** in 1829. Perhaps at a later date they would have made it **Easy Street**. 'Living on Easy Street' as an expression appears to derive from a story by George V. Hobart, *It's Up To You* (1902).

Some 'street' expressions have not survived. To turn the corner of **Bolt Street** once meant to run away. Of a heavy drinker it could once be said that all his money went down **Beer Street**. **Gutter Alley** and **Gutter Lane** were alternative names for the throat, based on both the obvious meaning of 'gutter' and the Latin *guttur*, 'throat'.

13
SIGNING A NAME

VISITORS to Britain have for centuries been making favourable comments about the public houses they find on all sides. Britain has some fifty-five thousand 'pubs'. The earlier terms 'inn' and 'tavern' appear to have referred originally to different kinds of pub. The inn was obliged to remain open at all hours in order to receive guests. Taverns were for casual refreshment and were obliged to close at a certain hour. But the two terms became confused at an early date, and few modern writers on the subject use them consistently with their original meanings. Both have in any case been replaced by 'pub' in normal speech, so we will refer to pubs and their names throughout this chapter.

Pubs carry on a tradition of convivial hospitality which began to be established in the Middle Ages. Many writers have written eloquently about their charms, but we must concern ourselves here with their names. These are often distinctive and intriguing in themselves but they have, of course, another famous characteristic. Each name is usually accompanied by its visual representation, its sign. Pub names and signs together add to the interest of any journey through Britain, and this interest can only be deepened when one looks into the past to see how and why the names and signs arose.

The ale-stake

The classic writers on signboard lore, Larwood and Hotten, conclude that our medieval ancestors must have imitated the Romans when they began to make use of trade signs. The Romans certainly identified their various tradesmen by symbols. A tavern keeper would tie a bunch of evergreens to a pole, the 'ale-stake', and display it in the street. He was crudely honouring Bacchus, the god of wine, who was always shown with ivy and vine leaves. The **Bush** appeared in medieval England as a pub sign and is still to be found as such.

The Bush is technically a generic sign, rather like the three balls that symbolise any pawnbroker or the red and white striped pole that still sometimes announces the presence of a barber. In a street where each establishment carries on a different trade such signs are adequate, but the custom whereby particular trades were associated with special streets seems to have begun early. As soon as there were several butchers, bakers or whatever next door to one another in a medieval street it became necessary to distinguish them more individually. Today in such a situation we would do it very simply, by showing the different shop names. At a time when hardly anybody could read, shops needed names for spoken use but signs that could be used for visual identification.

It is important to realise that for several centuries city streets in Britain were filled with signs of all kinds, not just pub signs. All tradesmen needed them, and even private householders found them necessary. This was an age when there were no numbered houses, and one's address was a descriptive phrase that made use of any convenient landmark. Many people found it easier to display a personal sign outside their houses so that they could speak of living 'at the sign of the **Star**' or something similar. Some surnames derive from these sign names, which came into use at the end of the surname period.

Influence of emblems

But did the use of signs consciously imitate the Romans? They could just as easily have come upon the scene as a natural reflection of medieval life. People could not read or write but they could recognise simple pictures. One might say that they were trained to do so. One of the greatest educational influences of the era was the Church, which itself used a system of name signs.

These name signs are still to be seen in churches

In his *Introduction to Inn Signs*, Eric R. Delderfield writes:

In the coaching era there were two inns at Stony Stratford (Bucks), the Cock and the Bull, and between them a fierce rivalry existed. As the coaches arrived from different directions, the gossip of the road was exchanged, and lost nothing in the telling. So much so that anything which resembled a gross exaggeration or was obviously distorted became known as a 'Cock and Bull story'.

Mr Delderfield has at least provided an excellent example of a cock-and-bull story, which has come to mean 'a foolish story told as if it were true'. The expression was in use long before the coaching era, and there is strong linguistic evidence which connects it with the French *coq à l'âne*. It originally referred to any story which passed incoherently from one subject to another.

but few of us are now very adept at 'reading' them. The medieval church-goer, by contrast, would look at a stained-glass window which showed a woman holding a basket of fruit or flowers and know immediately that this was St Dorothy. A nearby statue of a man holding a key or keys was St Peter. The saints were known by their *emblems* which performed much the same function as name plates might have done. By the end of the 14th century many of these emblems had become standardised throughout western Europe.

Some of them were highly individual, others had more in common with the Bush in that they were symbolic in a general way. A book might be held not only by the Evangelists but by any saint who had a reputation for learning or devotion to the liturgy. A sword was a symbol of execution and a palm indicated martyrdom by other means. All of these and many more the ordinary person was able to interpret. He went to church often and was frequently told the stories behind the emblems. They came to form a simple kind of hieroglyphic language.

Today we think of pictures of any kind as adjuncts to words and names. If we see a pub with even the simplest of signs outside it, such as a **Red Lion** or **Plough,** we still expect to see the name written with it. A complex sign outside a private

---

After being originally christened The Hospice, and degenerating into its present name, The Ostrich, no wonder the house hangs its head today.

Cecil Aldin   *Old Inns*

---

house, say, with a sheaf of rye to be seen and a hare near it, the sun shining in the background, would baffle us completely. Even if we knew that the people living there were called **Harrison** we would still not make the 'hare-rye-sun' connection. A few centuries ago we would have been far more practised in deciphering such 'silent names', as Camden calls them when he gives the Harrison example. We would have had to be, for the signs of the time did not bother to give the verbal forms of the names.

Mistaken interpretations

This is not to say that all men would immediately have seen the point of the Harrison rebus. There is ample evidence that many signs have been misinterpreted in the past. The mistakes began with the saintly emblems, with new explanations for them being invented by fertile minds. St Denis was usually shown holding his head in his hands, for example, as a reminder that he had been decapitated. A myth soon arose to the effect that he had walked from Montmartre to the place of his burial carrying his head.

Out in the street the signs were often poorly painted, and artists might not manage to convey the impression they wished. A sign which was meant to announce the **Coach and Horses** pub might become the **Coach and Dogs** by a brutal piece of art criticism. A **Black Swan** could likewise become the **Muddy** or **Mucky Duck.** The **Heedless Virgin,** corrupted by folk-etymology to **Headless Virgin** and shown on a sign as a decapitated saint, could accidentally or deliberately be interpreted as the **Silent Woman,** implying an 'at last!'.

Misinterpretation of this kind sometimes led to establishments being known simultaneously by more than one name. The **Rose,** in Bristol, was also known to local people as the **Cauliflower.** The **Swan and Lyre** could be referred to as the **Goose and Gridiron.** When the alternative name became widely known it was sometimes thought desirable to keep it and create a new sign that intentionally matched it.

Influence of heraldry

Another kind of name sign that came into being for practical reasons during the Middle Ages was the coat of arms. Men went into battle heavily armed and were difficult to recognise. It became the custom for them to adorn their shields and to decorate their helmets with distinctive crests. As an idea this was not new, for the Greeks and Romans had fought behind shields painted with animals and the like, but these do not seem to have become conventional symbols, always associated with one family. Coats of arms accompanied the development of surnames in Britain, becoming hereditary in the same way.

It would have been logical for coats of arms to take over the designs used on seals, which were used to authenticate documents in Britain from the 11th century onwards, but the opposite seems to have happened. The seals were again name signs, the upper-class equivalent of the X that was used as the mark of more humble men who could not write. At first they were freely chosen signs used by individuals, but they later reproduced the coats of arms. As F. J. Grant says in *The Manual of Heraldry*: 'but for the fact that few persons were able to write and had to authenticate all deeds and transactions they entered on with their seals, we should not now have these records of the early armorial designs.'

General illiteracy, then, led to names being represented pictorially at all levels of medieval society. Sign names were to remain in practical use for several centuries. They are now little more than decorative fossils, whether coats of arms or pub signs, but they attract in both forms enthusiastic modern students. It is the pub signs with which we are now concerned but that does not mean that we can immediately put heraldry to one side. A large number of pub signs, and therefore pub names, derive from coats of arms. The **Red Lion** and **White Hart** are probably the best known of these, the first referring to the coat of John of Gaunt, the second to that of Richard II. The word 'arms' itself was later to become so strongly associated with pub names that it became almost a synonym for 'inn', 'tavern' or 'pub'. Modern names such as the **Junction Arms, Bricklayers' Arms, Platelayers' Arms** and **Welldiggers' Arms** show the trend.

Sign names

There is a marked difference between most of the pub names that came into existence before the late 18th century and those that have appeared since then. The earlier names may well have been the names of the signs themselves. When the Knights Templars established a hostel for pilgrims and others and identified it by a sign that showed an angel, it is unlikely that they thought in terms of 'naming' what was in effect a primitive pub. They would have wanted an appropriate sign to indicate that the hostel was under divine protection and which was easily recognisable as a generic symbol. The name **Angel** would only occur later, when people shortened the phrase 'at the sign of the Angel' or 'the Angel sign' to 'the Angel'.

Similarly, the signs that indicated loyalty to the throne were meant to do precisely that, but not

---

At Grantham, in Lincolnshire, from the eccentricity of the lord of the manor, who formerly possessed the majority of the houses in the town, there is at the present time the following inns that have the word 'Blue' attached to their signs: viz.—Blue Boat, Blue Sheep, Blue Bull, Blue Ram, Blue Lion, Blue Bell, Blue Cow, Blue Boar, Blue Horse and Blue Inn.

By way of completing this catalogue, a wag, whose house belonged to himself, and who resided near the residence of his lordship, a few years ago actually had the Blue Ass placed on his sign.

The Mirror, 1833 quoted by Rowland Watson   *A Scrapbook of Inns*

necessarily to create such names as the **Crown, Sceptre, King's Arms** and **Queen's Arms.** Such signs were especially useful in being widely known. The names that derived from them could be classed as descriptive, but once again descriptive of the signs rather than the places.

Many heraldic signs were subjected to a kind of visual folk-etymology. What was perhaps meant to be interpreted as the **Warwick Arms** became the **Bear and Ragged Staff.** The **Prince of Wales** might emerge by a similar process as the **Feathers.** Such names seem to indicate that familiar as certain famous coats must have been in former times, ordinary men could not interpret them as easily as the saintly emblems. These names also show quite clearly that the signs came first, the names afterwards.

One class of pub names, however, which appeared early definitely began as names and were then deliberately converted into visual form. These were often surnames which ended in '-ton' and were easy to illustrate by means of the tun, the large cask in which beer was stored. A lute, thorn, ash tree and the like could be shown with it to pun on **Luton, Thornton, Ashton,** etc. The pub names would nevertheless emerge as the **Lute and Tun** type. The **Tun and Arrows,** for instance, was meant to be the **Bolt in Tun** for **Bolton.** The **Hand and Cock** was similarly the sign used by a publican called **Hancock.** In spite of the punning intention, these remain descriptive names.

Shop sign names

Names chosen in modern times differ from the original sign names in that the names almost always come first, the signs afterwards. A point was reached where the signs were in danger of being abandoned altogether, the names having taken complete precedence. Before this happened, however, the density of signs and names in large cities had become very great, and the signs constituted a public nuisance. They blotted out the daylight from the narrow streets, made a continual creaking noise by swinging back and forth, and occasionally caused accidents. There was a notorious incident in London in 1718, when a heavy sign-board pulled down the wall to which it was attached, killing some passers-by.

The density of sign names had also caused them to change in kind. The early signs had always been familiar objects or symbols, but there was only a limited supply of these and they were quickly used

up. Partly in an effort to avoid duplication, sign names were formed by deliberately combining elements, such as the **Whale and Crow,** the **Frying Pan and Drum.** Such names could also arise, however, when a publican or shopkeeper went to a new establishment. He would want to take his personal sign with him but retain the goodwill associated with the existing sign, so he would combine the two.

In a famous *Spectator* essay of 1710 Addison commented on street signs of his time and gave in passing another possible explanation of the combination names:

'Our streets are filled with **Blue Boars, Black Swans** and **Red Lions,** not to mention **Flying Pigs** and **Hogs in Armour,** with many creatures more extraordinary than any in the deserts of Africa. . . . I should forbid that creatures of jarring and incongruous natures should be joined together in the same sign; such as the **Bell and the Neat's Tongue,** the **Dog and the Gridiron.** The **Fox and the Goose** may be supposed to have met, but what has the **Fox and the Seven Stars** to do together? And when did **Lamb and Dolphin** ever meet except upon a signpost? I must, however, observe to you upon this subject that it is usual for a young tradesman at his first setting up to add to his own sign that of the master whom he served, as the husband after marriage gives a place to his mistress's arms in his own coat. . . .'

Addison uses heraldic terms metaphorically, of course, but at the back of many shop and tavernkeepers' minds must have been the wish to become known by a sign that would act in the same way as a coat of arms.

The Pelican at Speenhamland
It stands upon a hill.
You know it is The Pelican
By its enormous bill.

quoted by Cecil Aldin   *Old Inns*

Appropriate sign names

A century before Addison wrote his essay Thomas Heywood had lightheartedly commented on the way different pub signs attracted different kinds of customer. The gentry, he wrote, would go to the **King's Head,** the bankrupt to the **World's End,** the gardener to the **Rose,** the churchmen to the **Mitre,** etc. An extended version of this appeared in the *Roxburgh Ballads*. It was said, for instance, that the drunkards by noon would go to the **Man in the Moon,** while

> The Weavers will dine at the **Shuttle,**
> The Glovers will unto the **Glove,**
> The Maidens all to the **Maidenhead,**
> And true lovers unto the **Dove.**

Addison turned the whole idea round and commented on the relationship between the namer and the sign name: 'I can give a shrewd guess at the humour of the inhabitant by the sign that hangs before his door. A surly, choleric fellow generally makes choice of a **Bear,** as men of milder dispositions frequently live at the **Lamb.'**

'What are we?' said Mr Pecksniff, 'but coaches? Some of us are slow coaches; some of us are fast coaches. We start from The Mother's Arms, and we run to The Dust Shovel.'

Charles Dickens   *Martin Chuzzlewit*

There is obviously a serious point underlying both of these approaches to sign names, or any names for that matter, but the majority of signs in Addison's time gave little indication that they had been carefully chosen. The sheer size of a sign became the most important factor in some cases, or the extravagance of its supporting ironwork. All the time they were becoming more purely decorative, since standards of literacy were rising and names could be interpreted in their linguistic form.

By the 1760s official action was taken against street signs. In many areas it was forbidden to have signs that projected into the streets. Number names of houses and shops were to become compulsory before long, again making the sign names superfluous. Inevitably they began to disappear from the streets, and might have done so totally but for their survival as pub signs, and in a different way as trade marks. Pub signs survived for several reasons. From the 15th century onwards publicans had been required to display signs by law, so that the tradition of signs and sign names was particularly strong in their trade. The shopkeepers had never been under such an obligation. There was also a difference for a long time between taverns in the cities and inns elsewhere. For the inns on the coaching roads a sign was not lost among a hundred others but was something of a landmark in itself. Even today signs are still more frequent in the country than in the towns. Finally, the withdrawal of street sign names by the shopkeepers gave a new kind of meaning to those that remained. The mere presence of a sign now had the same generic significance as the early ale-stake as well as a more individual meaning.

Types of pub names

All that has been said so far about the general background to pub signs has been necessary in order to explain pub names as they exist today. The nomenclature has unique characteristics which can only be explained by reference to a time when it was desired not so much to create a name as to allow a locative phrase, 'at the sign of . . .', to come into being. In modern times the usual processes that affect name systems have come into operation. Many names are transferred to new pubs because they are felt to be unambiguously pub names. Others are created to fit into the traditions established by the early names. The **Air Hostess** and the like are converted names, while the **Sherlock Holmes** and **Sir Walter Scott** are normal transfers. The pub signs give visual support to the names.

Other categories of names are also found. Names that described the pubs themselves rather than the signs naturally became more common when projecting signboards were banned, but a few had existed previously. Publicans sometimes looked at the characteristics of the buildings they occupied and described these in the name. The **White House, Red House, Blue House** and the like may have been deliberately arrived at by painting the buildings for the purpose, or they may simply have reflected what was there. This was almost certainly the case with names such as the **Green Lattice,** a lattice being fixed across a pub's open windows to give those inside the building some privacy. When the lattices gave way to the more usual windows the word was likely to be misunderstood. In at least one instance a **Green Lettuce** later came into being.

By metonymy objects directly associated with the pub could be used for its name. The **Brass Knocker** is one kind of example, while the food offered inside the pub accounts for names like **Round of Beef, Shoulder of Mutton, Boar's Head, Cheshire Cheese** and so on. Drink was obviously not forgotten and led to the **Jug and Glass, Foaming Tankard, Malt and**

Hops, **Full Quart** and many more. The **Black Jack,** for instance, was a primitive kind of leather bottle, sometimes lined with metal. A fashionable drink of the past is remembered in the **Punch Bowl** and other names that mention 'punch', though the nearest pub of this name I can actually get to derives its name from The Devil's Punch Bowl, a metaphorically named hollow in the hills.

The inn-keepers

Even nearer, however, is one of my 'locals', the **Swan.** In the early 19th century it was kept by John Locke who had a wife 'absolutely incomparable in the preparation of stewed eels, and not to be despised in the art of cooking a good beef-steak or a mutton-chop'. So wrote William Hone in 1838, while a few years earlier Theodore Hook sat in a punt on the Thames and wrote a poem about the pub. He also mentioned the inn-keeper's wife, being struck by her 'bright blue eyes' as much as her cooking.

A pub's dependence on its landlord and landlady has long been recognised. In many areas it leads to the unofficial renaming of a pub by its publican's name. Edinburgh, for example, formerly had many establishments known by such names as **Lucky Middlemass's Tavern** and **Jenny Ha's Change House.** 'Lucky' was a pleasant way of addressing a woman, especially a grandmother, and it became the specific term for the keeper of an ale-house. Jenny Ha's was a reference to another 'lucky', Janet Hall.

It is largely due to the inn-keepers, one imagines, that the pub has survived as a national institution in Britain. They have helped to give familiar names like the **Rose and Crown,** the **Bell, George and Dragon, Wheatsheaf, Coach and Horses, Talbot** and **Ship** a very special meaning, an accumulated goodwill built up by centuries of relaxed social gatherings. There are not many names among the millions in existence to which such a remark could apply.

Other pub names

Mention of landlords and their ladies has taken us inside the pubs, and while we are there we can look at some of the names we find. Often, for instance, the individual rooms have names. The well-known **Shakespeare Hotel** in Stratford-on-Avon has rooms named after the plays. A member of The Names Society once told me that she was a little discon-certed, when staying there with her husband, to

learn that they would spend the night in a room called **The Taming of the Shrew.** The **Mouth,** a pub mentioned by Taylor, the Water Poet, had rooms called the **Pomegranate,** the **Portcullis, Three Tuns, Cross Keys, Vine, King's Head, Crown, Dolphin** and **Bell,** all of which could occur as pub names in their own right.

Also within a pub are to be found the vast number of names for the various drinks. Gin, for instance, has also been known at various times as **Cuckold's Comfort, Ladies' Delight, Gripe Water, Eyewater, Blue Ruin, Mother's Ruin, Flash of Lightning, Lap, Last Shift** and **No Mistake**. These are only a few of its nicknames. Beer has also come in for unofficial renaming, ranging from **Jungle Juice** to **Belly Vengeance** and **Dragon's Milk.** If one adds the nicknames of the inn-keepers, such as **Mother Louse** who kept an ale-house near Oxford in the 18th century, it is clear that one could fill a book very easily with pub names and those names that are connected with pubs.

Australian pub names

A list of popular and curious pub names, together with their explanations, is at the end of this chapter. They give a general idea of the types of names found in Britain today. But Britain is not alone in having pubs. They appeared in Australia at the end of the 18th century, for instance, and spread throughout that continent. In many places there pubs came before private houses, and in their relatively short history they have played a remarkable part in the country's social development. Pubs have served as churches, town halls, post offices, surgeries, and theatres. The first Australian zoo was at the **Sir Joseph Banks** in Botany Bay. The whole story is well told in Paul McGuire's *Inns of Australia.*

McGuire remarks specifically that 'most' Austral-ian pub names 'were brought from Britain', but his book makes it quite clear that they quickly took on their own characteristics. One of the first pubs in New South Wales, for instance, was the **Three Jolly Settlers.** The **Bulletin** in Sydney was named after the Australian weekly newspaper as soon as it appeared, which may have been an innovation in pub-naming. There are pubs in Britain with names like **Express** and **Mail** but they were named after coaches.

One man who arrived in Australia in a ship called the **Buffalo** founded a pub called the **Buffalo's Head.** A model of the ship's figurehead was used as a sign. Pub signs therefore established themselves in

Australia along with the names, but the many photographs in McGuire's book make it clear that not many pubs used them. They had none of the long history behind them to make them traditional, and they served little practical purpose. The fact that they were used at all merely reflected the vague feeling of British settlers that pubs should have a sign.

The Buffalo's Head, mentioned above, later became the **Black Bull** and acquired a double-sided signboard. A peaceful bull was shown on one side, a raging bull on the other. An inscription read:

> The bull is tame, so fear him not
> So long as you can pay your shot.
> When money's gone, and credit's bad,
> That's what makes the bull go mad.

Name, sign and inscription have unfortunately since been removed.

Australian **Halfway Houses** sprang up spontaneously (and optimistically in some cases) and cannot be said to be transfers from Britain. Another entirely Australian pub name, in origin at least, is the **Tiger** in Tantanoola. The tiger turned out to be a wolf, now stuffed and displayed in the bar. A man who traded on the 'tiger's' reputation for sheep stealing in order to establish a private butchery in the bush was later sent to prison for six years. Two other pub names, **McDonald's** and the **Glenrowan,** have now become totally Australian and Ned Kelly's.

Inside the pubs the food and drink appears to have taken on a national flavour as well. At **Scott's,** which was a club rather than a pub, one could eat Kangaroo Tail Soup, Curried Bandicoot, Parroqueet Patties and Aspic of Native Pigeon. In more ordinary establishments drinks—or 'throat-scrapers' and 'eye-openers'—with names like **Spider** (lemon-ade and brandy), **Maiden** (peppermint and cloves) and **Catherine Hayes** (claret, sugar and orange) were consumed. All in all it seems safe to say that Australian pubs, and the names that were attached to them in various ways, were well and truly Australian from the beginning.

Conclusions

Pub names have something for everybody. My own special interest lies in their complex relationship with the signs that accompany them. The only parallels that come to mind are certain American place names such as **Straddlebug Mountain** and **Ucross** which derive from brand marks on cattle. For others the appeal lies in the anecdotal explanations of many a curious name. And who could not be curious, for instance, about a name like the **Drunken Duck**? This pub in Westmorland is famous for the story of a former landlady who once found her ducks lying in the road. She thought they were dead and began to prepare them for dinner, but they turned out to be in a drunken stupor. Beer had drained into their feeding-ditch. The ducks were reprieved and allowed to sober up, and one hopes that they lived long and happily.

The Cooney brothers encircled me in the back bar of the Ultima Thule [a pub in Australia]. This had recently been renamed the Whingeing Pom, in deference to the disposition of its clientele.

Howard Jacobson   *Redback*

A cocktail by any other name

It is possible that 'cocktail' began as the proper name of a particular mixed drink, then went on to become the general term. Whatever its origin, it remains a fanciful word for something that traditionally attracts fanciful names. The following are a small selection.

Amour
Angel's Kiss
Appendicitis
Atta Boy
Banco
Between the Sheets
Biter
Black Baby
Blonde
Blood Transfusion
Blue Monday
Boomerang
Brainstorm
Buster Brown
Cameron's Kick
Caresse
Cat's Eye
Champs-Elysée
Charleston
Clap of Thunder
Clover Club
Corpse Reviver
Cowboy
Damn the Weather
Depth Bomb
Devils
Earthquake
Eclipse
Elektra
Elixir
Eye-Opener
Fair and Warmer
Fascinator
Favourite
Five Fifteen
Flu
Forty-Seven
Four Flush
Fourth Degree
Gimlet
Gin N Sin
Glad Eye
Gloom Chaser
Gloom Raiser
Good Night Ladies
Grand Slam
Great Secret

Green-Eyed Monster
Hanky-Panky
Hasty
Hell
Hesitation
Hole in One
Honeymoon
Hoopla
Hoots Mon
Hula Hula
Hundred Per Cent
Hurricane
Income Tax
Jabberwock
Jack in the Box
Jupiter
Kicker
Knickerbocker
Knock Out
Last Round
Leap Year
Leave it to Me
Lovers' Delight
Lucifer
Macaroni
Maiden's Blush
Maiden's Prayer
Manhattan
Marmalade
Merry Widow
Moonlight
Moonraker
Moonshine
Morning After
Mule
Mule's Hind Leg
New Life
Nineteenth Hole
Nine-Twenty
Oh Henry
One Exciting Night
Paradise
Perfect
Ping-Pong
Poker
Pooh Bah
Poop Deck

Presto
Prohibition
Queen of Sheba
Reinvigorator
Resolute
Rolls Royce
Rusty Nail
S.O.S.
Screwdriver
Self-Starter
Sensation
Seventh Heaven
Sidecar
Six Cylinder
Slipstream
Snowball
Soul Kiss
Stinger
Strike's Off
Sweet Potato
Swizzles
Tempter
Third Degree
Third Rail
Thunder
T.N.T.
Torpedo
Tropical
Twelve-Mile Limit
Twelve Miles Out
Twentieth Century
Upstairs
Velocity
Welcome Stranger
Whizz Bang
Whoopee
Widow's Kiss
Wow

Roger Hannahs of Wilmington, Delaware, once suggested in *Word Ways* that new cocktails could be called *Rabbit Punch* and *Marriage on the Rocks*

A selection of pub names past and present

Many names have more than one possible origin and these are indicated. For heraldic names the immediate source rather than the ultimate origin is given.

Some ten thousand British pub names are fully explained in *A Dictionary of Pub Names*, by Leslie Dunkling and Gordon Wright (Dent, 1994).

Adam and Eve popular figures in medieval pageants; arms of Fruiterers' Company.

Air Balloon often commemorates first ascent at Versailles in 1783 with animals as passengers.

Alice Hawthorn a famous racehorse.

Alma for the Battle of Alma, 1854, in the Crimea. A river name.

Anchor an easily illustrated sign; often a retired seaman as landlord.

Axe and Compass arms of Carpenters' Company.

Bag O'Nails reputedly a corruption of Bacchanals; actually the sign of an ironmonger.

Bear where bear-baiting took place; occurs in many coats of arms.

Beehive a convenient 'object sign'. One pub so named had a living sign, occupied by a swarm of bees.

Bell used by bell-ringers or bell-makers; near a bell-tower.

Bible and Crown a common toast of the Cavaliers.

Bird in Hand a joking reference to the proverb, especially if a Bush was near by; a falcon on a gauntlet is common in heraldry.

Bleeding Heart a reference to the Virgin Mary; arms of the Douglas family.

Blue Boar arms of Richard, Duke of York. Corrupted to **Blue Pig** in one instance.

Blue Boys Bridewell boys—orphans and foundlings—dressed in blue; scholars of Christ's Hospital; postilions of George IV (whose coach stopped at an inn of this name).

Blue Vinny a Dorset cheese.

Brockley Jack a notorious highwayman.

Bull often because bull-baiting took place before it was forbidden in 1835.

Bull and Mouth commemorates Henry VIII's victory at Boulogne Mouth, or is a corruption of 'bowl and mouth'.

Canopus after a flying-boat.

Cardinal's Error referring to Wolsey's suppression of Tonbridge Priory.

Case is Altered local anecdotes account for different instances, eg a pub replaces something less desirable; departure of a military camp causes loss of trade; new landlord cancels outstanding debts. Ingenious but highly unlikely explanations include a corruption of Casey's Altar or *Casa de Saltar* ('house of dancing').

Castle and Ball perhaps a corruption of Castle and Bull in arms of Marlborough family.

Cat and Fiddle usually a joking reference to the nursery rhyme. Corruptions of *La Chatte Fidèle* ('the faithful cat'); *Caton le Fidèle* (the governor of Calais) and *Catherine la Fidèle* (Catherine of Aragon) have also been suggested.

Cat I' Th' Window a Catherine Wheel window; from a stuffed cat placed in the window.

Charles XII a racehorse.

Chequers formerly emblem of money-changers; indication that draughts or chess could be played; common element in coats of arms; from a simple decorated post used as a sign.

Church Inn near a church, though Defoe described one inn of this name as the Devil's Chapel, with a larger congregation than the church itself.

Clickers for the shoemakers.

Clipper's Arms referring both to a ship and sheep-clippers.

Coach and Eight in one instance the reference is to rowing.

Cock and Bottle the 'cock' being a spigot, indicating that draught and bottled beer was sold.

Comet a stage-coach name.

Compleat Angler for the book by Izaak Walton, 1653.

Cow and Snuffers occurs in an early play as a satirical example of a pub name and perhaps taken from there. Another source says it was the result of a bet to find an incongruous name.

Cromwell's Head an oblique reference to the Restoration.

Crooked Billet a shepherd's crook; a weapon; a yoke; bishop's crosier; part of tankard; arms of Neville family.

Cross Foxes arms of Williams-Wynn family.

Crown formerly Crown property; showing allegiance to king.

Cutty Sark the short shirt worn by men and women in the Border Country; name of ship.

Curiosity for its collection of curiosities.

Daniel Lambert a man who died in 1809 weighing fifty-two stone.

Dirty Dick Nathaniel Bentley was so called in the 18th century. He lived as a hermit after his bride-to-be died on wedding-day.

Discovery after Captain Scott's ship.

Doff Cockers an invitation to locals to take off their leather gaiters.

Dog and Duck spaniels were set to chase ducks on nearby ponds.

Dolphin and Crown arms of French Dauphin.

Duke of York after the battleship in one instance.

Eagle and Child arms of Earls of Derby.

Eagle and Lion arms of Queen Mary.

Eclipse usually transferred from the racehorse rather than an actual event.

Elephant and Castle for the Cutlers' Company; often falsely said to be corruption of *Infanta de Castile*.

Falcon a frequent element in coats of arms; formerly a popular bookseller's sign.

Falstaff after Shakespeare's much-loved rogue.

Fifteen Balls Cornish coat of arms.

Fighting Cocks for a 'sport' abolished in Great Britain in 1849.

First and Last usually refers to location of pub at edge of town or village.

Fish and Ring a reference to St Kentigern's having his ring returned to him by a fish when he dropped it into a stream.

Five Alls usually a king, parson, lawyer and soldier who say they rule, pray, plead and fight for all, plus a taxpayer who pays for all, or a devil who takes all, etc.

Fleece for those in woollen industry.

Flower Pot such signs often showed lilies originally, referring to the Virgin Mary.

Flying Bull after Fly and Bull, two stage-coach names.

Flying Dutchman usually after the racehorse of this name.

Flying Horse Pegasus; from roundabout on nearby fairground.

Fox and Grapes Aesop's fable; two signs combined.

Frighted Horse formerly Freighted Horse, a pack-horse (?).

Gate near a church gate, toll-gate, prison gate or gate-keeper's lodge.

George and Dragon to proclaim English patriotism.

Goat in Boots as a caricature of a Welshman; sometimes explained as corruption of Dutch *Goden Boode*, a reference to Mercury.

Goat and Compasses arms of Wine Coopers' Company; a legend that it is a corruption of 'God encompasseth us' is widely believed.

Green Man for foresters and woodmen; for Robin Hood; for May King, Jack-in-the-green.

Greyhound usually a stage-coach name.

Gunners nickname of Arsenal Football Club.

Hammers nickname of West Ham United Football Club.

Hat and Feathers early 17th-century reference to fashion in plumed hats.

Hole in the Wall local anecdotes account for the name, eg a debtors' prison that became a pub had a hole through which food was passed; pub is reached by passing under viaduct arch that looks like a hole in the wall.

Honest Lawyer a joke name, usually showing a headless lawyer unable to speak.

Intrepid Fox after Charles Fox, not the animal.

Iron Devil plausibly a corruption of *hirondelle* ('swallow') on arms of Arundel family.

Jacob's Well a biblical joke, for 'whosoever drinketh of this water shall thirst again'.

Key for locksmiths; Jane Keye kept an inn of this name in the seventeenth century.

Labour in Vain originally religious, for Psalm 127 says: 'Except the Lord build the house, they labour in vain that build it.'

Lamb and Flag formerly a religious reference to the Holy Lamb with nimbus and banner; arms of Merchant Taylors.

Lamb and Lark proverbially one should 'go to bed with the lamb and rise with the lark'.

Leather Bottle formerly much used by shepherds.

Lion and Antelope arms of Henry V.

Lion and Bull arms of Edward V.

Lion and Unicorn arms of James I.

Little John variant of Robin Hood, itself often used as a pub name.

Little Wonder a racehorse.

Live and Let Live usually a comment by a landlord on competition which he considers unfair.

Mad Cat probably from a badly painted heraldic fox.

Mall Tavern from the game of pall mall (or pell mell), played with a mallet and ball.

Man with a Load of Mischief a famous sign reputedly by Hogarth shows him with a woman, a monkey and a magpie among other things.

Master Robert a steeplechaser.

Mermaid a popular sign, easy to illustrate.

Moon and Sun a rebus for the Monson family.

Mother Redcap a legendary woman who lived to be 120 'by drinking good ale'.

Nag's Head one sign shows a woman's head; usually a horse.

Naked Man formerly a tailor's sign; sometimes meant to be Adam; in one case said to be for a tree struck by lightning that then resembled a man.

New Inn usually of great age.

Noah's Ark formerly sign of dealer in animals.

No. Ten and other examples such as No. Five, No. Seven refer to houses that had only number names when granted a licence.

Oliver Twist one pub of this name is in Oliver Road, which has a bend or twist in it.

Ordinary Fellow in honour of King George V, who once described himself in this way.

Pewter Platter for Pewterers' Company; to show that food is obtainable.

Pig and Whistle almost certainly a corruption, but origin not clear. A 'peg' was a measure of drink, a 'piggin' a drinking-vessel. 'Wassail' in one of its several

---

A remark by Sherlock Holmes to a German spy, who says that he will shout for help:

'My dear Sir, if you did anything so foolish you would probably enlarge the limited titles of our village inns by giving us The Dangling Prussian as a sign post.'

A. Conan Doyle   *His Last Bow*

> Professor W. E. Kershaw points out that in rural areas the sign Cock and Bottle is far more likely to refer to a haycock, a small heap of hay, and a 'bottle' of hay, where *bottle* refers to a bundle, not a glass container.

meanings may have been origin of 'whistle'.

Pin and Bowl where ninepins and bowls could be played.

Pride of the Valley a reference to Earl Lloyd George.

Printer's Devil frequented by printers' apprentices.

Ram arms of Cloth Workers.

Ram Jam a kind of drink; legend says landlady made to ram and jam holes in barrel with her thumbs by trickster who left without paying bill.

Rampant Cat a reference to a heraldic lion by irreverent locals.

Red Cat for a badly painted lion.

Ring o' Bells usually for hand-bell ringers.

Rising Sun heraldic reference to House of York.

Rose Revived reference to Restoration of Charles II; a Rose re-opened after closure.

Royal Mortar probably Royal Martyr.

Running Footman whose job was to run before a coach to clear the way.

Saracen's Head variant of Turk's

Head when Crusades made the Turks common topic of conversation.

Sedan Chair introduced to England in 1623.

Seven Stars a reference to the Virgin Mary; the Plough constellation.

Ship an easy to illustrate sign, popular everywhere; in some instances meant to be The Ark.

Ship and Shovel used by coal-heavers who came from nearby ships and left their shovels at the door.

Silent Whistle a former Railway Hotel where branch line was closed.

Silver Bullet a locomotive name.

Sky Blue in honour of the local football club colour (Coventry).

Smoker a racehorse name.

Star referring to Star of Bethlehem or to the Virgin Mary; a simple visual symbol.

Stewpony corruption of Estepona, birthplace of landlord's wife.

Swan and Antelope arms of Henry IV.

Swan With Two Necks probably badly painted sign of two swans originally. Often explained as

'swan with two nicks' on bill to show that it belonged to Vintners, but this would have made a difficult-to-identify sign.

Tabard a sleeveless garment worn outdoors by monks, soldiers, etc.

Talbot breed of hunting-dog used in arms of Earl of Shrewsbury.

The Sparkfold name of a hunt.

Three Compasses arms of Carpenters and Masons; sometimes accompanied by advice 'to keep within compass'.

Three Tuns arms of Vintners, said to be an unlucky sign associated with tragedy.

Tumble-Down Dick a reference to Richard Cromwell; to an 18th-century dance; to Dick Turpin.

Two Angels arms of Richard II.

Unicorn formerly sign of goldsmith or apothecary.

Waltzing Weasel weasels actually 'waltz' round their victims.

Why Not a racehorse name.

World Upside Down popular when Australia was being discovered.

Yorker a cricketing reference to the type of delivery perfected by Spofforth, the bowler.

In the year 1775, there stood upon the borders of Epping Forest, at a distance of about twelve miles from London, a house of public entertainment called the Maypole; which fact was demonstrated to all such travellers as could neither read nor write (and sixty years ago a vast number both of travellers and stay-at-homes were in this condition) by the emblem reared on the roadside over against the house, a fair young ash, thirty feet in height, and straight as any arrow that ever English yeoman drew.

Charles Dickens   *Barnaby Rudge*

14
HOME-MADE NAMES

IT HAS often been said that man has a 'need to name'. House names may sometimes owe their existence to this aspect of human nature, but they reflect also something that is less often mentioned—man's 'right to name'. An inventor who creates something new is thought to have the right to name it; a botanist has the right to name the new species he has identified. Whatever the legal technicalities, it is now usually looked upon as a mother's right to name the children. The situation where someone finds that he has this right to name does not often occur, and when it does it is not lightly thrown away. It is not surprising that many householders in Britain—for it seems to be in the English suburbs where house-naming most frequently occurs—decide to use their prerogative and name their own houses.

Most houses, of course, already have a number name, and full use is often made of it. The previous owner of my former house had **Seven** made up in wrought iron and displayed it on the gate. I thought it an excellent name and gave it even more prominence on the wall. Most suburban streets show similar examples of number names that have been put into verbal form and carved or painted on attractive boards. Higher number names can be dealt with in **One Three Six** style.

Touches of individuality are often added to number names by varying the spelling. **Numbawun, Nyneteign** and the like show a perfectly understandable determination to individualise common names. Synonyms of number names sometimes occur, as in **Gross House** and **Century House,** and they appear in translated form as **Douze** (12) or whatever. Associations of a number can lead to names like **Sunset Strip** for '77'. An occasional name is added as a phrasal complement to the existing number name, the outstanding example being **Ornot** shown alongside '2B'.

Number names can be humanised, then, if this is felt to be necessary, but possibly the common objection to them is caused by the fact that they are imposed from outside by an anonymous authority. The house-owner feels that his right to name is being usurped. In some areas, especially those where all the houses are privately owned, the objection to imposed names may extend to the street names. Residents rightly feel that they, and not the local authority, have the right to choose the name. In other areas where there is a mixture of privately owned houses and council houses, house names may be used as an outward sign that the houses concerned *are* privately owned. As it happens, tenants of council houses could almost certainly bestow names on them if they wished. They would probably not be allowed to fix name-boards to the walls, but they could put them on posts in the garden. The only problems then would be the comments of the neighbours about snobbishness.

Snobbish names

The fairly widespread feeling that it is snobbish to name a house has partly come about because of inappropriate names that have been given. Flora Thompson smiles gently at **Balmoral** in Chestnut Avenue in her *Lark Rise to Candleford*, a book which itself led to **Lark Rise** becoming a popular house name. And to stay with literature—which is safer for the moment—one thinks naturally of **Dotheboys Hall.** Nicholas Nickleby (Knuckleboy as he was for Mrs Squeers) was given a lesson about house names when he arrived in Yorkshire.

'Is it much farther to Dotheboys Hall, sir?' asked Nicholas.
'About three mile from here,' replied Squeers. 'But you needn't call it a Hall down here.'
Nicholas coughed, as if he would like to know why.
'The fact is, it ain't a Hall,' observed Squeers drily.
'Oh, indeed!' said Nicholas, whom this piece

of intelligence much astonished.

'No,' replied Squeers. 'We call it a Hall up in London, because it sounds better, but they don't know it by that name in these parts. A man may call his house an island if he likes; there's no Act of Parliament against that, I believe?'

'I believe not, sir,' replied Nicholas.

'Hall' carries a definite suggestion of historic grandeur, but the English language manages to make even 'house' snobbish if it becomes a house-name element. Just as the street I live in would be downgraded by being called **Speer Street** rather than **Speer Road,** so my house would be considerably overgraded if I called it **Speer House.** 'Cottage' is still defined in the dictionary as 'a small or humble dwelling', but it probably has a positive cash value if it can be applied with reasonable appropriateness to a house.

The charge of snobbishness about house names is usually applied when a house also has a number name. If a house has no other kind of identification, the need for a name is accepted. Even then, villagers are likely to smile to themselves when a newcomer puts up a board with his own choice of name over the house he has just bought. If the house has been there for some time it will already have a name. This will remain in general use, or the name of the new owner may become attached to it. Local people will not easily allow a stranger to affect their linguistic habits.

A house which has no number name is normally in the country rather than the town, which gives it immediate status in the eyes of many town-dwellers. It is also often larger than the typical suburban 'semi'. Accusations of snobbishness aimed at someone who has added a name to his house are therefore accusations of misrepresentation. As with Squeers, it is felt, an attempt is being made to profit unfairly by favourable associations.

Defensive names

A defensive reaction to this situation can be seen in many house names which actually belittle the houses concerned. Favoured words like 'manor', 'grange' and 'cottage' are left aside and a house becomes **The Shack, The Igloo, The Hut, Little House. The Bothy** is less obvious, but its specific sense was once a one-roomed hut in which unmarried labourers lodged together. **The Hole** and **The Hovel** are hardly more complimentary, and the Australian **Wurley,** 'an Aboriginal's hut', is again modest to say the least.

A similar type of name refuses to comment on a pleasant view or something of the kind, emphasising instead the house's exposed position. **Windy Walls, Windswept, All Winds, High Winds, Wild Winds** and dozens of others have an admirable honesty about them that would have horrified Squeers. In Bermuda there is a **Rudewinds.** Bermuda, one should mention, has no number name system for its houses and is something of a happy hunting ground for house name enthusiasts. I have not had the pleasure of a personal visit, but the *Bermuda Telephone Directory* is one of my favourite books.

Other 'windy' house names include **Bicarbonate** and **Dambreezee,** the latter occurring in several spellings. There is no joking, however, with **Cold Blow, Gale Force, Western Gales.** It should not be forgotten that the winds themselves have names, **Zephyr** being the best known. This occurs as a house name but is complimentary, since the west wind is normally light and pleasant. **Mistral,** a cold northwest wind in France, has been borrowed as an English house name, and a correspondent who lives in Edinburgh tells me that his house name, **Snelsmore,** is a wind in that area.

Bleak House is hardly a complimentary name, though it has acquired a new meaning thanks to Dickens. He did not invent it, for old directories show that many such houses were in existence before he wrote his novel, but he chose the name with a sure touch. It is hard to imagine a starker name. It has the naturalness of country speech about it, though, not the appearance of consciously invented names. The latter can be seen in **Dryrotia, Dry-Az-Ell, Lean Tu** and **Isor** ('eye-sore') which relieve the negativeness with a touch of humour.

An anthropologist might want to link this deliberate denigration of a house with the custom in some tribes of naming a child negatively. The usual wish is to convince the gods that the child is worthless, for if the opposite impression is given the child might be snatched away from the parents in an early death. In British society the gods are the evil spirits of rumour and gossip who will drag down anyone who tries to stand higher than the rest. The house name is therefore made into an acknowledgement of lowliness, either of the house or its occupants. This may seem extraordinary, but the house names sometimes appear to support such an argument. **On the Rocks, Overdraft, Skynt, Stony Broke, Haz-a-Bill, The Bank's, Little Beside** and many similar names show a healthy contempt for, but an awareness of, keeping up appearances. A pair of jerry-built houses proclaim **Ibindun** and **Sovi.** Other names publicly announce that inside the house there is **Chaos, Bedlam, Pandemonium, Panic.** More names which have a confessional quality include **Drifters' Lodge, Fools' Haven, Hardheads, Hustlers' Haunt, Paupers' Perch, The Monsters** and **Ellinside.**

An alternative explanation for such names is that the householders are extroverts who are not so much naming a house as putting up a notice for the public to appreciate. A 'graffito instinct', as one might call it, is emerging. It is seen even more clearly in house names which have nothing to do with the house and very little to do with the householder, unless they can be said to reflect his philosophy of life. **Rejoice** and **Wiworry** say such house names, or as D. H. Lawrence discovered in Australia, **Wyework.** They may also throw out a greeting: **Ahoy, Cheers, Hey There, Yoo Hoo.** Next door to the last named, in Bermuda, is **Yoo Hoo Too.**

Houses with names like these need to be publicly situated, perhaps in a seaside town that attracts many visitors. They tend to be in such towns for another reason; the householders there are exposed to nomenclatures where frivolity is a tradition. The names of small boats and beach-huts are especially humorous. In quieter suburbs statement-type house names are neighbourly invitations, such as **Kumincyde, Popinagen, Popova** and **Havachat,** or they are quiet murmurs of satisfaction: **This'll Do, Thistledew, Sootsus, Dunbyus, Welerned.**

A small group of these names are rather aggressive. **Llamedos** on a house in Loughborough is not a Welsh name but a back-spelling. It was chosen, so I was told on the doorstep, because the family were feeling generally fed-up when they moved in. Mrs E. Luhman has written to me in the past about the time she and her husband moved into a bungalow in Essex. A local busybody descended on them 'and after many questions as to who we were and where we previously lived, loftily enquired "What are you going to call this place?" My husband, who was by then exasperated, replied, "We were thinking of calling it **Oppit.**" So Oppit it became.'

Other correspondents have written to me about **Fujia,** a reference to the householder's being all right regardless of Jack's condition, and a dual-purpose house name, **Wypyafeet.**

We were saying earlier that naming a house says in effect that the house is privately owned. Some people feel that the point needs emphasising: **Itzmyne, Myholme, Myonwna Lodge, Ourome, Ourn, Jusferus.** Link names such as **Barholme,** where the family name is Bar, **Ednaville, Helenscot, Lynsdale, Silvanest**—for a De Silva family in Bermuda—serve

a similar purpose. **Morgan's Cottage,** actually based on the wife's first name, caused her to be addressed as Mrs Morgan by the neighbours, with a moment of embarrassment all round when she explained that she was Mrs Dunstan.

These link names do not always emphasise ownership. They can become in-jokes for those who happen to know the owner's name. Thus, a **Bird Song** in Middlesex picks up on the surname Bird, **Cornucopia** on Le Cornu (in Jersey), **Deer Leigh** on Deering, **Emblur** on Bulmer, **Little Parkin** on Parr, **Seltac** on Castle, **The Eddy** on Edwards, **The Huddle** on Huddy, **The Nuttery** on Nutt. **Little Manor** is a clever link with the surname Littman.

House-owners' names can also lead to house names without actually being linked to them. **Sixpenny House** was almost inevitable for the Tanner family in pre-decimal currency days, though the surname's origin was nothing to do with money. A Robin and Marion decided they had to live in **Sherwood,** and families with animal surnames, such as Fox and Lyon, are likely to live in **The Lair** or **The Den.**

Blends

It is in the house name system that blends come into their own. A blend is the special type of link that is built up with parts of more than one name, especially the names of the family members. These names clearly have very great significance as a group to the family concerned, and it is natural that people should think of symbolically combining them to represent the family group.

A simple blend may 'marry' the first names of the husband and wife. Barry and Wendy form the name **Barwen;** Mary and Tony decide on **Marony.** Less often the two family names are blended to give names like **Shorrlin** from Shortland and Ling, **Kenbarry** from Kenyon and Barry. One trouble with blended names is that they often fail to conform to the normal rules of the language. It is quite obvious that **Lynmar** *is* a blend, from the daughters' names in this case. Similarly, **Margrek, Dorsyd, Lespau** and the like stick out like linguistic sore thumbs.

By contrast, blends can resemble words too closely and convey a meaning which is not intended. **Maveric,** for instance, and **Maudlyn** come far too close for comfort to 'maverick' and 'maudlin'. It is even possible for the namers to form a real word without knowing it. In *English House Names* I quoted the example of a Renee and Albert who called

'We shall 'ave to call this little 'ouse by a name. I was thinking of 'Ome Cottage. But I dunno whether 'Ome Cottage is quite the thing like. It's got eleven bedrooms, y'see,' said Kipps. 'I don't see 'ow you call it a cottage with more bedrooms than four. Prop'ly speaking, it's a Large Villa. Prop'ly it's almost a Big 'Ouse. Leastways a 'Ouse.'

'Well,' said Ann, 'if you must call it Villa—Home Villa.'

Kipps meditated.

''Ow about Eureka Villa?' he said.

'What's Eureka?'

'It's a name,' he said.

Ann meditated. 'It seems silly like to 'ave a name that don't mean much'.

'Perhaps it does,' said Kipps. 'Though it's what people 'ave to do.'

He became meditative. 'I got it!' he cried.

'Not Ooreka!' said Ann.

'No. There used to be a 'ouse at Hastings opposite our school—St Ann's. Now **that**—*'*

'No,' said Mrs Kipps with decision. 'Thanking you kindly, but I don't have no butcher-boys making game of me . . .'

H. G. Wells   *Kipps*

their house **Renal,** not realising that this means 'of the kidneys'.

Blended house names often confuse the passerby, who is likely to be an amateur etymologist. Some householders have overheard remarkable explanations of the names they themselves formed, with people stating confidently that they have visited the places so named. Mrs M. Evans also told me in a letter about the vicar's interpretation of **Maralan,** which derived from Margery and Alan. 'Ah! Latin *mare*, "sea", and Welsh *a-lan*, "high".' Mrs Evans adds: 'As we were in the middle of a coalfield, with a view of coal-tips, I was speechless.'

A name blending more than two names may take only the initial letter of each. In **Kahne Lodge** the first word is for a Kathleen, Amber, Harry and Norman Ellis. An Australian **Kenjarra** is felt to honour John, Eric, Kenneth, Audrey, Joyce, Ross and Keith. One cannot help feeling that the most successful names of this type manage to build in more than one meaning. **Montrose** can thus be a transferred place name and a blend of Tom, Rose, Sheila and Tony at the same time.

It is not only family names that form the basis of blended names. **Tarrazona** is a reminder of two hotels where the householders spent their honeymoon; **Neldean** is from the song 'Nellie Dean' made

famous by Gertie Gitana; **Lacoa** commemorates Los Angeles, City of Angels, for someone who lived there for several years; **Hillside** includes elements from two previous house names; **Duke Leigh** is for HMS *Duke of York* and a naval base. If the last example seems a very masculine one it is only fitting, for it seems to be the husband who more often than not names the house.

But why, one may ask, do some people instinctively turn to the idea of blending names while others would never dream of doing it? Whatever the conscious reason for choosing a name of this type there appear to be signs of name magic revealing themselves again. For me at least there is a parallel between blending names and the practice of mixing ingredients of special significance to arrive at a powerful potion. I do neither of these things personally, but the more I look at the naming practices of my fellow men, the more I detect these deep-rooted beliefs in name magic.

Transferred house names

Surveys I have made on large estates in the Midlands and South of England show that 32 per cent of suburban house names are transferred from other nomenclatures. The largest group consists of transferred place names, which are usually borrowed because of sentimental associations. The place mentioned may be a birthplace, where a couple met, became engaged, spent a holiday or honeymoon, or formerly lived. An Italian place name I once asked about was where the son of the family had been killed during the war. When you see tears in someone's eyes on an occasion like that you become aware of a name's private meaning in a way that no amount of abstract thinking could achieve.

> A house which was 'bought for a song' in the village of Angmering, Sussex, was named *Arches*. The owner was the music-hall entertainer Bud Flanagan who, together with his partner, Chesney Allen, made a fortune from their song 'Underneath the Arches'.

Other reasons for place name transfer—leaving aside the large country-houses which are known by the name of the nearest village—include a liking for a song (**Sorrento**), a wish to honour a clan chief (**Rossdhu**), a combination of favourite hymn tune and holiday associations (**Melita**). Often it is only the namer who can explain the thought process that led to the transferred name, as with **Clairvaux** 'because it is associated with St Bernard and our wedding day was his feast day'; **Pitcairn** because the couple met on a ship the day it arrived there; **Culloden** because the English wife and Scottish husband thought it appropriate to use the name of a battlefield where their nations once fought. I admit to having made completely wrong guesses about two other place names that have been used as house names—**Littleover** and **Knockmore**. Both turned out to have been chosen for the usual sentimental reasons, though I had thought the first a member of the 'money reference' group, the second a 'statement' name.

Transferred field names form another worthwhile group of house names. **Copstone, Pottersfield, Stone Brigg, The Gowter, The Yeld, Venborough, The Wainams** and **The Spawns** are some examples. It seems fitting that fields which are built on should at least leave their names in the area. Many live on by becoming street names; others have to wait for householders with a feeling for the past to rescue them from old documents. Street names themselves

lead to house names, as do ship names, pub names, any names that exist. One couple met in a hospital ward, so the name of the ward became their house name. Famous racehorses such as **Arkle** and **Bandalore** have brought winnings to many and given house names to a few grateful backers. **Tia Maria** was suggested by a liqueur bottle, **Sunderland** not directly by the place but by the name of an aircraft flown during the war. Finally, some house names—but not as many as one might expect—are simply the family names of the people living there.

Descriptive house names

The householders who link and transfer names are probably sentimentalists; the down-to-earth prefer a no-nonsense, factual name. The house is on a hill, so let it be **Hilltop** or **Hillside.** It's a **Corner House,** has **Twin Chimneys, Blue Shutters** or is at the **Heathside:** the house names itself.

House names like these are obviously very sensible if they are given to houses which have no number names. They are the nearest verbal equivalent to number names—utility names. Activity names such as **The Vicarage** belong here, and little more need be said about them.

> *To his matter-of-fact home, which was called Stone Lodge, Mr Gradgrind ('Facts alone are wanted in life') directed his steps.*
>
> Charles Dickens   *Hard Times*

Other descriptions are by no means as functional. **Sunnyside** and **Dawnside** can hardly be put into the same category as **Barnside.** Nor are the metonymic descriptions which make use of flowers or trees that happen to be growing in the garden as practical as the **Blue Gates** type of name. **Roseleigh** and **Oak House** show the most common elements of this kind of name. Animals and birds are often mentioned in house names, including **Dog Cottage.** This is one instance where the use of 'house' would have been humorous instead of snobbish.

Many names are actually of the **Woodside** type in that they describe the house's position in relation to something nearby, but the connecting element is omitted. **Rill Cottage** and **Bonny Brook** are examples of such names. The use of 'view' in a name implies nearness to whatever can be seen, but once again such names are not functionally descriptive. **Castle View** and the like are outward descriptions which by no means identify the houses concerned. Such names are really as vague as **Sunset View.**

Examples of environmental descriptions have already been given with the 'wind' names. 'Sunny' names are of the same kind, though clearly more positive in outlook. Names like **Sunshine** and **Sunnyhurst** may slip into the commendatory class, expressing what is hoped for rather than describing a real situation. They are commendatory in another sense when they are used for seaside boarding-houses along with such names as **Seascape** and **Seaview.**

We must consider as descriptive names those which describe the occupants of a house. The number of people in the family is often indicated as in **Izaners, Triodene, The Foursome, Fyve Fold, Us Lot.** The fact that the householder is retired is indicated in many names, especially the **Dunroamin** type, eg **Dunskruin** for a retired prison warder. Many converted names are also a direct reflection of the occupants' pastimes. **Extra Cover, Double Oxer** and **The Bunker** are probably as effective as any descriptions could be of someone's cricket, show-jumping and golf interests. Music-lovers are likely to choose names such as **Harmony** or transfer the names of composers or pieces of music to their homes. A love of literature leads to transfers from characters and titles of novels, but conversions such as **Brillig,** from the Lewis Carroll poem, also occur. One **House at Pooh Corner,** however, is because of a nearby sewage-farm.

Sometimes the house names which say most about the occupants are not those which do so deliberately. Names like **Cosynest** and **Merriland, Sheerluck** and **Joys** are especially revealing of attitudes and philosophies, though names of all kinds do this to some extent. An astute door-to-door salesman, one would think, might be able to plan his opening remarks on the basis of the house name, which hints strongly at the character of the namer.

Apart from the category of name that is chosen, its form can reveal still more about the namer. Names in foreign languages are especially interesting in this respect. Why was **Chez Nous,** for instance, once *the* typical English house name, when many English people would have had no idea how to pronounce it and would not have been able to translate it? *Chez* represents an Old French *chiese,* Latin *casa,* originally a 'shepherd's hut'. *Chez nous*

is a curious fossil in modern French, to be translated 'at our house', but it is even more curious that it should have appeared in countless English streets. It is now disappearing, though occasionally made a joke of in the form **Shay Noo.**

All the name was meant to do for the occupants of the house, we must assume, was to show knowledge of a foreign language. This would in turn hint at a good education and foreign travel. Knowledge of foreign languages and travelling abroad are no longer the status symbols they once were, though an amazing number of **Casa Nostras** have appeared since package tours began.

'How do I find the blasted house?'
'The name's on the door.'
'What is the name?'
'Wee Holme.'
'My God!' said Frederick Mulliner. 'It only needed that!'

P. G. Wodehouse   *Portrait of a Disciplinarian*

Names in Welsh, Gaelic, Manx, Cornish, Maori and Australian Aboriginal are obviously different in character. They show a national pride which is nothing to do with impressing the neighbours. Latin names are of several sub-categories, such as religious, botanical and learned. With these, and with Greek names, one is somehow far less suspicious of an urge to impress others. The names usually have some point to them and genuinely reflect the background or interests of the namers. Names in other languages—and The Names Society's files contain house names in at least forty-five languages—are often linguistic souvenirs after residence abroad or a sign that one of the occupants of the house is from the country concerned. Since they are so rarely understood by passers-by, they contrast strongly with the public-statement type of name we were looking at earlier.

Another form a name may take is a back-spelling. The motivation behind such names is difficult to understand but they undoubtedly please many people. Those who are reluctant to put their family name above the porch in its normal form are often quite happy to put it there spelt backwards. I suggest you try reversing your own name to get an idea of the dreadful results this usually achieves. **Gnilknud** is no worse than many which are to be found in suburban streets.

As house names, however, they are part of the rich variety of names that are there for the consideration of a suburban stroller. They add the final personal touches to the historical anecdotes contained in place names, street names, pub names and the like. They have what one might call a language of their own which one must be prepared to study a little. It amply repays the effort.

Beach-hut, caravan and houseboat names

Those who do not live in suburban streets need not feel left out. A holiday stroll along the beach can often be enlivened by the names of those mini-houses, the beach-huts. Monstrous puns and jokes strike exactly the right note as the children play noisily in the background: **RR's by the Sea, Strip and Dip, The Winkle, Avarest, Taconap, Linga-Longa, Thut, Bikini Bay, Lang May Your Lum Reek, Brewden, Dormat, Bunk House** and **Hereur.** I once paid an out-of-season visit to a caravan site in order to collect similar names there. This led to my being arrested by a police dog (whose superb name turned out to be **Justice**), but I managed to note down such caravan names as **Brief Encounter, Cara Mia, Kip Inn, Pent House** (a marvellous comment on the confined space), **Tin Ribs** and **Leisure Daze.**

Houseboats provide a further field for investigation. Kelsie Harder has aroused my envy with a report of some name-collecting he did in the Valley

---

Following the ancient custom by which the Englishman strives to preserve the sanctity of his castle from strange visitors by refusing to give it a street number, hiding it instead under a name like Mon Repos, Sea View, The Birches, Dunrovin, Jusweetu, and other similar whimsies, the demesne of Mr Hogsbotham was apparently known simply as The Snuggery.

Leslie Charteris   *Follow the Saint*

---

of Kashmir, which has many houseboats bearing English names. Floating along on a lake in such a beautiful place must make one's investigations particularly pleasant. The names Professor Harder collected included many transferred girls' names, flower names and bird names. **Cutty Sark, Miss England, Highland Queen, HMS Pinafore, Dream Boat** and **Buckingham Palace** hint at the wider range of names used.

Sabine Grossenwahn, divorced niece of Boone Havock, whose Louisiana-plantation-style bungalow was known as Alimony Hall.

Sinclair Lewis   *Cass Timberlane*

The houseboats are often let to tourists, and carry announcements to that effect. On one occasion when Mr Khrushchev was in Srinagar a river-boat procession was arranged which passed by two such boats. They carried large signs which read: '**Miss America:** Running hot and cold: Ready for Possession' and '**Miss England:** Sanitary fitted: Ready For Occupation.' Mr Khrushchev is said to have been highly amused.

Let Miss England bring us back to that country for a brief summary of its house names. They are thick on the ground in the South, but thin out as one travels northwards. There are more of them on the coast than inland. They are mainly transferred, linked or are descriptive, but they are also a fine repository of folk-humour. The humorous names are again found mainly in the South. Northern names are more dignified, as are Welsh and Cornish names.

As a naming system, house names have their own characteristics, which I hope have emerged in this chapter. They have a distinctive quality, a unique taste. Perhaps this is what we should expect. They are, after all, home-made names.

The house was called Dilkhush, 'to make the heart glad'; that was as common a name for a house in India as Fairview or Mon Repos in Europe.

Rumer Godden   *Kingfishers Catch Fire*

A house by any other name

The words listed below have all been used by house-namers as replacements for the word *house* itself.

Abode formerly a temporary residence, a place where one waited.

Adobe technically a house built with adobe bricks, which are made from sun-dried earth and straw.

Ark figuratively, a place of refuge.

Asylum an inviolable shelter, but jokingly used for 'a mad house'.

Berth usually used by ex-sailors in the sense of 'a comfortable place'.

Billet used by ex-soldiers. *Billet* is French 'note', and the original reference was to the official notice which required a house-holder to lodge a soldier.

Booth a temporary dwelling.

Bothy originally a hut for unmarried workmen.

Box from a 'shooting box', a small country house.

Bungalow originally a Bengal house.

Burrow often used by families called Fox.

Cabin

Cartref Welsh 'home'.

Casa Spanish 'house'.

Castle Castlette is also jokingly used.

Châlet

Château French 'castle', also used for country house.

Corner Used in the sense of 'secluded place'.

Cot a cottage. Dialectal cote also occurs.

Cottage

Court jokingly used because the house-holder 'holds court' there.

Cover in the sense of shelter.

Croft a small-holding.

Curatage used for a house where a curator or curate lives.

Deanery sometimes also used by families called Dean.

Den a place of retreat. Favoured by families named Lion/Lyon.

Dive used jokingly to indicate that much (disreputable) drinking takes place there.

Domus Latin 'home'. Usually in the phrase *dulce domum*, 'home sweet home'.

Fold a pen for animals, but used with Christian reference, eg John 10:16 'There shall be one fold and one shepherd'.

Folly for a costly structure showing the builder's, or buyer's, foolishness.

Grange originally a granary, now a country house.

Hacienda Spanish 'country house (plus estate)'.

Hall residence of a territorial proprietor.

Hame Scottish 'home'.

Harbourage a shelter.

Haunt a place of frequent abode.

Haven

Hermitage used for a solitary house, or by occupants who prefer their own company.

Hive for a house swarming with people.

Hole for an untidy house.

Holm(e) flat ground near a river, but used as a spelling variant of 'home'.

Home

Homestead implying a fairly large house and estate.

Hoose Dialectal 'house'.

Hovel

Hut

Igloo Eskimo 'house', used for a cold house.

Inn used for a house that welcomes guests.

Keep a stronghold.

Kiosk technically a Turkish or Persian summer house, rather than a newspaper stand. Used for a very small house.

Kot modern variant of 'cot'.

Lair presumably a place where those who feel hunted can be safe.

Lean-to a building with rafters resting against another building.

Lodge especially a keeper's house on an estate.

Maison French 'house'. *Mini-maison* has also been used.

Maisonette

Manor also in joke names such as *Bedside Manor*.

Manse a Scottish ecclesiastical residence.

Mansion

Nest

Neuk a Scottish form of 'nook'.

Nook a sheltered place.

Ohm used for 'home' by an electrician.

Palace

Parsonage

Penthouse originally a lean-to. Now an additional structure on a roof, suggestive of luxury. Jokingly used for a house, caravan, etc., where people are pent in.

Place perhaps from references to 'my place'.

Port a shelter from storms.

Presbytery a priest's house.

Rectory

Residence

Rest ie resting-place.

Retreat

Roost used especially for a house which has many women living in it, a hen-house.

Shack

Shanty a cabin.

Shebang the original meaning of the American slang term was a hut or shed.

Shebeen a low-quality public-house in Ireland, used as a house name to suggest conviviality.

Shieling also *Shealing*. Originally a hut erected near pasture land in Scotland.

Shelter

Studio

Ty Welsh 'house', used in names like *Ty Ni*, 'our house'.

Vicarage

Villa a superior mansion.

Ville French 'town', but used erroneously for villa.

Warren for a house likened to a rabbit warren.

Wurly the hut of an Australian Aboriginal.

A selection of house names

Alcrest from the phrase '*after labour comes rest*'.

Allways husband used to close letters to his wife with this version of 'always'.

Almost There

Aroma opposite a brewery.

Arden a wartime sign 'Warden' lost its initial letter and was taken to be a house name.

Aurora goddess of the dawn.

Bachelor's Adventure on a holiday cottage.

Bali Hai a house on a hill.

Banshee House a 'banshee' is a female elf thought to wail under the windows of a house when someone is about to die.

Bar None for a home in the style of a ranch house.

Barn Yesterday a converted barn.

Bassetts 'all-sorts' in family (four adopted children).

Beam Ends

Beau Nidle

Bedside Manor the home of a retired doctor.

Belleigh Acres a pun on 'belly-achers', ie 'complainers', a name inspired by unfriendly neighbours.

Bendova home of a retired schoolteacher.

Bethany Biblical, 'house of poverty or affliction'.

Billion Bill and Marion live there.

Birdholme 'holme' means an islet, but is often used as a synonym of 'home' in house names.

Birdhurst 'hurst' can mean hillock or wood.

Bonanza Spanish 'prosperity'.

Boogaroph the opposite of **Kumincyde**.

Brouhaha French 'indistinct noise'.

Brytome 'bright home'.

Buffers on a converted railway carriage.

Ca d'oro name of a Venetian palace ('house of gold'). A sign on the gate of the suburban version says: 'Beware of the Doges'.

Cartref Welsh 'home'.

Chattings

Chippings can refer to a kind of sparrow or squirrel.

Clover used metaphorically, 'to be in clover'.

Cobblers

Cobwebs 'currently owned by Woolwich Equitable Building Society'.

Conkers for the horse-chestnuts that fall into the garden.

Copper Coin all that remained after paying for house.

Copper Leaves a retired policeman lives there.

Copper View opposite the police station.

Copsclose next door to the police station.

Cowries little shells found on nearby beach.

Crackers 'to have bought this house'.

Deriter a back-spelling.

Deroda a back-spelling.

Diddums Den

Dinnawurri another version of **Wyeworrie**.

Dokomin

Doo Town in Tasmania, where all the houses have names like **Yule Doo, Av Ta Doo, Zip Eddie Doo, Doodle Doo, Doo Us, How Doo You Doo, Didgeri Doo.**

Dulce Domum Latin 'home sweet home'.

Dunbolyn A. P. Freeman, the former Kent bowler, lived here.

Dunkillin home of a retired surgeon.

Dunravin home of a retired vicar.

Dunrobin home of a retired lawyer.

Dunwistairs a bungalow.

Elasrofton a back-spelling.

Eleven Plus for the number name **11B**.

Elveston an anagram of 'lovenest'.

Emange M and G.

Emoclew a common back-spelling. Does one receive the reverse of welcome when calling there?

End in View at the end of a lane, inhabitants retired.

Eureka Greek 'I have found it'.

Fair Dinkum to show Australian connections.

Fir Teen the number name 13.

Foon Hai Chinese 'happiness', transferred from a Chow.

Forbidden Fruit on a holiday bungalow.

Fortitoo the number name 42.

Fost Un first house in Foston Avenue.

Four Walls Mr and Mrs Walls and their two children live there.

French Leave a holiday house.

Genista Mrs Broom lives there.

Gnuwun 'new one'.

Gorldy Woods 'worldly goods'.

Halcyon Days 'calm days', a reference to a fabled bird.

Halfdan a Danish wife.

Hangover Hall in Temperance Road.

Happy Landing

Happy Ours

Harfa House a semi-detached house.

Heimat a place name transferred by a trampoline enthusiast.

Hen House a reference to the number of daughters in family.

Highlight

High Loaning 'loaning' is a piece of uncultivated ground on which cows are milked, but the mortgage is also referred to.

Hindquarters for the Hind family.

Hobbs 'half owned by building society'.

Holmleigh usually a fancy spelling of 'homely'.

Hysteria next door to a house called **Wistaria**.

Isor a house which is an 'eye-sore'.

Itzit

Jacquaboo the daughter is Jacqueline, the son's nickname is Boo.

Jayceepayde

Justintime

Justinuff

Kayaness K and S live there.

Kef the enjoyment of idleness, a state of dreamy intoxication usually induced by drugs. An Arabic word.

Koldazel

Kon Tiki because they drifted there.

Kosinuk for 'cosy nook'.

Ladsani a father and two sons.

Lautrec because it has 'two loos'.

Little Boredom Mr Bore lives there.

Loggerheads

Long Odds

Lucky Dip a seaside bungalow.

Majority the number of the house is 21.

Mascot 'mother's cottage' but also 'anything which brings luck'.

Mews Cottage Whiskers is the name of the occupant.

Mini Bung

Moonshine house first seen in moonlight, and son interested in astronomy.

Morning Feeling Mr Munday lives there.

Mutters the neighbours' reaction when they moved in.

Mylzaway a house which is miles away from anywhere.

Myob '*m*ind *y*our *o*wn *b*usiness'.

Nycere it's 'nice here'.

Obu Garret

Offbeat a retired policeman lives there.

Onaroc a reference to *Luke* 6:48: 'He is like a man which built an house, and digged deep, and laid the foundation on a rock.'

On the Rocks

Osterglay back-slang for Gloucester.

Owzat a cricketer who was stumped for a name.

Pan Yan the occupants of the house are always in 'a pickle'.

Peelers a converted police station.

Pennings because of letters written to builders.

Poodleville for the dog.

Popova

Pretty Penny

Pro Tem Latin 'for the time', ie until a number name is allocated.

Raylvu

Ringside a retired boxer.

Robins Nest the Robinsons live there and hope not to fall out.

Rolyat the Taylor family lives there.

Roundabout Friday from the builder's favourite saying.

Round the Bend for a corner house.

Ruff Roof

Rumbling Winds

Seaview on a house in London, forty miles from the sea.

7777777 the number of the house is 49.

Sherkin

Shieling a rough hut erected on pasture-land in Scotland, or the pasture-land itself.

Shilly Chalet

Sixpence the Tanner family lives there.

SJ619714 the National Grid reference of the house.

Sky Lark on a holiday cottage.

Spite Cottage because of a 'spite wall' built to spoil the neighbour's view.

Spooks across the road from a cemetery.

Stocking Cottage 'stocking land' has been cleared of stocks.

St Onrow a blend of John*ston* and *Row*berry.

Straw Hat a thatched cottage.

Stumbledon when houses were scarce.

Sunny Jim a pun on Sonny Jim, used to address any young boy whose name is not known.

Taintours on a Council estate.

Tamesis an older form of Thames.

Ten Minutes a home ten minutes' walk from the station.

Testoon a coin name used by a numismatist.

The Chimes the Bell family live there.

The Filling for a house sandwiched between others.

The Ginger House because of its orange-brown tiles.

The Halfyard former field name, from a measure of land.

The Hardies next door to **The Laurels**.

The Hive the Honey family live there.

The Jays sometimes refers to birds that visit the garden, more often to members of the family whose first names begin with 'J'. Also a metaphorical reference to people who chatter a great deal.

The Keep the Norman family live there.

The Marbles in Elgin Road.

The Moorings home of the Moore family.

The Pride the Lyons family live there.

The Rashers the Gammon family

live there.

The Ripples it has a corrugated iron roof.

The Speck one meaning of the word 'speck' is a small piece of ground.

The Stumps a dentist lives there.

39 Steps

The Toucans Mr and Mrs Cann live there.

The Tops

Three-O for the number name 30.

Tiedam a back-spelling.

Tivuli a back-spelling.

Top Notch

Touche Bouais Jersey French 'touch wood' because the number is 13.

Touch Me Pipes from a Cornish miner's expression meaning 'to rest and have a smoke'.

Traynes near the railway.

Tre-Pol-Pen to show that the occupiers are Cornish.

Triangle House for the Corner family.

Troy Hector is the husband's name.

Tuksumduin

Tusikso the number is 260.

Tu-Threes the number is 33.

Twa Lums for the 'two chimneys'.

Tympcasa tympana (which the owner plays) + *casa*, 'house'.

Uno (United Nations Organization) husband and wife of two nationalities, children born in other countries.

Uprising Twenties the number is 21.

Up Si Daisy

Valhalla in Teutonic mythology the hall where Odin held court.

Venetia named for the Venetian blinds.

Weemskat a dialectical form of 'we're broke'.

Well Away a holiday bungalow.

Wevernder

Whooff for the dog.

Widdershins also withershins, for a house facing in the opposite direction from those round it.

Wiktro '*w*ell *it* *k*eeps *the* *r*ain *o*ff'.

Wom dialectal for 'home'.

Wun Tun the number of the house is 100.

Popular house names

In 1988 the Halifax Building Society ran a computer check on over fifteen million addresses of investors and borrowers. The most popular house names in Britain, revealed by the survey, are listed below.

1	The Bungalow	4485	36	West View	697	76	Willow Cottage	444	116	Hollybank	340
2	The Cottage	4049	37	The Haven	690	77	White Lodge	443		The Cedars	340
3	Rose Cottage	2936	38	Grey Stones	687	78	Wind Rush	437		The Manor
4	The School		39	Orchard Cottage	679	79	Conifers	435		House	340
	House	2038	40	High Field	673	80	Park View	427	119	Meadowcroft	338
5	Hillcrest	1607	41	The Rectory	661	81	April Cottage	425	120	Mill Cottage	336
6	The Lodge	1595	42	The Grange	623		Garden Cottage	425	121	Beech House	335
7	Woodlands	1391	43	The Nook	616	83	The Oaks	422	122	Brooklands	333
8	The Coach		44	The Homestead	595	84	Bridge House	421	123	Little Orchard	330
	House	1205	45	Brookside	592	85	Fairfield	417	124	Primrose
9	Hillside	1162	46	Mill House	571	86	Fairways	416		Cottage	326
10	The Gables	1138	47	Lyndhurst	565		White Gates	416	125	Beech Croft	325
11	The Old School		48	Holly Cottage	556	88	The Mount	409	126	Cherrytree
	House	1080	49	New House	552	89	Park House	401		Cottage	323
12	The Vicarage	1059	50	Lynwood	549	90	Lyndale	396	127	Hill Croft	322
13	Sunnyside	1045	51	Greenways	542	91	Hazeldene	394	128	Holly House	320
14	The Croft	1024	52	Station House	540	92	The Pines	393	129	Chapel House	319
	Treetops	1024	53	Sunny Bank	538	93	Braeside	392	130	Oak Leigh	318
16	Ivy Cottage	1012	54	Rose Bank	526	94	Belmont	390	131	River Dell	317
17	Greenacres	1005	55	The Elms	525	95	Church Cottage	388	132	Glen Dale	312
18	Fair View	1002	56	Mayfield	519		Rosedene	388		Green Acre	312
19	The Willows	973	57	Oak Dene	518	97	Cherry Trees	387		Highlands	312
20	The Firs	902	58	Cartref	507	98	The Old Post		135	Vine Cottage	311
21	The Old Rectory	877		Oaklands	507		Office	386	136	Cross Ways	310
22	The Old		60	The Orchard	504	99	Oak Cottage	385	137	The Birches	309
	Vicarage	852	61	Pear Tree		100	Beechwood	384	138	Ash Lea	306
23	The Hollies	842		Cottage	503	101	Lilac Cottage	381		Ivy House	306
24	The Laurels	804	62	Tanglewood	502	102	Corner Cottage	375	140	The Hawthorns	304
25	Wood Side	799	63	Meadow Wood	495	103	Spring Cottage	369	141	Fern Lea	303
26	Hill View	789	64	Avalon	494	104	The Paddock	366		New Bungalow	303
27	Orchard House	783	65	The Poplars	492	105	Field House	360	143	Bank House	301
	Yew Tree		66	The Barn	485	106	Brook Cottage	358		Braemar	301
	Cottage	783	67	The Spinney	483	107	Byways	357	145	West Winds	300
29	Wayside	763	68	The Manse	481		High Trees	357	146	West Field	299
30	The White		69	Cornerways	472	109	Lynton	355	147	Brook Field	297
	Cottage	742		New Lands	472		Manor Cottage	355		Jasmine Cottage	297
31	South View	726	71	Brook House	467		Manor House	355		North Lodge	297
32	Windy Ridge	725	72	Hilltop	453	112	Mount Pleasant	351		Stone Leigh	297
33	The Beeches	723	73	The Limes	450	113	Tall Trees	348		Woodstock	297
34	Spring Field	722	74	Hill House	447	114	Wood View	344			
35	Four Winds	706	75	Keepers Cottage	445	115	Avondale	343			

I moved into Windows, as I called my home, on April 1. It wasn't the expanse of glass that led me to that name. Its christening derived from 'my life as an open book'. For twenty years I had lived behind transparencies.

Tallulah Bankhead   *Tallulah – My Autobiography*

15
TRADING A NAME

O N SEVERAL occasions in previous chapters the question of the 'image' created by a name has been mentioned. Personal names, place names and street names, as we have seen, have all been changed in order to create a different impression of the named entity. In our last chapter we had the example of **Dotheboys Hall** being used for business purposes more than as a house name. When we come to deal with trade names as a group, therefore, we are not moving into a totally new world.

Trade names share the basic characteristics of other nomenclatures and the same categories of names are found. The relative importance of those categories, however, is different. As with house names there are many blends, but invented names play a far greater role in the trade name system than in any other nomenclature we have yet examined.

Types of trade name

The reason for the importance of invented trade names will quickly emerge: first it is as well to distinguish between those trade names which were originally meant to identify one business enterprise rather than another, and those names which are designed to further business *in themselves*. **Guinness** is an example of the former, **Lux** of the latter. Guinness is a transferred surname, representing the Irish *Mag Aonghusa* or *Mag Aonghuis*, 'son of Angus'. **Angus** in turn is usually explained as 'one choice', with 'one' being used in the sense 'unique'. Having passed from family name to company name, Guinness was further transferred to the product, but there was never at any time an intention to make use of an intrinsic 'meaning' in the name in order to attract business.

Lux, however, was clearly a conscious attempt at bringing a name into being that would help to associate the product bearing it with certain desirable concepts, 'luxury' and 'luck'. These ideas are suggested without being stated, while the name itself retains a brevity and force useful for advertising purposes. When one notes, too, that its form almost certainly ensures that it will remain a name and not slip into the general vocabulary, it is seen to combine most of the features a trade name needs. The name even has a respectable etymological background, since *lux* is Latin for 'light'.

Early trade names

In earlier times the respectability of products was thought to be assured if their names were based on Latin and Greek or made historical allusions. A soap powder being advertised in 1907, for instance, was **Phenozone,** which apparently relied on the public's understanding of the 'shining' allusion in the Greek prefix. Madame Downing of Charing Cross Road in London was offering a corset a few years earlier to male readers of the magazine *Society*. She called it **The Kitchener.** Lord Kitchener was still alive at the time and one wonders what he thought of this use of his name. To go with the corset gentlemen of the time were offered a hat known as the **Sans Souci.**

The last example shows how startlingly unsuitable a product name could be at this period. *Sans Souci* is certainly a famous name, and it is sometimes found today as a suburban house name. At least it has some point when it is so used. Frederick the Great gave this name to his palace at Potsdam, which made it well known to European high society. Voltaire, who often visited him there, had his doubts about the name, saying that in spite of its meaning ('without care') 'a certain renowned king was sometimes consumed by care when he was there'. Thackeray made a rather similar comment in his *Roundabout Papers*: 'Sans Souci indeed! It is mighty well writing, "Sans Souci" over the gate, but where is the gate through which Care has not slipped?'

It is difficult to see how such historical and

In the 19th century, pomposity and prolixity were admired to some extent. This was reflected in many of the trade names of the time. As usual Charles Dickens could be relied upon to note the phenomenon and make fun of it. In *Nicholas Nickleby* Mr Bonney is talking of a proposed new company. It is to be the *United Metropolitan Improved Hot Muffin and Crumpet Baking and Punctual Delivery Company*.

'Why,' says Mr Bonney, 'the very name will get the shares up to a premium in ten days.'

literary associations, which would have been known to relatively few, could have been thought suitable for a hat. Perhaps the namer thought only of the literal meaning of the words, which he assumed the middle-class public would recognise or would never admit to not recognising. The hat seems to have been a soft one, so that it didn't matter if it became crumpled. It could be carried or worn 'without care'.

Such a thought process is likely to lead to a highly unsatisfactory trade name because it satisfies the namer rather than the people at whom the name ought to be directed. It was probably such names that Claude Hopkins had in mind when he wrote in 1923: 'The question of a name is of serious importance in laying the foundation of a new undertaking. Some names have become the chief factors of success. Some have lost for their originators four-fifths of the trade they developed.' Hopkins's comment needs a great deal of expansion. It applies in particular to converted and invented names, which must be chosen with minute care, but transferred surnames have certain points operating in their favour. In the case of a product a family name can carry with it an implicit guarantee. The name transfer suggests a complete identification of the producer with his product, and hints that a pride in the latter is linked with his fundamental self-respect. There is an uncompromising honesty in pinning one's own name to a business or product that will offset neutral qualities in the name itself. **Dunkling,** for instance, would hardly recommend itself as a linguistic unit to someone who was looking for a

trade name, but a former namesake of mine who founded a jeweller's shop in Australia was right to use his name for trade purposes. By doing so he made a statement of good intent.

Surnames as trade names

The fact that **Dunkling** is established as a trade name, in one part of the English-speaking world at least, raises an interesting point. If I wanted to set up business as a jeweller in Australia I might not be allowed to use my rightful name for business purposes. I could be legally restrained from doing so if I implied by means of my name that I was connected with the established business. In Britain Messrs Wright, Layman and Umney Ltd, for instance, obtained injunctions against a Mr Wright which stopped the latter trading under a name containing Wright or Wright's. The company claimed that it had a wide reputation in certain goods under the name **Wright's,** and Mr Wright's similar goods would naturally be confused with theirs.

Surnames occur frequently as trade names, but the use of first names is less common. They are mostly seen as shop names, especially those of hairdressers, but they do not seem to be popular for products launched nationally. Ford tried it with a car called the **Edsel,** the name that Henry Ford had chosen for his son. Many attributed the failure of that particular model to the nature of the name Edsel itself.

When they first began to appear on the social scene, automobiles were given names like *Fidelity, Utility, Safety, Safeway, Gadabout, Bugmobile, Fool Proof*. Compare these with the more recent *Mustang, Cobra, Wildcat, Panther, Cougar, Meteor, Comet* and *Starfire*.

D. B. Graham has commented that modern names convey life-styles. He cites (in his article 'Of Edsels and Marauders') names like *Rambler, Ambassador, Marquis, VIP, Cutlass, Rebel, Valiant, Maverick, Lark, Caprice, Boss, Judge, Grabber, Swinger, Spoiler* and *Marauder*.

Other names become trade names, especially popular place names such as **Oxford** and **Cambridge,** but there appears to be a definite preference in modern trade-naming to form new names by various processes. One problem with transferred names is that they are by their very nature shared with another entity. The trade name ideal lies in uniqueness. There are other ideals, of course. The name should catch the attention and be memorable. It should also work below the conscious level of the person who is exposed to it and appeal to the motives which really do cause him to buy a product, though he might be reluctant to admit it. As Vance Packard suggested by the title of his book some years ago, product names should be *Hidden Persuaders*.

Lipstick names

A few years ago, Jill Skirrow looked at the names of some lipsticks that were then on sale to see what characteristics they revealed. The namers, she decided, had thought deeply about what was at the back of a woman's mind when she went into a shop to buy lipstick. She would be thinking about making herself look young, hence **Young Pink.** There would be thoughts of kissing, and **Snow Kissed Coral** could remind her of these thoughts while pretending to talk of something else. 'Snow' would also be suggesting coolness to her, with 'purity' lurking in the background, while 'coral' threw out hints of the South Seas. The combination of ideas in Snow Kissed Coral is illogical if one stops to think about it, but the namers knew that very few customers would try to analyse it. Even if they did it would not matter. As a slight obscurity will sometimes be used by a poet to make the reader or listener pay more attention, so an illogicality in a name may make customers notice it more.

The woman buying lipstick is presumably anxious to emphasise her femininity, the namers think, so they tempt her with **Moods of Red, Porcelain Pink, Tiger Rose, Quiet Flame, E. S. Pink.** Moods of Red, Jill Skirrow says, would appeal to the 'vampire instinct' in a woman, and I must accept her word for it. The 'porcelain' reference certainly suggests high quality and fragility, and E. S. Pink plays on 'extra sensory perception', flattering the feminine illusion about intuition. Tiger Rose and Quiet Flame show the male idea of a woman who wants to be docile yet passionate, and may even reflect the idea some women have of themselves.

The moistness of a lipstick is emphasised in **Dewy**

Peach, the 'peach' probably linking with the idea of a 'peach of a girl'. **Pink-Whisper** cleverly introduces a suggestion of intimate conversations and softness, while focusing the customer's attention on her mouth. **Gilt-Edged Pink** and **All Girl Gold** cater for the dreams of wealth that are lurking at the back of many a young feminine mind. Perhaps Miss Skirrow goes too far, however, in suggesting that 'gilt-edged' will also hint at excitement because of 'guilt'. The same is no doubt true when she says that names like **Bare Blush** and **Itsy Bitsy Pink** have partly been chosen because the lips are especially used to pronounce them. If she *is* right, then the namers have been too subtle, for when these names are most influencing the customer they are probably not being spoken aloud.

The creators of trade names have long been known for their punning. Some results of their efforts noted by Ellen T. Crawley, editor of the *Trade Names Dictionary*, are:

Lip Lip Hooray for a lip-stick collection.
Line Tamers, Waist-a-way and *Sweet Add-a-line* for foundation garments.
Bee Bop for an insecticide.
Prints Charming for stationery.
Eye-gene for eye-drops.
Sweeping Beauty for a make-up brush.
W'eyes Guise for false eyelashes.

Lipstick names make a particularly interesting study because the namers are forced to be right up to date in the associations they build into a name. The customers will not be loyal to a particular lipstick for very long, and it is not really possible for the manufacturers to decide on a few names that they will then try to establish for all time. The namers are faced with a challenging situation in which customers will be running their eyes over a great many similar lipsticks, ready to indulge their whim of the moment in deciding which one to buy. While a customer is examining one colour rather than another, the lipstick names will be doing their work, planting suggestions in her mind. I suspect that they plant them in a man's mind too, for even I find myself going back to certain names again and again as I run my eye down the list. **Apricot Dazzle,** for example, attracts me very much as a name, though I can't begin to analyse why. I don't even like apricots.

Hotel names

At about the same time as Miss Skirrow was making her analysis of lipstick names, I was conducting an experiment into hotel names. I asked a large number of people to look at several names. I then asked them to indicate which hotel of those mentioned they thought they would stay at if they had no other information but the name on which to base a judgment.

Names like **Grand Hotel** and **Queens Hotel** were rejected by many because they 'sounded expensive', but they were chosen by others because the names suggested luxury. The **Seaview Hotel** type of name did rather better than the **Sunshine Hotel** type, the former apparently being taken at its face value, the latter regarded with suspicion. Names which I planted experimentally to see whether they would make an appeal were ignored even more completely than I had expected. These were of the **Summerjoy Hotel, Magic Carpet Hotel** variety. Modern-looking names like **Hotel Two** failed to appeal to young or old, while **White Hermitage Hotel** made a quiet showing with older informants. By far the most popular name, particularly with women, was **Little Orchard Hotel.** I was conducting my survey in the centre of a city and presumably their choice revealed an emotional need for a rural retreat.

Poetical names

'Emotional need' is rather a key phrase in this context. Trade names of the kind we have been discussing are not meant to be prosaic descriptions, satisfying the mind with the facts they supply. If they are to be successful they must be like poetry, and the advertising men who suggest new names are commercial poets in their way. A typical poetical device, for instance, is the deliberate exploitation of polysemy—the different meanings that can be suggested simultaneously by the same word. This is constantly used in trade names. In *Trade Name Creation* Jean Praninskas quotes the example of a popular American detergent, **All.** This manages to suggest that it gets all the dirt out of clothes, that it can be used in all machines for all fabrics, does all cleaning jobs and does the work all by itself. For a

simple word of three letters it is surely doing a great deal for the product it identifies. Its conversion to a trade name was a brilliant piece of inspiration.

Other poetical devices seen in trade names include rhyme, hyperbole, personification and metaphor. **Merry Cherry,** another lipstick name, shows the usual end rhyme, but one should include here the initial repetition of sound known as 'alliteration'. **Coca Cola** is an obvious example. Hyperbole is exaggeration that is not meant to be interpreted literally, so **Magi-Stik** does not really lay claim to occult powers. By personification a machine or device can be turned into a human servant, a **Handy Man** or **Brewmaster.** Metaphor simply compares the product being named with something having associated qualities, such as the speed and grace of a **Jaguar.**

Other trade name devices

But if one kind of trade name is a miniature poem, making intensive and subtle use of the language, another kind prefers to play games with the language. The various possibilities for playfulness are seen in names like **Helpee Selfee, Eat-A-Voo, Choc-A-Lot, Get Set** and **Ab-Scent.** Helpee Selfee manages to say to Americans that it is a laundry by implying that it has Chinese connections, although the same name elsewhere might suggest a self-service Chinese eating-place. These national associations are probably worthy of a special study in themselves. We have already noted the value of a Russianised name to a ballet-dancer and a French name to a hairdresser. There are presumably many other ways in which vague national associations can be exploited.

Eat-A-Voo plays on the established 'rendezvous' element in many a restaurant name. Apart from making it clear that an eating-house is referred to the name also emphasises a down-to-earth attitude. 'Never mind the fancy foreign names,' it seems to say, 'we're more concerned with the real business of providing a good meal.' As with all jokey names, there is a suggestion that the namer means to entertain and establish a relaxed atmosphere.

Choc-A-Lot identifies the product and adds a further enticement with its suggestion of quantity. Get Set takes a familiar phrase and deliberately reinterprets it. The reference is to a hair preparation and the joke obviously has point to it. What the name brilliantly implies is that having had one's hair set with this product the customer will then be ready to 'go' in the best sense. Ab-Scent is a deodorant, and the name is etymologically satisfying as well as being a pleasant pun.

Trade name spellings

A problem created by trade names is referred to by my former colleague, Dr Sven Jacobson, in *Unorthodox Spelling in American Trademarks*. As is well known, the lack of relationship between the sounds of English and English spelling already causes great difficulty to children who are learning to read. This difficulty is aggravated when children, and adults for that matter, are constantly exposed to spellings in trade names of the **Sox** and **Kwik** kind. Louise Pound commented on 'The Kraze for "K"' as long ago as 1925 in an article in *American Speech*. Other trade name crazes, as Sven Jacobson points out, include the use of hyphens in names like **Tys-Ezy** (plastic straps), **Sto-A-Way** (tables) and **Shat-R-Proof** (safety glass); the use of letter pronunciations in **E-Z-Chek** (brake gauges) and **Trip-L-Bub-L** (chewing-gum); the use of 'x' for '-cks' in **Clix** (light switches) and **Hanx** (paper handkerchiefs); the use of 'z' for 's', as in **Stripzit** (paint-stripper) and **Kilzum** (insecticide).

Names like **Kehr-Fully Made,** used by Kehr Products Co., and the **Get It Dunn Safely** of Dunn Products are obviously not deliberately reformed spellings. They simply profit by a similarity of sounds that is suggested by existing names. It might be claimed that such names add to the orthographic confusion, but the language itself tolerates such an amazing variety of forms that a few more will probably do no harm. Consider how the same sound is represented, for example, in words like meet, meat, mien, me, seize and foetus.

Trade names are in any case virtually forced to resort to spelling variations as the search for new names becomes more difficult. At least 25 000 new consumer products and services come into being in the English-speaking world each year, and each of them needs a new name. They are not in the happy position of being able to borrow names from a small central stock, nor do they inherit names by family tradition. Their names must not resemble those already in existence for similar products, and there are many other restrictions placed on them.

The most notable restriction, however, is undoubtedly that of transfer within the system. What would be considered to be natural duplication elsewhere—when several namers independently arrive at the same name—is also banned. All names must be registered, and only one namer is allowed to be credited with a name in a distinctive business area. As far as possible, therefore, there is an insistence that a name should be truly individual.

This situation has already led, in the relatively short history of legally registered trade names, to there being more trade names on record than there are words in the English language. In 1961 Lippincott and Margulies, the American industrial design and marketing consultants, stated that a half-million trade names were already registered. At that time there were rather less entries in the mammoth *New English Dictionary*. Supplementary volumes of the dictionary have since been published, but it is inconceivable that the vocabulary of English increases at the rate of fifty or more words a day, which is the rate at which trade names multiply. Many of these names are then pounded into the minds of the public by the use of highly sophisticated techniques. Our medieval ancestors were educated by signs and pictures; we are forcibly given a literal education by way of trade names and advertising slogans.

According to Garson Kanin, in *Moviola*, the actor Ricardo Cortez, born Jacob Kranz, took his stage name from a brand of cigars.

Trademarks still supply a visual accompaniment to many names, but these are becoming design abstractions rather than meaningful symbols. Few companies today try to find a **Nipper** who will sit and

The names of some of Shakespeare's more famous characters have been transferred to products. *Falstaff* aptly names an American beer, and *Hamlet* now means a cigar to British television audiences. *Romeos*, inevitably, have become prophylactics, and *Juliet* lends her name to a bra. It is also possible to buy *Lear* cigarettes, *Macbeth* glassware and *Miranda* rubber gloves, though the last-named, especially, comes close to being sacrilege.

Famous Brand Names, Emblems and Trade-Marks, by Marjorie Stiling, tells the stories behind many familiar names. *Maxwell House* was the name of a luxurious hotel in Nashville used by presidents, diplomats and the European nobility. It was there that Joel Cheek first tried out his new blend of coffee, subsequently using the hotel name for the coffee itself. *Quaker Oats* were named by a man who was not a Quaker himself, but was impressed by the human qualities the Quakers displayed.

listen to 'His Master's Voice' with an appealingly attentive ear, though such emotion-rousers add their own touch of aptness to any name. The tendency now is to favour initials and display them in an interesting way, but one suspects that the results often satisfy professional designers rather more than they satisfy the public. A display of graphical ingenuity is wasted if it is mere self-indulgence.

These initial names are unsatisfying in linguistic terms as well as visual, but as company names they are not obliged, perhaps, to create a public image. The companies concerned present themselves to the public by a wide variety of product and brand names, and a modern multi-national company, which has probably acquired many smaller businesses, is likely to own a very large number of names indeed. The latter represent a new phenomenon, a company nomenclature. This in turn must come to play an important part in the lives of employees, affecting their general use of language. The time will certainly come, if it has not done so already, when larger companies will be obliged to prepare dictionaries of these corporate languages for the benefit of employees.

Trade number names

With a few notable exceptions, trade-namers seem to have steered clear of number names. There is the very well-known **4711,** to which one may add examples like **7-Up** and **Vat 69.** Heinz showed a few years ago that '57' could be given an individual meaning, for that number always appeared in their advertising. Had it been converted to a number name at that point it would have been synonymous with **Heinz** itself. Number names are certain to come into their own before long, given the general situation of dwindling supplies of other names and ever-pressing needs. The first in the field will have a distinct advantage, being able to make use of numbers which carry a favourable meaning to many people. Latecomers might have to contend with **900424214** or something of the sort.

As it happens, it would not be as difficult to establish that number name as it might at first seem. Most of us these days successfully cope with several seven-digit number names, otherwise known as telephone numbers. We think of a certain person and the row of numbers comes into our minds. For anyone in a business where the customers need to telephone, the adoption of the telephone number as a trade name would seem to have several advantages. An advertising jingle could then be devised to fix the number name firmly in the mind.

A point that seems to have been missed where number names are concerned is that they have various verbal translations. The monstrous-looking nine-digit group quoted above could become 'nine hundred, four two, four two, one four' rather than 'nine hundred million, four hundred and twenty-four thousand, two hundred and fourteen'. The former breakdown enables a simple mnemonic to be constructed: 'Nine hundred four two, four two, plus one four you.' It would be possible to fit those words to a catchy little tune and have the entire number name nationally known in a few weeks by means of television advertisements.

The trade-namer is not yet in the position of having to accept arbitrary sets of numbers emerging from a computer as name suggestions, though he has for some years now been turning to a computer for new names. A computer can certainly supply combinations of letters that are 'names' of a kind, but the need is for names that will evoke an emotional response. These are needed, at least, in all those commercial areas where the buying of one product rather than another is likely to be a spur of the moment decision as far as the customer is concerned. Naturally there are many other instances where the price and quality of a product are what count, or where a particular product is uniquely associated with one name. When a customer is in what might be called a 'generic situation' the names come into their own. The customer is thinking: 'I need some soap, or a vacuum-cleaner, or whatever.' The trade name's job is to replace that generic, *without becoming a generic term itself.*

In *Names* Paul Dickson quotes the following names of shops: *Great Expectations* (maternity store); *Embraceable Zoo* (toy animals); *Another One Bites the Crust* (pizza house); *Shop Lefters* (left-handed objects); *Sew It Seams* (dress materials); *Moby Discs* (records); *Disguise the Limit* (costume rentals); *The Way We Wore* (second-hand clothing); *Wok Around the Clock* (Chinese takeaway).

The latter point is reached if a person is able to speak of 'hoovering' the carpet and then use an **Electrolux** or other make of machine to do the job; if he thinks of 'cola' as a kind of drink which equally well describes both **Coca Cola** and **Pepsi Cola**. 'Launderette' may still be technically a trade name, but it has passed into the ordinary language and no longer suggests a particular company. Whoever formed the term forgot to leave a name-identifying element within it, a dash of strangeness that would have enabled it to stand outside the main vocabulary.

These generic replacement names are going to be the ones that are more and more difficult to find in the future. Praninskas concludes that industry 'will see to it that the names of their new products are created by literary artists', and there is much to be said for that argument. It is quite clear, for example, that Dickens would have made a superb creator of trade names. Many trade names discussed in this chapter also reveal, I would have thought, a high literary quality. Namers have already learned a great deal from the techniques of the imaginative writers.

What they need to study now, however, is not literature. Their way ahead lies in a study of other nomenclatures, where a million ordinary people have brought names into being. Transfer *within* the trade name system may not be possible, but transfer into it from other non-commercial systems—avoiding the over-worked first name, surname and place name nomenclatures—is not only possible but increasingly necessary.

There must be relatively few trade-namers, but we are all affected by their work. I have not made a full study of my children's speech, but in spite of restricted television viewing it is quite clear that they are familiar with a large number of commercial names. In the course of a few days I was personally able to write down 400 product names with which I was familiar, including those of many products—such as cigarettes—that I would never dream of using. However, these trade names are part of our lives and language.

Pleasures of trade names

For my own part I try to make the best of the situation and enjoy trade names. I am happy to read the yellow pages of the telephone directories to find **Thun-Thoots** and **Teeny Poons,** which are children's sun-suits and feeding-spoons. I like the **Mity Tidy** shelves and the **Kant Mis** fly-swatters, the **Bug-Shok** insecticide and the delightful **Slug-A-Bug.** I cannot wear **Enna Jettick** shoes, which are for ladies, or **Top Secret,** a hair-tint which presumably calls for a better supply of hair than I can boast, but their names are welcome.

I enjoy, too, the names of shops. The Greater Cincinnati telephone directory lists beauty salons called **Pamper Hut, Kut-N-Kurl, Magic Mirror Beauty Shop.** Some British equivalents are **Beyond the Fringe, The Pretty Interlude** and **The Cameo.** Antique shops are another pleasant group: **The Shop of the Yellow Frog, Granny's Attic, Passers Buy, The Tarrystone, Past Perfect.** A member of The Names Society, Sidney Allinson, reports on Canadian names such as **The Salvation Navy Store, Poise 'N' Ivy, The Bra-Bar, Juicy Lucy's, The Fig Leaf, Leg Liberation, The Wearhouse** and **Undie-world,** all of which sell clothes in Toronto. Meanwhile, the *boutique* game continues in London and elsewhere, with **Bootique, Beautique, Shoetique, Fruitique, Motique** (car accessories), **Junktique, Bespotique** (tailor's) and **Fishtique.**

Some of these names you may consider to be dreadful, but their collective message is clear. Trade name creators have not yet run out of ideas, and the English language is alive and well.

Nigel Green writes from Leatherhead, Surrey, to add to the list of humorous American names for insecticides. Products used in the war against cockroaches, he says, include a borax powder called **Croak-a-Roach.** There is also such a thing as a **Roach Motel:** 'Roaches check in but don't check out.'

Trade names

Some indications of the various ways in which companies or products have been named are provided by the following examples, many of which are derived from *Dictionary of Trade Name Origins*, by Adrian Room:

Adidas a company founded by Adolph Dassler (1900-78), known to his friends as Adi. He added the first three letters of his last name to his pet name to form the trade name.

Aeroflot Soviet 'air-fleet'.

Agfa from the initial letters of *Aktiengesellschaft für Anilinfabrikation* ('limited company for dye manufacture').

Alka-Seltzer the Alka is an abbreviation of 'alkaline'; Seltzer in general terms refers to fizzy water, or *Selterser wasser*, 'water from Nieder Selters, Germany'.

Ampex founder of the company was Alexander Matthew Poniatoff, who added -ex to his initials (from the word 'excellent').

Andrews Liver Salt from the church of St Andrew, near the head offices of the company.

Aspirin from German *acetylirte Spirsäure* ('acetylated spiraeic acid') plus the chemical suffix -in.

Audi a company formed by August Horch. His last name translated into Latin gave *audi*, 'hear!'.

Avro the aircraft company was founded by A. V. Roe. The origin of the trade name is thus clear: it is less clear why Mr Roe's parents named him Alliott Verdon.

Babycham originally for the 'baby chamois' used as an emblem, though a link with 'champagne' rather than a goatlike antelope was inevitable in the minds of customers.

Bakelite invented by a Belgian-American L. H. Baekeland, who added the chemical suffix -ite to part of his name.

Bata the shoe company was founded by the Czech, Tomas Bata.

Bejam from the initials of Brian (brother), Eric (father), John Apthorp (founder of company), Millie and Marion (mother and sister).

Berlei founded by Fred Burley.

Birds Eye from the name of Clarence Birdseye (1886-1956) who devised process for freezing foods in small packages.

Biro invented by the Hungarian Lázló Biró.

BMW made by the *Bayerische Motoren Werke*, Bavarian Motor Works.

Bostik ultimately from Boston (Massachusetts) and 'stick'. The original company was the Boston Blacking Co.

Bovril Latin *bos, bovis* 'ox' gives the first two letters. 'Vril' was a word invented by Edward Bulwer-Lytton in his novel *The Coming Race* (1871). It meant 'an electric fluid, the common origin of forces in matter'. Professor Weekley was probably correct in assuming that this word in turn was derived from Latin *virilis* 'manly'.

Brillo from the word 'brilliant' rather than the Italian *brillo*, 'drunk'.

Cadillac manufactured in Detroit (a small town near Bordeaux), which was founded by a Frenchman who was Sieur de Cadillac.

Calor Latin 'heat'.

C & A founded by the Dutch brothers *C*lemens *and A*ugust Brenninkmeyer.

Carlsberg originally the name of the brewery near Copenhagen which stood on a hill (Danish *berg*). Carl was the name of the brewer's son.

Castrol the product was originally based on castor oil, obtained from castor beans.

Cherry Blossom originally used for a soap, sold in tins such as those later used for the shoe polish.

Coca Cola from the coca shrub and cola nut.

Cow Gum from the name of Peter Brusey Cow, one-time owner of the company.

Cuticura Latin *cutis* 'skin' and *cura* 'care'.

Dan-Air from *Da*vies and *N*ewman Ltd, which established an air service; nothing to do with Denmark and the Danes.

Dorothy Perkins the trade name was borrowed from the name of the rose.

Drambuie from Gaelic *dram* 'drink' and *buidh* 'yellow'.

Durex a name which came 'out of the air' to the chairman of the company in 1929. Adrian Room links it with words such as 'endurable' rather than Latin *duresco* 'harden'.

Fanta from the German word *fantasie* 'fantasia'.

Findus an abbreviation of *F*ruit *Indus*tries.

Frisbee from the name of the Frisbie Bakery in Connecticut. Its pie tins could be thrown much as modern frisbees.

Golden Wonder from the variety of potato, which is, however, not suitable for making crisps.

Granada borrowed from the Spanish province when the group's chairman went on holiday there.

Harpic the inventor was *Har*ry *Pic*kup.

Hovis suggested in a competition to find a suitable trade name by Herbert Grime in 1890. He based it on Latin *hominis vis* 'strength of man'.

Kenwood the company was founded by Ken Wood.

Kia-Ora Maori 'good health'.

Kiwi the shoe polish was marketed by an Australian who named it in honour of his New Zealand wife.

Kodak invented by George Eastman, the photographic pioneer. His favourite letter was K.

Lec originally the Longford Engineering Company.

Lego Danish *leg godt* 'play well'.

Lemon Hart from the name of an 18th-century wine merchant,

Lemon Hart. Lemon is more usual as an English last name, deriving ultimately from 'beloved man' or 'sweetheart'.

Lucky Strike introduced during the Gold Rush of the mid-19th century.

Mars the company was established by an American, Forrest Mars.

Mazda name of the Persian god of light.

Meccano from the phrase 'mechanics made easy'.

MG for Morris Garages, set up by William Morris, later Lord Nuffield.

Nivea the feminine of Latin *niveus* 'snowy'.

Ovaltine originally 'Ovomaltine' from Latin *ovum* 'egg', 'malt' and -ine. Shortened to Ovaltine when introduced to Britain from Switzerland.

Pepsi Cola influenced by Coca Cola and intended to relieve dys*pepsi*a.

Perspex Latin *perspexi* 'I looked through'.

Quink from 'quick-drying ink'.

Rawlplug invented by John Rawlings.

Rentokil originally meant to be Entokil, from Greek *entoma* 'insects' and 'kill'. The initial R- was added because a name like Entokil was already registered.

Ribena the Latin botanical term for the blackcurrant is *Ribes nigrum,* which suggested this name.

Rolex an arbitrary word of no meaning, invented by Hans Wilsdorf.

Ronson founded by Louis V. Aronson.

Ryvita 'Rye' plus Latin *vita* 'life'.

Schweppes the business was begun by a German, Jacob Schweppe.

7-Up originally called Bib-label Lithiated Lemon-Lime Soda. Its inventor then considered, and rejected, six alternative names

before deciding on 7-Up.

Shell the founder of the company, Marcus Samuel, imported shells in the early 19th century.

Sony based on Latin *son* 'sound'.

SR the initials on the toothpaste stand for sodium ricinoleate.

Tesco founded by Sir John Cohen, one of whose earliest suppliers was T. E. Stockwell. The latter's initials plus the first two letters of Cohen led to Tesco.

Typhoo invented by John Sumner in 1863, but of no meaning.

Uhu the German word for 'eagle owl'. Such birds live in the Black Forest, where the German manufacturers of Uhu have a factory.

Volvo Latin 'I roll'. Originally the name of a company making ball-bearings.

Wimpy J. Wellington Wimpy was a hamburger-loving character in the Popeye cartoon strips.

Names of hairdressers

Hairdressers in Britain and Australia are rather fond of giving their establishments punny names. Here is a selection of them taken from telephone directories.

Ahead of Time	Crimpers	Hairpin	Mirror Image	Sophisticut
Ali Barber	Crowning Glory	Hairport	Mad Hackers	Soul Scissors
All Ways Ahead	Curls and Capers	Hair Today	Mane Line	Split Ends
Aristocuts	Curl Up And Dry	Hair We Are	Mop Shop	Streaks Ahead
As You Like It	Curl Up and Dye	Hair We Go	New Wave	Sweeny Todd's
Back 'n' Front	Cut Above	Hazel Nutz	Nuts	Szizzers
Barbery, The	Cute Cuts	Head First	One Step Ahead	Through the Looking
Basin Cut	Cut Loose	Head High	Perm Factory	Glass
Beyond the Fringe	Cut 'n' Dried	Headlines	Prime Cuts	Topknots
Blow Your Top	Cutting Corners	Headmasters	Rollers	Tops
Boldilocks	Cutting It Fine	Head Quarters	Roots	Topsy Turvy
Bubbles	Cutting Room	Heads together	Rough Cut	Trimmers
Busy Scissors	Do Yer Nut	Heads You Win	Scalpers	Trimplicity
By George	Fringe Benefits	Headway	Shady Lady	Undercutters
Champu	Frizzy Lizzy	High Lights	Shampers	Unwind Ltd
Chick Hairdresser	Golden Scissors	Hot Gossip	Shear Genius	Uppercuts
Classy Clippers	Goldilocks	Jet Set	Shear Pleasure	Vanity Fair
Clear Cut	Hair Dinkum	Klever Kutz	Sheik Look	Vizzage
Clikkers Hair Studio	Hair Doo	Knots 'n' Tangles	Sherlocks	Wavelengths
Clip Joint	Hair Force	Krinkles	Shylocks	Y Knot Hair Care
Clipso	Hairizon	Last Tangle	Simply Scissors	
Comb Corner	Hairmania	Light Waves	Smart Set	
Crazy Curl	Hair 'n' Now	Look Ahead	Snip in Time	
Cream of the Crop	Hairobics	Lucy Locketts	Snippets	

16
NO END OF NAMES

I BORROW my chapter title from Browning. It seems suitable for a chapter in which I want to emphasise that the names enthusiast draws his materials from a well that never runs dry. This book is obliged to be finite; the subject is not.

In ranging over a wide variety of name topics this chapter is likely to resemble a typical issue of *Viz.*, the newsletter of The Names Society. A discussion about names of all kinds went on in its pages for nearly ten years, until rising costs and a lack of voluntary help caused it to cease publication. It was not immediately known as *Viz.* when it began in 1969: that was naturally one of the subjects that came up for discussion—what to call a magazine devoted to names. Suggestions included **Onoma** and **Names**—which were already being used for similar publications—**The Nominist, Nomen, Name, The Onomatologist, Nomina, Namely, The Nomenclator, Philonoma, Nomenalia** and **Notamina.**

Other magazine names

Viz. was only one of countless small magazines that are non-commercial labours of love. Poetry magazines abound, for instance, and have names like **Poetmeat, Nightrain, Bean Train, Wild Dog, Long Hair, Software, Fish Sheets, Circle, Circuit, Nomad** and **Stand.** It would be easy to write a verse about them, for one finds a **Twice, Nice, Vice** and **Spice,** a **Choice** and **Voice, Ambit** and **Gambit.** An ever-increasing band of enthusiasts also collect science-fiction magazines, which usually have names that are suitably out of this world. Some examples are **Bweek, Zot, Erk! Reverb Howl, Kangaroo Feathers, Egg, The Hog on Ice, Son of Fat Albert.** A few have names that could easily be absorbed into the English suburbs as house names, however. **Shangri-La** would certainly be at home there, as would **Soitgoze. Curse You** might cause a few mutterings among the neighbours, but **Powermad** might merely strike them as an honest statement.

What charming names the groups have these days—The Necrophiliacs, The Jam, The Scum, Medea and her Babes, Sore Throat.

Margaret Drabble   *The Middle Ground*

'Alternative' publications in recent years have included **Wipe,** printed entirely on toilet paper, and **Arse,** published by the Architects' Revolutionary Socialist Enclave.

Pop group names

Names that share many of the magazine name characteristics are those of the pop groups. In pre-pop days there were names like **The Andrews Sisters,** which followed the direct description tradition of the theatre. A dash of self-publicity led to **The Supremes, The Magnificent Men, The Spellbinders.**

Another reminder of trade names in the sixties and seventies comes with respelt names, used by famous groups such as **The Beatles** and **The Monkees.** A vaguely religious set of names was discernible in 1968 such as **The Righteous Brothers, The Apostolic Intervention, The Angels** and **The Spiritual Five.** Names that with a slight change of form could easily have appeared on the covers of poetry magazines were also to be found, and some have endured well: **The Searchers, The Seekers, The Shadows, Saturday's Children.**

Names that showed an aggressive reaction to the Establishment were very similar to those of the alternative and 'underground' magazines. These were the groups called **The Enemies, The Animals, The Rejects, The Freak-Outs, The Barbarians** and the like. The science-fiction magazines translated into pop groups names such as **The Grateful Dead,**

Launce: I think Crab my dog be the sourest-natured dog that lives: my mother weeping, my father wailing, my sister crying, our maid howling, our cat wringing her hands, and all our house in a great perplexity; yet did not this cruel-hearted cur shed one tear.

William Shakespeare   *The Two Gentlemen of Verona*

'Has she a dog?'

'A cocker spaniel, Mr I., called Benjy.'

'Conciliate that dog, Bert. Omit no word or act that will lead to a 'rapprochement' between yourself and it. The kindly chirrup. The friendly bone. The constant pat on the head or ribs. There is no surer way to a woman's heart than to get in solid with her dog.'

P. G. Wodehouse   *Cocktail Time*

3½, The Mindbenders, U. F.O., The Leathercoated Minds, The Happenings, The Mind Expanders. All of these are meant to be attention-catchers, and some perform that function well. But names like **The Strawberry Alarm Clock** and **The Nitty Gritty Dirt Band**—the latter being rare in that it condescends to admit a connection with music—are like certain paintings. They are fine as exhibition pieces, but would be difficult to live with.

But we shall all, no doubt, get thoroughly used to such names as time passes. There is evidence on all sides of a new adventurousness in names which seems likely to affect a great many nomenclatures. Newly formed football clubs, for instance, are leaving aside traditional name elements such as 'Wanderers', 'Rovers', 'United' and 'Athletic'. There are already local teams called the **Alley Cats, Eskimoes, Stags** and **Juggernauts.** Before very long another generation will be wanting to show *its* individuality, and we must wait to see how that affects names.

Meanwhile, we can look back once again at some of the names given in the past. One area of great interest is the living world that surrounds man, the world of animals and plants. Another is that of man's various forms of transport—ships, locomotives, cars and the like, all man-made objects which are often felt to develop a personality of their own. There is enough material in those areas to fill another book of this size, so we must be brief.

Animal names

By animal names I mean the proper names of individual animals rather than the generic names of species used by a zoologist. We could all write down the names of several individual animals who are as well known to us as people. In many cases a pet is considered to be one of the family. Other animals are internationally famous. **Lassie** is better known in Germany, for instance, than **Leslie,** as I often discovered.

A special group of animal names have become part of the English language. We can refer to a tom cat called **Percy** without it seeming strange, for 'tom' is no longer felt to be a form of **Thomas** in that context. Historians who are cat-owners will know that before Tom came on the scene, **Gib**—from **Gilbert**—was the usual name for a male cat. A 'tabby' looks suspiciously like a corruption of 'tib cat', which in some dialects remains the female equivalent of tom cat, but it has a different origin. Tabby is a striped taffeta and derives from the Arabic name of the place where it was made. A tabby cat was earlier described as 'tabby-coloured'. **Tib** was once the name of a low-class woman, the female equivalent of **Tom,** and was probably a diminutive of **Isabel.**

In medieval times cats and dogs were no doubt referred to by generic names and no others. These days individual names are bestowed on a wide range of pets and often display all the ingenuity we find in other nomenclatures. **Dora,** for instance, was owned by Annabel Bool and therefore known more fully as **Adorabool. Ocky** was **Octavius** on formal occasions and received that name because it was its owner's eighth cat. **Polly,** a corgi, was named from a resemblance to a television announcer of that name, and **Nelson** belonged to a **Hardy** family. Among my own favourite names are **Curlicue** for a curly tailed mongrel, **Edom** for a cat ('over Edom will I cast out my shoe'—Psalm 60), **Worthington** for a Basset hound and **Rover** for a budgerigar. The last example was intended to be an ice-breaker at parties.

Adrian Room's booklet on *Pet Names* gives many more examples, some of which have already become minor classics. **Keith** and **Prowse** for a pair of cats are probably the best known, the agency of that name being famous for its advertising slogan: 'You want the best seats, we have them.' But children do a great deal of pet-naming and are not usually quite so subtle. They like incident names or descriptive names especially. My own children were probably typical when they named their white rabbit **Flash** because he was off 'like a flash' the first time they put him down.

Needless to say, these informal pet names are usually different from the registered titles of pedigree animals. I use the word 'title' deliberately, for they are often of the **Duchess of Bolcord, Lady of Arvon** type. A Kennel Club *Stud Book* I have by me shows that even formal names can be interesting, however. Among the bulldogs listed are **Abracadabra, Boom-De-Ay, Bully Boy, Derby Day, Queer Street, Rev. Dismal Doom, Bubbles, Cigarette, How Nice** and **Trifle.** There is even a bitch called **Buttercup,** though this would strike most of us as a typical name for a cow. Perhaps it was a humorous mis-naming, for many owners see no need to be too serious in the names they give. Chows with names like **Chin Chin** and **Yum Yum Victoria** are listed, and there is a Japanese spaniel called **Stoneo Brokeo. Spot XXVIII** is not without a certain humour, and has point in being basically the kind of shoutable name that is necessary for daily use.

She would save a slice for Sunny, the cat—his drawing-room name Sung-Yen had undergone a kitchen change into Sunny.

Virginia Woolf   *Between the Acts*

The Buttercup example reminds us of non-domestic animal names, of which once again there are countless thousands. Some of them are worthy of special note. R. D. Blackmore mentions a cow called **Dewlips**, which has a definite charm, and the quinquemammalian cow called **Sanctity** discovered by a member of The Names Society who once looked into the subject would always belong in the Top Ten.

Cows usually get suitably feminine names given to them, such as **Candy** and **Marigold,** but **Bullyface, Beefy, Droopy, Hoppy** and **Tango** are among other names that have been bestowed. One cow name that later became nationally known as a trade name was **Carnation.**

National attention was focused in Belgium a few years ago on the name of a donkey. A farmer who was protesting about agricultural policy arrived in Brussels with a donkey who bore the same name as the then minister of agriculture. This kind of satirical naming would probably not be allowed in Britain: it would be considered unfair to donkeys. I see from a show catalogue that British donkeys actually receive names like **Mrs Donk,** which is a fascinating generic link name, **Jack the Ripper, Mockbeggar Gussie** and **The Vicar of Bray.**

Who but Stevenson could have named a donkey Modestine?

John Steinbeck   *The Pastures of Heaven*

Different kinds of horses receive names of different kinds, as one would expect. There was formerly a special point to the names of dray-horses, which always worked in pairs. Their partnership was often recognised in pairs of names like **Thunder** and **Lightning, Crown** and **Anchor, Might** and **Main, Time** and **Tide, Rhyme** and **Reason, Pomp** and **Circumstance.** No rules governed such names, such as those which have long been imposed by the Jockey Club on namers of racehorses. The restrictions do not prevent the creation of interesting names for the latter, however. Many are what could be called 'notional blends', a group we have not yet mentioned in connection with any other names.

Notional blends lead to names like **Mickey Mouse** by **Lightning Artist** out of **Cinema, Watchdog** by **Warden of the Marches** out of **Beagle.** A phonetic link may also be present, as in **Dial O** by **Diomedes** out of **No Reply,** and puns are possible: **Sea Pier** by **Duke of Buckingham** out of **Mollusca.** In the 1930s **Buchan** and **Short Story** had many bookish offspring, such as **Portfolio, Bookseller, Bibliograph** and **Birthday Book.**

Once the names come into being, by whatever means, they can exert a great influence on amateur punters. Horses are often backed because their names seem significant to a particular person at a particular time. The names are taken to be omens, in other words. We do not seem to be able to escape name magic wherever we look. One cannot help wondering, in passing, how much money has been lost to all but the bookmakers on poor horses that happen to have had brilliant names.

The new miracle of Nature [an orchid] may stand in need of a new specific name, and what so convenient as that of its discoverer? 'Johnsmithia'! There have been worse names.

H. G. Wells   *The Flowering of the Strange Orchid*

Flower names

If we turn now to flowers, our expectation might lie in the direction of lovely names rather than friendly ones. Oscar Wilde probably spoke for many people when he made Lord Henry, in *The Picture of Dorian Gray*, say:

'Yesterday I cut an orchid for my buttonhole. . . . In a thoughtless moment I asked one of the gardeners what it was called. He told me it was a fine specimen of **Robinsoniana,** or something dreadful of that kind. It is a sad truth, but we have lost the faculty of giving lovely names to things.'

We have not lost this faculty, as it happens, but one can see what Wilde meant. One has only to glance at a list of botanical names to understand also the remark of the nineteenth-century pamphleteer, Alphonse Karr, that 'botany is the art of insulting flowers in Latin and Greek'. The attractive names of flowers tend to be the folk names: **Sweet William, Jack-Go-To-Bed-At-Noon, Gill-Over-The-Ground, Good King Henry, Bitter Sweet, Morning Glory, Youth-And-Old-Age, Nancy Pretty** (or **None so Pretty**), **Old Man's Beard, Mourning Bride, Coral Bells.** The last named, to take one example, translates into the botanical name *Heuchera sanguinea*.

The botanists might argue, however, that scientific accuracy is of more importance to them than aesthetics. Historically speaking, it was logical for them to turn to classical languages that were internationally understood in order to create descriptive names. Those names may seem barbarous to the average person, but still more people would no doubt be offended if botanists made use of that other international language which begins '1, 2, 3'.

There are many signs that those who name cultivated varieties of flowers, such as the rose, make an attempt to find a name that suggests beauty. Rose varieties include **First Love, Maiden's Blush, Coral Dawn, Alpine Glow, Burning Love, Elegance, Golden Showers, Passion** and **Wildfire** as well as the famous **Peace.** (See also page 12.) Oddities occur, nevertheless. It is strange to find **Atombombe,** for instance, named in 1954 and presumably referring to a mushroom shape. One wonders also whether the reasons for choosing names like **Grumpy** and **Radar** really justified attaching them to roses. A number name that has been used for a rose, **Forty-Niner,** named in 1949, seems to fit in quite well with the names around it.

Scientists now say that there is some point in treating a plant as one would treat an animal, talking to it affectionately in order to make it grow better. We are therefore probably not far from the day when house plants will be named individually by their owners. Until that day comes, plant names remain at the generic level. It is probably just as well, for even at that level there are hundreds of thousands of names.

Apple names

The above statement about the vast quantity of names may be too general to impress itself upon the mind. Let us take a specific example. Whether we are gardeners or not, we all eat an apple from time to time. How many different kinds of apple are there? **Cox's, Granny Smith, Golden Delicious**—any more?

The *National Apple Register of the United Kingdom* lists 6000 more, together with another 1600 names that have been used as alternative descriptions for the same 6000 cultivars. To be fair, many of these variant names are slight respellings of one another, abbreviations and so on. Translations of English names into other languages are also treated as variants. Nevertheless, the Golden Delicious, for instance, has also been known as the **Arany Delicious, Stark Golden Delicious** and **Yellow Delicious,** and other apples have a long string of such genuine synonyms. **King of the Pippins** has such aliases as **George I, Hampshire Yellow, Pike's Pearmain, Princess Pippin, Seek No Further** and **Winter Gold Pearmain.** This is the kind of complexity that lies beneath not only 'apple' but most of the generic terms we use every day.

The apples that were popular in the 17th century were rather different from those in the shops today.

One was the **Api,** or **Lady Apple,** carried by ladies in their pockets because it was very small and had no odour. It had been found growing wild in the Forest of Apis, in Brittany, and is known to have been in Louis XIII's garden by 1628. The **Catshead,** which 'took the name of the likenesse' according to a 17th-century writer, was later to be much used for apple dumplings. Particularly interesting were **Costards,** which at one time were sold for a shilling a hundred by costardmongers (the later costermongers). 'Costard' became a slang word for the head and occurred in the phrase 'cowardy costard', later corrupted to 'custard'. As an apple name it had originally referred to the apple's ribbed appearance (Latin *costa,* 'rib').

Another apple name well known in the 17th century was the **Nonpareil,** 'having no equal; peerless'. The word is unlikely to occur in a normal English conversation today, but it might well have done so in Shakespeare's day. He himself uses it in several of his plays—Miranda is said to be a nonpareil in her father's eyes, for instance. If there is ever a comprehensive *Dictionary of Names* which lists names that occur in several nomenclatures, 'Nonpareil' will be a typical entry. It names birds and moths, houses and a size of printing type among other things. In 1580 it became the name of a British warship, though this was renamed the **Nonsuch** in 1603.

Ship names

Since brevity is essential in this chapter, we must allow this mention of ship names to lead us into the world of transport, which we mentioned earlier as another area of great naming interest. We move from the world of living things to one where inanimate objects are constantly being personified. Captain T. D. Manning and Commander C. F. Walker introduce the subject well in their *British Warship Names:*

'. . . of all creations of men's hands, the ship—and especially the sailing ship—is surely the nearest approach to a living entity, possessing individual traits which distinguish her from her sisters, even of the same class. Small wonder, then, that the sailor, ever a sentimentalist at heart, has always endowed his vessel with an almost human personality and given her a name; or that, deprived as he is for long periods of the society of womankind, that personality should

invariably be feminine—though by some illogical thought process he does not demand that the name should follow suit, and sees nothing incongruous in referring to an **Agamemnon** or a **Benbow** as "she".'

The Royal Navy has established over several centuries a stock of names that can be transferred from ship to ship. In this way names such as **Victory, Warspite, Orion, Ajax** and **Greyhound** have figured in great naval combats at widely differing periods. Because the ships were specifically built for these combats from the 16th century onwards, their names were often suitably war-like. **Warspite** probably represents 'war despite', showing contemptuous disregard for the danger of battle. **Dreadnought** speaks for itself, as do **Triumph, Repulse, Revenge** and **Defiance, Swiftsure** is thought to be another contraction, this time of 'swift pursuer'.

In our discussion of place names in the New World we saw the influence of both Charles I and Charles II. The latter turned his attention also to his ships when he returned to England, immediately renaming the **Naseby,** which commemorated a Roundhead victory, the **Royal Charles.** Other ships became, for obvious reasons, **Royal Oak, Royal Escape** and **Happy Return.** The **Cleveland** was named after the Duchess of Cleveland, one of his mistresses. His highly subjective naming continued even with the **Loyal London,** which was paid for by the citizens of the city. The ship was sunk, but later raised and rebuilt. It spite of many hints thrown out by Charles, Londoners were less willing on this occasion to provide the funds. Charles struck out the 'Loyal' and allowed only 'London' to remain as the ship's name.

As Jean E. Taggart points out, in her *Motorboat, Yacht or Canoe—You Name It,* the United States Navy now has a logical system for naming ships according to their class. Battleships are named for the states, aircraft carriers are named for famous historical fighting ships, or for important battles. Cruisers take the names of American cities or territories if they are larger. People are commemorated in the names of destroyers, frigates, submarines, etc.

The Taggart book contains much interesting information about ships, but the best book on the subject by far was published in 1974 by Don H. Kennedy. It is called simply *Ship Names,* and on almost every page there is something that I would like to re-quote here. For those interested in ships the book is essential. I would go further and say that anyone who is thinking of writing a book about any

Ships are not always able to live up to their names. An article in the magazine *Yachting* once pointed out that the *Tarry Not* sailed from Maine in November one year with a cargo of Christmas trees. It arrived in Philadelphia in February. *Big Bonanza* was sold for debt four times in thirteen years, and *Brilliant Sailor* held a record for taking longer to cross the Atlantic than any other ship of its kind. A ship called *Prohibition* had a captain who, notoriously, was hardly ever sober.

naming system should study it closely. Among the Names Society's collection of over six hundred books on names it seems to me to be the one which most satisfyingly deals with a single nomenclature.

Ships have often been given nicknames, especially when their official names are difficult to pronounce. Some examples from the British navy:

Agamemnon 'Eggs and Bacon'
Amphitrite ''Am and tripe'
Ariadne 'Hairy Annie'
Belle Poule 'Bell Pull'
Bellerophon 'Billy Ruffian'
Belliqueux 'Billy Squeaks'
Cyclops 'Cyclebox'
Daedalus 'Deadlies'
Dedaigneuse 'Dead Nose'
Niobe 'Nobby'
Polyphemus 'Polly Infamous'
Temeraire 'Trim yer 'air'
Ville de Milan 'Wheel 'em along'

A reading of *Ship Names* makes it clear that we can safely say that all categories of names are represented on the high seas. There was even, at one time, a remarkable example of a physical blend name to add to the notional blends we found in racehorse names. The **Zulu** and **Nubian** were two destroyers that were both damaged in the First World War. A composite ship was assembled in 1917 using the forepart of *Zulu* and the after portion of *Nubian*. It was then named **Zubian.**

Some ship names, such as **Mayflower, Titanic, Mauretania** and **Cutty Sark** are world famous: at the other end of the scale completely are the names of yachts and smaller boats. Whereas modern ships like the great liners need dignified names, private vessels of all kinds allow whimsicality and humour to appear in their names. *Lloyd's Register of Yachts* for 1968, for instance, lists such examples as **Miss Conduct,**

Miss Demena, Bung Ho, C'est La Vie (which I have seen elsewhere in the form **Sail La Vie),** **Annelory** and **Fairynuff.** The last named roughly translates a name I saw on a French chalet, **Sam Sufy** (*ça me suffit*).

Among other names from various sources are **Miss Mie, Miss Fitz, What Next, Bossy Boots, Koliwobbles, Q. Jumper, Tung Tide, Hare-Azing, Codswallop** and **Honey Don't.** I particularly like the names which link with the generic class name. 'Catamaran' is actually an adaptation of a Tamil word meaning a 'tied tree', but to many punsters who own one it is simply another kind of 'cat'. The names therefore emerge as **Nauticat, Kitti, Wild Cat, Cat Nap, Whiskers Two, Pussy Willow, Puss Face, Seamew, Sly Puss, Dupli-Cat, Show'er Puss** and **Pussy Galore.** 'Solo' class yachts receive names like **Solow, So-So, Soliloquy, Imalone, Solace, Slo Koche, Seule, Lone, So-Long, By Me Sen, Soloist.** In the 'Finn' class one finds names like **Huckleberry Finn, Tail Finn, Finale, Dolfinn, Finnigan, Finess** and **Finnisterre.** Even the National 'Flying Fifteen' class does not defeat the jokers. The two 'fs' in the title are picked up in names of the **Ffancy Ffree** type.

All kinds of names occur, not just the jokey ones, and the standard generally is very high indeed. That is to say that if the namers decide to be witty they are usually very witty, often making learned or polyglot allusions. If they decide to be descriptive, convert words into names, link, transfer or invent names, they also seem to do these things well. There are not many nomenclatures where one finds names of the **Sailbad The Sinner** standard.

Train and locomotive names

The care with which boat-owners do their naming reflects the great enthusiasm the boats themselves arouse. An equal amount of enthusiasm is generated for some people by locomotives and trains, though this phenomenon appears to be almost exclusively

British. Perhaps only an Englishman (Cecil J. Allen) could write that many of the trains described in his book 'have become old friends to me', or that 'the route between Victoria and Dover is anything but easy *from the locomotive point of view*' (my italics). Both remarks occur in *Titled Trains of Great Britain*, a loving account of such trains as the **Broadsman, Flying Scotsman, Master Cutler, White Rose, Mancunian, Red Rose, Welsh Dragon, Capitals Limited, Granite City, Statesman** and **Red Dragon.** The *Statesman* was named because it connected with the sailings of the **United States.** The 'Limited' in *Capitals Limited* perhaps referred to the limited number of stops, or first class seats, and the other names all contain references to the places served.

Apart from named trains, most of the larger steam locomotives once had individual names. The practice was established in the early days of Stephenson's **Rocket** and pioneers such as **Novelty, Sanspareil, Invicta** and **Northumbrian,** but when **Locomotion** commenced work in 1825 it also bore the number name, **No. 1.** The many railway companies that sprang up had their own ideas about identifying locomotives, some considering number names quite sufficient, but the Great Western Railway consistently gave verbal names to its express passenger locomotives from the earliest days. When the railways were grouped into four companies in 1923 such names came back into general favour. Everything was set for the small boys (I was among them) who would later gaze upon the powerful giants with considerable awe and carefully underline those names in little books. Later still, 'enthusiasts' were to go much further, removing the nameplates from the driving wheel splashers completely if the opportunity presented itself.

Locomotive names were often grouped thematically as 'halls', 'castles', 'clans', 'granges', 'manors', 'counties', etc. The LNER named some Pacific locomotives after famous racehorses, though this led to the sight of **Sandwich, Spearmint** and **Pretty Polly** standing at the heads of trains and looking rather sheepish. As more and more locomotives were named, so the names were drawn from yet more sources. Many names were those which seem to be free-floating, likely to turn up in almost any nomenclature: **Atlas, Bonaventure, Pathfinder, Blue Peter, Vanguard, Meteor, Sunbeam.** Some names looked back to the immediate source of locomotive names, the stage coaches. These had borne names like **Vivid, Lightning, High Flyer, Nimrod, Royal Sovereign, Talisman, Vixen, Arrow, Dart, Comet, Red Rover.**

A famous mail-coach bore the name **Quicksilver.**

We see once again how the world of names consists of countless overlapping nomenclatures. It is impossible to look through a book such as H. C. Casserley's *British Locomotive Names of the Twentieth Century* and not be reminded of ship names, place names, surnames, animal names and a dozen other kinds of name. One feels, too, that every name will have its day sooner or later. The stage coach **Red Rover** may have slipped into obscurity, but its name lives on as a pub name and as the name for a London Transport ticket. **Blue Peter** has earned a new kind of fame in Britain as the name of a television programme. Such names call for an individual approach which allows one to trace their path of transfer into different naming systems after their initial establishment as names. **Blue Peter,** for instance, possibly began as a French place name, **Beaupreau,** 'beautiful meadow'. A fabric made there, a kind of linen, was used to make flags. The fabric was called *beaupers* or *bewpers* in English. Professor Weekley suggested that the second part of this word may have been mistaken for **Piers,** which is another form of **Peter.** 'Beau' could then have been changed to 'blue' to suit the actual colour of the flag. Many well-authenticated instances of similar word and name changes caused by folk etymology are recorded.

The railways as a whole were sources of very many names. Nicknames for the railway companies soon came into being, usually being based on the company initials. The London, Midland and Scottish was known by such names as **Ell of a Mess, Let Me Sleep** and **Lord's My Shepherd.** The Great Western became **Go When Ready** or **God's Wonderful Railway,** while the LNER was **Late and Never Early. The Bluebell Line** and **Cuckoo Line** were well known branches of the Southern Railway, and the Waterloo and City line became **The Drain.** Much the same kind of process in the USA led to names like the **Apple Butter Route, Spud Drag, Original Ham and Egg Route, Bums' Own** and **Pennsy.**

Frank McKenna, in his *Glossary of Railwaymen's Talk*, mentions nicknames that were used by the railwaymen themselves. The footplatemen from Yeovil, for instance, were known as the **Apple Corps;** the **Master Cutler** was less reverently known as **The Knife and Fork;** an efficient fireman was **Terror of the Tongs;** the Leeds–Carlisle main line was the **Burma Road** because it was difficult to negotiate. One wonders whether many other occupations, other than military, have produced such collections of names. Mining language must include many examples. Geordie pitmen certainly used to name newly opened 'districts', according to one of my correspondents. **Spion Kop** was named after the battle for that hill had just taken place, and grim irony caused **White City** to be transferred below ground.

Lorry names

In many parts of the world individual vehicles are named, and Philip Riley has written an interesting article about the names of lorries in Malta. He thinks that the custom of giving names began when handcarts were the normal conveyers of goods. They had no registration plates but needed to be identified in some way. It became usual to display on them the nicknames of their owners.

The modern lorries which carry on the tradition of naming 'are almost exclusively privately owned', Mr Riley says, which hints at ownership proclamation as the main reason for them. Most of the names are in English, the language used for educational purposes, but there is interference in the spelling of many names due to the influence of Maltese or Italian. A large group of names—which are apparently carefully painted in 'a spiked and ornate lettering, usually in bright red, yellow and green'— are the names of saints. These may be the patrons of villages where the drivers live or the patron saints of the drivers themselves. Other religious names refer to the Virgin Mary or may be statements of faith: **In God We Trust.**

Another large group of names draws its inspiration from the entertainment world. Song titles such as **Sonny Boy, High Noon, Congratulations,** **Thunderball** and **April Love** appear, and singers such as **Sandie Shaw** and **Cliff Richard** are honoured. Films have an influence, and **Peter Sellers, Steve McQueen, James Dean** are among those stars who drive round Maltese streets. **James Bond** (together with **007**) and **Goldfinger** are there with them.

A wide range of transferred names is called upon, and lorries called **Wilson** and **Kennedy** are seen beside **New York, Victoria, Melbourne, California** and **Germany.** A few lorry owners continue the former tradition of transferring their own nicknames, such as **Happy** or **Blue Boy.** One group Mr Riley describes as 'prowess names, designed to enhance the owners' reputations'. He includes here such names as **Big Boy, Let Me Pass, Roadmaster, Hercules, King of the Road,** and **Super Power,** which reflect drivers' attitudes with which we are all only too familiar. Some of the animal names, such as **Tiger** and **Lion,** might belong in this group, which are another form of personal trade names in a sense. A few names hint at prowess beyond the realm of driving, Mr Riley suggests. He mentions names like **Lucky Lips** and **Kiss Me,** though these now have a curious innocence about them. They take us back to the 'sauciness' of seaside resorts just after the war.

Names take us everywhere, in fact. Not only into our social history, though they do that particularly well, but into every aspect of human activity. They take us everywhere English is spoken, showing the cultural differences that have evolved over centuries among peoples who often had a common origin.

This chapter, however, and those that have preceded it, are meant to have made that point. I have the consoling thought at the back of my mind that if the words I have written have failed to do it, the names will in any case have spoken for themselves.

Edwin D. Lawson writes about the unofficial naming of American B.29 bombers by their crews during World War Two. Officially the bombers were identified by call-names such as *Z Square 20*. When they arrived overseas their nose-cones were usually decorated and nicknames bestowed. As Professor Lawson says, such naming no doubt helped the crews to feel more in control of an anarchic situation. Typical nicknames given to the bombers were *Ancient Mariner, Teaser, Slick Dick, Flying Jackass, Special Delivery, American Beauty, Four Roses, Miss Hap, Dreamboat, Gravel Gertie, Flagship 500, Kansas Farmer, Double Exposure, Lucky 'Leven, Jokers Wild, Beaubomber, Devil's Delight, Wichita Witch, Satan's Sister, Lady in Dis-dress.*

OSCULATORY ONOMASTICS

IN AN *Observer* article in March 1990, Amanda Atha mentioned that British people now kiss each other 'by way of saying hello' far more than they did before the 1960s. She thought that social kissing had become rather a subtle art, with different kinds of salutation which deserved names of their own. She suggested some possibilities, including the:

Royal Cheek—one cheek slightly turned towards the other person; actual contact slight or non-existent

Side Slip—both faces poised a few inches apart

Double Squeak—a Side Slip accompanied by 'a noise halfway between a grunt and a moo'

Flesh Press—cheeks in contact but no actual kiss

Croydon Peck—an actual pecking kiss on both cheeks.

Ms Atha was by no means the first writer to suggest names for different kisses. Barton Holyday, whose play *The Marriage of the Arts* was performed at Oxford in 1630, refers interestingly to 'the different manners of a *French, Spanish* and *Dutch kiss.*' Unfortunately, we can only guess at how these kisses differed. Even the French kiss to which he refers was unlikely to have been of the modern tongue-probing kind. Such a kiss has only been generally known by that name since the 1920s. The French, incidentally, do not return the linguistic compliment and describe a more innocent kind of kiss as 'English'.

Sinclair Lewis has a husband and wife jokingly describe the different kinds of kisses to which the wife has been subjected at a party in *Cass Timberlane*. They give them names such as the *Solid Brother-in-Law,* the *Allergic-to-Lipstick,* the *Short Interrogative,* the *Long Interrogative,* the *Vampire-Minatory.* They also mention the so-called *Butterfly Kiss,* which is usually not a kiss in the normal sense, but a fluttering of the eye-lashes against the partner's cheek. The variant *Eye-lash Kiss* referred to in *The Art of Kissing* (1936), by Hugh Morris, involves a mingling of the eye-lashes. The same author describes kisses which he calls the *French Soul*, the *Vacuum* (both partners suck inwards), the *Spiritual* (eye-contact only), the *Nip* (a bite), the *Surprise* (used to wake a partner who is asleep).

There is clearly scope here for a pair of research students to conduct a full-scale study in the field of Osculatory Onomastics —the names of kisses, smacks, busses, salutes and pecks. The latter would include the well-known *Paternal* or *Avuncular peck* on the forehead. There is also the more sinister *Judas kiss* and the modern sporting commentator's *Kiss of Death*. Rarer varieties include the *Deputy Kiss,* as Charles Dickens would no doubt have named it. Sam Weller says to Mary in *The Pickwick Papers*: 'Put your lips to this here tumbler, and then I can kiss you by deputy.' Ben Jonson, of course, had thought of the idea two hundred years earlier:

'Or leave a kiss but in the cup
And I'll not look for wine.'

A truly Dickensian invention was the *Keyhole Kiss,* fully described in *David Copperfield*. The young David has been locked in his room by his horrid step-father, and Peggotty, the family-servant, comes to comfort him. They conduct their conversation on either side of the door, until, as David says: 'Peggotty fell to kissing the key-hole, as she couldn't kiss me. We both kissed the keyhole with the greatest affection.'

Popular dog names

The list below shows the most frequently-used names for dogs in the USA, as revealed by a computer-based study of some 25 000 dog licences.

1 Lady	36 Mickey	71 Barney	Samantha	141 Jackie	Jet
2 King	37 Tammy	72 Sassy	107 Major	Mimi	Judy
3 Duke	38 Cindy	73 Bobo	Tony	Pixie	Ricky
4 Peppy	39 Pierre	Joe	109 Bonnie	Ringo	Sarge
5 Prince	40 Tiny	Mike	Bozo	Tanya	Tootsie
6 Pepper	41 Max	76 Rocky	Thor	146 Honey	Whiskers
7 Snoopy	42 Skippy	77 Snowball	112 Cleo	Killer	Wolf
8 Princess	43 Fifi	78 Benji	Pete	Pudgie	183 Chipper
9 Heidi	44 Champ	Peanuts	114 Boy	Suzette	Hans
10 Sam	45 Fritz	80 Laddie	Casey	150 Chip	Lisa
Coco	46 Brownie	81 Scottie	Mandy	Dino	Molly
12 Butch	47 Caesar	82 Bridget	Shep	Freckles	Skip
13 Penny	48 Boots	Lassie	118 Peaches	Frosty	Spotty
14 Rusty	49 Kelly	84 Baby	Pee Wee	Pookie	Sunshine
15 Sandy	50 Buttons	Jack	Terry	Rebel	Whitey
Susie	Tina	86 Midnight	121 Bandit	Roscoe	191 Bruce
17 Duchess	52 Sparky	Patches	Red	157 Fritzie	Cuddles
18 Blackie	53 Daisy	Poncho	Satan	Goldie	Foxy
19 Ginger	54 Gigi	89 Happy	Timmy	Spike	Heather
20 Queenie	Nicky	90 Jojo	Tinker	Tramp	Peggy
21 Rex	56 Spot	Mac	126 Chichi	161 Beau	Queen
22 Candy	57 Gypsy	Rags	127 Cricket	Dobie	Shaft
23 Buffy	Taffy	93 Brutus	Sport	Rover	Spooky
24 Mitzie	59 Tuffy	Bullet	129 Bobby	164 Hobo	Tasha
25 Tiger	60 Corky	Samson	Sadie	Joey	200 Girl
26 Smokey	Skipper	Shadow	Thunder	Randy	Kojak
27 Charlie	62 Misty	97 Dolly	132 Holly	Shannon	Lance
28 Chico	Frisky	Gretchen	Lobo	168 Babe	Patsy
29 Brandy	64 Cookie	99 Pal	Ralph	Jody	Peanut
30 Sheba	65 Buster	100 Maggie	Shawn	Patty	Pokey
31 Fluffy	Dusty	101 Poochie	136 Bambi	Star	Snow
32 Missy	Muffin	Sugar	Blue	Tracey	
Toby	68 Buddy	103 Baron	Duffy	173 Bootsie	
34 Lucky	Teddy	George	Sammy	Ebony	
Trixie	70 Bruno	Gidget	Trouble	Jenny	

Amongst the more individual dog names revealed by the computer print-out were the following:

Adonis	Beowulf	Bus	Daddy	Froggy	Igloo
Alabuster	Bicky	Cat	Dawg	Gangster	Inkspot
Ambrosia	Bikini	Champagne	Ding	Garbo	Jam
Arf-Arf	Bitch	Charm	Disco	Genius	Jelly Bean
Asphalt	Blacktooth	Cheater	Dollar	Groucho	Judge
Attila	Bliss	Chimney	Donut	Guinness	Lamb Chop
Avanti	Blood	Chimp	Droopy	Handsome	Lap
Baby Sister	Bogart	Chop	Dumbo	Havoc	Lash
Bacchus	Bounce	Chump	Evil	Hayyou	Leed
Bad Boy	Boz	Cloud	Fag	Hitler	Legs
Banshee	Breezy	Cop	Fate	Hornet	Lemon
Barker	Brick	Cowboy	Fearless	Hot Dog	Limbo
Bee	Bugger	Cue	Flake	Hound	Lollipop
Bent	Bully	Cupcake	Flea-bag	Huggy	Lover Boy

Macwoof	Munch	Poorboy	Ripple	Shivers	Tornado
Magic	Mustard	Popcorn	Rug	Shrimp	Trip
Midas	Mystery	Pounce	Sabre	Slave	Twit
Might	Nanoo	Puddycat	Scamper	Slipper	Underdog
Milky	Nibbles	Pussy	Scoop	Smudge	Venus
Mink	Nuisance	Radar	Scout	Sniffy	Willow
Monster	Nutmeg	Rap	Scratch	Snuggles	Wobbles
Moonshine	Orange	Ratso	Sentry	Sultan	Woman
Mozart	Outlaw	Rembrandt	Shandy	Tailstar	Woof
Mudball	Pardner	Restless	Sheik	Teeny	Yippy
Muggins	Playboy	Rich	Sheriff	Titan	Zulu

Popular cat names

A survey of British cat names, commissioned by Spillers Top Cat and carried out by the British Market Research Bureau, revealed the following most popular names:

1 Sooty	Sandy	21 Charlie	Sukie	Katie	Scamp
2 Smokie	Tinker	Lucky	Tammy	Kizzy	Shandy
3 Brandy	13 Blackie	Rusty	33 Bumble	Mickey	Sherry
Fluffy	Susie	Snowy	Cindy	Nelson	Simon
Tiger	Toby	25 Candy	Daisy	Oliver	Tabitha
6 Tibbie	Whisky	Cat	Dusty	Penny	Topsy
Tiggie	17 Ginger	Flossie	Fred	Pepper	Twiggy
Tom	Lucy	Mitzi	Frisky	Pickles	
9 Kitty	Tim	Puss	Honey	Purdy	
Sam	Tiny	Sally	Jerry	Sammy	

Some of the other names revealed by the survey were as follows:

Arthur	Fifi	Moggy	Scruffy	Sparky	Titch
Ashes	Fudge	Moody	Sebastian	Spats	Treacle
Bagpuss	Ginny	Mousse	Silky	Spike	Troubles
Basher	Halfpenny	Mrs Puss	Smudge	Tabby	Tumble
Benjy	Heidi	Muffin	Smutty	Tatty	Twopence
Benny	Herby	Muggins	Sneeze	Teapot	Vesta
Boofy	Inky	Noddy	Snudge	Tibbles	Whiskers
Boots	Jambo	Panda	Soda	Tiddle	Womble
Chairman Miaou	Japonica Troggs	Pepsi	Softy	Tinkie	Zebedee
Cheeky	Jason	Pippa			
Chichi	Jaybee	Pipsqueak			
Chumpers	Jemima	Podge			
Cloe	Jenny	Polly			
Crackers	Joe	Poochy			
Czumczusz	Katkin	Puss Puss			
Dandy	Libby	Pussy Cat			
Domino	Lydia la Poose	Puzzle			
Eric	Lulu	Raffles			
Ernie	Madam	Refus			
Fats	Marmalade	Sauté			
Felix	Maxwell	Scampi			

One of these kittens I bought for a rupee and called her Billi, which is the Urdu for a cat. She was a savage little creature, but in the end she came to depend on me for everything.

Francis Brett Young   *Marching on Tanga*

Dog names in fiction

Novelists sometimes comment on the dog names that occur in their stories. A selection of such comments is given below. (In G. B. Stern's *Dogs in an Omnibus*, the author imagines the names that dogs might give to humans—names like Legs-in-Authority, Savoury-Legs, Green-Silk-Legs, Equestrian-Legs, Shapely Legs, Master-Legs, Supreme-Legs, Chubby-Legs.)

'This is Ahab, that's Jezebel,' said Evie, who was one of those who name animals after the less successful characters of Old Testament history.
E. M. Forster   *Howard's End*

I enjoy interrupting my intellectual preoccupations to talk and play with Bashan. And what do I say to him? Mostly his own name, the two syllables which are of the utmost personal interest because they refer to himself and have an electric effect upon his whole being. I rouse and stimulate his sense of his own ego by impressing upon him – varying my tone and emphasis – that he *is* Bashan and that Bashan is his name. By continuing this for a while I can actually produce in him a state of ecstasy, a sort of intoxication with his own identity.
Thomas Mann   *A Man and his Dog*

'My dog Blast, th' only one saved out o' a litter o' pups as was blowed up when a keg o' minin' powder loosed off in th' store-keeper's hut.'
Rudyard Kipling   *On Greenhow Hill*

Dog was the doctor's golden labrador, so called because the family had never bothered to give him a name. Marshall, who believed that animals had souls which could be developed by human contact, had been greatly concerned by the problem of Dog. A dog with no name could hardly have a developing soul. He solved this problem by elevating the word dog to the status of a name.
Judith Woolf   *Emma With Objects*

Dog, which being interpreted cabbalistically backwards, signifies God.
Aldous Huxley   *Antic Hay*

The choice fell upon Feng Hou. That is the name to which, since it is hers and she is all caprice and individuality, she refuses to answer. (The name of a Pekinese spaniel, which 'should, of course, be Chinese and also easily pronounceable'.)
E. V. Lucas   *The More I See of Men . . .*

'If you name him by his character I should say Hamlet would be as good as anything.'
'Hamlet'll do,' said Jeremy comfortably. 'I've never heard of a dog called that, but it's easy to say.'
Hugh Walpole   *Jeremy*

Miss Belle Cunningham—'It's a touching habit', Lucille Christian interrupted, 'papa has of naming dogs after young ladies he used to admire when he was young.'
Robert Penn Warren *Night Rider*

'I'd change his name.'
'You don't like Nietzsche?'
'No,' said Helena dryly. 'I'd call him something like Rover.'
Mary McCarthy *The Group*

For years they had a black cocker spaniel which they had named Nigger without any thought except that black dogs *do* get called Nigger.
'Makes it worse, calling a *dog* that. We coloured people don't like the word 'nigger', and when you act like dogs and us are just the same. . . .'
Neil was angry. 'All right, all right, we'll change it! We'll call the mutt "Prince"!'
Sinclair Lewis   *Kingsblood Royal*

He had a black spot at the root of his spine.
'He ought to be called Spot,' said one. But that was too ordinary. It was a great question what to call him.
'Call him Rex—the King,' said my mother. We took the name in all seriousness.
'Rex—the King!' We thought it was just right. Not for years did I realise that it was a sarcasm on my mother's part.

It wasn't a successful name, really. Because my father, and all the people in the street, failed completely to pronounce the monosyllable Rex. They all said Rax. And it always distressed me. It always suggested to me seaweed, and rack-and-ruin. Poor Rex!
D. H. Lawrence   *Rex*

. . . a young wire-haired fox-terrier, for whom no more original name had been found than 'Spot'. It is true that he had a spot.
Arnold Bennett   *The Old Wives' Tale*

In some versions of the great drama of Punch there is a small dog—a modern innovation—supposed to be the private property of that gentleman, whose name is always Toby.
Charles Dickens   *The Old Curiosity Shop*

Charles rubbed Tweed behind his ears. 'What did you call the puppies?'
'This one's Dee. The others were Don, Tay, Garry, Spey and Clyde. All after Scottish rivers.'
Leonora Starr   *Corrie*

Ulysses—'Is that what you call him? Why?'
'Well, he seemed on the evidence to have led a roving life, and judging by the example we saw, it must have been adventurous.'
Georgette Heyer   *Arabella*

'What shall we call him? Harlequin?'
'No, that's too long, and it must mean something that's lost and all alone,' said Dot. 'Rover would do, only it's so common.'
'Vagabond, Tramp, Waif or Stray,' suggested Donovan.
'Oh—Waif—that's beautiful, and so nice to say.'
'Yes, a thing tossed up by chance; it'll just suit the beggar.'
Edna Lyall   *Donovan*

A selection of yacht names

Names that speak for themselves

About Time II	Coweslip	Gigolette	Luffabuoy	Op-A-Bout	Teas Maid
Addynuff	Craft E	Gloo Pot	Luff Divine	Owdonabit	Tempers Fugit
Adorabelle	Crusado	Golden B Hind	Luffinapuff	Pen-Y-Less	Tern Up
Allgo	Cuffuffle	Gonpotee	Luft Behind	Petard	The Pickle
Anuddha-Buddha	Daisy Dampwash	Goonlight	Maida Mistake	Phlappjack	Thou Swell
Any End Up	Dambreezy	Gozunda	Maid Tumesshure	Phlash	Tishoo
Anything	Dammit	Happikat	Mark 10:31	Pink Djin	To Be True
Appydaze	Dashtwet	Hei Yu	Maykway	Plane Crazy Too	Tomfoolery
Aquadisiac	Dinah Mite	Hell's Belles	Mea Tu	Potemkin	Too Fax
Avago	Dinah Mo	Helluvathing	Merry Hell	Puff-N-Blow	Too-She
Azygos	Drip Dri	Herr Kut	Mighty Mo	Red-E	Tri-N-Ges
Baise Mon Cul	D Sea Bee	Hot N Bothered	Miss B Haven	Redrump	Tsmyne
Bald 'Ed	Dumbelle	Hot Potato	Miss Carry	Reef Not	Tuchango
Bawdstif	Du-U-Mynd	Howdedo	Miss Conduct	Rock-N-Roll	Twilgo
Beezneez	Eb 'n' Flo	Hows Trix	Miss Doings	Rose Cheeks	Tyne E
B'Jabbers	Elcat	Icanopit	Miss Fire	Rosy Lee	Ucantu
Black Azelle	Fair Kop	I.C.U.	Miss Isle	Sa-Cas-Tic	Ul-C
Blew Moon	Fantabulous	Idunit	Miss Myth	Sail La Vie	Up-N-Atom
Blow Mee	Fast Lady	Infradip	Mister Sea	Sally Forth	Uskanopit
Blow-U-Jack	Fijit	Itsallgo	Moanalot	Scilly Whim	Utoo
Blu Away	First Luff	Jack's O.K.	Mrs. Frequently	Scubeedoo	Wacker Bilt
Bluebottle	Flamin-Go	Jest As Well	My Goodness	Seafari	Waltzing Matilda
Blue Over	Flipincid	Jesterjob	Nap Kin	Sheeza B	Water Lou
Bluesology	Fluffy Bottam	Joka	Nautitoo	Shoestring	Weatherornot
Bosunover	Flying Sorcerer	Ketchup	Neveready	Sin King	We We
Branestawm	Foggy Dew	K'Fuffle	Nhit Wit	Sir Fon	Windkist
Bright 'Un	Forsail	Kippin	Nnay Llas	Sir Loin	Wotahope
Brillig	Fred N Sign	Koliwobbles	No Idea	Slo-Mo-Shun	Wotawetun
Buzz Off	Freelove II	Konfewshun	Nowt	Smart E	Wot-You-Fink
Captain Cat	Frivulus	Koolkat	Nu Name	Soopurr	Wunnalot
Cham-Pu	Gaylee	Kriky	Nut Case	So Wet	Wych Syde
Chancalot	Geewiz	La-Goon	Nyctea	Spraymate	Y Dewin
Clewless	Gercher	La Poussiquette	Odzanends	Sudden Sally	Y Knot
Codswallop	Get Weaving	L For Leather	Oh-Ah	Sue Perb	Zom B
Co Mo Shun	Giggles	Loopey Llew	Ooops	Sweet Fanny	Z-Victor-One

Class names

FLYING FIFTEEN				
Craffty	Fflipinelle	Boffin	Sumfinn	
Eleffant	Fflotsam	Chafin	Tiffin	
Family Fun	Ffluff	Chin Fin		
Ffab	Ffolly	Coffinn	FLYING DUTCHMAN	
Ffanfare	Ffortissimo	Enuffin	Dutch Uncle	
Ffascination	Ffreak	Fickanfinn	Fair Phantom	
Ffelicity	Ffroff	Finantonic	Flying Chum	
Ffickle	Ffun	Finbad	Flying Fish	
Ffifi	Fifty Fifty	Finnatical	Flying Phantom	
Ffillipp	Flip Flop	Finnomenon	Flying Scotsman	
Fflagon	Nymff	Finny Hill	Ghost	
Ffirty Ffour	Sstutter	Laarfinn	Jinx	
Ffizzle		Micky Finn	Sea Myth	
Fflambuoyant	FINN	Muffin	Spectre	
Fflame	Affinity	Parafinalia	The Dutchess	
	Beefin	Skyfinn	Zeelust	

Names that reflect special interests

Arch Maid	Katy Did	Some Chicken	Hot Toddy
Bright Eyes	Latin Lover	Ta Baby	Lash Up
Concubine	Lust	Tangle Legs	Opening Time
Crumpet	Meremaid	Taylor Maid	Pale Ale
Cuddle	Mini The Minx	Tease	Pick Me Up
Curvaceous	My Posie	Tempt Me	Pie Eyed
Dabchick	My Spare Lady	Temptress	Pink Gin
Dancing Girl	Naughtilass	Testbed	Pinta
Dead Sexy	Nickers	Tiller Girl	Plastered
Easy Virtue	Nifty Chick	Wayward Lady	Quick One
Enterprising Lady	Oui Oui		Rum Baba
Fast Lady	Painted Lady	Beer Bottle	Say When
Flirt	Poppet	Bottoms Up	Scotch Mist
Geisha	Popsitoo	Brandy Bottle	Shandy
Girl Friend	Provocative	Brewer's Droop	Sippers
Glamour Girl	Saucy Puss	Bubbly	Soaked
Heart Throb	Sea Mistress	Bung Ho	Souced
Honeybunch	Sea Wife	Cheers	Sozzled
Honey Don't	Sexy	Corkscrew	Spree
Hot Tomato	Shady Lady	Foaming Ale	Still Sober
Hunnibun	She's Fast	Gin And Tonic	Too Tipsy
Jezebel	Slap N Tickle	Half Pint	Whisky
Jucy Lucy	Slick Chick	Hangover	Yo-Ho-Ho

Her name was Diana—Diana not of Ephesus but of Bremen. This ridiculously unsuitable name struck one as an impertinence towards the memory of the most charming of goddesses; for apart from the fact that the old craft was physically incapable of engaging in any sort of chase, there was a gang of four children belonged to her.

Joseph Conrad   *Falk*

The captain informed us he had named his ship the Bonnetta, out of gratitude to Providence, for once when he was sailing to America with a good number of passengers, the ship in which he then sailed was becalmed for five weeks, and during all that time numbers of the fish Bonnetta swam close to her, and were caught for food.

James Boswell   *Journal of a Tour to the Hebrides*

Hat names

Albert Jones, of Coulsdon, Surrey, has sent me his collection of hat names, pointing out that they form a particularly interesting group. As an admirer of Charles Dickens, I was pleased to see the name *Dolly Varden* in the list. The *Oxford English Dictionary* defines this as 'a large hat, worn by women, with one side bent downwards, and abundantly trimmed with flowers.' This is curious, since Dickens himself talks of Dolly wearing 'a little straw hat trimmed with cherry-coloured ribbons, and worn the merest trifle on one side—just enough, in short, to make it the wickedest and most provoking head-dress that ever malicious milliner devised.'

Dickens seems to have hats very much in mind when writing *Barnaby Rudge*. Apart from Dolly's hat, he refers to *slouch hats, flapped hats* and *three-cornered hats*. He mentions that Joe's recruiting sergeant 'had decorated his hat with sundry parti-coloured streamers, which made a very lively appearance,' and describes the blue cockades worn in the hats of Lord George Gordon's followers.

As for Dolly Varden, she is by no means the only fictional character to have given a name to a hat. *Trilby* O'Ferral is the young model who is groomed as a singer by the sinister Svengali in George du Maurier's novel, *Trilby* (1894). It was when the latter became a stage play that the actress playing the part appeared wearing a soft felt hat of the type that we now call a trilby. The *fedora* was named in a similar way after being seen in Sardou's play *Fédora* (1882). The Scottish *tammy*, or *Tam O'Shanter*, derives its name from Robert Burns's poetic hero of that name.

Other hats take their names from real people. In the 1930s Englishmen talked about wearing an *Anthony Eden*, a black felt homburg popularised by the then Foreign Secretary. In the 19th century men might have sported a *Bendigo*. This was a kind of fur cap worn by the Nottingham prize-fighter William Thompson, whose ring-name was Bendigo. The American equivalent would perhaps have been the *Davy Crockett*.

The origin of *bowler* is much disputed, but Brewer's *Dictionary of Phrase and Fable* is convinced that it was first made from felt supplied by the Bowler brothers. As for the *Robin Hood*, this name has been applied to the hat traditionally seen on that folk-hero.

Some hat names are simply transferred place names. Examples are *balaclava, balmoral, busby, derby, dunstable, glengarry, homburg* and *panama*. The last-named is said to have been first made in Ecuador, South America, but it was widely used in Panama, Central America.

Jokey hat names are rare, but in the 19th century there was a hat known as the *wideawake* because it had no 'nap'.

Further hat names from Mr Jones's collection: *Africander felt, baseball cap, basinet, bearskin, beret, billycock, biretta, boater, bonnet, bycoket, calotte, cap, capeline, casque, castor, cheese cutter, chef's hat, chimney pot, cloche, coif, coolie hat, coronet, cowboy hat, cowl, crown, crush hat, curch, deerstalker, dunce's hat, fez, forage cap, garrison cap, gibus, hard hat, helmet, hood, jockey cap, kaffiyeh, kepi, leghorn, liberty cap, mantilla, mitre, mobcap, morion, mortar board, mutch, pagri, peak cap, petasus, pileus, pill box, pixie hat, plumed hat, pork pie, shako, side cap, skull cap, sombrero, sou'wester, stephane, stetson, stove pipe, tarboosh, ten gallon, terai, top hat, topi, toque, trencher cap, tricorne, tuque, turban, Tyrolean, witch's hat, yarmulka.*

The veteran and retired actor-manager swept off the black hat which was one of the classic sights of Folkestone and Piccadilly. Throughout the races and tribes of the world, with their various and multitudinous head-dresses (Sir Rudolph was wont to explain), no hat similar in height, breadth and length was like the hat specially made for and worn by himself. Sir Rudolph's hat was a fourth-dimension hat. It was black, and at a casual glance appeared to be a bowler hat; but its crown was the shape of an acorn.

Henry Williamson   *The Dream of Fair Women*

17
NAME GAMES

AS WE have seen in previous chapters, names offer plenty of material for the serious student of history, language, psychology, sociology and the like who wants to make a scholarly investigation. But names also offer scope for a less serious approach. It is easy to play games with them in various ways, to treat them light-heartedly.

In the formal sense of playing an actual game, my children were fond of some simple name games that could be played on a car journey. One of these we knew as *Animal Names*. They looked at names of all kinds—street names, place names, shop names, pub names, etc—and scored a point for each animal they saw. If they saw **Oxford** they would score one point, the **Fox and Goose** would given them two points, and so on. I would personally allow a point, and perhaps give a bonus, if the 'rat' in **Stratford** was pointed out, and if names are scarce one can also allow puns. I might give a point for 'eel' in **Ealing**, for instance (in addition to the 'ling' that is there), if the child claiming the point knew that he was making a pun. If there are younger children who cannot yet read, one can allow them to score a point for any advertisement, pub sign and the like that shows an animal. They can also look for real dogs, cats, horses or whatever in streets or fields.

A simple street name game for a journey through a city makes use of the street name elements listed on pages 195 and 196. In my family we usually guess how many different words for 'street' we will see between the beginning and end of our journey, but there are many possible variations. One is to look for street names which have both parts beginning with the same letter, as in **Aragon Avenue.**

For longer journeys I once devised for the children's section of a national newspaper a place name game based on name elements. For common elements such as '-ton' or '-by', one point can be allowed. To these can be added three points for a tree, as in **Oakwell**, three for a river, as in **Burton-on-Trent**, and three for a first name, as in **Peter-borough**. Five points can be given for colours, as in

Mr Cruncher himself always spoke of the year of our Lord as Anna Dominoes: apparently under the impression that the Christian era dated from the invention of a popular game, by a lady who had bestowed her name upon it.

Charles Dickens   *A Tale of Two Cities*

Redhill, fruits, as in **Appledore,** and the animals of **Molesey** and the like. Place names containing a number up to ten, such as **Seven Oaks**, score that number of points, but larger numbers score a maximum of ten points.

A more sophisticated game could easily be devised using the list of place name elements on pages 174 and 175, and there is no need to wait for a long journey. A map in a classroom or at home makes an effective substitute. It is not long before children start to ask questions as to why places have the names they do, and a good teacher will instantly respond to such a cue.

In a less formal sense, adults often play games with their own names, and it is surprising what one can do. Anagrams and name rebus have long been popular, and there are translations to be made, pronunciations to be changed, name files to compile, variant spellings to collect, and in certain cases, select clubs to join. From the point of view of name games, 'what's in a name?' turns out to have a host of new answers.

Onomancy

Yet more answers to that question are possible if one believes in some kind of name magic. Since ancient times people have believed that it is possible to predict a person's future and discover hidden character traits by studying that person's name. Several methods of divination have been used, all of which come under the general heading of 'onomancy'. In name terms onomancy is roughly the equivalent of astrology.

The basic tenet of those who practise onomancy is that a person's name *is* that person, the name is not just a kind of label. Such a belief is common in many primitive societies of the world, often leading to a situation where individuals refuse to reveal their names to those outside the family circle. They fear that anyone who knows their name will have power over their innermost spirit.

In civilised societies people are only too willing to reveal their names; indeed they often spend their lives trying to make their names known as widely as possible. But as several of the literary quotations I have used in this book reveal (and as the letters from my correspondents constantly confirm), the belief that a name *is* a person is widely held. This belief is usually revealed unconsciously, but many will know what Addie means in William Faulkner's story *As I Lay Dying*:

'I would think about his name until after a while I could see the word as a shape, a vessel, and I would watch him liquefy and flow into it like cold molasses flowing out of the darkness into the vessel.'

It follows that if a name *is* the person who bears it, then the investigation of a name is like an investigation of the person. Once that point is accepted, there are at least four ways in which the investigation can be made.

Name meanings: Roman generals would try to find a soldier who had a good name (one which indicated he was likely to be victorious in life) and put him at the head of the troops as they marched into battle. In Roman times, the meaning of a name was usually more immediately apparent than it is today, but if it is possible to discover the original meaning of one's first name and surname, a symbolic interpretation can be made.

Anagrams: Rearranging the letters of a person's name in order to find meaningful phrases was a popular after-dinner diversion in the 17th century, and has been taken more seriously at different times. The French King Louis XIII, for instance, appointed an official anagrammatist. He was able to find (allowing for the common interchange of 'i' and 'j') the phrase *c'est l'enfer qui m'a créé*, 'it was hell which created me', in the name of Frère Jacques Clement, the man who assassinated Henry III. Most

people will want to find rather happier omens in their own names.

Numerology: This method of divination gives each letter of a name a numerical value and arrives at three figures, a total for the vowels, a total for the consonants and a total for the name. These figures are then interpreted in their turn, though there is disagreement among the various writers on the subject as to what the figures mean.

Alphabet mysticism: This system again takes note of the letters which form a name, but makes a direct interpretation of what each letter means (see following pages).

There is no doubt that we interpret names in modern times, though not necessarily using the methods outlined above. We constantly make judgements about the age, ethnic background, religion and social standing of people we come across on the basis of their names. They make similar judgements about us.

Such modern interpretations are largely justified, as it happens. Changes in name fashions do often make it possible to guess a person's age by his name, and the parents' choice of names *can* reveal quite a lot about their social position, religion and even political beliefs. We are naturally on more dangerous ground when we make subjective judgements about pleasant or unpleasant names and assume that the name-bearers will be like their names. Yet this commonly happens, and we share the indignation of Nicholas Nickleby when he learns from Newman that the name of the beautiful girl with whom he has fallen in love is Miss Bobster, rhyming with lobster. Not that Dickens allows this to be the case, of course. It turns out that Newman has made a mistake, and the girl concerned is really Madeline Bray.

As for onomancy, attitudes to it will clearly vary from person to person. Some, like the ancients, will take it very seriously, as they do astrology. Others will treat it as little more than a party game, and then be surprised, as I have often observed, by what their names reveal.

In case you would like to try a name interpretation for yourself—establish a 'name-print'—I provide letter meanings on the following pages. I have taken them from my book on the subject of name magic, *Our Secret Names* (see Bibliography for details). If you are with a group of friends, it may be quicker to restrict the interpretation to their initials.

. . . .

A

This letter is universally acknowledged to be a symbol of excellence and achievement. It is therefore a sign that a high standard can be reached in the name-bearer's chosen field. It also indicates an insistence on excellence in others, which often means a strongly developed critical faculty. How openly this criticism is expressed depends on other aspects of the name-print. This is also a letter of initiation, showing a person who is keen to do new things. When it is the first letter of a name it is a sign of ambition. Occurring elsewhere in the name it can indicate an unfortunate tendency to be negative about other people's ideas and wishes. As the dominant letter of a name-print, it shows a very great potential for a successful life.

B

This letter indicates the ability to compromise. It reveals a faculty for accepting a majority view and abiding by a general decision. In a positive sense the letter indicates maturity and tact. It has a negative side, which could be interpreted as a lack of will-power or determination. As a dominant letter it hints very clearly at a good team-member, but not a leader. The letter is also connected with domesticity.

C

A sign of steadiness and consistency, both in terms of physical effort that can be applied and emotional commitment that can be made. This letter indicates a good employee, who will eventually settle in one job for many years. More importantly, perhaps, it reveals a steadiness and lack of change in emotional relationships. This positive reliability is counterbalanced to some extent by a certain dullness and lack of imagination.

D

A rather negative symbol which must be fought against by the name-bearer, particularly if it is the dominant letter. It indicates a tendency to give in and not fight for survival. It is the letter of laziness, also of small-mindedness. More positively, the letter is associated with travel, but even this may be a metaphoric kind of travelling, a flight of fancy which represents an attempt to escape from problems. Other elements in the name-print will be able to overcome the influence of this letter, but the name-bearer should guard against apathy and indifference.

E

A symbol of recovery, showing the ability to get back to normal after physical or emotional setbacks. An essential characteristic in most people's name-prints, it includes a certain amount of optimism. When things are going well the letter indicates that the name-bearer will be looking ahead and making plans for improvements. The negative side of the letter can be summed up by the word 'muteness'. This is a tendency to let others have their say but not to speak about one's own views. Nevertheless, as a dominant letter it shows someone who will be able to cope resolutely with the ups and downs of life.

F

The letter contains an indication of violence—perhaps a deep-rooted but strongly suppressed wish to be involved in violent action. It hints at a sadistic streak, which may, nevertheless, be kept tightly under control. Here, too, are signs of a contempt for rules and regulations, and a willingness on occasions to go beyond the law. As a dominant letter F is dangerous, but it can virtually be cancelled out by other personality factors. Coupled with ambition, however, it can lead to ruthlessness. Uncontrolled, the name-bearer will be given to violent changes of mood and sudden rages.

G

Movement is the essential concept contained in this letter. It indicates a restlessness of mind and body, a dissatisfaction with a settled situation. This will be nagging constantly at the name-bearer, causing thoughts of a new job or new partner to be lurking in the mind. As a dominant letter G clearly indicates someone who would be happiest travelling about, and a job which involves mobility would be satisfying. In human relationships the name-bearer may find it difficult to remain faithful to one person. More positively, this letter also hints at speed of thought and action.

H

A determination to achieve success and wealth is the keynote of this letter. It also indicates a yearning for world recognition rather than the satisfaction of personal self-respect quietly enjoyed. This personality trait in its most disagreeable form can lead to the yes-man who will demean himself in any way in order to gain advancement. In a woman it can lead to a deliberate exploitation of bodily attraction. Properly controlled, however, this characteristic can lead to dedicated hard work over a long period, provided that appreciation is expressed constantly by others.

I

This, of course, is the letter which indicates egotism, a supreme interest in one's own affairs at the expense of others. As an element in a complete character-reading it plays a necessary part, for everyone must protect personal interests to some extent. (Absence of this letter in a name-print should therefore be considered significant.) When I dominates a name-print the effect will most clearly be seen on a name-bearer who is young. Others are likely to find such a person oppressively self-centred. Some are able to control this characteristic in themselves, or at least control its public display. But a person who is dominated by I and who appears to be sitting quietly, listening to others, is almost certainly considering how his own interests can be advanced as a result of the conversation.

J

A sign of fair-mindedness and a well-balanced outlook. It indicates a faculty of judgement which others will value. Also inherent in this letter is a concern for the past. Memories are important, and a person whose name-print is dominated by J will probably keep a diary and collect souvenirs. J mostly reveals characteristics that will be valued by others, but the total name-print needs a dynamic element to help counteract the rather static quality that it also suggests.

K

This letter refers exclusively to money and the acquisition of wealth. Other letters contain indications of success, and may well include financial success, but here we are dealing with a naked need for money and the power associated with it. As a dominating letter in a name-print it gives a clear indication of someone who values worldly goods above all else. Coupled with such factors as ambition and ability, it will lead to riches. Lacking the opportunity to acquire wealth, the name-bearer is likely to become soured, being unable to apply other sets of values.

L

A sign of co-ordination, both physical and mental, but perhaps one or the other in an individual. Physical co-ordination may well lead to success in sport or other activities when young. The facility for mental organisation will be very useful for an administrator. The drawback of this letter lies in indecision, for a while the name-bearer may be able to cause a group of people to contribute their various skills to a common undertaking, policy decisions at the outset may cause him great problems. Nevertheless, a name-print dominated by this letter shows ability to cope with complex situations.

M

A concern for outward appearance and an appreciation of beauty are amongst the main indications contained in this letter. The former trait may lead the name-bearer to conceal inner thoughts and feelings as much as possible. A certain amount of such concealment is a good ingredient in a well-balanced personality, but it must not be taken to excess. Appreciation of beauty is also useful in many ways, but ideally the domination of a name-print by M should be balanced by indications of sensitivity and deeper understanding. In a negative way, this letter gives signs of snobbishness and pettiness. When coupled with critical ability it hints at a person with highly developed artistic skills.

N

This letter indicates lack of confidence, and a name-print in which it is a dominant letter will usually indicate a worrier, always uncertain about the future. It reveals a slightly pessimistic outlook which may come to the fore on occasions. At other times it can be kept in check by more positive characteristics. A person whose name is dominated by N may also be uncertain emotionally, afraid to make a complete commitment to another person. The basic lack of self-confidence will often be hidden by a superficial show of supreme self-confidence which crumbles away upon close examination.

O

An indicator of emotion, hinting at sensitivity and depth of feeling. A very useful ingredient in a name-print, and only a problem when dominating it too markedly. The problem may lie in an extreme sensitivity to other people's comments and opinions, so that the name-bearer is too easily hurt. The same sensitivity, however, will be an asset when dealing with other people's emotional problems. This letter in a name shows a capacity for delicacy, both in human relationships and in physical movement.

P

This is a conformist's letter, showing someone who is content to merge with the crowd, or finds it safer to do so. There may also be a wish for personal recognition shown in the name-print, but this need for the support of others may lead to an unwillingness to take risks. This letter usefully counterbalances more rebellious influences, but as a dominating letter it can hint at obscurity for the name-bearer. In a woman the letter may indicate loss of personal identity in a marriage or other relationship.

Q

An indication of a temperamental person, someone who is subject to sudden, but short-lived, changes of mood. But this letter also reveals someone who is constantly enquiring into the world about him. It shows the eternal curiosity of the life-long student. As a dominant letter it hints strongly at someone who becomes knowledgeable, and who passes that knowledge on to others. For Q also indicates a facility for communication, either in speech or print.

R

Probably the best letter of all, reflecting sound common sense, a special concern for education and a well-balanced adjustment to life. As a dominating letter this may not suggest a person who will be wealthy or surrounded by possessions, but it hints very strongly at inner richness and contentment. People who have the qualities symbolised by this letter are essential supports to those who are less stable. The appearance of the letter in any name-print should be welcomed as an indication of a solidly-founded character and personality. Those who have R as a dominating letter will be valued friends and colleagues.

S

This letter is associated with moral goodness and virtue. It contains its own opposite; in other words, it can hint at either sharp awareness of what is right or wrong, both in the name-bearer's own behaviour and in his or her judgements of other people's behaviour. If the name-bearer does anything which is wrong, there will be an expectation of punishment—a need for punishment. Certain types of people whose name-prints are dominated by S will be very difficult to live with because of the high moral example and rigid code of behaviour they set themselves.

T

This letter is an indication of fickleness and lack of permanent commitment. It also signifies impatience, an inability to wait for events to take their natural course. A person whose name-print has T as a dominant letter feels under a constant pressure to get things done now, which makes him valuable in certain working environments. The obsession with time will also have a negative effect, making the person worry unduly about growing old. Minute exactness will not concern this name-bearer, though he or she will be able to concentrate on the job in hand for a short period. Soon, however, it will have to be set aside for something new.

U

The sign of a protective person who is able to take care of others. It is also an indication, however, of someone who needs to feel protected by a familiar environment. There is no easy adjustment to new people or situations. Superficially the name-bearer may seem at ease, but beneath the surface there will be worries. Intellectually, the person whose name-print is dominated by U will be capable of absorbing a great deal of varied information. It is mostly a very positive letter, marred only by a certain streak of intellectual snobbishness.

V

A letter of psychic and spiritual importance. It indicates a person whose perception of events goes beyond the normal. This is the letter of instinct, by which things are known by no logical process. Other people will also respond to a mysterious quality in the name-bearer's personality. This response will either be strongly positive or strongly negative, and it may well defy logical explanation. As a dominant letter, V reveals a person of great psychic potential, which may be lying dormant.

W

A letter hinting at solidarity and strength of character. When W dominates a name-print there are strong qualities of self-control in the name-bearer. These may not yet have been tested by events, but they are there in the background. This letter also speaks of an active person who is able to get on with a job. It is an indication of a realist, who is able to turn an abstract concept into something concrete. A W person may be thought of as rather dull and old-fashioned by some people, but others will greatly value his or her dependability.

X

A secretive and mysterious nature is indicated by this letter. This may have been overruled by other character traits, but the name-bearer's natural tendency would be to be uncommunicative about thoughts and feelings. At the same time the letter indicates a need for physical contact with others, especially those of the opposite sex. One partner is unlikely to satisfy someone whose name-print is dominated by this letter.

Y

This letter indicates a concern for others. It hints at a quiet personality, ready to take second place to someone who is a more natural leader. A Y in the name-print reveals someone who looks for a permanent relationship in which mutual support will be given consistently. There may be a lack of excitement and fire, but this is someone who can be relied upon. As a dominant letter Y is rather dangerous because it suggests almost total anonymity, the name-bearer failing to establish a personal identity. As a feature of personality it may well make the name-bearer reasonably popular, as a good listener is popular, but it should be tempered with a degree of self-assertion.

Z

An indication of someone who appreciates the unusual and is particularly glad to get out of a rut, socially or professionally. It is the mark of an individual who will stand out in a crowd. The name-bearer will be happiest in a job which allows personal recognition. Negative associations with the letter include a degree of untidiness, and occasionally a lack of clear communication in speech or writing. The name-bearer will also work at a rather slow speed.

Love letters

By using onomancy you can also find out how much two people have in common with one another, and which personality traits they share. The simple love-letter test outlined below also indicates how their relationship is likely to fare over a long period.

First of all, write down the first name and last name of each person, like this:

SARAH WILLIAMS
DAVID LAWSON

(If the two people share a name, eg parent and child, make use of the middle names instead.)

Now consider each letter of the top name in turn. If it occurs in the name underneath, cross it out in both names and write it down separately, like this:

$ARAH WILLIAMS   S
DAVID LAW$ON

Do this with each letter in the top name:

$ARAH WILLIAMS   SA
DAVID LAW$ON

When you come to a letter that does not occur in the name below, ignore it and pass on to the next one:

$ARAH WILLIAMS   SAA
DAVID LAW$ON

With these two names, this is the eventual result:

$ARAH WILLIAMS   SAAWIL
DAVID LAW$ON

The letters common to both names indicate the personality traits that they have in common (see the meaning of each letter under 'Alphabet Mysticism' above). The number of letters shared indicates the kind of relationship they are likely to have, as follows:

Letters in common

1   the two people have almost nothing in common, but perhaps 'opposites attract'.
2   these two people will find it difficult to sustain a long-term relationship without working at it very hard.
3   the relationship between these two people is likely to become more difficult as time passes.
4   these two people could probably survive together quite well.
5   there is a good chance for a harmonious relationship between these two people.
6   these two people should be able to live and work together quite happily.
7   these two people make a very well matched pair.
7+ an ideal couple.

It was a favourite superstition of Uncle Matthew's that if you wrote somebody's name on a piece of paper and put it in a drawer, that person would die within the year. The drawers at Alconleigh were full of little slips of paper bearing the names of those whom my uncle wanted out of the way. The spell hardly ever seemed to work.

Nancy Mitford   *Love in a Cold Climate*

Rebus

A name rebus can look like this: **Eur U** which example is meant to be decoded as 'Lo! "u" is past "eur"', or **Louis Pasteur.** Similarly, **Aristophanes, Lord Tennyson, King Solomon** and **George Washington** are to be found—by those who are ingenious enough—in the following:

Ar	Y	M	Gt
Hes	L/D Xn	K	Ge/Gew H

Two simple rebus that are among my own favourites have a satisfying visual appearance. It was J. Bryan who told me of the horse named **Potoooooooo,** and Mark Lower quotes **ABCDEFGHIJKMNOPQRSTUVWXYZ** in his 19th-century *Essays on English Surnames.* The number of 'o's' is important in the first, of course, as is the letter that is missing from the second.

Pictorial rebus have already been mentioned in connection with sign names, and it can be amusing to think of a way to illustrate one's own name. A suggestion for **Dunkling** was long ago given indirectly, I regret to say, by the boy who sat next to me at school. He delighted in calling out at quiet moments: 'Doesn't dung cling!' Other names may hint at a more pleasant illustration, particularly if it is the bearer of the name who is thinking about it. We tend to play unkind games with other people's names rather than our own. I am reminded of the entry in a parish register by the sexton who dug a grave for a Mr **Button**. He wrote simply: 'To making one button hole: 4s 6d.'

Other name games

Some names translate well into other languages. Joe Green, for example, looks altogether better as Giuseppe Verdi. My former colleague René **Quinault** becomes Mr **Cinema** in Germany, where they pronounce his name as *Kino.* In a vaguely similar way, a Greek friend tells me that shifting the stress on his surname, **Melas,** changes him from Mr **Black** to Mr **Honey.** I can think of no English names that would change their meaning so drastically by an altered pronunciation, but some could perhaps be improved in sound. With some English surnames different families do in fact make use of different pronunciations.

There are those who are greatly offended by what they consider to be a mispronunciation of their name, and even more so by a misspelling. Several correspondents of mine have a more light-hearted approach. They keep a little notebook in which they collect variations of their own name. Their enthusiastic greeting of yet another form takes away all traces of irritation. One can go further and deliberately pun on one's own name. In the past many families did this when they adopted mottoes. The **Manns,** for example, adopted the phrase *Homo sum,* 'I am a man', and the *Festina lente,* 'hasten slowly', of the **Onslow** family is well known.

Another name game of a sort is to compile what might be called a 'name file'. The idea is to collect together all the information one can about one's own surname, including details of other people who have borne the name. Biographical dictionaries and encyclopedias can be consulted, but if no one famous has found his way into the reference books it may be necessary to write around to namesakes mentioned in telephone and other directories. There are those who claim to be the unique bearers of a particular surname, but this rarely turns out to be true when one looks into the matter. A name file, then, is a 'clan scrapbook' in a sense. It makes an interesting

A correspondent in Oxford draws my attention to a kind of name game that was first used in the education of Jewish children. It can be adapted from Hebrew to English, and consists of finding a personal text in the scriptures. Such a text must begin with the first letter of one's name, and end with its last letter. The other letters of the name should be included in the text, preferably in order.

For her own name my correspondent cited a verse in Psalm 51 (in the American Prayer Book version): '*C*reate in me a clean *heart*, O God, and renew a *r*ight spirit withi*n* m*e*.' This seems to link well with the original meaning of **Catherine,** 'pure'.

For **Leslie** the Authorised Version yields: '*L*ord, my h*e*art i*s* not haughty, nor mine eyes *l*ofty: ne*i*ther do I exercise myself in great matters, or in things too high for m*e*.' I am happy to accept that, with all modesty, as my own personal text.

personal name project and may suggest something to educationists for classroom work.

There is a slight connection between the 'name file' idea and the Jim Smith Society, which we mentioned previously. Membership of that band is obviously open to all Jim Smiths, and for a fortunate few entry into another happy band may be possible. This is the 'My Name Is A Poem Club', open to those who have names like **Jane Cane, Newton Hooton** and **Nancy Clancy**. The president of the club, according to latest information, is **Hugh Blue**. Such names might be described as collectors' items, for there are many people around who do collect unusual names, eagerly noting those that appear in newspaper reports and the like.

A great collector of the past was N. I. Bowditch, who published his *Suffolk Surnames* in 1858, and an edition seven times larger in 1861. The latter contains a very large number of unusual names that were to be found in America, especially Suffolk County, at the time. Bowditch rarely gives the origin of the names, but strings anecdotes together in a fast and furious way. One moment he is recounting how **Ottiwell Wood** spelt out his name ('*O* double *t*, *i* double *u*, *e* double *l*, double *u*, double *o*, *d*'), and immediately he remarks on the confusion of the sexes in Mr **Maddam**, Mr **Shee** and the like.

More recently we have had the published collections of John Train, in *Remarkable Names of Real People* and *Even More Remarkable Names of Real People*. Mr Train scored by adding a line or two about the persons named: **Chief (Clayton) Crook** is a police chief in Ohio, **Wong Bong Fong** lives in Hong Kong, **Mr Vice**, of New Orleans, has been arrested 890 times and convicted on 421 occasions.

In a sense, autograph hunting is a collection of unusual names. Children can also enjoy collecting what I call nymographs. The object is to collect the signatures of people who bear as many different first names as possible. Only one signature per name is needed, but if one does happen to meet famous people, their signatures can be substituted for the more ordinary bearers of the same first names. The advantage of nymograph rather than autograph collecting is that one can start immediately, and every person met is a potential contributor.

Name pieces

Amongst those who do collect names, many are tempted to make humorous use of them in literary pieces. These may take the form of short stories or

poems, and a few examples will quickly make the point. A. A. Willis, for example, who used to write for *Punch* as 'A.A.', showed what a really clever writer could do with place names. In the middle of a longer article on the subject which appeared in *Punch* in October 1936, the following occurs:

'By way of light relief from cold classification, I have also compiled from village names a little modern romance. It is a love story of **Harold Wood** (Essex) and **Daisy Hill** (Lancashire), **Loversall** (Yorkshire) with **Pettings** (Kent). Follows naturally **Church** (Westmorland) with **Ring O' Bells** (Lancashire) for the **Bride** (Isle of Man). **Honeymoor** (Herefordshire) is obviously a honeymoon cut short—no doubt because the **New House** (Sussex) was **Fulready** (Warwickshire). Follows even more naturally **Nursling** (Hampshire) with **Cradle End** (Hertfordshire) and **Bapchild** (Kent). After a while Harold, being already very **Clubworthy** (Devon), takes to **Club Moor** (Lancashire), so he and Daisy begin to **Bicker** (Lincolnshire) and even **Wrangle** (also Lincolnshire), and are soon at **Loggerheads** (Staffordshire). She is thus left to her own **Devizes** (Wiltshire) with the result that there presently appears **Bill Brook** (Staffordshire), a **Lover** (Wiltshire) for her to **Skipwith** (Yorkshire). This should be the **Finish** (Ireland), but as I don't play with Irish names and anyway it's a modern romance, Harold treats this as a **Cause** (Shropshire) for Divorce (which unfortunately I **Havant** (Hampshire) been able to find anywhere), and all three end up in **Court** (Somerset).'

Miss Muriel Smith has made use of her extensive knowledge of apple names to compose a similar story incorporating them. In the full version Miss Smith managed to build in no less than 365 different names. The story begins as follows:

'**Mrs Toogood**, whose daughter **Alice** was a **Little Beauty**, but rather a **Coquette**, despaired of ever seeing a **Golden/Ring** on the **Lady's Finger**, although she had been **Queen** of the **May, Dainty** as a **Fairy**, with **Brown Eyes, Golden Cluster** of curls, **Pink Cheek, Sweet** expression (her **Family** called her **Smiler**) and had roused **Great Expectations** when she was a **Pretty Maid** of **Three Years Old**, a mere **Baby**, not out of the **Nursery**.'

In Miss Smith's epic, Alice eventually elopes with **Shannon**, an **Irish Giant**. Another rousing tale, based on the names of moths and assembled by

Pauline Quemby, traces the adventures of **Grisette**, a **Small Quaker**, who is saved by a **Cosmopolitan** gentleman from the **False Mocha**. The highlight of this story occurs when a **Scarce Dagger** is plunged into Mocha's heart, causing his blood to flow out in a **Small Rivulet**. The landlord of the inn where this takes place then exclaims: 'Look what tha's done to ma **Ruddy Carpet**.'

Names in verse

From such compositions it is but a short step to writing verses about names. Even great poets like Pope, for instance, could dash off a piece in a lighter moment about a name. In his case he chose to theorise about the name of the **Kit-Cat** Club:

> Whence deathless **Kit-Cat** took its name
> Few critics can unriddle;
> Some say from Pastry Cook it came,
> And some from **Cat and Fiddle** . . .

Pope goes on to give an explanation of the name that is more obscure than the name itself, which derives from Christopher **(Kit) Catling**, the keeper of the pie-house where the Club originally met.

In a similarly relaxed moment, Dryden played with his cousin's surname, **Creed**. After a discussion one evening about the origin of names he is said to have composed the following lines spontaneously:

> So much religion in your name doth dwell
> Your soul must needs with piety excel.
> Thus names, like well-wrought pictures drawn of old,
> Their owners' natures and their story told.
> Your name but half expresses, for in you
> Belief and practice do together go.
> My prayers shall be, while this short life endures,
> These may go hand in hand, with you and yours;
> Till faith hereafter is in vision drowned,
> And practice is with endless glory crowned.

By the 19th century James Smith was able to take up this theme of names and natures in his *Comic Miscellanies* and say that 'surnames seem given by the rule of contraries'. Sample verses from his long poem will illustrate his theme:

> Mr **Child**, in a passion, knock'd down **Mr Rock**,
> Mr **Stone** like an aspen-leaf shivers;
> Miss **Poole** used to dance, but she stands like a stock,
> Ever since she became Mrs **Rivers**.

> Mr **Swift** hobbles onward, no mortal knows how,
> He moves as though cords had entwined him,
> Mr **Metcalfe** ran off, upon meeting a cow,
> With pale Mr **Turnbull** behind him.
> Mr **Barker's** as mute as a fish in the sea,
> Mr **Miles** never moves on a journey,
> Mr **Gotobed** sits up till half after three,
> Mr **Makepiece** was bred an attorney.
> Mr **Gardener** can't tell a flower from a root.
> Mr **Wilde** with timidity draws back,
> Mr **Ryder** performs all his journeys on foot,
> Mr **Foote** all his journeys on horseback.

Smith turned his attention to a variety of name topics, not to mention allied subjects such as heraldry. He makes his contribution to the large body of poems about pub names, and is one of the very few writers I can think of who has tackled street names. Once again he was concerned with misnomers, this time of London streets:

> From Park Land to Wapping, by day and by night,
> I've many a year been a roamer,
> And find that no lawyer can London indict,
> Each street, ev'ry lane's a misnomer.
> I find **Broad Street**, St Giles's, a poor narrow nook,
> **Battle Bridge** is unconscious of slaughter,
> **Duke's Place** cannot muster the ghost of a duke,
> And **Brook Street** is wanting in water.

Several more verses follow in a similar vein, and Smith does have the grace to admit that, even if he has proved 'That London's one mighty mis-nomer' it is in 'verse not quite equal to Homer'.

Name jokes

Jokes and minor anecdotes based on names have been circulating for a very long time, as William Camden once again makes clear. His *Remains Concerning Britain* contains a whole chapter on name puns, and in this we learn that the Romans, for instance, jokingly changed the name of **Tiberius Nero** because of his drinking habits. They made him **Biberius Mero**, or a 'mere imbiber' if one uses 'mere' in its early sense of undiluted wine. Camden also quotes the famous joke about the Angles ('not Angles but Angels'), which must be almost as well known as 'Thou art **Peter** [which means 'stone' or 'rock'] and upon this rock I will build my church.' Before this the Apostle had been called **Cephas**, the

Aramaic equivalent of 'rock', though his real name was Simon.

Archie Armstrong wrote at roughly the same time as Camden, in the early 17th century, but he was far less learned in his *Banquet of Jests and Merry Tales*. His name jokes are not the kind to raise even a smile today, though he was popular at the time. A typical Armstrong joke is about the demand that was current in certain quarters to change Christmas to Christ-tide in order to avoid the Catholic reference to 'mass'. **Thomas**, Archie says, and one can almost feel him holding his sides, is worried in case he has to become **Thomside**. One anecdote in the book does provide additional evidence, if any were needed, about the badly painted name boards that were displayed in 17th-century

streets. On a board which had been taken to be a monster, Armstrong says that it is a sign that the painter was an ass.

By the 19th century the standard of name joke had improved somewhat. Bowditch writes of a doctor who, when he learnt that a Mr **Vowell** had just died, instantly remarked that he 'was glad it wasn't *u* or *i*'.

In modern times the best witticisms are probably to be found in the names themselves rather than in anecdotes about them. Personally, I still enjoy coming across a retired teacher of mathematics who is living in a house called **After Math**, and learning that there is a book on chess called *Pawnography*. Surely that is the way the names game should really be played?

Anagrams

A true anagram should use all the letters of one's full name once only, eg William Shakespeare gives 'We all make his praise', Margaret Thatcher gives 'that great charmer'. First names often have their own anagrams, however. In the 17th century the words

derived from the names would probably have been thought to give clues to the characters of the name-bearers. Some examples are given below. Names are in bold type and anagrams follow.

Abel able, bale
Adrian radian
Agnes geans
Aidan naiad
Alan anal
Alban banal
Alberta ratable
Aldred ladder
Alec lace
Alfred flared
Algernon non-glare
Alister realist, saltier
Alma lama
Almeric claimer, miracle, reclaim
Alvin anvil
Amy may, yam
Andrew dawner, wander, warden, warned
Anna nana
Annie inane
Astrid triads
Avis visa
Bella be-all, label
Bernard brander
Bertha bather, breath
Betsy bytes
Blake bleak
Boris biros

Brenda bander
Brian bairn, brain
Bridie birdie
Caleb cable
Candide candied
Carlos carols, corals
Carmel calmer
Carole oracle
Caroline acrolein
Cary racy
Cathy yacht
Catrine certain
Charles larches
Chester retches
Claire éclair, lacier
Clare clear
Claud ducal
Clea lace
Cleo cole
Clio coil
Cornelia creolian
Cornelius reclusion
Cressida sidecars
Cyril lyric
Dai aid
Damien maiden, median
Damon nomad
Dane dean

Daniel lead-in, nailed
Darien rained
Dave veda
Dean Dane
Deirdre ridered
Delia ailed, ideal
Della ladle
Denis dines, snide
Dennis sinned
Diana naiad
Dodie diode
Don nod
Dora road
Dorian ordain, inroad
Earl real
Edna dean
Edward warded
Edwin widen, wined
Electra treacle
Elias aisle
Ellis lisle
Elmira mailer
Elsa seal, sale
Elvis evils, lives, veils
Emil lime, mile
Eric rice
Erin rein
Ernest enters, nester, resent, tenser

Ernestine internees
Esther threes
Evan nave, vane
Evelyn evenly
Ewan anew, wane, wean
Ezra raze
Freda fared
Freya faery
Geraint granite, ingrate, tearing
Gerald glared
Geraldine realigned
Gerard grader, regard
Gerda grade, raged
Gina gain
Glenda angled, dangle
Glynis singly
Graeme meagre
Greta great
Hester threes
Horst short
Hortensia senhorita
Ida aid
Ifan fain, naif
Isla ails, sail
Isolde soiled
Israel sailer, serial
Ivan vain
Karl lark
Kay yak
Laban banal
Lana anal
Lance clean
Laura aural
Laurel allure
Leah hale, heal
Leander learned
Lena lean
Leon lone
Lewis wiles
Lil ill
Lisa ails, sail

Lissa sails
Lloyd dolly
Lois oils, soil
Lorena loaner
Loretta retotal
Lothar harlot
Lucian uncial
Luther hurtle
Lydia daily
Mabel amble, blame
Marian airman, marina
Marianne Armenian
Marina airman
Marlon normal
Mary army
May yam
Medusa amused
Meg gem
Megan mange
Melissa aimless
Miles limes, slime, smile
Mina main
Mirabel balmier
Moira Maori
Mona moan
Morna manor
Munro mourn
Nancy canny
Nat ant, tan
Ned den, end
Neil line, Nile
Nigel ingle
Noel lone
Nora roan
Norma manor, Roman
Oberon Borneo
Olaf foal, loaf
Olga gaol, goal
Omar roam
Osbert sorbet

Otto toot
Pat apt, tap
Patsy pasty
Pearl paler
Pedro doper, roped
Perseus peruses
Petra pater, prate, taper
Rab bar, bra
Regan anger, range
Rhoda hoard
Rocky corky
Rodney yonder
Rosa oars, soar
Rosalind ordinals
Rose Eros, roes, sore
Rosetta rotates, toaster
Ruby bury
Ruth hurt
Sadie aside, ideas, aides
Seamus amuses, assume
Selina aliens, saline
Selma lames, males, meals
Seward waders
Silas sails, sisal
Simeon monies
Simone monies
Sorel loser, roles
Stan ants, tans
Sterling ringlets, tinglers
Steven events
Stewart swatter
Susie issue
Tabitha habitat
Teresa Easter, eaters, reseat, teaser
Tessa sates, seats
Thelma hamlet
Theresa heaters, reheats
Vera rave, aver
Vida avid
Zelda lazed

At a tavern one night
Messrs Moore, Strange and Wright
Met to drink, and their good thoughts
exchange;
Says Moore, 'Of us three
Everyone will agree
There's only one fool, and that's
Strange.'

Says Strange, rather sore,
'I'm sure there's one Moore,
A most terrible knave, and a fright,
Who cheated his mother,
His sister and brother . . .'
'Oh, yes,' replied Moore, 'that is Wright.'

Anon

A page from a name collector's notebook

The names below were collected by the late George F. Hubbard of New York. All are or were borne by real people.

Henrietta Addition
Cyretha Adshade
Nancy Ancey
Etta Apple
Oscar Asparagus
Orville Awe
Sterling Blazy
Duckworth Byrd
George A. Canary
Columbus Cohen
May Day
Richard Dinners
Upson Downs
Mark Rile Dull
Loveless Eary
Luscious Easter
Lilley Easy
Ireland England
Alice Everyday
Remington P. Fairlamb
Wanda Farr
Thaddeus Figlock
Charmaine Fretwell
Courter Shannon Fryrear
Yetta Gang
Bess Goddykoontz
Henry Honeychurch Gorringe
Gussie Greengrass
Tommy Gunn
Thomas Hailstones
Ima Hogg
Arabelle Hong
Louise Hospital
Rutgers I. Hurry
Mel Manny Immergut
Inez Innes
Melvin Intriligator
Chester Irony
Lizzie Izabichie
Hannah Isabell Jelly
Watermelon Johnson
Amazing Grace Jones
Boisfeuillet Jones
Halo Jones
Pinkbloom Jones
Love Joy
Pleasant Kidd
Maude Kissin
Rosella Kellyhouse Klink
Zeno Klinker
Royal Knights
Bent Korner

Michael Leftoff
Joan Longnecker
Logwell Lurvey
Hunt A. Lusk
Sistine Madonna McClung
Raven McDavid
Pictorial McEvoy
Mussolini McGee
Spanish McGee
Phoebe McKeeby
Miriam Mates
Marybelle Merryweather
Lilla Mews
James Middlemiss
Maid Marion Montgomery
Malcolm Moos
Seeley Wintersmith Mudd
Harriet Bigelow Neithercut
Savage Nettles
Olney W. Nicewonger
Penny Nichols
Melvin Mackenzie Noseworthy
Louise Noun
Belle Nuddle
Fluid Nunn
June Moon Olives
Ichabod Onion
Memory Orange
Ada Garland Outhouse
Freelove Outhouse
Zoltan Ovary
Mollie Panter-Downes
Sirjohn Papageorge
Hector Piazza
Human Piper
Penelope Plum
Omar Shakespeare Pound
Alto Quack
Florence A. Quaintance
Nellie Quartermouth
Alberta Lachicotte Quattlebaum
Pearline Queen

Flora Rose Quick
Freeze Quick
John B. Quick
Wanton Rideout
Pius Riffle
Harry Rockmaker
Sarepta Rockstool
Dewey Rose
Rose Rose
Violla Rubber
Little Green Russian
Louis Shady
Laurence Sickman
Bess Sinks
Ester Slobody
Adelina Sloog
G. E. Kidder Smith
Sory Smith
Burt Softness
Minnie Starlight
Sally Sunshine
Daily Swindle
Rose Throne
Yelberton Abraham Tittle
Milton Trueheart
Thomas Turned
Britus Twitty
Nell Upole
Albertina Unsold
Viola Unstrung
Sue Verb
Pleasant Vice
Carrington Visor
Melvin Vowels
Burson Wynkoop
Thereon Yawn
Herbert Yells
Romeo Yench
Berma Yerkey
Homer Yook
Ida Yu
April Zipes

The 'Joe Green phenonemon' occurs when names are translated, losing something of their mystique in the process. The Giuseppe Verdi—Joe Green example is well-known: Casanova, Einstein, Racine and Stalin fare little better as Newhouse, Onestone, Root and Steel.

Surname Groups

Names can be collected in other ways. In the *Book of Smith*, for instance, Elsdon C. Smith published his impressive collection of -smith surnames. The following are a small selection:

Ainsmith	Boltsmith	Highsmith
Aldersmith	Bowsmith	Hoopersmith
Allinsmith	Brooksmith	Joysmith
Anchorsmith	Brownsmith	Knifesmith
Armsmith	Bucklesmith	Locksmith
Arrowsmith	Clocksmith	Naesmith
Axsmith	Coopersmith	Platesmith
Balismith	Coppersmith	Sharesmith
Barretsmith	Fieldsmith	Shoesmith
Bauersmith	Finesmith	Silversmith
Bellsmith	Fostersmith	Sixsmith
Billsmith	Garnersmith	Tinsmith
Blacksmith	Gildsmith	Whitesmith
Bladesmith	Goldsmith	Wildsmith
Bocksmith	Greensmith	Youngsmith

Another collector of surnames was C. L. Lordan. In the 19th century he published his curious booklet: *Of Certain English Surnames And Their Occasional Odd Phases When Seen In Groups*. After a lyrical Introduction in praise of directories, he gave a long list of the -man surnames he had unearthed, which included the interesting . . .

Acreman	Boothman	Doleman
Aleman	Bootyman	Dollman
Allman	Bonnyman	Duckman
Ambleman	Borrowman	Eastman
Ampleman	Bowman	Fairman
Angleman	Brickman	Fatman
Ashman	Brightman	Ferryman
Badman	Buckman	Fitman
Bandman	Bussman	Flatman
Bannerman	Carman	Footman
Barleyman	Cashman	Foreman
Beachman	Castleman	Fortyman
Beatman	Chapman	Freeman
Beautyman	Cloudman	Gasman
Beeman	Cloutman	Ginman
Bellman	Coldman	Goatman
Berryman	Coleman	Goodman
Bigman	Cotman	Gutman
Blackman	Couchman	Gutterman
Blankman	Crossman	Hackman
Bleakman	Dayman	Halfman
Blythman	Deadman	Hardman
Bodman	Dearman	Headman
Bogman	Dickman	Hellman
Boorman	Dishman	Henchman

Heman	Masterman	Slyman
Hillman	Meatman	Smallman
Holeman	Merriman	Snowman
Hollowman	Newman	Spademan
Hollyman	Norman	Strangeman
Homiman	Oldman	Swearman
Honeyman	Overman	Sugarman
Hoofman	Pennyman	Truman
Horniman	Pieman	Twentyman
Houseman	Poorman	Twoman
Hugman	Potman	Wagman
Illman	Prettyman	Walkman
Ironman	Proudman	Warman
Jarman	Pullman	Wellman
Jollyman	Quarterman	Whatman
Kingsman	Redman	Whenman
Lackman	Richman	Wildman
Ladyman	Rugman	Wineman
Laidman	Sackman	Woodman
Lawman	Sandman	Workman
Longman	Sellerman	Yeoman
Loveman	Sickman	Youngman
Lowman	Silliman	
Maryman	Slowman	

Those who enjoy making this kind of collection might make a start with surnames ending in -son, -land, -house, -ton, -field, -wood, -well and -ing.

As for Lordan, his main interest really lay in grouping surnames thematically. The 'Money' surnames he had unearthed included Crown, Dollar, Ducat, Farthing, Florin, Guinea, Halfpenny, Mark, Noble, Penny, Pound, Shilling, Tenpenny, Twentymark and Twopenny, as well as the more general Argent, Bullion, Cash, Lucre, Mammon, Money, Price, Riches and Treasure. Under 'Love' he listed Catchlove, Cutlove, Dearlove, Freelove, Fullolove, Love, Loveband, Lovechild, Loveday, Lovefit, Lovegood, Lovegrove, Lovejoy, Lovekin, Lovelace, Loveladd, Lovelady, Loveless, Lovelock, Lovely, Loveman, Lover, Loverage, Lovering, Lovewell, Loveys, Manlove, Marklove, Menlove, Newlove, Proudlove, Spendlove, Sweatlove, Sweetlove, Truelove, Wellbeloved. To these he added Hymen, Marriage, Marry, Wedd, Wedlock.

Perhaps Lordan's most ingenious group of surnames were those he classified as 'Imperative Verbs'. He had managed to find over 150 examples, allowing himself a little licence in the spelling. Thus, along with such obvious names as Dare, Read and Waddle he included Wherritt, Sitwell and Shuffell.

It is clear that Mr Lordan's hobby provided him with a great deal of innocent fun. The nearest telephone directory awaits those who would like to try it for themselves.

Hairy Names

In *Buried Treasure*, a story by P. G. Wodehouse, two men who are rivals at moustache-growing name their own moustaches. Wodehouse compares them to 'ancient heroes bestowing names on their favourite swords'. There may be men in real life who give an individual name to a moustache or beard: one suspects that there are far more who do not realise that their facial growth already has a name. Different beard and moustache *styles* have been identified since at least the 17th century. A knowledgeable modern moustache-spotter, therefore, could distinguish between a *Box car, Captain, Chevron, Colman, Consort, Eleven-a-side, General, Guardsman, Handlebar, Horseshoe, Kaiser, Major, Mephistopholes, Mexican, Military, Mistletoe, Old Bill, Painter's brush, Pencil line, Pyramidal, Sergeant-major, Soup strainer, Toothbrush, Walrus, Wing* and *Zapata*.

Beards and side-whiskers have received an even wider range of names. Modern beards tend to be boringly unimaginative: our ancestors were able to observe a passing parade of beard-styles with names like *Anchor, Artillery, Assyrian, Aureole, Balbo, Bodkin, Breakwater, Burnsides, Cads, Captain Kettle set, Cathedral, Ducktail, Dundrearies, Forked, Full, Goatee, Half, Hammer cut, Imperial, Ladykillers, Lavatory brush, Marquisotte, Masonic, Miner's, Mutton chops, Napoleon III, Needle, Neptunian, Old Dutch, Olympian, Parted, Pencil, Piccadilly weepers, Pique-devant, Pisa, Polar beaver, Rimmers, Roman T, Royale, Saucer, Screw, Shenandoah, Sideburns, Spade, Square-cut, Stiletto, Sugar loaf, Swallow tail, Tile, Tyburn collar, Uncle Sam* and *Vandyke*.

All the above are illustrated and discussed in detail in the *Guinness Book of Beards and Moustaches*, by Leslie Dunkling and John Foley. The book contains many ideas for men who would like their faces to look more interesting: other readers should enjoy the hilarious social history of male 'face-fittings'.

Surname Puns

Mark Anthony Lower, in his *Essay on Family Nomenclature*, 4th edition, 1875, has a chapter on surname puns which includes the following:

AIRE
In St Giles's Church, Cripplegate, on the tomb of Mr Aire:
Methinks this was a wondrous death,
That Aire should die for want of breath!

BERRY
An epitaph on Mr John Berry:
  How! how! who's buried here?
  JOHN BERRY: Is't the younger?
  No, it is the *elder*-Berry.
  An elder-Berry *buried* surely
    must
  Rather spring up and live than
    turn to dust:
  So may our Berry, whom stern
    Death hath slain,
  Be only *buried* to rise up again.

BUTTON
A sexton's bill for digging the grave of Miles Button: 'To making a *Button-hole*, 4s. 6d.'

This Mr Button was the subject of an extended witticism after his death. Local wags were fond of asking which grave was the deepest, longest and broadest in the churchyard while yet being the smallest. The answer was: the grave of Miles Button. It had Miles below, was Miles in length and breadth, yet was still only a button-hole.

EKINS
The godfathers of one Jeremiah Ekins were James Nott and John Butt, after whom he was baptized with both their Christian and surnames. The effect of his name is very singular: James Nott John Butt Jeremiah Ekins.

GUNN
A certain Alexander Gunn was dismissed from his post at the custom-house in Edinburgh. This was duly recorded in official records as: 'A. Gunn was discharged for making a false report.'

HOGG
Sir Nicholas Bacon was one day trying a criminal, one Hogg, who asked the learned judge to spare his life, on account of his kindred to him—'because my name is Hogg and your lordship's is Bacon.' The judge pointed out that 'Hog is not bacon until it be well hanged.'

LETTSOM
An 18th-century physician used to sign his name as I. Lettsom. One of his waggish patients therefore composed the following:
  When any patient calls in haste,
  I physics, bleeds, and sweats 'em;
  If after that they choose to die,
  Why, what cares I?
                    I. Lettsom

Further Reading

Since the original publication of this book the author has expanded on some of the topics it raises in the following:

First Names First (history, sociology and psychology of first names) Dent/Universe 1977, Gale Research 1982

Dictionary of First Names (with William Gosling), Dent/Facts on File, 1983; Signet 1985; 4th edition Dent, 1994

Our Secret Names (onomancy and the interpretation of names) Sidgwick & Jackson, 1981; Prentice-Hall 1982

Name Your Baby, Faber and Faber, 2nd edition, 1994

Scottish Christian Names, Johnston and Bacon, 2nd edition 1988

Dictionary of Pub Names (with Gordon Wright), Routledge & Kegan Paul 1987, (paperback) Dent 1994

Dictionary of Days Routledge/Facts on File, 1988

Dictionary of Epithets and Terms of Address Routledge, 1990

The following books usefully deal with various aspects of names:

Algeo, John *On Defining the Proper Name*, University of Florida, 1973

Bebbington, Gillian *London Street Names*, Batsford, 1972

Camden, William *Remains Concerning Britain* (17th century comments on personal names), reprinted E.P. Publishing, 1974

Casserley, H.C. *British Locomotive Names of the 20th Century*, Ian Allan, 1967

Chichley Plowden, C. *A Manual of Plant Names*, Allen & Unwin, 1972

Cottle, Basil *The Penguin Dictionary of Surnames*, Penguin, 1967

Darton, Mike *The Dictionary of Scottish Place Names*, Lochar Publishing, 1990

Dickson, Paul *Names*, Delacorte Press, 1986

Disraeli, Isaac *Curiosities of Literature* (includes essays on various name topics), Moxon, 1849

Dynes, Cecily *The Great Australian and New Zealand Book of Baby Names*, Angus & Robertson, 1984

Ekwall, Eilert *English River Names*, OUP, 1968

Evans, Cleveland Kent *Unusual and Most Popular Baby Names*, Publications International, 1991

Field, John *English Field Names*, David & Charles, 1972

Field, John *Place Names of Great Britain and Ireland*, David & Charles, 1980

Freeman, William *Dictionary of Fictional Characters*, Dent, 1967

Guppy, Henry B. *Homes of Family Names in Great Britain*, Harrison, 1980

Hanks, Patrick & Hodges, Flavia *Dictionary of First Names*, OUP, 1990

Hanks, Patrick & Hodges, Flavia *Dictionary of Surnames*, OUP, 1988

Harder, Kelsie B. *Illustrated Dictionary of Place Names*, Van Nostrand Reinhold, 1976

Kennedy, Don *Ship Names*, University Press of Virginia, 1964

Lawson, Edwin D. *Personal Names and Naming* (a bibliography), Greenwood Press, 1987

Mills, A.D. *Dictionary of English Place-Names*, OUP, 1991

Odelain, O. & Ségineau, R. *Dictionary of Proper Names and Places in the Bible*, Robert Hale, 1982

Payton, Geoffrey *Payton's Proper Names*, Warne, 1969

Pringle, David *Imaginary People*, (fictional characters), Grafton Books, 1987

Rees, Nigel & Noble, Vernon *A Who's Who of Nicknames*, George Allen & Unwin, 1985

Room, Adrian *Dictionary of Coin Names*, Routledge & Kegan Paul, 1987

Room, Adrian *Place Names of the World*, David & Charles, 1974

Room, Adrian *Dictionary of Trade Name Origins*, Routledge & Kegan Paul, 1982

Room, Adrian *Dictionary of Astronomical Names*, Routledge, 1988

Smith, Elsdon C. *Personal Names - A Bibliography*, Gale 1965

Smith, Elsdon C. *Treasury of Name Lore*, Harper & Row, 1967

Smith, Muriel *National Apple Register of the United Kingdom*, Ministry of Agriculture & Food, 1971

Stewart, George R. *Names on the Land*, Houghton Mifflin, 1967

Stewart, George R. *American Place Names*, OUP, 1970

The publications of the English Place Name Society provide detailed information about English place names. They also give a great deal of incidental information about early forms of surnames.

Names Index

A 89
Aa 141
Aab 141
Aablaster 141
Aackerman 141
Aafers 141
Aal 141
Aanensen 141
Aansell 141
Aargan 141
Aarkins 141
Aaron 21, 31, 43, 45, 47, 48, 50, 55, 57, 141
Abbas 112
Abbey 36, 55, 92
Abbie 36, 57
Abbinett 135
Abbs 136
Abd al-Basit 111
Abd al-Haqq 111
Abdul 111
Abdullah 112
Abel 35
Abenaa 114
Aberdeenshire 173
Abiel 35
Abigail 25, 36, 43, 52, 57, 79, 91-2, 102
Abir 112
Abishag 43
Abner 35
ABORIGINAL PLACE NAMES 165
Abraham 35, 43, 47, 49, 57, 106, 255
Absalom 35
Abuza 149
Accord 182
Achilles 99
Achurch 135
Acreman 256
Acres 135
Acton 133, 143
Ad 99
Ada 36, 51, 53, 57, 255
Adah 42
Adair 34
Adam 21, 25, 31, 43, 47-8, 50, 55, 57, 90, 117, 124, 138
Adams 124, 141, 162
Adamson 124, 138
Adarene 99
Adcock 124
Addems 134
Addis Ababa 186
Addison 124
Addition 255
ADDRESS, TERMS OF 29
Addy 124, 137
Adela 36, 43, 57
Adelaide 36, 57
Adele 36, 57
Adelina 36, 255
Adeline 36
Adelle 36, 57
Aditya 110
Adkins 124
Adlard 125
Adlai 35
Adlestrop 176
Admiral 22
Adnams 133
Adney 99
Adnil 91
Adolf 82
Adolph 89
Adrian 31, 48, 55, 57
Adrienne 36, 57
Adshade 255
Adshead 133

Adwoa 114
Aelfred 82
Afghanistan 183
Afra 112
AFRICAN GIVEN NAMES 114
Afua 115
Afy 100
Agar 137
Agatha 25, 90, 124
Agg 46
Aggass 124
Aglaia 96
Agnes 21, 25, 36, 43, 46, 51, 53, 57, 83, 90, 91, 99, 116, 124, 167
Agneta 36
Agnew 127
Agnew 142
Ah San 109
Ah Si 109
Ahab 35
Aherne 127
Ahimaaz 91
Ahmet 117
Aholibamah 43
Aidan 31, 34, 57
Aiden 57
Ailbhe 31
Aileen 41, 57
Ailsa 42
Aim 46
Aimee 36, 57
Aine 41
Ainsmith 256
Aire 257
Airedale 19
Aisha 41, 112
Aisling 41
Aitchison 138
Aitken 124, 138
Aitkins 124
Ajax 99
Ajit 110
Akbar 112
Akehurst 137
Akers 136
Akiko 109
Akira 109
Akosua 114
Akram 112
Akua 114
Al 21
Alabama 184
Alan 31, 43, 47, 48-9, 50, 55, 57, 124
Alana 36, 42, 55, 57
Alannah 146
Alasdair 34
Alaska 184
Alastair 27, 31, 57
Albach-Retty 149
Albericus 178
Albert 31, 47-9, 57, 93
Alberta 255
Albertina 255
Alberto 104
Albutt 137
Alcock 124
Alden 141
Alder 136
Aldermanbury 169
Aldersmith 256
Alderton 141
Aldo 117
Aldous 137
Aldworth 136
Alec 31, 57
Aled 35
Aleman 256
Alessandra 117
Alex 31, 57
Alexander 31, 45, 47-9, 50, 55, 57, 96, 116, 124, 138, 142

Alexanderina 89
Alexandra 36, 52, 54-5, 57, 79, 93
Alexandru 117
Alexey 117
Alexia 36, 57
Alexina 42
Alexis 36, 54, 57, 116
Alf 21, 82, 96, 99
Alfie 31, 57
Alflatt 125
Alford 129, 134
Alfred 118, 31, 43, 47-9, 57, 90
Alfredo 117
Algar 43
Algeria 183
Algernon 25, 93, 96, 106
Algiers 183, 186
Ali 112
Alias 22
ALIASES 143
Alice 36, 43, 51-3, 55, 57, 88, 96, 255
Alicia 36, 54-5, 57
Alick 57
Alisha 36, 57
Alison 36, 52, 55, 57, 88
Alissa 36, 57
Alistair 27, 31, 48, 57
Alister 57
Alker 135
Allah 111
Allan 31, 57, 124, 136, 138, 141
Allanson 124
Allbones 131
Allbutt 137
Allcorn 137
Allcott 135
Allegra 99
Allen 124, 141
Allen 31, 49, 57
Allerton 141, 172
Alleyn 124
Allington 137
Allinsmith 256
Allinson 124
Allison 36, 54, 57
Allman 133, 256
Allnatt 125
Allwright 118
Allyson 57
Alma 26, 53, 58, 90
Almeric 99
Almond 22, 135
Alonzo 33
Alpha 22
ALPHABET MYSTICISM 245-49
Alphonso 33
Alpin 34
Alston 129, 137
Althea 58
Alto 255
Alton 134
Alty 135
Alun 35, 58
Alvah 35
Alvar 125
Alvarez 126
Alvaro 126
Alvin 33
Alwin 43, 125
Alwyn 58
Alyson 58
Alyssa 36, 54
Amabel 36
Amanda 21, 36, 52, 54-5, 58, 90
Amarjit 110
Amaryllis 104
Amaziah 43
Amazing 255

Amber 36, 45, 54, 58
Ambleman 256
Ambler 137
Ambreen 111
Ambrose 31, 58
Ambrosine 58
Amelia 21, 36, 51, 53, 58, 93
America 178
AMERICAN BOMBER NAMES 236
AMERICAN INDIAN GIVEN NAMES 113
AMERICAN INDIAN PLACE NAMES 165, 182
AMERICAN STATES, NAMES OF 184-5
AMERICAN SURNAMES 123
Americus 178
Amerigo 178
Amery 124, 134
Ames 21, 124
Amesbury 136
Amethyst 45
Amey 135
Amice 43, 124
Amies 124, 136
Amin 112
Aminah 112
Amis 124, 136
Amison 124
Amity 43
Amma 115
Amon 35
Amorous 22
Amos 35, 47, 58, 99
Amphlett 137
Ampleman 256
Amsterdam 186
Amy 25, 36, 46, 51-2, 54-5, 58, 89
Ana 117
Anagnostopoulos 142
Anaktuvuk Pass 183
Anand 110
Ananias 35, 91
Anastasia 36, 58
Anatole 96
Ancey 255
Anchor 22
Anchorsmith 256
Andante 99
Anders 117
Anderson 124, 138, 141
André 33, 50, 58
Andrea 36, 52, 54-5, 58
Andreas 116-7
Andrew 18, 31, 47-9, 50, 55, 58, 120, 124
Andrews 120, 124
Andrey 117
Andrzej 117
Angel 22
Angela 36, 52, 53, 54-5, 58, 103
Angeles 143
Angelica 96
Angelina 58
Angeline 58
Angharad 42, 58
Angleman 256
Anglesey 173
ANGLO-SAXON CLAN NAMES 168
ANGLO-SAXON PERSONAL NAMES 118, 125
ANGLO-SAXON

PLACE NAMES 169
ANGRIEST FIRST NAME 91
Anguish 131
Angus 4, 34, 55, 58, 83, 96, 173
Anika 36, 58
Anil 110
'ANIMAL' FIRST NAMES 45, 89
ANIMAL NAMES 230-1
Anita 21, 36, 58, 116
Ankara 19, 186
Ankers 133
Ann 21, 26-7, 36, 51-5, 58, 80, 84, 110
Ann-Marie 36, 58, 100
Anna 36, 51-2, 54, 58, 96, 116-7
Annabel 36, 58
Annabelle 36, 58, 99
Annable 136
Annamarie 58
Annamarie 58
Annapolis 179
Annarenia 86
Anne 26-7, 36, 52-5, 58, 88, 95-6, 110
Anne Marie 36, 53-4, 58
Annemarie 36, 58
Annette 36
Annett 136
Annette 58
Annice 36
Annie 21, 27, 46, 51, 53, 58, 96, 100
Anning 134
Annis 36, 58, 124
Annison 124
Annmarie 58
Annunciata 100
Anon 22
Anouska 58
Anson 124
Antell 134
Anthea 45, 58
Anthony 31, 47-9, 50, 55, 58, 93
Antigua 178
Antoine 33, 116
Antoinette 58
Antonia 42, 58
Antonin 117
Antônio 50, 117
Antony 31, 58
Antrim 173
Antwan 33, 50
Anu 116
Anwen 42
Anxious Bay 181
Anya 58
Anyan 135
Aoife 58
Ap Rhys 122
Apaminondas 44
Aphrodite 100
apHugh 152
Aplin 136
Apperley 135
Apple 22, 255
Applebachsville 182
Applegarth 134
APPLES, NAMES OF 9, 232-3
Appleyard 137
April 21, 36, 58, 85, 90, 255
Arabelle 255
Arawinda 113
Arch 137
Archer 130
Archibald 90, 96
Ardern 133
Argent 256

Argentina 183
Argyll 173
Aria 22
Ariel 35, 54
Aris 136
Aristides 44
Ariya 113
Ariyadasa 113
Ariyapala 113
Ariyaratna 113
Ariyasiri 113
Arizona 184
Arjuna 113
Ark 22
Arkansas 184
Arkell 134
Arkle 136
Arleena 100
Arlene 53, 58, 100
Arley 140
Arlott 132
Armagh 173
Armand 124
Arment 124
Armitage 137
Armsmith 256
Armstrong 119, 132, 138
Arnatt 136
Arney 136
Arni 116
Arnold 31, 33, 45, 58
Arran 34, 58
Arron 58
Arrow 22, 100, 170
Arrowsmith 130, 256
Arscott 134
Arthur 100
Arthur 138
Arthur 31, 47-9, 50, 55, 58, 89, 93
Arthurton 136
Arturo 117
Arty 21
Arub 112
Arun 110
Aruna 110
Arwel 35
Arwenna 42
Arwyn 35
Asa 35
Asanka 113
Ascunción 186
Ash 136
Ashby 129
Ashby-de-la-Zouch 139
Asher 35
Ashleigh 36, 52, 55, 58
Ashley 31, 48, 52, 54-5, 58, 82, 136
Ashman 136, 256
Ashraf 112
Ashton 58
Ashwell 135
Asia 54
Aslam 112
Asparagus 255
Aspinall 135
Aspinwall 135
Astaire 142
Astbury 133
Aston 133
Astra 90
Athaliah 42
Athens 19, 186
Atherton 135
Athol 34
Atkin 124
Atkins 124
Atkinson 124
Atthow 136
Attica 19
Attila 116
Attoe 136
Attrill 135

Aubrey 58
Audrey 36, 51-3, 58, 93, 100, 103, 118
Audubon 123
Augusta 168, 179
Augustine 43, 124
Aulay 34
Aurelia 45
Aurelie 116
Aurolyn 88
Aurora 90, 100
Austen 58, 124
Austerlitz 142
Austin 31, 50, 58, 124
Australia 183
Austria 183
Autumn 22, 36
Averay 125
Averil 59
Averill 136
Aves 137
Avis 43, 59
Avoca 180
Avon 170, 174
Avril 36, 59, 85, 90
Awdry 137
Awe 255
Awen 35
Axe 170
Axsmith 256
Ayana 41
Ayanna 41
Ayesha 41, 112
Ayles 135
Ayling 137
Aylmer 125
Aylwin 125, 137
Aymes 124
Aynsley 136
Ayrshire 173
Ayşe 117
Azariah 35
Azel 35
Azhar 112
Azile 91
Aziz 112, 151
Azizah 111
Azubah 42

Baba 113
Babbage 134
Babcock's Grove 183
Baber 136
Babi 113
Babiya 113
Baby 22
Bacchus 130
Back 136
Backer 130
Bacon 130
Baden 47
Badman 136, 256
Badnocks 172
Badr 112
Badrick 125
Bagg 136
Baghdad 186
Bagnall 136
Bahrain 183
Bailey 130
Baillie 138
Baird 138
Baker 130, 141, 149, 162
Bakewell 136
Bal 131
Balaam 35
Balaclava 19
Balász 116
Baldey 125
Baldry 137
Balfour 138
Baline 149
Balismith 256
Baljit 110

Balkwill 134
Ballam 134
Ballantyne 138
Ballard 132, 135
Ballinger 134
Balman 125, 134
Balmforth 137
Balsdon 134
Balston 125
Baluchistan 183
Bamber 135
Bamforth 137
Bandman 256
Bandula 113
Bane 127
Banffshire 173
Banfield 135
Bangkok 186
Banham 136
Banks 129
Bannerman 256
Banwell 136
Barabbas 35
Barak 35
Barbara 36, 43, 46, 51-5, 59, 96
Barber 130
Barbour 138
Barclay 138
Bardon 127
Barebone 89
Barfoot 135
Barford 136
Bargo Brush 182
Barham 137
Barış 117
Bark 134
Barker 130
Barleyman 256
Barling 135
Barnabas 31
Barnaby 31, 59
Barnsley 134
Barnstable 136
Barnum 123
Barr 138
Barraclough 137
Barretsmith 256
Barrie 59
Barrington 59, 136
Barrowcliff 136
Barry 21, 27, 31, 48, 55, 59, 93
Barryman 133
Bart 116
Bartholomew 35, 59, 124, 138
Bartle 124
Bartlet 124
Bartlett 124
Barton 129
Bartram 136
Baruch 35, 123
Barzillai 35
Basford 133
Basham 134
Bashir 112
Basil 31, 59, 90, 100
Basimah 112
Baskerville 133
Baskeyfield 136
Basnett 133
Bass 132
Basset 132
Bastable 134
Bastin 134
Bate 124
Bateman 124
Bater 134
Bates 124
Bateson 124
Bather 136
Batho 136
Bathsheba 42
Batkin 124, 136
Batt 124, 136
Battams 133
Batten 124
Batterham 136
Battersby 135
Battiest 180
Battle 181
Batts 136
Batty 124, 131, 137
Battye 137
Bauer 126
Bauersmith 256
Baughan 140

Baxter 130, 138
Bayliss 130
Bays 133
Bayya 113
Bazeley 136
Bazley 136
Be-Courteous 43
Bea 21
BEACH-HUT
    NAMES 215
Beachman 256
Beadle 134
Beak 137
Beales 136
Beanes 136
Beard Belcher 132
Beardall 136
Beardmore 136
BEARDS, NAMES
    OF 257
Beardsley 134
Beat 46
Beata 117
Beate 117
Beathag 42
Beatman 256
Beaton 124
Beatrix 36, 59
Beatrice 36, 46, 51, 53, 59, 95, 96, 100, 117, 124, 138
Beatrix 36, 59
Beattie 134, 138
Beatty 124, 142
Beaty 134, 142
Beauchamp 121
Beaulieu 170
Beaumont 170
Beaurepaire 177
Beautyman 256
Bebb 138
Bebbington 133
Bebi 113
Becher 35
Beck 136
Becky 36, 59
Beddall 134
Beddoes 136
Bedfordshire 133, 173
Bedloe 125
Bedworth 151
Beeby 134
Beecroft 136
Beedell 134
Beedle 149
Beeman 256
Beer 134, 162
Beet 124
Beeton 124
Beever 137
Beevers 137
Beevors 137
Begley 127
Behan 127
Beijing 186
Bela 35
Belcham 134
Belcher 145
Belfast 168
Belgium 183
Belgrave 170
Belgrove 133
Belinda 36, 55, 59
Bell 21, 132, 138, 138, 141, 143, 162
Bella 95
Bellairs 136
Bellamy 132
Bellars 136
Belle 53, 99, 255
Bellis 138
Bellman 256
Bellsmith 256
Belper 177
Belsey 135
Belteshazzar 43
Bemrose 135
Ben 21, 48, 59
Benbow 136
Bendall 137
Benedict 25, 31, 43, 59, 124
Benjamin 31, 43, 47-9, 55, 59, 79, 82, 96, 116
Benn 124
Bennett 124, 141, 162

Bennie 21, 33
Benning 133
Benny 133
Benson 124
Benstead 135
Bensted 135
Bent 135, 255
Bentall 134
Bentham 137
Bentley 129
Benton 129
Beornred 169
Berengaria 79
Berg 126
Berger 126
Berkshire 133, 173
Berma 255
Bernadette 36, 41, 59
Bernadine 97
Bernard 25, 31, 43, 47-9, 55, 59, 89, 90, 149
Bernice 42, 59, 89
Berridge 135
Berriman 133, 145
Berrow 135
Berry 22, 89, 257
Berryman 127, 256
Bert 59, 96
Bertha 51, 53, 59, 94-5
Bertie 31, 47, 59
Bertram 31, 47, 59
Berwickshire 173
Beryl 36, 43, 51-2, 59
Besent 134
Besley 134
Bess 21, 43, 255
Bessie 53, 90
Best 138
Beta 22
Beth 36, 43, 59
Bethan 42
Bethany 36, 59, 181
Bethell 124
Bethesda 180
Betsy 36, 51, 59, 93, 107
Bett 135
Better 138
Bettinson 136
Betty 25, 36, 43, 51-3, 59, 107
Beulah 43, 59
Bevan 4, 124, 127
Bevelina 93
Beverley 36, 52, 55, 59, 80
Beverly 21, 36, 53-4, 59, 80
Bevin 124
Bewick 136
Bewley 170
Beynon 138
Bianca 37, 45, 54-5, 59, 116
Biba 111
Bibby 124, 135
BIBLICAL FIRST
    NAMES 35, 42
BIBLICAL NAME,
    MOST
    FREQUENT 91
Bice 133
Bickford 136
Bickle 134
Bickle 149
Bicknell 136
Biddick 133
Biddle 134
Bigelow 255
Biggin 134
Biggs 132
Bigman 256
Bill 21, 59, 85, 89
Billington 141, 172
Billion 131
Billsmith 256
Billy 59
Billyard 136
Bing 21, 135
Binge 136
Bingley 136
Binning 136
Binns 137
Birch 146
Bird 162

Birgitta 117
Birgitte 117
Birtles 133
Bisdee 136
Bithiah 42
Björn 89, 116
Black 132, 138, 141, 162
Blackbird 131-2
Blackfoot 114
Blackman 135, 256
Blackpool 168
Blackshaw 133
Blacksmith 256
Blackwell 129
Blades 135
Bladesmith 256
Blaine 59
Blair 34, 59, 138
Blaise 21
Blake 96, 132
Blakemore 136
Blakeway 137
Blakey 137
Blanche 37, 45, 53, 59, 84, 93-4
Blandford 134
Blanket 131
Blankley 135
Blankman 256
Blarney 133
Blatchford 134
Blatherwick 136
Blazey 255
Bleakman 256
Bleasdale 135
Bleazard 135
Bleddyn 35
Blencowe 135
BLENDED HOUSE
    NAMES 211
Blenkin 137
Blenkiron 137
Bletsoe 135
Blezard 135
Blezzard 135
Blight 151
Bliss 90
Blodwen 59
Blossom 22, 43, 59
Blowers 137
Blowey 134
Bloye 134
Blue 22
Blue Mountain 182
Blue's Point 182
Bluebell 43
Blundell 132
Blunt 132
Blythman 256
Bo 117
Boaden 133
Boagaerde 142
Boam 134
Board 136
Boase 133
Boaz 35
Bob 85
Bobbie 37, 59
Bobby 59
Bobby-May 100
Bocksmith 256
Boddington 137
Boddy 136
Boden 136
Bodenham 135
Bodle 137
Bodman 256
Body 131
Boffey 133
Boffin 140
Bogarde 142
Bogman 256
Boisfeuillet 255
Bolam 136
Bold 22
Bolitho 133
Bolivia 183
Bolshaw 133
Bolt 134, 142
Bolton 129
Boltsmith 256
BOMBERS, NAMES
    OF B.29 236
Bone 131
Bonfield 135
Bong Bong 182
Boniface 137

Bonita 59
Bonney 135
Bonnie 21, 37, 59, 82
Bonnyman 256
Bonus 22
Boon 136
Boorman 135, 256
Boosey 131
Boothman 256
Bootyman 256
Border 135
Borlase 133
Borman 135
Borrett 137
Borrowman 256
Borton 136
Bosanquet 127
Bosomworth 137
Bossey 132
Boston 179
BOTANICAL
    NAMES 169
Botany Bay 181
Botham 140
Bothwick 136
Bott 136
Botterill 137
Botting 137
Bottom 140
Bottomley 137
Botulf 179
Boucher 137
Boughey 136
Boughton 133
Bould 136
Boulden 135
Boulter 137
Boulton 136
Boum-Boum 142
Boumphrey 124
Bouncehorn 172
Bounds 135
Boundy 134
Bourner 137
Bovey 134
Bowditch 134
Bowdler 136
Bowell 131
Bowering 136
Bowers 136
Bowes 137
Bowman 130, 256
Bowmer 134
Bowser 135
Bowsmith 256
Boy 22
Boyd 31, 45, 59, 100, 127, 138
Boyle 127
Bracegirdle 133
Bracher 137
Brackenbury 135
Bradford 129, 141, 172
Bradley 31, 55, 59, 129
Bradock 133
Bradridge 134
Bradshaw 129
Brafield 136
Brag 134
Bragg 132
Brained 22
Bramall 137
Branca 117
Brandee 91
Brandi 54, 91
Brandon 31, 50, 129
Brandt 126
Brandy 91
Branson 135
Brasher 30
Brasnett 136
Brass 151
Braund 134
Braxton 100
Brayden 55
Brayley 134
Brazier 133
Brazil 183
Breach 137
Breakspear 136
Breakwell 136
Brear 137
Brears 137
Breary 133
Breayley 134

Breconshire 173
Breedlove 180
Brenchley 135
Brenda 37, 52-4, 59
Brendan 31, 55, 59
Brendon 59, 133
Brennan 127, 132
Brent 26, 31, 59, 132
Brenton 133
Bret 31
Bretherton 135
Breton 129
Brett 31, 55, 59, 129
Brewer 130
Brewis 136
Brewster 130, 141
Bria 54
Brian 27, 31, 43, 47-9, 50, 55, 59
Briana 54
Brice 135
Brickell 134
Brickman 256
Briddon 134
Bridge 22
Bridges 129
Bridget 37, 41, 51, 59
Bridgman 134
Bridstow 169
Brigham 137
Bright 162
Brightman 133, 256
Brightmore 125
Brimacombe 134
Brimble 136
Brindle 135
Brindley 136
Brine 134
Brisbourne 136
Bristow 135
Britannia 59
British Columbia 178
BRITISH PLACE
    NAMES 166
Briton 22
Britt 129
Brittany 37, 54-5, 59
Britten 129, 136
Britteridge 141, 172
Britton 129
Britus 255
Broadbent 137, 149
Broadberry 136
Broadhead 137
Broadhurst 133
Broadley 135
Brocksopp 134
Broderick 34
Brodie 136, 138
Broken Hill 182
Brolly 131
Bromage 135
Bromwich 136
Bronia 79
Bronte 143
Bronwen 42
Brook 37
Brooke 37, 55
Brooks 129
Brooksmith 256
Broom 134
Broomfield 135
Broomhead 134
Broster 133
Brough 149
Broughall 136
Broughton 135
Brown 80, 132, 138, 141, 148, 162
Browne 141
Browning 134
Brownjohn 151
Brownlow 135
Brownsmith 256
Bruce 34, 49, 50, 55, 60, 127, 134, 138
Brumby 135
Brunger 125
Bruno 117
Brunt 136
Brunwin 125
Brussels 186
Brutus 44
Bryan 27, 31, 60
Bryant 33, 162
Bryn 35
Brynmor 35

Bryony 37, 43, 60, 79
Bub 144
Bubb 134
Buccaneer Bay 180
Buchanan 138
Buck 89
Buckeridge 133
Bucket 151
Buckinghamshire
    133, 173
Bucklesmith 256
Buckley 129
Buckman 256
Buckmaster 133
Bucknell 134
Bud 131
Budd 135
Budge 133
Buenos Aires 186
Bugg 134, 144, 148
Bugler 134
Bulcock 135
Bull 80, 129
Buller 136
Bullion 256
Bullman 134
Bullmore 133
Bullock 151
Bulmer 137
Bunce 133
Buncombe 180
Buncombe County 19
Bunn 136
Bunny 21
Bunt 133
Bunyan 139
Burbidge 137
Burce 149
Burch 136
Burchard 125
Burdikin 134
Burdon 134
Burgoin 134
Burgoyne 134
Burke 122, 127
Burkill 135
Burkitt 135
Burma 183
Burnaby 135
Burnard 133
Burnett 132, 138
Burns 127, 134, 138, 139
Burrage 125
Burrough 134
Burrow 134
Burson 255
Bursteye 172
Burston 136
Burt 255
Burton 129
Burward 125
Bushby 136
Bushra 112
Buss 135
Bussman 256
Buster 22
Buswell 136
Butcher 130
Bute 173
Butler 130
Butlin 136
Butter 22
Butterfield 137
Butters 135
Butterworth 135
Buttery 136
Button 137, 141, 257
Butts 151
Byard 134
Byford 134
BYNAMES 119
Byrd 137, 255
Byron 31, 33, 46, 60, 92, 136

Cabot 179
Cade 135
Cadillac 142
Cadle 135
Cadwallader 136
Caernarvonshire 173
Caesar 21, 137
Çağdaş 117
Çağri 117
Cain 35, 162
Caines 134

Cair Luel 167
Cairns 136, 138
Cairo 186
Caithness 173
Caitlin 37, 54-5, 60
Cake 134
Calcutt 136
Calder 138
Caldwell 129, 135, 138
Caleb 35, 50
California 184
Calla 100
Callender 134
Callow 135
Callwood 133
Calum 34, 60
Calver 137
Calvin 31, 33, 60
Cambridgeshire 133, 173
Camero 126
Cameroon 183
Camilla 37, 41, 60
Camille 41, 97, 116
Cammack 135
Campbell 27, 34, 127, 138, 141
Campion 130
Campkin 135
Canada 183
Canary 255
Canary Islands 19
Canberra 186
Candace 37, 54, 91
Candice 37, 54, 60
Candida 37, 45
Candy 21, 91, 97
Cannell 136
Cannibal Plateau 181
Cannings 168
Cant 134
Cantrell 136
Cantrill 136
Cape Anna 179
Cape Banks 181
Cape Catastrophe 181
Cape Cod 179
Cape Elizabeth 179
Cape James 179
Capes 135
CAPITAL CITIES, NAMES OF 186
Capstick 137
Captain 22
CAR NAMES 221
Cara 37, 60
Caracas 186
CARAVAN NAMES 215
Cardell 133
Cardew 127
Cardiganshire 173
Cardwell 135
Careen 82
Careless 137, 139
Carey 60, 136
Carina 37, 60
Carissa 37
Carl 31, 48-9, 50, 60
Carla 37, 52, 60
Carless 132, 139
Carleton 60
Carley 37, 60
Carlie 37, 60
Carling 91
Carlisle 167
Carlos 33
Carlson 126
Carlton 33, 60, 129
Carly 37, 52, 55, 60
Carlyon 133, 151
Carman 256
Carmarthen 167
Carmarthenshire 173
Carmel 37, 41-2, 60, 90
Carmen 37, 41, 60, 117
Carmichael 136, 138
Carnation 86, 99
Carne 133
Carnegie 123
Carol 27, 37, 52-5, 60, 90-1, 115
Carole 21, 27, 37, 53-5, 60

Carolina 37, 179
Caroline 37, 51-2, 55, 60, 84-5, 100, 116
Carolus 143
Carolyn 37, 45, 53-4, 60
Carolynn 37
Caron 60
Carpenter 120, 130, 149
Carrick 127
Carrie 37, 53, 60, 88, 100
Carrington 255
Carroll 143
Carruthers 134, 138
Carson 126
Carter 130, 141, 162
Cartier 179
Cartmell 135
Cartridge 137
Cartwright 130
Carver 130, 136, 141
Carveth 133
Carwyn 35
Cary 136
Carys 42
Casanove 255
Casco 183
Case 124, 136
Casey 53
Cash 124, 133, 256
Cashman 256
Cass 124
Cassandra 37, 45, 54-5, 60, 97, 124
Cassey 37, 60
Cassia 42
Cassie 37, 97
Cassius 44
Casson 124
Casswell 135
Castillo 126
Castle 129, 130
Castleman 130, 256
Castro 126
CAT NAMES, MOST POPULAR 239
Catarina 117
Catchlove 256
Catchpole 130
Cater 130
Caterina 117
Cathal 34
Catherine 24, 37, 51-5, 60, 90, 92, 104
Cathleen 60
Cathryn 60
Cathy 60
Catlin 124
Catling 137
Catlow 135
Caton 124, 134
Catrin 42
Catrina 60
Catriona 42, 60
Catterall 135
Cattermole 137
Cattling 124
Caunce 135
Cave 132
Cawrse 133
Cawsey 134
Ceabba 177
Cecil 25, 31, 47, 60, 90
Cecilia 60, 117
Cecily 124
Cedric 31, 33, 60, 100
Ceinwen 42
Celeste 94
Celia 21, 37, 60, 88, 90, 90
Celine 37
CELTIC PLACE NAMES 166
Cemal 117
Cemlyn 35
Century 130
Cephas 35
Ceri 35, 37, 60
Cerian 42
Ceridwen 60
Cerise 90, 94
Cerys 42
Cesare 117

Ceylon 19
Chad 31
Chadfield 134
Chafer 130
Chaffe 134
Chaffer 130
Chalker 130
Chalkley 135
Challand 136
Challen 137
Challender 130
Challinor 130
Challis 134
Chalmers 130, 138
Chamberlain 130
Chambers 130
Chammings 134
Champion 130
Chandler 130
Chandra 41, 113
Chandradasa 113
Chandrapala 113
Chandraratna 113
Chandrasiri 113
Chanel 41, 60, 90
Chanelle 60
Chang 108
Chanise 41
Channel 90
Channin 134
Channing 134
Chantal 37, 60, 116
Chantel 37, 60
Chantelle 37, 60
Chantler 135
Chaplin 130
Chapman 130, 256
Chard 136
Charde 41
Charis 97
Charisma 37
Charity 37, 43, 60, 89, 98, 110
Charleen 37, 60
Charlene 37, 52, 60
Charles 25
Charles 31, 47-9, 50, 60, 97
Charley 100
Charlie 60
Charline 37, 60
Charlotte 37, 51-3, 60, 84, 94-5, 116
Charlton 169
Charlwood 137
Charmaine 37, 60, 255
Charmian 37, 61
Charnings 134
Charnley 135
Charnock 135
Charterhouse 170
Chartreuse 170
Chatham 180
Chattaway 137, 140
Chatterton 135
Chauchoin 149
Chaundler 130
Chaundy 136
Chave 134
Chavez 126
Chell 137
Chelsea 37, 52, 54-5, 61
Chelsie 37
Cheney 135
Chennells 135
Chenoweth 133
Cherie 37, 61
Cheriton 134, 169
Chernyshev 144
Cherry 21, 37, 43, 61, 97, 100
Cheryl 37, 54-5, 61, 80, 90
Cheshire 133, 136, 173
Chessman 131
Chester 144
Chester 21, 162, 255
Chesterfield 168
Chesters 133
Chettle 136
Chew 136
Chicago 165
Chilcott 134
Chile 183
Chilton 141, 172

China 183
CHINESE GIVEN NAMES 108-109
Chiswick 170
Chito Hajo 114
Chitty 137
Chivers 133
Chloe 37, 52, 55, 61, 97
Chlorian 95
Chobham 177
Chokichi 109
Cholmondeley 121
Chorlton 169
Chowen 134
Chown 134
Chris 21
Christa 37
Christal 94
Christensen 126
Christian 18, 31, 44, 50, 55, 61, 81, 116, 124, 151
CHRISTIAN NAMES 43
Christie 124, 138
Christina 37, 54, 61, 104
Christine 37, 52-5, 61, 90, 116
Christison 124
Christmas 91
Christopher 31, 47-9, 50, 55, 61, 90, 124
Christy 37, 42, 124, 134
Chubb 134, 148, 162
Chugg 134
Churches 136
Churchill 123, 129
Churchman 137
Chuter 137
Chuzzlewit 151
Ciara 41
Ciaran 34
Cincinnatus 44
Cinderella 37
Cindy 37, 61
Cintron 37
Cirencester 170
Clack 119
Clair 37, 61
Claire 37, 52, 55, 61, 90, 116
CLAN NAMES 119
CLAN NAMES, ANGLO-SAXON 168
CLAN NICKNAMES 158, 162
Clapham 137
Clapp 136
Clapton 136
Clara 37, 51, 53, 61
Clare 37, 61, 94, 136
Clarence 31, 49, 61, 100, 102
Claribel 94
Clarice 61
Claridge 133
Clarinda 94
Clarissa 79
Clark 31, 61, 121, 130, 138, 141, 162
Clarke 79, 130, 141
CLASSICAL FIRST NAMES 45
Claud 21, 61, 101
Claude 61
Claudette 61
Claudia 37, 61, 117
Claudine 101
Claxton 136
Clayton 61, 129
Clear 133
Cledwyn 35
Cleeton 136
Clement 93, 124
Clementina 93
Clementine 93
Clements 124
Clementson 124
Clemms 124
Clemow 133
Clempson 124
Clemretta 180

Clemson 124
Cleodolinda 94
Cleopatra 107
Cleveland 174
Cleverdon 134
Clewes 134
Clewlow 137
Clews 134
Cliff 21
Clifford 26, 31, 47, 49, 61, 123, 129
Clift 135
Clifton 129
Clinch 135
Clint 61, 90
Clinton 33, 135
Clive 31, 48, 61
Clocksmith 256
Clod 119
Clothier 136
Cloudman 256
Clough 137
Cloutman 256
Clowes 137
Cluett 134
Clulow 137
Clumsy 119
Clutterbuck 135
Clwyd 174
Clyde 34
Clyma 133
Clymo 133
Coad 133
Coaker 134
Coate 136
Coatsworth 134
Cobbald 125
Cobbity 182
Cobbledick 133
Cobbold 137
Cobden 135
Cobeldick 133
Cobley 135
Cockburn 136
Cockeram 134
Cockram 134
Cockshott 137
COCKTAIL NAMES 205
Coco 90
Cocozza 149
Codd 135
Codling 137
Cody 31, 50
Coffee 115
Coffin 131
Cogan 136
Coggan 136
Coggins 136
Cohen 126, 255
Coke 130
Colclough 137
Coldman 256
Cole 124
Coleman 43, 256
Coles 162
Colette 37
Colette 61
Colin 18, 31, 48, 55, 61
Colleen 37, 53-4, 61
Collen 133
Collett 124
Collette 61
Colley 124, 138
Collie 131
Collier 130
Collinge 135
Collingham 136
Collins 124, 141
Collinson 124
Collis 124
Collishaw 135
Colm 34
Colombia 183
Colombo 178
Colorado 184
'COLOUR' FIRST NAMES 45
COLOURFUL FIRST NAMES 90
Colson 137

Colwill 134
Coma 22
Comely 135
Comfort 101
Common 136
Compton 129, 137
Comus 101
Concord 182
Coney 135
Coneybeare 134
Congdon 133
Connecticut 184
Connibear 134
Connie 61
Connor 34, 48, 61
Conquest 162
Conrad 31, 61, 101
Constance 21, 37, 43, 51, 61, 124
Constantinople 94
CONVERTED NAMES 22
Conway 129
Conybear 134
Cook 130, 141, 179
Cooke 130, 141
Cooling 135
Coombe 134
Cooper 130, 141, 149
Coopersmith 256
Copeman 136
Copenhagen 186
Copestake 134
Copp 134
Coppard 137
Coppersmith 256
Cora 61
Coral 21, 37, 45, 61, 101
Corbishley 137
Cordelia 97
Corderey 133
Corderoy 133
Corey 33, 37, 50, 61
Corfield 136
Corin 37, 61
Corine 37
Corinna 37, 45, 61
Corinne 37, 61
Corinthia 102
Corke 137
Corky 22
Cormac 34
Corner 136
Corney 135
Cornford 137
Cornish 129
Cornock 135
Cornwall 129, 133, 173
Cornwallis 129
Cornwell 129
Corona 22
Corp 136
Correy 37
Corrie 37, 102
Corrine 37, 61
Corringham 136
Cory 37
Cosh 136
Cosmin 117
Cosmo 34
Cossey 136
Cotle 149
Cotman 256
Cottingham 135
Cottle 137
Cotton 129, 162
Couch 133
Couchman 256
Coulson 124
Coultrip 135
Counsell 136
Coupland 135
Courter 255
Courtice 134
Courtney 37, 54-5, 61
Coveney 135
Coverdale 137
Coward 135
Cowen 136
Cowing 136
Cowling 133

Cowper 130
Cox 162
Coxall 133
Coy 22, 139
Cracknell 137
Crackston 141, 172
Crago 133
Cragoe 133
Craig 27, 31, 48-9, 50, 55, 61, 80, 136, 138
Crampton 147
Crane 149,
Cranfield 133
Crang 134
Cranidge 135
Crapper 137
Crawford 34, 129, 138
Crawley 147
Crawshaw 137
Craze 133
Crazy Snake 114
Creaser 137
Cresbard 180
Cricetti 149
Crichton 138
CRIMINAL NICKNAMES 158
Crimp 134
Crippen 132
Cripps 132
Crisp 132
Crispin 25, 132
Cristillo 149
Critchley 135
Crockford 133
Crocombe 134
Crocus 22
Crofts 137
Crompton 135
Cromwell 172
Cronk 132
Crookes 134
Croom 136
Croome 135
Cropley 135
Cropper 135
Crosby 129
Cross 162
Crossman 136, 256
Crowhurst 135
Crowle 133
Crowles 138
Crown 256
Cruikshank 132, 138
Cruise 122
Crump 132, 147
Crumpton 147
Crupp 147
Crusoe 147
Cruz 126
Crystal 21, 37, 45, 54, 61, 97
Cubitt 136
Cuckow 132
Cuffee 115
Cuffy 115
Culley 136
Cullimore 135
Culshaw 135
Cumberland 134, 136, 173, 179
Cumberledge 137
Cumbria 174
Cuming 134
Cumming 138
Cundy 133
Cunha 149
Cunliffe 135
Cunningham 127, 138
Cupit 134
Cureton 136
Curling 135
Curnow 133
Currall 137
Currer 143
Currie 138
Curson 136
Curtis 33, 61, 132
Cuss 124, 137
Cussans 124
Cusse 137
Cust 124
Custance 124
Custard 131
Cutforth 135

Cuthbert 25, 81, 83, 90, 118, 135
Cutlove 256
Cutteridge 125
Cutting 137
Cutts 134
Cynewulf 169
Cynthia 37, 45, 54, 61, 101, 103
Cyretha 255
Cyril 47, 61, 90, 102
Cyrus 35
Cytherea 97

Dabbs 125
Daffodil 43
Dafydd 35
Dagger 135
Dahlia 61
Dailey 140
Daily 255
Dainty 136
Daisuke 109
Daisy 37, 43, 51, 61, 94
Dakins 124
Dalach 140
Dalby 135
Dale 31, 49, 50, 55, 61
Daley 31, 61, 140
Dalgleish 138
Daliya 112
Daljit 110
Dalley 140
Dally 145
Dallyn 134
Dalton 129
Daly 127, 140
Dalzell 134
Dalziel 134, 138
Damaris 42
Damerell 134
Damian 31, 48, 55, 61, 117
Damien 31, 61
Damodar 110
Damon 33
Damon 61
Dampier 136
Dan 21
Danby 137, 183
Dancer 133
Dand 136
Dandy 124
Dane 61
Daniel 31, 43, 47-9, 50, 55, 62, 85, 116, 124
Daniela 62
Daniella 37, 62
Danielle 37, 52, 54-5, 62
Daniels 124, 149
Danke 22
Dannatt 135
Dannet 124
Dannson 124
Danny 62
Daphne 37, 43, 62
Dara 113
Darch 134
Dare 134, 256
Daren 62
Darian 50
Darin 62
Darius 33, 35, 50
Dark 22, 135
Darlene 53-4, 62
Darnell 33, 135
Darran 62
Darrel 62
Darrell 33, 62
Darren 27, 31, 45, 48, 62, 80
Darrin 62
Darrington 133
Darron 62
Darryl 31, 49, 50, 62
Dart 134
Darvell 133
Darvill 133
Darwin 118, 125, 136
Daryl 31, 62
Daryll 31, 62
Daubney 135
Daved 86
Davenport 129

David 31, 43, 47-9, 50, 55, 62, 88, 90-1, 122, 124
Derbyshire 134, 173
Davidge 124,
Davidson 124, 138, 141
Davies 122, 124, 141, 149
Davina 37, 62
Davindar 110
Davine 37
Davinia 37
Davis 124, 141
Davison 124
Davitt 124
Dawe 124
Dawes 124
Dawkins 124, 135
Dawn 21, 37, 52, 54, 62, 90, 102
Dawson 124, 138
Dawyer 137
Day 80, 124, 130, 162, 255
Dayman 256
Dayment 134
DAYS, NAMES OF 13-18
de Courcy 151
de Witt 180
Deadman 131, 256
Deakin 137
Dean 31, 48, 55, 62
DeAndre 50
Deanna 37, 62
Dearden 135
Dearlove 256
Dearman 256
Debbie 37, 62, 155
Debenham 137
Debora 62
Deborah 27, 37, 43, 45, 51-2, 54-5, 62, 79, 89, 93, 104, 155
Debra 37, 45, 62
Decimus 25, 89
Deck 137
Declan 34, 62
Dee 111
Deeley 136
DEFINITIONS OF 'NAME' 6
Deinol 35
Deion 86
Deirdre 41, 62, 94, 101
Delain 146
Delaware 184
Delhi 186
Delia 21, 45, 62, 101, 117
Delicia 90, 97
Delicious 90
Delilah 42
Della 62
Delphine 62
Delroy 31, 62
Delyth 42
Demain 137
Demaine 137
Demetrius 33
Demsky 142
Denbighshire 173
Denby 137
Dence 129
Dench 129
Dene 62
Denholm 34
Denis 31, 43, 62, 124
Denise 37, 52-4, 62
Denison 124, 137
Denman 136
Denmark 183
Dennett 124
Denning 136
Dennis 31, 47-9, 50, 55, 62, 116, 124, 129
Denniss 124
Denns 129
Denny 62, 124
Densem 134
Densham 134
Denton 129
Denzil 62
Deon 33
Deontae 50

Dequan 50
Derek 31, 47-8, 50, 62
Derick 62
Derman 43
Dermot 34, 62
Derrick 33, 50, 62, 136
Derry 136
DESCRIPTIVE HOUSE NAMES 213
DESCRIPTIVE NICKNAMES 157
DESCRIPTIVE SURNAMES 132
Desforges 135
Deshawn 33
Desiree 37, 54, 97
Desmond 31, 62
Despair 22
Destiny 54
Dethick 170
Devil 131
Devin 33, 50
Devindra 110
Devon 33, 62, 173
Devonshire 134
Devonte 50
Dewar 138
Dewey 255
Dewhurst 135
Dewi 35, 62
Dexter 62, 135
Dharma 113
Dharmadasa 113
Dharmapala 113
Dharmaratna 113
Dhorea 146
Diamond 22, 45, 54
Diana 37, 45, 53-4, 62, 79
Diane 21, 37, 52-4, 62
Dianne 37, 55, 62
Diarmid 34
Diarmuid 34
Diaz 126
Dibag 110
Dibb 137
Dibble 135
Dick 21, 84-5, 107, 138
Dick Tracy 91
Dick-less Tracy 91
Dickens 123-4
Dicker 134
Dickie 138
Dickinson 124
Dickman 256
Dicks 136
Dickson 124, 138
Diederick 31
Diego 126
Digby 62
Diggers' Rest 182
Dili 113
Dilip 113
Dilipa 113
Dilipa Manaranjani 113
Dillamore 133
Dillon 122
Dilnot 135
Diment 136
DIMINUTIVES, FIRST NAME 43
Dimmock 133
Dimock 133
Dimond 134
Dinah 21, 42-3, 51, 62, 101
Dingle 133
Dinners 255
Dinning 136
Dino 117
Dinsdale 137
Dion 33, 62
Dione 41
Dionne 41, 62
Diplock 137
Dirk 31, 62, 97
Disastrous 94
Dishman 256
District of Columbia 178
Ditton 170

Dix 124
Dixon 124
Dmitriy 117
Dobbie 125
Dobbs 125, 135
Dobie 125
Doble 134
Dobson 125
Docherty 127
Doctor 22
Dodd 125
Dodds 138
Dodge 125
Dodgson 125, 143
Dodo 35, 90
Dods 138
Dodson 125
Doel 137
DOG NAMES, FICTIONAL 240
DOG NAMES, MOST POPULAR 238
Doggett 132-3
Doidge 134
Doleman 256
Dolin 142
Dollar 255
Dollman 256
Dolly 94
Dolores 37, 53, 62, 94, 98, 117
Dolphin 22, 129
Domingos 117
Dominic 31, 63, 102
Dominican Republic 183
Dominick 31
Dominique 37, 50, 54, 63, 90
Dominy 134
Dommett 134
Don 21, 63, 168, 170
Donal 34
Donald 31, 47-9, 50, 55, 63, 124, 134, 138, 162
Donaldson 124, 138
Doncaster 136, 168
Done 133
Donkey 112
Donna 37, 52-5, 63
Donte 50
Dook 135
Dooley 133
Doolittle 137, 145
Dora 53, 63, 107
Dorcas 42, 63
Dore 170
Doreen 46, 51-2, 63
Dorey 134
Doria 94
Dorian 33, 63
Dorinda 97
Doris 21, 37, 51-3, 63, 79, 93-4
Dormer 133
Dorothea 63, 94
Dorothy 37, 51-3, 63, 146
Dors 142
Dorset 173
Dorsetshire 134
Dorsey 142
Dotey 141
Dottery 172
Doug 21
Dougal 45
Douglas 21, 26, 31, 45, 47-9, 50, 55, 63, 127, 138, 142
Dover 133, 170
Dowdeswell 135
Dowell 135
Down 173
Downs 129, 255
Dows 135
Dowse 135
Dowsett 134
Dowson 124
Doyle 127
Drabble 134
Drackley 135
Drage 136
Drake 162, 179
Drakes 135
Draper 130
Draycott 135

Drew 21, 63
Drewery 135
Drewitt 135
Drewry 135
Dring 135
Drinkall 135
Dronfield 134
Drudge 135
Drummond 34, 122, 138
Drunkard 119
Drury 135
Drysdale 138
Dudley 129
Duane 21, 31, 63, 101
Dublin 168, 186
Ducat 256
Duce 255
Duck 131, 137
Duckham 138
Duckman 256
Duckmanton 136
Duckworth 135, 255
Dudding 135
Dudley 31, 63
Due West 180
Duff 138
Duffel 19
Duffield 136
Dufty 147
Dugald 34
Dugald 45
Duggan 138
Duggleby 137
Duke 22
Dukinfield 149
Dulcie 63, 91
Dull 255
Dumbrell 137
Dumbrill 137
Dumfriesshire 173
Dumpling 144
Dunbar 173
Dunbarton 173
Duncan 31, 45, 63, 92, 127, 138, 141
Dunclent 128
Duncombe 133
Dunderdale 135
Dunford 134
Dungey 135
Dunkley 136
Dunklin 128
Dunkling 112, 128, 144, 221
Dunklyn 128
Dunlop 138
Dunn 132, 138
Dunstable 101
Dunstan 101, 133
Dunstone 133
DuPage Center 183
Durand 124
Durant 124
Durden 134
Durgin 149
Durham 129, 134, 173
Durose 137
Durrah 112
Durrance 124
Durrant 124, 162
Durston 136
Dustin 21, 31, 50, 155
Dusty 22
Dutch 129
DUTCH GIVEN NAMES 116
Dutchman 129
Duton 133
Dutton 129
Duxbury 135
Dwayne 31, 49, 50, 63
Dwelly 132
Dwight 133, 149
Dyball 136
Dye 136
Dyer 127, 130
Dyfan 35
Dyfed 174
Dykes 138
Dylan 35, 50, 55, 63
Dyment 136
Dymond 134
Dyson 124, 137
Dzhugashvili 142

Eade 124
Eady 124
Eamonn 34, 63
Eanwulf 169
Eardley 137
Earl 21, 33, 46, 49, 63, 134
Earle 49, 134
Earley 140
EARLIEST PLACE NAMES 165
Early 140
EARLY TRADE NAMES 220
Earnley 140
Earnshaw 137
Earthquake 181
Earthy 131
Eary 255
East Lothian 173
Easter 255
Easterbrook 134
Eastham 135
Eastman 125, 256
Easy 255
Eaton 129, 141, 172
Eatwell 137
Eaves 135
Eayres 135
Eayrs 135
Ebenezer 35
Ebony 22, 41, 54
Eccles 135
Ecga 177
Eckley 135
Ecuador 183
Edda 90
Eddie 63, 101
Eddis 124
Eddison 124, 136
Eddols 125
Eddy 125, 133
Eden 63, 133
Edgar 31, 43, 47, 49, 63, 118, 138
Edginton 136
Edinburgh 167
Edis 124
Edison 123-4
Edit 116
Edith 37, 43, 51-3, 63, 84, 97, 124-5
Edkins 137
Edmans 133
Edmond 31, 63, 124
Edmonds 124
Edmondson 124
Edmons 124
Edmund 27, 31, 43, 47, 63, 97, 118, 124
Edmunds 124, 138, 141
Edna 42, 51, 53, 63, 90
Edney 135
Edouard 116
Edrich 125
Edryd 35
Edsel 221
Edward 31, 43, 47-9, 50, 55, 63, 93, 101, 118, 124, 138
Edwardes 124
Edwards 122, 124, 138, 141
Edwin 31, 47, 49, 63
Edwina 37, 42, 63
Edyta 117
Eels 131
Egbert 81
Eggins 134
Eggleston 134
Egham 177
Eglah 43
Eglantine 43
Eglinton 136
Egoniaga 182
Egstrom 149
Eibhlin 41
Eifion 35
Eiji 109
Eileen 21, 41, 51-2, 63, 101
Eilidh 42
Eilir 35
Einahnuhto Hills 182
Einar 116

Einion 138
Einstein 255
Eirlys 42
Eisenhower 123
Ekalaka 179
Ekins 135, 257
El Salvador 183
Elaine 37, 52-4, 63
Elbourn 133
Elbow 183
Elder 22
Elderberry 22
Eleanor 37, 46, 51-3, 63, 93, 124
Electra 45
Elen 42
Elena 37, 63, 117
Eleonora 117
Eleri 42
Eley 134
Elfed 35
Elfreda 63
Elgan 35
Elgey 137
Elgie 137
Elhanan 35
Eli 31, 35, 47
Eliakim 35
Elias 124
Eliezer 35
Elif 117
Elijah 35, 47, 63
Elin 42
Elinor 37, 63
Eliot 31, 124
Eliott 31
Elis 35
Elisabet 117
Elisabeth 37, 63, 117
Elise 55
Elisha 35, 63
Eliza 43, 46, 51, 63
Elizabeth 25-7, 37, 43, 51-5, 63, 79, 83, 92, 95, 97, 107, 124, 138
Elkanah 35
Elkington 137
Ella 21, 46, 53, 63
Ellacott 124
Ellaway 138
Ellen 37, 51, 63, 84, 101, 124
Ellerby 137
Ellerton 137
Ellicott 124
Ellinor 124
Elliot 31, 63, 119, 124, 138
Elliott 31, 63, 124
Ellis 63, 124, 141, 143
Ellison 124
Elm 22
Elmer 46, 49
Elmitt 135
Elnathan 35
Eloisa 79
Eloise 37, 63
Elphee 125
Elroy 31
Else 134
Elsegood 125
Elsey 125
Elsie 37, 43, 51-3, 63
Elsmore 137
Elson 124
Elspeth 37, 42
Elston 134
Eluned 42
Elvey 125
Elvidge 135
Elvira 90
Elvis 31, 45, 63
Elwood 125
Elworthy 134
Elwyn 35
Elżbieta 117
Embleton 136
Embrey 135
Emerson 123
Emerson 124
Emery 124
Emett 124
Emilie 37, 116
Emily 37, 51-4, 63, 84, 97
Emit 22
Emma 21, 37, 43, 51-

3, 55, 63, 82, 97, 124
Emma-Jayne 63
Emma-Louise 63
Emmeline 63
Emmott 137
Emrys 35, 64
Emyr 35
Ena 64
Encounter Bay 181
Enda 34
Endacott 134
Energetic 22
Enfys 42, 90
England 129, 183, 255
English 141, 129
ENGLISH RIVER NAMES 175-6
Enid 64, 90
Enoch 35, 64, 101
Enos 35
Ensor 134
Entwisle 135
Entwistle 135
Enzo 117
Eoghan 34
Eoin 34
Ephraim 35
Epping 169
Epton 135
Er 35, 91
Erastus 35
Erema 101
Eric 31, 47-8, 50, 64, 83
Erica 37, 54, 64
Erik 31, 88, 117
Erika 37, 64
Erin 37, 54-5, 64
Erlam 133
Erna 21
Ernest 21, 31, 33, 47, 49, 64, 97, 103
Ernie 64
Errol 45, 64
Erskine 34
Erwin 125
Eryl 35
Esam 136
Esau 35
Esk 170
Esma 117
Esme 42, 64
Esquire 22
Essex 134, 137, 173
Estabrook 134
Estella 64
Estelle 38, 64, 90, 93
Ester 255
Esther 21, 38, 43, 51, 53, 64, 90-1
Etchells 133
Ethan 35
Ethanac 180
Ethel 38, 51, 53, 64, 90, 94-5
Etheldreda 38
Etheridge 137
Ethiopia 183
Ethna 41
Etta 21, 255
Euan 64
Eugen 117
Eugene 31, 49, 64
Eugenie 97
Eugenius 31
Eugeniy 117
Eunice 42, 64
Euphemia 101, 103
Eurig 35
Euros 35
Eusdean 97
Eustace 102
Eva 21, 38, 51, 53, 64, 116-7, 133
Evan 4, 21, 124
Evangeline 97
Evangelist 22
Evans 124, 141
Eve 38, 43, 64, 91, 93, 134
Eveleigh 134
Eveline 64
Evely 134
Evelyn 38, 51-3, 64, 102

Everall 136
Everard 43
Everbe 102
Evered 136
Evershed 137
Everyday 255
Evison 135
Evon 24
Ewa 117
Ewan 34, 64
Ewart 64
Ewer 136
Ewing 138
Exe 168, 170
Exeter 168
Eye 131
Eylem 117
Ezekiel 35
Ezer 35
Ezra 35
Faber 123
Fabia 117
Fafa 90
Fag 135
Failes 136
Faint-not 43
Fairbairn 136
Fairchild 132, 134
Fairclough 135
Fairfax 132
Fairhead 134
Fairlamb 255
Fairly 22
Fairman 256
Fairthorne 133
Faith 43, 110
Falconer 130
Falkner 130
Fallows 137
Falmouth 183
Falstaff 224
FAMILY NAMES 118
FAMOUS NICKNAMES 163
FANCIFUL SPELLINGS OF FIRST NAMES 45
Fancy 102
Fanny 51, 53, 64, 94, 102
Farah 112
Farewell 22
Farinola 149
Farley 129
Farmer 130
Farnham 176
Farnsworth 136
Farquhar 34, 138
Farquharson 138
Farr 255
Farrall 137
Farrar 130
Farrell 127
Farthing 136, 256
Faruq 112
FASTEST FIRST NAMES 89
Fateful 22
Fatima 112
Fatma 117
Fatman 256
Faulder 134
Faulkner 130
Fawkes 135
Fay 38, 64, 102, 135
Faye 21, 38, 64
Fazakerley 135
Fear 131, 136
Fearn 134
Fearon 130, 134
Feather 22, 130, 137
Featherstonehaugh 121
Feaveryear 137
Feaviour 137
Felgate 134
Felicia 41
Felicity 25, 38, 43, 64
Felipe 117
Felix 21, 31, 64, 97, 117
Felixstowe 169
Felony 92
Felton 136
Fenella 42, 64, 94
Fenner 134

Fensom 133
Fenton 129, 136
Fergal 34
Fergus 34, 64
Ferguson 127, 131, 138, 141
Fermanagh 173
Fern 38, 43, 64, 137
Fernandez 126
Fernando 117, 126
Ferrari 89
Ferryman 256
Fewings 134
ffaringdon 151
ffinch-ffarowmere 121
ffion 42
ffoulkes 151
ffrench 151
Fiancé 22
FICTIONAL CHARACTERS, NAMES OF 147
Fidelma 41
FIELD NAMES 171
Fields 129
Fieldsmith 256
Fife 173
Fifett 134
Fight-the-good-fight-of-faith 43
Figlock 255
Figueroa 126
Filbee 136
File 135
Filipa 117
Filkins 124
Filmer 135
Finbow 137
Fincham 137
Finching 151
Findlay 127, 138
Finesmith 256
Finish 172
Finland 183
Finlay 34, 138
Finlayson 138
Finn 135
FINNISH GIVEN NAMES 116
Fiona 25, 38, 55, 64, 102
Fionnghal 42
Firkins 137
FIRST NAME DIMINUTIVES 43
FIRST NAME, ANGRIEST 91
FIRST NAME, FUNNIEST 89
FIRST NAME, MOST ALCOHOLIC 91
FIRST NAME, MOST COMMON ANANYM 91
FIRST NAME, MOST HESITANT 91
FIRST NAME, MOST MYSTERIOUS 89
FIRST NAME, MOST ORIGINAL 90
FIRST NAME, MOST POPULAR DAY 91
FIRST NAME, MOST RIOTOUS 90
FIRST NAME, MOST STERTOROUS 90
FIRST NAME, MOST SURPRISING 90
FIRST NAME, MOST UNEXPECTED 90
FIRST NAME, MOST VALUABLE 89
FIRST NAME, ODDEST 89
FIRST NAME, RUDEST 89

FIRST NAME, SWEETEST 91
FIRST NAME, TASTIEST 90
FIRST NAME, WINDIEST 91
FIRST NAMES - REASONS FOR CHOICE 78
FIRST NAMES WITH FANCIFUL SPELLINGS 45
FIRST NAMES, ANIMAL 89
FIRST NAMES, BIBLICAL 42
FIRST NAMES, CLASSICAL 45
FIRST NAMES, COLOURFUL 90
FIRST NAMES, FASTEST 89
FIRST NAMES, FLOWER NAMES USED AS 43
FIRST NAMES, FLOWERY 90
FIRST NAMES, FRUITIEST 89
FIRST NAMES, INSECT 89
FIRST NAMES, IRISH 41
FIRST NAMES, MONTH NAMES AS 90
FIRST NAMES, MUSICAL 90
FIRST NAMES, NUMERICAL 89
FIRST NAMES, NUMERICAL 89
FIRST NAMES, ODOROUS 90
FIRST NAMES, PLACE NAMES AS 89
FIRST NAMES, PURITAN 43
FIRST NAMES, RACIALLY MARKED 89
FIRST NAMES, SCOTTISH 42
FIRST NAMES, SEXIEST 90
FIRST NAMES, SUPERLATIVE 89
FIRST NAMES, TIME OF DAY 90
FIRST NAMES, UNLUCKIEST 89
FIRST NAMES, WELSH 42
Firth 137
Fischer 126
Fish 135
Fisher 130, 138
Fisk 137
Fiske 137
Fitchett 134
Fitman 256
Fitt 135
Fitter 137
Fitz-Adam 151
Fitzgerald 149
Fitzsimmons 149
Flament 129
Flanders 129
Flannan 34
Flatman 137, 256
Flatt 136
Flaude 102
Flavia 45
Fleeming 129
Flement 129
Fleming 129, 134, 138
Fletcher 130, 141
Fleur 38, 64, 82, 85
Flinders 129, 179
Flintshire 173
Flook 135
Flora 38, 64, 94, 102, 116, 255
Florabelle 93
Florence 30, 38, 51-3,

64, 84, 89, 90, 94, 102, 255
Flores 126
Florey 136
Florica 117
Florida 184
Florin 117, 256
Florinda 102
Florrie 30, 94
FLOWER NAMES 232
FLOWER NAMES USED AS FIRST NAMES 43
FLOWERY FIRST NAMES 90
Floyd 33, 49, 136
Fluck 135, 142
Fluid 255
Flurry 94
Fluvanna 180
Flux 135
Fly-fornication 43
Foal 131
Foale 134
Fogden 137
Folashade 41
Folkard 134
Foll 133
Follows 137
Fooks 134
Foot 134
Footit 135
Footitt 136
Footman 256
Forbes 34, 127, 138
Ford 21
Foreman 256
Forester 130
Forman 135
Forrest 135, 138
Forrester 137
Forryan 135
Forshaw 135
Forster 130
Forsyte 7
Forsyth 138
Fortescue 132
Forty 131
Forty Fort 180
Fortyman 256
Fortynine Creek 180
Foss 134
Fostersmith 256
Foulke 134
Foulkes 138
Fountain 133
Fountaine 133
Fowke 134
Fowler 130
Fowles 136
Fox 162
Foxton 137
Fraidah 112
France 129, 183
Frances 24, 27, 38, 51-5, 64, 129
Francesca 38, 64
Francine 64, 88
Francis 24, 25, 31, 47, 49, 55, 64, 129, 155, 162
Francisca 117
Francisco 117
Francome 137
Frank 21, 31, 47-9, 50, 55, 64, 155
Frankie 64
Frankcombe 137
Frankish 129
Franklin 46, 64, 123
Franklyn 64
František 117
Fraser 34, 64, 138, 141
Freada 86
Frearson 135
Fred 28, 47, 49, 64, 83, 96, 102
Freda 21, 64, 90
Frederica 28
Frederick 31, 47-9, 50, 64
Frederick County 179
Fredericksburg 179
Free 22
Freebody 133

Freedom 22
Freegard 137
Freelove 256
Freeman 256
Freestone 135
Freeth 137
Freethy 127, 133
Freeze 255
Fremlin 135
French 129
FRENCH GIVEN NAMES 116
Fretwell 134, 255
Frewer 125
Frewin 125
Friar 22
Friedman 126
Friend 22, 134
Frisby 135
Frobisher 130
Frogley 133
Frohock 133
Frontenac 182
Frontignac 182
Froome 133
Frow 135
Frøydis 117
FRÜITIEST FIRST NAMES 89
Fry 132
Frye 132
Fryrear 255
Fulcher 137
Fulepet 170
Fulks 149
Fullard 133
Fuller 130, 141
Fullman 131
Fullolove 256
Fulton 138
Funnell 137
FUNNIEST FIRST NAME 89
Furber 133
Furneaux 134
Furphy 127
Furse 134
Furtherfits 172
Furze 134
Fyson 133

Garside 137
Gary 31, 48-9, 50, 55, 64
Garza 126
Gascoigne 129
Gascoyne 129
Gaskain 129
Gaskin 129
Gasman 256
Gatehouse 134
Gates 137
Gateshead 169
Gaunt 135
Gavin 31, 48, 55, 65
Gawain 31
Gay 21, 38, 65, 132
Gayatri 110
Gaye 38
Gayford 136
Gayle 38, 65
Gaynor 38, 65, 80
Gaza 19
Gazard 135
Gaze 136
Geach 133
Geake 133
Geary 135
Geddes 138
Gedge 136
Geldard 137
Gelder 137
Gelien 149
Gelisa 41
Gelsthorpe 136
Gem 22
Gemma 38, 52, 65
Gemmell 138
Gemson 124
General 22
Genevieve 90
Genge 134
Gent 134
Gentle 22
Geoffrey 31, 43, 47-8, 55, 65, 107, 124
George 20, 25, 27, 31, 47-9, 50, 55, 65, 83, 92, 94, 117, 123, 255
Georgetown 186
Georgette 38
Georgia 38, 52, 55, 65, 179, 181, 184-5
Georgina 38, 55, 65, 117
Georgine 38
Geraint 35
Gerald 31, 43, 47-9, 50, 65, 98, 124
Geraldine 38, 53, 65
Gerard 31, 65, 124
Gerhart 98
Gerlad 35
Germaine 65, 129
German 129, 134
GERMAN GIVEN NAMES 116
Germany 183
Germing 129
Gerontius 31
Gerrard 65
Gerry 21, 133
Gershom 35
Gertrude 38, 51, 53, 65, 90, 101
Gervais 124
Gervas 124
Gervase 43
Gervis 124
Gerwyn 35
Gethin 35
Ghey 137
Gianetta 94
Gibb 124, 138
Gibbard 136
Gibbin 124
Gibbons 124
Gibbs 124
Giblett 136
Gibson 124, 138
Giddy 132
Gideon 35
Gidley 134
Gilbart 124
Gilbert 31, 65, 124
Gilbertson 124
Gilbey 124
Gilchrist 34, 138

Gilda 21
Gildsmith 256
Giles 31, 65
Gilham 125
Gilhespy 136
Gill 124
Gillam 125
Gillard 134
Gillbard 133
Gillespie 138
Gillett 124
Gillian 38, 52, 65, 125
Gilliart 135
Gilliatt 135
Gillingham 134
Gillott 124
Gillyatt 135
Gilmour 138
Gilpin 124
Gilson 124
Gimson 124, 135
Gina 38, 65
Ginger 45, 133
Ginman 256
Gipp 119
Gipps 124
Gippsland 182
Gipsy 22
Giulia 102
Giuseppe 117
GIVEN NAMES, AFRICAN 114
GIVEN NAMES, AMERICAN INDIAN 113
GIVEN NAMES, CHINESE 108-109
GIVEN NAMES, DUTCH 116
GIVEN NAMES, FINNISH 116
GIVEN NAMES, FRENCH 116
GIVEN NAMES, GERMAN 116
GIVEN NAMES, HINDU 110
GIVEN NAMES, HUNGARIAN 116
GIVEN NAMES, ICELANDIC 116
GIVEN NAMES, ITALIAN 117
GIVEN NAMES, JAPANESE 109
GIVEN NAMES, MUSLIM 111
GIVEN NAMES, NETSILIK 111
GIVEN NAMES, NORWEGIAN 117
GIVEN NAMES, POLISH 117
GIVEN NAMES, PORTUGUESE 117
GIVEN NAMES, ROMANIAN 117
GIVEN NAMES, RUSSIAN 116-17
GIVEN NAMES, RUSSIAN 117
GIVEN NAMES, SIKH 110
GIVEN NAMES, SLOVAKIAN 117
GIVEN NAMES, SPANISH 117
GIVEN NAMES, SRI LANKAN 112
GIVEN NAMES, SWEDISH 117
GIVEN NAMES, TURKISH 117
Gladness 22
Gladwin 43, 125
Gladys 21, 38, 46, 51, 53, 65, 93, 94, 155
Glamorgan 173
Glasson 133
Gleave 133
Gledhill 19
Glen 31, 65, 138
Glen Ellyn 183
Glenda 38, 65

Glendinning 136
Glenis 65
Glenn 31, 55, 65
Glenys 65
Gloria 21, 30, 38, 41, 53-4, 65
Glory 22
Gloucester 168, 170
Gloucestershire 134, 173
Glover 130
Gloyn 134
Glubb 151
Glyn 32, 65
Glyndwr 35
Glynis 65
Glynn 32
Goacher 137
Goatman 256
God 25
Godden 135
Goddier 133
Goddykoontz 255
Godfrey 32, 65
Godman 43
Godsall 135
Godsell 135
Godwin 43, 125
Goergetown 179
Goff 136
Goffage 149
Gohachiro 109
Golby 136
Goldbard 125
Goldberg 126
Goldbogen 149
Goldburg 125
Golden 22
Goldfish 149
Goldhawk 125
Goldsmith 130, 256
Goldstein 126
Goldstraw 137
Goldsworthy 133
Goldwin 125
Goliath 35
Gomesano 126
Gomez 126
Gomm 133
Gomo 126
Gontil 117
Gönül 117
Gonzales 126
Gonzalo 126
Gooch 136, 143
Good 138
Good Works 44
Goodbody 138
Goode 136
Gooderham 137
Goodfellow 132, 138
Goodfriend 138
Goodhew 135, 138
Goodier 133
Goodlad 138
Goodliffe 125
Goodman 132, 138, 141, 256
Goodrich 125
Goodson 138
Goodswen 138
Goodwill 137-8
Goodwin 125
Goodyear 135
Goolden 132
Goose 135
Gora 126
Gordon 32, 47-8, 65, 138
Gorfinckel 148
Gornall 135
Gorringe 137, 255
Gorst 135
Gorwyn 134
Gosden 137
Gosling 131
Gotobed 139
Gott 137
Gottfried 21
Gough 127
Goulder 136
Goulding 135
Goulter 135
Gow 138
Gowan 123
Gower 135
Gowlett 134

Grace 38, 43, 51, 53, 65, 102, 255
Graeme 32, 65
Graham 26, 32, 48, 55, 65, 138, 141
Grahame 65
Graig 127
Grainger 137
Grainne 41
Granger 137
Grant 27, 32, 65, 132, 138, 141, 151
Grantchester 169
Granville 65
Graton 134
Grave 130
Gray 132, 138, 141
Great Badminton 19
Great Fryup 172
Greece 183
Greed 136
Green 129, 141, 149, 255
Greenacre 136
Greenaway 137
Greengrass 255
Greenhalgh 135
Greenhill 137
Greenhouse 140
Greensmith 256
Greenwell 134
Greer 124
Gregory 32, 49, 50, 55, 65, 102, 124
Gregson 124, 135
Greig 124, 138
Gren 152
Grendon 134
Grenville 65
Gresty 133
Greta 24, 65
Grey 132, 144, 151
Grierson 124, 138
Grieve 130
Grieve 138
Griffiths 141
Grigg 124, 133
Grigson 124
Grim 177
Grimes 137
Grimsbury 177
Grimsdyke 177
Grimsey 137
Grimshaw 135
Grimwood 137
Grissel 83
Grist 137
Grose 133
Gross 126
Grossel 149
Ground 133
Grounds 133
Grove 129, 137
Growcott 136
Grubb 148
Gruffydd 35
Grummitt 135
Grushko 144
Guilding 137
Guillaume 18, 116
Guinea 256
Guinea Coast 19
Guinevere 80
Guinness 4, 127
Gulliver 132, 136
Gulsevin 117
Gumboil 131
Gumm 142
Gummer 125
Gunn 136, 255, 257
Gunnar 116-7
Guppy 134
Gurmit 110
Gussie 255
Gustafsson 142
Gustave 21
Guthbjörg 116
Guthrie 138
Guthrun 116
Gutierrez 126
Gutman 256
Gutterman 256
Guy 32, 49, 65, 102
Gwen 65
Gwendolen 65
Gwendoline 51-2, 65
Gwendolyn 41, 65
Gwent 174

Gwilt 136
Gwilym 35
Gwyn 35
Gwynedd 174
Gwyneth 65
Gwynfor 35
Gwynne 138
Gwynneth 65
Gyda 86
Gynn 133
Gyorgy 116
Gyte 134

Haas 126
Habakkuk 43
Habib 112
Hack 135
Hacking 135
Hackman 256
Haddad 123
Hadfield 134
Hadingham 137
Hadley 137
Hadrian 65
Haffenden 137
Hafiz 112
Hafoc 169
Haggai 35
Haggar 133
Haggard 139
Hagger 133
Haggett 136
Hahn 126
Haigh 137
Haile 21
Hailstones 255
Hainsworth 137
Haiti 183
Hakin 135
Hal 102
Halcyon 22
Hales 136
Haley 137
Halfacre 133
Halfman 256
Halford 137
Halfpenny 256
Halil 117
Hall 79, 138, 141
Halliwell 135, 169
Halls 134
Hallworth 133
Halo 255
Halsall 135
Halse 134
Halverstadt 149
Ham 35, 131
Hambleton 137
Hamblin 124
Hambly 133
Hambrook 135
Hamburg 172
Hames 134
Hamilton 127, 138, 141
Hamish 34, 65
Hamlet 124, 224
Hamley 124
Hamlyn 124, 134
Hammersley 137
Hammond 124
Hamnet 124
Hamo 124
Hampshire 135, 137, 173
Hampson 124
Hampton 129
Hamson 124
Hana 117
Hananaiah 91
Hananiah 35
Hancock 123-4
Hancorn 135
Handford 134
Hands 137
Handshaker 131
Handsome 80
Handy 22
Hanif 112
Hank 21
Hankey 133
Hankin 124, 135
Hanks 135
Hann 134
Hanna 116

Hannaford 134
Hannah 7, 38, 43, 51-2, 54-5, 65, 112, 255
Hans 21
Hansen 126
Hansford 134
Hanson 124, 126, 137
Happy 22
Harare 186
Harbans 110
Harber 137
Hardcastle 137
Harden 135
Hardie 138
Harding 43
Hardman 135, 256
Hardstaff 136
Hardy 132
Harker 137
Harland 137
Harle 136
Harman 124
Harmon 124
Harold 32, 47, 48-9, 65, 90, 102, 118
Harper 130, 138
Harpham 136
Harradine 133
Harrianne 45
Harriet 38, 51-3, 65, 95, 102, 255
Harriman 124
Harris 124, 141, 162
Harrison 55, 124, 141, 149
Harrow-on-the-Hill 169
Harry 32, 47, 49, 65, 84, 98, 102, 107, 138, 255
Hartle 134
Hartley 129, 149
Hartman 126
Hartnell 134
Hartnoll 134
Hartop 133
Hartridge 135
Harvey 32, 65, 124, 138
Harvie 124
Hasan 112
Hashim 112
Hasler 134
Hassall 133
Hassell 133
Hastings 129, 168
HAT NAMES 243
Hatch 136
Hatfield 129
Hatherell 135
Hathway 137
Hatt 136
Hauxton 169
Havana 19
Havard 137
Hawaii 182, 184
Haward 137
Hawke 124, 133
Hawken 133
Hawkesbury 169
Hawkey 133
Hawking 137
Hawkins 124
Hawksworth 169
Hawley 134
Haworth 135
Hawthorne 123
Hay 135, 138
Hayden 32, 55, 65
Haydn 32, 65
Haydock 135
Haydon 32, 65
Hayes 129
Hayfa 112
Hayhurst 135
Hayley 38, 52, 55, 66, 80, 85
Hayman 134
Hayne 133
Hayter 134
Haythornthwaite 135
Hayward 130
Hazel 21, 38, 43, 52-3, 66
Head 137
Heading 136
Headington 133
Headman 256

Headon 134
Healey-Kay 142
Health 134
Heaman 134
Heard 134
Hearle 133
Heath 129
Heather 38, 43, 52, 54-5, 66, 90
Heatley 136
Heaver 137
Hebditch 136
Hebron 137
Hector 32, 47, 66, 96, 255
Heddon 134
Hedrick 149
Heemstra 149
Hefin 35
Heggadon 134
Heidi 21, 36, 38, 66
Heighway 136
Helen 21, 38, 51-3, 55, 66, 101, 103
Helena 38, 66
Helene 66
Heler 137
Helga 116
Helliwell 137
Hellman 256
Helm 22
Helmer 134
Helmheard 169
Helmi 116
Heman 35
Hembrow 136
Hemchman 256
Hindle 135
Hindmarsh 136
HINDU GIVEN NAMES 110
Hingley 137
Hinni 113
Hinton 129, 136
Hiram 21, 35
Hirst 137
Hitchcock 137
Hitchens 124
Hitler 115
Hjalmar 103
Hoadley 137
Hoar-Stevens 149
Hoare 132
Hoath 137
Hobart 124-5
Hobby 135
Hobden 137
Hobgen 137
Hobley 136
Hobson 137
Hockenhall 133
Hockenhull 133
Hockey 136
Hockley 134
Hocknell 133
Hockridge 134
Hod 35
Hoddell 135
Hodge 133
Hodges 125
Hodgkins 137
Hodgkinson 125
Hodgkiss 125
Hodgson 125
Hodiah 35
Hodson 125
Hoffman 126
Hogben 135
Hogbin 135
Hogg 131, 136, 138, 148, 255, 257
Hoggins 151
Hogsbotham 151
Hohn 146
Holbeck 141
Holbrook 129, 136
Holder 135
Holdom 133
Holdsworth 137
Holdwater 144
Holebeck 172
Holeman 256
Hollamby 135
Holland 162
Hollands 135
Hollenbeck 149
Hollick 137
Holliday 137

Hewson 124, 135
Hext 134
Hey 137
Heygate 136
Heyward 134
Heywood 134
Hezekiah 35
Hiawatha 180
Hick 137
Hicken 137
Hickie 124
Hickin 137
Hickmott 135
Hicks 124, 149
Hickson 124, 133
Hickton 136
Hide 137
Hideo 109
Hides 135
Higgins 124
Higgs 124
High Harpers 172
Highsmith 256
Higman 133
Hignell 135
Higson 135
Hilary 38, 52, 66
Hilda 38, 51, 66
Hildred 135
Hill 129, 138, 141
Hillary 38
Hillman 256
Hillson 134
Hilson 134
Hilton 129
Hinchcliff 137
Hinchcliffe 137
Headington 133
Hemus 137
Henderson 124, 138, 141
Hendry 124
Hendy 132
Henery 86
Henley 137
Henman 256
Henrietta 26, 38, 51, 66, 255
Henry 26-7, 32, 43, 47-9, 50, 55, 66, 89, 98, 104, 124, 255
Henryson 124
Henshall 133
Henson 135
Henstock 134
Henwood 133
Hep 103
Hephzibah 103
Heppell 134
Hepple 134
Hepworth 137
Herbert 27, 32, 43, 47, 49, 66, 90, 255
Herbie 21
Hercule 10, 98
Hercules 96
Herd 130
Herdman 136
Herefordshire 135, 173
Heriot 124
Herman 34, 49, 90, 124, 126
Hernandez 126
Hernando 126
Herod 35
Heron 22
Herrick 136
Herring 135
Herrod 136
Hertfordshire 135, 173
Hervey 124
Heseltine 137
Hesketh 135
Hesmondhalgh 135
Hess 126
Hesse 126
Hetuhamy 113
Hetuwa 113
Heulwen 42
Hewer 137
Hewes 124
Hewett 124
Hewitson 124, 134
Hewlet 124

Hollie 38, 66
Hollier 135
Hollingsworth 137
Hollington 137
Hollins 137
Hollinshead 133
Hollow 133
Holloway 129
Holly 21, 43, 52, 66
Hollyman 131, 256
Holmes 129, 162
Holness 135
Holroyd 137
Holt 129
Holtom 136-7
Holy 38
Holyday 137
Homa 84
Home 22, 136
Homer 134, 255
Honduras 183
Hone 136
Honess 135
Honey 21
Honeybum 144
Honeychurch 255
Honeyfield 134
Honeyman 256
Honeysett 137
Hong 255
Honniball 134
Honor 21, 99
Honour 43, 136
Hood 138
Hoofman 256
Hook 137
Hooke 141
Hookway 134
Hooley 133
Hooper 130
Hoopersmith 256
Hoover 123, 126
Hope 21, 38, 43, 66, 81, 110, 138
Hopkins 125, 141
Hopkinson 125
Hopley 133
Hopps 134
Horace 21, 27, 47, 66, 90
Horatio 103
Horatius 44
Hornby 149
Horne 162
Horniman 256
Hornsby 136
Horrocks 135
Horsey 136
Horsfall 137
Horsley 137
Horton 129
Horwood 133
Hospital 255
Hotchkiss 125, 136
HOTEL NAMES 223
Hotten 133
Houlbrook 133
Houldsworth 137
Houlihan 18
Hounsell 134
Hounslow 169
Housden 134
House 129
HOUSE NAMES 209-19
HOUSE NAMES, MOST POPULAR 219
HOUSEBOAT NAMES 215
Houseman 137, 256
Housley 134
Houston 129
Hovick 149
Howard 26, 32, 49, 66, 144
Howel 124
Howell 4, 124
Howes 136
Howett 136
Howey 136
Howie 136, 138
Howitt 136
Howkins 124
Howland 141, 172
Howse 137
Howson 124, 137

Hoyes 135
Hoyles 135
Huband 137
Hubbard 124
Huber 123
Hubert 32, 66, 124
Huddleston 135
Hudson 124, 162
Huggett 124
Huggins 124, 136
Hugh 21, 32, 43, 47, 66, 97, 103, 124
Hughes 122, 124, 141
Hugill 137
Hugman 256
Hugo 66
Hulbert 125, 137
Hulland 134
Hullett 124
Hullis 124
Human 131, 255
Humberside 174
Humbley 135
Humperdinck 142
Humphrey 124
Humphreys 124
Humphries 124
Hundred 180
HUNGARIAN GIVEN NAMES 116
Hungary 183
Hunstanton 171
Hunt 130, 255
Hunter 130, 138, 141, 162
Huntingdon 173
Huntingdonshire 173
Hurd 136
Hurley 136
Hurrell 134
Hurren 137
Hurry 133, 255
Hurt 136
Huskinson 136
Hussain 112
Hutch 162
Hutchings 124
Hutchins 124, 162
Hutchinson 124, 162
Hutchison 138
Hutley 134
Hutt 136
Hutton 129, 135
Huw 35, 66
Huxham 134
Huxley 133
Huxtable 134
Hyacinth 103
Hyde 137
Hylton 66
Hymen 22, 256
Hyslop 138

Iain 27, 66
Ian 27, 32, 48, 55, 66
Ibbotson 124, 137
Ibison 135
Ibrahim 112
Ibson 124
Iceland 183
ICELANDIC GIVEN NAMES 116
Ichabod 35, 103, 255
Ichiro 109
Icky 103
Ida 21, 53, 66, 90, 103
Idaho 184
Iddon 135
Idler 119
Idobel 38
Iesha 41
Iestyn 35
Ieuan 35
Ifan 35
If-Christ-had-not-died-for-thee-thou-hadst-been-damned 89
Igor 21, 117
Iles 135
Ilhan 117
Illinois 184
Illman 256
Ima 21, 255
Immanuel 35
Immergut 255

Imogen 38, 66
Ina 42, 103
Inas 112
INCIDENT NICKNAMES 156
INCIDENT PLACE NAMES 181
INDEX PAGES 1-36
India 38, 41, 66, 183
Indiana 184
Indigreat 183
Indira 110
Indonesia 183
Inez 38, 255
Ing 133
Ingall 135
Ingate 137
Inge 135
Ingle 135
Ingleby 137
Inglis 129, 138
Ingolia 149
Ingram 136
Ingrid 38
Inions 136
INITIALS 79
INKS, NAMES OF 9
Innes 42, 127, 138, 255
INSECT FIRST NAMES 89
Inskip 133
Instone 136
Intriligator 255
INVENTED NAMES 21
Inverness-shire 173
Iolo 35
Iona 21, 42, 66
Iowa 184
Iqbal 112
Ira 35
Iran 183
Iraq 183
Ireland 129, 183, 255
Irena 117
Irene 38, 51-3, 66, 88, 103
Irina 117
Iris 21
Iris 38, 43, 51-2, 66
Irish 129, 134
IRISH FIRST NAMES 34, 41
IRISH SURNAMES 121
Ironman 256
Irony 255
Irvona 180
Isaac 34, 47, 49, 66, 82
Isaacs 134
Isabel 21, 38, 51, 66, 117, 124
Isabell 255
Isabella 38, 51, 66, 179
Isabelle 38, 66
Isaiah 66
Isgar 136
Ishmael 36, 66
Iskowitz 149
Isla 21, 42, 66
Islamabad 186
Isle of Muck 28
Isle of Wight 173
Ismay 42
Ismet 117
Isobel 66, 92
Israel 47, 183
Isted 137
István 116
Ita 41
ITALIAN GIVEN NAMES 117
Italy 183
Ivan 32, 66
Ivanhoe 149
Ivatt 133
Iveson 137
Ivey 133
Ivor 21, 32, 66, 90
Ivory 22, 135
Ivory Coast 183
Ivy 38, 43, 51, 66, 79, 81
Iwan 35
Izabela 117

Izabichie 255
Izzard 133

Jabal 36
Jacalyn 25
Jack 18, 21, 32, 47-9, 55, 66, 84, 103, 138
Jackalin 25
Jackaline 25
Jackie 66, 98
Jackman 134
Jacks 136
Jackson 79, 124, 138, 141
Jaclyn 25, 66
Jaclynn 25
Jacob 124, 18, 32, 43, 47-9, 50, 55, 66, 124
Jacobs 124
Jacobson 124
Jacoby 149
Jacolyn 25
Jacqualine 25
Jacqualyn 25
Jacqualynn 25
Jacquelean 25
Jacquelene 25
Jacquelin 25
Jacqueline 25, 38, 52-5, 66, 98
Jacquelyn 25, 66
Jacquelyne 25
Jacquelynn 25
Jacques 18, 32, 137
Jaculine 25
Jade 22, 38, 45, 52, 55, 66
Jael 42
Jafar 112
Jagger 137
Jaggs 124
Jago 127
Jaguar 89
Jaime 38, 66, 126
Jakarta 186
Jake 32, 48, 55, 66
Jakelyn 25
Jaleesa 41
Jaleisa 41
Jalen 50
Jalesa 41
Jalisa 41, 54
Jamaica 183
Jamal 34, 50
James 32, 47-9, 50, 55, 66, 85, 90, 104, 113, 122, 124, 141, 255
Jameson 134
Jamie 32, 38, 48, 54, 66
Jamieson 124, 134, 138
Jamilah 112
Jan 66, 116-7
Jana 117
Janae 41
Janay 41
Janaye 41
Jane 38,
Jane 46, 51-3, 55, 66, 83-4, 95, 102-3, 111, 133
Janet 38, 52-5, 66, 92
Janette 67
Janice 27, 38, 52-5, 67
Janie 103
Janine 38, 67
Janis 38, 67
Jannine 38, 67
János 116
January 94
Japan 183
JAPANESE GIVEN NAMES 109
Japheth 36
Jaqueline 25, 67
Jaquelline 25
Jardine 151
Jared 32, 36, 50
Jarman 129, 256
Jarmila 117
Jaroslav 117
Jarrad 36
Jarrard 124, 135

Jarrod 32
Jarrom 135
Jarvie 124
Jarvis 124
Jasmine 38, 52, 54-5, 67
Jason 32, 48, 50, 55, 67, 78-9, 82
Jasper 103, 133
Javal 149
Jay 21, 67
Jayne 38, 45, 67
Jean 21, 38, 51-3, 67, 93
Jeanette 38, 67
Jeanne 38, 67, 100
Jeannette 38, 67
Jeans 22
Jeavons 137
Jedaiah 36
Jeeves 124
Jeffcoate 137
Jefferies 124
Jefferson 123-4
Jeffery 67
Jeffrey 32, 48-9, 50, 55, 67, 124
Jeffs 133
Jehoshaphat 43
Jehudi 36
Jelbart 133
Jelbert 133
Jelisa 41
Jellicoe 30
Jellis 135
Jelly 30, 131, 255
Jemima 51, 67, 80, 103
Jemimah 42, 45
Jemma 38, 67
Jenifer 67
Jenkin 133
Jenkins 124, 149
Jenna 38, 67
Jenni 116
Jennie 38, 53, 67
Jennifer 38, 52, 54-5, 67, 83, 90, 146
Jennings 124
Jennison 124
Jenny 38, 51, 67
Jensen 126
Jephcott 137
Jephson 124
Jepp 124
Jepson 124, 133
Jeremiah 32, 138
Jeremy 32, 47-8, 50, 67
Jermaine 34, 67, 89
Jermyn 129
Jeroboam 36
Jeroen 116
Jerome 49, 50, 67
Jerram 134
Jerrold 124
Jerry 21, 32, 49
Jerusalem 186
Jerzy 117
Jeshua 32
Jesse 32, 47, 50, 55, 67
Jessica 38, 52, 54-5, 67, 78, 85, 106
Jessie 42, 51, 67
Jesson 135
Jesty 134
Jesus 32, 91
Jesus-Christ-came-into-the-world-to-save 89
Jet 45
Jethro 36
Jevons 137
Jewel 22, 46
JEWEL NAMES 43
Jewett 124
Jezebel 42
Jill 38, 55, 67, 155
Jillian 38, 55, 67
Jillings 137
Jillisa 41
Jim 21, 67, 85, 113
JIM SMITH SOCIETY 147
Jimmy 32
Jimpson 124

Jin 46
Jiří 117
Jifo 109
Jitindra 110
Jitka 117
Jo 107
Jo-Ann 38, 67
Jo-Anne 38, 67, 103
Joab 36
Joakim 117
Joan 21, 25, 51-5, 67, 84, 100, 104, 255
Joana 117
Joanna 38, 51, 67, 103
Joanne 27, 38, 52-5, 67, 79, 103
João 117
Job 36, 98
Jobling 136
Jocasta 103
Jocelyn 38, 43, 67
Jock 18
Jocke 103
Jodhpur 19
Jodi 38, 67
Jodie 38, 52, 55, 67
Jody 38, 67
Joe 21, 67, 255
Joel 32, 67
Joginder 110
Johan 117
Johanan 91
Johanna 38, 67
Johanne 67
JOHANNESBURG STREET NAMES 193-4
John 25, 27, 32, 47-9, 50, 55, 67, 78, 84, 89, 91, 93, 97, 104, 120, 122, 124, 255
Johnathan 67
Johnny 67
Johns 124
Johnson 124, 141, 162, 255
Johnston 134, 138, 141
Johnstone 138, 151
Joie 22
Joke 89
JOKE NAMES 21
Jolene 67
Jolliffe 132, 135
Jolly 22, 132
Jollyman 256
Jolyan 124
Jolyon 67
Jon 116-7
Jon 32, 67
Jonah 36, 45, 103
Jonas 67, 133
Jonathan 32, 43, 47-8, 50, 55, 67
Jonathon 67
Jones 79, 122, 124, 141, 149, 255
Jonina 116
Jonna 116
Jonothon 86
Jordan 32, 48, 50, 55, 67, 183
Jordana 67
Jordison 137
Jorge 117
Jorgensen 123
Jory 127
José 117, 133
Josef 117
Joseph 25, 32, 43, 47-9, 50, 55, 68, 91
Josephine 38, 68, 107
Josh 68
Joshua 32, 43, 47-8, 50, 68, 82, 91
Joshuah 55
Josiah 36, 47
Josie 38, 68
Joule 134
Jowett 124, 137
Joy 21, 38, 43, 68, 102, 255
Joyce 38, 51-4, 68, 255
Joyes 137
Ju Ao 108

Juan 117
Juanita 68
Jubb 137
Juby 137
Judah 36
Judas 36
Jude 36
Judit 116
Judith 38, 51-5, 68, 88
Judkins 136
Judson 137
Judy 38, 53-4, 68, 88
Juha 116
Juju 111
Jules 21
Julia 38, 51-3, 68, 84, 116
Julian 32, 48, 68, 124, 133
Juliana 38, 117, 124
Julie 38, 52-5, 68, 89, 103
Julien 124
Juliet 38, 68, 224
Juliette 68
Julius 32
Julyan 124, 133
June 38, 52, 68, 85, 90, 255
Junior 104
Junior 22, 104
Junko 109
Jupe 137
Just 22
Justin 21, 32, 48, 50, 55, 68
Justina 68
Justine 38, 68
Jyrki 116

KABALARIANS 146
Kábul 186
Kaisa 116
Kaiser 22
Kaitlyn 54
Kalvaitis 123
Kamil 112
Kamilah 112
Kaminsky 142
Kanako 109
Kane 32, 55, 162
Kanisha 54
Kansas 184
Kanti 110
Kapil 110
Kappelhoff 149
Kara 38, 68
Karel 117
Karen 27, 38, 45, 52-5, 68
Kari 116
Karimah 112
Karin 38, 68, 116-7
Karina 38, 68
Karl 32, 48, 68, 117
Karla 38, 68
Karly 68
Karon 68
Karyn 68
Kashmir 183
Katarzyna 117
Kate 38, 51-2, 55, 68
Katharina 38
Katharine 24, 38, 68, 124
Katherina 116
Katherine 38, 52-5, 68
Katheryne 86
Kathleen 38, 51-5, 68
Kathrin 116
Kathrine 68
Kathryn 38, 68
Kathy 53-4
Kathy 68
Katie 38, 52, 54, 68
Katina 41
Katrin 116
Katrina 38, 68
Katrine 42
Katsutoshi 109
Katy 38, 68
Katz 126
Kaufman 126
Kaumeyer 149
Kaur 110
Kay 21, 38, 55, 68,

138
Kaye 38, 68, 142, 145
Kayla 54-5
Kaylea 38, 68
Kaylee 38, 68
Kayleigh 38, 52, 68, 85
Kayley 38, 68, 85
Kaylie 38, 68
Kazuko 109
Kazuo 109
Keast 133
Keaton 149
Keeble 137
Keedwell 136
Keel 136
Keeley 38, 68
Keelie 38
Keeling 137
Keely 38, 68
Keen 132
Keep 133
Keetley 135
Keevil 137
Keightley 135
Keir 34
Keirl 136
Keisha 41
Keith 26, 32, 48-9, 50, 55, 68
Kellaway 134
Keller 126
Kellett 135
Kelli 38
Kellie 38, 55, 68
Kellogg 130
Kelly 38, 52, 54-5, 68, 80, 82, 85, 127, 141, 162
Kellyhouse 255
Kelsey 38, 54, 68
Kelvin 32, 68
Kemal 117
Kemble 137
Kemp 130
Kempson 133
Kemsley 134
Ken 21
Kendra 41, 54
Kendrew 137
Kenichi 109
Kenji 109
Kennedy 127, 138
Kennerley 133
Kenneth 32, 47-9, 50, 55, 68
Kenny 68
Kenrick 125
Kent 84, 135, 173
Kentaro 109
Kentucky 184
Kenward 125
Kenway 125
Kenworthy 137
Kenya 41, 89
Kenyatta 41
Kenyetta 41
Kenyon 135
Kerenhappuch 42
Kerensa 98
Keri 38, 68
Kerkin 133
Kermode 127
Kerr 127, 141
Kerri 38, 68
Kerrich 125
Kerrie 38, 55, 69, 80
Kerrison 136
Kerry 38, 45, 52, 69, 90
Kerslake 134
Kerstin 117
Kestle 133
Keswick 170
Ketley 134
Kettle 162
Kettlewell 137
Kettley 134
Keturah 42
Kevan 69
Kevern 133
Kevin 32, 48-9, 50, 69
Keynes 134
Keyte 137
Keyworth 136
Keziah 41-3

Khadija 54, 111
Khaki 22
Khalid 112
Khalig 111
Khartoum 186
Kiana 54
Kiara 54
Kidd 137-8, 162, 255
Kidder 255
Kidner 136
Kieran 32, 48, 55, 69
Kieron 69
Kierra 54
Kiesler 149
Killer 131
Killick 137
Kilminster 135
Kilmister 135
Kilshaw 135
Kilts 180
Kilvington 137
Kim 38, 53-5, 69, 116
Kima 116
Kimball 10, 116
Kimber 133
Kimberley 38, 55, 69, 104
Kimberly 38, 54, 69
Kimmo 116
Kincardineshire 173
Kinch 137
King 138, 141, 149, 162
Kingham 133
Kingman 134
Kingsley 69, 135
Kingsman 256
Kingsnorth 135
Kingston 136, 169, 186
Kingwell 134
Kinross-shire 173
Kinsey 133
Kipling 137, 167
Kirby 129
Kircudbrightshire 173
Kiribaba 113
Kiribabi 113
Kirk 32, 69
Kirkby Overblow 172
Kirkman 135
Kirkup 134
Kirrkomaki 123
Kirsten 21, 39, 69
Kirstie 42, 69, 104
Kirsty 39, 52, 69
Kirton 134
Kish 36
Kisser 131
KISSES, NAMES OF 237
Kissin 255
Kissing Point 182
Kitchener 135
Kitson 124
Kitt 124
Kitto 133
Kittow 133
Kitts 124
Kitty 21, 51, 104
Kizzie 41
Kizzy 41, 69
Klein 126
Kleinville 182
Kline 126
Klink 255
Klinker 255
Knaggs 137
Knapman 134
Knapp 129, 137
Kneebone 133
Knibb 137
Knickerbocker 123
Knifesmith 256
Knifton 134
Knight 130, 162
Knightsbridge 169
Knott 134
Knowles 129
Koch 126
Kodak 180
Kofi 115
Konigsberg 149
Korah 36
Korea 184
Korina 37, 39

Korner 255
Kovacs 123
Kowalsky 123
Kramer 126
Krause 126
Krishna 117
Kristen 54
Kristian 32, 69, 88
Kristin 54, 116
Kristina 39, 69, 117
Kristine 45, 117
Kristopher 32
Kristy 39, 55, 69
Kruger 126
Krystyna 117
Krysztof 117
Kuala Lumpur 186
Kubelsky 149
Kujnir-Herescu 149
Kuldip 110
Kumakichi 109
Kurt 32, 69
Kuwait 183, 186
Kuznetsov 123
Kwabena 114
Kwadwo 114
Kwaku 114
Kwame 115
Kwasi 114
Kyla 85
Kyle 32, 48, 50, 69
Kylie 39, 55, 69, 85
Kynaston 136
Kyoko 109

La Fayette 123
La Paz 186
Laban 36
Lacey 39, 69, 135
Lachicotte 255
Lachlan 34, 55
Lackman 256
Laddie 22
Ladds 135
Lady 22
Ladyman 256
Laetitia 104
Lafayette 46
Lagden 134
Lagos 186
Laidler 136
Laidman 256
Lain 136
Laing 138
Laity 133
Lake 129
Lake Victoria 166
Lakeisha 41, 54
Lakin 137
Lala 90
Lamar 34
Lamb 162
Lambrick 125
Lambshead 134
Laming 135
Lamming 135
Lamond 34
Lamont 34, 138
Lamorna 7
Lamplough 137
Lamplugh 137
Lana 39, 69
Lanarkshire 173
Lancashire 135, 173
Lancaster 168
Lance 21, 32, 69
Land 136
Lander 130, 133
Lane 129
Lanfear 133
Lang 126, 132, 134, 138
Langehanke 149
Langemore 141
Langford 129
Langley 129
Langman 134
Langridge 135
Langworthy 134
Lanning 98
Lanny 98
Lanyon 133
Lara 39, 69
Larcombe 134
Larisa 117
Larita 95
Larkin 124, 135
Larking 135

Larkins 124
Larry 49, 50, 69
Lars 117
Larsen 126
Larson 126
Larwood 136
Lashawn 41
Laslett 135
Lassie 112
Last 22, 137
LAST NAMES 118
László 116
Latanya 41
Latasha 41
Latham 141
Latif 112
Latisha 41
Latona 41
Latonya 41, 89
Latoya 41, 54
Latrice 41
Laura 21, 39, 43, 51-5, 69, 84, 89, 117
Laurel 39, 43, 69
Lauren 39, 52, 54-5, 69
Laurence 24, 32, 47-8, 69, 124, 255
Lauretta 104
Laurie 69, 107, 124, 138
Lavender 22, 130
Laverack 137
Laverick 137
Lavington 135
Lavinia 69
Law 124, 138
Lawana 95
Lawless 140
Lawley 136
Lawman 256
Lawrence 24, 32, 49, 50, 69, 124
Lawrenson 135
Lawrie 124, 138
Lawry 133
Lawson 69, 124, 138
Lay 133
Laycock 137
Lazarus 36
Lazienki 144
Lea 39, 69
Leach 130, 149, 162
Leadbeater 130, 135
Leadbetter 130, 135
Leadbitter 130
Leah 39, 43, 69, 133
Leak 137
Leake 137
Leakey 144
Lean 133
Leanne 39, 52, 55, 69
Leaper 137
Lear 35, 134, 224
Leather 133
Leaver 135
Leavers 136
Leavey 125
Leavold 125
Lebanon 183
Lecia 88
Leckenby 137
Ledbrook 137
Lee 21, 32, 48, 69, 80-1, 129, 141
Leech 130
Leeder 136
Leeds 136
Leela 110
Lees 162
Lefevre 123
Leftoff 255
Legg 134, 162
Leggett 135
Leggott 135
Leicestershire 135, 173
Leigh 39, 55, 69, 80-1
Leigh-Ann 69
Leigh-Anne 69
Leighanne 69
Leighton 21, 32, 69, 137
Leila 39, 69, 104
Leister 141, 172
Leivers 136
Lemmer 125

Lemon 80, 132
Lemuel 36
Lena 21, 39, 69
Leney 135
Lenin 104, 142
Lenka 117
Lennart 117
Lennox 138
Lent 170
Lenton 135
Leo 45, 69, 89
Leon 32, 49, 69
Leona 39, 69
Leonard 32, 45, 47-9, 50, 69, 89
Leonie 39, 69, 90
Leonor 117
Leppard 137
Leroy 32, 49, 69
Lerwill 134
Lesbos 19
Lese 137
Lesley 24, 39, 52, 55, 69, 81
Leslie 24, 26, 32, 47-8, 69, 81-2, 112, 138
Lethbridge 134
Letheren 134
Lettice 21
Lettsom 257
Lever 135
Levi 36, 126
Levine 126
Levitch 142
Levy 21, 126
Lewell 136
Lewin 125
Lewis 32, 48-9, 69, 124, 141-3
Ley 134
Liam 32, 48, 69
Liane 69
Lianne 39, 70
Libby 21, 124
Liberace 142
Liberia 183
Libero 104
Liberty 22
Liddicoat 133
Lidstone 134
Light 135
Lila 39, 70
Lilac 22
Lili 111
Lilian 39, 51-2, 70
Lilith 42
Lill 135
Lilla 255
Lilley 135, 255
Lilleyman 125
Lillian 39, 53, 70
Lillie 53
Lilly 51
Lily 39, 43, 51, 70, 104
Limb 134
Limbrick 135
Limer 137
Lina 112
Lincoln 123, 129, 172
Lincolnshire 135, 173
Linda 39, 43, 52-5, 70, 90, 116
Lindley 136
Lindop 137
Lindsay 39, 52, 70, 138
Lindsey 39, 54, 70
LINK PLACE NAMES 180
Linnell 136
Linsay 39
Linsey 39, 70
Lionel 21, 32, 45, 70, 89, 104
LIPSTICK NAMES 222
Lisa 21, 39, 52, 54-5, 70
Lister 130
Litchfield 134
LITERARY NICKNAMES 164
LITERARY SURNAMES 151
Little 22, 138, 162, 255

Littlechild 134
Littlejohn 124, 133
Littlejohns 134
Littler 133
Litwin 125
Liv 88
Livesey 135
Liveseley 135
Liz 43, 83
Liza 39, 43, 46, 70
Lizzie 51, 104, 255
Llewellyn 124
Llinos 42
Lloyd 32, 70, 127
Llyr 35
Loaring 129
Lobb 133
Loch Ness 167
Locksmith 256
Lodder 134
Loder 134
Lodge 137
Logan 138
Loggerhead 145
Logwell 255
Lois 21, 39, 42, Lois 53, 70
Lokuduya 112
Lokuputa 113
Lola 70
Lolita 104
Lolly 94
Lombardo 123
Lona 42
Londinos 167
London 94, 166, 169, 173, 186
LONDON STREET NAMES 190-3, 196-97
Londonderry 173
Long 132, 162
Long Ditton 170
Longbottom 137
Longden 134
Longfellow 123
Longley 137
Longman 256
Longnecker 255
Longton 135
Longworth 135
Lonsdale 135
Lonsley 133
Look 136
Looker 135
Loosemoor 134
Loosley 136
Loosmoor 134
Lope 126
Lopez 126
Lor 46
Lora 42
Loraine 39, 70
Lord 22
Loren 70
Loretta 70
Lori 21, 39, 54
Lorimer 130
Loring 129
Lorna 10, 25, 39, 70, 104
Lorne 21
Lorraine 39, 52-3, 55, 70, 80, 129
Lorry 133
Loseby 135
Lotta 21
Louch 136
Louis 21, 26, 32, 43, 49, 70, 98, 124, 255
Louisa 39, 51, 53, 70, 84, 104
Louise 26, 39, 52-3, 70, 79, 84, 104, 143, 255
Louisiana 179, 184
Lovatt 137
Love 135, 255-6
LOVE NAMES 8
Loveband 256
Lovechild 256
Loveday 256
Lovefit 256
Lovegod 125
Lovegood 256
Lovegrove 136, 256

Loveguard 125
Lovejoy 104, 256
Lovekin 256
Lovelace 132, 256
Loveladd 256
Lovelady 256
Loveless 255-6
Lovelock 256
Lovely 256
Loveman 256
Lover 256
Loverage 256
Lovering 134, 256
Loverman 256
Loverock 137
Lovewell 256
Lovey 22
Loveybond 136
Loveys 256
Lovibond 136
Loving 180
Low 22, 46, 138
Lowanna 98
Lowis 124
Lowman 256
Lowri 42
Lowry 124
Loxton 136
Lucas 70, 124
Lucia 39, 70, 104
Lucie 39, 70
Lucien 70
Lucille 39, 70
Lucinda 39, 70
Luck 124, 135
Luckett 124, 136
Luckin 124
Lucking 134
Lucky 22
Lucre 256
Lucy 39, 51-3, 55, 70, 104, 155
Ludlam 134
Ludmila 117
Ludovic 34
Ludwig 34, 143
Lug 133
Luguvallium 167
Luis 117
Luísa 117
Luke 21, 32, 47-8, 55, 70, 124
Lukin 124
Lulham 146
Lulu 53, 104
Lumb 137
Lumsden 136, 138
Lundenceaster 168
Lune 168
Lupe 126
Lurvey 255
Lusaka 186
Luscious 255
Luscombe 134
Lush 131
Lusk 255
Lusty 135
Luther 180
Lutley 136
Lutwidge 143
Luxembourg 184
Luxton 134
Lycurgus 44
Lydia 39, 42, 51, 70, 93
Lyford 133
Lyle 133
Lymer 137
Lyn 39, 70
Lynam 134
Lynda 39, 45, 70
Lyndon 70
Lyndsay 39, 70
Lyndsey 39, 70
Lynette 39, 55, 70
Lynn 21, 27, 39, 52-5, 70, 135
Lynne 27
Lynne 39, 52-5, 70
Lynsay 39
Lynsey 39, 52, 70
Lyon 135, 138
Lysander 44
Lythgoe 135

Ma 22
Maachah 43
Maarbjerg 152

Maaz 91
Mabbot 124
Mabbs 124
Mabel 39, 46, 51, 53, 70, 105, 124
Mably 133
MacAngus 4
Macansh 4
Macaulay 135
Macbeth 124
MacDonald 141
MacGenis 4
MacGinnis 4
MacGuinness 4
Machigonne 183
Machin 124, 130
MacInnes 4
Macintosh 122
Mack 136
Mackaness 136
Mackay 138, 141
Mackenzie 138, 141, 255
Mackie 138
Mackinder 135
Mackinnes 4
Mackinness 4
Mackintosh 138
Mackley 135
Maclaine 142
Maclaren 134, 138
Maclean 138, 141
Macleod 138, 141
Macmillan 138, 141
Macnab 138
Macpherson 138
Macrae 138
Maddaford 133
Maddison 124
Maddiver 133
Maddy 135
Madelaine 70
Madeleine 39, 55, 70
Madeley 136
Madeline 39, 70
Maden 135
Madge 24, 104, 134
Madison 55, 124
Madonna 255
Mads 117
MAGAZINE NAMES 229
Magdalen 124
Magdalene 39, 42
Magennies 4
Maggot 101
Maggots End 172
Maggs 124
MAGIC, NAME 9
Maginnis 56
Maginniss 4
Magnet 22
Magnus 34, 116
Magor 133
Magson 124
Maguinness 4
Mahershalalhashbaz 89
Mai 42
Maid 255
MAIDEN NAMES 144
Maidens 135
Mailes 135
Main 136
Maine 185
Mainwaring 121, 135
Mair 42, 138
Mairead 41
Mairi 42
Maisie 24, 39, 70
Maitland 104, 138
Majella 41
Major 22, 133
Makbule 117
Makepeace 43, 104, 134
Makins 124
Makinson 124
Makoto 109
Malachi 36
Malawi 183
Malchiah 36
Malcolm 138
Malcolm 25, 32, 45, 48, 55, 70, 138, 255

Malden 133
Maldonaldo 126
Malik 112
Malikah 112
Malkiat 110
Malkin 137
Mallam 134
Malleson 124
Mallett 124, 136
Mallinder 134
Mallinson 137
Mallory 132
Malta 183
Malvina 42
Mami 109
Mammett 124
Mammon 256
Manasseh 36
Manchester 174
Mandi 45
Mandy 39, 52, 70, 80
Manjit 110
Manleigh 139
Manley 134, 139
Manlove 256
Manly 139
Mann 80, 126
Manners 137, 140
Mannington 137
Manny 255
Mansell 136
Manuel 117
Manwaring 135
MAORI PLACE NAMES 165
Mapp 124
Mappin 124
Mapson 124
Mapstone 136
Mar'ann 46
Maradick 152
Marah 105
Marc 32, 70
Marcel 116
Marchant 130
Marchington 134
Marcia 39, 43, 53-4, 70
Marcus 32, 34, 50, 70
Mardell 135
Marfell 135
Marfleet 136
Margaret 18, 24, 27, 39, 45, 51-5, 70, 84, 90, 105, 124
Margareta 117
Margarine 86
Marge 105
Margerison 124, 135
Margerson 135
Margery 70
Margeson 141
Margetson 124
Marginson 135
Margot 39, 70, 85
Margrèt 116
Margretts 124
Marguerite 39, 70, 98, 105
Mari Dunum 167
Maria 18, 39, 51-2, 54-5, 70, 83, 116-17
Mariah 54
Marian 18, 39, 71, 146
Marianne 39, 71, 117
Marie 39, 52-4, 71, 100, 116
Marieke 116
Marietta 105
Mariette 45
Marilyn 39, 52-5, 71, 90
Marina 39, 71
Mario 117
Marion 39, 52-3, 55, 71, 124, 255
Marisa 42
Marissa 71
Marius 21
Marjoribanks 121
Marjorie 43, 51-3, 71, 101, 105
Marjory 71
Mark 21, 32, 47-9, 50, 55, 71, 79, 90, 116, 255-6

Markham 136
Markk 86
Marklove 256
Markova 142
Marks 126, 142
Markus 116-17
Marlena 41
Marlene 39, 53, 71
Marloes 116
Marlon 34, 71
Marples 134
Marquis 50
Marriage 134, 256
Marriner 149
Marriott 124
Marrison 124
Marry 256
Marryat 124
Marsha 71
Marshall 130, 138, 141
Marsland 133
Marson 137
Martell 124
Martens 124
Martha 39, 42, 46, 51, 53, 71, 105
Martin 21, 32, 47-9, 50, 71, 79, 117, 124, 138, 141, 162
Martina 39, 71, 117
Martindale 134
Martine 39, 71
Martinet 124
Martinez 126
Martinson 124
Martland 135
Martyn 32, 71
Marvin 34, 49, 105
Mary 21, 27, 39, 43, 51-5, 71, 81, 83-4, 91, 95, 124
Mary Ann 46, 51, 79, 124
Mary Anne 93
Mary Therese 93
Maryat 124
Marybelle 255
Maryland 179, 185
Maryman 256
Masayoshi 109
Mashiter 135
Mask 135
Maskell 134
Maskery 134
Maskrey 134
Maslen 133
Mason 123, 130
Massachussetts 185
Masterman 256
Mastin 136
Masud 112
Matcham 135
Mates 255
Mathams 134
Matheson 124, 138
Mathew 71
Mathieson 124, 138
Matilda 39, 51, 71, 124
Matson 124, 137
Matt 21
Matterson 124, 137
Matthew 32, 47-9, 50, 55, 71, 78, 89, 105, 124, 146
Matthews 124
Matthias 116, 138
Matthieu 116
Matti 116
Mattin 124
Mattison 137
Matts 135
Maud 21, 39, 43, 51, 53, 71, 90, 105
Maude 255
Maudlin 22
Maudling 124
Maudsley 135
Maudson 124
Mault 124
Maunder 133
Maundrell 137
Maura 41
Maureen 39, 52-5, 71
Maurice 32, 34, 43, 47-9, 50, 71, 124
Mauritania 183

Mavis 25, 39, 52, 71
Maw 136
Mawdsley 135
Mawer 136
Mawle 136
Mawson 124, 137
Max 21, 32, 71
Maximilian 32, 71
Maxine 39, 71
Maxted 135
Maxwell 32, 34, 71, 133, 138
May 21, 27, 39, 43, 46, 51, 53, 71, 90, 162, 255
Maya 54
Maycock 124
Mayday 22
Mayer 126, 137
Mayfield 129
Mayhew 124
Mayie 46
Maykin 124
Maylam 135
Mayne 133
Mayo 134
Mayor 135
McAdam 138
McArthur 138
McClean 138
McClung 255
McCormick 123
McCulla 143
McCulloch 138
McDavid 255
McDonald 138
McDougall 138
McEvoy 255
McEwan 138
McEwen 138
McFarlane 127, 138
McGee 255
McGowan 121
McGregor 122, 127, 138
McIntosh 127, 138
McIntyre 127, 138
McKay 127, 138
McKeeby 255
McKenzie 127, 138
McKie 138
McLaren 138
McLean 127
McLeod 127, 138
McMath 149
McMillan 127, 138
McNab 138
McNaughton 138
McNeil 138
McNeill 138
McPherson 127, 138
McRae 138
Meaden 134
Meadmore 135
Meadows 129
Meaker 136
'MEANINGS' OF NAMES 7
Measag 105
Measures 136
Meatman 256
Meatyard 134
Medford 137
MEDIEVAL STREET NAMES 189
Medina 126
Medium 22
Medora 96
Meech 134
Meek 22
Meen 137
Meeson 134
Meg 105
Megan 39, 52, 54-5, 71
Meggeson 124
Megginson 137
Meggison 137
Meggs 124
Meghan 39
Megson 137
Meikle 138
Meironwen 42
Mel 21, 255
Melancthon 180
Melanie 39, 45, 52, 55, 71, 82, 90, 92,

105, 116
Melech 36
Melfyn 35
Melhuish 134
Melinda 39, 55, 71, 91
Meliora 95
Melissa 39, 45, 52, 54-5, 71, 89, 91
Melita 91
Mellings 136
Melluish 134
Mellyora 95
Melody 21, 39, 71, 105
Melsome 137,
Melton 129,
Melvin 32, 71, 255
Melvyn 32, 71
Memory 22, 255
Memory Cove 181
Menika 113
Meniki 113
Menlove 256
Mentasta 182
Menzies 138
Mercer 130
Mercy 21, 43, 98, 105, 110
Merdegrave 170
Meredith 39, 95, 122
Mereid 42
Meriel 42, 71
Merionethshire 173
Merle 71
Merrell 137
Merrikin 136
Merrills 136
Merriman 256
Merryweather 255
Merseyside 174
Mertijn 116
Mervin 43
Mervyn 71
Mesha 36
Mesnieres 140
Message 137
Metherall 134
Metherell 134
Metson 134
Meunier 144
Mew 135
Mews 255
Mexico 183
Meyer 126
Micah 36
Michael 32, 43, 47-9, 50, 55, 71, 90-1, 93, 107, 116, 124, 255
Michaela 39, 71
Michaella 71
Michele 39 71
Michell 124
Michelle 39, 52, 54-5, 71, 84, 90
Michi 109
Michieson 124
Michigan 185
Micklewhite 149
MIDDLE NAMES 26
Middlemas 136
Middlemiss 136, 173
Middlesex 136, 173
Middleton 138, 149
Midgley 137
Midlothian 173
Midsummer 22
Midwinter 136
Miguel 117
Mihika 113
Mika 116
Mikaela 55
Mike 21
Miklós 116
Milan 19
Milbank 134
Milborrow 125
Mildon 134
Mildred 39, 41, 53, 71, 90, 105
Miles 21, 32, 71
Milk 136
Mill 134
Millar 138
Millbank 134
Mille 89

Milledge 134
Millen 135
Miller 130, 138, 141, 144, 162
Millichamp 136
Millie 89
Milligan 138
Millington 136
Millman 134
Mills 129, 130
Milly 71
Milman 134
Milne 135, 138
Milner 130
Milsom 137
Milton 34, 71, 129, 255
Mima 109
Mimi 90, 105, 111
Mimosa 22
Minako 109
Minchin 135
Mine 22
Minett 135
Minna 116
Minnehaha 98, 182
Minnesota 185
Minnie 21, 46, 51, 53, 255
Minns 136
Minoru 109
Minshall 133
Minshull 133
Minter 135-6, 141
Mintey 137
Minton 136
Minty 137
Mira 105
Mirabell 95
Miranda 25, 39, 71, 224
Miriam 39, 43, 53, 71, 91, 98, 105, 255
Miroslav 117
Miroslava 117
Misao 109
Miser 119
MISLEADING SURNAMES 131
Missing 135
Mississippi 185
Missouri 185
Mister 22
Misty 71
Mitchell 32, 55, 71, 124, 138, 141
Mitchelson 124
Mitchison 124
Mobbs 124
MODIFIERS, PERSONAL NAME 29
Moffat 138
Mogford 134
Mogg 124
Moggs 124
Mohammed 111
Mohan 110
Mohani 110
Mohinder 110
Moir 138
Moira 21, 39, 71, 105
Mold 124
Mole Hill 183
Mollie 39, 71, 255
Mollison 124
Molly 21, 39, 46, 72, 92, 95, 103, 105
Molnar 144
Molyneux 135
Mona 21
Monaco 183
Money 131, 256
Moneypenny 131, 152
Mongolia 183
Monica 39, 72, 105
Monika 117
Monique 41, 54
Monkman 137
Monmouthshire 138, 173
Monnington 135
Montague 72, 147
Montana 185

Montevideo 186
Montgomery 45, 136, 255
Montgomeryshire 173
MONTH NAMES AS FIRST NAMES 90
Montreal 182
Moody 105, 131-2
Moon 255
Moore 132, 141, 162, 254
Moorhouse 137
Moos 255
Morag 42
Morales 126
Moray 173
Morcock 124
Morcom 133
Mordecai 36, 138
Mordred 98
Moreno 126
Morgan 35, 122, 141, 162
Morkam 133
Morphett 135
Morrice 124
Morris 72, 124, 141, 149
Morrison 124, 136, 138, 141, 149
Morse 124, 137
Morson 124
Morter 162
Mortimer 106
Mortimore 134
Mortin 134
Morton 129, 138
Morven 42
Moseley 129
Moses 21, 36, 47, 138
Mossman 133
Mossop 134
MOST ALCOHOLIC FIRST NAME 91
MOST COMMON ANANYM FIRST NAME 91
MOST COMMON SURNAMES 141
MOST FREQUENT BIBLICAL NAME 91
MOST HESITANT FIRST NAME 91
MOST MYSTERI-OUS FIRST NAME 89
MOST ORIGINAL FIRST NAME 90
MOST POPULAR DAY FIRST NAME 91
MOST RIOTOUS FIRST NAME 90
MOST STERTO-ROUS FIRST NAME 90
MOST SURPRIS-ING FIRST NAME 90
MOST UNEX-PECTED FIRST NAME 90
MOST VALUABLE FIRST NAME 89
Mott 125, 134
Mottershead 133
Mottram 137
Mould 124
Mouldy 152
Moule 137
Moulson 124
Moult 124
Mounfield 133
Mounsey 134
Mountain 183
Mountfield 133
MOUSTACHES, NAMES OF 257
Mowbray 136
Moxon 124, 137
Moyle 133
Moza 36
Mozart 152
Muchbetter 152
Muck 28
Mudd 255
Muddy 105

Mudge 134
Mueller 126
Mugford 134
Muggleston 134
Muhammad 111
Muir 138
Muirhead 138
Mulder 144
Mullen 126
Muller 144
Mulliner 130
Mullinger 136
Mullins 141
Mullock 133
Mulluch 36
Muna 112
Munckton 134
Mundy 127
Mungo 34
Munn 137
Munro 127
Munroe 138
Munslow 136
Murcott 137
Murder 22, 181
Murdoch 34, 138
Murfin 134
Murfitt 133
Murgatroyd 137
Muriel 39, 51, 72, 93, 105-6
Murphy 127, 141, 162
Murray 34, 72, 127, 138, 141
Murrumbidgee 165
Murton 135
MUSICAL FIRST NAMES 90
MUSLIM GIVEN NAMES 111
Mussolini 255
Musson 135
Mustapha 21
Mustill 133
Mutton 133
Muzzammil 112
Myatt 137
Mycroft 10
Myers 126, 137
Myfanwy 42
Mykula 143
Myra 72
Myrddin Caer Myrddin 167
Myron 34
Myrtle 43, 72, 90
Mystic 22
Mytton 137

Naamah 42
Nabal 36
Nabil 112
Nabu 36
Nada 112
Nadezhda 117
Nadia 39, 72
Nadimah 112
Nadin 134
Nadine 39, 72, 90, 116
Nadirah 112
Nadya 112
Naessmith 256
Nagataka 109
Nahor 36, 90
Nahum 36
Nairnshire 173
Nairobi 186
Najmah 112
Naked 181
Nakia 41
Nakita 41
Nalinika Jayanadani 113
NAME ANAGRAMS 245, 253-4
NAME CALLING 29
NAME COLLECT-ING 255-6
'NAME', DEFINITIONS OF 6
NAME GAMES 244, 250
NAME JOKES 252-3
NAME MAGIC 9
NAME REBUS 250
NAME SUBSTI-TUTES, PERSONAL 8
NAME VERSES 252
NAME-PRINTS' 10
NAMES OF FICTIONAL CHARACTERS 147
NAMES, BIBLICAL FIRST 35
NAMES, CONVERTED 22
NAMES, INVENTED 21
NAMES, IRISH FIRST 34
NAMES, JOKE 21
NAMES, LOVE 8
NAMES, MIDDLE 26
NAMES, NUMBER 20
NAMES, SCOTTISH FIRST 34
NAMES, TYPES OF 6
NAMES, UNUSUAL FIRST 22
NAMES, WELSH FIRST 35
NAMES, 'MEANINGS' OF 7
NAMESAKES 147
Nance 127, 133
Nancekeville 134
Nancekivell 134
Nancy 39, 51, 53-4, 72, 93, 95, 100, 106, 255
Nancy Jane 88
Nani 111
Nankevil 134
Nannie 100
Nao 109
Naomi 39, 43, 52, 55, 72
Naphtali 36
Napper 133
Narelle 55
Naresh 110
Nasha 112
Nasimah 112
Nat 21
Natalie 25, 39, 52, 55, 72, 85, 90-1, 155
Natallia 146
Natalya 117
Natasha 39, 53, 55, 72, 91
Nathan 32, 43, 48-9, 50, 55, 72
Nathaniel 32, 47, 72
Nawal 112
Nayana Priyadharshani 112
Naylor 130
Neal 32, 72, 86, 124
Neame 135
Neat 139
Nebraska 185
Nebuchadnezzar 36, 43
Ned 46
Negus 127, 133
Nehemiah 36
Neighbour 136
Neil 21, 32, 48, 55, 72, 138
Neilson 124, 138
Neithercut 255
Nell 255
Nellie 27, 51, 53, 72, 255
Nelly 51
Nelson 72, 124, 141, 146
Neola 180
Nerissa 106
Nerys 42
Nesling 137
Nessie 167
Nesta 42
Netherlands 183
Netherway 134

NETSILIK GIVEN NAMES 111
Nettles 255
Nevada 185
Nevell 136
Nevil 32, 72
Neville 26, 32, 72
Nevin 136
Nevins 136
New 135
New England 178
New Hampshire 185
New Jersey 185
New Mexico 185
New York 179, 185, 189
New Zealand 183
Newall 133
Newby 135
Newcombe 134
Newey 137
Newhouse 255
Newington 137
Newitt 136
Newlove 256
Newman 256
Newsholme 137
Newsome 137
Newson 137
Newth 137
Newton 129
Newton's Station 183
Nia 42
Niall 32, 34, 72
Niamh 41
Nibbs 124
Niblett 135
Nibson 124
Nice 139
Niceville 182
Nicewonger 255
Nichola 39, 72
Nicholas 18, 32, 47-8, 50, 55, 72, 116, 124, 155
Nichols 255
Nicholson 124, 138
Nick 21
Nickells 124
Nickless 137
NICKNAMES 153
NICKNAMES, CLAN 158, 162
NICKNAMES, CRIMINAL 158
NICKNAMES, DESCRIPTIVE 157
NICKNAMES, FAMOUS 163
NICKNAMES, INCIDENT 156
NICKNAMES, LITERARY 164
NICKNAMES, OBSOLETE 160-1
NICKNAMES, POLITICAL 159
NICKNAMES, REASONS FOR 155
NICKNAMES, SELF-GENERATED 163
NICKNAMES, TRADITIONAL 158
NICKNAMES, WELSH 154
Nicknocks 172
Nicks 124
Nickson 124
Nicky 39, 45, 72
Nicol 138
Nicola 39, 52, 72
Nicolas 72
Nicolay 117
Nicole 39, 54-5, 72, 116
Nicoletta 39
Nicolette 39, 72
Nicoll 138
Nicolson 124, 138
Nicosia 186
Nielsen 126
Nigel 32, 48, 72, 106, 124
Niger 183

Nigeria 183
Nikki 39, 72
Nils 117
Nimal 113
Nimala 113
Nimali 113
Nimalka 113
Nina 39, 72
Ninaview 180
Ninel 91
Nini 111
Niranjan 110
Nisbet 138
Nisbett 138
Nixon 124
Noah 21, 36, 43, 72, 106
Nobbs 125
Noble 132, 137, 256
Noboru 109
Nobottle 172
Nock 136
Noden 133
Noel 25, 32, 72, 85, 91, 115
Noelle 91
Nolan 72, 127
Nora 21, 39, 51, 72, 90
Norah 39, 72
Norbury 133
Noreen 72
Norfolk 136, 169, 173
Norma 39, 52-3, 72, 90
Norman 32, 43, 47-9, 72, 129, 256
NORMAN NAMES 43
NORMAN PLACE NAMES 170
Normand 129
Nornabell 137
Norrish 134
North Carolina 185
North Dakota 185
Northam 134
Northamptonshire 136, 173
Northey 85
Northmore 134
Northumberland 136
Norway 183
NORWEGIAN GIVEN NAMES 117
Norwood 129, 136
Noseworthy 255
Nosworthy 134
Nottage 134
Nottingham 137
Nottinghamshire 136
Noun 255
Nova 22, 72
Novak 126, 149
Nuala 41
Nuddle 255
NUMBER NAMES 20
NUMBER NAMES, TRADE 225
NUMERICAL FIRST NAMES 89
NUMEROLOGY 245
Nunn 255
Nureyev 142
Nurse 136
Nutter 135

O Dalaigh 140
O'Brien 127
O'Byrne 127
O'Connor 127
O'Daly 140
O'Higgins 149
O'Neill 127
O'Reilly 127
Oak 22
Oakden 134
Oakes 133
Oakley 129
Oana 117
Oates 133
Oats 133
Obadiah 98
Obadiah 36
Obed 36

OBSOLETE NICKNAMES 160-1
OCCUPATIONAL SURNAMES 130
Ocean 22
Ockey 135
Ockleman 149
Octavia 20, 85, 89, 90
Odd 89
ODDEST FIRST NAME 89
Odger 133
Odgers 133
Odling 136
ODOROUS FIRST NAMES 90
Ody 137
Offen 135
Ogard 139
Ogilvie 138
Ogilvy 138
Ogle 136
Ohio 181, 185
Okel 133
Okla 84
Oklahoma 185
Olafia 116
Olave 34
Old 133
OLD ENGLISH PERSONAL NAMES 43, 125
Oldacres 135
Olden 149
Oldham 172
Oldman 256
Oldreave 134
Oldreive 134
Olean 180
Oleg 117
Olga 39, 72, 117, 155
Oliphant 136
Olivant 136
Olive 21, 40, 43, 51-2, 72, 105-6
Oliver 21, 32, 43, 47-8, 72, 138
Olives 255
Olivia 40, 55, 72, 83
Ollerton 135
Olney 255
Olof 117
Olsen 126
Olson 126
Olver 133
Olwen 42, 72
Olwyn 72
Omar 255
Omar 34
Omega 22
Onesiphorous 43
Onestone 255
Onion 107, 138, 255
Onions 136, 138
Only 22
ONOMANCY 244-49
Onyx 45, 90
Oonagh 72
Opal 43, 106
Ophelia 21
Opie 127, 133
Oppy 133
Optima 182
Oram 136
Orange 22, 80, 255
Orangeburg 179
Orchard 135
Ordway 125
Oregon 185
Oren 36
Organ 135
Orgee 135
Oriana 90
Oriel 43
Original 25, 90
Orkney 173
Orla 42
Ormond 138
Ormston 136
Orpe 137
Orpen 135
Orph 106
Orpheus 106
Orpin 135
Orr 138
Orrick 125

Orson 21, 45, 89, 135
Ortiz 126
Orville 255
Osbert 127
Oscar 32, 49, 72, 255
Óskar 116
Osker 86
Oslo 186
Osmer 125
Osmund 43
Ossi 116
Oswald 118
Oswin 125
Other 22
Otis 21
Ottawa 186
Otter Point 180
Otto 89
Ouch 139
Ouida 143
Oulton 133
Ouse 170
Outhouse 255
Outhwaite 137
Outram 134
Outridge 125
Ovary 255
Overell 135
Overett 162
Overman 256
Overton 136
Owain 35
Owen 21, 32, 47, 72, 98, 122
Owner 22,
Oxfordshire 136, 173,
Oyler 135

Packham 137
Padaiah 36
Padbury 136
Paddock 136
Paddon 134
Paddy 21, 91
Padfield 136
Padma 113
Padman 113
Padraic 34
Pagan 124
Page 130
Paget 130, 135
Paige 40, 72, 130
Pain 139
Paine 124, 139
Pakistan 183
Palanuik 149
Palethorpe 136
Palfrey 134
Paling 136
Palk 134
Pallister 134
Pamela 25, 40, 51-2, 54-5, 72, 91, 106
Pandora 98
Paniers 135
Pankhurst 137
Pannel 124
Pannell 134
Panniers 135
Pansy 43, 72
Pantall 135
Panter-Downes 255
Panther 136
Papageorge 255
PAPER, NAMES OF 9
Paradise 182
Paraguay 184
Paramatta Rangi 165
Paramjit 110
Parfitt 132
Parham 137
Paris 94, 186
Parish 134
Park 138
Parker 130, 141, 162
Parkhouse 134
Parkin 124
Parkins 135
Parkinson 124
Parks 124
Parnaby 137
Parnell 124
Parr 124
Parrish 134
Parrot 124
Parry 124
Parslow 135

Parson 130
Parsons 130, 162
Parton 137
Pascoe 127, 133
Pasquale 117
Pat 21, 46
Patchett 136
Pate 131
Paterson 124, 138, 141
Patience 43, 81
Patinson 134
Patmore 134
Paton 124, 138
Patrice 41
Patricia 40, 51-5, 72, 97, 117, 155, 162
Patrick 32, 48-9, 50, 55, 72, 91, 116, 124, 162
Patten 135
Patterson 124, 138
Pattinson 124
Pattison 124
Patty 21
Paul 21, 32, 48-9, 50, 55, 73, 79, 90, 107
Paula 40, 52, 73
Paulette 40, 73
Pauline 40, 52-3, 73, 116
Paulson 136
Pavey 134
Paxman 136
Paxton 136
Payling 136
Payne 124, 139
Paynter 133
Peabody 143
Peace 22
Peach 134
Peacock 129
Pearcey 134
Pearl 21, 40, 43, 46, 73
Pearline 255
Pearn 133
Pears 124, 162
Pearse 124
Pearson 124, 162
Pease 134
Peat 134
Peatfield 136
Pedi 113
Pediya 113
Pedlar 133
Pedler 133
Pedro 117
Peebleshire 173
Peel 137, 152
Peggy 24, 40, 51, 73
Pegler 135
Pegrum 134
Pegson 124
Peking 186
Pell 136
Pemberton 135
Pembrokeshire 173
PEN NAMES 142
Pendell 137
Pender 133
Pendle 137
Pendle Hill 166
Pendlebury 135
Pendleton 129
Penelope 40, 55, 73, 255
Penfold 137
Pengelly 127, 133
Pengilly 133
Penhill 166
Penn 123
Penna 133
Pennifold 137
Pennsylvania 180, 185
Penny 21, 40, 73, 255-6
Pennyman 256
Penrice 137
Penrose 127, 133
Pensil 152
Penson 135
Penwarden 134
Pepper 22, 130
Percival 32, 47, 73, 90
Percy 26-7, 32, 46-7,

73, 107
Perdita 98
Peregrine 10, 32
Perez 126
Perfect 132
Perham 136
Perkin 134
Perkins 124
Perrin 124, 134
Perrot 124
Perry 32, 73, 124
Pershing 123
Persis 21, 98
Perske 149
Person 124
PERSONAL NAME
    MODIFIERS 29
PERSONAL NAME
    SUBSTITUTES 8,
    29
PERSONAL
    NAMES, ANGLO
    SAXON 118, 125
PERSONAL
    NAMES, OLD
    ENGLISH 43, 125
PERSONAL
    NAMES,
    SCANDINAVIAN
    118
PERSONAL-NAME
    WORDS 18-19
Perthshire 173
Peru 184
Peta 73
Petard 145
Petch 137
Peter 21, 32, 46-9,
    50, 55, 73, 106,
    116, 124, 133
Peterborough 173
Peters 124
Peterson 124, 141
Pether 136
Petherbridge 134
Petherick 134
Pethick 133
Petr 117
Petra 73, 117
Petrina 73
Petronella 124
Petru 117
Pettengale 129
Pettingale 129
Pettingell 129
Pettipher 136
Pettit 132
Petula 73
Petunia 45
Petur 116
Pheasants 22
Phelan 89
Phelps 124
Phil 21
Philadelphia 188
Phileas 10
Philip 32, 47-9, 50,
    55, 73, 90-1, 124
Philippa 40, 73, 78
Philippines 184
Philips 138
Philipson 136
Phillip 32, 73
Phillippa 124
Phillips 122, 124,
    141
Phillipson 124
Philp 133
Philpot 124
Phintias 33
Phippen 124
Phipps 124
Phoebe 40, 51, 73,
    98, 106, 155, 255
Phyllis 101
Phyllis 40, 51-4, 73
Piara 110
Piazza 255
Pick 136
Pickersgill 137
Pickett 137
Pickin 136
Pickles 22
Pickup 135
Pickwell 136
Pickwick 147
Pictorial 255
Piddle 144

Pidduck 135
Pidgeon 152
Pieman 256
Pierce 124
Pierre 116
Piers 21, 32, 43, 73
Pike 162
Pilcher 135
Pilgrim 134
Pilkington 135
Pilling 135
Pimblett 135
Pimlott 133
Pina 113
Pinch 133
Pinches 136
Pinchin 137
Pinhay 134
Pinhey 134
Pinkbloom 255
Pinkie 22
Piper 130, 255
Pirangeli 149
Piroska 116
Pitchford 136
Pither 133
Pitock 135
Pitsner 152
Pius 255
PLACE NAME
    CHANGES 183
PLACE NAME
    ELEMENTS 174-5
PLACE NAMES AS
    FIRST NAMES 89
PLACE NAMES,
    ABORIGINAL 165
PLACE NAMES,
    AMERICAN
    INDIAN 165, 182
PLACE NAMES,
    ANGLO-SAXON
    169
PLACE NAMES,
    BRITISH 166
PLACE NAMES,
    CELTIC 166
PLACE NAMES,
    EARLIEST 165
PLACE NAMES,
    INCIDENT 181
PLACE NAMES,
    LINK 180
PLACE NAMES,
    MAORI 165
PLACE NAMES,
    NORMAN 170
PLACE NAMES,
    PRE-CELTIC 165
PLACE NAMES,
    ROYALTY IN 178
PLACE NAMES,
    SCANDINAVIAN
    170
PLACE NAMES,
    TRANSFERRED
    177
PLACE-NAME
    WORDS 19
PLACKETT 134
Plaistowe 133
Platesmith 256
Pleasant 22, 255
Pledger 134
Plews 137
Plum 255
Plumbly 136
Plummer 130
Plumtree 136
Plym 177
Plymouth 177, 179
Pochin 135
Pocklington 136
Podiduya 113
Podmore 136
Poel 124
Poggs 124
Poisin 42
Polakoff-Baidarov
    149
Poland 184
POLISH GIVEN
    NAMES 117
POLITICAL
    NICKNAMES 159
Polkinghorne 133
Polkingthorne 143
Poll 46, 136

Pollitt 135
Pollock 138
Polly 21, 46, 73, 88
Pollyanna 10
Pomeroy 134
Pomfret 135
Poopy 144
Poore 135
Poorman 256
POP GROUP
    NAMES 229
Pople 136
Popplewell 137
Poppy 21, 40, 43, 73
Porrett 137
Porritt 137
Portland 183
Portsmouth 135
Portugal 129, 184
PORTUGUESE
    GIVEN NAMES
    117
Poskitt 137
Postlethwaite 135
Potman 256
Pottenger 136
Potter 130
Potticary 135
Potts 124, 152
Pound 255-6
Pow 136
Powell 4, 124
Powlesland 134
Pownall 133
Powys 174
Poyey 133
Pratt 132, 149
PRE-CELTIC
    PLACE NAMES
    165
Prebble 135
Precious 137
Preece 124
Prem 113
Prema 113
Prescott 129
President 22
Preston 129
Prettejohn 134
Pretty 95, 135
Pretty Sally's 182
Prettyford 95
Prettyjohn 134
Prettyman 132, 256
Price 122, 124, 141,
    144, 256
Prickett 124
Priday 135
Priest 141
Priestner 133
Prima 20
Primrose 43, 45, 73
Prin 106
Princess 22, 106
Pring 134
Pringle 136, 138
Priscilla 40, 51, 73
Prishchipenko 144
Prisk 133
Pritam 110
Pritchard 124
Pritchett 124
Probert 125
Probyn 125
Proctor 130
Prodham 137
PROLIFIC NAMER
    90
Pronty 143
Prospect Park 183
Proud 134
Proudfoot 132
Proudlove 256
Proudman 256
Prower 141
Prowse 132
Prudence 25, 43, 92
Prudom 137
Prunty 143
Psmith 145
Psyche 79
PSYCHOLOGICAL
    EFFECTS OF
    SURNAMES 145
PSYCHOLOGY OF
    SIGNATURES
    150
PUB NAMES 198-

208
Puckeridge 137
Puddifoot 132
Puddy 136
Pugh 124, 152
Pugsley 134
Pullen 132
Pullman 123, 256
Pumphrey 124
Punjab 183
Punya 113
Purdy 136
Purfleet 168
PURITAN FIRST
    NAMES 43
Purkis 133
Purnell 124
Purser 137
Pursglove 134
Purslove 134
Purssell 133
Purves 138
Purvis 138
Puttergill 129
Puttock 137
Puuenuhe 181
Pyatt 137
Pybus 137
Pym 134

Qasim 112
Quack 255
Quail 131
Quaintance 255
Quance 134
Quarles 152
Quartermaine 132
Quarterman 256
Quartermouth 255
Quatlebaum 255
Quaver 22
Queen 22, 255
Queenborough 169
Queenie 73
Quelch 134
Quenby 133
Quenell 125
Quentin 34, 73
Quested 135
Quibell 136
Quick 255
Quiggin 127
Quilp 146
Quilter 134
Quinney 137
Quinny 137
Quirk 127
Quito 186
Quraishi 111

Rabat 186
Rabbets 134
Rabbi 22
Rabiah 112
Rabjohns 134
Rachael 40, 73
Rachel 40, 43, 45,
    51-5, 73, 95
Racine 255
Racket 129
Raddall 133
Raddle 133
Radley 136
Radnorshire 173
Radu 117
Radway 135
Rae 73, 138
Rafferty 127
Rafiq 112
Rafter 127
Ragnhild 117
Rain 106
Rainbow 22, 98, 137
Rainford 135
Rains 134
Rainy 22
Rajesh 110
Rajinder 110
Ralegh 121
Raleigh 121, 172
Ralph 124
Ralph 32, 43, 47, 49,
    73, 89, 97, 124
Ram 36, 110
Ramble 22

Ramindar 111
Ramirez 126
Ramon 73, 117, 126
Ramona 106
Ramos 124
Ramsay 34, 138
Ramsbottom 135
Ramsden 137
Ramsey 129
Ranby 136
Rance 106
Rand 124
Randal 32, 124
Randall 32, 49, 50,
    124
Randolph 89, 118,
    124
Rands 124
Randy 32
Rangitoto 165
Rangoon 186
Ranjit 111
Rank 132, 147
Rankin 124, 138
Ransome 124
Raper 22
Raphael 36, 73
Rapley 137
Rapson 133
Rasheda 41
Rashid 112
Rashida 41
Rathbone 133
Ratigan 127
Ratty 103
Raughley 121
Rauly 121
Ravel 106
Raven 22, 41, 54,
    134, 255
Ravenscroft 133
Ravenshaw 136
Ravinder 111
Raw 137
Rawcliffe 135
Rawdon 10
Rawkins 124
Rawle 124, 136
Rawleigh 121
Rawleyegh 121
Rawley 121
Rawlings 124
Rawlins 124
Rawlinson 124, 135
Rawlison 124
Rawson 124
Ray 21, 49, 73
Rayley 121
Raymond 32, 47-9,
    50, 55, 73
Raymont 134
Raymount 134
Rayner 146
Read 132, 256
Reading 168
Readman 137
Reagh 127
Reakes 136
Reavey 127
Rebecca 40, 51-5, 73,
    84, 104
Rebekah 40, 43, 73
Reddaway 134
Reddicliffe 134
Redgate 136
Redman 130, 256
Redmayne 137
Redvers 47
Redway 125
Reece 35, 73, 124
Reed 132
Reeson 136
Reeve 130
Reg 21
Regina 40, 73
Reginald 32, 47-8,
    73, 81, 89, 106
Reid 138, 141, 145
Reilly 127
Reiss 73
Rena 73
Rene 73
Renee 40, 53-5, 73
Renehan 127

Renfrewshire 173
Renita 41
Rennell 124
Rennie 124, 138
Rennison 124, 137
Rennit 147
Renshaw 134
Renton 136
Renwick 136
Rere 90
Retallack 133
Retallick 133
Retter 134
Reuben 32, 47, 73
Revell 134
Revill 134
Rew 134
Rex 21, 32, 73
Reyes 126
Reynald 124
Reynolds 124, 149,
    162
Reynoldson 124
Rhett 10
Rhiain 42
Rhian 73
Rhiannon 42, 55, 73
Rhoades 136
Rhoda 21, 42, 73
Rhode Island 185
Rhodes 162
Rhodri 35
Rhona 42, 73
Rhonda 54, 73
Rhude 172
Rhys 35, 55, 73, 124
Ria 73
Rice 22, 124
Rich 89
Richard 32, 43, 47-9,
    50, 55, 73, 85, 89,
    98, 106, 124, 255
Richards 122, 124,
    162
Richardson 124, 138
Riches 256
Richman 256
Richmond 138
Rick 21, 106
Rickard 133
Rickett 133
Ricketts 124, 135
Rickie 32
Ricky 45, 74, 82
Ridd 134
Rideout 255
Rider 137, 162
Riding 135
Ridout 134
Riffle 255
Rigdale 141, 172
Rigden 135
Riggall 136
Righton 135
Riitta 116
Rile 255
Rimmer 135, 147
Ring 127
Ringer 136
Rioty 90
Rippon 136
Rishworth 137
Rising 136
Rita 40, 52, 74, 83
Ritchie 98, 127, 138
Rivanna 181
RIVER NAMES
    170-1
RIVER NAMES,
    ENGLISH 175-6
Rivera 126
Rivett 136
Rix 124, 136
Roadley 136
Roads 133
Robb 138
Robbie 74, 125
Robbins 125
Robens 125
Robert 25-6, 32, 43,
    47-9, 50, 55, 74,
    88, 90, 125
Roberta 26, 40, 74,
    88
Roberts 122, 125,
    141
Robertshaw 137
Robertson 125, 138,

141, 149
Robey 125
Robin 33, 40, 48, 53-
    4, 74, 93, 95, 106
Robina 74
Robinetta 95
Robinson 10, 125,
    141, 147
Robson 125, 138
Robyn 21, 40, 55, 74
Rochelle 40, 74
Rockefeller 123
Rockmaker 255
Rockmeteller 106
Rockstool 255
Rodda 133
Roddam 136
Roddis 136
Rodenhurst 136
Roderick 33, 74, 104,
    107
Rodger 138
Rodmell 137
Rodney 33, 74
Rodrigo 126
Rodriguez 126, 141
Roebuck 137
Roger 33, 43, 47-9,
    50, 74, 125
Rogers 125, 141
Rogerson 125, 135,
Roggenfelder 123
Rohini 110
Roisin 74
Roland 33, 43, 74
Rolt 147
Romain 129
Roman 117
Romania 184
ROMANIAN GIVEN
    NAMES 117
Romayne 129
Rome 129, 186
Romeo 7, 224 255
Romero 126
Rona 74
Ronald 33, 48-9, 50,
    55, 74
Ronan 34
Ronnie 74
Rood 136
Roofe 136
Room 129
Roome 129
Roose 133
Roosevelt 34, 123
Root 134
Root 255
Rory 33, 74
Rosa 40, 74, 117
Rosaleen 40
Rosalie 40, 74
Rosalind 40, 74,
    107
Rosaline 40
Rosalyn 40, 74
Rosamond 43, 74
Rosamund 74, 95
Rosanna 40
Rosanna 51
Rosanna 74
Rosanne 40
Rosbotham 135
Rosbottom 135
Rose 21, 40, 43, 46,
    51, 53, 74, 80, 255
Roseanne 74
Rosebotham 135
Rosebud 22, 81
Roseline 40
Rosella 255
Roselyn 74
Rosemarie 74
Rosemary 40, 52, 55,
    74
ROSES, NAMES OF
    12
Rosetta 21, 40, 74
Roseveare 133
Rosewarne 133
Rosh 36
Rosie 21, 40, 74
Rosina 40, 74
Rosita 40
Roskelly 133
Roskilly 133
Roslyn 40, 55, 74
Ross 33, 55, 74, 127,

134, 138, 141
Ross and Cromarty 173
Rossall 135
Rossell 135
Rosser 138
Rossiter 134
Rothwell 135
Rounthwaite 137
Rouse 133
Routhwaite 137
Routledge 134
Routley 134
Rowan 34, 74
Rowarth 134
Rowe 147
Rowena 74
Rowland 33, 74, 129
Rowles 136
Rowlingson 133
Rowntree 137
Rowse 133
Roxana 40, 90
Roxanne 40, 74
Roxburghshire 173
Roy 33, 45, 47-9, 74
Royal Knights 255
ROYALTY IN PLACE NAMES 178
Royce 135
Royston 33, 74
Rubber 255
Ruby 21, 40, 43, 74, 105
Ruddle 137
RUDEST FIRST NAME 89
Rudyard 167
Rudyard Lake 167
Ruffle 134
Rufus 36
Rugby 19
Rugg 136
Rugman 135, 256
Ruiz 126
Rum Cay 178
Rumbold 135
Rumming 137
Rumpe 144
Rundle 133
Runnalls 133
Runyon 107
Rupert 33, 74, 90, 99
Ruscoe 133
Rushworth 137
Russ 21, 137
Russell 33, 45, 48-9, 55, 74, 132, 138, 141, 162
Russian 255
RUSSIAN GIVEN NAMES 116-17
Ruston 133
Rutgers 255
Ruth 40, 43, 51, 53-4, 74, 99, 104
Rutherford 138
Rutland 173
Rutlandshire 135
Ruy 126
Ryan 33, 48, 50, 55, 74, 83, 127
Ryder 138
Ryding 135
Rymer 135

S 26, 89
Saajid 111
Sabah 112
Sabin 136
Sabina 74, 116
Sabrina 40, 74
Saburo 109
Sacandaga 182
Sachiko 109
Sackman 256
Saddler 130
Sade 41
Sadie 40, 74, 103
Sadiq 112
Sadun 113
Safe-deliverance 43
Saffron 22
Sagar 135
Saint 134
Sajid 111
Sakae 109

Sakura 109
Saliha 111
Salik 117
Salim 112
Saliva 95
Sallie 40
Sallis 133
Sally 21, 25, 40, 51-3, 55, 74, 83, 88, 103, 111, 255
Sally-Ann 74
Sallyanne 74
Salma 112
Salmon 131
Salome 21, 42
Salop 174
Salter 130
Salthouse 135
Sam 47, 55, 74
Sama 113
Samadara Hasarangani 113
Samantha 40, 52-3, 55, 74, 82, 90
Sammy 74
Samson 36, 141
Samuel 33, 43, 47-9, 55, 74
Samways 134
San Marino 184
San Salvador 182, 186
Sanchez 126
Sancho 126
Sandbach 133
Sander 116
Sandercock 133
Sanders 124
Sanderson 124
Sandie 40, 75
Sandman 256
Sandra 40, 52-5, 75, 107, 116
Sandry 133
Sands 136
Sandy 21, 40, 75
Sankey 136
Santiago 126, 186
Sapphire 22
Sar'ann 46
Sara 21, 40, 75, 116
Sarah 21, 25, 40, 43, 51-5, 75, 80, 91, 95, 99
Sarah Ann 46
Sarah-Jane 75
Sarah-Jayne 75
Sarcee 114
Sardeson 136
Sare 133
Sarepta 255
Sargent 130
Sargisson 136
Sass 94
Satish 110
Satu 116
Saudi Arabia 184
Saul 36, 43
Saunders 124
Saunderson 124
Savage 132, 255
Savannah 22
Savill 134
Savin 136
Savory 136
Sawridge 114
Sawyer 131
Say 136
Sayers 137
Scales 136
SCANDINAVIAN PERSONAL NAMES 118
SCANDINAVIAN PLACE NAMES 170
Scantlebury 133
Scarborough 136
Scarlett 21, 82
Scarp 146
Scarth 137
Schaefer 126
Schluderpacheru 149
Schmidt 123
Schneider 126
Schoen 126
Scholes 135
Scholey 136

Schoolcraft 180
Schrift 149
Schroeder 126
Schultz 126
Schwabe 149
Schwartz 126, 149
Schwenkville 182
Scicolone 149
Scoley 136
Scollan 129
Scoones 135
Scotland 129, 184
Scott 27, 33, 46, 48-9, 50, 55, 75, 80, 89, 129, 138, 141
SCOTTISH FIRST NAMES 34, 42
SCOTTISH SURNAMES 122
Scotton 135
Scragg 133
Scrimshaw 136
Scrimshire 136
Scriven 136
Scrivener 133
Scroggs 133
Scrooge 147
Scruby 134
Scudamore 135
Scutt 134
Scutts 129
Seal 134
Sealey 136
Sealy 136
Seamus 34
Sean 21, 33-4, 50, 55, 75, 131
Sear 133
Sears 135
Searson 136
Seath 135
Seavers 125
Seaward 135
Sebastian 33, 75, 116
Seccombe 133
Seddon 135
Sedgwick 137
Sedman 137
Seeley 136
Sefton 135
Segar 135
Selby 136
Seldon 134
Selena 40, 75
Selene 107
SELF-GENERATED NICKNAMES 163
Selim 117
Selina 40, 51, 75
Selkirkshire 173
Sellars 137
Sellek 134
Sellerman 256
Sellers 137
Selwyn 75, 82, 135
Sena 113
Senga 42, 91
Senior 22
Sepala 113
Sepalika 113
Sephton 135
Seppanen 123
Septimus 25, 89
Seraiah 36
Sercombe 134
Serena 75, 85
Serendip 19
Serge 21
Sergeant 22, 136
Sergey 117
Seth 36, 43, 47
Seventy-Six 180
Severs 137
Sewa 111
Seward 134
Sexauer 148
SEXIEST FIRST NAMES 90
Seyoyah Creek 182
Sha-Bosh-Kung Bay 182
Shabbona 182
Shackel 133
Shackerley 169
Shacklady 135
Shackleton 137
Shacklock 134
Shadae 41

Shady 255
Shah 111
Shakelady 135
Shakespeare 132, 255
Shallow 146
Sham 22
Shambelly 172
Shameless 119
Shane 33, 55, 75, 80
Shanece 41
Shanel 90
Shanell 90
Shanice 41
Shaniece 41
Shaniqua 54
Shanise 41
Shanks 136, 138
Shannell 90
Shannon 40-1, 54-5, 75, 255
Shapland 134
Shaquille 50
Shardae 41
Shardai 41
Sharday 41
Sharde 41
Shared 22
Sharesmith 256
Sharif 112
Sharland 134
Sharlene 40, 75
Sharon 40, 43, 45, 52-5, 75, 80
Sharp 132, 138
Sharples 135
Sharpley 136
Sharratt 137
Sharrock 135
Sharron 75
Shatwell 152
Shaun 33, 48, 55, 75
Shave 134
Shavington-cum-Gresty 172
Shaw 129, 138, 141
Shawn 33, 75
Shayla 41
Shayne 75
Sheard 137
Sheba 42
Shed 22
Sheelagh 75
Sheen 133
Sheena 40, 75
Sheffield 135
Sheila 42, 51-4, 75
Shelagh 75
Shelah 36
Shelby 54
Sheldrake 137
Sheldrick 137
Shelemaiah 36
Shelley 40, 75, 137
Shelly 40, 75
Shelmerdine 151
Shelton 129
Shem 36
Shemaiah 36
Shemilt 137
Shenice 41
Shenise 41
Shenton 137
Shephatiah 36
Shepherd 131, 138
Sheppard 131
Shepperson 133
Sheree 40, 75
Sheri 40
Sherill 134
Sheringham 136
Sherratt 137
Sherri 45
Sherrie 40, 75
Sherry 53-4, 91
Sherwill 134
Sherwin 134
Sheryl 40, 75
Shetland 173
Shield 136
Shields 135
Shilling 256
Shiloh 180
Shingo 109
SHIP NAMES 178
SHIP NAMES 178, 233-4, 242
Shipley 129
Shipman 135

Shipp 135
Shipton 170
Shipway 135
Shirley 8, 21, 40, 52-4, 75, 82, 137
Shirt 134
Shoebotham 137
Shoebottom 137
Shoesmith 256
Shona 42, 75
Shone 133
Shopland 134
Shore 133
Shorland 134
Shorrock 135
Short 120, 132
Short Leg 119
Shorter 135
Shorthouse 132
Shortt 121
Shotton 134
Shreeve 136
Shrimpton 136
Shropshire 136, 173
Shuffell 256
Shufflebottom 131, 140, 149
Shuker 136
Shunsuke 109
Shute 134
Shuzo 109
Sian 40, 42, 75
Sickman 255-6
Sid 107
Siddons 136
Siddorn 133
Sidebottom 134
Sidford 137
Sidney 26, 33, 47-8, 75, 90
Sidsel 117
Siegfried 107
Siena 88
Sierra 41, 54
Sierra Leone 184
Siggers 125
SIGNATURES, PSYCHOLOGY OF 150
Sigourney 75
SIKH GIVEN NAMES 110
Silcock 135
Silida 113
Silidi 113
Silliman 256
Silva 126
Silvana 90
Silver 22
Silversmith 256
Silvery 22
Sim 134
Simen 117
Simeon 33, 75, 91
Simi 111
Simm 134
Simmonds 125
Simms 125
Simon 33, 47-8, 55, 75, 84, 91, 125
Simone 40, 55, 75, 90
Simpkins 125
Simple 132
Simpson 125, 138, 141
Sims 125
Sinclair 127, 138
Sind 186
Sinden 137
Sindh 186
Sine 40
Sinead 42, 75
Singapore 184
Singer 131, 136
Singh 110
Singleton 135
Sinks 255
Sinott 149
Siobhan 40, 42, 75
Sioned 42
Sir 22, 75
Sirell 135
Sirene 85
Sirett 133
Siri 88
Sirjohn 255
Sisi 90, 111

Sisley 124
Sisson 124
Sistine 255
Sitwell 256
Sixsmith 256
Sjoke 149
Skeels 133
Skegg 132
Skelton 129
Skerrett 135
Skewes 133
Skidmore 134
Skikne 149
Skinner 131, 152
Skipton 170
Skull Creek 182
Skyrme 135
Slader 134
Slater 131
Slatter 131
Slee 134
Slim 22
Sling 119
Slipper 136
Slipslop 146
Sloan 138
Slobody 255
Slocock 133
SLOGAN NAMES 43
Sloog 255
Sloper 137
SLOVAKIAN GIVEN NAMES 117
Slowman 256
Slugget 134
Slye 149
Slyman 256
Smale 134
Small 132
Smallbridge 134
Smallman 256
Smallridge 134
Smaridge 134
Smart 22, 132
Smedley 134
Smellie 131
Smerdon 134
Smithers 131, 137
Smithin 137
Smithology 123
Smithson 152
Smoker 131
Smollett 132
Smyth 134
Smythe 131, 145
Sneath 136
Snell 132
Snelson 133
Sniktaw 179
Snoreham in Ruins 172
Snoring 137
Snow 132, 162
Snowdrop 22, 43
Snowman 256
Snyder 126
Soame 136
Sob Lake 181
Sobani 113
SOBRIQUETS 153
Soby 134
Sofia 186
Softness 255
Sohan 111
Soida 113
Solley 135
Solomon 36, 43, 75, 135
Solon 44
Soma 113
Somerset 136, 173
Somerville 138
Sonia 40, 75
Sonja 40
Sonny 21-2
Sonya 40, 75
Soper 134
Sophia 40, 51, 53, 75, 83, 95
Sophie 40, 52, 55, 75, 116
Sophronia 89

Sophy 103-4
Sorcha 42
Sorrell 132, 134
Sory 255
Sorya 149
Soso 90
Soule 141
South 135
South Carolina 185
South Dakota 185
Southgate 137
Southon 135
Southwell 135
Spademan 256
Spain 129, 184
Spalton 134
Spanier 129
Spanish 255
SPANISH GIVEN NAMES 117
SPANISH SURNAMES 123
Spargo 133
Sparkes 137
Sparrow 162
Speechley 135
Speed 136
Spenceley 137
Spencer 33, 75, 131
Spendlove 256
Spensley 137
Sperling 43
Sperring 136
Spice 131
Spicer 134
Spiers 137
Spink 136
Spinks 136
Spittle 131
Spokane 179
Spokes 136
Spooner 131
Spotterswood 134
Sprake 134
Spratt 136
Spriggs 135
Sproston 133
Spurgeon 134
Spurle 134
Spurrell 134
Spurrett 136
Squance 134
Squeaky Creek 179
Squinter 119
Squire 22, 131
Squirrell 137
Sri Lanka 19
SRI LANKAN GIVEN NAMES 112
St John 107
St Kitt's 178
St Maur 132
Stace 135
Stacey 36, 40, 48, 52, 54, 75
Staci 40
Stacie 40
Stacy 36, 40, 75
Stacy's Corner 183
Stafford 129
Staffordshire 136, 173
STAGE NAMES 142, 149
Stainer 149
Staines 134
Stainthorpe 137
Staite 135
Staley 134
Stalin 142, 255
Stallard 136
Stamp 136
Stan 21
Stanbra 136
Stanbridge 133
Stanbury 134
Stand-fast-on-high 43
Standish 141, 172
Stanford 129
Stanhope 107
Staniforth 134
Stanisław 117
Stank End 172
Stanley 33, 46-9, 75, 129, 132
Stannard 137
Stansfield 137, 149

Stanton 129, 133
Stanworth 135
Staples 136
Stapleton 129
Star 22
Starbuck 152
Stares 135
Starkie 135
Starlight 255
Starling 136
Startford 133
Stavely 137
Stay 137
Steeds 136
Steel 138, 255
Steele 131, 162
Stefan 75, 116
Stefania 116-7
Stefanie 40, 75, 116
Steggall 137
Stein 126
Stelfox 133
Stella 40, 46, 53, 75, 90
Stendall 136
Stenson 125
Stephanie 40, 52, 54-5, 75, 116
Stephen 24, 33, 47-8, 55, 75, 90, 110, 125, 138
Stephens 125
Stephenson 125
Sterling 255
Steven 24, 33, 48-9, 50, 55, 76, 110
Stevens 125
Stevenson 125, 138
Stewart 33, 76, 127, 136, 138, 141, 147
Stickles 135
Stidolph 125
Stidston 134
Stimpson 136
Stinchcombe 135
Stingray Harbour 181
Stinking-saddle-blanket 114
Stinton 137
Stirling 138
Stirlingshire 173
Stobart 136
Stobert 136
Stock 134
Stockdale 133
Stockhill 137
Stockill 137
Stockton 133
Stoddard 137
Stoddart 138
Stokell 137
Stokes 129
Stonehouse 137
Stoneman 134
Stoppard 134
Stops 136
Storer 134
Storm 91
Storr 136
Story 141
Stowe 136
Strachan 138
Strang 132
Strange 140, 254
Strangeman 256
Stranger 22
Stratton 129
Straughan 136
Straw 136
Strawson 136
Streaker 139
Streek 139
STREET NAMES 187-197
Stride 135
Striker 140
Stringer 131
Strong 132
Struthers 138
Strutt 134
Stuart 33, 48, 55, 76, 135, 138
Stubbins 136
Stuble 136
Stuckey 136
Studley 134
Stunt 135
Stuppies 135

Sturdy 137
Sturgeon 137
Sturt 137
Stuyvesant-Knox 151
Subligna 180
SUBSTITUTES, PERSONAL NAME 8, 29
Such 139
Suckabone 182
Sudan 184
Suddaby 137
Sudu 113
Sududuya 113
Sue 21, 76, 92, 255
Suffolk 137, 169, 173
Sugarman 256
Sugden 137
Suggett 137
Suggitt 137
Suicide 181
Sukey 88
Sulayman 112
Sullarton 138
Sullivan 127, 162
Sully 136
Sultan 112
Sumitra 110
Summerfield 133
Summerhayes 136
Sunderland 137
Sunil 113
Sunny 22
Sunnyfarebrother 152
Sunshine 22, 255
Sunter 137
SUPERLATIVE FIRST NAMES 89
SUPERLATIVE SURNAMES 138
Surjit 111
SURNAME CHANGES 144
SURNAMES AS TRADE NAMES 221
SURNAMES, AMERICAN 123
SURNAMES, DESCRIPTIVE 132
SURNAMES, DISTRIBUTION BY COUNTY 133
SURNAMES, HISTORY OF 118
SURNAMES, IRISH 121
SURNAMES, LITERARY 151
SURNAMES, MISLEADING 131
SURNAMES, MOST COMMON 141
SURNAMES, OCCUPATIONAL 130
SURNAMES, PSYCHOLOGICAL EFFECTS OF 145
SURNAMES, SCOTTISH 122
SURNAMES, SPANISH 123
SURNAMES, SUPERLATIVE 138
SURNAMES, WELSH 122
Surprise 90
Surrey 137, 173
Surtees 134
Susan 40, 51-5, 76, 90, 92, 95
Susanna 43 76
Susannah 40, 51, 76
Susanne 40, 76
Susi 111
Susie 76
Sussex 137, 169, 173
Suter 137
Sutherland 127, 138, 173, 179
Sutton 129
Suzanna 76
Suzanne 52-5, 76, 116
Svein 117

Svetlana 117
Swaffer 135
Swaffield 134
Swan 138
Swanton 136
Swaran 111
Swarbrick 135
Swearing Creek 180
Swearman 256
Sweatlove 256
Sweden 184
SWEDISH GIVEN NAMES 117
Sweet 136
SWEETEST FIRST NAME 91
Sweeting 134
Sweetlove 256
Swetnam 137
Swift 22, 132
Swindle 131
Swindle 255
Swinton 133
Switzerland 184
Swynnerton 152
Sydney 33, 49, 76, 179
Syed 111
Sylvania 180
Sylvia 40, 45, 51-2, 76, 88, 95
Symes 134
Symonds 125
Syratt 133
Syren 22

Taber 134
Tabitha 42, 104
Tabor 134
Tacey 89
Tacy 89
Tadeus 117
Tag 124
Tagg 134
Tait 132, 138
Taizo 109
Takeshi 109
Talbot 132
Tamar 42
Tamar 43, 76
Tamara 40, 76
Tamasa 170
Tamblin 125
Tamblyn 133
Tame 133
Tameke 41
Tamika 89
Tamike 41
Tamiko 41
Tamlin 125
Tammie 40
Tammy 40, 54, 76
Tampling 125
Tamsin 40, 76
Tancock 134
Tandy 137
Tanganyika 184
Tania 40, 55, 76
Tanisha 41, 54
Tanner 131
Tansy 107
Tanya 21, 40, 76
Tanzania 184
Tapley 133
Tapping 133
Tara 40, 76
Tarn 134
Taro 109
Tarr 136
Tasha 41
Tasman 179
Tassell 135
TASTIEST FIRST NAME 90
Tatchell 136
Tatham 137
Tatisceff 149
Tattam 133
Tattersall 135
Tatyana 117
Taumata 165
Taunton 137
Taupo Nui A Tia 182
Taverner 134
Tawana 41
Tawanna 41
Taylor 50, 54, 55, 131, 138, 141, 162

Tazewell 136
Teak 80
Teal 137
Teale 137
Teate 144
Ted 46
Teddy 21
Teek illey 136
Tehran 186
Telfer 136
Telford 136
Tempest 22, 91
Temple 136
Templeman 136
Templeton 138
Tennant 138
Tennessee 185
Tennison 137
Tennyson 124
Tenpenny 256
Tenville 41
Terence 33, 48, 55, 76
Teresa 27, 40, 52, 76, 117
TERMS OF ADDRESS 29
Terrance 34
Terrell 34, 50
Terrence 50, 76
Terri 40, 76
Terrie 40, 76
Terry 33, 40, 45, 76
Tessa 40, 76
Tester 137
Tetsy 107
Tett 107
Tetty 107
Tevin 50
Texas 185
Texhoma 180
Thackery 138
Thackray 138
Thackwray 138
Thaddeus 255
Thailand 184
Thames 170
Thames Ditton 170
Thara 112
Thatcher 131
The Neck 183
The Paroo 182
The-Lord-is-near 43
Thelma 25, 40, 76, 99
Theo 76
Theodora 37, 40, 76, 107
Theodore 33, 49, 95, 107
Theophania 40
Theophilus 99
Thereon 255
Theresa 27, 40, 53-4, 76
Therese 81
Theyer 135
Thibaud 116
Thirkell 135
Thistle 22
Thoday 133
Thom 138
Thomas 25, 33, 47-9, 50, 55, 76, 79, 97, 107, 113, 116, 122, 125, 141, 255
Thomasin 40
Thomason 125
Thomlinson 134
Thompson 125, 141, 149
Thompstone 133
Thomson 138, 141
Thora 42
Thoreau 123
Thorington 134
Thorn 22
Thornber 138
Thornhill 133
Thornton 129
Thoroughgood 132
Threlfall 135
Throne 255
Thrower 131, 136
Thunder 143
Thurlby 136
Thurman 137
Thurston 129

Thwaites 138
Tiara 41, 54
Tibbetts 137
Tibbs 124
Tibor 116
Tice 137
Tichelar 123
Tickhill 139
Tickle 133, 139
Tickler 123
Tickner 135
Tidy 137, 139
Tierney 149
Tierra 41, 54
Tiffany 40-1, 54, 76, 78
Tilbrook 134
Till 135
Tiller 131
Tilley 124, 141, 172
Tillison 124
Tillman 131
Tillotson 124
Timberlake 133
TIME OF DAY FIRST NAMES 90
Timothy 33, 47-9, 50, 55, 76, 78
Timperley 133
Tina 40, 52, 54, 76
Tinker 138, 141
Tinkler 134
Tinney 133
Tinsmith 256
Tippett 133
Tipping 137
Tipton 129, 136
Tirzah 42
Titcombe 137
Titley 136
Tittle 255
Tittmus 135
Titus 21
Tiw 169
Tiza 46
Tize 46
TO-NAMES 153
Tob 36
Tobias 33, 36, 76, 107
Tobikuma 109
Tobitt 137
Toby 33, 76
Tod 138
Todd 33, 50, 76, 89, 131, 138
Toddman 131
Tofield 133
Tofts 134
Tokyo 186
Toll 133
Toller 131
Tolley 124, 137
Tom 21, 47, 76, 84, 107, 113, 133
Tomás 117
Tomasz 117
Tombs 125, 131
Tomes 133
Tomi 116
Tomika 41
Tomkin 135
Tomkinson 137
Tomlinson 125
Tommie 34
Tommy 21, 76, 255
Tompkins 125, 133
Tompsett 135
Toms 134
Tomsett 125
Tongue 137
Toni 40, 76
Tonia 40, 76
Tonkin 133
Tonkins 125
Tonks 125
Tono 181
Tony 33, 76, 99
Toogood 136
Tooley 136
Toon 135
Toone 135
Topaz 107
Tope 134
Topp 134
Topping 134-5
Topsy 21

Torao 109
Torpenhow Hill 166
Torquil 34, 93
Torr 137
Torres 126
Tortoiseshell 131
Toru 109
Towes 137
Towndrow 134
Towneley 119
Townend 138
Townley 152
Townroe 134
Townrow 134
Townsend 129
Townson 135
Toy 139
Toya 41
Tozer 134
Tracey 24, 40, 52, 55, 76, 79, 80
Tracie 76
Tracy 24, 40, 52, 54, 76, 80, 82, 91
TRADE NAMES 220-8
TRADITIONAL NICKNAMES 158
Trafford 136
TRAIN AND LOCOMOTIVE NAMES 234-5
Trainer 131
TRANSFERRED HOUSE NAMES 212-3
TRANSFERRED PLACE NAMES 177
Tranter 131
Trapp 131
Travers 131
Travis 33, 50, 55
Trease 127
Treasure 22, 136, 256
Trebilcock 133
Tregarvan 95
Tregear 133
Tregellas 133
Tregelles 133
Tregoning 133
Treleaven 133
Treloar 133
Tremain 133
Tremaine 127
Tremayne 133
Trembath 133
Tremlett 134
Trerise 133
Tresidder 133
Trethewey 133
Trevail 133
Trevean 127
Trevelyan 133
Trever 86
Trevor 33, 48, 55, 76, 107, 127, 141
Treweeke 133
Trewen 127
Trewhella 133
Trewin 133
Trey 50
Tribe 137
Trick 134
Tricker 137
Trickett 133
Trilby 19
Trina 76
Trinder 131
Trinidad 184
Tripcony 133
Tripoli 186
Trippas 137
Trissie 96
Tristan 76, 107
Tristram 89
Trollope 131
Trotman 135
Trott 134
Trotter 131
Trounson 133
Trowbridge 134
Troy 21, 33, 55, 76
Trude 134
Trudgen 133
Trudgeon 133
Trudgian 133
Trudi 40, 76

Trudy 40, 76
True 22
Trueheart 255
Truelove 137, 256
Trueman 133
Truman 256
Trumble 125
Truscott 133
Truscott-Jones 149
Truswell 136
Truth or Consequences 180
Tucker 131
Tuckett 134
Tudge 135
Tudor 21, 138
Tuesley 169
Tuff 135
Tuffin 134
Tuffley 135
Tulip 84
Tullia 117
Tully 134
Tunnicliff 137
Tupper 162
TURKISH GIVEN NAMES 117
Turnbull 132, 138
Turned 255
Turnell 136
Turner 131, 138, 141, 149, 162
Turnock 137
Turrill 136
Turton 134
Turvill 135
Tustain 136
Tuti 111
Tutt 139
Tutta 139
Tuvim 149
Tweeke 134
Tweedy 137
Tween 134
Twentyman 256
Twentymark 256
Twitchin 135
Twitty 255
Twoman 256
Twopenny 256
Tyack 133
Tyacke 133
Tyerman 137
Tyler 33, 50, 76, 131
Tyley 136
Tym 134
Tymm 134
Tyne and Wear 174
TYPE-FACES, NAMES OF 9
TYPES OF NAMES 6
Tyreman 137
Tyrer 135
Tyrone 33-4, 76, 173
Tyrrell 133
Tyson 76

Udall 134
Ukkuwa 113
Ulla 116-7
Ullah 111
Ullman 149
Ullyatt 136
Ultima 20
Ulyanov 142
Ulysses 106
Umpleby 138
Una 25, 42, 76
Unable-to-buy 114
Underhay 134
Underhill 134
Undy 172
Unicume 135
UNLUCKIEST FIRST NAMES 89
Unsold 255
Unstrung 255
UNUSUAL FIRST NAMES 22
Unworth 135
Upeksha 113
Upole 255
Upson 255
Upton 21
Uren 133
Uri 36
Uriah 36
Uriel 36

Urmston 133
Urquhart 138
Ursula 40, 45, 77, 89
Urszula 117
Usha 110
Usher 136
Usherwood 135
Utah 185
Utley 138
Utopia 182
Utting 136
Uzma 112
Uzziah 36
Uzziel 36

Václav 117
Valda 77
Vale 22, 135
Valentine 21, 77
Valentino 142
Valerie 40, 52, 77, 97
Vallance 134
Vallee 149
Van Rosevelt 123
Vancouver 179
Vanda 77
Vandermeer 126
Vanessa 25, 40, 55, 77
Vanstone 134
Varley 138
Varney 133
Vasile 117
Vaughan 33, 77, 127, 140
Vawser 133
Vazquez 126
Veli 116
Vellenoweth 133
Venezuela 184
Venner 134
Venning 133
Ventress 137
Ventris 137
Venus 45
Vera 40, 51-2, 77, 117
Verb 255
Vergette 136
Verity 40, 43, 77, 138
Vermont 185
Vernon 33, 77, 99, 105
Veronica 40, 77
Verrall 137
Verran 133
Vesa 116
Vespa 95
Vessy 127
Vest 22
Viccars 133
Vice 255
Vicesimus 89
Vick 135
Vicki 40, 77
Vickie 77
Vicky 40, 45, 77
Victor 33, 47, 77, 93, 107
Victoria 21, 40, 45-6, 52, 54-5, 77, 93, 179
Vida 77
Vietnam 184
Vigar 136
Vigors 136
Vijay 110
Vikki 40, 45, 77
Vimpany 135
Vincent 33, 77
Vinson 135
Vinter 136
Viola 43, 107, 255
Violet 40, 43, 51-2, 77, 99

Violet Town 182
Violla 255
Virgil 92
Virgin 22, 96
Virginia 40, 53, 55, 77, 96, 155
VIRTUE NAMES 43
Visor 255
Vivian 77, 133
Vivien 77, 96
Vivienne 40, 77
Vladimir 117
Vlk 146
Voaden 134
Vodden 134
Von Losch 149
Von Nordenwall 149
Vooght 134
Vosper 133
Vowels 255
Vowles 136
Vurginia 185
Vyse 135

Wacher 135
Waddell 138-9
Waddingham 136
Waddle 139, 256
Wade 21, 77, 149
Wadland 134
Wadley 135
Wadsley 136
Wadsworth 138
Wager 134
Wagman 256
Wagner 126
Wagstaff 149
Wagstaffe 132
Waimakiriri 182
Wainwright 131
Wakeford 137
Wakeham 134
Wakely 134
Walburn 134
Walby 135
Walch 129
Walden 134
Walder 137
Wales 138, 184
Walker 131, 138, 141, 162
Walkman 256
Wallace 34, 129, 138, 141
Wallasek 149
Wallbank 135
Waller 131
Walles 129
Wallis 129
Wallwin 134
Walmsley 135
Walrond 136
Walsh 129, 135
Walsman 129
Walter 21, 33, 43, 47, 49, 50, 77, 125
Walters 125, 162
Walton 129
Wanamaker 123
Wanda 21, 41, 77, 255
Wanlace 136
Wanless 136
Wanton 255
Ward 131, 141, 162
Warden 137
Warder 136
Ware 129, 134
Wareham 134
Wareing 135
Waring 135
Warman 256
Warminster 169
Warnborough 169
Warnes 136
Warr 133

Warren 21, 33, 43, 49, 77, 80, 129, 141, 162, 172
Warrilow 137
Warwick 136
Warwickshire 137, 173
Washington 46, 106, 129, 172, 185-6, 189
Wass 136
Waterfall 134
Waterhouse 134
Waterman 135
Watermelon 255
Waters 149, 162
Waterson 134
Watkins 125
Watkinson 125, 138
Watman 43
Watson 125, 138, 141, 162
Watt 138
Watts 125
Waycott 134
Wayman 133
Wayne 33, 48, 55, 77, 80
Wearmouth 134
Wearne 133
Weatherhead 138
Weaver 131
Webb 131, 149, 162
Webber 131
Weber 126
Webster 131, 138
Wedale 139
Wedd 256
Weddell 136
Weddle 136
Wedgwood 152
Wednesbury 169
Weedon 169
Weekley 140
Weekly 140
Weeney 135
Weetman 137
Weighell 137
Weighill 137
Weightman 136
Weintrop 149
Weir 127, 138
Weiss 126
Welburn 137
Welch 129
Welford 137
Wellbeloved 256
Wellburn 137
Wellings 136
Wellington 133, 186
Wellish 129
Wellman 256
Wells 129, 149
Wellsman 129
WELSH FIRST NAMES 35, 42
WELSH NICKNAMES 154
WELSH SURNAMES 122
Welson 135
Wenden 134
Wendon 134
Wendy 25, 40, 52, 54-5, 77, 116
Wenham 137
Wennell 125
Went 135
Were 134
Werner 126
Werrett 135
Wescott 136
Wesley 33, 77, 129
West Lothian 173

West Midlands 174
West Virginia 185
Westacott 134
Westaway 134
Westbrook 129
Westcott 134
Westerby 136
Western 134
Westley 77, 136
Westmorland 134, 173
Westoby 136
Westren 134
Wetton 134
Wey 165
Weybridge 165
Weymouth 165
Whalebelly 136
WHAT'S YOUR NAME? 23
Whatley 137
Whatman 125, 256
Whearty 127
Wheatcroft 134
Wheaton 134
Wheeler 131, 162
Wheelton 133
Whelan 127
Whenman 256
Wherrit 256
Whetter 133
Whinnet 133
Whipp 135
Whisky 131
Whitaker 129
Whitbread 132
Whitcher 135
White 138, 141, 162
Whiteaway 134
Whitebread 135
Whitehouse 132
Whitehurst 137
Whitelegg 133
Whiteley 138
Whiteside 135
Whitesmith 256
Whiteway 134
Whitley 138
Whitlock 134
Whitlow 133
Whitmore 137
Whitnee 41
Whitney 41, 54, 136
Whitni 41
Whitnie 41
Whitsed 136
Whittany 41
Whittard 125
Whittingham 134
Whittleton 136
Whittney 41
Whitton 136
Whitwell 137
Whyte 138
Wibberley 134
Wickens 137
Wickett 133
Widdicombe 134
Widdop 138
Widdows 136
Widdup 138
Wigley 134
Wigtownshire 173
Wilberforce 137
Wilberfoss 137
Wilbur 83
Wilcock 125
Wilcox 125
Wild 80
Wilday 137
Wilde 132
Wilder 133, 141
Wildman 256
Wildsmith 256
Wiles 135
Wilford 135

Wilfred 107
Wilfred 33
Wilfred 47
Wilfred 77
Wilkie 125
Wilkie 133
Wilkins 125
Wilkinson 125
Will 21
Willday 137
Willets 137
Willetts 137
Willey 136
William 18, 33, 43, 47-9, 50, 55, 77, 86, 99, 120, 122, 125, 162
Williams 122, 125, 141
Williamsburg 179
Williamson 125, 138
Willie 21, 33, 47, 77, 89, 90
Willing 134
Willis 125
Willison 133
Willoughby 129
Willow 77
Willows 136
Wills 125
Wilmer 125, 133
Wilsdon 136
Wilshaw 137
Wilson 77, 125, 138, 141, 162
Wiltshire 137, 173
Winbolt 125
Winbow 125
Winder 135
Windermere 171
WINDIEST FIRST NAME 91
Wineman 256
Winifred 27-8, 40, 51-2, 77, 101
Winmer 125
Winn 136
Winnall 137
Winney 125
Winnie 77
Winslade 136
Winslow 141, 172
Winsom 102
Winson 134
Winstanley 135
Winston 33-4, 45, 77, 129
Winstone 136
Wint 137
Wintersmith 255
Wintle 135
Wintour 135
Winwood 137
Wisconsin 185
Wise 132
Witchell 135
Withecombe 134
Witherden 135
Witheridge 134
Withers 143
Withey 136
Witheycombe 134
Withy 136
Witney 136
Witt 135
Witter 133
Witty 137
Woddall 133
Woden 169, 178
Wogan 127
Wohlbruck 149
Woking 176
Wolton 137
Wombwell 136
Wonnacott 134
Wood 138, 141, 162

Wooddisse 137
Woodhams 137
Woodhead 138
Woodings 137
Woodland 136
Woodley 133
Woodman 256
Woods 129, 162
Woodward 131
Woof 131
Wookey 136
Woolage 132
Woolcock 133
Woolgar 125
Woolgrove 136
Woolhouse 136
Woollam 133
Woollams 133
Woolland 134
Woollard 137
Woollatt 135
Woolston 136
Woombill 136
Woomera 165
Wooster 133
Worcestershire 137, 173
WORDS FROM PERSONAL NAMES 18-19
WORDS FROM PLACE NAMES 19
Workman 137, 256
Worledge 132
Wormington 137
Wormleighton 135
Worsley 135
Worsnop 149
Worthington 129
Worthy 22
Wortley 136
Wotton 129, 134
Wragg 134
Wrathall 138
Wray 137
Wrayford 134
Wreford 134
Wren 137, 162
Wrenn 132, 137
Wright 131, 138, 141, 145, 162, 221, 254
Wrighton 136
Wrightson 137
Wrixon 134
Wroot 136
Wroth 134
Wulmar 43
Wumond 43
Wych 133
Wyles 135
Wylie 138
Wyllie 138
Wyman 118, 125, 136
Wyn 35
Wynkoop 255
Wynn 127
Wyoming 185

Xavier 50

Yaa 115
YACHT NAMES 241-2
Yackandandah 182
Yah 91
Yahweh 25, 91
Yapp 132
Yarnold 137
Yarrow 133
Yarwood 133
Yasmin 40, 77, 112
Yates 129
Yaw 115

Yawn 255
Yeandle 136
Yeend 135
Yehudi 36
Yelberton 255
Yelland 133
Yells 255
Yemen 184
Yench 255
Yeoman 256
Yerkey 255
Yetta 255
Ying Hua 108
Yoelson 149
Yolanda 41, 77
Yonwin 125
Yook 255
York 94, 129, 136
Yorkshire 137
Yorkshire 173
Young 141, 145
Young-man-afraid-of-his-horses 114
Young-man-whose-very-horses-are-feared 114
Young 138
Younger 136
Youngman 256
Youngmay 125
Youngsmith 256
Yugoslavia 184
Yuko 109
Yul 21
Yule 149
Yuriko 109
Yuriy 117
Yves 40
Yvette 40, 77
Yvonne 24, 40, 43, 52, 77

Zabad 36
Zabdiel 36
Zachary 33, 50, 77
Zadok 36
Zahid 112
Zahrah 112
Zak 77
Zambia 184
Zanzibar 184
Zara 40, 77
Zaynab 111
Zebadiah 36
Zebedee 36
Zechariah 36, 91
Zedekiah 36
Zelda 90
Zena 77
Zeno 255
Zephaniah 36
Zero 89
Zilpah 42
Zimmerman 126, 149
Zinah 112
Zinnia 45
Zipes 255
Zipporah 42
Zizi 111
Zoe 40, 52, 77, 155
Zola 89
Zoltan 116, 255
Zouch 139
Zowie 40, 77
Zuriel 36
Zurrap 141
Zursman 141
Zuzi 111
Zyers 141
Zyscherk 141
Zytogorski 141
Zywyno 141
Zyznarski 141
Zyzyk 141
Zzaman 141
Zzoha 141
Zzuppichine 141